משנה

ArtScroll Judaica Classics®

Rabbi Nosson Scherman / Rabbi Meir Zlotowitz

General Editors

THE GIFT OF

Published by
Mesorah Publications, ltd

SHABBOS

Ideas and Insights of the

SFAS EMES

on the tefillos, seudos and hashkafah of Shabbos

Anthologized and Adapted
by Rabbi Yosef Stern

FIRST EDITION
First Impression . . . August 2005

Published and Distributed by
MESORAH PUBLICATIONS, Ltd.
4401 Second Avenue
Brooklyn, New York 11232

Distributed in Europe by
LEHMANNS
Unit E, Viking Business Park
Rolling Mill Road
Jarrow, Tyne & Wear NE32 3DP
England

Distributed in Australia & New Zealand by
GOLDS WORLD OF JUDAICA
3-13 William Street
Balaclava, Melbourne 3183
Victoria Australia

Distributed in Israel by
SIFRIATI / A. GITLER — BOOKS
6 Hayarkon Street
Bnei Brak 51127

Distributed in South Africa by
KOLLEL BOOKSHOP
Shop 8A Norwood Hypermarket
Norwood 2196, Johannesburg, South Africa

ARTSCROLL JUDAICA CLASSICS®
THE GIFT OF SHABBOS

4401 Second Avenue / Brooklyn, N.Y. 11232 / (718) 921-9000 / www.artscroll.com

---

ISBN:
1-4226-0014-9 (hard cover)

Typography by CompuScribe at ArtScroll Studios, Ltd.
4401 Second Avenue / Brooklyn, N.Y. 11232 / (718) 921-9000

Printed in the United States of America by Noble Book Press Corp.
Bound by Sefercraft Quality Bookbinders, Ltd., Brooklyn, N.Y.

This volume of
Sfas Emes
is dedicated by

Dr. Yedidiah and Mrs. Aviva Ghatan

in loving memory of

R' Zakarya Ghatan

ר׳ זכרי׳ה בן ידידי׳ה ז״ל

a gentle and sensitive individual
who was sincere with all those who knew him.
He naturally refrained from *lashon hara*
and greeted everyone gracefully
Although his children were reared
in the spiritually challenging
environment of Tehran, Iran,
he had the *zechus* that
all of his descendants are
Torah-observant Jews.
May it be the will of *Hashem*
that our mother enjoy good health
and continue to reap
Yiddishe nachas
from all of her descendants.

מכתב ברכה מאת כש"ת אדמו"ר מגור זצוק"ל
לספרי הקודם על שלש רגלים

ב"ה ה' שמות תשנ"ב לפ"ק

לכב' ידידי היקר והנכבד הרה"ג חו"ב נותן טעם לשבח הרב דוד אלעווסקי שליט"א

שלום רב!

בנידון הספר המבאר את השפ"א לסוכות אשר חיבר הרב יוסף שטערן שליט"א — הנה כידוע לך אינני נותן הסכמות באופן עקרוני. ובפרט כאשר השפה האנגלית אינה שגורה בפי לא שייך בכלל שאני אעבור ע"ז ואסכים עליו. אבל כפי ששמעתי מכם שאנשים חשובים שבחו את הספר הנני מצרף גם ברכתי להרב המחבר שליט"א שיצליח.

והנני בזה ידידך הדורש"ט

פנחס מנחם אלטר

Rabbi CHAIM P. SCHEINBERG
Rosh Hayeshiva "TORAH-ORE"
and Morah Hora'ah of Kiryat Mattersdorf

הרב חיים פינחס שיינברג
ראש ישיבת "תורה-אור"
ומורה הוראה דקרית מטרסדורף

יום ד׳ לש״ק פ׳ כי תצא, י״א אלול תשנ״ה.
פעיה״ק ירושלים תובב״א.

מכתב ברכה

שונה תורתינו הקדושה מספרי אומות העולם, באשר התורה באה לידי תכליתה כשהיא מלמדת לאדם את האמת, ויש בזה שני חלקים דהיי׳ א׳ ידיעה האמת, וב׳ המעשה שהיא חיי האמת, שעם כל הקושי הכרוכה בקנין ידיעת התורה ע״י עמל רב במחשבה בחריפות ביישוב הדעת, מ״מ עוד יותר קשה לאדם ללחום עם יצרו ולחיות את כל אורחות חייו על פי דעת התורה.

ובדורינו מצינו של״ע ירד קרן התורה פלאים ממה שהי׳ בדורות הקודמים, בזה שנלקו הלבבות בטמטום עצום מרב כל, וקשה מאד לעורר את הלבבות הסתמים והאטומים לשאיפת התורה והאמת, וכדי לחזור ולקרבן נצרך שפה מיוחדת המדברת אליהן בהסברת פנים ומושכן אחרי התורה.

וספרי "שפת אמת" הצליחו מאד בזה בדורינו בכוללם יחד את שני הענינים, הא׳ ה"אמת", והב׳ ה"שפה" המשתף גם את הלב בעבודה, ומעוררה לקיים את המעשה, ונמצא שמתוך הספרים האדם מתעורר לשלימות בין באמונה פשוטה ותמה בקיום המצוות, ובין בידיעה בתורה בעמקות ובחריפות, ועי״ז גם יכול לעשות את המצוות בהבנה ובטעם בכל הלב ובכל הנפש החפצה.

וכידוע בגלל דקותן של הענינים, לפעמים קשה אפי׳ לגדולים לעמוד על בוריין במקורן, ולכן עוד יותר קשה למסרן בשפה אחרת, וכדי לעשות כן דרושה מלאכת אומנות יתירה.

וב״ה זכה האי גברא רבא איש האשכולות ש״ב **הרה״ג רבי יוסף שטרן שליט״א**, רב דביהכ״נ אגודת אחים בפלעטבוש נ.י., שכבר נתפרסם כסופר מהיר המנצח על עבודה זו בהצלחה מרובה, והספרים הראשונים של ליקוטים והסברים בלשון ענגליש על המועדים ועל ליל הסדר כבר נתקבלו ברבים בחשק עז, ועכשיו שלח את ידו לעניני הימים הנוראים וחנוכה ופורים, ומתכונן בע״ה להמשיך אח״כ בשפת אמת על התורה.

ועל כן כל המסייעו בעבודתו הכבירה הוא ממזכי ומחזיקי תורה לרבים, שהיא זכות גדולה לברכה ולהצלחה בכל הענינים הרוחניים והגשמיים כמבואר ברז״ל.

ותפלתינו שזכותו של השפת אמת זצ״ל תעמוד לסייע שיתקבלו הספרים החדשים לא פחות ועוד יותר ממה שנתקבלו הראשונים, ושהנ״ל ימשיך בעבודתו עבודת הקודש ללמוד וללמד תורה ברבים בכל האופנים כיד ה׳ הטוב עליו מתוך הרחבת הדעת, ושיעמיד דורות ישרים אשר מהם ירוו׳ רב נחת אמיתית, ושיפוצו מעיינותיו חוצה, ושנזכה לראות בהרמת קרן התורה לאמיתה והיראה הטהורה בהכרת האמת, בביאת משיח צדקינו ובבנין בית המקדש במהרה בימינו אמן.

הכו״ח לכבוד התורה ולומדי׳,

חיים פינחס שיינברג

חיים פינחס שיינברג

רחוב פנים מאירות 2, ירושלים, ת. ד. 6979, טל. 371513-(02), ישראל
2, Panim Meirot St., Jerusalem, P. O. B. 6979, Tel (02)-371513, Israel

מכתב ברכה מאת כ״ק האדמו״ר מנאוואמינסק לספרי הקודם על הגדה של פסח

(718) 436-1133

RABBI YAAKOV PERLOW
1569 - 47TH STREET
BROOKLYN, N.Y. 11219

יעקב פרלוב
ביהמ״ד עדת יעקב נאוואמינסק
ברוקלין, נ.י.

בס״ד יום ד׳ כ׳ אדר א׳ תשנ״ה

כבוד מעלת ידידי הרב המופלג והנעלה
מו״ה יוסף פעלדמאן שליט״א, שלום ורב טוב.

תשואות חן חן לו על עבודתו הפוריה להוציא בשנה
האחרונה לפני רבים בהצלחה את משנתו הקדושה והנשגבה
של רבינו השפת אמת זצ״ל. כמעשהו על שלש רגלים
כן מעשהו כעת על הגדה של פסח, השכיל והצליח לתרגם
ולהביע את אמרותיו הטהורים של קדוש ישראל ותפארתו
למען ישתו רבים מבאר המים בכל לשון שאזנם שומעת.
יתן השם אלקים את הברכה ויזכה להפיץ אורה ויראת שמים
בקרבת ישראל לאורך ימים טובים. כעתירת נפש ידידו הדו״ש
ומברכו ברכת השלומים וכל טוב סלה
יעקב פרלוב

RABBI NAFTALI JAEGER
ROSH HAYESHIVA

בס"ד

מוצאי ש"ק תשס"ה "וברך אתה בדרך הימני" (רש"י דברים תכ"ג)

עוז נפשי הרה"ג הרב יוסף נ"י יאיר ויזרח כשמש הנודע בהרבצת התשובה שלו ומקרב נפשות תחת כנפי השכינה מול ספר שפת אמת - ענין שבת בשפה המדוברת וכתב אחז"ל מתנה טובה יש לי בבית גנזי ושבת שמה (שבת י') והודיע לנו השפ"א דאם צ"ע החידוש הרי"ם צ"ע דבמתנה מתנה היינו כדאמרי מאן דיהיב מתנה בעין יפה יהיב ולכן אע"פ דהמוכר ד"מ לא מכר לו את הדרך אבל הנותן ד"מ צריך ליתן לו דרך כו' (ב"ב ע"א) כי המוכר דעתו רק לקבל המעות אבל הנותן רוצה שיהיה למקבל המתנה לכן נותן לו הדרך כדי שיוכל לקבל את המתנה (עפ"י רשב"ם ...) וכן הוא בכל דבר רוחני שהקב"ה לא רק נותן לנו המתנה (תשובה ומצוות כו') אלא גם הדרך - ההתקשרות לקיימם. והרב ר' יוסף נ"י לא רק נתן לנו מתנה שבנים הי"ט את דברי השפ"א אלא גם את הדרך להבנתו לירד עד לעומק דבריו הק' כדי להאיר לנו את הדרך ... הרגשתי שכל אחד שילמד ילך בה. מטעם השבת בבחי' "שמו נאו כי טלה" ספרו יזכה לטעום וכתב אתמהי גברא ואתמהי רמ"ע דספריו הקודמים

ובוודאי אין צריך לדידי להוסיף אלא כדי למלאות רצוני ונראה ד"ה שכל כוונתו לשם שמים להרבות תשובה ויראת שמים שהשם לכן אמינא לפעלו שרא ייפה וברכתי ברכת הדיוט שיזכה תמיד ללמוד וללמד להרחיב גבולות דקדושה מתוך מנוחה ושמחה

הכו"ח לכבוד התשובה ולומדי'

נפתלי הלוי יעגר

שאר ישוב
SH'OR YOSHUV
INSTITUTE

ONE CEDARLAWN AVENUE • LAWRENCE, NEW YORK 11559 • (516) 239-9002 • FAX: (516) 239-9003

Publisher's Preface

To publish this work is a high honor. *Sfas Emes* is a name that has evoked respect and awe for a hundred years, as a commentary on the Talmud and as a collection of penetrating insights on the Torah and Festivals. One of the last generation's great *roshei yeshiva* said:

> "There is hardly a Torah commentary that I have not studied, but always I come back to the *Sfas Emes*. Every year I go through it again and I never fail to see new ideas that I never noticed before."

Rabbi Yosef Stern is one of the countless *talmidei chachamim* whose fascination with *Sfas Emes* has enriched his own life and, through him, the lives of many who attend his classes and lectures. Now, he goes a giant step further. He has taken the major ideas of the *Sfas Emes* on Shabbos and presented them in clear, cogent, stimulating essays, topic by topic. At the very least, this book will vastly enrich all who read it. At best, it will introduce many of its readers to the original, so that they too will mine its vast storehouse of ideas and comments.

This book is not a translation, for the *Sfas Emes* cannot be translated. It pulls together strands of thought on individual topics from the over thirty years of comment collected in the original, and weaves the ideas into a clear and coherent tapestry. To those familiar with the *Sfas Emes,* it will be a reminder, a refresher, and a treasury of insights they may have overlooked. To those unfamiliar with it, the book will be an electrifying adventure in Torah thought.

We express our appreciation to Rabbi Stern for undertaking this challenging work.

We likewise are grateful to all those whose talents have been harnessed in producing a work so significant. They may all be proud to have made an important contribution to the Torah growth of countless people.

Rabbis Meir Zlotowitz/Nosson Scherman

6 Av 5765
August 2005

Table of Contents

Author's Preface

◆§ SOME GUIDELINES TO LEARNING SFAS EMES

Before undertaking to study the teachings of *Sfas Emes* (either in this *sefer*, or ideally in the original text), it might be useful to consider some caveats:

- ❑ We have by no means presented an exhaustive anthology of all the *Sfas Emes'* thoughts regarding Shabbos. Anyone familiar with the structure of *Sfas Emes* is aware that virtually every one of the thousands of *divrei Torah* communicated by the *Sfas Emes* contained references to some aspect of Shabbos. For example, there are some 369 references to the concept of *neshamah yeseirah* alone. It is estimated that even a fairly complete coverage of the *Sfas Emes'* insights on Shabbos would require at least two thousand pages! Rather than present a truncated version of everything that the *Sfas Emes* wrote regarding Shabbos in one volume, we chose to explore in depth a few seminal topics (such as *Menuchah* and *Melachah*) and, simultaneously, consider the association between these concepts and other aspects of Shabbos, including *neshamah yeseirah, Kiddush* and the manna.
- ❑ We were greatly assisted in our search for sources by a CD-ROM that contains the entire text of *Sfas Emes al HaTorah*. The reader desiring to explore some of these topics in greater depth (or to embark upon a new area of the *Sfas Emes'* encyclopedic writings) might want to obtain a copy of this invaluable research tool from DBS, the publishers of The Computerized Torah Library, 55 Malchei Israel St., Jerusalem, Israel 94395 (tel. 02-5384258).

❑ As we indicated in the introduction to previous volumes of the *Sfas Emes* series, this *sefer* definitely should not be read all at once. In fact, the reader might be best served by sampling a few *divrei Torah* of each topic and then determine which of these areas he seeks to pursue in further detail.

❑ It is also important to emphasize that we have not endeavored to translate the *Sfas Emes'* esoteric and soaring sacred rhetoric. Moreover, we have not preserved the sequence in which his teachings were presented. Instead, we sought to present this great *gadol's* teachings in such a manner that the reader will be motivated to integrate them into their *derech ha'chaim* (as well as study the *Sfas Emes* in its original text).

❑ As is the case with many classic *sefarim*, some of their teachings are subject to varying interpretations. We have made efforts to adhere as much as possible to the simplest meaning of every *dvar Torah*. We acknowledge however, that other students of *Sfas Emes* may interpret differently some of the material in his original writings from which this *sefer* has been extracted.

❑ The reader is also encouraged to read the section entitled, "Some Themes from the *Sfas Emes'* Writings. In this section many of the concepts permeating the writings of the *Sfas Emes* are explored further, wherever possible utilizing the *Sfas Emes'* own words.

Acknowledgments

This *sefer* would not have been possible without the assistance of many distinguished individuals.

◆§ The sponsor:

Dr. and Mrs. Eliot Y. Ghatan whose generosity made this volume possible. Dr. and Mrs. Ghatan are renowned for their outstanding acts of *chesed* both professionally (while practicing medicine) and personally. It is well-known that through their *hachnasas orchim* and *tzedakah*, they exemplify the words of *Pirkei Avos*, יְהִי בֵיתְךָ פָּתוּחַ לָרְוָחָה וְיִהְיוּ. עֲנִיִּים בְּנֵי בֵיתֶךָ, *Let your house be open wide and treat the poor as members of your household* (1:5).

In the merit of their outstanding *mitzvos* and *maasim tovim*, may they enjoy only *nachas* from their children. We pray that the publication of this *sefer* may be an eternal *zechus* for the *neshamah* of Dr. Ghatan's father, ר׳ זכרי׳ בן ידידי׳, in whose memory The *Gift of Shabbos* is dedicated.

◆§ The facilitator of this project

My unforgettable brother-in-law, Rabbi Yehoshua Mosak, *z"l*, who despite his advanced terminal illness was extremely instrumental in arranging the sponsorship of this *sefer*.

In the words of *Yirmeyahu HaNavi* (used to describe Hashem's boundless love for the Jewish People), כִּי מִדֵּי דַבְּרִי בּוֹ זָכֹר אֶזְכְּרֶנּוּ עוֹד עַל כֵּן הָמוּ מֵעַי לוֹ, *Whenever I speak about him, I remember him again. Therefore, my inner self yearns for him* (31:19). Whenever I am able to speak (or think) about him, these thoughts evoke many poignant memories, which includes memories of more than a decade of *mesirus nefesh*, disseminating Torah in Norfolk, Virginia and Dallas, Texas. Rabbi Mosak's pioneering *kiruv* efforts contributed significantly to the subsequent development of these cities as Torah centers of note. To this day, his *talmidim* recall the lasting impact he left on them.

Memories also of his incredible integrity even while working in the business world. Rabbi Mosak's high ethical standards and his outstanding *yiras Shamayim* led him to spurn several lucrative opportunities for self-enrichment that he felt were inappropriate for a *ben Torah*.

Memories of how he was נוֹשֵׂא בְּעוֹל עִם חֲבֵרוֹ, deeply immersed in the suffering of everyone but himself. When *parnassah* was scarce, he *davened* (and invested great effort) so that others would find employment. During his terminal illness, he was greatly concerned about another patient who was stricken with a similar disease. Before returning to his own home after his first surgery (and after having received his terminal prognosis), he first traveled to another hospital to give *chizuk* to this patient.

Above all, memories of how Rabbi Mosak was *mekadesh shem Shamayim* during his final illness. The most hardened health professionals, who had been inspired by his unswerving *emunah* — despite the bleak prognosis that he had been given — were moved to tears when they heard of his passing.

During this most challenging phase of his life, Rabbi Mosak actually composed a *sefer* (based largely on the Torah thoughts of Rav Henoch Leibowitz, *shelita*).

As the *navi* continues, הָמוּ מֵעַי לוֹ, *my inner self yearns for him.* Anyone who was present in Rabbi Mosak's *succah* on the final Hoshanah Rabbah of his life (after he had just been released following a particularly difficult hospital stay) and witnessed the extraordinary *simchah* with which he recited the *berachos* of לֵישֵׁב בַּסּוּכָּה and שֶׁהֶחֱיָנוּ will always yearn for the time of *techiyas hameisim* when we will be reunited in body as well as in spirit with this outstanding *eved Hashem.* Anyone who witnessed how Rabbi Mosak just weeks before his *petirah* overcame intense pain to walk to *shul* (on a weekday morning) will derive renewed appreciation for *tefillah b'tzibbur.*

Despite his profound involvement in communal affairs, Rabbi Mosak was at all times, an unusually devoted husband and father. Regardless of having spent many years away from the vibrant Torah centers of the East Coast, he (along with his *eishes chayil, shetichyeh),* nonetheless, merited to rear children and grandchildren who are *bnei Torah* and *yirei Hashem.* For them, we pray (in the words of the final phrase of the *pasuk)* רַחֵם אֲרַחֲמֶנּוּ, *I will have compassion for them,* that Hashem, in His infinite compassion will grant them only *simchos.*

◆§ My family

My Parents :

According to *Chazal* (*Kiddushin* 30b) parents are partners with *HaKadosh Baruch Hu* in our creation. My father's *z"l, ahavas HaTorah,* his deeply imbued *yiras Shamayim,* and his unstinting *emunas chachamim* will never be forgotten. His and my mother's *mesirus nefesh* for the *chinuch* of their children and their legendary *hachnasas orchim* will always be profoundly appreciated. My brother, Elchonon, *shelita,* and I will always be inspired by memories of this *eidele Yid* who left this world while preparing to *daven* on the second day of Pesach ten years ago, *yehi zichro baruch.*

These outstanding traits are perpetuated so well by my mother, *shetichyeh, leorech yamim tovim.* May *HaKadosh Baruch Hu* grant her the *zechiyah* to enjoy in good health many generations of descendants immersed in Torah and *yiras Shamayim.*

My Parents-in-law:

The impact of my father-in-law, Rav Shmuel Scheinberg *z"l,* on countless *talmidim* during four decades of *harbotzas HaTorah* can not be overestimated.

As an adolescent, he left behind the comparative tranquility of America to travel with great *mesirus nefesh* to study Torah at the feet of *gedolei HaTorah,* such as Rav Eliezer Yehudah Finkel, *zt"l,* and Rav Yeruchom Levovitz, *zt"l.* Returning to America, he became one of Rav

Aharon Kotler's, *zt"l*, initial fourteen *talmidim* (in White Plains, N.Y.), and later was instrumental in acquiring *Bais Hamedrash Govohah's* first building in Lakewood, New Jersey.

Despite the challenges of rearing and supporting a large family, Rav Scheinberg chose to devote his considerable talents primarily to *chinuch*, shaping and influencing many hundreds of *talmidim* in Yeshivas Rabbi Yaakov Yosef and in Yeshivas Rabbi Yitzchok Elchonon. Many *talmidim's* entire lifestyle, as well their *derech ha'limud* were profoundly affected by their beloved *Rebbi*. His final contribution, the establishment of *Yeshivas Migdal Torah* (renamed *Nachlas Shmuel* in his memory) devoted to the education of the children of English-speaking expatriates living in *Eretz Yisrael* has already had an impact on Torah education.

Notwithstanding his involvement in *harbotzas HaTorah*, Rav Scheinberg was above all a devoted *mechanech* and mentor to his own children. *Baruch Hashem*, his sons, Rav Meir, *shelita*, and Rav Avrohom Yonah, *shelita*, as well as all other family members, continue in the *derech ha'chaim* that they derived from him.

All of these accomplishments would have been impossible without the support and participation of my mother-in-law, Rebbetzin Scheinberg, *shetichyeh*. May *HaKadosh Baruch Hu* grant her *arichus yomim veshanim*, in good health, to reap continued *Torahdik nachas* from all of her descendants.

Acharon acharon chaviv, my wife, *shetichyeh*. Without the atmosphere of *ahavas haTorah* and *yiras Shamayim* that she has fostered in our home, our dream of completing this *sefer* would never have reached fruition. Her involvement in and her constant encouragement to continue writing, in the face of many other responsibilities, were instrumental in bringing us to this point.

May Hashem grant us the opportunity to enjoy, דוֹרֵי דוֹרוֹת many generations of יוֹדְעֵי שְׁמֶךָ וְלֹמְדֵי תוֹרָתֶךָ לִשְׁמָהּ.

I would also like to take this opportunity to thank our children for their computer assistance throughout this project. Their tremendous assistance in preparing the Index is greatly appreciated.

◆§ My editor

It is has been a true privilege to collaborate again with Mrs. Ethel Gottlieb. Her dedicated and highly professional workmanship is manifest in every aspect of the book. Her cogent questions helped clarify many difficult passages of this *sefer*. No detail (such as improving sentence syntax, rearranging sequence of material, and validating sources) was too tedious for her. In fact, the *sefer's* name, *The Gift of Shabbos*, was based on a suggestion of hers.

May she enjoy only *Yiddisheh nachas* from her family.

❧ The staff of Mesorah Publications

Rabbi Nosson Scherman's encouragement and support for this *sefer* (as well as previous volumes of the *Sfas Emes)* is profoundly appreciated. May Hashem grant him (and his family) *arichus yamim veshanim*, so that he may continue to disseminate Torah to the vast reaches of *Klal Yisrael* whose lives have been so enriched by Mesorah Publications.

Thank you to the staff of Mesorah Publications, including Mrs. Esther Fierstein, Mrs. Chumie Lipschitz, Ms. Sury Reinhold and Ms. Sara Rivka Spira. A particular *yasher koach* is due to Mendy Herzberg, who shepherded this *sefer* through its final phases. Many logistical and technical issues were simplified through his expertise.

We thank Rav Dovid Olewski, of the Gerer *Bais Din* who continues to serve as an invaluable liaison to the Gerer *kehillah*.

To the members of Congregation Agudath Achim of Midwood, and its President Michael Reminick, where I am privileged to serve as their *rav*.

To my friends Reb Mordy Kriger (author of the *Chasdei Hashem* series), and Reb Shmuel Bernstein for their constant encouragement and support. We owe a *yasher koach* to Dr. Yaakov Nagelblatt for making available to us the Friday evening *siddur*, with an anthologized commentary (based largely on *Sfas Emes*) by Rav Yehudah Aryeh Leib Haine, *z"l*, a descendant of the *Sfas Emes*.

Of course, the ultimate tribute is due to *HaKadosh Baruch Hu*. Without *siyata d'Shemayah*, no step in life no matter how minuscule may be successfully undertaken. Our every breath, our health, our *parnassah*, our families, are all in place only because of His constant *hashgachah pratis*. May He continue to bless our efforts so that, in the words of the *tefillah* recited at a *siyum*:

כְּשֵׁם שֶׁזָּכִינוּ לְסַיֵּים סֵפֶר זוּ, כֵּן נִזְכֶּה לִלְמוֹד וּלְסַיֵּים שְׁאָר סְפָרִים, *Just as we merited to complete this sefer, so too, we should merit to study and complete other sefarim.*

Yosef Stern

מוצאי ש״ק נחמו ומוצאי ט״ו באב

Some themes from the Sfas Emes' writings

In this section, we will attempt to clarify some of the basic themes that permeate the *Sfas Emes'* writings, especially those that are cited in this *sefer*. Wherever possible, this objective will be accomplished by using the *Sfas Emes'* own language (accompanied by a free and expanded translation in English).

✥ The inner (Divine) Spark (nekudah ha'penimiyus)

ואותו נקודה חיות שמתלבש באיזה מקום להחיותו זו הנקודה אין לה שיעור כי היא למעלה מן הזמן והטבע ועל נקודה זו נאמר הוא מקומו של עולם ואין עולמו מקומו ... מאוד הוא יותר ממקום התלבשות ... כי כן בכל דבר נקודה פנימיות אין לה ,מדה וגבול וכן בנשמת אדם שאין לה שיעור ... ושבת היא התגלות הפנימיות ... לכן הוא נחלה בלי מצרים

The (Divine) Spark of life that is contained in every entity sustains it and keeps it alive. This spark is beyond any limitations of time and is not subject to any natural constraints. It is in reference to this spark that *Chazal* write that "Hashem is the *Makom* (*Place)* of the universe and the universe is not His *makom*" (cf. *Rashi, Shemos* 33:21).

Dovid HaMelech alludes to this Divine Spark by writing, , *for everything that has been created, I see a (finite end). Your mitzvos are exceedingly broad* (*Tehillim* 119:96). The term *meod, exceedingly* implies that this Divine Spark (which is "nurtured" through our *mitzvos*) can "occupy" (in a spiritual sense) an area greater than that of its casing (the word used by *Sfas Emes* is *hislavshus / levush).*

This concept applies to the realm of space, especially as it pertains to *Eretz Yisrael*, which is compared to a deer. "Just as a deer's hide can not contain its skin,"[1] so too, as long as *Klal Yisrael* earns the distinction of

1. Once a deer's hide has been removed, it contracts and can no longer be stretched to cover the area it had previously occupied.

living in *Eretz Yisrael,* the land expands to meet its inhabitants' needs (in other words,there are no physical constraints to anything sacred).

The same concept — that there are no physical dimensions to anything sacred containing the *nekudah ha'penimis* — pertains to the soul. There is simply no limit to the spiritual levels that the soul can attain. Just as any mass — any geographical area — can expand beyond its natural base to accommodate the spiritual levels attained by its inhabitants, so too, the soul's (which is called an *olam katon, a small universe)* capacity to grow is proportionate to the level of our spiritual ambitions.

While the concept of *nekudah ha'penimiyus* pertains all week long,it is especially true on Shabbos, a day when this inner Divine Spark, normally latent, comes to the surface. It may be for this reason that those who observe Shabbos are rewarded with a (spiritual) inheritance that is beyond any natural limits (*nachalah beli metzarim).*
(Adapted from *Bereishis* 5640)

בשעה שהקדימו ישראל נעשה לנשמע באו ס״ר מה״ש לכל א׳ מישראל קשרו לו ב׳ כתרים א׳ של נעשה ואחד של נשמע ... אחד מה שניתן בו נקודה פנימיות ... ועוד שנית מאיר עליו מלמעלה הארה עליונה למעלה מהשגתו וב׳ הארות אלו הם תלוין זה בזה ...

In this *dvar Torah,* we will demonstrate the capacity of *Klal Yisrael* to not only fully exploit its inner capacity for greatness (based on the Divine Spark) but also, on certain occasions (such as the Giving of the Torah), to actually exceed this innate capacity and to achieve unimaginable levels of greatness.

When the Jewish People said *naaseh* before *nishmah,* the angels came and tied two crowns on each individual's head, one (of the crowns) corresponding to *naaseh* and the other to *nishmah.*

The significance of granting every Jew two crowns may be explained in the following manner: Whereas the first crown represents the capacity of every individual to exploit their Divine inner Spark to its fullest, the second crown alludes to the extraordinary assistance rendered by *HaKadosh Baruch Hu* to achieve beyond our capacity. (Just as a crown is placed — or tied — above the head, so too, *Klal Yisrael* enjoyed then the capacity to attain levels of *daas Hashem* that were well beyond their ordinary capacity.) The term *kashru, they tied,* gives us an indication of the innate connection that every Jew has not only with his innate potential for good, but also with his potential to achieve and soar to levels of *kedushah* beyond his head.(Adapted from *Shavuos* 5635)

◆§ Shoresh (heavenly roots)

The concept of *shoresh,* that there is an inexorable relationship between any of Hashem's creations on earth and its counterpart in heaven, is discussed frequently in *Sfas Emes.* To illustrate this concept, we have adapted one of the earliest references to this concept (from *Bereishis* 5641).

It is well-known that every object on earth has its roots in heaven. For example, *Chazal* (*Bereishis Rabbah* 10:6) write that every blade of grass on earth has a *mazal* (in this context, probably referring to an angel) in heaven that strikes it and says "you must grow".

With this premise, we can appreciate what happened to the waters that were above the firmament. (מַיִם אֲשֶׁר מֵעַל לָרָקִיעַ). While it is generally known that when Hashem created the firmament, the waters *below* (i.e., the water on earth) attained a certain level of *kedushah* by being poured alongside the *mizbeiach* during the *nisuch ha'mayim* ceremony. One wonders what happened to the waters that now remained *above* the firmament. However, based upon the foregoing assumption that everything below enjoys heavenly roots above, we suggest simply that the waters above are the counterparts and *shoresh* in heaven of the waters below on earth. Consequently, when we pour water alongside the Altar on Succos (or in the form of salt placed on every *korban*), we are placing *both* the waters below as well as the waters above on the *Mizbeiach.*

Utilizing this approach, we may appreciate why the Torah does not explicitly discuss the creation of angels. We suggest that *malachim* may comprise the heavenly component of every thing that had been created on earth. Thus, the creation of angels may be inferred from the creation of everything that emerged during the *sheshesh yemei hamaaseh,* Six Days of Creation.

It is on Shabbos, a day that is described as *porais succas sholom, He spreads His canopy of completion (perfection, sheleimus),* that our presence on earth is best linked to its heavenly roots. In fact, when we greet the angels every Friday evening with the expression, *shalom aleichem,* we are alluding to the *sheleimus* that we now enjoy as they "descend" from heaven to join us here on earth.

◆ Ohr ha'ganuz (evoking the first light of Creation)

דמקודם הי׳ בריאת האור וירא וכו׳, האור כי טוב ויבדל גנזו לצדיקים כמש״כ חז״ל ובכל יום כי וירא כי טוב והיינו בתורה שנק׳ אור וטוב כמש״כ מה רב טובך כו׳, צפנת מה שגנז האור בתוך הבריאה ... ולכן בשבת לא כ׳ וירא כי טוב כי בשבת הוא כולו אור וטוב כמש״כ חז״ל בשבת יעשה כולו תורה

It is well-known that *HaKadosh Baruch Hu* hid the first light of Creation. As the Torah says, וַיַּרְא אֱלֹקִים אֶת הָאוֹר כִּי טוֹב וַיַּבְדֵּל אֱלֹקִים בֵּין הָאוֹר, *God saw that the light was good and God separated the light* (i.e., He hid it from public view and designated it for the enjoyment of the righteous in the World to Come) (*Bereishis* 1:4).

Yet despite the apparent concealment of this light from mankind, we note that the same expression that is used to describe the creation of light, *tov, good,* is repeated throughout the Six Days of Creation (וַיַּרְא אֱלֹקִים אֶת הָאוֹר כִּי טוֹב, *God saw the light that it was good*). From this apparent dichotomy, we may deduce that while the first light of Creation was hidden, it may be found again, in particular through diligent study of Torah, which is described as both being a "light" (כִּי תוֹרָה אוֹר) and as being the epitome of good (כִּי לֶקַח טוֹב נָתַתִּי לָכֶם תּוֹרָתִי עַל תַּעֲזֹבוּ) . In fact, by studying Torah, we can detect that first light of Creation in all of Hashem's Creations. As Dovid *HaMelech* writes, מָה רַב טוּבְךָ אֲשֶׁר צָפַנְתָּ, *how great is Your Goodness (*i.e., the first light of Creation, which is described as being "good") *which You hid* (in the world that You created) (cf. *Tehillim* 31:20). Moreover, the *ohr ha'ganuz* of each day of Creation that can be elicited through *limud haTorah* is unique. As we read in *Mishlei*, וָאֶהְיֶה שַׁעֲשֻׁעִים יוֹם יוֹם, *I (the Torah) was a delight every day* (8:30). What greater delight than eliciting (through *limud haTorah*) the unique light of Creation that is obscured in the material world that each day of the Six Days of Creation brings.

Extending our analysis, we note that — unlike any of the other days — in reference to Shabbos, the Torah does not write that God pronounced the light to be good. On Shabbos, a day that is suffused by the sacred light of the Torah (as *Chazal* in *Tanna D'Bei Eliyahu* write, שַׁבָּת יַעֲשֶׂה כֻּלּוֹ תּוֹרָה, *Shabbos is a day that is entirely devoted to Torah study)*, we don't have to seek the light of Creation. It is only during the *shesesh yemei hamaaseh* that we are given the challenge of finding that light amidst the material world that Hashem created through the Torah that we study. (Adapted from *Bereishis* 5646)

⧼ Studying Torah despite our (initial) lack of comprehension or pleasure

---

זהו נק׳ עמל בתורה ... אפילו אינו מבין מ״מ מייגע עצמו בתורה שחביב בעיניו להגות במאמרו יתברך אפילו שאינו זוכה להשיג הטעם ... לכן כתב המהר״ל שמברכין לעסוק בדברי תורה שגם שא״י להשיג מ״מ עוסק הוא בתורה ... שלא בירכו בתורה תחלה ... קודם שמשיג רק מתאוה להגות בדברי קודש דברי אלקים חיים.

While the true student of Torah derives boundless enjoyment from his study, it is our obligation to delve into Torah even *prior* to our achieving any understanding. The reason is simply because the Torah is the Word of Hashem with which He entrusted *Klal Yisrael*. When *Chazal* refer to *ameilus baTorah, toiling in Torah,* they may be referring to our sacred commitment to study Torah even prior to appreciating the reason for its commandments. In fact, even after proceeding to a more advanced level of Torah study, we still do not comprehend even one-thousandth of its immense profundity.

As the *Maharal* notes, we recite (prior to studying Torah) the blessing of לַעֲסוֹק בְּדִבְרֵי תוֹרָה, *to immerse ourselves in the words of Torah.* Whether or not we comprehend the Torah that we study, we thank Him for the opportunity to immerse ourselves in Torah. Utilizing this approach, we attain new insight into a renowned Gemara (*Nedarim* 81a) stating that the destruction of the *Bais HaMikdash* was caused עַל שֶׁלֹּא בֵּרְכוּ בַּתּוֹרָה תְּחִילָּה, *because they did not recite the blessing on the Torah at first.* While it is relatively simple to express our appreciation for the Torah *after* having obtained some understanding of its teachings, the generation of the *Churban* failed to express its gratitude (by reciting *birchas haTorah)* *before (techilah)* understanding Hashem's Word.

Utilizing this approach, we can appreciate why the Torah promises material rewards to be enjoyed in This World for those who follow Hashem's Statutes. As the Torah states, אִם בְּחֻקֹּתַי תֵּלֵכוּ ... וְנָתַתִּי גִשְׁמֵיכֶם בְּעִתָּם, *If you will follow My Statutes then I will grant your rain* (and all other material blessings) *in their appropriate time* (*Vayikra* 26:3-4).

While it is generally true that *sechar mitzvah behai almah lechah, there is no reward for the performance of mitzvos in This World*, that is only true when *mitzvos* are performed (and the Torah is studied) from a purely intellectual viewpoint. If, however, we study Torah because of our desire to cling to Hashem (and to negate ourselves to Him), regardless of our lack of rational comprehension, it follows, almost as a matter of course, that as such dedicated servants of Hashem, we enjoy His Blessings even in This World. (Adapted from *Bechukosai* 5649)

◆§ Kavod hatorah (the honor due Torah and its students)

הרי אמרו הלומד מחבירו אות א׳ צריך לנהוג בו כבוד. ומה נעשה אל התורה בעצמה אשר מלמדה אותנו תמיד איך לעבוד את ה׳, ומה הכבוד אל התורה להגות בה יומם ולילה ... כי באמת התורה אין לה שיעור ויש לכל פרשה ולכל פסוק ולכל תיבה ולכל אות כמה עולמות עליונים מיוחדים ... אבל הקב״ה הניח לנו פאה ועוללות ... וכפי מה שאדם יודע זאת ומחזר על העוללות כעני ואביון אז התורה מרוממת אותו

The following is an adapted translation of an outstanding excerpt of *Sfas Emes* extolling the Torah and pleading that we grant the Torah the honor that it is due.

Our Rabbis relate that if one learns even one word of Torah from his peer he must demonstrate respect to him. It follows then that we certainly must respect the Torah itself, which is always teaching us how to serve Hashem. How do we honor the Torah? By immersing ourselves in its teachings at all times (day and night).

Rashi describes our attempts at studying Torah as being comparable to an individual who is gleaning *olelos* (the last pickings of the grapes which are reserved for the paupers who make the rounds of the vineyards). By using that metaphor, *Rashi* is implying that our comprehension of Torah is little more than a small fragment of the Torah's immense and limitless treasures. Indeed, every portion, every *pasuk* every word, and even every letter of the Torah has a cosmic impact beyond our imagination. Just as the pauper can only obtain gleanings of the harvest, so too, *HaKadosoh Baruch Hu* permitted us a few insights into His infinite Torah.

The mere fact that we are conscious of our limitations and that we are well-aware of how little of the Torah we truly comprehend, is in itself a great source of merit and serves to elevate us spiritually. When our forefathers stood at Mt. Sinai, the Torah emphasizes that they were בְּתַחְתִּית הָהָר, *at the bottom of the mountain* (*Shemos* 19:17). By realizing that they were at the "foothills" of Torah (far from its pinnacle), the Jewish People merited to "scale the mountain" and reach its peak spiritually (and, in fact, they received the Torah at Sinai).

Another aspect of *kavod haTorah* is to search for the light (connoting, impact) of the Torah in every possible place. In fact, there isn't a place where the impact of the Torah is not felt. Similarly, every occurrence may be understood in the light of the Torah. If we search for the meaning of all that happens to us from the perspective of the Torah then the Torah will raise our spiritual aspirations. (*Succos* 5664)

Bais Shammai and Bais Hillel (machlokes leshem shamayim (an argument for Hashem's sake)

וידוע ששמאי עמד ביותר על קו הדין ודקדוק המשפט בפרטות אבל התורה בכלל נמשכת אחר דעת הלל ... לעתיד יהי׳ הלכה כב״ש ... כי כמו שעלה במחשה כן יהי׳ כך בנתיים בעו״הז מתנהג בשיתוף מדת הרחמים

[Author's note: In this segment we will cite two somewhat diverse approaches of the *Sfas Emes* regarding the many disputes of the House of Shammai and the House of Hillel. Other scholars may have other approaches in their pursuit of a general approach to the *machlokes* of these Torah giants. (Refer to *Leor HaHalachah,* by Rav Shlomo Yosef Zevin, *zt"l*, for an in-depth discussion of this question. Also discussed is his original approach that these two schools of *Halachah* are disputing whether to emphasize the potential ramifications of a situation (*b'koach*) if no action is taken, as *Bais Shammai* prefers, or to focus on the present reality (*b'poel*) rather any eventual consequences.) However, this much is clear — it is absolutely erroneous to depict Shammai (or his school) as a mean-spirited zealot. In fact, it is Shammai himself who teaches us הֱוֵי מְקַבֵּל אֶת כָּל הָאָדָם בְּסֵבֶר פָּנִים יָפוֹת, *greet every person with a pleasant countenance.*]

On one hand, we suggest that *Bais Shammai* — described by *Chazal* as being "more incisive" (of course, *Bais Hillel* was also very incisive) — focused on the specifics (*perat*) of each Halachic situation, while *Bais Hillel's* approach was to evaluate each situation in the context of the entire Torah (*klal*). (Adapted from *Korach* 5638)

In order to appreciate an alternative approach to the disputes between the Schools of Shammai and Hillel, we recall the *Chazal* stating that Hashem originally "intended" to create the universe with the attribute of *din, strict justice,* which was subsequently mitigated by His addition of the attribute of mercy. While *Bais Shammai* emphasized the attribute of *din* (and consequently was generally more stringent), *Bais Hillel's* approach was to rule on the basis of the attribute of mercy, which was later added to the universe. According to the *Ari Hakadosh, ztl,* while in This World we generally rule like the School of Hillel, in the Future World the *halachah* will follow the school of *Shammai.* This statement can be understood in the context of the *Chazal* cited previously, that the universe was originally intended to be created on the basis of strict justice. Just as at its inception the universe was based on *middas hadin,* the attribute favored by *Bais Shammai,* so too, in the Future World the universe will eventually revert to its original design. It is only in This World — the period between the original plan for the universe and its ultimate destiny — that we follow the opinion of *Bais Hillel,* based on *middas ha'rachamim.* (*Korach* 5647)

◆§ Timtum halev (stifling one's potential for greatness)

כי עיקר הגאולה הוא בנפש שמתקשר בגוף וצריך גאולה שיוכל להיות נפרד מהגשמיות ... וע״י מינים מטמאים ונטמתם וכ׳ שא״י להפרד הנפש מהגוף ע״י איסורים הללו

When referring to the prohibition against eating *sheratzim, vermin,* the Torah draws an association between the Exodus and the prohibition of eating non-kosher food. וְלֹא תְטַמְּאוּ אֶת נַפְשֹׁתֵיכֶם ... כִּי אֲנִי ה׳ הַמַּעֲלֶה אֶתְכֶם מֵאֶרֶץ מִצְרַיִם, *Do not defile yourself because I am Hashem Who elevated you from the land of Egypt* (*Vayikra* 11:44). By exploring the association between *yetzias Mitzrayim* and *maachlos asuros (prohibited food),* we may also derive a better understanding of the concept of *timtum haleiv, the (spiritual) blockage* associated with non-kosher food.

Firstly, let us expand upon the concept of *geulah, redemption.* From the Torah's perspective, we are not merely referring to *physical* liberation, but equally so to the redemption of the *soul* from its virtual incarceration by the body and its physical cravings. By abstaining from non-kosher food, we allow the soul to emerge as a force in its own right. In the Torah's words, *I elevated you through the liberation from Egypt* so that your soul could become totally free of its dependence upon the body. However, by partaking of non-kosher food we expose ourselves to *timtum haleiv, the blocking of our heart* so that our soul is no longer free to render its own moral decisions. (*Shemini* 5647)

Sparks of the luchos

ואיתא שברי לוחות מונחים בארון והיינו כי בודאי המתנה שנתן לנו הקב״ה לא הי׳ למגן ואם כי אז לא היינו ראויים לקבל ונגנז בארון ונשברו הלוחות לתקן כל אלה השברים ... כמו פיזור וגלות בנ״י בכל הארצות השברים כדי ללקוט אתו השברים

We conclude this introductory section discussing popular themes that permeate the *Sfas Emes'* writings with a particularly esoteric and beautiful *dvar Torah.*

While we always assume that the first *luchos* lost all of their significance when Moshe shattered them, in reality, the Tablets never disappeared. On the contrary, the letters engraved on the Tablets and the Tablets themselves simply separated. As our Rabbis relate, the letters are פּוֹרְחוֹת בָּאֲוִיר, *flying in the atmosphere,* almost being preserved as a trust for the Jewish people till they are ready to benefit from their luminescence, while the body of the *luchos* (in the form of fragmented pieces) were placed in the Ark alongside the Second Tablets. Moreover, it is well-known that any Divine Gift, once granted is never taken back. Thus, we may deduce that while the physical form of the *luchos* may have changed, their impact remains if we only exploit their potential.

While no longer existing as an intact cohesive unit, the fragments of the *luchos* on earth and their counterpart, the letters of the tablets in heaven, remain available to us — if we only take advantage of the opportunity. If we merit, we can benefit greatly from the spiritual aura of the *luchos* — both the fragments on earth and their spiritual presence in heaven, the letters themselves. In fact, one of the functions of the *galus* is for *Klal Yisrael* to elicit the aura of the *luchos* (by evoking the *kedushah* latent in the letters or in the fragments) . Wherever the Jewish people may have been dispersed, they may enjoy the opportunity to elicit some of the *kedushah* of the first *luchos* which were also dispersed throughout the universe.

The *Ari Hakadosh* suggested that Aharon's words to the mob seeking to erect the Golden Calf, חג לה׳ מחר, tomorrow will be a holiday for Hashem (*Shemos* 32:5), may be literally true. While the 17th of Tammuz, the day when the *egel* was erected was then a tragic moment of epic proportions, tomorrow, in the Future World, once we have elicited and been influenced by the full impact of the *luchos'* remains, this day will become a *yom tov.* אמן כן יהי רצון. *(Adapted from Balak 5648, 5660).*

The Gift of Shabbos

לָדַעַת כִּי אֲנִי ה' מְקַדִּשְׁכֶם

To inform [you] that I am H*ASHEM*, *Who makes you holy* (*Shemos* 31:13).

אָמַר לוֹ הַקָּדוֹשׁ בָּרוּךְ הוּא לְמֹשֶׁה מֹשֶׁה מַתָּנָה טוֹבָה יֵשׁ לִי בְּבֵית גְּנָזַי וְשַׁבָּת שְׁמָהּ וַאֲנִי מְבַקֵּשׁ לִיתְּנָהּ לְיִשְׂרָאֵל לֵךְ וְהוֹדִיעַ אוֹתָם

H*ASHEM said to Moshe, "I have a good gift in My treasure house, whose name is Shabbos. I seek to grant this gift to the Jewish people. Go and tell them [about the significance of this gift]"* (*Beitzah* 16a).

In this chapter we will explore the nature of the gift of Shabbos and consider why Hashem insisted that Moshe inform *Klal Yisrael* in advance about His intention to grant them the Shabbos. We will also attempt to understand the relationship between Shabbos and Hashem's treasure house. In addition, the expression, "I seek to grant this gift" — implying that Hashem had not yet given the Shabbos to *Klal Yisrael* -- requires clarification. The foregoing conversation between Hashem and Moshe occurred immediately *before* the sin of the Golden Calf. By that time, Hashem had already spoken to *Klal Yisrael* about Shabbos on several occasions (e.g. at Marah, in reference to the manna, and most notably at Sinai).

The Nature Of The Gift Of Shabbos

Divine Assistance to Achieve Beyond Our Capabilities

והנה שבת הוא מתנה מן השמים וכן אמרו מתנה טובה יש לי. ונח הי׳ בחי׳ שבת כמ״ש בזוה״ק. את האלהים התהלך נח והוא בחי׳ השבת שנק׳ מתנה כדאיתא בזוה״ק נח הוא שבת. ואפשר שזה הוא משרז״ל עלה במחשבה לבראו במדה״ד וראה שאין העולם מתקיים ושיתף עמו מדה״ר. היינו הסיוע שיש בש״ק שנמשך הארה מעולם העליון למעלה מן הטבע. דהא כתיב ברא אלקים משמע שבמעשה נברא במדה״ד רק שהקדים ושיתף מדה״ר היינו שיהי׳ דביקות להבריאה בעולם הרחמים והוא על ידי השבת ולכן אמר השבת כ׳ אלה תולדות כו׳ ביום ברוא ה׳ אלקים.

The *Zohar,* by stating that Noach represents the same attributes as Shabbos, offers a clue as to the nature of the gift of Shabbos. Despite his many virtues (refer to *Bereishis* 6:9 where Noach is described as a תָּמִים, a perfect individual), Noach was unable to achieve his full potential without Divine assistance. In fact, the *pasuk* (ibid.) describing his many virtues, which concludes, אֶת הָאֱלֹהִים הִתְהַלֶּךְ נֹחַ, *Noach walked with God,* means that with Hashem's active assistance, Noach was able to attain his full potential. By equating Noach and Shabbos, the *Zohar* is suggesting that every Shabbos, we receive an infusion of סייעתא דשמיא, Divine Help, enabling us to reach spiritual levels unattainable during the week. Just as Noach, despite all his personal achievements, was ultimately the beneficiary of an unrequited Divine gift (see *Bereishis* 6:8, וְנֹחַ מָצָא חֵן בְּעֵינֵי ה׳, *Noach found favor in* HASHEM*'s eyes*), so too, despite the levels of *kedushah* achieved during the six weekdays, we require the Divine gift of Shabbos to attain our full potential.

The Divine gift of Shabbos is as ancient as the universe itself and is rooted in the very first Shabbos. As *Rashi* (ibid. 1:1) writes, Hashem originally intended to create the universe with the Attribute of Justice (מִדַּת הַדִּין) and only later "diluted" this Attribute with an infusion of Divine Mercy (מִדַּת הָרַחֲמִים).[1] This mitigation of strict justice with an outpouring of mercy occurred on the first Shabbos of Creation — and in fact, is the first manifestation of the gift of Shabbos. It is entirely appropriate that the expression עֲשׂוֹת ה׳ אֱלֹהִים (*Bereishis* 2:4) describing Creation as a synthesis of the Attribute of Justice (אֱלֹהִים) and Mercy (ה׳) is first utilized after discussion of the first Shabbos. This outpouring of Divine Mercy is among the greatest blessings of Shabbos. When the Torah writes, וַיְבָרֶךְ אֱלֹהִים אֶת יוֹם הַשְּׁבִיעִי, *God blessed the seventh day* (ibid. 2:3), it may be referring to the ability of the deserving Jew, who by virtue of his efforts at self-perfection all week long is able to come closer to Hashem every Shabbos and benefit from the outpouring of Divine assistance granted to us every Shabbos.

(Adapted from *Noach* 5647, 5663)

אח״כ וממדבר מתנה שיש ג״כ דרך אפילו לאינם ראוים שיזכו במתנת לזו הבאר ע״י הביטול שנמשכים אחר הקב״ה באמונה. וזה מי הבאר שנפתח בע״ש כי שבת נק׳ מתנה טובה ולכן בשבת הביטול כל מלאכות בחי׳ ממדבר מתנה כנ״ל.

To corroborate this approach to the concept of מַתְּנַת שַׁבָּת (the gift of Shabbos), let us consider other instances in which the Torah utilizes the term מַתָּנָה. For example, when describing the Well of Miriam — which homiletically refers to the wellsprings of Torah (refer to *Avos* 6:2) — the Torah describes its water as וּמִמִּדְבָּר מַתָּנָה, *a gift from the Wilderness* (*Bamidbar* 21:18). Even those individuals who lack the necessary prerequisites to acquire Torah knowledge (refer to *Pirkei Avos* 6:6 which states 48 desirable attributes which are conducive to acquiring Torah knowledge) are still able to benefit from a Divine grant of Torah as long as they remain steadfastly loyal to Hashem. According to *Chazal* the

1. The Creation was with *middas hadin* and Hashem then connected that *briah* to the attribute of *rachamim* through Shabbos, which in a sense was a different world. Shabbos was the conduit to *rachamim*, and this in itself is a *matanah*.

most opportune time to partake of this Divine gift of Torah knowledge is on Shabbos, a day which itself is described as a מַתָּנָה טוֹבָה, a great Divine gift. As *Pirkei Avos* (5:8) reminds us, the opening of the well (פִּי הַבְּאֵר) of Torah was created on *erev Shabbos* at twilight, so that everyone — even those who ordinarily would be unable to enjoy the Torah's treasures — may partake of its pristine waters on Shabbos.

(*Chukas* 5652)

אבל הכהן כתיב עבודת מתנה אתן.

Similarly, the Divine Service performed exclusively by the *Kohen Gadol* is described as עֲבֹדַת מַתָּנָה, *a service that is a* [Divine] *gift* (*Bamidbar* 18:7). Despite the many personal attributes of the *Kohen Gadol*, his ability to successfully enter the Holy of Holies and not only persevere but also act as an effective emissary of *Klal Yisrael* is entirely due to a gift of Hashem. (*Korach* 5657)

והוא ג"כ בחי' השבת שכ' בזוה"ק דקרח חלק על שבת. דשבת הוא מתנה טובה.

Utilizing this approach (which emphasizes that Hashem granted us Shabbos as a gift because of our immense potential rather than because of our merit) we can appreciate why, according to the *Zohar*, Korach not only disputed the legitimacy of Moshe and Aharon's mission but also disputed the concept of *shemiras Shabbos*. From Korach's perspective, merit, rather than Divine approval, was the sole criterion in choosing a Jewish leader. He reasoned (incorrectly) that he and his adherents merited the positions currently held by Moshe and Aharon. Not only was Korach's assertion a tragically flawed one — that he deserved to lead *Klal Yisrael* more than Moshe and Aharon — but also the very notion that Jewish leaders are selected on the basis of self-proclaimed qualifications without first receiving Hashem's approval is totally without foundation. This can be demonstrated from the institution of Shabbos itself, which was given to *Klal Yisrael* as a gift despite our total lack of merit. Well aware of the nature of the gift of Shabbos and perceiving this concept as a threat to his contention that merit alone mattered in the designation of Jewish leaders, Korach began to question the significance of Shabbos. (*Korach* 5659)

ובעבדת קרח כתיב קרואי מועד היא הקדושה שבישראל כמ״ש מקדש ישראל והזמנים ישראל דקדשינהו לזמנים. אבל קדושת השבת למעלה מזה. ולכן איתא דקרח חלק על שבת.

It is significant that Korach chose to question the institution of Shabbos rather than the Festivals. In fact, his followers are described as קְרִאֵי מוֹעֵד, *those summoned for meeting* (*Bamidbar* 16:2), which may be homiletically interpreted as "those individuals who proclaimed the Festivals." Korach had no reason to dispute the existence of *Yamim Tovim* — sacred occasions that could be observed once the *Sanhedrin*, representing the best of *Klal Yisrael*, proclaimed the New Moon. If anything, the existence of *Yamim Tovim* appeared, at first, to support his notion that only merit should be considered in the selection of Jewish leaders. However, Shabbos, which arrives regularly at the conclusion of every week without any involvement of *Klal Yisrael*, proves that Hashem's designation of a certain time as being sacred — or of certain individuals as being *Klal Yisrael's* leaders — was all that mattered. (*Korach* 5661)

❧ Earning the Gift of Shabbos

וכמ״ש במ״א בשם מו״ז ז״ל פי׳ יגעתי ומצאתי תאמין שע״י היגיעה זוכין למציאה ומתנה. שאינו בשכל אנושי. רק שהקדוש ברוך הוא נותן התורה במתנה כפי יגיעת האדם. וכן הוא בחי׳ שבת מתנה טובה ...

Refer to our previous *dvar Torah* stating that, every Shabbos, Hashem grants us the gift of being able to achieve spiritual levels well beyond our ordinary capabilities. However, the gift of Shabbos is not entirely unrequited, nor is it enjoyed in equal measure by all of its recipients. Just as the great Divine gift of Torah can only be attained through a combination of two factors — effort (יְגִיעָה), followed by Hashem's Assistance — enabling us to comprehend what we attempted to master through own efforts (a concept known as סִיַּיעְתָּא דִשְׁמַיָּא, refer to *Megillah* 6a), so too, the gift of Shabbos is enjoyed in direct proportion to our efforts during the weekdays to attain the highest possible spiritual level.

(*Ki Sisa* 5654)

⌁§ The Gift of Retention

שבת שנאמר עליו מתנה טובה יש לי
הוא הסיוע מלמעלה והוא בחי׳ זכור.

To appreciate better the nature of Shabbos' gift and especially the relationship that we have established between the gift of Shabbos and that of Torah (refer to the previous *dvar Torah*), we recall the Gemara's (*Megillah* 6a) suggestion that while the ability to cogently analyze the teachings of the Talmud may be attained through diligent study, retention of one's learning, on the other hand, is nothing but a Divine gift. The Shabbos is aptly described in the *Aseres HaDibros* with the term זָכוֹר, *remember*! There is no occasion better suited to recall the teachings of Torah (and the very purpose of our existence in This World) than Shabbos. (Adapted from *Ki Sisa* 5657)

⌁§ Returning to the Spirit of the First *Luchos*

וצריך שלא להיות דבר המפסיק בינתים. וסמיך לפרשת השבת
ויתן אל משה. כמ״ש במ״א כי בשבת יש הארה מלוחות
הראשונים. שזהו כוחו של מרע״ה דכ׳ ומשה יקח את האהל.
ובשבת מחזירן לבנ״י ומתחדש אותו הארה בכל שבת.

In the previous passage, we suggested that an important aspect of the gift of Shabbos is the renewed ability to retain the Torah that one has studied. This concept can be best appreciated by recalling that every Shabbos, Hashem restores *Klal Yisrael* to the exalted level that it enjoyed at the time that it received the First *Luchos*. At that moment, we enjoyed so close a relationship with Hashem that every word that we heard from Him would never be forgotten. The gift of retention was particularly true for the first two of the *Aseres HaDibros* which the Jewish people heard directly from Hashem (cf. *Yalkut Shir HaShirim* 981). It was only when *Klal Yisrael* requested that Moshe act as an intermediary to convey the remaining commandments to them that the Jewish people began to forget the Torah that they had learned. In later generations, *Klal*

Yisrael reflect wistfully and long for the day when they will receive the Torah *directly* from Hashem as they did, at first, at Sinai. In the words of *Shir HaShirim* (1:2), יִשָּׁקֵנִי מִנְּשִׁיקוֹת פִּיהוּ, *Let Him kiss me from the kisses of His Mouth* (i.e., let us receive the Torah *directly* from Hashem). According to the *Midrash* (ibid.), Hashem responds that this intimate bond that once existed at Sinai can not be enjoyed again in This World. Not until we merit the treasures of *Olam Haba* can *Klal Yisrael* regain the intimacy it enjoyed at the giving of the First *Luchos*.

On Shabbos, a day described as a microcosm of the World to Come (refer to the following *dvar Torah*), *Klal Yisrael* is able to some extent to return to the lofty levels that it attained at Sinai before sinning, and even to the relationship that it enjoyed with Hashem when it listened to the first two commandments. Just as those first two precepts outlining the fundamentals tenets of Torah, אָנֹכִי ה׳ אֱלֹהֶיךָ, *I am* HASHEM, *your God*, were never forgotten, so too, the Torah that we study every Shabbos will always be retained.

As further support for our thesis that the intimacy (and retention level) of the First *Luchos* is restored every Shabbos, we note the juxtaposition of the passage describing Shabbos (concluding with the term וַיִּנָּפַשׁ, *Shemos* 31:16-17) and the next *pasuk* beginning with the phrase, וַיִּתֵּן אֶל מֹשֶׁה, *He gave Moshe* (31:18), which describes the majestic state of the First *Luchos* as they existed just prior to the sin of the *Egel* (Golden Calf). We may deduce from the association between these two *pesukim* that every Shabbos the aura and full glory of the First *Luchos* is enjoyed by *Klal Yisrael*. (*Ki Sisa* 5661)

◆§ The Gift of Torah

ובאמת זה מתנת אלקים כמ״ש ישמח משה במתנת חלקו. וכ׳ ויתן אל משה. והטעם כי עבד נאמן קראת לו. כי התחתונים מקבלים הכל ע״י יסורים כדאיתא ג׳ מתנות כו׳ וכולן ע״י יסורים. כי צריכין נסיון להיות מוכנים לקבל. אבל משה עבד נאמן לכן ניתן לו במתנה. ובשבת קודש מחזיר מרע״ה לבני ישראל ג״כ זה הכח. לכן נק׳ שבת מתנה טובה.

Extending the theme of our previous *dvar Torah* in which we stated that every Shabbos *Klal Yisrael* returns to the exalted spiritual level that it attained at *Matan Torah* (when it received the First *Luchos*), we suggest that on Shabbos we ascend to the lofty heights of resembling *malachim.* Just as at the time of the giving of the Torah, the Jewish people had transcended *all* of the physical limitations of mortals and were poised to become virtually on the level of *malachim* (cf. *Tehillim* 82:6, אֲנִי אָמַרְתִּי אֱלֹהִים אַתֶּם וּבְנֵי עֶלְיוֹן כֻּלְּכֶם, *I said* (at the time of *Matan Torah*) *that you are angels and children of the Most High*), so too, every Shabbos when we return to the levels we achieved at *Matan Torah* we assume again angel-like characteristics.

The most significant ramification of becoming *malachim* again is our renewed ability to study Torah. Whereas all week long, true greatness in Torah can only be achieved through enormous effort, a concept known as יִסוּרִין, on Shabbos we may study Torah with the same proficiency as *malachim.* This new-found capacity for greatness in Torah that is enjoyed by *Klal Yisrael* every Shabbos is a Divine gift given to us every Shabbos.

What better Divine emissary to bestow this gift upon *Klal Yisrael* than Moshe *Rabbeinu* – since he had not participated in the sin of the *Egel* -- who never lost the angel-like status that all of us once enjoyed at Sinai. For Moshe, Torah was *always* a Divine gift, to be enjoyed without first suffering יִסוּרִין. As we pray every Shabbos, יִשְׂמַח מֹשֶׁה בְּמַתְּנַת חֶלְקוֹ, *Moshe will rejoice in the gift that is his portion.* On Shabbos, the day when we approach the level of *kedushah* that we enjoyed at Sinai, Moshe shares with us his gift of studying Torah without struggle. What greater gift can there be than our renewed capacity to study Torah without facing the limitations that confront us all week. (*Vayikra* 5655)

◆§ A Taste of *Olam Haba*

כי הנה בכל דבר יש סוד ה׳ כמ״ש גדולים מעשה ה׳ אך שנתלבש בבחי׳ עולם שנה נפש והסוד הוא כמ״ש רב טובך אשר צפנת ליריאיך והוא בחי׳ עוה״ב וע״ז אמרו חז״ל כל ישראל יש להם חלק לעוה״ב. אך הברית הוא התקשרות ודעת שיוכלו הצדיקים להתדבק בזה הסוד בהיותם בעוה״ז ג״כ. וזהו ובריתו להודיעם. ואמרו חז״ל על שבת מתנה טובה יש לי לך והודיעם כו׳

Chazal (*Berachos* 57b) describe Shabbos as a microcosm of the World to Come (*Olam Haba*). It would seem that the spiritual treasures of *Olam Haba* are far too profound for anyone in *Olam Hazeh* to appreciate.

Only through the gift of Shabbos are we able to grasp a small measure of the *kedushah* of *Olam Haba* every week.

In order to comprehend how Shabbos facilitates *Klal Yisrael's* exposure to the spiritual light of *Olam Haba,* we recall that the *Shechinah* is present in every aspect of every life. While the full Presence of Hashem can only be perceived in the luminescence of the Future World, even in This World any Jew can potentially feel His Presence. As stated in the introduction to *Pirkei Avos*: כָּל יִשְׂרָאֵל יֵשׁ לָהֶם חֵלֶק לָעוֹלָם הַבָּא, *"Every Jew has a share* (even while in This World) *in* appreciating and perceiving the spiritual treasures of *Olam Haba."* However, we are generally unable to elicit the Presence of Hashem because of the many factors that serve to veil His immense *kedushah.* For example, the *Shechinah* is often obscured in the very universe that Hashem created. An individual could actually become so absorbed in the natural world that he may overlook its Creator. Similarly, the human body with its intricate physiology can actually lead its beholder to develop a closer relationship with Hashem, or (ח״ו) to become so absorbed in its many details that one forgets the Creator of man. Finally, the daily routine of time — day following day seemingly without interruption — can actually alienate the unthinking and superficial individual from Hashem Who created time. To prevent His Creations from losing sight of their Creator because of their obsession with the splendid universe that He created (or the perfect human body or the infinite symmetry of the march of time), Hashem ensured that there would always be a reminder of His Presence in each of these three entities. Specifically, the rite of circumcision reminds mortals of the immense *kedushah* that the human body can potentially achieve by controlling one's passions. The most sacred site on earth, the *Beis HaMikdash,* where *Klal Yisrael* could perceive the *Shechinah* with unusual clarity, helped ensure that we would never lose sight of the *Shechinah* in this world that He had created. Finally, it is through the Divine gift of Shabbos that the humdrum routine of daily life never allows us to forget the Creator of the Universe. It is only through Shabbos — a day devoted to remembering the Creator — that we recall that the very institution of time was set into motion by Hashem. Once we become prescient enough to detect the *Shechinah* in the universe that He created, we are prepared to bask in the preview of *Olam Haba* that we enjoy every Shabbos.[1]

1. Indeed, *Olam Haba* is described as the perfect ambiance in which the *tzaddikim,* liberated from all the material burdens of This World, repose in the Presence of Hashem (*Berachos* 17a, צדיקים יושבין ונהנין מזיו השכינה).

This theme — that Hashem has preserved in His universe several potent reminders of His Presence — is succinctly stated by David in the following words of *Tehillim* (25:14): סוֹד ה׳ לִירֵאָיו וּבְרִיתוֹ לְהוֹדִיעָם — "The Hidden Presence of Hashem is only perceived by those who fear Him. However, through His covenant (those *mitzvos* that are identified as a ברית, *covenant* (*milah*, the *Beis HaMikdash*, and Shabbos) it is possible to know Him" (to detect His Presence even in *Olam Hazeh*). (*Vayeira* 5647)

והענין דשבת הוא מעין עוה״ב כי בעוה״ז חסר השלימות כמ״ש במ״א. ולכן שבת צריך הכנה. וזהו הודעה שקודם המתנה להיות מוכן לקבל הארה שלמעלה מעוה״ז.

Assuming that Shabbos is a foretaste of the Future World, we can appreciate why Hashem insisted that Moshe *Rabbeinu* inform *Klal Yisrael* (לֵךְ וְהוֹדִיעַ אוֹתָם) in advance about Shabbos. In order to benefit from a gift that is so removed from anything that we have in This World, it is necessary to be properly prepared. (*Pinchas* 5646)

Preparing for *Olam Haba*

הענין כי שבת הוא מעין עוה״ב. יום שכולו שבת. והשי״ת שנתן לנו המצות נתן לנו הכלים וההכנות שנוכל לקבל המצות. והשבת הוא הידיעה והתקשרות להכין להשגת עוה״ב יום שכולו שבת.

In the previous *dvar Torah* we suggested that those who truly benefit from Shabbos are able to perceive the Presence of Hashem and to enjoy a foretaste of *Olam Haba* while still in This World. Extending this approach, we propose that not only do we enjoy a scintilla of the Future World every Shabbos, but also that the gift of Shabbos — which itself is a taste of *Olam Haba* — prepares us for the *Olam Haba* which we will eventually enjoy. In this light the expression, לֵךְ וְהוֹדִיעַ אוֹתָם, *Go and tell them* (refer to the Introduction to this chapter for the full text of this *Chazal*), does not necessarily mean that Moshe should inform *Klal Yisrael* about Shabbos, rather that the Shabbos itself is a form of יְדִיעָה, as we shall elaborate. Assuming that the term יָדַע connotes far more than intellectual knowledge, and also implies an emotional bond and connection (a concept known as הִתְקַשְׁרוּת), we may interpret Hashem's request, לֵךְ וְהוֹדִיעַ אוֹתָם, as a plea to Moshe that he provide the Jewish people with the קֶשֶׁר — the close emotional bond with Hashem while we are still living in This World — which will enable us to eventually appreciate *Olam Haba*. The most effective means of developing this bond is the Shabbos day, which itself is a minute indication of the spiritual closeness and awesome *kedushah* of *Olam Haba*. By Moshe revealing and teaching (לֵךְ וְהוֹדִיעַ) *Klal Yisrael* about the profundities of the institution of Shabbos they will be brought closer to Hashem. The *pasuk* cited in the Introduction, לָדַעַת כִּי אֲנִי ה' מְקַדִּשְׁכֶם — *To inform [you] that I am* HASHEM*, Who makes you holy*, assumes an additional meaning in light of this approach. By observing the Shabbos you will attain the closeness to Hashem (known as דַּעַת) which will lead to the time in the World to Come — the time described by *Chazal* as a day that is "completely Shabbos" — when your entire personality will be sanctified by Him. (*Ki Sisa* 5642)

⚜ Returning to One's Roots

אבל באמת זו המתנה טובה נתן לנו הקב"ה מעולם. והוא דכתיב ויפח באפיו נשמת חיים. רק השבת הוא הדעת שנוכל להוציא מכח אל הפועל להתדבק בזו המתנה. וזהו שנאמר לדעת. צריך להודיע.

It seems surprising that the supernatural *kedushah* of Shabbos, which seemingly transcends all limitations of time, should be confined to one day. In response, we suggest that the underlying purpose of Shabbos — and the primary effect of the gift of Shabbos — is not limited to Shabbos itself, but rather enables us to return to our sacred roots. By observing Shabbos, we are able to surmount all of the temporal limitations of *Olam Hazeh* and retrieve the gifts that Hashem gave to *Klal Yisrael*. Firstly, the soul itself, originally implanted by Hashem into the first man — and frequently corrupted by our misguided behavior — is purified every Shabbos. On Shabbos, described by Hashem as a time of דַּעַת, a time in which we reconnect with Hashem (refer to the previous *dvar Torah*), we are able to overcome all of the obstacles placed in the way of our spiritual development all week and to restore the original pure *neshamah* implanted by Hashem. (*Sfas Emes* explains the concept of דַּעַת as the ability to appreciate and develop an association which can be internalized from the gift of Shabbos.)

According to *Pirkei Avos* (3:18) there are two other gifts — the Torah itself and the special relationship with *Klal Yisrael* and Hashem — that are characterized by the term דַעַת (נוֹדַעַת). Every Shabbos, the day blessed with the gift of דַעַת, we not only reestablish our ties with Hashem but we also benefit again from Hashem's original gifts — the Divine Soul, His loving relationship with His People, and the Torah.

(*Toldos* 5653)

◆§ Hashem's Gift of Peace

בענין הבארות. פי׳ מו״ז ז״ל עשק ושטנה בחי׳ עבודת ימי המעשה. ואח״כ זוכין בשבת לרחובות. והיא מתנה מן השמים כדאיתא על שבת מתנה טובה יש לי כו׳. ונראה שלכך אין עליו מריבה וערעורים. הואיל ובא הכח עליון. וז״ש כי עתה הרחיב ה׳ לנו. וכ״כ על שבת פורס סוכת שלום עלינו. ואין מגע נכרי בשבת. והיא בחי׳ הנשמה יתירה שבא בשבת סיוע משורש הנשמה.

To appreciate another dimension of the gift of Shabbos, we recall the constant friction between Yitzchak's shepherds and the shepherds of Gerar, with each party contending that they were the legitimate owners of certain wells. Whereas in the first two instances, the Torah reports that they quarreled, when Yitzchak's servants discovered a viable source of water a third time, the shepherds of Gerar did not offer any opposition. To commemorate the turmoil and controversy that marked the first two wells, they were named appropriately, עֵשֶׂק (referring to the bitter quarrel that ensued between Yitzchak's shepherds and those of Gerar) and שִׂטְנָה (accusations alluding to the many unjust accusations made by Yitzchak's enemies). However, the third well, whose status was beyond question, was aptly named רְחבוֹת (related to רחב, to widen or expand) in tribute to Hashem Who allowed Yitzchak to now live in an open environment, free of controversy, and to prosper during his stay in Gerar. We may draw an analogy between these three wells and the relationship between the weekdays and Shabbos. Just as Yitzchak's search for water was at first beset by controversy, so too, during the first six days of the week we need to contend with adversaries, such as the *yetzer hara* or the dedicated enemies of *Klal Yisrael* whose sole motive is to antagonize the Jewish people. However, the analogy closes on a happier note. Just as Yitzchak eventually enjoyed a harmonious relationship with his neighbors, so too, on Shabbos, the day when we are blessed with the נְשָׁמָה יְתֵירָה, Hashem grants us His gift of peace — enabling us to develop a harmonious relationship with all of our adversaries. As we pray every Friday evening, פּוֹרֵשׂ סֻכַּת שָׁלוֹם, [HASHEM] *spreads His canopy of peace [over us].* On this hallowed day, *Klal Yisrael* is able to rest peacefully, knowing that with Hashem's help, it will prevail over any force that jeopardizes its viability. (Adapted from *Toldos* 5645)

◈ The Gift of *Sheleimus* (Perfection)

וכן שבת נק׳ שלום והיא מתנה טובה כמ״ש פורס סוכת שלום עלינו כי בכל ימי המעשה נברא דבר מיוחד וכמו כן כל הברואים יש בכל אחד ענין מיוחד לא ראי זה כראי זו ולכן נחסר השלימות. ושבת הוא כלל כל הבריאה.

Refer to our previous *dvar Torah* in which we suggested that *Klal Yisrael* benefits from the סֻכַּת שָׁלוֹם, *canopy of peace* — the harmonious environment which Hashem shares with us every Shabbos. Here we will expand on this theme and suggest that the expression סֻכַּת שָׁלוֹם refers not only to the peaceful ambiance permeating the Shabbos day but also to the fundamental concept of שְׁלֵימוּת, *perfection,* that can be achieved on *Shabbos Kodesh.*

In This World, perfection — the ability to perceive the entire universe created by Hashem as an integrated whole — is difficult to achieve. Already at the time of Creation, Hashem determined to bring into being a universe consisting of many different entities, each created independently of all other aspects of His Creation. To underscore the unique purpose assigned to every component of His Universe, Hashem designated a distinct time for the creation of each aspect of *Maaseh Bereishis* (e.g., the heavenly luminaries were created on the fourth day, fish and fowl on the fifth day of Creation, etc.). It is only on Shabbos, when Hashem had completed the process of Creation, that the perfect harmony of the entire universe working together to fulfill the Divine Will can be appreciated.

When the first man was created, Hashem intended that this perfect individual – created directly by Him, whose soul was implanted by the *Shechinah* Himself – should contain within himself the outstanding characteristics of *all* of Hashem's creations. Had Adam not sinned, he would have been the embodiment of *sheleimus* – one individual whose personality integrated *every* aspect of Creation. Just as the dazzling light of Creation – which Hashem hid from our view – enabled its beneficiaries to perceive the entire universe as an integrated whole, so too, on the Shabbos, when we bask again in that light (refer to our *dvar Torah* entitled "The First Light of Creation"), we are able to perceive the בְּרִיאָה (Creation) from an entirely different perspective – globally rather than limited to our ordinary narrow focus. What greater gift than *sheleimus* – the ability to transcend all of our limitations and appreciate the universe in its totality, a gift we enjoy every Shabbos.

(*Pinchas* 5659)

◆§ The Source of All of Hashem's Gifts

כמה מתנות טובות נתן הבורא ית' לבנ"י ותורה וכל המצות. אכן האמת השבת הוא כולל הכל. והוא השורש של כל המתנות טובות. והשורש נקרא בית גנזיו של הקב"ה.

Shabbos is by no means Hashem's only gift to *Klal Yisrael.* The Torah itself and all of its *mitzvos* are priceless Divine gifts. In fact, Hashem is perpetually showering us with His manifold kindnesses. Our very lives and our *parnassah* are nothing but a gift from Hashem. However, by stating that the Shabbos can be found in Hashem's treasure house, a place that is so remote and hidden from our perception, *Chazal* are alluding to the source of all our Divine gifts, the Shabbos. All of the other gifts that sustain and nurture us are derived from the gift of Shabbos. By using the term מַתָּנָה, derived from נוֹתֵן, *to give, Chazal* are implying that Shabbos, more than other Divine gifts, is transmitted from Hashem *directly* to *Klal Yisrael* (as taken from the Giver's "Hand" and placed directly into the recipient's hand). All of His other gifts are derived from Shabbos. (*Ki Sisa* 5640)

☙ A New Gift Every Shabbos

ובכל שבת ושבת הוא מתנה חדשה. וצריך האדם להכין עצמו ולידע להיות מוכן לקבל מתנה זו ... וצריכין לקנות שביתה זו בכניסת היום והוא ענין קבלת שבת.

In the passage introducing this section we cited a *Gemara* which discusses Hashem's desire to grant the Shabbos to the Jewish people. From the *pasuk* utilized by the Gemara (*Shemos* 31:13), it is clear that this Divine wish was voiced shortly before the sin of the Golden Calf. It seems surprising that, at that comparatively late stage — many weeks after the *mitzvah* of Shabbos was incorporated into the *Aseres HaDibros* and several months after *Klal Yisrael* had first learned about Shabbos when they received the manna — Hashem should imply that He had not yet granted the Shabbos to the people. Apparently the Gemara is not referring to the original *mitzvah* of Shabbos which had already been granted to *Klal Yisrael* on numerous occasions, but rather to the *renewal* of Shabbos every week. Hashem not only granted *Klal Yisrael* the Shabbos, but also endowed *Klal Yisrael* with the capacity to be worthy recipients and absorb and integrate the many gifts that He presents us with every Shabbos. Hashem, Whose capacity to bless *Klal Yisrael* knows no limits, showers His people with new gifts (material and spiritual) every Shabbos, which we readily accept.

This theme is reflected in the plea repeated throughout the Shabbos *davening*, וְהַנְחִילֵנוּ ה׳ אֱלֹהֵינוּ שַׁבָּת קָדְשֶׁךָ, *Allow us to inherit Your sacred (day) of Shabbos.* This passage does not refer to the concept of Shabbos itself which was bequeathed to *Klal Yisrael* at Sinai, but rather to the gift of Shabbos — the weekly renewal of our bond with the Shabbos day. By voicing this prayer, we are asking Hashem that we be fully prepared to absorb the unique blessings that He bestows upon *Klal Yisrael* every Shabbos. With this approach, we can appreciate the concept of the *Kabbalos Shabbos* service — a collection of prayers in which we become the conduits that "accept" the Shabbos. While the institution of Shabbos is not in any way contingent upon our acceptance, by taking it upon ourselves every Friday night, *Klal Yisrael* is preparing itself to absorb the extraordinary *berachos* that each new Shabbos brings. The theme of *Kabbalos Shabbos* — preparing to accept each Shabbos' special *berachos* — is also reflected in *Halachah*. In certain instances, we are required to actually delineate a certain place where we intend to be at the beginning of Shabbos. (For example, an individual is permitted — under certain extenuating circumstances — to sail on Shabbos if had arrived on the ship prior to Shabbos and remained there at Shabbos' inception. Likewise, an individual may walk an additional two-thousand cubits beyond the ordinarily permissible limit on Shabbos [a concept known as תְּחוּם שַׁבָּת] if at the beginning of Shabbos he stood at a point located two-thousand cubits from the city limits.) By designating a site where one begins the Shabbos, one is not merely passively waiting for Shabbos to arrive but, instead, is actually demonstrating that he is anticipating the arrival of another Shabbos with its own set of *berachos*. (*Vayishlach* 5648)

◆§ The Gift of *Erev Shabbos*

והלא במרה איפקדו אשבת ... אבל נראה כי עתה ניתן להם במתנה השבת ... הנותן בעין יפה נותן ... הוא הכנת יום הששי שיש אז הארות לבנ״י שיוכלו לקבל השבת.

To appreciate another dimension of the "gift of Shabbos," we recall the question of *Tosafos* (*Shabbos* 87b ד״ה כאשר) who wonders why the Gemara (ibid.) describes the Shabbos observed by the Jewish people after the arrival of the manna as the "first Shabbos" when, in reality, *Klal Yis-rael* had already been informed about Shabbos at the time when Moshe sweetened the bitter waters of Marah (refer to *Rashi, Shemos* 15:25).

In response, we distinguish between the *mitzvah* of Shabbos which, indeed, was related to the Jewish people at an earlier time, and the *gift* of Shabbos which was granted to us in conjunction with the manna. Our approach is supported by the manner in which the Torah describes Shabbos in the context of the manna: רְאוּ כִּי ה׳ נֹתֵן לָכֶם הַשַּׁבָּת, *Behold, HASHEM has given you the* [*gift of*] *Shabbos* (*Shemos* 16:29).

Let us explore further the parameters of the gift of Shabbos granted to *Klal Yisrael* along with the manna. According to the Talmud (*Bava Basra* 65a), anyone who grants a gift does so generously (בְּעַיִן יָפָה). In particular, the Gemara rules that an individual who receives a well as a gift is also entitled to a path leading to the well. Applying the Gemara's ruling homiletically, we suggest that when Hashem offered *Klal Yisrael* the gift of Shabbos, He simultaneously presented them with the path that is necessary for the gift's proper utilization — *erev Shabbos.* By preparing on *erev Shabbos* — the pathway to *Shabbos Kodesh* — one can fully exploit the Shabbos.

Our entire approach can be corroborated by the sequence of *pesukim* used by Moshe *Rabbeinu* to describe the gift of Shabbos — *Behold, HASHEM has given you the Shabbos. Therefore, He has given you on the sixth day a double portion [of manna]* (*Shemos* 16:29). (*Beshalach* 5643)

The Gift of *Achdus* (Unity)

ונראה דזה סמיכות פרשת מועדות למצות ונקדשתי. דהנה מקראי קודש הם בכח התאחדות בנ״י. וכמו כן שבת איתא דהוא רזא דאחד. אך השבת היא מתנה לבנ״י דקדושת שבת מביא האחדות בלבות בנ״י. כיון דקדושה ויחוד תלוין זה בזה.

Every Shabbos, *Klal Yisrael* is blessed with the gift of *achdus* (unity) which enables us to unite for the purpose of consecrating Hashem's Name (קִדּוּשׁ הַשֵּׁם). As we recite immediately before *Borchu* on Friday night, בְּרָזָא דְאֶחָד— on Shabbos Hashem grants us the ability to unite as one nation to proclaim His Oneness.

Our contention that Shabbos is conducive to unity among *Klal Yisrael* is corroborated by the juxtaposition of the *mitzvah* of Shabbos (and *Yom Tov*) to that of *Kiddush Hashem* (sanctifying Hashem's Name). Just as *Kiddush Hashem* is best performed in the presence of ten Jews united for a common purpose (generally to recite *Kedushah* or *Kaddish*), so too, the Shabbos itself serves to unify *Klal Yisrael* so that it can better sanctify His Name. (*Emor* 5655)

Testifying to Hashem's Existence

וגם בשבת דהוא סהדותא חל על בנ״י נשמה יתירה שיוכלו להכיר ולהעיד על הבורא ית״ש. ועל שבת אמרו מתנה טובה יש לי בבית גנזי.

What greater gift is there than being able to bear witness by our actions and words to the existence of Hashem and to His creation of heaven and earth? By ceasing all of our mundane workday activity in favor of the overwhelming spirituality of *Shabbos Kodesh,* we are testifying to the Divine origins of the Universe. For *Klal Yisrael,* testifying about *HaKadosh Baruch Hu* is not merely a requirement but rather a great privilege. We rejoice that Hashem granted us the capacity to be able to testify through word and deed about the *Shechinah.*

(*Shavuos* 5661)

Hashem's Treasure House

In this section we will not only discuss alternative interpretations of the expression בְּבֵית גְּנָזַי, *My treasure house,* but also attempt to discover the true source and origin of the "gift of Shabbos."

◆§ Enjoying the First Light of Creation

והוא מאור שנברא בראשון שהי׳ מאיר מסוף העולם ועד סופו וגנזו הקב״ה לצדיקים. ובשבת יש הארה מאור הגנוז וכמ״ש מתנה טובה יש לי כו׳ ולכן נקרא מתנה שאין זה בכח מעשה האדם.

We *recall* Rashi's comment (*Bereishis* 1:4) that the light created by Hashem on the first day of Creation was far too spiritually imposing for mankind's use. Consequently, Hashem "hid" this dazzling light from mankind's view, preserving it in His "treasure house" for the *tzaddikim's* use in the World to Come. Every Shabbos, a day which is a microcosm of *Olam Haba,* Hashem shares a few rays of the Hidden Light of Creation — described by *Chazal* as אוֹר הַגָּנוּז — from His storehouse of spiritual treasures with *Klal Yisrael.* What greater gift than for the Jewish people to merit every Shabbos, during their sojourn in This World, a treasure ordinarily reserved for *tzaddikim* in the World to Come? (Refer to our earlier comment that every Shabbos is an unrequited gift granted by Hashem to *Klal Yisrael* — despite our evident unworthiness of this priceless Divine present.) (*Chanukah* 5654)

☙ A Taste of the Manna

והנה בשבת מתגלה מתנה טובה שבבית גנזיו. ולכן יתכן לומר כי בעונג שבת יש בו מעין טעמי המן. כי צנצנת המן נגנז היינו שנשאר ממנו משהו לדורות ואחז״ל לא ניתנה תורה אלא לאוכלי המן. ולכן אכלו בנ״י המן לחם שמלאכי השרת אוכלים אותו. והוא מזון מצד הנשמה. ומכל אלה התיקונים נשאר גם לדורות. כמ״ש הלא העומר כו׳ למשמרת. ונראה שבש״ק שהוא מתנה טובה מבית גנזיו. מתגלה בעונג שבת הארה מן המן כי הנשמה יתירה שיורדת בש״ק. בזכותה מתגלה מזון הנשמה בשבת קודש.

Perhaps the expression בְּבֵית גְּנָזַי (My treasure house) refers to a remnant of the manna's taste that is enjoyed by the Jewish people every Shabbos. When Hashem instructed Moshe (*Shemos* 16:32-34) to place a container of manna in the Holy of Holies (קֹדֶשׁ קָדָשִׁים) beside the *Aron* – a site that contains His most revered treasures – His intention was to preserve the memory of the manna for future generations that were long removed from the time when the manna descended, not to hide the manna from public view. Every Shabbos when *Klal Yisrael* joyously partakes of its meals (a *mitzvah* known as עוֹנֶג שַׁבָּת), Hashem allows us (if we are deserving) to perceive, in some fashion, a sample of the manna's flavor in our ordinary food. This sacred taste is truly a Divine gift presented to us every Shabbos directly from Hashem's treasure house. (Adapted from *Beshalach* 5647)

Expanding on the above theme, we recall that the manna which had always nurtured the angels (refer to *Yoma* 75b) essentially sustained the *neshamah* of *Klal Yisrael*. The extraordinary generation of Jews that had participated in *Yetzias Mitzrayim* eventually achieved such an exalted spiritual level that it could persevere on the basis of its *neshamah*, without resorting much to the mundane food that is ordinarily necessary for the body's continued survival. While we are certainly far removed from the exalted level of *kedushah* enjoyed by the Wilderness Generation (דּוֹר הַמִּדְבָּר), nonetheless, every Shabbos, when our lives are graced by the hallowed presence of the *neshamah yeseirah*, we too, in some small measure, are able to "partake" of the taste of the manna while enjoying our Shabbos meals. (*Beshalach* 5647, 5650)

◆§ A Place Untainted by Sin

נראה שבשבת לא קלקלו ע״י החטא. ולכך שבת מעין עוה״ב כמ״ש בלוחות ראשונות חירות כו׳. וכן איתא בחטא אדם הראשון שנתקבל בשבת. ג״כ כנ״ל שלא הגיע החטא לבחי׳ שבת. והוא ששבת במקום הגניזה כמ״ש מתנה טובה יש לי בבית גנזי כו׳ וכיון שנגנז לא הגיע קלקול החטא לשבת כנ״ל.

Perhaps the term בְּבֵית גְּנָזַי (My treasure house) refers to the lofty level achieved by the Jewish people before they sinned by erecting the Golden Calf. As a result of this tragic error, the Jewish people descended precipitously from the lofty heights that they had reached when proclaiming נַעֲשֶׂה וְנִשְׁמַע (*we will do and we will listen*) at *Har Sinai.* However, on Shabbos, a day so hallowed and so removed from This World — as indicated by the concept of Hashem's treasure house, implying eternal value that cannot be corrupted by our sins — we are able to return, albeit temporarily, to the great heights that we once attained.

We find an earlier precedent for the eternal purity of Shabbos, to the extent that its *kedushah* remains intact despite our sins, from the pardon that Adam was granted on Shabbos. Despite having sinned on *erev Shabbos,* the first man's expulsion order requiring him to immediately depart *Gan Eden* was suspended until Shabbos ended and Adam's *teshuvah* from his grievous sin was accepted on Shabbos. (*Ki Sisa* 5632)

מול זה בא הבורא ית׳ לנחם את בני ישראל ולהגיד להם כי השבת עודנו ניתן להם כמו שהי׳ להם מקודם החטא. וז״ש מתנה טובה יש לי בבית גנזי שהשבת ניתן לבנ״י באופן שהוא גנוז שלא יכול להיות מגע סט״א כלל.

With this approach, we may also resolve the question that we raised in a previous *dvar Torah* (entitled, "A New Gift Every Shabbos"), that despite the implication of this *Midrash* that Hashem was revealing to *Klal Yisrael* the *mitzvah* of Shabbos for the first time, in reality, this *mitzvah* had already been taught to *Klal Yisrael* on numerous other occasions — especially at Sinai and Marah. Based on the foregoing assertion that every Shabbos *Klal Yisrael* returns to the lofty heights they achieved at Sinai by proclaiming *Naaseh V'Nishma,* we suggest that Hashem is informing the Jewish people that Shabbos remains in its pure, intact form — untainted by the sin of the Golden Calf.[1]

(*Ki Sisa* 5637)

לכן בש״ק מחזירין לישראל הכתרים ... דאיתא שבת ניתן בצינעא. והוא עצמו כנ״ל כי לוחות הראשונות שהיו בפרהסיא ובקולות שלט בהן עין רע.

א״כ הם ב׳ מפתחות שבת הוא מפתח שנפתח מן השמים כמ״ש מתנה טובה יש לי בבית גנזי שנפתח שער הפנימית.

When the Jewish people accepted the Torah, they were each granted two crowns, corresponding to their dual pledge of *Naaseh* and *Nishma.* As a result of attaining such an unprecedented spiritual level, *Klal Yisrael* was able to bask in the light that Hashem had hidden from mankind (אוֹר הַגָּנוּז) and reserved for the *tzaddikim* since the beginning of time. While their participation in the sin of the Golden Calf had the effect of no longer allowing them to bask in this glorious light [refer to *Shemos* 33:6, וַיִּתְנַצְּלוּ בְנֵי יִשְׂרָאֵל אֶת עֶדְיָם מֵהַר חוֹרֵב, *The Jewish people removed the crowns they had received at Mount Chorev (Sinai)*"], on Shabbos, *Klal Yisrael* is able to enjoy this treasure again. Our *aveiros* can only "tarnish" those aspects of Jewish life that are observed by *Klal Yisrael* while they are residing in This World (i.e. their quality of observance of virtually every *mitzvah* was affected by the grievous sin of the *Egel*). However, on Shabbos which is insulated (גָּנוּז, *hidden*) and protected from the corrupting influences of *Olam Hazeh,* we are able to return to the lofty heights that we enjoyed before sinning. On Shabbos, we once again enjoy the first light of Creation. This same theme that *Klal Yisrael* is able to return to its previous levels of *kedushah* every Shabbos is alluded to by Yechezkel (46:1) who refers to the "gates of the inner courtyard" of the Third (future) *Beis HaMikdash* which will be

1. Just as a precious jewel is preserved in a treasure house to maintain its luster, so too, the Shabbos was preserved in Hashem's treasure house to sustain and protect it.

opened every Shabbos – a reference not only to the dimensions of the future *Beis HaMikdash* but also to the inner gates of spirituality that we enjoy on Shabbos. (*Ki Sisa* 5642, Adapted from *Masei* 5659)

☙ Unlike Anything in the Natural World

פי׳ בבית גנזי שהיא למעלה מהטבע ואינה יכולה להתגלות בעולם כמו אור הגנוז לצדיקים ... וכמו כן מלאכת המשכן. אם כי הוא שורש מעשה בראשית וכמו בששת ימי בראשית נחלבש האור בטבע ואח״כ קדושת שבת למעלה מהתלבשות הטבע. כמו כן בכל מלאכת המשכן נתלבש האור במלאכה זו והשבת למעלה מזה ההתלבשות.

The term בְּבֵית גְּנָזַי (My treasure house) conveys the image of a totally inaccessible vault holding treasures too valuable to be exposed to human contact. Nothing better describes the Shabbos than the metaphor, treasure house. On one hand, Shabbos is the source of all of the week's *berachos* (similar to a vault containing valued treasures). On the other hand, none of the *berachos* that *Klal Yisrael* enjoys during the week – which are derived from Shabbos – are visible on Shabbos. On this day, saturated with spirituality, anything that is even remotely associated with the natural world (טֶבַע) has no place. Thus, the manna, despite its Heavenly Source (refer to *Yoma* 75b describing the manna as the sustenance of angels), and since it appeared to *Klal Yisrael* in a natural form, cannot descend on Shabbos, a day that is totally spiritual. Similarly, the construction of the *Mishkan* had to yield to the *kedushah* of Shabbos. Despite its intense sanctity, the *Mishkan* was still a part of This World. *Chazal* compare the *Mishkan* and the *melachos* associated with its construction to the Creation of Heaven and Earth. Just as Hashem rested on Shabbos from the process of imbuing this world with His *kedushah*, so too, the *Mishkan* – a place on earth where His *kedushah* is most manifest – must yield to the supernatural nature of *Shabbos Kodesh.*

Perhaps the closest analogy to the immense supernatural *kedushah* of Shabbos, described by *Chazal* as emanating from Hashem's remote treasure house, is the hidden light of Creation (אוֹר הַגָּנוּז), deemed to be too sacred to be enjoyed by mortals in This World. In fact, *Chazal* describe both concepts — the treasure house containing the gift of Shabbos and the First Light of Creation — with the same term גָנוּז, hidden from the perspective of the natural world.

In light of this discussion the choice of Moshe as the agent to convey the gift of Shabbos to *Klal Yisrael* can be particularly appreciated (refer to the introduction to this essay). What better bearer of this supernatural gift than Moshe, who personified the essence of Torah which of course transcends all natural limitations. (*Ki Sisa* 5658)

☙ A Source of *Yiras Shamayim* (Fear of Hashem)

ויראת ה׳ נק׳ אוצר ורמז ליום השבת ירא שבת שאחז״ל עליו מתנה טובה בבית גנזי.

By using the term בְּבֵית גְּנָזַי (My treasure house), which usually connotes something that is so valuable that it is carefully guarded, to describe the heavenly source of the gift of Shabbos which Hashem shares with *Klal Yisrael, Chazal* are alluding to the ultimate purpose of all the other *middos* (character traits) that we seek to develop to attain *yiras Shamayim,* fear of Hashem — an attribute that is enhanced as a result of *shemiras Shabbos.* As Yeshayah (33:6) notes, after enumerating many of the virtues that are critical for the Torah Jew's success (such as wisdom and faith), יִרְאַת ה׳ הִיא אוֹצָרוֹ, Fear of Hashem enjoys the unique distinction of being "lodged" in Hashem's treasure house. In fact, all other attributes that we seek to acquire (love of Hashem, the *middah* of *emes,* truth) are simply means of ultimately acquiring the most significant of all *middos* — fear of Hashem. *Chazal* (*Shabbos* 31b) expand upon this theme by describing the individual who, despite acquiring a great deal of Torah knowledge, lacks *yiras Shamayim,* as one who erects a gate for a home that he does not own. So too, Torah study should lead to increased fear of Hashem, which is the true objective of Jewish life. One who has not attained *yiras Shamayim,* fear of Hashem, despite his other positive attributes, possesses the means to the objective without any credible opportunity to reach the objective.

By rearranging the letters that comprise the first word of the Torah, בְּרֵאשִׁית, to read יָרֵא שַׁבָּת – fear of Hashem is enhanced through observance of Shabbos (as the *Zohar HaKadosh* explains) – we adduce additional support for our assertion that Shabbos is a priceless opportunity to nurture that most valuable of all *middos*, יִרְאַת שָׁמַיִם.

(*Shemini* 5654)

◆§ The Gift of *Ahavas Hashem* (Loving Hashem)

וזה פורס סוכת שלום כי בשבת יש הארה מהשי״ת במתנה בלי עבודה כמ״ש מתנה גנוזה כו׳ ... שע״י היראה יזכה אדם לבחי׳ אהבה הבא במתנה ... וכן בכל ש״ק שזוכין ע״י ימי העבודה לבחי׳ שבת שהוא אהבה ומתנה מהשי״ת כנ״ל.

In the previous *dvar Torah,* we emphasized that by observing Shabbos we can enhance our *yiras Shamayim.* Besides being a source of fear of Hashem, the Shabbos day may also help bring its observers closer to the exalted level of אַהֲבַת ה׳, *love of Hashem.* As we pray every Friday night, פּוֹרֵשׂ סֻכַּת שָׁלוֹם, on Shabbos Hashem spreads His canopy of peace over *Klal Yisrael.* Whereas all week long it is difficult to attain our spiritual objectives without us first taking the initiative, on Shabbos, a day which itself is a Divine gift, we benefit from Hashem's blessings which He bestows upon us from His Heavenly abode. Just as a canopy shields those who are standing below it from harm, so too, on Shabbos Hashem protects *Klal Yisrael* and showers us with His Heavenly blessings. (Refer to our previous *dvar Torah* entitled, "Divine Assistance to Achieve Beyond Our Capabilities," p. 16.)

However, the gift of Shabbos, enabling us to reach spiritual levels unattainable (and unimaginable) during the week (and especially the *middah* of *ahavas Hashem*), is directly proportionate to the effort that we invest into our Divine service during the week days. In particular, the *yiras Shamayim* that we demonstrate during the week is particularly conducive to reaching our objective of receiving a Divine "infusion" of *ahavas Hashem* every Shabbos. (Adapted from *Pinchas* 5631)

ואהבת את ה״א מקשים החוקרים איך שייך ציווי על אהבה. אבל באמת היא מתנה מן השמים וע״י תורה ומצות יכולין לעורר האהבה. והנה שבת נק׳ מתנת טובה כי השבת הוא בחי׳ אהבה.

By assuming that our *ahavas Hashem* is greatly facilitated by Hashem's magnanimity – whereby He grants us the capacity to love Him – we can respond effectively to the question raised by some philosophers who wonder about the feasibility of observing the Biblical Commandment of וְאָהַבְתָּ אֵת ה׳ אֱלֹהֶיךָ, *You should love* H*ASHEM*, *your God* (*Devarim* 6:5). "How can any one be *commanded* to love?" However, in light of our approach that *ahavas Hashem* is made possible through a Divine gift of the capacity to love – a gift which is often granted to us on Shabbos as reward for the great spiritual strides that we accomplished during the week – this question is readily resolved. Just as Hashem insists that we love Him, He also facilitates this process by granting us the capacity for *ahavas Hashem*. (*Va'eschanan* 5648)

The Berachah of Shabbos

◆§ Heavenly Source of Everything on Earth

ויכל ביום השי׳ כי השבת היא המודדת חיות לכל הדברים כי ויכל הוא מדה כמש״כ וכל בשליש. בת יכיל. והשבת עצמה אין לה מדה וגבול כי היא מתוספות שלמעלה מהטבע כמש״כ לעיל כמה פעמים ... והשבת הוא עיקר הברכה ע״י שהוא שורש הכל כנ״ל והיא נותנת ברכה לכל הימים דכ׳ ויברך את יום השביעי פי׳ שכל הברכות הם האמצעות השבת. וכ׳ והחיות רצוא ושוב. וכמ״כ בכל הימים כשבא שבת שבים כל הברואים לשורשם ועי״ז יש חיות חדש כמש״כ הספר אוה״ח שבכל שבת יש חיות חדש על ו׳ הימים.

By blessing Shabbos, as it says, וַיְבָרֶךְ אֱלֹהִים אֶת יוֹם הַשְּׁבִיעִי, *And God blessed the seventh day* (*Bereishis* 2:3), Hashem is not only blessing *this* day but through the Shabbos is blessing the entire week. In fact, the term אֶת יוֹם הַשְּׁבִיעִי may be interpreted as meaning *with the seventh day*.[1] In other words, it is through the seventh day that the entire week is blessed.

1. The word אֶת is interpreted elsewhere in *Tanach* as *with*, i.e., אֶת יַעֲקֹב אִישׁ וּבֵיתוֹ, *with Jacob, each man and his household* (*Shemos* 1:1).

To comprehend why the entire week derives its *berachos* through the Shabbos, we suggest that Shabbos is the root (*shoresh*) of all Creation. This approach is supported by the term וַיְכַל, *completed*, as the *pasuk* states, וַיְכַל אֱלֹהִים בַּיּוֹם הַשְּׁבִיעִי מְלַאכְתּוֹ אֲשֶׁר עָשָׂה, which is usually translated: *God completed on the seventh day His work that He had performed* (ibid. 2:2). However, the term וַיְכַל may also mean, *he measured.*[1] In other words, on the first Shabbos, Hashem apportioned to each day its proper place and share of Hashem's blessings that it would enjoy. Once we have established that Shabbos is the source (and the "lifeblood") of each day of Creation, we can appreciate why it is also the source of all *berachos.* Assuming that everything that exists derives its *berachah* from its origin (*shoresh*), we deduce that if its origin is blessed, it too will be blessed.

Using this approach, we can gain additional comprehension of the *pasuk*, וְהַחַיּוֹת רָצוֹא וָשׁוֹב, *The Chayos ran to and fro* (*Yechezkel* 1:14), which may be (homiletically) translated, "all that lives, flows and then returns." The days of the week, after running their full course (רָצוֹא) return (וָשׁוֹב) to their sacred roots, the Shabbos, from which they attain their renewed strength. (Adapted from *Bereishis* 5640)

והנה בשבת קודש יורד הקדושה לאדם. והוא ישלח עזרך מקודש. הנשמה יתירה. ומציון יסעדך הוא ימי המעשה. ושבת נותן ברכה לכל הימים א״כ יש בקדושת השבת שורש לכל הימים ואותן השרשים הם הציונים שיש בהם רמזים לקדושה אף שאינו קודש ממש. וכ׳ ויברך ויקדש בשבת. גוף הקדושה של שבת וגם להיות ברכה ושישפיעו ממנו נחלים מיוחדים לכל הימים.

The relationship between the blessings of Shabbos and the entire week may be alluded to in the renowned *pasuk*, יִשְׁלַח עֶזְרְךָ מִקֹּדֶשׁ וּמִצִּיּוֹן יִסְעָדֶךָּ, *May He dispatch your help from the Sanctuary, and support you from Zion* (*Tehillim* 20:3). This may be translated homiletically: "He will send your assistance from the sacred source (מִקֹּדֶשׁ) of the Shabbos day, and He will sustain you even from the allusions to *kedushah*[2] (the

1. Refer to *Yeshayahu* (40:12), וְכָל בַּשָּׁלִשׁ, *He measures*, and to *Melachim I* (7:26), בַּת יָכִיל, *it measured [two thousand] bas*, for similar usage of this term.

2. According to this approach, the term צִיּוֹן is interpreted as if read as צִיּוּן, a marker or allusion to another concept — הַצִּיבִי לָךְ צִיֻּנִים, *Make road markers for yourself* (*Yirmiyah* 31:20).

weekdays whose own *kedushah* is rooted in Shabbos, and great as it is, is only an allusion to the enormous *kedushah* of Shabbos). Returning to the first reference to Shabbos' *berachos* (in the וַיְכֻלּוּ portion) describing the conclusion of Creation, the Torah not only emphasizes that Hashem sanctified the Shabbos in its own right (וַיְקַדֵּשׁ אֹתוֹ), but it also says, וַיְבָרֶךְ אֱלֹהִים אֶת יוֹם הַשְּׁבִיעִי, *God blessed the seventh day,* allowing it to become a source of blessing for the entire week.[1] (*Kedoshim* 5637)

⌘ The Original Source

נקראים ימי המעשה חפנים שהם השפע בא ע״י שליח מדרגא לדרגא אחרת ... ומ״מ עיקר השכר מקבלין ע״י העמל בימי המעשה וז״ש ממלא חפנים שבכח ימי המעשה זוכין אל השבת.

To appreciate yet another dimension of Shabbos' *berachah,* we refer to the following *pasuk* in *Koheles* (4:6) and, in particular, to *Chazal's* interpretation of this verse. Shlomo *HaMelech* writes, טוֹב מְלֹא כַף נָחַת מִמְּלֹא חָפְנַיִם עָמָל וּרְעוּת רוּחַ, *Better one handful (spoon) of satisfaction than two fistfuls of toil and frustration.* Whereas on Shabbos, Hashem's *berachos* are derived from "the hand / spoon" (the Heavenly Source through which He dispenses His bounty), during the week it may appear as if the *berachos* are diverted through a secondary source ("two fistfuls") before being enjoyed by *Klal Yisrael.*[2]

On the other hand, without the effort invested in *avodas Hashem* during the week, we would never be able to earn the *berachos* of Shabbos. This thought may also be derived from the foregoing *pasuk* — it is good when the "spoonful of satisfaction" (enjoyed on Shabbos) is derived from the hard work of the week.

(Adapted from *Vayikra* 5649)

1. Seemingly, the *Sfas Emes* interprets the term *berachah* (בְּרָכָה) as being related to *bereichah* (בְּרֵכָה), *a pool* or *stream of water.* Just as a stream of water has many tributaries linking the original source to remote locations, so too, the blessings of Shabbos sustain each of the weekdays.

2. All *berachos* emanate from Hashem, but they are channeled through various natural forces and *malachim* until we can benefit from them.

◆§ The Divine Spark

כי בכל דבר יש נקודה חיות מחי החיים. רק שבעוה״ז נסתר הפנימיות. וזה המבוקש מאיש ישראל לעורר ולגלות הפנימיות שיש בכל דבר ע״י המצות. שבכל מעשה נמצא ממצות הש״י עשה או ל״ת. וע״י המצות מקרב כל המעשים אליו ית׳... וכן בשבת כ׳ ויברך כי זה היא בחי׳ שבת להיבטל ולהיכלל לנקודה הנ״ל ושם שורה ברכה.

Expanding upon the theme of the previous *dvar Torah* that the *berachos* of Shabbos emananate *directly* from Hashem without being first channeled through any intermediate source, we suggest that there is a Divine Spark latent in every material entity. By observing the *mitzvos* associated with that particular entity we are able to evoke that Spark. What greater *berachah* than to elicit the spiritual core that is contained within everything material. This thought is transmitted by Moshe *Rabbeinu* when he defines Hashem's blessings in the following manner: אֶת הַבְּרָכָה אֲשֶׁר תִּשְׁמְעוּ, *The blessing that you hearken* (*Devarim* 11:27) — the blessing occurs when you hear and evoke the presence of Hashem in everything. The *pasuk* continues, אֶל מִצְוֹת ה׳ אֱלֹהֵיכֶם, *to the commandments of Hashem, your God* — through the *mitzvos* of Hashem you will be able to find the source of all *berachos* and the Divine Spark in everything. There is hardly an object that can not be utilized for a sacred purpose, and in particular for either a positive or negative commandment.

By blessing the Shabbos day, Hashem is indicating that there is no more opportune time to find His presence in the material world (and to negate everything material to its spark of spirituality than by dedicating it to a sacred purpose) than Shabbos. On Shabbos, we are able to detect the spark of *kedushah* in the most secular of entities and that is another aspect of this day's *berachos*. (*Re'eh* 5631)

◆§ The Ideal Receptacle for the Week's *Berachos*

דאיתא אין כלי מחזיק ברכה אלא שלום. ולכן כתיב ויברך כו׳ את יום השביעי שבת שנקרא שלום ומיני׳ מתברכין כל שיתא יומין. ולא נתן הקב״ה ברכת כל יום ביומו כי אין מחזיקין ברכה ימי המעשה רק השבת שהוא שלום.

By recalling the renowned statement of the *Zohar* that *Shalom* is one of the names of Shabbos (refer to our chapters on *Shabbos Shalom, Menuchah*), we can further appreciate why Shabbos is the source of all of the week's *berachos*. There is a well-known *Chazal* (*Uktzin* 3:12) stating that *shalom*, the attribute of peace, is the perfect receptacle for Hashem's *berachos*. How appropriate that Hashem chose Shabbos, the day that is imbued with the attribute of *shalom*, as the vehicle through which the entire week is blessed. (*Naso* 5650)

◆§ The Dual *Berachah* (Connecting to Our Heavenly Roots)

כי החלק שלמטה אינו שלום רק בהתדבקות לחלק שלמעלה ... וזה הי׳ תכלית כל המשכן להיות כלי מחזיק ברכה לכל העולם. וכמו כן שבת בזמן שכל מעשי׳ כפולים. לחם משנה. מזמור שיר.

It is noteworthy that many aspects of Shabbos are presented to us in a "double" form. Thus, the *mitzvah* of *Zachor* is complemented with *Shamor*, we partake of a *lechem mishneh* (double bread — refer to our chapter on the topic) and even Psalm 92, dedicated to Shabbos, commences with a double expression of praise, מִזְמוֹר שִׁיר לְיוֹם הַשַּׁבָּת. This is no mere coincidence, but on the contrary, alludes to the very nature of Shabbos' *berachos*.

To appreciate the relationship between the *berachos* of Shabbos and the dual nature of many of its *mitzvos*, we recall that every entity that exists here on earth in a physical sense also enjoys spiritual "roots" in heaven. With this in mind, we suggest that it is the individual or entity that is able to successfully link his physical presence on earth with his heavenly spiritual roots that is the true source of *berachah*. The fact that many of Shabbos' *mitzvos* are observed in a "double" fashion suggests that Shabbos, more than any other day, is the ideal opportunity to link together our physical presence with our spiritual roots in heaven. Consequently, it is Shabbos, the day when we return to our spiritual antecedents, that is the source of blessings for the entire week.[1] (*Pekudei* 5660)

1. Just as Shabbos, the day when our physical presence is linked to its spiritual roots, is the prime source of *berachos*, so too, Moshe *Rabbeinu*, who perhaps more than any other individual

‍◆ Reaching Our Potential (Finding Our Place)

וזה ענין שבת קודש עי"ז שורה ברכה ומעורר חיות פנימי שבו ונמצא שאין האדם מוסיף דבר רק שמעמיד עצמו במקומו כנ"ל.

Whereas in previous *divrei Torah* we have focused largely on the impact of Shabbos' *berachos* on the universe itself, we now suggest that one of the greatest *berachos* of Shabbos is the innate capacity of every individual to find his true "place" (niche) on that blessed day.

To appreciate this aspect of Shabbos' *berachos* we need to consider what Hashem desires from us. Rather than insist that we attempt to attain strides well beyond our capacity, Hashem prefers that we simply "find our place" and use the enormous potential that He has granted us to its fullest.[1] To be most effective,this process must be implemented in the proper sequence — first finding our unique niche and only then meriting to reach our potential. It is only by first finding ourselves that we can consequently exploit our abilities to serve Hashem and study His Torah.[2]

No better opportunity exists for any individual to find his true place in life than on Shabbos.[3] Once this initial task has been achieved, then the true measure of Shabbos' *berachos* may be enjoyed as we begin to evoke our latent talents. (*Haazinu* 5634)

was able to "connect" to his heavenly roots, was best suited to bless the Jewish people. Similarly, the *Beis HaMikdash*, the site on earth most closely linked to its heavenly cognate (*Beis HaMikdash Shel Maalah*), is a potent source of *berachah* for the entire universe.

It is also noteworthy that just as Shabbos, the source of *berachah* for the entire week, is observed through many *mitzvos* which have a "dual identity" (refer to the text), so too, the *Mishkan*, the source of *berachah* for the entire universe, is described by the Torah in double terms (cf. *Shemos* 38:21, הַמִּשְׁכָּן מִשְׁכַּן). Similarly, Moshe *Rabbeinu*, who more than any other individual was a source of blessing for his people, enjoyed a distinction that was virtually unique. When Hashem appears to him in the burning bush, He repeats Moshe's name (cf. *Shemos* 3:4, מֹשֶׁה מֹשֶׁה).

1. As we recite in the daily *tefillah*, נְשָׁמָה שֶׁנָּתַתָּ בִּי טְהוֹרָה הִיא, *the soul that You placed in me is pure* (and enjoys enormous potential to serve You).

2. The renowned statement of *Chazal*, יָגַעְתִּי וּמָצָאתִי, *I have labored and I found* (*Megillah* 6b), may be understood in this light. By endeavoring to locate one's niche, one will then undoubtedly find enormous reserves of hidden potential .

3. AUTHOR'S NOTE: The *pasuk*, אַל יֵצֵא אִישׁ מִמְּקֹמוֹ בַּיּוֹם הַשְּׁבִיעִי, *Let no man leave his place on the seventh day* (*Shemos* 16:29) (a verse frequently discussed in the writings of *Sfas Emes*), may in a homiletical sense support this interpretation of Shabbos' *berachos*. No one needs to leave his place on Shabbos. On the contrary, it is by finding one's proper niche that one can fully exploit Shabbos' *berachos*.

◆§ The Weekly Renewal of *Berachos*

ז״ש ויתן לך האלקים וכו׳ חז״ל יתן ויחזור ויתן. והוא הברכה המתחדש תמיד מלמעלה. ובפרטות הוא בש״ק דמיני׳ מתברכין כל שיתא יומין. ובכל שבת ושבת מתחדש שורש הברכה.

Whereas in the previous *dvar Torah* we demonstrated that Shabbos is the source of all *berachos,* we now extend this analysis and suggest that every Shabbos these *berachos* are renewed for the week that lies ahead. The concept that *berachos* are not a one-time phenomenon but rather are constantly renewed is best illustrated by the words which introduce Yitzchak's *berachos* to Yaakov: וְיִתֶּן לְךָ הָאֱלֹהִים, *And may God give you* (*Bereishis* 27:28). By prefacing his *berachos* with the seemingly redundant term "and," Yitzchak is emphasizing that Hashem's *berachos* are constantly being replenished. As *Rashi* notes, יתן ויחזור ויתן, *he will give and give again* – continuously.

While this concept pertains to all of Hashem's *berachos,* it is particularly true in reference to the *berachos* of Shabbos which is the *shoresh* of the entire week's blessings. Despite His munificent blessings on the first Shabbos, Hashem renews His *berachos* every Shabbos for the week ahead. (*Toldos* 5653)

וחז״ל דרשו היום סתם על שבת דכתי׳ בי׳ ג״פ היום. וי״ל כנ״ל כי התחדשות הבריאה בשבת עלי׳ לכל הברואים לשורשם והיא בחי׳ היום כנ״ל. ולכן ויברך אלקים כו׳ יום השביעי כו׳.

To corroborate our contention that it is on Shabbos that Hashem renews the universe and infuses it with enough life to last another week, we turn to the beginning of *Parashas Re'eh,* where the Torah says, רְאֵה אָנֹכִי נֹתֵן לִפְנֵיכֶם הַיּוֹם בְּרָכָה וּקְלָלָה, *See, I place before you today a blessing and a curse* (*Devarim* 11:26). While the term הַיּוֹם, *today,* may refer to every day (suggesting that Hashem renews the universe and its many blessings every day), it particularly alludes to the Shabbos day which is described three times in the same *pasuk* (cf. *Shemos* 16:25) as הַיּוֹם, *the day.* It is on Shabbos, the ultimate and greatest of days, and the root of all *berachos,* that Hashem blesses and renews His universe.

In fact, in the first instance when the Torah describes the blessings of Shabbos it writes, וַיְבָרֶךְ אֱלֹהִים אֶת יוֹם הַשְּׁבִיעִי, *God blessed the seventh day*, implying that it is this greatest of days (יום) that is the source of all renewal and blessings. (*Re'eh* 5634)

◆§ *Berachos* in the Future World

וכן תמיד בכל שבת נמשך ברכה מהשורש טוב הצפון לששת ימים. עד שיזכו בנ״י במעשיהם לעשות כל השבת ברית עולם. פי׳ להמשיך כל ההארה מהשורש לכל הימים ואז יהי׳ יום שכולו שבת לעתיד לבוא ב״ב אמן.

Whereas in This World, we receive a sufficient outpouring of Divine blessings every Shabbos to sustain us during the week ahead, and then we renew our *berachos* the following Shabbos for yet another week, eventually we will merit through our *mitzvos* and *maasim tovim* that the entire week will become as great a source (*shoresh*) of *berachos* as Shabbos itself. It is about this blessed time that the Mishnah writes, לְיוֹם שֶׁכֻּלּוֹ שַׁבָּת, *the day that is entirely Shabbos* (*Tamid* 7:4). When the Torah describes Shabbos as being a בְּרִית עוֹלָם, *an eternal covenant* (*Shemos* 31:16), it may be alluding to the time when every weekday will be as potent a source of *berachah* as Shabbos is in This World. What had been a temporary phenomenon, confined to one day each week, will be transformed into a permanent and blessed state of affairs. (*Yisro* 5636)

◆§ Serving to Enhance Hashem's Glory (*Kavod Shamayim*)

ויכלו השמים כו׳ שנעשו כלים. דכל מה שברא הקב״ה לכבודו ברא. ולכן בשבת ע״י הביטול שנתבטל הבריאה אליו ית׳ שלא יהי׳ דבר נפרד בפ״ע. ונתברר שהכל הכנה להיות כלי לתשמישו ית׳ אז שורה ברכה כמאמר חז״ל כלי מחזיק ברכה והוא השבת שנקרא שלום. ומזה מתקיים בכל שבת.

In the first *dvar Torah* of this chapter we suggested that the term וַיְכֻלּוּ may mean to measure. According to the *Midrash* (*Yalkut Bereishis* 16), this term may also be related to כֵּלִים, *vessels.* At the completion of the creation of heaven and earth and with the advent of the first Shabbos, all of heaven and earth was transformed into one unified and harmonious body whose sole function was to serve as a vehicle (כְּלִי) to enhance the glory of Hashem. Whereas during the Six Days of Creation each individual aspect of Creation was featured prominently, once Shabbos arrived, the completed universe shone in its full splendor. With the advent of Shabbos, every individual aspect of the universe coalesced to become part of a united whole and a receptacle for *kavod Shamayim.*

What greater source of *berachah* than being a means of enhancing Hashem's glory. (*Bereishis* 5645)

☙ Demonstrating *Berachah* Through *Oneg Shabbos*

כי מצות עונג שבת הוא לברר כי כל הברכה ופרנסה בימי השבוע הוא רק בכח השבת וזה הג׳ סעודות של שבת וחז״ל דרשו מג״פ היום בפ׳ המן. וגם בפ׳ זו כ׳ ויכל ביום השביעי וישבות ביום השביעי ויברך את יום השביעי ... א״כ מלאכת ימי המעשה מתקשר אז להשבת וזה סעודת ליל שבת. וישבות הוא יום השבת וסעודת שחרית שהיא התעלות הכל אל השורש לכן נאמר בו שביתה ויברך הוא סעודה ג׳ שנותן ברכה על שבת הבאה. ונק׳ סעודות שהם סועדין ומפרנסין לכל הימים.

To demonstrate our full conviction that the entire week's *berachah* stems from Shabbos, we eat three meals and delight in the Shabbos day (refer to our chapters on *Oneg Shabbos* and *Shalosh Seudos).* The term סְעוּדָה [*seudah*], meal, is derived from סעד, meaning to support and sustain. Every Shabbos we voice our firm belief that our *berachos* are made possible and enhanced through Shabbos and by observing the three *seudos.*

More specifically, the first meal held on Friday night, the time when the universe reached completion, celebrates the negation of the individual identities of each of the Six Days of Creation to the Shabbos. Referring to the first meal, the Torah writes וַיְכֻל (*Bereishis* 2:2) — the universe became a כְּלִי, *a receptacle* for Hashem's *kavod.* The second meal of Shabbos, observed by day, reminds us of how the entire universe returns to its sacred roots every Shabbos. As the Torah writes,

וַיִּשְׁבֹּת (ibid.) — the universe ceased to exist by itself (but instead returned to its source). Of the third meal, which is eaten when one week yields to another, the Torah writes, וַיְבָרֶךְ, *and He blessed* (ibid. 2:3). At that time the Shabbos becomes a source of *berachah* for the week ahead.

(*Bereishis* 5645)

◆§ Serving Hashem Without Coercion

כי ימי המעשה הוא שליטת מדריגה על מדריגה שהבריאה כך הי׳ גבוה על גבוה שומר וזה שליט על זה. כענין שאמרו כל עשב יש לו מזל שמכה ואומר לו גדל ונק׳ ימי המעשה מלשון כפי׳ שאין שום אחד רוצה להיות כפוף. ומעשה בראשית הם כולם מהופכים זה מזה ובע״כ עושין כ״א היפוך מהותו והכל עדות על הבורא ית״ש ... השבת ניתן לבני ישראל שהם בני חורין ויכולין לקבל ברכת השבת וז״ש ישמחו במלכותך שומרי שבת.

To appreciate another dimension of Shabbos' *berachah* we turn to one of the first recorded instances where a father blesses some of his children and curses others. Perhaps by carefully studying the distinction between the fate of those who were blessed and those who were cursed, we will obtain additional insight into the nature of a *berachah.*

When Noach seeks to curse Cham and Canaan for their inappropriate behavior, he condemns them to slavery (refer to *Bereishis* 9:25). There is no greater *berachah* than enjoying true freedom, and conversely, no greater curse than to be denied that freedom.

In a similar vein, the distinction between the six days of the week and Shabbos may be one of free-willed Divine service versus coercion. Whereas during the week, all of Hashem's creations may be coerced into following Hashem's design for the universe,[1] on Shabbos, when the full glory of the *Shechinah* is revealed, the entire natural world serves Hashem with free will and a sense of joy. This distinction between the coercion of the six weekdays and Shabbos' free-willed service of Hashem is also reflected in the names used to describe each of these occasions. We typically refer to the weekdays as the שֵׁשֶׁת יְמֵי הַמַּעֲשֶׂה, *the Six Days of Creation.* We suggest that the term מַעֲשֶׂה is related to מְעוּשֶׂה, *to*

1. Cf. *Bereishis Rabbah* 10:6 which states that every blade of grass has a *malach* which compels it to grow.

be coerced,[1] alluding to the fact that Hashem may compel the natural world to fulfill His Will during the weekdays. We may perceive the universe as an elaborate hierarchy in which each level of creation supervises the level immediately below it and ensures that each one performs its designated function.

On Shabbos, however, the universe of its own free will and with great joy serves Hashem. This changed status is also reflected in one of Shabbos' names. According to the *Zohar, Shalom* is one of the names of Shabbos. On this day of peace and harmony, every component of Hashem's universe subordinates its own interests in favor of serving Hashem's design for a unified universe. What greater source of *berachah* than the feeling of *shalom* that reigns every Shabbos. As our Rabbis relate, לֹא מָצָא הקב״ה כְּלִי מַחֲזִיק בְּרָכָה אֶלָּא הַשָּׁלוֹם, *Hashem found no better receptacle for His blessings than the attribute of peace* (*Uktzin* 3:12). What greater *berachah* than serving Hashem without coercion and with great joy, as we recite during the *Musaf* service, יִשְׂמְחוּ בְמַלְכוּתְךָ שׁוֹמְרֵי שַׁבָּת, *They shall rejoice in Your Kingship, those who observe the Sabbath.* On the day when all of nature joyously recognizes Hashem's sovereignty, we, *Klal Yisrael,* observe Shabbos. (*Noach* 5663)

⊰ The All-Inclusive Day (*Kollel*)

כי ארץ ישראל הוא המקום הכולל כל המקומות כדכתיב מציון מכלל יופי ... וכמו כן בנפש המילה שלא נקרא אאע״ה תמים עד שמל. והוא כולל כל הנפש ... וכמו כן שבת כולל כל הזמן וששת ימי המעשה ונקרא שלום ובו הברכה על כל הזמנים. ובאמת בכל דבר יש בו נקודה שמשם נמשך דביקות אל השורש למעלה וזו הנקודה היא גנוז כמ״ש סוד ה׳ ליריאיו לכן סוד המילה ערלה חפיא עליה ונתגלה רק לבני ישראל וכן בש״ק אות היא ביני כו׳ וגוי שמל או ששבת חייב מיתה. וכ״כ מכנף הארץ כו׳. שהיא הנקודה שמכנף ומאחד הכל צבי לצדיק שהוא היסוד עולם והוא נסתר כדכתיב רזי לי כו׳.

The *mekubalim* (scholars of *Kabbalah*) frequently speak of three distinct spheres: זְמַן (*time*), עוֹלָם (*universe/place*) and נֶפֶשׁ (*soul*). Moreover, in

1. Cf. *Gittin* 88b, discussing a גט מעושה, a divorce that is obtained under duress.

each sphere, there is always one element that is particularly significant and embodies everything that lies within that sphere, a concept known as the *kollel* (the all-inclusive factor).

For example, in the realm of place (עוֹלָם), there is no site more sacred and that itself embodies the outstanding feature of every place on earth than *Eretz Yisrael* (and in particular, *the Beis HaMikdash*.) Similarly, in reference to the human personality (נֶפֶשׁ), there is no greater source of *kedushah* than the ritual of *bris milah* which consecrates the entire human body.[1]

In this vein, we suggest that Shabbos is the source of the entire week's *berachah* because it is the day that embodies in itself (or is *kollel*) the *kedushah* of the entire week[2] (in the realm of זְמַן).

Extending this concept even further, we recall that everything that exists on earth has heavenly roots (*shoresh*). We suggest that it is through this *kollel*, this one aspect that symbolizes everything else, that the realms of space, time and the soul can connect to their respective heavenly roots. Just as the universe is linked to its Creator through the *Beis HaMikdash*, and the soul reaches its full spiritual potential through the *bris milah*, so is it through Shabbos that the weekdays in their present physical form can find their roots in heaven.

Drawing the analogy between the realms of *olam*, *zeman* and *nefesh* even further, we suggest that the inner spark in each of these spheres (*Eretz Yisrael*, Shabbos and *bris milah*) is often shrouded and hidden from public view. For example, the *bris milah* is hidden by the *orlah* (foreskin) which must be excised before the *kedushah* of the *bris milah* permeates the entire body. In general, the rite of *bris milah* attests to *Klal Yisrael's* uniqueness. Similarly, the true *kedushah* of the *Beis HaMikdash* is hidden from any mortal and can only be appreciated by Hashem. As *Yeshayahu* (24:16) notes, רָזִי לִי, which may be interpreted, *this secret* (the full effect of the *Beis HaMikdash*) *is Mine*. In a similar vein, the Shabbos is a sign of the extraordinary relationship between *Klal Yisrael* and Hashem, as the Torah states: כִּי אוֹת הִוא בֵּינִי וּבֵינֵיכֶם, *for it is a sign between Me and you* (*Shemos* 31:13).[3] (*Lech Lecha* 5648)

1. In another version the *Sfas Emes* suggests that the *tzaddik* is the exalted soul that embodies everything that the *nefesh* can accomplish. (*Chayei Sarah* 5658)

2. Refer to *Sfas Emes Chayei Sarah* 5658 where he suggests that *Yom Tov* as well as Shabbos may be described as *kollel*, the time that embodies all other time. This is particularly true in light of the *Chazal* (*Zohar, Parashas Emor*) implying that every *Yom Tov* we benefit from the אוֹר הַגָּנוּז, the original dazzling light which permeated the entire universe for the first three days of Creation (see *Rashi, Bereishis* 1:14). Any moment when we enjoy that primeval light is of such significance that it truly embodies the entire concept of *zeman*.

3. Refer to *Sanhedrin* 58b, עכו״ם שֶׁשָּׁבַת חַיָּיב מִיתָה.

◆§ A Double *Berachah*

וכמו בשבת קודש זכור ושמור כאחד וכן שם שבת השבתה ושביתה כמ"ש וישבות ועל שניהם ויברך את יום השביעי.

To appreciate the full impact of Shabbos' *berachah,* let us turn to the first place where this concept is mentioned in the Torah. When discussing the first Shabbos, the Torah says, ... וַיְכַל אֱלֹהִים בַּיּוֹם הַשְּׁבִיעִי ... וַיִּשְׁבֹּת בַּיּוֹם הַשְּׁבִיעִי, *God completed His work by the seventh day ... and He rested on the seventh day* (*Bereishis* 2:2). Apparently, two distinct events occurred on that first Shabbos. On one hand, Hashem completed the process of creation, an *active* event, and subsequently He rested, which is a *passive* occurrence (not continuing the process of creation). When the Torah writes, וַיְבָרֶךְ אֱלֹהִים אֶת יוֹם הַשְּׁבִיעִי, *God blessed the seventh day* (ibid. v. 3), it is referring to each of these phenomena — the passive as well as the active component. In other words, Hashem blessed both the universe's completion which occurred on Shabbos, as well as the rest (and the cessation of *melachah*) that the Shabbos brings.

To reinforce this theme that the Shabbos is a source of *berachah* in an active as well as a passive manner, we recall that in the *Aseres HaDibros* the *mitzvah* of Shabbos is presented in a twofold manner as *Zachor,* which refers to the positive aspects of Shabbos, and *Shamor,* which is the source for the prohibition of *melachah* (refer to our chapter on this topic). Both components of the Shabbos day are of great importance and each of these aspects of Shabbos are blessed.[1]

(*Lech Lecha* 5662)

---

1. This dual aspect of Jewish life and the blessings that accrue to our observance of the positive and negative aspects of *mitzvos* is by no means confined to the *mitzvah* of Shabbos. When the Talmud (*Menachos* 43b) requires us to recite a hundred blessings every day, it may be alluding to a twofold process that we experience every day — leaving behind the evil (סוּר מֵרָע) and beginning a new and good life (עֲשֵׂה טוֹב). The *Zohar* notes that the *gematria* of לֶךְ לְךָ, through which Hashem introduces Himself to Avraham and commands him to leave behind his entire past, is equivalent to 100 which corresponds to the aforementioned 100 *berachos.* To commence this new phase of life (which led to the formation of the Jewish nation) Avraham had to undergo a double process — leaving behind the material (and often superficial) world of his ancestors and clinging to a new spiritual life dominated by the true values of Torah. To accomplish this dual goal, this *tzaddik* not only had to leave behind the fifty gates of defilement (חֲמִשִּׁים שַׁעֲרֵי טוּמְאָה) but also successfully penetrate fifty levels of *kedushah.*

⟡ Blessing the Week as well as Shabbos Itself

ומעין זה הוא ימי המעשה שהם הכנה לשבת לכן יש בשבת לחם משנה וכל מעשי שבת כפולין שהשבת מקבל ברכה גם לימי המעשה.

It is significant that virtually every aspect of Shabbos is celebrated in a "double" fashion (as previously mentioned). Thus, the *mitzvah* of Shabbos is stated as both *Zachor* and *Shamor* (refer to our chapter on this topic), and we utilize two loaves of bread during every Shabbos meal (refer to our chapter on *lechem mishneh*). This phenomenon may be based upon the double impact of Shabbos – leaving its blessing on the week ahead as well on the Shabbos day itself.[1] (*Vayechi* 5653)

⟡ Earned *Berachos*

דכ׳ ששת ימים תעבוד. ואם היינו מקיימין העבודה כראוי. אז ויום השביעי כו׳ לה׳.

In previous *divrei Torah* we have emphasized that the *berachah* of *Shabbos* leaves a lasting impact on the week ahead. In reality, the relationship between Shabbos' *berachos* and the weekdays is twofold. On one hand, Shabbos is the source of *berachah* for the week ahead. However, the converse is also true. In the merit of our *avodas Hashem* during the week we earn the *berachos* of Shabbos. In fact, the renowned *pasuk*, שֵׁשֶׁת יָמִים תַּעֲבֹד וְעָשִׂיתָ כָּל מְלַאכְתֶּךָ, *Six days shall you work and accomplish all your work* (*Shemos* 20:9), may be interpreted in the following manner: Six days you should serve Hashem and in that merit you will enjoy the blessings of Shabbos. (*Yisro* 5636)

1. Similarly, the name *Yissachar* (spelled with two "*shins*") alludes to the double reward associated with this learned son of Yaakov. On one hand, he was entitled to ample reward of his own on the basis of his proficiency in Torah and diligent study. On the other hand, he also was the conduit through which his brother Zevulun, who supported his studies, would be blessed.

This relationship between Yissachar and Zevulun resembles that of Shabbos and the weekdays in which the more spiritual occasion (or individual) shares its/his blessing with those who are involved in the pursuit of material goods.

◆§ Derived from Hashem's Satisfaction (*Ratzon*)

וזה האות שרצה בנו הקב"ה במה שנתן לנו השבת. לומר כי הברכה והקדושה בשבת הכל תלוי כפי הרצון שמעלין בנ"י במעשיהם. לכן אומרים בקידוש היום ורצה בנו.

Whereas in the previous *dvar Torah,* we demonstrated that the *berachah* of Shabbos is contingent upon our efforts at *avodas Hashem* during the previous week, we now proceed even further and suggest that the blessings of this great day result from the satisfaction (*ratzon*) that Hashem derives from our activities during the previous week. Just as the first Shabbos did not come into effect until Hashem derived great satisfaction from His just-completed universe [as the Torah states, וַיַּרְא אֱלֹהִים אֶת כָּל אֲשֶׁר עָשָׂה וְהִנֵּה טוֹב מְאֹד, *God saw all that He had made, and behold it was very good* (*Bereishis* 1:31)], so too (on our own level, of course), the *berachah* that we obtain from every Shabbos is contingent upon the *nachas* that Hashem derives from our actions during the past week. As we recite in *Kiddush,* וְרָצָה בָנוּ וְשַׁבַּת קָדְשׁוֹ בְּאַהֲבָה וּבְרָצוֹן הִנְחִילָנוּ, [*Hashem*] *was satisfied with us and* [*consequently*] *bequeathed to us with love and goodwill His sacred day, Shabbos.*

(*Yisro* 5654)

◆§ Derived from Our Unity

וכתיב לפניכם כי נקודה זו הכללית יורדת לכללות בנ"י כשמתאחדין להיות אחד. לכן ביום השביעי דמתאחדין בי' שורה הברכה והיום הוא שבת כמ"ש במ"א.

Another important catalyst in enabling us to enjoy the many *berachos* associated with Shabbos is the sense of unity permeating the ranks of *Klal Yisrael* on Shabbos.

In a previous *dvar Torah* (entitled, "The Weekly Renewal of *Berachos,*") we suggested that the *pasuk,* רְאֵה אָנֹכִי נֹתֵן לִפְנֵיכֶם הַיּוֹם בְּרָכָה וּקְלָלָה, *See, I place before you today a blessing and a curse* (*Devarim* 11:26), may refer to Shabbos which is described by the Torah as being הַיּוֹם, *the day*. This *pasuk*, though commencing with the singular רְאֵה, *see*, concludes in the plural form, לִפְנֵיכֶם, *before you*. It is to the united *Klal Yisrael* that Hashem pleads that we avail ourselves of the opportunity to earn His blessings. There is no better opportunity to enjoy these blessings than on Shabbos, the day that embodies unity.

(*Re'eh* 5638)

◆ Above Angels

אנכי נותן לפניכם כו׳. והלא ברכה וקללה נמצא לכל העולם. אך לבנ״י אנכי נותן דייקא שיהי׳ תלוי הברכה והקללה בשמירת התורה ומצות ... דהשבת ג״כ אות ע״ז שנמשך הברכה מש״ק על ימי המעשה וזה ניתן לבנ״י כי ציווי המעשה ההנהגה ע״י הטבע והמלאכים. ולבנ״י ניתן בש״ק הברכה על כל ימי המעשה כנ״ל.

Returning to the *pasuk* cited in the previous *dvar Torah*, רְאֵה אָנֹכִי נֹתֵן לִפְנֵיכֶם הַיּוֹם בְּרָכָה וּקְלָלָה, *See, I place* [give] *before you today a blessing and a curse* (*Devarim* 11:26) — implying that only the Jewish people (לִפְנֵיכֶם) enjoy blessings and suffer from curses — we wonder, Isn't all of mankind subject to Hashem's blessings and curses? In response, we suggest that the answer lies in the first two words of this *pasuk*, אָנֹכִי נֹתֵן, *I am giving* – I am granting you the prerogative of meriting *berachos* based on your behavior. Whereas, to a large extent, mankind enjoys Hashem's blessings according to regular natural patterns set into motion by Hashem (and administered by His *malachim*), *Klal Yisrael* is empowered to *directly* control its fate through its observance of *mitzvos* and Torah study.

This capacity to be in control of our destiny based on our spiritual behavior is rooted in the *berachos* of Shabbos. It is on this day when we are not necessarily dependent on natural forces and even *malachim* that ordinarily implement Hashem's Will (but rather are *directly* under Hashem's *hashgachah*), that *Klal Yisrael* derives its blessings for the entire week. (*Re'eh* 5647)

◆§ Based on *Emunah*

וכן בזמנים שבתות וי״ט נק׳ אמונת עתיך שהם זמנים שמעלין הכל של השורש. ולכן נמשך על ידם ברכות לכל הזמנים. ולכן נק׳ סעודת שבת סעודתא דמהימנותא ונותן ברכה על כל ימי המעשה.

According to the *Midrash* (*Yalkut Shemos* 414) there is a clear association between the attribute of *emunah* and being a source of *berachos*. Thus, Moshe *Rabbeinu* is described as אִישׁ אֱמוּנוֹת רַב בְּרָכוֹת, *A man of integrity will increase blessings* (*Mishlei* 28:20), which teaches us that a man of faith merits many blessings.

To appreciate the association between *emunah* and *berachah*, we have to first define *emunah*,, particularly as it pertains to Moshe *Rabbeinu*. In the aftermath of the sin of the Golden Calf, Moshe was offered the opportunity to become a great nation in his own right — וְאֶעֱשֶׂה אוֹתְךָ לְגוֹי גָּדוֹל, *I shall make you a great nation* (*Shemos* 32:10). Rather than avail himself of Hashem's offer, Moshe prefers to plead for *Klal Yisrael's* survival. What greater act of *emunah* than to recognize one's true mission and place in life (הַמַּכִּיר אֶת מְקוֹמוֹ). By refusing Hashem's offer to become the founder of his own great nation, Moshe acknowledged that only the *Avos* could serve as the founding fathers of *Klal Yisrael*. The נֶאֱמָן, the true practitioner of *emunah*, is faithful and understands well the nature of his own mission, and even realizes that his soul on earth is intricately connected with its heavenly roots. Thus, accepting a mission that is beyond his capabilities or that encroaches upon another's role is perceived by him as being in opposition to his spiritual growth.

In the *dvar Torah* at the beginning of this chapter, we noted that all *berachos* have heavenly roots. It is only when an entity is able to evoke and connect to its spiritual roots in heaven that it is worthy of being blessed. How appropriate it was that Moshe, who understood the nature (and limitations) of his mission, was chosen to bless *Klal Yisrael*.

Every Shabbos when the universe, and all of us, return to our roots is an ideal opportunity to reap *berachos*. Our belief in the ability of Shabbos to generate *berachos* for the week ahead is reflected in the term selected to describe the Shabbos meals, סְעֻדָּתָא דִמְהֵימְנוּתָא, *meals of perfect faith*.

(*Pekudei* 5657)

◆§ Negating Mankind's First Curse

כמו כן הגזירה אחר החטא לעבוד את האדמה אשר לוקח משם והוא הגוף שנלקח מאדמה. וכשהגוף משכיל לשרת את הנפש באמונה יוצא מכלל ארור לכלל ברוך וכן הכנת ימי השבוע אל השבת שהשבת נותן ברכה לכל ימי השבוע לצאת מכלל ארור. ולכן סעודת שבת נק׳ סעודתא דמהימנותא. כי לפי האמונה שמאמינין בשבת ומבטלין כל המעשים אל השבת כך מקבלים ממנו הברכה כנ״ל.

To further appreciate the dimensions of Shabbos' *berachah,* let us turn to the first curse ever imposed on mankind. After sinning by partaking of the forbidden fruit, Adam is condemned לַעֲבֹד אֶת הָאֲדָמָה אֲשֶׁר לֻקַּח מִשָּׁם, *to serve/work the earth from which he had been taken* (*Bereishis* 3:23). We suggest that through these words, Adam was not only condemned to eke out a living by tilling the soil but also his soul (נְשָׁמָה) became subservient to his body (גוף), which had been created from the earth. Those foresighted individuals who take great pains that the body obey the soul's dictates, rather than the reverse, are able to reverse the curse that Adam received. For them, the spiritual requirements of the *neshamah,* rather than the physical cravings of the *guf,* prevail.

A similar relationship may be drawn between Shabbos and the weekdays. By preparing all week long for Shabbos, we not only are ready to absorb the *kedushah* of Shabbos but also the weekdays themselves are not necessarily affected by the curse that Adam received. By preparing all week long for Shabbos, the entire atmosphere of the week is transformed from one of a relentless search for material needs into a quest for ever-increasing levels of *kedushah.* If, in fact, one leads such a life in which our entire focus is one of preparing for Shabbos, then indeed each of the weekdays is blessed by its association with Shabbos.

To further illustrate this relationship, we recall that the meals of Shabbos are known as סְעֻדָּתָא דִמְהֵימְנוּתָא, *the meals of perfect faith.* The weekdays are blessed in direct proportion to the *emunah* that we have in the Shabbos, as reflected by our directing our efforts all week long towards the objective of being worthy of enjoying the *kedushah* of Shabbos. (*Chayei Sarah* 5662)

◆§ *Berachos* Without Barriers

כי בימי המעשה יש תערובות וכל נקודה קדושה א"י להתגלות רק ע"י הסתר וקליפה וסט"א. אבל בשבת קודש סט"א ערקת והברכה מתפשטת בלי תערובות ובטל העצבון. ולכן אחז"ל וביום שמחתכם הוא שבת.

During the weekdays every sacred entity is often veiled and obscured in an overall environment where good and evil are indistinct.[1] However, on Shabbos when the forces of evil are no longer in effect, we can enjoy Hashem's undiluted *berachos.*

In this context, we may appreciate why *Chazal* (*Yalkut Bamidbar* 725) describe Shabbos as יוֹם שִׂמְחַתְכֶם, *your day of joy.* There is no greater source of joy than being relieved of the constant torment of the *yetzer hara* and the opportunity to enjoy Hashem's *berachos* in their purest form. (*Tazria* 5654)

◆§ A Day of Listening

וכפי הכנה שלו לשמוע מצות הבורא זה השלימות. ובזה זוכה לקבל הברכות. ולכן השבת כ' בו ויברך כו' יום השביעי. כי בכל מ"ב הי' איזה בריאה וכשנגמר כל הבריאה אז האדם מוכן לקבל מצות ה' וזה השבת. וכן נאמר היום אם בקולו תשמעו היינו שבת שנק' היום. ולכן כל המלאכה בו בטלים. ושבת יעשה כולו תורה.

Of all the capacities which Hashem granted us, few are as critical as the gift of hearing. In fact, according to *Chazal* (*Bava Kamma* 85b), if an individual damages his peer's ability to hear to the extent that he becomes totally deaf, the defendant is obligated to compensate his *full* value (rather than merely for the loss of his ear).

1. In this context the *Sfas Emes* may be alluding to the blurring of good and evil that occurred after Adam partook of the Fruit of the Tree of Knowledge of Good and Evil.

As Torah Jews, the ability to hear involves far more than merely listening to mundane speech. On the contrary, it is the capacity to listen and absorb the Divine Word that is of critical importance. It is only when he is able to concentrate on listening carefully to Hashem's Word that man has reached his *sheleimus* (his capacity for perfection and his full potential). Consequently, the Torah specifies that we can best enjoy Hashem's blessings by *listening* to His *mitzvos* — אֶת הַבְּרָכָה אֲשֶׁר תִּשְׁמְעוּ אֶל מִצְוֹת ה׳ אֱלֹהֵיכֶם, *The blessing that you hearken to the commandments of Hashem, your God* (*Devarim* 11:27).[1]

It was only upon the arrival of the first Shabbos — when the entire universe (the material setting in which man could thrive and grow spiritually) was completed — that man enjoyed all of the prerequisites to listen to Hashem's Word. The tradition stating that the *pasuk*, הַיּוֹם אִם בְּקֹלוֹ תִשְׁמָעוּ, *Today, if we but listen to His call* (voice) (*Tehillim* 95:7), refers to Shabbos, may also be understood in this context. There is no better opportunity to concentrate on hearing Hashem's Voice than on Shabbos. The prohibition of performing *melachah* on Shabbos may be based on the same rationale — it is only by desisting from any physical activity that we can be fully focused on listening to Hashem. (Refer to our chapter on *Melachah* for extensive treatment of this topic.) In a similar vein, *Chazal* (*Tanna D'bei Eliyahu*) describe Shabbos as a day that is completely Torah. On this day when we totally yield any association with our physical routine of the weekdays, we are free to better understand Hashem's Will by listening and studying His Torah. In fact, the Torah was given on Shabbos, the day that is most conducive to listening to Hashem's teachings.

It is because of man's new-found capacity to listen to Hashem's Word, an ability which he derived upon the conclusion of the entire material world and the inception of the first Shabbos, that Hashem blessed the Shabbos. For us, too, it is only by listening to Hashem's teachings that we earn the *berachos* associated with Shabbos.

(*Re'eh* 5656).

1. While it is true that prior to the sin of the Golden Calf, it may have been possible to enjoy Hashem's blessings on the basis of our deeds alone, after that tragic event which demonstrated that our commitment of נַעֲשֶׂה וְנִשְׁמַע, *we will do and we will listen*, was flawed, we primarily derive our blessings from listening to the Word of Hashem.

◆§ Inhaling a Spiritual Fragrance

ויצחק שהוא שרש היראה ראה מהריח מי שראוי לברכו. והריח הוא מבחי' הנשמה כמ"ש חז"ל איזהו דבר שהנפש נהנה בו ולא הגוף זה הריח דכתיב כל הנשמה תהלל. כי הנשמה כ' בה ויפח באפיו נשמת חיים. ואיתא בגמרא על פ' שפתותיו שושנים כל דיבור שיצא מפי הקב"ה נתמלא כל העולם בשמים. ומעין זה הנשמה יש בה מזה הריח. וע"ז חל הברכה. וכמו כן שבת יומא דנשמתין. והנשמה יתירה הבאה בשבת מג"ע ממנה בא הריח. ולכן שורה בו נרכה ולכן מריחין בבשמים מוצ"ש לפי שנחסר זה הריח אחר השבת.

It is significant that before blessing Yaakov, Yitzchak first smelled the fragrance that emanated from his garment (see *Bereishis* 27:27). Apparently, a *tzaddik* of Yitzchak's stature could determine from the quality of the fragrance that he smelled whom to bless.

To appreciate the association between fragrance and *berachos,* we recall the Gemara (*Berachos* 43b) that derives the obligation of reciting a *berachah* on a fragrant smell from the *pasuk,* כֹּל הַנְּשָׁמָה תְּהַלֵּל יָהּ, *Let every soul praise God* (*Tehillim* 150:6 — implying that the soul rather than the body should praise God). Whereas the body can derive pleasure from food and drink, only the soul benefits from a fragrance.

Having established this relationship between the *neshamah* and fragrance, we can appreciate that by testing the fragrance that emanated from any individual who sought his *berachos,* Yitzchak was actually evaluating the quality of his spirituality and his suitability to be blessed. In Yaakov's case, as *Rashi* notes, Yitzchak detected the fragrant odor of *Gan Eden* emanating from his garments. Based on this observation, he felt that it was appropriate to bless his son.[1]

In a similar vein, *Chazal* (*Shabbos* 88b) note that when Hashem gave the *Aseres HaDibros* to *Klal Yisrael,* the entire universe was suffused with spices. In light of the association that we demonstrated between fragrance and the *neshamah,* we can appreciate that the source of the pleasant fragrance at *Matan Torah* is none other than *HaKadosh Baruch*

1. Similarly, *Chazal* (*Sanhedrin* 93b) note that *Mashiach* will enjoy the capacity to judge individuals on the basis of the fragrance that they emit. This too may refer to his keen ability to discern the spiritual essence of every individual with whom he interacts.

Hu, the Source of all spirituality, the One who implanted the first soul into the first man.

Every Shabbos, the day when *Klal Yisrael* enjoys the "fragrant" *neshamah yeseirah,* which emanates from *Gan Eden,* the Jewish people are richly deserving of Hashem's *berachos.*[1] (*Toldos* 5662)

◆§ Not Our Sole Motivation

לכן כתיב שבת שבתון שיהי׳ השביתה לשם השבת עצמו. ולא בעבור ברכת השבת לעובדין דחול.

Despite the many *berachos* that are derived from Shabbos, we should not base our observance of this sacred day on the premise of its potential benefit to us. As the Torah emphasizes, שַׁבַּת שַׁבָּתוֹן (which *Sfas Emes,* in this context, explains): Our observance of Shabbos should be for the sake of Shabbos (i.e., to commemorate that Hashem rested and every other aspect of Shabbos) rather than because of its many blessings. (*Ki Sisa* 5645)

◆§ Why Pesach Is Called Shabbos

ולכן פסח נק׳ שבת כדאיתא בשבת קודש דמתברכין מיני׳ כולהו יומין ומנא לא ירד בי׳ דאיהו שורש הברכה קודם שמתגשם כמ״ש בזוה״ק יתרו. כמו כן בפסח הברכה יורדת על כל ימי השנה בשורש.

Based on the foregoing discussion and especially our contention that all of the week's material *berachos* are rooted in Shabbos' sacred spiritual origins, we gain additional insight why Pesach is described by the Torah as being a Shabbos (cf. *Vayikra* 23:15). Just as on Shabbos we enjoy Hashem's *berachos* in their original pristine form — before they assume any material dimensions (become *megusham*) during the week ahead — so too, on Pesach, the time of *Yetzias Mitzrayim* (as well as the

1. By smelling fragrant spices on *motzei Shabbos* we compensate to some extent for the loss of the intense spirituality represented by Shabbos' *neshamah yeseirah.*

korban ha'omer), we enjoy the material *berachos* that Hashem will grant us in the coming harvest season in their original spiritual form (*shoresh*).

(*Pesach* 5647)

◆§ The *Berachos* of Shabbos and of Rosh Chodesh

וב׳ אלו הענינים הם ענין השבת והחודש דכתיב ביום השבת יפתח וביום החודש יפתח. דאיתא מחדש בטובו בכל יום מ״ב. והם בחי׳ שבת וחודש. כן השבת הוא מקור הברכה ונקרא טוב ובחי׳ הי״ב חדשים הם י״ב שערים שהשפע יורד על ידיהם להתחתונים לכן נקרא חודש שמשתנה כל חודש להתחדשות דרך אחר. והשבת הוא כלל כל השערים.

To appreciate the relationship between the *berachos* of Shabbos and those of Rosh Chodesh, we recall the renowned *pasuk*, וּבְיוֹם הַשַּׁבָּת יִפָּתֵחַ וּבְיוֹם הַחֹדֶשׁ יִפָּתֵחַ, (The gate of the future *Beis HaMikdash) will be opened on Shabbos and on the day of the New Moon it will be opened* (*Yechezkel* 46:1). This refers not only to a specific gate of the third *Beis HaMikdash* but also (homiletically) to the gates of heaven through which Hashem showers us with His abundant blessings.

Whereas Shabbos is the heavenly source of our blessings (מְקוֹר הַבְּרָכָה), the twelve months of the year (and especially the Rosh Chodesh of every month) are additional conduits through which these *berachos* are transmitted to us here on earth.

Moreover, every month represents not only a new beginning but also a different means through which Hashem channels His *berachos* to us. In fact, the term *chodesh* (related to *chadosh, new*) implies the fresh start and the new method through which Hashem conveys His blessings to us each month.

In, truth, Hashem's *berachos* are always being presented to *Klal Yisrael*. There is not a day in which we do not enjoy His blessings. However, on most occasions, these *berachos* are often hidden from us. We frequently are unable to completely appreciate Hashem's numerous kindnesses. However, on Shabbos and Rosh Chodesh, the days when the gates of the *Beis HaMikdash* (and of understanding Hashem's Blessings) are opened, we are able to more readily perceive the *berachos* that we always enjoy. (Adapted from *Masei* 5643)

◆ Simulating *Birchas Kohanim*

וכל הג׳ ברכות שבברכת כהנים הם ג״כ ... יברכך הוא הפרנסה דמיני׳ מתברכין שיתא יומין ולכן נתנו לחה״פ בכל שבת ובמקדש שמשם יוצא הברכה. יאר ה׳ הוא נרות שבת ובמקדש. שלום הוא פריסת סוכת שלום בשבת.

By examining some of the *mitzvos* of Shabbos, we may draw a parallel between *Birchas Kohanim* (the three-fold blessing through which *Kohanim* bless the Jewish people) and the *berachos* of this greatest of days. For example, the first of these blessings, יְבָרֶכְךָ, *may He bless you*, which according to *Chazal* (cf. *Rashi, Bamidbar* 6:24) alludes to prosperity, "that your possessions should be blessed," resembles the *berachah* of sustenance that every Shabbos brings. As the *Zohar* notes, Shabbos is the source of our *parnassah* for the entire week. This theme is also reflected in the *lechem hapanim* (showbread) which was placed on the Table (*Shulchan*) in the *Beis HaMikdash* every Shabbos. It demonstrated that our sustenance all week long is derived from the blessings of Shabbos.

The following *berachah*, יָאֵר, *may He enlighten/illuminate*, corresponds to the Shabbos lights and resembles the *Menorah* of the *Beis HaMikdash*. Finally, the concluding *berachah*, וְיָשֵׂם לְךָ שָׁלוֹם, *may He grant you peace*, corresponds to the overwhelming sense of serenity and peace that we enjoy every Shabbos. As we recite in the Friday evening service, הַפּוֹרֵשׂ סֻכַּת שָׁלוֹם עָלֵינוּ וְעַל כָּל עַמּוֹ יִשְׂרָאֵל, *He spreads the canopy of peace over us and all of His people, Israel.*[1] (*Emor* 5654)

◆ Three Meals – Three Blessings

ולכן הג׳ סעודות מיוחדים לאלה הג׳ בח״מ [ובליל ש״ק יתכן שהוא בחי׳ מזוני. וביום השבת חיי. ובסעודה ג׳ בני כפי מ״ש בתיקונים בכמה מקומות ע״ש ד׳ ס״ז סע״ב. ולכן בליל שבת בעי למיטעום מכלא דבי׳ שרי׳ ברכה במזוני כנ״ל] ומיני׳ מתברכין ימי המעשה ג״כ כנ״ל.

As we conclude this chapter on the *berachos* of Shabbos, we suggest that in addition to the overall blessed ambiance of Shabbos, there

1. The *Sfas Emes* suggests that the *ketores* (incense) offered on the Inner Altar (מזבח הזהב) corresponded to the third *berachah* of *shalom*.

are specific *berachos* that are most prominent at specific times throughout the Shabbos. It is well-known that enjoying ample *parnassah,* good health and children are the most prized of all *berachos.* We suggest that the three meals of Shabbos not only correspond to these *berachos* but also that each meal is a catalyst to help us attain these *berachos.* Consequently, it is by participating in the Friday night meal that we merit adequate sustenance all week long.[1] Similarly, by partaking of the Shabbos day meal we merit life, and through the third meal we enjoy the *berachah* of children.[2] (*Ki Savo* 5647)

1. The popular custom of tasting a sample of the Shabbos day meal on Friday night may be based on our desire to extend the *berachos* of the Friday meal to all the Shabbos meals and, by extension, to the entire week.

2. According to the *Sfas Emes,* the association between diligently participating in the third meal of Shabbos and meriting children is based on *Tikkunei Zohar* 67b.

Zachor V'Shamor

☙ Return to Sinai

ועל ב׳ אלו נאמר זכור ושמור שצריכין למצוא בש״ק הארה מקבלת התורה וזה זכור כמ״ש חז״ל מזה שבשבת ניתנה תורה. ושמור לגרש אל זר.
ושמור היא לשמור מן השכחה שכן כתיב השמר כו׳ ושמור נפשך מאוד פן תשכח כו׳. כי הטבע מסתיר ומשכח הפנימיות וזה שליט בימי המעשה. ובשבת נפתח לבנ״י הפנימיות והוא יומא דזכירה.
כי שבת יומא דזכירה כמ״ש זכור את יום השבת. ומתעורר בו נקודה החקוקה בנפשות בנ״י שא״א לבוא לידי שכחה.

Assuming that *Zachor, remember,* couched in positive terms, and *Shamor, safeguard,* stated in negative terms, are important not only in their own right but are also symbolic of *all* of the positive and negative commandments of the Torah, we can appreciate why the Torah describes the Shabbos using *both* of these expressions. Every Shabbos, a day which is a microcosm of the World to Come (refer to *Berachos* 57b and to our chapter on this topic), we are able to return to the lofty spiritual level that we enjoyed briefly at Sinai, when Hashem transmitted to us the first two commandments. Both the positive commandment, אָנֹכִי ה׳ אֱלֹהֶיךָ, *I am HASHEM your God,* as well as the negative commandment, לֹא יִהְיֶה לְךָ אֱלֹהִים אֲחֵרִים, *You shall not recognize the gods of others,* were transmitted *directly* by Hashem (whereas, according to many authorities, the other eight commandments were transmitted by Hashem to Moshe, who in turn taught them to the Jewish people). By describing Shabbos in terms of positive and negative commandments, the Torah is indicating that every Shabbos, to some extent, we recreate a bit of the aura of Sinai when Hashem presented *Klal Yisrael* with the first positive and negative commandments. Unlike the rest of the Torah, transmitted by Hashem to Moshe and subsequently by Moshe to *Klal Yisrael,* which the Jewish people are capable of forgetting, the first two *mitzvos* which comprise the fundamental beliefs of *Yidddishkeit* – as well as the positive and negative aspects of Shabbos – are deeply etched in the Jewish *neshamah* and can never be totally forgotten.[1]

Shabbos is not only a microcosm of the World to Come but also the day when the Torah was given to *Klal Yisrael.* As a result, every Shabbos *Klal Yisrael* approaches the level it enjoyed at Sinai before sinning, allowing it to draw strength from those two *mitzvos* that it heard directly from Hashem. The positive commandment of *Zachor* not only pertains to Shabbos, but also corresponds to the positive commandment we heard at Sinai – אָנֹכִי ה׳ אֱלֹהֶיךָ, *I am HASHEM, your God.* Every Shabbos, as we enjoy the enhanced presence of the *neshamah yeseirah* and *Klal Yisrael* forges an inseparable bond with Hashem, we feel closer to the aspect of Hashem's Presence in all of us (the Divine Spark which we first enjoyed at Sinai when we heard אָנֹכִי ה׳ אֱלֹהֶיךָ). In the spirit of *Shamor* (guarding), this Divine Spark cannot be diluted, as we heard in the second commandment, לֹא יִהְיֶה לְךָ אֱלֹהִים אֲחֵרִים, *You shall not recognize the gods of others,* which refers to any distractions or interests which would drive out Hashem's Presence that is lodged within all of us. By using the terms *Zachor* and *Shamor,* the Torah is alluding to the first two commandments, the positive and negative commandments whose influence is particularly felt every Shabbos. (*Va'eschanan* 5647, 5661)

By using the term *Zachor, remember,* in the context of Shabbos, the Torah is implying that Shabbos – and the many experiences associated with it – is so deeply etched in the *neshamah* of *Klal Yisrael* that it can never be totally forgotten. (Adapted from *Ki Sisa* 5661)

1. Similarly, commentators state that every Shabbos, *Klal Yisrael* experiences some of the aura of the First *Luchos.* While the Torah in its current state is derived from the Second *Luchos* (which remained intact while the first *Luchos* were shattered by Moshe), every Shabbos *Klal Yisrael,* to some extent, is able to return to the lofty level that it enjoyed when it received the First *Luchos.*

◆§ Enhancing the Shabbos and Guarding Shabbos' *Berachos*

זכור את יום השבת לקדשו הרי שהאדם יכול להוסיף קדושה לשבת. ושמור לשמור הברכה היורדת לאדם בש״ק.

Perhaps the simplest explanation for the Torah describing Shabbos as both an occasion to remember (*Zachor*) as well as a time to be safeguarded and preserved (*Shamor*) is that the Torah is referring to two aspects of this most sacred of days. On one hand, by remembering the Shabbos — by verbalizing the *kedushah* (sanctity) of Shabbos through *Kiddush*, the Shabbos *tefillos*, and even simply by talking about Shabbos — we can actually enhance the Shabbos. The power of *Klal Yisrael* to augment the sanctity of Shabbos may be deduced from a seemingly redundant term (which follows the *mitzvah* of זָכוֹר אֶת יוֹם הַשַּׁבָּת, *Remember the Shabbos day, Shemos* 20:7), לְקַדְּשׁוֹ, *to sanctify it. Klal Yisrael,* through its observance of Shabbos, actually supplements the *kedushah* that Hashem originally instilled in Shabbos. Just as we augment and "benefit" the Shabbos through our meticulous observance, so too, we are the beneficiaries of Shabbos' enhanced *kedushah* and of all the *berachos* that we receive on Shabbos. To ensure that we retain all the gains that we have achieved on Shabbos, the Torah implores us, *Shamor*, "preserve the Shabbos" — maintain the progress that you achieved on *Shabbos Kodesh*. (*Shemos* 5661)

ובוודאי לא כל אדם מוכן לזה. ומ״מ יש לכ״א מבנ״י חלק בקדושת שבת. ואמרו חז״ל זכור ושמור בדיבור אחד נאמרו. כל שישנו בשמירה ישנו בזכירה. כי זכירה הוא דבר גדול. ומ״מ כל השומר שבת כפשטו. יש לו חלק בזכירה.
כל שישנו בשמירה ישנו בזכירה. כי זכור נשמר לאנשים גדולי הערך אשר בהזכירם את יום השבת מוסיפין לו קדושה כמ״ש לקדשו. וזה הי׳ עפ״י מדריגה גבוה שהי׳ לבנ״י בקבלת התורה. עכ״ז גם ע״י השמירה ששומר עצמו אדם כדי שלא יפגום ח״ו בקדושת שבת ע״ז יש לו שייכות גם בזכירה.
שמור הוא הקדושה שיורדת בשבת וצריכין לשמור שלא לחלל הקדושה ... אבל זכור הוא הקדושה שצריכין בני ישראל להמשיך בשבת תוספות קדושה ע״י קידוש היום ותפלת שבת והוא מדריגה שלמעלה. אבל אחז״ל כל שישנו בשמירה ישנו בזכירה שע״י בחי׳ שמירה זוכין למדריגת זכור.

While it is certainly true that not every individual Jew enjoys the capacity to actually enhance the sanctity of Shabbos through his personal observance, nonetheless, every one of us has a portion of their own in the *kedushah* of Shabbos. By transmitting the *mitzvah* of Shabbos through the dual medium of *Zachor* and *Shamor*, the Torah is encouraging even the simplest Jew and assuring him that he too has a role to play in Shabbos. While the lofty spiritual level of *Zachor* — remembering Shabbos and consequently augmenting the *kedushah* of the day (refer to the previous essay where we discussed the concept of לְקַדְּשׁוֹ, *to sanctify it*) — may only pertain to some members of *Klal Yisrael*, *shemiras Shabbos*, simple observance of Shabbos, pertains to every Jew. By expressing *Shamor* alongside *Zachor*, the Torah is indicating that even if one has not yet attained the level of *Zachor*, by doing his utmost to observe the manifold details of Shabbos observance (*Shamor*), it is considered as if he has, to some extent, enhanced its *kedushah* as well. As *Chazal* (*Berachos* 20b) state, "Whoever observes *Shamor* is considered as if he observed *Zachor* as well." (*Yisro* 5651; *Shavuos* 5637, 5660)

◂§ ***Shamor*** **(Abstaining from This World) — A Prerequisite for *Zachor* (Eliciting the Inner Divine Spark)**

והוא כמו השבת דכתיב ביום השבת יפתח והוא מגלה הקדושה שנסתרת בימי המעשה ... כמ״ש זכור ושמור בדיבור אחד כל שישנו בשמירה ישנו בזכירה ...

Chazal express the relationship between guarding the Shabbos (*Shamor*) and remembering Shabbos (*Zachor*) in the following terms: כָּל שֶׁיֶשְׁנוֹ בִּשְׁמִירָה יֶשְׁנוֹ בִּזְכִירָה, *Whoever is included in guarding* (שְׁמִירָה) *the Shabbos is also included in remembering* (זְכִירָה) *the Shabbos* (*Berachos* 20b).[1] It is well-known that much of the *kedushah* that is hidden from us all week long is revealed on Shabbos. The prophet Yechezkel alludes

1. This *Chazal* is the source for the obligation of women to observe every aspect of Shabbos — even the positive commandments (*mitzvos asei*) such as *Kiddush*. While women are generally exempt from positive commandments which are time-bound (מִצְוַת עֲשֵׂה שֶׁהַזְּמַן גְּרָמָה), in this instance, since they are obligated to guard the Shabbos (*Shamor*) by observing all of its negative commmandments, they are also required to fulfill all of its positive commandments (*Zachor*). In this essay, we will emphasize the homiletical interpretations of this *Chazal*.

to the potential of Shabbos to evoke the *kedushah* that is veiled all week long by writing, *On the Shabbos day the gates* (of the Future Temple) *will be opened* (46:1). We suggest that he is not only referring to the gates of the *Beis HaMikdash* but also to the gates of *kedushah* that may appear to be remote all week long and yet are very accessible on Shabbos. However, there is an important prerequisite en route to the lofty objective of *kedushah* – abstaining from the material vices and the immorality of This World. It is only by meeting this important preliminary requirement – guarding oneself from inappropriate values (*shemirah*) – that we may eventually attain a full appreciation of Shabbos' immense *kedushah*. (*Lech Lecha* 5652)

ולכן זכור ושמור בדיבור א' נאמרו. ואמרו כל שישנו בשמירה ישנו בזכירה. הרוח הוא דכל מקום שיש זכירה שהוא התגלות המעין פנימי צריך שמירה. וכפי השמירה כך זוכין להתדבק בפנימיות המעין.

Just as *Shamor* – abstaining from values that are antithetical to the Torah – may be a *prerequisite* for *Zachor* – eliciting that inner Divine Spark that we all potentially enjoy – so too, another aspect of the *Shamor* concept is particularly critical. After eliciting and benefiting from that inner Divine Presence, it is imperative that we preserve all of the gains that we achieved over Shabbos. In particular, every Shabbos when we are able to tap our inner spiritual resources in a manner unlike anything comparable to during the week (*Zachor*), it is now necessary to carefully guard that newly-discovered inner spark to ensure that it is not tampered with (*Shamor*). When *Chazal* comment, "Whoever is included in *shemirah* is also included in *zechirah*," they may be alluding to the relationship between finding our vast inner potential and preserving it. Whoever is capable of preserving the Inner Spark is also capable of successfully eliciting and benefiting from it. (*Beha'aloscha* 5663; *Pinchas* 5651)

דבכל מקום שיש התגלות הפנימיות צריך שמירה כמו זכור ושמור לפי שבו נפתח שער הפנימי ... והכל מעין שהי' באדה"ר בג"ע שהוא שער הפנימי כתיב לעבדה ולשמרה והכל ענין אחד.

Consider some parallels to the foregoing *Zachor-Shamor* relationship, between developing a more intimate relationship with Hashem by eliciting one's inner potential and then taking great precautions to guard this new-found relationship. For example, the *Leviim* who sang Hashem's praises (a form of *Zachor* — verbalizing our tribute to Hashem), were also assigned the function of guarding the *Beis HaMikdash* (*Shamor*) where they attained this intimate relationship with Hashem. Perhaps, the original source for the *Zachor-Shamor* relationship can be found at the commencement of history when Adam was assigned the mission of guarding (*Shamor*) and developing the Garden of Eden (cf. *Bereishis* 2:15) — a positive form of Divine Service (*Zachor*). (*Beha'aloscha* 5663)

כי זכור ושמור בש״ק להסיר הערלה ושיתגלה הפנימיות.

One may also draw a parallel between these two aspects of Shabbos observance, *Zachor* and *Shamor*, and the two components of the *mitzvah* of *bris milah* — the *milah* itself, which involves the excision of the *orlah* (foreskin) and *periah* (uncovering of the thin membrane adhering to the glans). Just as the removal of the *orlah*, which is symbolic of lust and craving for material values, is followed by the *periah*, which enables the true inner self (*penimiyus*) of the individual to surface, so too, by abstaining from the passions of *Olam Hazeh* (*Shamor*), we merit to bask in the true inner radiance of Shabbos. (*Lech Lecha* 5665)

לכן מקדשין על היין לרמוז על התגלות הנשמה כנ״ל ולכן יין צריך שמירה ממגע נכרי

Both aspects of Shabbos — enjoying the hidden, innermost treasures (*Zachor*), as well as guarding our new-found accessibility to Hashem (*Shamor*) — may be found in the *mitzvah* of *Kiddush* performed through the medium of wine. On the one hand, wine symbolizes the hidden treasures and innermost secrets of the Torah which we can exploit on Shabbos, when we are blessed with the presence of the *neshamah yeseirah*, more than at any other time.[1] Thus, *Chazal* (*Berachos* 34b) use the expression, "Wine that has been preserved in its grapes since the Six Days of Creation," to allude to the Torah's most intimate secrets. However, as the expression "wine that has been preserved" implies, wine needs to be protected from inappropriate contact by a gentile. Likewise,

1. Refer to *Eiruvin* 65a, נִכְנַס יַיִן יָצָא סוֹד, "When wine enters , secrets emerge."

the Torah's most cherished secrets also need to be guarded from abuse (by inappropriate students). (Adapted from *Ki Sisa* 5653)

וז"ש ארץ יראה ושקטה. כי העצה בבחי' ארץ להיות התיקון גם בעוה"ז ע"י הקדמת היראה לאהבה כנ"ל. והוא בחי' זכור ושמור שזכירה הוא דביקות בחיות פנימיות. ושמור הוא יראה שלא לצאת מהגדר להיות נקי ומוכן לקיים המצות. [וכ' זכור ושמור בדבור אחד נאמרו כי ודאי משה רבינו ע"ה לא שינה מאמר השי"ת מזכור. רק כי דיבור ה' לכלל ישראל הוא אחר תיקון השלימות מצדם. ובחי' שמור הוא ההכנה להיות מוכן לקבל הקדושה. וז"ש מי שישנו בשמירה ישנו בזכירה.

To comprehend somewhat better the relationship between *Zachor* and *Shamor* and why *Shamor* is a prerequisite for *Zachor* -- we recall the *pasuk* describing *Matan Torah*, אֶרֶץ יָרְאָה וְשָׁקָטָה, *The earth feared and then it became calm* (*Tehillim* 76:9). In order for the universe to eventually become calm, it first had to fear. It was only by demonstrating its concern and fear of the consequences if the Jewish people would not accept the Torah (refer to *The Three Festivals*, pgs. 285-290 for a complete treatment of this topic), that the universe was then able to restore its previous equilibrium and sense of calm. So too, for the Jewish people to be able to evoke their latent inner potential emanating from the Divine Spark that they all enjoyed (a concept which we have identified in previous *divrei Torah* as being based on the theme of *Zachor*), it is necessary to first display fear and concern about the consequences of not properly observing Torah (*Shamor*). It was in the merit of that concern, which was perhaps the best possible preparation (*hachanah*) for the Giving of the Torah, that *Klal Yisrael* merited to reach the level of *Zachor* – of evoking their inner Divine Spark and their latent potential for *avodas Hashem*. (*Shavuos* 5631)

Based on this assertion that *Shamor* refers to the intense personal preparation necessary before we may benefit from our inner Divine Spark, we suggest that when Moshe *Rabbeinu* substitutes *Shamor* (*Safeguard the Shabbos day* – cf. *Devarim* 5:12) for *Zachor* (*Remember the Shabbos day*, the text given in the first rendition of the Ten Commandments, cf. *Shemos* 20:7), he is not inserting his own version of the Divine Command in place of Hashem's. On the contrary, Moshe is simply explaining to *Klal Yisrael* how to achieve the lofty spiritual level of *Zachor*, which enables us to elicit our inner spark of *kedushah* that emanates from Hashem. It is through *Shamor* – knowing that one enjoys great potential and determining to guard this enormous capacity for following the Divine Will from being corrupted through its involvement in matters of This World — that one may eventually attain the attribute of *Zachor,* actually being able to exploit the Divine Inner Spark embedded in all of us.

It is entirely possible that some individuals may never attain the coveted status of *Zachor.* This is particularly true if we assume that *Zachor* means that we are to reach the level of being to able to "internalize" a sense of *deveikus,* clinging to Hashem. As the term *Zachor* implies, my relationship with Hashem becomes so embedded in me that I can never forget my Creator. While it is possible that I may never attain so exalted a status, merely making the determination that whatever Divine Spark I enjoy will not be compromised, is in itself a great source of merit — so great that it may eventually allow me to internalize my relationship to Hashem and reach the level of *Zachor.* As *Chazal* state, "Whoever is included in *Shamor* — seeking to safeguard the Divine Spark — will also be included in *Zachor* — the realization and internalization of one's inner potential for spiritual greatness." (Ibid.)

☙ Following Avraham's Footsteps

שמעי בת כו׳ ושכחי עמך כו׳ משל למי שראה בירה דולקת כו׳ הציץ עליו בעל הבירה אני הוא בעל הבירה כו׳. עיקר תיקון האדם כפי מה ששוכח הבלי עולם כמ״ש שכחי עמך ולזכור כי נשתלח בעוה״ז לעשות שליחותו וזה בחי׳ זכור ושמור מ״ע ומל״ת הוא בחי׳ זכירה ושכחה ששניהם צריכין לאדם לשכוח הבלי עוה״ז ואז יכול לזכור ולהתדבק בעולם העליון וזה שרמזו מי שישנו בשמירה ישנו בזכירה ובאמת בשבת שכל ישראל שובתין ממלאכה והוא בחי׳ שכחה מעוה״ז לכן זוכין לנשמה יתירה זכירה ודביקות בעוה״ב בשבת קודש שהוא מעין עוה״ב. וזה זכור ושמור בשבת. אבל באמת השבת ללמד על הכלל כולו יצא. שאיש ישראל צריך לעולם לשמור ב׳ בחי׳ הנ״ל שמעי בת. ושכחי. ואברהם הי׳ הראשון שהשליך הבלי העולם וזכה למשוך אור בעולם ועליו נאמר מי העיר ממזרח כו׳, וזה הענין של בירה דולקת כי כל עוה״ז נברא רק כדי לשכוח ולבטל הבלי עולם.

In the previous *dvar Torah* we discussed that *Shamor* — guarding oneself from being immersed in the fleeting pleasures of *Olam Hazeh* — is a crucial prerequisite for *Zachor,* the intimacy with Hashem that we enjoy every Shabbos.

While abandoning the material pleasures of This World seems to be a formidable task, we are assisted in our pursuit by the shining example of Avraham *Avinu,* whose entire life was the embodiment of *Shamor V'Zachor,* as the following *Midrash* elucidates: It comments on the *pasuk,* שִׁמְעִי בַת וּרְאִי וְהַטִּי אָזְנֵךְ וְשִׁכְחִי עַמֵּךְ וּבֵית אָבִיךְ, *Listen, O maiden, and see, and incline your ear, and forget your people and your father's house* (*Tehillim* 45:11) that this alludes to Avraham *Avinu,* who was commanded by Hashem to forsake his father's home, as well as his birthplace and ancestral land. One can compare Avraham's relationship with Hashem to an individual who was traveling from place to place. Upon noticing a palace that was burning, this individual exclaims, "Is it possible that this palace has no owner?" The owner of the palace appears and proclaims, "I am the owner of the palace" (*Yalkut Bereishis* 62). Likewise, when Avraham was wondering, "Is it possible that the universe has no Master?" Hashem responded, "I am the Master of the universe."

By using the metaphor of a "burning palace," *Chazal* are simultaneously defining the primary objective of our lives as Torah-true Jews and also clarifying the concept of *Zachor* and *Shamor.* Let us assume that the palace represents This World and all of its material attractions. By showing Avraham a burning palace, Hashem is demonstrating to him and his descendants, the Jewish people, that despite the superficial allure of This World, the mission of *Klal Yisrael* is to overcome the temptation of *Olam Hazeh* rather than be captivated by it. By proclaiming His mastery over the very palace that is burning, Hashem is indicating His Wish that we "burn" (forsake) the many temptations of This World in favor of the true pleasures of *Olam Haba,* the World to Come. Despite our natural tendency to perceive This World as being the true palace, by allowing the palace to be consumed by flames, Hashem is teaching Avraham (and all future generations of Jews) that This World is not the palace, but rather, as *Avos* (4 :16) notes, merely *the corridor leading to the palace* of *Olam Haba.* In the *pasuk* introducing this *Midrash,* David *HaMelech* voices a similar theme — *Oh maiden!* (an allusion to the Jewish people), *forgot your people and your father's house.* Turn away from the superficial charm of This World and you will be amply rewarded in the Future World.

When *Chazal* draw an association between *Zachor* and *Shamor* they are not only referring to the two different terms that the Torah utilizes (in the two renditions of the *Aseres HaDibros*) to introduce the *mitzvah* of Shabbos, but also to the very essence of Torah life. By following Avraham's example and realizing that This World is not the true palace but merely a burning edifice (and at most a corridor to the Royal Palace of *Olam Haba*), we fulfill the spirit of *Shamor*. In fact, as a prerequisite for coming close to Hashem, Avraham was bidden to forget his past. So too, we leave behind This World before tasting the true pleasures of the World to Come. By clinging to Hashem like Avraham did – once he forsook the pleasures of This World – we merit to partake in the spirit of *Zachor* as well and enjoy an unusual degree of intimacy with Hashem.

By associating the duality of *Zachor* and *Shamor* with *Shabbos Kodesh* (despite their relevance to all of Torah), *Chazal* are indicating that there is no more opportune time to fulfill the spirit of *Zachor* and *Shamor* than on Shabbos. On this day, which is described as a microcosm of the World to Come, as we benefit from the presence of the *neshamah yeseirah*, we are particularly well-equipped to not only leave behind the fleeting pleasures of *Olam Hazeh*, but also to cling to Hashem as we will ultimately do in *Olam Haba*. However, as we read in the daily *Shacharis* service: כָּל דָּבָר שֶׁהָיָה בִּכְלַל וְיָצָא מִן הַכְּלָל לְלַמֵּד, לֹא לְלַמֵּד עַל עַצְמוֹ יָצָא, אֶלָּא לְלַמֵּד עַל הַכְּלָל כֻּלּוֹ יָצָא, *A concept that was included in a general principle and was then singled out as an exception to this principle – [this exemption] comes not only to teach about itself but also to teach us something about the entire generality*. By teaching us that the duality of *Zachor V'Shamor* applies on Shabbos – that by yielding the pleasures of This World we may merit unparalleled intimacy with Hashem (known as *deveikus*) – *Chazal* are encouraging us to lead our daily lives in the same manner. By recalling Avraham's lesson that all of *Olam Hazeh* is nothing more than a passing phenomenon ("burning palace"), and the true spiritual rewards remain for us in the World to Come, we merit to live every day in the spirit of *Zachor* and *Shamor*.

By associating Avraham's "discovery" of *HaKadosh Baruch Hu* with the vision of a burning palace and with the theme of *Zachor* and *Shamor*, *Chazal* are perhaps alluding to the special role played by the Shabbos lights (*neiros Shabbos*). Just as a fire not only destroys but also emits light, so too, Avraham *Avinu* not only abandoned his past but also became a true luminary to all of mankind. We, too, every Shabbos, are not only "burning" the old-discredited material values but are kindling the flames of our enthusiastic *avodas Hashem*. Whenever we kindle the Shabbos *licht* we are recalling both characteristics of fire — the destruction of evil and the nurturing of a new and intimate relationship with Hashem (refer to our chapter on "The Shabbos Lights"). (Adapted from *Lech Lecha* 5660)

בשם הרב הקדוש מפרשיסחא במ״ש רז״ל לעולם יכנוס אדם שתי פתחים ויתפלל שפתח אחד לצאת מעוה״ז ופתח השני לכנוס בעולם העליון עכ״ד. וב׳ אלו הם בחי׳ זכור ושמור בשבת ג״כ כמ״ש במ״א מזה.

In a similar vein, the great *chassidic* thinker, R' Simcha Bunim of Peshischa, explained the recommendation of *Chazal* (*Berachos* 8a) that one should enter through two "openings" (doorways) before commencing to *daven* — as an allusion to the requirement to leave the material confines of This World and then enter through the portals of the World to Come (at least in a spiritual sense) before even commencing to pray. Likewise, the spirit of *Zachor* and *Shamor* — abstaining from the materialism of This World prior to partaking of the spiritual pleasures of the World to Come — pertains not only to the observance of Shabbos, but also to the proper ambiance for *tefillah*. (*Vayeira* 5665)

Active and Passive Aspects of Shabbos (and of the Entire Torah)

ובימי המעשה הוא בחי׳ גליא והוא ימי מלחמה להלחם עם הסט״א שהטבע מסתיר ומעלים הקדושה אבל איש ישראל צריך להלחם ולברר ולהעיד כי כל הטבע הכל מאתו ית״ש בלבד. וזהו בנסוע הארון. כמו שרמזו בנסוע גי׳ יעקב. והוא בחי׳ ימי המעשה ... וב׳ אלו כלל כל התורה זכור ושמור מ״ע ומל״ת סור מרע בחי׳ המלחמה. ועשה טוב אין טוב אלא תורה בחי׳ שבת קודש יעשה כולו תורה ומיוחד רק לבנ״י ושם אין מגע נכרי ונק׳ יום מנוחה.

As indicated in the previous *dvar Torah*, the concepts of *Zachor* and *Shamor*, while particularly pertinent to Shabbos, are a paradigm for the entire Torah. Just as there exists a *passive* aspect to Shabbos (abstaining from *melachah*) as well as an *active* aspect (*Kiddush*, *oneg Shabbos*), so too, the Torah itself consists of positive commandments which are performed actively (the 248 *mitzvos asei*), symbolized by *Zachor*, as well as the negative commandments (365 *mitzvos lo sa'asei*), which we fulfill by refraining from violating Hashem's Will and are represented by *Shamor*.

According to *Chazal* (*Shabbos* 116a), the two *pesukim* beginning with וַיְהִי בִּנְסֹעַ הָאָרֹן, *When the Ark would journey*, and וּבְנֻחֹה, *And when it rested* (*Bamidbar* 10:35-36) comprise a distinct book of the Torah.[1] Perhaps the justification for this distinction is that they represent both aspects — refraining from evil (*Shamor*) as well as accomplishing good (*Zachor*). Whereas the first of these two *pesukim* emphasizes the battle against all of our foes, which certainly includes the *yetzer hara*, one of our deadliest enemies (*Shamor*), the second *pasuk*, וּבְנֻחֹה, alludes to the sense of rest and harmony that we derive from performing Hashem's positive commandments and especially from studying Torah (*Zachor*).

(*Beha'aloscha* 5660)

בשבת קודש זכור ושמור כאחד וכן שם שבת השבתה ושביתה כמ״ש ויכל וישבות ועל שניהם ויברך את יום השביעי.

הבחי׳ גם בשבת לשון השבתה ממלאכה וסט״א ערקית ולכן יש בו תוספות נשמה ושביתה והם בחי׳ זכור ושמור.

It is significant that both aspects of Shabbos — the active and passive — were blessed by Hashem. When describing the first Shabbos, the Torah not only mentions that Hashem blessed the seventh day, but also emphasizes two distinct events that occurred on that first Shabbos — "completion" of the universe (וַיְכַל אֱלֹהִים), as well as Hashem "resting" from Creation (וַיִּשְׁבֹּת מִכָּל מְלַאכְתּוֹ). Evidently, both aspects — the active phase, completion of Creation (*Zachor*), as well as the passive, no longer Creating (*Shamor*) — are equally significant and are both being blessed.

Even the concept of resting on Shabbos (which seemingly is a purely passive act of abstaining from *melachah*) contains a "positive aspect." By abstaining from *melachah*, we ensure that the *yetzer hara*, which thrives in an environment of materialism, becomes ineffective. Consequently, the more positive aspect of rest becomes apparent. Instead of being

1. While we generally assume that there are five books of the Torah, according to this approach of *Chazal* the book of *Bamidbar* actually consists of three distinct books, each with its own message. Consequently, the entire Torah is comprised of seven books.

threatened by the forces of evil, we now benefit from the addition of a potent spiritual force motivating us to do better – the *neshamah yeseirah*.

(*Lech Lecha* 5662; *Vayeishev* 5664)

וכן בש״ק שהוא נותן דעה באיש ישראל כמ״ש לדעת כי אני ה׳ מקדישכם. יש בו קידוש והבדלה זכור ושמור. השבתת מלאכה. ושביתה ומנוחה ודביקות אל השורש.

Exploring the concept of the active and passive components of Shabbos further, we notice that this theme permeates the entire spirit of Shabbos. Thus, the Shabbos is inaugurated with *Kiddush*, a positive/active statement of the sanctification of *Klal Yisrael*, and concludes with *Havdalah*, which emphasizes our separation from the rest of mankind, essentially a passive function. Even the concept of *shevisah*, "resting," contains both a passive component – abstaining from *melachah* – and a positive aspect – resting from *Olam Hazeh's* materialism so that we can return to our heavenly roots (refer to our chapter on *Menuchah* and the prohibition of *melachah* for further discussion of these concepts). (*Tazria* 5661)

ולכן הי׳ לו ב׳ שבטים. מנשה ע״ש כי נשני. ואפרים ע״ש התוספות. והם בחי׳ זכור ושמור.

The two reasons for the name given by Rachel *Imeinu* to Yosef *HaTzaddik*, as well as the names of Yosef's two children, Menasheh and Efrayim, also reflect this theme – the need to passively separate from evil (סוּר מֵרָע) before undertaking to do good (וַעֲשֵׂה טוֹב). Thus, Rachel emphasizes, אָסַף אֱלֹהִים אֶת חֶרְפָּתִי, *God has taken away my shame* (of not having any children), before praying יֹסֵף ה׳ לִי בֵּן אַחֵר, *May Hashem add on for me another son* (*Bereishis* 30:23-24). Before contemplating to attain greater levels of *avodas Hashem*, it is imperative that we "remove our shame" (our previous transgressions). Similarly, Yosef's first son was named Menasheh, related to נַשַּׁנִי, *forget* (ibid. 41:51). Only after forgetting and severing all ties with evil is it possible to contemplate fruitful and productive spiritual growth, as the name of Yosef's second son, Efrayim (related to הִפְרַנִי, *be fruitful*; 41:52), implies.

(*Tazria* 5661; *Vayeitzei* 5648)

◆§ Establishing and Implementing the Covenant (of Morality)

אלו בחי׳ זכור ושמור. המילה שניתן לאברהם והשמירה של יוסף הצדיק.

In accordance with our assertion in the previous *dvar Torah* that the concept of *Zachor* and *Shamor* pertains not only to Shabbos but rather is a paradigm for all of Torah, we suggest that the duality of *Zachor* and *Shamor* alludes to the Covenant of Morality that Hashem first established with Avraham *Avinu* at the time of his circumcision. By removing the *orlah,* which symbolized rampant immorality, Avraham was ensuring that his posterity would distance itself from immoral behavior. However, Avraham was commanded not only to establish the Covenant of Morality (*Bris Ha'Maor*) through his own sterling example but also to "guard the Covenant" (*Bereishis* 17:9). [The implementation of this role (symbolized by the *Shamor* concept) was left to Yosef *HaTzaddik* who by resisting the importuning of Potiphar's wife was a beacon of morality in the promiscuous society of Egypt.]

(*Vayeishev* 5662)

◆§ The Two Covenants – Morality and Speech

והוא ברית הלשון. מילה ברית המעור. ושבת כולל שניהם זכור ושמור.

In the previous *dvar Torah* we suggested that *Zachor* and *Shamor* represent both the establishment (between Avraham *Avinu* and Hashem) and the implementation (by Yosef *HaTzaddik*) of a Covenant of Morality. It is also possible that *Zachor* and *Shamor* represent the two covenants (refer to *Sefer Yetzirah*) that define a Jew's obligations — the *Bris HaMaor,* the Covenant of Morality, as well as the *Bris HaLashon,* the Covenant of Speech obligating us to guard our speech.

(*Chanukah* 5655)

ונראה דשניהם אמת כי יש בשבת זכור ושמור והוא בחי׳ יוסף ויהודה. והם בחי׳ סתים וגליא ברית המעור וברית הלשון. כי שבת סהדותא איקרי. והפה הוא בחי׳ התגלות שהפה נברא להודות לה׳ וזכור הוא באתכסיא. ולכן לא הכירו השבטים כוחו של יוסף. ויהודה כ׳ בי׳ אתה יודוך אחיך כי הארה שלו בהתגלות. ואיתא יוסף קידש ש״ש נסתר ניתוסף לו ה׳ משמו של הקב״ה ויהודה קידש ש״ש בפרהסיא נקרא כולו ע״ש של הקב״ה.

Elaborating upon this theme, we suggest that the two covenants represent two aspects of Shabbos. On one hand, there is a *visible* aspect of Shabbos whereby *Klal Yisrael* through its observance of Shabbos testifies that Hashem created heaven and earth. However, there also exists a *hidden* aspect of Shabbos that can only be appreciated by *Klal Yisrael* and *HaKadosh Baruch Hu*. As the Torah states: אוֹת הִיא בֵּינִי וּבֵינֵיכֶם, *It is a sign between Me and you* [*Bnei Yisrael*] (*Shemos* 31:13). While Shabbos is commemorated by *Klal Yisrael* here on earth, the true roots of Shabbos lie in Heaven. In a similar vein, the two covenants referred to previously, the Covenant of Morality and the Covenant of Speech, also represent these two aspects of Shabbos. While the Covenant of Speech seeks to define our *public* behavior, the Covenant of Morality alludes to Judaism's insistence upon adhering to its values, even regarding the most *private* and intimate matters (a concept known as *tznius*).

The relationship between the two *shevatim* who were the pillars of *Klal Yisrael* may also be explained in this manner. As *Chazal* (*Sotah* 10b) relate, whileYosef sanctified Hashem's Name in private by rebuffing the overtures of Potiphar's wife, Yehudah sanctified His Name in public by confessing publicly to his (unintentional) relationship with Tamar. *Zachor* and *Shamor* represent these two aspects of Shabbos. *Zachor*, "remembering," refers to a cognitive processs that is not always apparent. On the other hand, *Shamor*, refers to the more obvious aspects of Shabbos, abstaining from *melachah*, which is a very visible tribute to Hashem's creation of heaven and earth. (*Vayechi* 5656)

⁂ Hashem's Role / *Klal Yisrael's* Role

וכתיב בשבת ביני ובין בנ״י אות היא. א״כ השבת יש בו חלק להקב״ה וחלק לבנ״י. וב׳ אלו הם ב׳ בחי׳ הנ״ל. זכור ושמור. יוסף ויהודה.

In the previous *dvar Torah* we spoke about the hidden roots of Shabbos as well as its more visible manifestation. The dual aspect of Shabbos is implied in the *pasuk*, בֵּינִי וּבֵין בְּנֵי יִשְׂרָאֵל אוֹת הִיא לְעֹלָם, *Between Me and the Children of Israel it* (Shabbos) *is a sign forever* (*Shemos* 31:17). Evidently, there is a hidden aspect of Shabbos, known only to Hashem, as well as a more public, distinct role in which *Klal Yisrael* participates – *shemiras Shabbos. Zachor*, the hidden aspect of Shabbos and *Shamor*, the more visible observance of Shabbos, also reflect these two aspects of Shabbos. (*Vayechi* 5656)

◆§ The Tree of Life (*Zachor*) / The Road Towards the Tree of Life (*Shamor*)

ובשבת יש פתיחת השער והארת עץ החיים לכן יש בו זכור ושמור זכור בחי׳ מצות עשה דכתיב בהם אשר יעשה אותם האדם וחי בהם בחי׳ עץ החיים ושמור מל״ת לשמור דרך עץ החיים וכפי השמירה זוכין לזכירה.

To appreciate the association between *Zachor* and *Shamor*, we recall that after Adam's sin and his expulsion from *Gan Eden* he was barred from entering *Gan Eden*. To ensure that he would never return – and to guard the road leading to *Gan Eden* and the Tree of Life – Hashem posted the Cherubs (כְּרֻבִים) and the fiery blade of the revolving sword (לַהַט הַחֶרֶב הַמִּתְהַפֶּכֶת) to the east of Eden.

Every Shabbos, a day when we experience a taste of the spiritual pleasures of the World to Come, and when "the gates of Eden swing open," we can transcend the barriers that prevented mankind from entering *Gan Eden*. Every Shabbos, as we perform the positive commandments such as *Kiddush* (that symbolizes all *mitzvos asei*), which are described by the Torah as a source of life (אֲשֶׁר יַעֲשֶׂה אֹתָם הָאָדָם וָחַי בָּהֶם, *which man shall perform and by which he shall live, Vayikra* 18:5), we "approach" and come closer (in a spiritual sense) to the Tree of Life. However, to successfully reach the Tree of Life, we need to navigate through the obstacles blocking our entry into *Gan Eden*. To help us accomplish this prerequisite to entering *Gan Eden*, we observe the "negative commandments" (*mitzvos lo sa'asei*) of Shabbos. By abstaining from *melachah* on Shabbos – the *Shamor* aspect we are guarding the path to the Tree of Life and ensuring that we don't partake of the Tree of Life without proper preparation. (*Vayeira* 5662)

◆ The Tree of Life / The Tree of Knowledge

וזכור הוא בחי׳ עה״ח. ושמור עה״ד שצריך שמירה כמ״ש לשמור דרך עץ החיים. ובש״ק שנפתח שער הפנימי שאין תערובת פסולת לכן הם לאחרים.

In the previous *dvar Torah,* we suggested that *Zachor* and *Shamor* represent the Tree of Life and the path towards the Tree of Life, respectively. Extending the analogy between *Gan Eden* and Shabbos, we propose that *Zachor* symbolizes the Tree of Life (עֵץ הַחַיִּים) while *Shamor* represents the Tree of Knowledge (עֵץ הַדַּעַת). Whereas in This World, the fruit of the Tree of Knowledge of Good and Evil is "off-limits" to mankind because of the inevitable confusion of good and evil that would result from partaking of its fruit (such as happened to Adam after he partook of its fruit), in *Olam Haba,* where evil will no longer exist, both the fruit of the Tree of Knowledge as well as the fruit of the Tree of Life will be accessible to us (in a spiritual sense). This can be demonstrated from the prophecy of Yechezkel (37:16, designated as the *Haftorah* of *Parashas Vayigash*) in which he is commanded to hold two pieces of wood together, indicating that in the Future World any distinction between the Tree of Life and the Tree of Knowledge will no longer exist. Even in This World, every Shabbos, which is considered to be a microcosm of *Olam Haba* (blessed by the presence of the *neshamah yeseirah*) when all evil will disappear, we are permitted to enjoy the spiritual fruit of both the Tree of Knowledge and the Tree of Life. They are both represented through the dual concept of *Zachor* and *Shamor.* Whereas the fruit of the Tree of Life may be readily enjoyed (in particular, in the form of *limud Torah*) as indicated by the positive commandment of *Zachor* — the fruit of the Tree of Knowledge must be guarded carefully, in the spirit of *Shamor.* In fact, Hashem dispatched Cherubs and the fiery blade of the revolving sword to guard the path leading to the Tree of Life, where the Tree of Knowledge was located.

(*Vayigash* 5648)

⸎ Humbling the Body / Elevating the Soul

וכמו כן בשבת קודש זכור ושמור הם ב׳ בחי׳ הנ״ל. הכנעת הגוף לכן כל המלאכות בטלין בשבת וזהו בח״י שמור. וזכור הוא התגברות הנשמה.

While in previous *divrei Torah* we emphasized that by integrating the concept of *Zachor* and *Shamor* we are able not only to leave behind the material trappings of *Olam Hazeh* but also to enter another world — the lofty spiritual realm of the World to Come — here we will focus on the impact that both *Zachor* and *Shamor* have on us during our life span in This World. On one hand, every Shabbos, by abstaining from *melachah* — many of the material activities that we perform all week — in the spirit of *Shamor*, we negate the body (גוּף). Once we diminish the role of the material aspect of our lives, we are now prepared to appreciate in the spirit of *Zachor* the enhanced role of the soul (נְשָׁמָה). The *Zohar* summarizes this aspect of *Zachor* and *Shamor* by defining Shabbos as a "day of the soul and not the body." (*Vayishlach* 5654)[1]

וכ׳ משכו וקחו משכו ידיכם מע״ז וקחו צאן של מצוה. ויש בחי׳ שמור וזכור. כלל מל״ת ומ״ע. וב׳ כוחות אלו נמסרו לבנ״י. שיכולין למשוך מן הטבע והגשמיות. ושיכולין לעורר הקדושה ולהתדבק בהקב״ה.

With this approach, we can appreciate another dimension of the relationship between Shabbos and *Yetzias Mitzrayim*. This association of *Zachor* and *Shamor*, first diminishing the once-dominant role of the body (by curtailing our material pleasures) which, in turn, allows the soul's spirituality to prevail, was first formulated at the time of *Yetzias Mitzrayim*. Then Hashem insisted that *Klal Yisrael* first rid itself of all the Egyptians' pagan deities and only then sanctify itself by offering the *korban pesach*. (*Bo* 5662)

1. Refer to *Re'eh* 5662 where the *Sfas Emes* uses this approach to explain the relationship between fear of Hashem (*yiras Hashem*) and serving Him joyously (*simchah*). The role of fear of Hashem is similar to that of *Shamor* — humbling our body. On the other hand, by serving Hashem with joy we enable the soul to prevail.

והקב״ה נתן לנו ע״ז תרי״ג מצות. רמ״ח מ״ע להאיר כח הנשמה בגוף ע״י המ״ע כמ״ש וחי בהם. והמל״ת הם לשמור הגוף וחומר שלא יעשו פגם בנשמה ... לכן ענין מל״ת נגד שס״ה גידים שלא יסתמו דרך הילוך החיות וכח הנשמה. וב׳ הנ״ל הם בחי׳ זכור ושמור. וכל זה תלוי בזיכוך הגוף כמ״ש זכה נוחל. וע״ז אז״ל רצה הקב״ה לזכות את ישראל כו׳ הרבה להם תורה ומצות. ושבת הוא זכור ושמור כלל כל המצות.

Extending this theme a bit further, we suggest that the body itself can be used as a vehicle for *avodas Hashem* if it is properly influenced by the *neshamah*. By granting us both positive and negative commandments, the Torah is influencing the relationship between body and soul in two distinct ways. On one hand, the negative commandments prevent the body and its material pleasures from corrupting the soul. On the other hand, the positive commandments were given to enable some of the enlightened influence of the soul to affect the body. In fact, each of the 248 limbs of the body is nurtured by the positive commandment to which it corresponds. As the Torah writes, אֲשֶׁר יַעֲשֶׂה אֹתָם הָאָדָם וָחַי בָּהֶם, *which man shall perform and by which he shall live* (*Vayikra* 18:5), which refers to the *mitzvos*. Similarly, *Chazal* (*Makkos* 3:16) suggest that Hashem offered *Klal Yisrael* many *mitzvos* (and a vast Torah to study) לְזַכּוֹת אֶת יִשְׂרָאֵל, which may be interpreted, "for the purpose of purifying (the body as well as the soul of) the Jewish people." *Zachor* and *Shamor* — which we have already established represent not only two aspects of Shabbos but all of the Torah's positive and negative commandments — leave a great impact on both the body and soul. While the negative commandments, if observed properly, prevent the body from corrupting the soul, the positive commandments enable the soul to influence the body for good. (*Tazria* 5653)

שמור וזכור ובשמור כתי׳ וזכרת כי עבד היית. כי הנה השבת הוא שביתת ממלאכה והוא תיקון הגוף להיות בן חורין מהתקשרוה בהבלי עולם. וזה בחי׳ שמור. וזכור הוא בחי׳ עשה טוב ... וכאשר חכמים הגידו כי בשבת א״צ אות תפילין.

Utilizing this approach, we can appreciate why *tefillin* are not worn on Shabbos. In essence, whatever would ordinarily be accomplished by observing the *mitzvah* of *tefillin* is achieved through the Shabbos itself. The function of the arm-*tefillin* to perfect our body and release it from the material impulses that it is otherwise subordinated to, is performed by the *Shamor* aspect of Shabbos which releases us from the vanities of This World. [In fact, in the second rendition of the *Aseres HaDibros* (in *Parashas Va'eschanan*), associated with *Shamor*, the Torah relates Shabbos to *Yetzias Mitzrayim*, the seminal moment when we were liberated from the defiled environment of Pharaoh's Egypt.] Similarly, the function of the *tefillin shel rosh* (head-*tefillin*) is to sanctify our speech and thoughts (as it says in *Shemos* 13:9: *So that* H*ASHEM's Torah may be in your mouth*), and is fulfilled through the *Zachor* aspect of Shabbos, which reminds us of *Matan Torah*[1] – the moment when *Klal Yisrael's* thoughts, words, and bodies were infused with *kedushah*.

(Adapted from *Va'eschanan* 5651)

◈ Yetzias Mitzrayim (Shamor) / Kabbalas HaTorah (Zachor)

וב' אלו הם ג"כ בחי' זכור ושמור בש"ק. שמור נזכר בו יצ"מ וזכור הוא בחי' נשמה יתירה וזכירת ומתן תורה כמ"ש זכור בעצומו של יום מתן תורה.

Extending the theme that we discussed in the previous *dvar Torah*, we suggest that *Zachor* and *Shamor* represent two seminal events in Jewish history. Whereas *Shamor* reminds us of *Yetzias Mitzrayim* (the reason given for *shemiras Shabbos* in the second rendition of the *Aseres HaDibros* where the term *Shamor* is used), *Zachor* alludes to *Kabbalas HaTorah*. In fact, *Chazal* derive that the Torah was given on Shabbos from זָכוֹר אֶת יוֹם הַשַּׁבָּת, *Remember the Sabbath day* (*Shemos* 20:8).

Zachor and *Shamor* are not only of historical significance, helping us to recall *Yetzias Mitzrayim* and *Matan Torah*, but they also enable us to benefit from these events, as we shall elucidate. Every Shabbos, benefiting from the diminution of the *yetzer hara*, we perceive a release

1. From the *pasuk*, זָכוֹר אֶת יוֹם הַשַּׁבָּת, *Remember the Sabbath day* (*Shemos* 20:8), *Chazal* (*Shabbos* 86b) derive that the Torah was given on Shabbos.

from the effects of evil-doing, a form of *Yetzias Mitzrayim* (which symbolizes not only liberation from Egypt but also freedom from every force that oppresses or stifles us). As we enjoy the presence of the *neshamah yeseirah,* we sense some of the ambiance of *Matan Torah.*

(*Va'eschanan* 5659)

◆§ The Significance of *Zachor* and *Shamor* Being Said Simultaneously

אלו השפעות בשבת נעשין א׳ כמ״ש זכור ושמור בדבור אחד נאמרו הם בחי׳ מ״ע ומל״ת. ובש״ק הכל בקדושה שא״צ לבוא ע״י בירור התערובות. לכן בש״ק לא כתיב ערב.

According to *Chazal* (*Shevuos* 20b), the term *Zachor* used by the Torah to introduce the concept of Shabbos in the first rendition of the *Aseres HaDibros,* as well as *Shamor,* which the Torah uses in the second rendition (*Parashas Va'eschanan*) of the *Aseres HaDibros,* were said simultaneously. In light of our previous *divrei Torah* identifying *Shamor* with abstention from evil (and the material pleasures of *Olam Hazeh*), followed by *Zachor* and the development of an intimate relationship with Hashem, we can particularly appreciate why these two seminal terms were said at the same time. Whereas during the week, it is necessary to first engage the *yetzer hara* in intensive spiritual combat — by abstaining from evil and material vices no matter how tempting (*Shamor*) — before ascending to a loftier spiritual level (*Zachor*), on Shabbos these two processes occur at once. On this greatest of days, both the *Shamor* aspect of Shabbos (abstaining from evil), as well as the *Zachor* aspect (coming closer to Hashem) occur concurrently.

To corroborate our contention that every Shabbos the struggle against evil coincides with our quest for greater *kedushah,* we note that unlike the Six Days of Creation where *erev,* evening, always preceded *boker,* morning, when discussing the first Shabbos, the Torah only refers to יוֹם הַשְּׁבִיעִי, *the seventh day.* The evening is a period of darkness, where the light of the day has been superseded by darkness. In fact, the term *erev*

(עֶרֶב) is related to *taaroves* (תַּעֲרוֹבֶת, *mixture*), alluding to the confused mixture of good and evil that so often prevails in This World, especially during the six weekdays. On Shabbos, however, the confusion of good and evil dissipates. On Shabbos — the time when abstaining from evil (*Shamor*) occurs at the same time as accomplishing good (*Zachor*) — there is no darkness, no preliminary stage of *erev* that must precede *boker*, the clarity of the morning.

When *Chazal* (*Shabbos* 119b) describe the scene of the idyllic Jewish home where everything is completely prepared for Shabbos (the candles are lit, the beds have been made, the table has been set), they note that even the evil angel is forced to voice the blessing that the same scene should be replicated the following week. On Shabbos, the day when the obliteration of evil and the attainment of *kedushah* occur simultaneously, even the forces of evil bless the home of the Sabbath observer.

(*Vayeishev* 5649)

ושבת נמצא בו הארה מעץ החיים וז״ש טועמיה חיים זכו. וזה הנשמה יתירה היורדת בשבת לכן זכור ושמור בדבור אחד נאמרו כמ״ש והיו לאחדים שהוא מעין עוה״ב שאז יהיו לאחדים ממש.

Refer to our previous *dvar Torah* entitled, "The Tree of Life: The Tree of Knowledge" in which we suggested that *Zachor* represents the fruit of the Tree of Life while *Shamor* represents the fruit of the Tree of Knowledge. We also suggested there that in the Future World we will be able to enjoy the fruit of both trees (since any evil component of the Tree of Knowledge will no longer exist). With this contention, we gain new insight into the concept stated by *Chazal* that *Zachor* and *Shamor* were stated simultaneously. Whereas during the weekdays it may be necessary to abstain from evil as symbolized by the Tree of Knowledge, on Shabbos — when there is a lessening of evil influences — one may partake not only of the Tree of Life symbolized by *Zachor* but also from the Tree of Knowledge. *Zachor* and *Shamor* — both the fruit of the Tree of Knowledge and that of the Tree of Life — were said at the same time, indicating that on Shabbos, a microcosm of *Olam Haba*, both *Zachor* (Tree of Life) and *Shamor* (Tree of Knowledge) are identical.

(*Vayigash* 5648)

כי הנה כל הי״ב שבטים בירור התערובות טו״ר בעולם. והמה בענין ששת ימי המעשה ששה ימים וששה לילות כמ״ש ויהי ערב ויהי בוקר. ויוסף הוא בחי׳ השבת שהוא אחדות אחת. זכור ושמור בדיבור אחד נאמרו. מדת לילה ויום אחד הוא ביום השבת. וכתיב קמה אלומתי הוא בחי׳ הלולב צדיק כתמר יפרח וגבוה מכולם. תסובנה אלומותיכם כו׳ כי הכל נעשין אגודה אחת לסבב הלולב שהוא הצדיק.

We may attribute additional significance to the simultaneous rendition of *Zachor* and *Shamor*. We recall that as a result of Adam's sin (partaking of the fruit of the Tree of Knowledge of Good and Evil), the distinctions between good and evil would henceforth be blurred.[1] One of the primary missions of *Klal Yisrael* is to return the universe to its original state when the distinction between good and evil was recognizable. Two basic methods exist to accomplish this laudable objective: Firstly, by clarifying what is good and what is evil and then separating these two diametrically opposed concepts from each other. This was the preferred approach of Yosef's brothers. In fact, one of Yosef's dreams where they were standing in the field and preparing sheaves of grain (see *Bereishis* 37:7) illustrates a process which involves isolating the chaff from the grain. This is also the method that we assume during the workweek, which consists of six days and six nights (corresponding to the twelve tribes, Yosef's brothers). This approach is based on a clear delineation between good and evil, or between day (representing good) and night (evil).

However, Yosef utilized a different approach in combating evil. Instead of isolating the forces of evil, he brought them into the fold of those who perform good. This can be deduced from the conclusion of Yosef's dream when the brothers' sheaves turn around and pay homage to Yosef. This scene embodies the message of *achdus*, unity. In an environment of true *achdus*, we are all alike. Any previous distinction between good and evil no longer exists. This unity is achieved every Succos when the Four Species (including the *aravah* which represents the Jew who is totally lacking in Torah and *mitzvos*) are all bound to the *lulav*, which represents the *tzaddik*.[2] In an environment of such unity, there are no longer distinctions between good and evil, as all evil yields to good and ceases to exist.

1. Refer to *The Three Festivals*, pg. 69, for further discussion of this theme.

2. Refer to *Tehillim* 92:13 where the *tzaddik* is compared to a date palm, the source of the *lulav*.

Whereas *Shamor* represents the negation of evil, or at least the separation of good from evil, *Zachor* represents the ideal when evil no longer exists. During the week, *Shamor* is a necessary prerequisite for the eventual elimination of evil. However, on Shabbos when *Zachor* and *Shamor* were said simultaneously, the separation of evil and the bringing of these forces under the influence of the forces of good (such as the *tzaddikim* of each generation) occur at the same time. As further proof of our contention that on Shabbos the forces of evil cease (rather than act in a separate capacity), we recall that on Shabbos the Torah makes no distinction between day and night (unlike every day of the Six Days of Creation where the Torah writes, "It was evening and it was morning"), indicating that even evil, symbolized by night, comes under the embrace of good. (Adapted from *Succos* 5648)

מ״מ מי ששומר עצמו וחיותו ורצונו שלא להשתמש בו לעניני עוה״ז כדי שיהי׳ עיקר הרצון נקי לקיים מצותו ית׳. הוא בכלל זכור ג״כ שבדיבור אחד נאמרו כנ״ל. ומרע״ה במשנה תורה פירש הכנת בנ״י ג״כ איך לבוא לבחי׳ זכור כנ״ל.

Refer to our previous *dvar Torah* (entitled "Eliciting the Divine Spark", p. 44) in which we suggested that by observing *Shamor* – by determining that the Divine Spark in our midst be used appropriately and not be abused – we may merit to attain the level of *Zachor*, whereby we can benefit from the inner yearning to cling to Hashem (*deveikus*) that we possess. While it seems almost impossible to leap from the level of *Shamor*, of merely guarding the Divine Spark, to *Zachor* – actually benefiting from its Presence – *Chazal* note that *Shamor* and *Zachor* were said with one *dibbur* (Divine Statement), שָׁמוֹר וְזָכוֹר בְּדִבּוּר אֶחָד.

Homiletically, we may interpret the term *dibbur* as referring to the words of the Torah. While ordinarily it is impossible to advance from *Shamor* to *Zachor*, if the entire universe is governed on the basis of the Torah – as was the case at the time of *Matan Torah* – then this becomes possible. It is significant that *Onkelos* translates וַיֵּרֶד ה׳ עַל הַר סִינַי as וְאִתְגְּלִי ה׳, "Hashem *revealed* Himself on Mt. Sinai" (*Shemos* 19:20). In a universe dominated by Torah (which itself contains many hidden treasures), our Divine Spark, ordinarily recessed below the surface, may come to the forefront. In particular, when Hashem's Presence is revealed throughout the universe (as occurred at the time of the Giving of the Torah), it is possible to evoke the Divine Spirit embedded in our midst. By translating the term וַיֵּרֶד (descended) as וְאִתְגְּלִי (revealed), *Onkelos* may be indicating that when Hashem's Presence is manifest throughout the universe, it is also possible to evoke the Divine Spark in ourselves, and by doing so to reach the exalted levels of *Zachor* and *Shamor*. In such a blessed and sanctified universe, one may ascend in rapid succession from the potential of *Shamor* to the fulfillment of our potential that *Zachor* implies. (Adapted from *Shavuos* 5631)

וכן בענין רמ״ח ושס״ה שהם ב׳ מדרגות אברים וגידים כמ״ש שם בזוהר. אבל בשבת זכור ושמור בדיבור א׳ נאמרו. כי בשבת מ״ע ומל״ת באחדות ושולט בו שם ישראל.

If we assume that *Zachor* and *Shamor* represent positive and negative commandments respectively, we may derive additional insight from the coincidence of *Zachor* and *Shamor*. As we know, the 248 positive commandments correspond to the 248 limbs of the human body, each of which is imbued with the spiritual light engendered by that *mitzvah*. On the other hand, the 365 negative commandments correspond to the 365 sinews of the human body. We may perceive sinews (consisting of hard material) as buffers that often shield us from the full impact of a crushing fall. By observing the 365 negative commandments corresponding to those sinews, we ensure that they will not act as an impediment and spiritual barrier to the light of Torah infusing our entire personality. Whereas during the week the battle against evil must come first, and subsequently we bask in the light of Torah and *mitzvos* that permeates our entire body, on Shabbos when *Zachor* (corresponding to the positive commandments) and *Shamor* (corresponding to the negative commandments) were said simultaneously, it is not necessary to mount a separate attempt to battle evil. The struggle against the *yetzer hara* (similar to that waged by Yaakov against Esav's *malach*) recedes on Shabbos and we are able to immediately bask in the full light of Torah and *mitzvos*.

(Adapted from *Devarim* 5653)

◆§ Our Shabbos (*Zachor*) / Our Master's Shabbos (*Shamor*)

ולכן כיון שביצ״מ נכנסנו להיות עבדי ה׳ כמ״ש עבדי הם אשר הוצאתי כו׳ לכן יש לנו חלק בשביתת האדון ית״ש. ולכן יש בקבלת שבת ונשמה יתירה כמה חילוקים כדאיתא בזוה״ק שיש מקבל בבחי׳ בן ועבד ואפי׳ אם אנו כחמורים אעפ״כ הוא בכלל חמורך אנחנו. ובשעת קבלת התורה לא היו צריכין לשום טעם למה צוה לנו השבת שהיו אז במעלה עליונה כדכתי׳ אני אמרתי אלקים אתם. אבל עתה אחר החטא התחיל אלה שינוים בכמה מדרגות עבדך אמתך בהמתך. ומ״מ בכלל שייך לנו השבת מצד העבדות עכ״פ. וגם בבחי׳ בהמה כתי׳ בהמה הייתי עמך שאפי׳ במדרגה השפלה אעפ״כ כתי׳ עמך.

Perhaps the distinction between *Zachor* and *Shamor* is best indicated by the text of the *Aseres HaDibros* where these terms originate. In *Parashas Va'eschanan* the Torah commands us to observe Shabbos to acknowledge that Hashem liberated us from Mitzrayim, and consequently became our master. As a servants of *HaKadosh Baruch Hu*, it is only appropriate that we rest when He does. Moreover, by specifying that not only free men but also servants, and even their oxen and donkeys, rest on Shabbos, the Torah is alluding that no matter how low our spiritual level may be — even if we have sunk to the level of donkeys[1] — nonetheless, we should rest on Shabbos. Even today, we can benefit from the *kedushah* of Shabbos, to some extent, regardless of our current spiritual level.

On the other hand, at the time of *Kabbalas HaTorah*, when we had achieved a spiritual level virtually identical to that of angels, it was not necessary to justify our observance of Shabbos on the basis of Hashem, our Master's Shabbos. At the time of *Matan Torah* we intrinsically deserved the Shabbos. Much as Hashem ceased creating on Shabbos, so too, we abstained from *melachah*. It was only later when the chasm between us and Hashem grew so much greater (as a result of our sins) that it became necessary to justify *shemiras Shabbos* in terms of a servant/master relationship.

1. Cf. *Shabbos* 112b where the term חֲמוֹרִים is used to describe *Klal Yisrael's* inferior spiritual status vis-a-vis previous generations — וְאִם רִאשׁוֹנִים בְּנֵי אֲנָשִׁים אָנוּ כַּחֲמוֹרִים.

This distinction between our intrinsic Shabbos and our later observance of Shabbos is also reflected in the terms *Zachor* and *Shamor*. Whereas *Zachor* implies an inherent observance of Shabbos (simply to remember the Shabbos and you will be able to relate to its *kedushah*), *Shamor* is, in effect, a Divine plea to guard ourselves against slipping further away from the sanctity of Shabbos — a very pertinent request in the aftermath of *Klal Yisrael's* involvement in the sin of the Golden Calf. In the *parashah* of *Shamor*, the Torah offers the possibility of Shabbos being observed at various levels, since it is imperative that we not totally detach ourselves from the Shabbos regardless of the level of our *kedushah*. However (as we have indicated frequently throughout this chapter), *Chazal* perceive *Shamor* not as an end in itself but rather as a prelude to *Zachor*, as they relate, "Whoever is required to observe *Shamor* is also required to observe *Zachor*" (*Shevuos* 20b). By observing *Shamor* — albeit on a a reduced level — we will eventually merit to return to the level where we fully observe *Zachor*. In the interim, we pride ourselves and rejoice at the opportunity to observe Shabbos, even if it is only on the basis of it being our Master's day of rest. As we say in the *Shemoneh Esrei*, "Those who guard Shabbos (*shomrei Shabbos*) rejoice in Your Kingdom." As servants (indicated by the term *shomrei Shabbos*), we rejoice that we enjoy the opportunity to share the Shabbos of our King and Master. (*Va'eschanan* 5650)

Servants of Hashem

וזהו בחי׳ זכור ושמור שמור בחי׳ עבד כמ״ש הטעם וזכרת כי עבד היית כו׳ ע״כ צוך כו׳ לעשות את כו׳ השבת לקיים גזירת המלך. וזכור בחי׳ בן כמ״ש הטעם כי ששת ימים עשה כו׳. הרי מבאר הטעם של השבת והוא בן לחפשא בגניזין דמלכא. וב׳ הדיברות ראשונים ואחרונים ניתנו בהר סיני עבד ובן. ועיקר חביבות עבודת איש ישראל בבחי׳ עבד כמ״ש עבדי אתה. וכן אומרים ישמחו במלכותך שומרי שבת. הגם דבחי׳ שמור למטה מבחי׳ זכור. אעפ״כ צריכין אנחנו לשמוח בבחי׳ זו. כי בן ירושה הוא ואין הבן יכול להשתנות. אבל בחי׳ עבד הוא בכח מעשה האדם להכניע עצמו תחת מלכות שמים ובזה אנו שמחים.

Our relationship with *Hakadosh Baruch Hu* assumes two forms: First, we are *servants* of Hashem (עֲבָדִים), as the Torah writes, כִּי לִי בְנֵי יִשְׂרָאֵל

עֲבָדִים, *For the Children of Israel are servants to Me* (*Vayikra* 25:55). In addition, we are *children* (בָּנִים) of Hashem — בָּנִים אַתֶּם לַה׳ אֱלֹהֵיכֶם, *You are children to HASHEM, your God* (*Devarim* 14:1).

This dual status that we all enjoy, servants and children, is reflected in the different forms of *avodas Hashem* undertaken by Yaakov's children, Yehudah and Yosef. Whereas Yosef's *kedushah* was derived from his status as Yaakov's son [אֵלֶּה תֹּלְדוֹת יַעֲקֹב יוֹסֵף, *These are the generations of Yaakov, Yosef* (cf. *Bereishis* 37:2); also, בֵּן פֹּרָת יוֹסֵף, *Yosef is a fruitful son* (cf. ibid. 49:22)], Yehudah fills the distinguished role of being a servant of Hashem. The same distinction between being a servant of Hashem and a son is found in the illustrious descendants of both Yosef and Yehudah (David and his dynasty who devotedly serve *Klal Yisrael*), who will facilitate the Final Redemption. Thus, the descendant of Yosef (who will die in battle defending *Klal Yisrael* against the enemy's onslaught) known as *Mashiach* ben Yosef is described as a precious son of Hashem (*Yirmiyahu* 31:19, הֲבֵן יַקִּיר לִי אֶפְרַיִם), while the *Mashiach* descended from Yehudah is described as Hashem's servant (*Yeshayahu* 52:13, הִנֵּה יַשְׂכִּיל עַבְדִּי).

The dual relationship of the Jewish people to Hashem — as both servants and children — is also reflected in the *Zachor* and *Shamor* concept.[1] Unlike a servant whose primary function is to subordinate himself to his master — as we do by observing the many restrictions of Shabbos included in *Shamor* — as children of Hashem, we do more than simply not defy Him. On the contrary, we develop an intimate relationship with Him by practicing the many positive commandments of Shabbos.

We may deduce from the *parshiyos* in which *Zachor* and *Shamor* are written that they represent these two distinct relationships with Hashem, that of the son and the servant respectively. Whereas in the *parashah* beginning with *Zachor* the Torah states the reason for celebrating Shabbos (because Hashem created heaven and earth in six days and rested on the seventh day), in the portion discussing the *Shamor* concept, no reason is given for observing Shabbos. Rather, the Torah simply says, *And you shall remember that you were a slave in the land of*

1. While the *Sfas Emes* draws a parallel between the duality of serving Hashem as children as well as servants and the duality of Shabbos, *Zachor* and *Shamor*, he does not elaborate on this relationship. The following remarks seeking to clarify this relationship are the author's.

Egypt therefore H*ASHEM*, *your God, has commanded you to make the Sabbath day"* (*Devarim* 5:12). A servant requires no reason to justify his obedience. It is enough for him to be told that it is his master's desire that a particular command be fulfilled.

Let us consider briefly the comparative virtues of being a servant and a son of Hashem. On one hand, no servant can match the love and enthusiasm with which a son serves his father. On the other hand, a servant enjoys the virtue of being consistently loyal to his master. Even if his enthusiasm diminishes, as a servant, he knows that he must dutifully serve his master. So too, as servants of Hashem, we negate any wishes that we may have that are contrary to the Divine Will.

In some respects, the role of a servant is even greater than that of a son. Unlike the distinction of being a son, which in essence results from Divine selection (just as a child of a natural father derives that distinction through genetics), one has to earn the distinction of being a true servant of Hashem. According to Yeshayahu (49:3), Hashem accords the Jewish people the distinction of being "My servants, in whom I take pride." Similarly, *Klal Yisrael* itself rejoices in its status of being Hashem's servants. As we read in the Shabbos *Musaf*: "They rejoice in Your Kingdom those who are *shomeri Shabbos*." Rather than rejoice in our status of observing, *Zachor* (seemingly a loftier level than *Shamor*), we take delight in being Hashem's servants, in fulfillment of *Shamor*.

(*Behar* 5660)

ויוסף ויהודה. הם ב׳ בחי׳ הנ״ל. ביוסף כתיב תולדות יעקב יוסף ובן פורת יוסף. ויהודה קיבל המלכות והוא בחי׳ עבד. ולכן יש משיח בן יוסף הבן יקיר לי אפרים. ויש משיח בן דוד ועליו נאמר הנה ישכיל עבדי . והשבת כולל ב׳ בחי׳ הנ״ל. והם בחי׳ זכור ושמור.

Utilizing this approach, we can appreciate why Shabbos is called both an inheritance (נַחֲלָה) and a gift (מַתָּנָה – refer to our extensive chapter on the theme, "The Gift of Shabbos"). As children of Hashem, we benefit from His inheritance. As His servants, we merit His gift as a reward for fulfillment of His Will.

(Adapted from *Vayeishev* 5653)

◆§ Two Aspects of *Gilui Shechinah* (Divine Revelation on Earth)

ויהודה המכין למטה כח החרישה שיוכל אח״כ לירד השפע מן השמים ובכח יוסף נגמר הפעולה ונקרא קוצר. אכן לעתיד יהי׳ אחדות למטה כמו למעלה ואז יהיה יהודה עיקר ... ואיתא כי שבת הוא מעין עוה״ב לכן בשבת זכור ושמור בדיבור אחד נאמרו והם ב׳ בחי׳ הנ״ל. ויתכן לרמוז בחריש ובקציר תשבות על ב׳ בחי׳ הנ״ל יהודה ויוסף זכור ושמור. שמור הוא בלב. זכור בפה בהתגלות. וזה הרמז עזור לשובתים בשביעי בחריש ובקציר עולמים כי הם ב׳ עולמות.

To gain yet additional insight into the duality of *Zachor* and *Shamor*, we refer to the *Midrash* (*Yalkut Bereishis* 150) that interprets the *pasuk*, וְנִגַּשׁ חוֹרֵשׁ בַּקֹּצֵר, *The plower of the field will approach the reaper* (*Amos* 9:13), as referring to the symbiotic relationship that will exist in the Future World between Yehudah and Yosef. Whereas in This World, Yosef and Yehudah adopted divergent approaches in their quest to make this universe a conducive environment for the *Shechinah* to be perceived, in the Future World their divergent paths will converge. Just as it is necessary to first plow so that the seeds will eventually sprout, so too, Yehudah perceived his role as preparing This World for the revelation of Hashem. Although plowing is necessary for the growth of vegetation, it is only when the crop is blessed with abundant rainfall that it can be nurtured to its maximum growth potential and eventually be harvested. Similarly, Yosef as the reaper was able through his many merits to consummate what Yehudah had initiated. Whereas Yehudah prepared This World for the *Shechinah*, Yosef was able through his *zechusim* to actually bring the Divine Presence onto earth. Just as a harvester can not gather his crop until the grain has been saturated with abundant rainfall from heaven, so too, Yosef *HaTzaddik* followed up on Yehudah's "plowing" with his own efforts, which led to the revelation of the Divine Presence on earth.

This relationship between the preparatory efforts (plowing) for the Divine Revelation and the subsequent visible manifestation (harvesting) of the *Shechinah* not only characterizes the efforts of Yehudah and Yosef to bring the *Shechinah* to Earth, but also helps us to appreciate the dual nature of Shabbos' observance. As the term *Shamor* (literally meaning to "guard") indicates, the first phase of *avodas Hashem* is in one's heart, "cultivating and nurturing" within us the *middos* that will eventually enable us to articulate *divrei Torah.* The second phase, *Zachor,* actually speaking the sacred thoughts of the Torah (such as the *Kiddush* which is derived from *Zachor,* cf. *Pesachim* 106a), is only possible after successfully completing the initial phase of *Shamor* – preparing internally for the moment when we can voice openly the sacred thoughts that had been preserved in our heart.

Utilizing this approach, we can gain new insight into the statement of *Chazal* that *Zachor* and *Shamor* were said simultaneously (refer to the previous *dvar Torah* where we offered various approaches to explain the significance of this phenomenon). Whereas in This World a great deal of preparation (*Shamor*) is necessary before we are able to verbalize the sacred Torah thoughts within our heart, in the Future World where Hashem's Presence will be apparent in the universe, it will be possible to simultaneously achieve the spiritual levels of *Shamor* (preparing in one's heart for the *Shechinah*) and *Zachor* (actually perceiving the *Shechinah*). Every Shabbos, a day which is a microcosm of the exalted *kedushah* that we will enjoy in the Future World, we are able to transcend the gap that often exists between the preparation for the *Shechinah*, which we undertake within our hearts, and the actual Divine Revelation (and the capacity to speak *divrei Torah*).

We find allusions to this approach that on Shabbos we are able to fuse the preparatory phase (plowing) and the subsequent Revelation of the *Shechinah* (harvesting) both in the Torah itself and in the Sabbath *zemiros.* The *pasuk,* בֶּחָרִישׁ וּבַקָּצִיר תִּשְׁבֹּת, *You should rest from plowing and harvesting* (*Shemos* 34:21, and refer to *Makkos* 8b for halachic interpretations of this *pasuk*), may allude to the unique opportunity that we enjoy on Shabbos to ascend swiftly from the initial stage of plowing to the final phase of harvesting. Similarly, we sing in the *zemiros,* עֱזוֹר לַשּׁוֹבְתִים בַּשְּׁבִיעִי בֶּחָרִישׁ וּבַקָּצִיר עוֹלָמִים, *Always help those who cease from plowing and harvesting on the Seventh.* Based on the foregoing commentary, the final term of this phrase, עוֹלָמִים, which literally means *worlds* (and is translated in the song as "always"), may allude to the two divergent worlds, *Olam Hazeh* and *Olam Haba,* which converge on Shabbos. Just as in the Future Universe there will be no lag between "plowing" and "harvesting," so too every Shabbos, when both worlds converge, we can move immediately from plowing to harvesting. (*Vayigash* 5652)

ויהודה בחי׳ שמור ויוסף בחי׳ זכור כי בזוה״ק איתא כי יוסף בחי׳ השבת. ובספרים איתא בברכת יהודה אתה יודוך כו׳ כי הוא בחי׳ שבת ע״ש ברקאנטי ורבינו בחיי. ושניהם אמת כי הם בחי׳ זכור ושמור בדיבור אחד נאמרו. והוא בחי׳ לחם משנה בשבת. לחם עוני לחם מן הארץ בחי׳ יהודה. ושמנה לחמו לחם מן השמים בחי׳ יוסף. דכתיב וישבות ביום השביעי אח״כ. ויברך ויקדש. השביתה הוא הכנת הכלי להיות העולם מוכן לקבל ברכה וקדושה והוא בחי׳ מנוחה. ובחי׳ יהודה הודאה הוא במקום שיש מחלוקת. מודים מכלל דפליגי. כי בעוה״ז הנפרד אין ניכר מלכות שמים מכח הטבע.

Let us develop further the association between Yehudah and Yosef and its relationship to the duality of Shabbos — *Zachor* and *Shamor* — which was discussed in the previous *dvar Torah.* It seems from the sacred Kabbalistic works that both Yehudah and Yosef represent various aspects of Shabbos. In reality, both the approach that Yehudah and Yosef correspond to *Zachor* and *Shamor* as well as the Kabbalistic approach are correct, as we shall demonstrate.

To appreciate that aspect of Shabbos represented by Yehudah, we recall that Yaakov *Avinu* prefaces his blessing to Yehudah with the words, יְהוּדָה אַתָּה יוֹדוּךָ, *Yehudah you will acknowledge* (cf. *Bereishis* 49:8). The very concept of acknowledgment implies that there had previously been dissension and doubt which is now terminated by the admission. (As *Chazal* relate, מודים מכלל דפליגי, "If we use the term *modim* (to admit) this implies that there had been controversy.") In This World, where much of mankind does not acknowledge *HaKadosh Baruch Hu,* Yehudah's role was to lead *Klal Yisrael* to acknowledge the *Shechinah.* It is entirely appropriate that Jewish kings were selected from the ranks of Yehudah's descendants, inasmuch as a primary function of Jewish monarchs is to motivate and inspire their subjects to acknowledge Hashem.

Yosef's role, on the other hand, was to connect his brothers with their heavenly roots — almost to lead them beyond the confines of This World into *Olam Haba.*[1]

This association between Yehudah consecrating This World and Yosef

1. To support the *Sfas Emes'* contention that Yosef's role was to inspire his brothers to an even higher level of *avodas Hashem* and to connect them to their heavenly roots, we note Yaakov's description of Yosef as נְזִיר אֶחָיו, the brother who was separated (and coronated for a higher mission) from among his brothers.

leading his brethren to the spiritual treasures of *Olam Haba* plays an important role in many aspects of Shabbos. For example, the Double Bread (*lechem mishneh*) that we have every Shabbos may symbolize that our sustenance is derived from two distinct sources: One is by exploiting This World (as Yehudah did, a concept known as *lechem min ha'aretz*), and two, by turning to Hashem for His direct intervention (similar to Yosef's role in linking his brothers to their heavenly roots, known as *lechem min ha'shamayim*. Refer to our chapter on *Lechem Mishneh* for in-depth discussion of these concepts).

Similarly, when discussing the first Shabbos, the Torah emphasizes that Hashem "rested " from all of His work and only then notes that He blessed and sanctified the Shabbos. By resting from all of His material creation on Shabbos, Hashem prepared the universe to be so spiritual in order that His blessings could then be showered from heaven onto earth. As the *pasuk* continues, *HASHEM blessed the seventh day and He sanctified the seventh day* (*Shemos* 20:11).

Correspondingly, *Shamor* and *Zachor* represent this two-fold process. By guarding and preserving This World first (*Shamor*), it is then possible to reach an intimate relationship with Hashem and enjoy the blessings that He bestows upon us (*Zachor*). (*Vayigash* 5657)

Hidden and Visible Presence of the *Shechinah*

והנה שבת כולל ג"כ ב' בחי' הנ"ל והם בחי' זכור ושמור. ונראה לבאר ההפרש בין שם שדי לשבת. כי ש' הוא השפע המצומצם בי"ד עתים. וז"ש לעולמו די שיהי' בבחי' זמן ועת לכל חפץ בהתלבשות הטבע. אך שבת השפע מיוחד לכנ"י. וזה ש' בת. וזה רמזו חז"ל באמרם שבת א"צ תפילין שהם עצמם אות. כי ע"י התפילין יוכל להתגלות הפנימיות שבאדם. ובשבת מתגלה בכח האדם בעצמו. וזה ניתן רק לבנ"י. וזה רמזו חז"ל במאמר שבת לכל יש בן זוג שהוא כלי הצימצום. והי' התשובה כנס"י יהי' בן זוגך כנ"ל.

Expanding upon the theme which we developed in the previous *dvar Torah*, we suggest that *Zachor* and *Shamor* represent two aspects of Divine Revelation. On one hand, the *Shechinah* is veiled within the universe that He created. As Hashem's universe unfolded, it became increasingly difficult to perceive His Presence. This attribute, whereby Hashem hides His Presence, is known as the *middah* of *tzimtzum.* The Name *Shakkai* is often utilized to convey Hashem's hidden Presence. On the other hand, when revealing Himself to *Klal Yisrael,* Hashem allows us to attain a degree of intimacy with Him unlike that of other nations.

These two aspects of Divine Revelation — the hidden Presence of the *Shechinah* as well as the more visible manifestation of His *kedushah* — can both be found in the *mitzvos* of *tefillin* and *mezuzah.* In each of these instances, Hashem's Name is not only inscribed *within* (in the *parshiyos,* Torah segments that are contained within the casing of these sacred artifacts), but is also present on the *outside* (in the form of the word *Shakkai* written on the outside of the *mezuzah's* case and the letters of Hashem's Name that comprise the various knots of the *tefillin* and are engraved onto the head-*tefillin*).

In light of the foregoing discussion, we suggest that the same distinction exists between Shabbos and the six days of the week. Whereas all week long the universe is governed by the principle of *tzimtzum* (Hashem's Presence is frequently obscured in the universe that He created), on Shabbos we benefit from His more direct Presence. It is significant that the terms Shabbos and *Shakkai,* the Name of Hashem used to connote His Hidden Presence, both begin with the same letter, a ש, which represents the שֶׁפַע (abundant) *berachos* that flow from Hashem. However, a major distinction exists between these two concepts, as indicated by the final two letters of each term. *Shakkai* continues with a ד and a י, two letters whose *gematria* (numerical equivalent) equals 14, which correspond to the fourteen different phases of the natural world described by Shlomo *HaMelech* (each beginning with the term עֵת, *time,* cf. *Koheles* 3:2-8). It is through these various aspects of the natural world that Hashem channels His *berachos* during the שֵׁשֶׁת יְמֵי הַמַּעֲשֶׂה. However, in the term Shabbos the ש is succeeded with a ב and a ת, two letters which spell בַּת, *daughter,* alluding to the unique relationship and intimacy that *Klal Yisrael* enjoys with Hashem, especially on Shabbos. When *Chazal* (*Yalkut Bereishis* 16) related that *Klal Yisrael* becomes a בֶּן זוּג, *partner of Hashem,* on Shabbos, they are referring to the *direct* manner in which He bestows His *berachos* on us on Shabbos.

(Adapted from *Vaeira* 5652)

Upon further contemplation, we realize that both aspects of Hashem's Presence are present on Shabbos. On one hand, Shabbos is the culmination of the six weekdays in which His Presence is veiled. On the other hand, Shabbos is a unique opportunity for *Klal Yisrael* to enjoy Hashem's Presence in a more direct fashion. By observing both aspects of Shabbos, *Zachor* and *Shamor,* we are acknowledging the duality of this special day — the culmination of the week in which Hashem's Presence, though very much present, may be veiled, and the unique intimacy with the *Shechinah* that *Klal Yisrael* enjoys on Shabbos.

◆§ Visible and Hidden

ובשבת קודש מתנה מבית גנזי יש הארה מחלק הנסתר. ולכן יש בו נשמה יתירה. ולכן כל מעשיו כפולים כמ״ש חז״ל זכור ושמור. לחם משנה. מזמור שיר. רמוז לב׳ בחי׳ הנ״ל.

Whereas in the previous *dvar Torah* we discussed the visible and hidden Presence of the *Shechinah,* here we suggest that every member of *Klal Yisrael,* besides his visible presence in This World, enjoys spiritual roots in heaven that can be exploited on sacred occasions such as Shabbos.[1] On Shabbos, which is described as a gift from Hashem's hidden treasure house (refer to our chapter on this topic), we are able to not only benefit from our obvious spiritual potential but also from the hidden potential that we haven't realized all week long. *Chazal* note that many aspects of Shabbos are celebrated in "pairs", rather than individually. Not only *Zachor* and *Shamor* but also the requirement that we partake of the Double Bread (*lechem mishneh;* refer to our chapter on this topic), the two lambs that are offered as the *korban* of Shabbos, as well as the Psalm devoted to Shabbos, is introduced with the double expression *mizmor shir.* These "double" concepts all allude to the dual nature of this most sacred of days — a visible presence here on earth, as well as hidden roots in heaven that we are able to exploit on Shabbos.

(*Terumah* 5655)

1. In fact, according to the *Zohar, HaKadosh Baruch Hu's* benevolence (שפע), the Jewish people, and the Torah not only "appear" to us in a visible form in This World, but also enjoy a hidden aspect that is generally beyond our comprehension. While there are aspects of שפע ה׳ that we can readily appreciate, there are other elements of Hashem's benevolence that we cannot fathom. Similarly, when *Chazal* describe Moshe *Rabbeinu* as being half man and half like an angel, they are alluding to his ability to plumb some of the Torah's deepest mysteries that are beyond our grasp.

וזהו רמז ז׳ כפולות כדאיתא במד׳ כל מעשה שבת כפולים זכור ושמור משנה לחם שני כבשים כו׳. וזה עצמו ענין לחם משנה דכתיב בשבת שהחלק שלמטה מתאחד בשורש שלמעלה. לכן נקרא שבת שלום שמחבר עליונים לתחתונים ויש עליות נשמות למעלה וירידת נשמה יתירה למטה.

Expanding on this theme, we find other indications that every Shabbos our soul on earth is linked to its heavenly roots. For example, Shabbos is frequently described, especially in the *Zohar*, as *Shabbos Shalom*, the Shabbos of peace (refer to our chapter on this topic). On a day when our soul here on earth connects to its source in heaven — while simultaneously the *neshamah yeseirah* descends from heaven to join us here on earth — there is such "synergy" and harmony between the soul as it appears here on earth and its heavenly roots that we can truly speak of a sense of serenity and peace — *Shabbos Shalom*.

Extending this analysis even more profoundly, the duality of Shabbos — whereby our presence on earth is linked to its heavenly roots — is alluded to by the seven *berachos* of the Shabbos *Shemoneh Esrei*, which may correspond to the seven letters of the *aleph-beis* that are known as double letters. By reciting as many *berachos* as there are double letters in the *aleph-beis* we are alluding to our capacity to magnify the power of Shabbos by linking its presence here with its roots in heaven.

(*Beha'aloscha* 5651)

◆§ Enjoying the First Light of Creation

והענין הוא כמ״ש חז״ל על יום השבת כי כל מעשיו כפולין לחם משנה זכור ושמור כו׳. כי יש בו שלימות העוה״ז והארה עליונה כמו שכ׳ חז״ל אמרה שבת לכל יש בן זוג כו׳ כנס״י יהי׳ בן זוגך. א״כ יורד בש״ק הארה מיום העליון אור שבעת הימים ונחשב השבת לב׳ מדריגות.

In the previous *dvar Torah*, we suggested that *Zachor* and *Shamor* correspond to our visible potential, as well as the capacity to draw on our latent spiritual roots that have not yet been exploited. Extending this theme a bit further, we suggest that not only the Jewish people but also the Shabbos day itself enjoys a "double dimension." On one hand, Shabbos is the most perfect moment of *Olam Hazeh,* marking the completion of the Creation process. On the other hand, the Shabbos day connects to its own heavenly roots (just as the Jewish soul seeks out its source in Heaven). Although the dazzling spiritual light by which the universe was created was hidden, the Shabbos day itself connects each week to its heavenly roots, allowing us as well to bask in the light of Creation. (Adapted from *Shemini* 5640)

◆§ *Zachor* With Our Mouth/ *Shamor* With Our Heart

דהנה כבר ניתן השבת זכור ושמור ומה ענין מצות השבת שנית. ויתכן כי השבת יש בו כמה מדריגות זו למעלה מזו כפי תיקון ועמידת בני ישראל. ויש בו בחי׳ מעשה דיבור ומחשבה. זכור ושמור זכירה בפה ושמירה בלב. ועתה הוא במעשה כמ״ש לעשות. כי בשעת קבלת התורה כתיב אמרתי אלהים אתם כו׳ והיו למעלה מעשי׳ גשמיות. ואחר החטא כתי׳ אך את שבתותי תשמורו. אך הוא לשון מיעוט שהוא מדריגה שלמטה ממה שהי׳ להם קודם החטא.

As is well-known, we serve Hashem with our heart, our gift of speech, and finally by implementing our thoughts and words into actual deeds. By describing the Sabbath as "a sign forever between Me and the Jewish people" (*Shemos* 31:17), the Torah is suggesting that the Shabbos can be enjoyed by the Jewish people at various levels depending upon their state of spiritual preparation. Consequently, at the time of *Matan Torah,* when *Klal Yisrael* approached the spirtual state of *malachim,* the *mitzvah* of Shabbos was presented to them in terms of *Zachor* and *Shamor,* which symbolize the mouth (power of speech) and the heart respectively. At that moment in Jewish history, it may have been sufficient to remind *Klal Yisrael* to guard the spirit of Shabbos in their hearts (*Shamor*) and to remember Shabbos (*Zachor*) by speaking about the day's *kedushah.* However, after the sin of the Golden Calf, Hashem determined to present Shabbos to *Klal Yisrael* in yet another form, this time emphasizing the practical application of the manifold laws of Shabbos. Thus, we read at the beginning of *Parashas Vayakhel, These are the matters that* HASHEM *commanded (you) to do them"* (cf. *Shemos* 35:1). To indicate that under ideal circumstances *Zachor* and *Shamor* may have been sufficient, the Torah prefaces the portion that discusses the observance of Shabbos after the sin of the Golden Calf with the term אַךְ, *only* (cf. *Shemos* 31:13). This term is traditionally interpreted as a *miut*, an expression that indicates a diminished spiritual level compared to previous references to the Shabbos. Whereas Shabbos was primarily observed in the realm of thought and speech, now, in the aftermath of the Golden Calf, it became necessary to explicitly teach *Klal Yisrael* about the observance of Shabbos in deeds. (*Vayakhel* 5649)

בש״ק ע״י זכור ושמור זכירה בפה שמירה בלב. והם בחי׳ תורה ותפלה.

Returning to our previous contention that *Zachor* and *Shamor* reflect the mouth (speech) and heart (emotions) respectively, we suggest that the association between speech and emotions is not unique to Shabbos, rather it is a crucial relationship for the proper observance of the entire Torah. The basis for our contention is the *pasuk* which states, כִּי קָרוֹב אֵלֶיךָ הַדָּבָר מְאֹד בְּפִיךָ וּבִלְבָבְךָ לַעֲשׂתוֹ, *Rather, the matter is very near to you – in your mouth and your heart –to perform it* (*Devarim* 30:14). This means that it is within the capacity of your mouth and heart to fulfill the *mitzvos* of the Torah. Evidently, the capacity to fulfill *mitzvos* is channeled through the heart and mouth. The relationship between Torah and *tefillah* may also be perceived in this manner. While the Torah is primarily associated with speech (one should verbalize the *divrei Torah* that one is studying), *tefillah* (while also verbalized) is described as a form of Divine service that emanates from the heart (refer to *Devarim* 11:13). (*Nitzavim* 5660)

וע״ז אומרים בתפלת שבת ושני לוחות אבנים הוריד בידו וכתוב בהם שמירת שבת. דיש זכור ושמור זכור בפה שמור בלב וכתיבות הלוחות הוא החקיקה בלבות בנ״י כמ״ש כתבם על לוח לבך וע״י החטא לא יכלו לקבל הלוחות.

Assuming that the term *Shamor* refers to the heart, we derive new insight into a phrase that we recite in the Shabbos *Shacharis tefillah*: וְכָתוּב בָּהֶם שְׁמִירַת שַׁבָּת, *On which is inscribed* [the *Luchos*] *the observance of* [the comandment to guard] *the Shabbos*. While the *mitzvah* of Shabbos was indeeed engraved on the *Luchos*, it was also engraved on the hearts of the recipients of the *Luchos*, *Klal Yisrael*.[1] This can be derived from the term *shemiras Shabbos* (the observance of the Shabbos) which, as we stated, corresponds to the heart (*Shamor*). When Moshe was compelled to shatter the *Luchos*, as a result of the Jewish people's sin, the words of Torah could no longer be safely inscribed on their hearts.

(*Yom Kippur* 5655)

◆§ Heart (*Shamor*) and Mind (*Zachor*)

וזה הי' בחי' יהודה בכלל ישראל. מלך במלחמה בחי' הלב. ויוסף הוא בחי' המוח בחי' גאולה. כי עיקר הגאולה בנפש. כשהנשמה והמוחין מאירין לאדם ואז שקטה מלחמת הלב ונעשה לב אחד. וע"ז כ' בשמחתו לא יתערב זר לכשמתמלא בשמחת הנפש מתבטל לב כסיל. לכן בשבת קודש דיש נשמה יתירה המאירה לנפש האדם. סט"א ערקית. ושבת הוא יום שמחה כמ"ש ח"ל ביום שמחתכם אלו השבתות לפי שהנשמה מאירה באדם.

Whereas in the previous *dvar Torah* we suggested that *Zachor* and *Shamor* represent the mouth (speech) and heart (emotions) respectively, here we suggest that *Zachor* and *Shamor* correspond to the mind (intellect) and heart, as we shall elucidate.

Shlomo *HaMelech* speaks of the vast discrepancy that exists between the heart of a wise man (חָכָם) and that of a fool (כְּסִיל) (refer to *Koheles* 10:2). In truth, this struggle occurs within each of us as we are torn between the wise and the foolish heart within each person. While it is certainly true that intellect as well as the emotions play a major role in affecting our behavior, nonetheless, the heart's role is often dominant. In fact, we may compare the role of the heart, the seat of our emotions, to that of a general commanding his troops in battle. Without the leadership role assumed by the general, the troops would lack direction and their opponents would prevail. So too, without the dominant role of the heart, our intellect alone would never be sufficient to lead in our quest for *avodas Hashem*.

1. Refer to *Mishlei* (3:3), כָּתְבֵם עַל לוּחַ לִבֶּךָ, *inscribe them on the tablet of your heart*, for another instance where words are described as being engraved on "the tablets" of a heart.

This struggle between the "wise heart" and "the foolish heart" within us continues all week unabated. However, on *Shabbos kodesh,* with the infusion of the *neshamah yeseirah* and the additional insight into Torah that we enjoy, it is enough to resolve the conflicts between the "two hearts" within us. With the presence of the *neshamah yeseirah* mediating between the "two hearts," the *yetzer hara* simply yields in his attempt to influence and try to subvert Hashem's Will.

Refer to our previous *divrei Torah* in which we discussed the distinct roles of Yosef and Yehudah, and the relationship between their respective roles and the concepts of *Zachor* and *Shamor.* In a somewhat similar vein, we suggest here, that Yehudah, the ancestor of David *HaMelech* and of the Davidic dynasty, assumes the role of the heart, the emotional component of every Jew. Just as the heart acts in a leading role marshaling the troops in the great battle between the heart of the wise man (the *yetzer hatov*) and the heart of the fool (the *yetzer hara*), so too, every Jewish king leads his troops to war. Yosef's role, on the other hand, was similar to that of the intellect. As important as emotions are, one can never attain clarity and true comprehension without using one's mind. Just as Yosef *Ha-Tzaddik* supported his brothers (and Yosef's descendant *Mashiach* ben Yosef will facilitate *Klal Yisrael's* Final Redemption; refer to *Succah* 52a), so too, the human mind may provide such clarity that any disputes between the "two hearts" (symbolized by the *yetzer hara* and *yetzer hatov*) within every Jew are resolved. This is particularly true every Shabbos due to the intellectul stimulus provided by the *neshamah yeseirah,* which allows us to prevail over the "heart of the fool," the *yetzer hara.*

These two factors that play so great a role in the internal battle within every Jew as he seeks to fulfill the Divine Will — heart and mind — are also contained within the "duality" of *Zachor* and *Shamor.* While the intellect (mind) *remembers* (*Zachor*), it is through the heart, the seat of our emotions, that we are able to *preserve* (*Shamor*) and retain the spiritual gains that we attained through our intellect. Alluding to the harmony that occurs every Shabbos when the struggle within every heart is resolved through the arrival of the *neshamah yeseirah, Chazal* state (*Shevuos* 20b) that *Zachor,* the intellectual phase of Jewish life, as well as *Shamor,* the emotional aspect, were related simultaneously. In other words, while the desires of the heart often conflict with the rational reasoning of the intellect, on Shabbos we may enjoy perfect harmony between head and heart, between *Zachor* and *Shamor.*

(Adapted from *Vayigash* 5660)

וכתיב שכולם מתאימות שצריך להיות המעשה נמשך אחר הדעת ולא להתחכם יותר מדאי. ואותן הנשמרים שיהי׳ הדעת כפי המעשה נשמר עליהם שכולם מתאימות וז״ש שלא הקדימו וכו׳, וכמו כן בש״ק זכור ושמור יש ב׳ אלו [כמ״ש בזוהר פינחס דשמירה בלב בחי׳ תש״י נגד הלב וזכירה במוחא ביום שבת.

A relationship similar to the one between the intellect and the emotions exists between thought and deed. *Chazal* (*Shir HaShirim Rabbah* 6:6) praise the Jewish warriors who battled Midian as individuals who never donned the head-*tefillin* before the arm-*tefillin*, an allusion to the fact that their deeds were not only motivated by the heart but also by their intellect. On Shabbos, by juxtaposing *Zachor* and *Shamor*, the Torah is ensuring that our deeds, which often are based on our emotions, are also guided by our intellect. (Adapted from *Matos* 5646)

וב׳ אלו מתחדשין ביום השבת. בחי׳ זכור ושמור. מוח ולב עבודה בלב. ולכן יש ב׳ לבבות כי בחי׳ עבד יש עובד ע״מ לקבל פרס ויש עבד לשמו ית׳. וזה הרבותא לי בנ״י עבדים לי לשמי. וע״ז העבודה מבקשין וטהר לבנו לעבדך באמת.

Extending the analogy between the head and heart and *Zachor* and *Shamor* even further, we recall a previous *dvar Torah* in which we suggested that *Zachor* alludes to our relationship as Hashem's children while *Shamor* corresponds to our role as Hashem's servants. That approach perceiving *Zachor* and *Shamor* as representing various approaches in *avodas Hashem* may correspond to the foregoing approach emphasizing the head and heart. While a son may be blessed (by virtue of birth) with an intellect similar to that of his father, a servant earns a reputation for loyalty and devotion by serving his master wholeheartedly. In fact, we find that *avodas Hashem* is associated with the heart. Every Shabbos we plead, וְטַהֵר לִבֵּנוּ לְעָבְדְךָ בֶּאֱמֶת, *Purify our heart to serve You in truth.*[1] (*Behar* 5661)

1. Assuming that the concept of serving Hashem is achieved through one's heart (*avodas ha'lev*), we can appreciate why the Torah speaks frequently of serving Hashem with our *hearts* (using the plural form). Just as servants display different degrees of loyalty, some serving their master strictly to earn their wages and others being totally committed to him, so too among *avdei Hashem* we encounter different levels of commitment. However, the Torah takes pride that as servants of Hashem we are motivated solely by altruistic reasons — as stated in *Vayikra* (25:55), כִּי לִי בְנֵי יִשְׂרָאֵל עֲבָדִים, *For the Children of Israel are servants to Me* (for My sake).

וזה ויגש אליו יהודה. ליוסף שהוא בחי׳ מוח ונשמה. והוא בחי׳ שבת שבו זכור ושמור בדיבור אחד. ולכן אז כל סט״א ערקית. וזכור ושמור הם ב׳ הארות הנ״ל כמ״ש במ״א שמירה בלב זכירה בפה ובמוח.

The opening *pasuk* of *Parashas Vayigash* in which Yehudah approaches Yosef to plead for Binyamin's release alludes to many of the themes that we have just discussed. By approaching Yosef, Yehudah, who symbolizes the heart of *Klal Yisrael* (and the *Shamor* aspect of Shabbos), seeks a rapprochement with Yosef, who symbolizes the intellect and the attribute of *Zachor*. (*Vayigash* 5665; *Yisro* 5647)

⇐§ Removal of Evil / Revelation of Good

במ״א האלקי מקרוב אני ולא מרחוק שאלקותו ית״ש בא ע״י קירוב מדרגות הקדושה זהו בחי׳ מ״ע זכור. וע״י ריחוק הסט״א ועולמות הנפרדים זה בחי׳ מל״ת שמור.

By using the dual expression *Zachor* and *Shamor*, the Torah is alluding to two distinct approaches that enable us to come closer to Hashem. Firstly, we try to diminish the influence of the *yetzer hara* through our meticulous observance of all of the negative commandments of the Torah, in the spirit of *Shamor*. Having distanced ourselves from evil, we can now draw closer to Hashem, an objective enhanced by the positive commandments of the Torah in the spirit of *Zachor*. When the prophet proclaims, *Am I a God from close and not a God from a distance* (*Yirmiyahu* 23:23), he may be alluding to these two different methods of coming closer to Hashem — first by distancing oneself from evil and subsequently by coming close to *kedushah*. (*Acharei* 5661)

בש״ק דמתאחדין ברזא דאחד לכן סט״א ערקית ויורד הקדושה לבנ״י. יום מנוחה וקדושה לעמך נתת. מנוחה בחי׳ שמור גדר ערוה וקדושה בחי׳ זכור להמשיך קדושת שבת בפה בקידוש היום.

We reiterate this two-fold approach to Shabbos when we recite in the

Minchah prayers, יוֹם מְנוּחָה וּקְדֻשָּׁה לְעַמְּךָ נָתַתָּ, *You have given Your people a day of rest and sanctity.* Whereas the concept of a "day of rest" addresses that aspect of Shabbos that emphasizes our relief from the *yetzer hara,* this is not enough. Once the forces of evil depart, it is now possible to enjoy the other aspect of Shabbos, its immense *kedushah.* This sequential relationship between purging the *yetzer hara* and then coming closer to the vast *kedushah* that the Torah allows us to enjoy is also indicated by the renowned *Chazal* (cited by *Rashi* [*Vayikra* 19:2] at the beginning of *Parashas Kedoshim*), "Whenever one finds a fence against immorality one finds *kedushah.*" By first battling immorality, we subsequently merit a state of *kedushah.*

(*Kedoshim* 5664)

והנה יוסף נק׳ ע״ש אסף אלקים את חרפתי. והוא רמז להסרת הערלה כדכ׳ חרפה היא לנו. ועי״ כן יש התגלות הקדושה. והוא רמוז ביוסף ה׳ לי בן אחר. שזה התוספות הבא מלמעלה אחר התעברות הסט״א. שכן הוא במילה שמתגלה אות ברית קודש בהסרת הערלה. וב׳ בחי׳ הנ״ל הם גם בשבת קודש. שנק׳ שבת ע״ש השביתה והחזרת הכל אל השורש. ונק׳ ג״כ ע״ש השבתת הסט״א כדאיתא דסט״א ערקת בשבת. ולכן יש התגלות נשמה יתירה שניתוסף בשבת. וב׳ בחי׳ הנ״ל הם בחי׳ זכור ושמור.

To appreciate this approach to *Zachor* and *Shamor* we recall the two reasons given for Yosef *HaTzaddik's* name. First, Rachel's shame (of being childless) has now been relieved. Second, is her plea for the future, that she should be blessed with more children. Similarly, on Shabbos we celebrate not only the dissipation of evil but also the extra dimension of *kedushah* associated with the *neshamah yeseirah.* By commemorating both aspects of Shabbos, *Zachor* as well as *Shamor,* we are acknowledging that both processes occur every Shabbos. In fact, the term Shabbos may reflect both themes, the cessation (שְׁבִיתָה) of the evil influence of the *yetzer hara,* as well as the return (שָׁב) of the *neshamah* to its spiritual roots (which follows the cessation of all *melachah* on Shabbos). (*Vayechi* 5652)

◆ The Divine Voice (*Kol*) / Hashem's Speech (*Dibbur*)

והנה בנ״י זכו במעשיהם וקבלת מלכותו. לשמוע קול הש״י וזה ג״כ זכור ושמור בדיבור אחד. ומי שישנו בשמירה ישנו בזכירה. כי שמירה צריך בבחי׳ דיבור הנ״ל שנעלם תוך מעשה בראשית. וכפי השמירה זוכין לזכירה הוא מקום שא״צ שמירה כנ״ל.

The distinction between *Zachor* and *Shamor* may also be explained on the basis of the relationship between *Kol* (the Voice of Hashem) and *Dibbur* (the Divine Word). While Torah and *mitzvos* were transmitted to *Klal Yisrael* in the form of *Dibbur* – Hashem's Word to Moshe *Rabbeinu* – even those individuals (or generations such as ours) that are not privileged to hear *directly* Hashem's Words as transmitted by His prophets, may still sense His Presence as a *Kol*, an inner voice embedded in their *neshamah* which yearns for the *Shechinah*. Thus the *Kol* is a far more inner phenomenon than *Dibbur*.[1]

By defining the *mitzvah* of Shabbos in terms of both *Zachor* and *Shamor*, the Torah is alluding to both aspects of the observance of Shabbos (and, by extension, of all *mitzvos*). On one hand, we can openly hear the *dvar Hashem*. Hashem speaks to us through His prophets and whenever we study His Torah. However, in such an environment – not quite as rarefied and as internal as the Voice of Hashem – there always is the risk of the *yetzer hara* (and other evil influences) persuading us to defy Hashem's Word. In such an environment, *shemirah* – guarding zealously one's hard-won gains – is essential. On the other hand, in an environment that is so hallowed that one can actually feel the Voice of Hashem prompting us to return to Him (*Kol*), *shemirah*, protecting us against contrary influences, is no longer as necessary. Under such circumstances where the *Kol Hashem* is very manifest – where we all can detect that inner spiritual presence in our lives – we can truly say that we have attained the spiritual level where *zechirah*, simply recalling and feeling intuitively the Presence of the *Shechinah* in our lives, is all that is required. (*Yisro* 5632)

1. For further discussion, refer to *Days of Awe*, pgs. 126 ff.

◆§ Forgetting This World (*Shamor*) / Remembering the World to Come (*Zachor*)

הארת הנשמה בגוף לכך יכולין לשכוח הבלי עולם. וב׳ אלו הם בחי׳ זכור ושמור. זכירה הארת הנשמה. שמירה שכחת הגוף והטבע הגשמיות ... פי׳ כשהקב״ה אמר אנכי ה״א נטע זה הכח בנפשות בנ״י נטיעה קיימת שא״א לשכוח. כי כל דברים הטבעיים יש בהם שכחה. כמ״ש התשכח אשה עולה. ומסיים גם אלה תשכחנה. שעכ״פ סופה להשכיח. כי שמים כעשן נמלחו והארץ כבגד תבלה. וסוף הגשמיות להתבטל מן העולם. אבל אנכי לא אשכחך שלא תוכל זו הנטיעה לבוא לידי שכחה. שהיא למעלה מן הטבע. רק איש ישראל צריך לייגע עצמו כל הימים לזכור זו הנטיעה ולשכוח מהבלי עולם. ועכ״פ ביום השבת שמתגלה הנשמה יתירה צריכין לשכוח בהבלי עולם.

As it is well-known, *Chazal* describe Shabbos as a microcosm of the World to Come. Just as in *Olam Haba,* all of the petty vanities of This World will be forgotten, so too, in order to truly appreciate the other-worldly atmosphere of Shabbos we need to forget (and we are in an excellent position to forget) the material pleasures of This World. While it is perfectly natural to remember what is significant and to forget what is trivial, in this instance, by writing *Zachor* and *Shamor* the Torah guides us regarding what we should forget and what we should recall. As a prerequisite to remembering (and appreciating) the Shabbos, it is necessary to first forget the material concerns of the weekdays. In effect, the commandment of שָׁמוֹר אֶת יוֹם הַשַּׁבָּת is the source for *Klal Yisrael's* valiant effort not only to abstain from performing *melachah* and speaking about material matters on Shabbos, but not even to *think* about such matters on this most hallowed of days. By disassociating oneself from even the thought of material matters on Shabbos — and forgetting This World — in the spirit of *Shamor,* we merit to appreciate the *Zachor* and to recall (*Zachor's* primary meaning) the other-worldly spiritual nature of Shabbos. As *Chazal* (*Berachos* 20b) relate,

כָּל שֶׁיֶּשְׁנוֹ בִּשְׁמִירָה יֶשְׁנוֹ בִּזְכִירָה, whoever participates in *Shamor* – by forgetting the material pleasures of This World every Shabbos – will benefit from the *Zachor*, recalling and appreciating the intense *kedushah* of Shabbos.

Extending this analysis a bit further, we suggest that the term *Zachor* means more than merely remembering. Rather, it connotes a sense of intuitive recall so that the matter at hand will never be forgotten [this interpretation is similar to that given to זָכוֹר אֵת אֲשֶׁר עָשָׂה לְךָ עֲמָלֵק, *Remember what Amalek did to you* (*Devarim* 25:17), which refers not only to a formal process of remembering Amalek's hatred but also to an instinctive loathing of Amalek's ideals]. By abandoning all the material pursuits of This World (*Shamor*), we attain a spiritual level so exalted that we can fulfill *Zachor* (זָכוֹר אֶת יוֹם הַשַּׁבָּת) in its fullest sense. In this way, Shabbos becomes so embedded in the *neshamah* of every Jew that we can be assured that the *kedushah* of this extraordinary day will never be forgotten. (*Yisro* 5657)

While it may seem almost impossible for anyone living in This World to forget *Olam Hazeh* (as the *mitzvah* of *Shamor* challenges us to do), in reality, the potential for such an extraordinary accomplishment lies within all of us. By implanting the Divine Soul, the *neshamah*, in all of us, Hashem is empowering us to emphasize spiritual matters over physical concerns . Our capacity to fulfill the *mitzvah* of *Shamor* is in direct proportion to the extent that we listen to the sage counsel of our *neshamah* rather than the importunings of the body. Thus, the *mitzvah* of *Shamor* may be interpreted in a broader sense – subordinate the body and its incessant demands to the spiritual quest of the soul.

Ultimately, in the Future World, the body and its physical cravings – and the material world – will yield to the soul and its quest for spirituality. The prophets indicate that even if heaven and earth in their present physical form will no longer exist, the Torah (and, of course, Hashem the Giver of the Torah) will remain (refer to *Yeshayahu* 51:6). While we are assured of the final outcome (predominance of the soul), our challenge is to attain some of this state of spiritual bliss while we live in This World. There is no more opportune time to enhance our soul and its spirituality and to diminish the capacity of our body to dominate us than on Shabbos. (*Yisro* 5661)

◆§ Remembering the Purpose of Our Creation (*Zachor*) / Forgetting *Olam Hazeh* (*Shamor*)

אמרו חז״ל בשבת ניתנה תורה זכור בעצומו של יום. דמכלל דכתיב זכור כו׳ השבת. אם כן שבת יומא דזכירה ומביא זכרון לאיש ישראל שיזכור על מה נשתלח בעולם. דעוה״ז עלמא דשכחה. דהטבע משכח. ובאמת עיקר השכחה הוא כדי לשכוח הבלי עולם והטבע. וזה זכור ושמור שכולל מ״ע ומל״ת שתכלית המצות לזכור את האדם שנברא רק לעשות רצון קונו. ותכלית מל״ת שבשמיעתן זוכין לשכוח הבלי עוה״ז. מ״ע מסייע אל הזכירה. ומל״ת אל השכחה.

Chazal relate that the *mitzvah* of *Zachor* (and all of the *Aseres HaDibros*) was said on Shabbos. Perhaps the reason for their insistence that this *mitzvah* was said on Shabbos was based on their belief that there is no day that is more conducive to remember what is truly critical than Shabbos. Thus, if Hashem commanded us to remember Shabbos, it is fair to assume that He did so on the day where we are most likely to recall His Word.

Expanding upon this theme, we suggest that Shabbos is not only a time that is conducive to recall the teachings of the Torah, but also an opportunity to recall the very purpose of our creation and our ultimate destiny when our soul will return to its Maker. In fact, a two-fold process occurs every Shabbos. Firstly, *Shamor* — symbolizing all of the negative commandments (לֹא תַעֲשֶׂה) of the Torah — motivates us to forget all of the material pleasures of *Olam Hazeh*. This is immediately followed by *Zachor* (representing all *mitzvos asei*) — a newly-found sense of awareness why we were created, which is to fulfill the Divine Will.

(*Yisro* 5662)

וכמו כן בשבת קודש שא״צ תפילין שהוא עצמו אות ומאיר בו הארת הנשמה לא יסיח דעתו. וזה בחי׳ זכור ושמור. לזכור השורש הנ״ל ולשמור שלא להרהר במלאכת עוה״ז כמ״ש בס׳ הבהיר שמור מן ההירהור.

Using this approach, we gain new insight into the *Chazal's* recommendation that we not even think about our weekday activities on

Shabbos (cf. *Sefer HaBahir* which interprets the term *Shamor* as a plea not to think about our weekday activities on Shabbos). On Shabbos, the day which is devoted to recalling the purpose of our creation, we should not be diverted by our customary preoccupation with material matters. Once we have successfully implemented the *Shamor* component, we are now prepared to seriously contemplate and recall the purpose of our creation and our ultimate destiny (*Zachor*).

With this purpose as our objective, we can also appreciate why we do not wear *tefillin* on Shabbos. Whereas the purpose of *tefillin* is to help us recall the rationale of our existence in This World and prevent us from becoming immersed in *Olam Hazeh*, on Shabbos this function is accomplished by the day of Shabbos itself. When the Torah (*Shemos* 31:13) describes Shabbos as an אוֹת, a Divine sign (using virtually the same language as by *tefillin*, לְאוֹת, cf. *Devarim* 6:8), it may be referring to the capacity of this sacred day to infuse the entire body with the light of the *neshamah*. In such an environment, we can be assured that the objective that is ordinarily accomplished by wearing *tefillin* — remembering our purpose in This World — is realized. (*Re'eh* 5664)

Remaining Distant / Coming Close

הרי הוא אומר שמש ומגן ה׳ אלקים. שמש הוא להאיר ומגן הוא לשמור שלא יתקרב אל האור מי שאינו ראוי. וה׳ מדה״ר. אלקים מדה״ד. ושניהם יש בהם שמש ומגן. ויש מי שזוכה לקבל בבחי׳ קירוב וע״ז נא׳ בנ״י עם קרובו. ויש שמקבל ע״י בחי׳ ריחוק. ושניהם אלו הם בחי׳ זכור ושמור. מ״ע ומל״ת. מ״ע הקירוב ומל״ת הריחוק. ורמזו כי בדיבור אחד נאמרו. שכל אחד כלול בחבירו התורה כולל שניהם.

Perhaps the term *Shamor* should be interpreted almost literally — "guard" — to prevent unauthorized access to Torah and *mitzvos* and especially the *mitzvah* of Shabbos. Just as the Jewish people are urged to observe Torah and *mitzvos*, so too, mankind is discouraged from observing *mitzvos*, with the exception of the seven Noachide commandments. This distinction between *Klal Yisrael* and mankind as a whole is true not only in reference to Shabbos but, to an extent, in reference to all *mitzvos*. This exclusion of non-Jews from most *mitzvos* was not intended to denigrate gentiles. On the contrary, by bringing *Klal Yisrael* closer to Him, Hashem enabled righteous individuals from the ranks of mankind to also find Him. If righteous gentiles were able to join the ranks of *Klal Yisrael,* it was because of the precedent set by Hashem who brought *Klal Yisrael* close to Him. Moreover, the process of *kiruv* frequently involves two distinct components – reaching out to *Klal Yisrael* who is committed to Hashem and His Torah, in the spirit of *Zachor*, and at the same time, in the spirit of *Shamor*, distancing Himself from those who are unworthy of receiving the Torah.

This perhaps conveys to us the necessity of keeping away from the Torah those who will not benefit from its teachings, as well as the importance of welcoming those who embrace Torah. *Tehillim* (84:12) describes the *Shechinah* as being both a shield and a sun. By depicting Hashem as the "sun," we are emphasizing the "dazzling" spiritual potential that Hashem transmitted through the Torah to *Klal Yisrael.* However, the *Shechinah* also serves as a "shield," keeping far away those who don't deserve to come close to the light of Torah.

Not only in reference to Shabbos but also in the larger context of the entire Torah, both dimensions – bringing close and keeping at a distance – are present. The role of positive commandments is that of *Zachor* to bring one close to Hashem. On the other hand, the negative commandments serve to keep at a safe distance those for whom closeness is inappropriate (*Shamor*).

By affirming that *Zachor* and *Shamor* were said simultaneously, *Chazal* are emphasizing the close association (the inseparability) of both these aspects of *Yiddishkeit.* (*Yisro* 5662)

◈ Peace On Earth / Peace In Heaven

פמליא של מעלה בחי׳ זכור. ושל מטה בחי׳ שמור. ושבת ג״כ שנק׳ שלום. לפי שכלול מזכור ושמור.

Assuming as we did in the previous *dvar Torah,* that *Zachor* refers to the intimate relationship enjoyed by those who are close to Hashem, while *Shamor* is the position assumed by those who remain at a distance, there is another connotation. These distinctions exist not only between *Klal Yisrael* and the world at large, but also among those who serve

Hashem on earth, the Jewish people, and Hashem's Heavenly servitors, the angels on high. While *Klal Yisrael*, standing at a distance on earth, observe the *Shechinah* in the spirit of *Shamor*, the *malachim* on high approach Him from a position of intimacy, *Zachor*. *Chazal* relate that those who study Torah *lishmah* (for its own sake) are able to bring harmony between *Klal Yisrael* serving Hashem on earth and the angels serving Him in heaven. There is no more opportune time to harmonize Hashem's servitors on high, who serve Him from close (*Zachor*) and His servants below, who stand at a distance (*Shamor*) than on Shabbos, a day which itself is the essence of *shalom*. (*Yisro* 5662)

Moshe and Aharon – Their Virtues

לא מצאתי לגוף טוב משתיקה והיא מדת אהרן כמ"ש וידום אהרן. ומרע"ה הוא הנשמה והמדבר. וב' האחים רומז לשפתים. כי השפה מיוחד לדיבור. ולהשתיקה ג"כ כמ"ש במ"א מזה. וכתיב משה ידבר. ושפתי כהן ישמרו דעת. ושניהם בחי' זכור ושמור. ומתאחדין בשבת קודש. שבת אחים גם יחד.

Perhaps the *mitzvos* of *Zachor* and *Shamor* correspond to Moshe and Aharon, who, each in their own unique manner, brought *Klal Yisrael* closer to Hashem. Firstly, the unique roles of Moshe and Aharon are alluded to by the *pasuk*, כִּי נֵר מִצְוָה וְתוֹרָה אוֹר, which homiletically means: "For a *mitzvah* is a receptacle of light and the Torah is the source of light itself" (cf. *Mishlei* 6:23). Whereas Aharon kindled the *Menorah*, which is a receptacle for the light, Moshe brought the Torah – the source of light itself – to *Klal Yisrael*. While Moshe enhanced the *neshamah* of *Klal Yisrael* by transmitting the Torah to them, Aharon demonstrated through his sacred lifestyle that even the body can be sacred. Consequently, he merited to wear the Priestly Garments, befitting someone whose very body is sacred.

Another distinction between these two great brothers was in the realm of *dibbur*, communication. Aharon's distinctive attribute was silence. Confronted with the tragedy of the sudden passing of his two children, Aharon remained silent (cf. וַיִּדֹּם אַהֲרֹן, *Vayikra* 10:3). Moshe's role, on the other hand, was to speak and transmit Hashem's Word to the Jewish people (cf. *Shemos* 19:19, *Moshe would speak and God would respond to him with a voice*).

The famed *pasuk* (*Malachi* 2:7), *For the lips of the Kohen should safeguard knowledge*, may allude to both Moshe and Aharon. Just as lips alternately open and close, so too, both Moshe, in his role as the Torah teacher speaking to *Klal Yisrael*, and Aharon, through appropriate and timely silence, preserved the Torah.[1] (*Tetzaveh* 5663)

◆§ Before and After Sinning (the Golden Calf)

כי קודם החטא נאמר זכור את יום השבת. והגם כי זכור ושמור בדבור אחד נאמרו. מ״מ שמור לא אידכר בשמא לגבי בחי׳ זכור שהוא העיקר. ובמתן תורה היו בנ״י בבחי׳ זכור. ושמור ממילא איכא. וכאן התחיל מצות שמירת שבת. וכאשר חכמים הגידו כל שישנו בשמירה ישנו בזכירה שע״י השמירה יכולין לבוא לבחי׳ זכירה. אבל מעלתן של בנ״י קודם החטא הי׳ למעלה מזה כמ״ש.

It is also possible that the terms *Zachor* and *Shamor* refer to different periods in the history of *Klal Yisrael*. Whereas *before* the sin of the *Egel* (the Golden Calf), the Jewish people were on a spiritual level so lofty that they deserved an intimate relationship with Hashem (implied by *Zachor*), *after* sinning they no longer enjoyed this close relationship. Now it was their function to focus on preserving the Shabbos by abstaining from performing *melachah* as derived from *Shamor*. While the prohibition of *melachah* on Shabbos certainly existed even before the sin of the Golden Calf, the Torah originally emphasized the *Zachor* aspect of Shabbos. Thus *Zachor*, rather than *Shamor*, is mentioned explicitly in the version of the *Aseres HaDibros* that we read in *Parashas Yisro*.

However, one should not assume that the Jewish people would never be able to return to their previous distinguished level of *Zachor*. By observing *Shamor*, *Klal Yisrael* can eventually return to *Zachor*. As *Chazal* relate, "Whoever is included in *Shamor* is included in *Zachor*."

(*Ki Sisa* 5657)

---

1. For further discussion of this concept refer to *The Three Festivals*, pg. 362.

◆§ *Zachor* – For All Mankind / *Shamor* – Only for *Klal Yisrael*

ושמור בדיבור א׳ נאמרו. ובזכור כ׳ כי ששת ימים כו׳ ע״כ ברך. ובשמור כ׳ וזכרת כו׳ עבד היית כו׳ ע״כ צוך כו׳ לעשות כו׳ השבת. והענין הוא כי בקבלת התורה הי׳ התגלות הקדושה והיו בנ״י מתוקנים והיו מוכנים לתקן כל הבריאה כמ״ש שעשרת הדברות היו תיקון עשרה מאמרות ... אכן ע״י עמלק הרשע שבלבל את בנ״י וכביכול נתמעט ע״י כבוד שמו הגדול והוא שגרם לבנ״י לחטא. ועי״ז הי׳ העצה ע״י בנ״י בלבד כי הי׳ מזיק להם התערובות כיון שלא נכפפו האומות וחזר להיות נסתר כבוד שמים בעולם. לכן נעשה השבת בבחי׳ יציאת מצרים בפרט לישראל כמ״ש ע״כ צוך כו׳.

Refer to our previous *dvar Torah* in which we suggested that while the spiritual level of *Zachor* could be maintained before *Klal Yisrael* had sinned, after sinning, our primary focus must be *Shamor*. Extending this theme, we suggest that prior to sinning, the concept of Shabbos – which at that point was primarily celebrated as a commemoration of Creation (which was the reason given for observing Shabbos in the first rendition of the *Aseres HaDibros*) – could be shared with all of mankind. At that point, it was not necessary to warn *Klal Yisrael* to guard Shabbos from the rest of mankind. However, after coming into contact with Amalek, who sorely affected *Klal Yisrael's* moral standing (refer to *Rashi, Devarim* 25:18, s.v. אשר), it was no longer possible for the Jewish people to attempt to influence all mankind. Such a mission involving extensive exposure with idolators would have jeopardized their *kedushah*. Instead, Shabbos is now primarily observed in commemoration of *Yetzias Mitzrayim* – an event that is only significant to *Klal Yisrael*. Under those circumstances, it is important to guard (*Shamor*) Shabbos from being observed by mankind. Our approach is supported by the Torah's insistence in the second rendition of the *Aseres HaDibros*, where the term *Shamor* is utilized: עַל כֵּן צִוְּךָ ה׳ אֱלֹהֶיךָ לַעֲשׂוֹת אֶת יוֹם הַשַּׁבָּת, *Therefore* HASHEM, *your God, has commanded you* (*Klal Yisrael*) *to make* (observe) *the Sabbath day* (*Devarim* 5:15). (*Va'eschanan* 5637)

◆§ The Days Before / The Days After

הם ג׳ ימים דקמי שבתא וג׳ ימים דבתר שבתא. דאיתא זכור מלפני׳ שמור מלאחרי׳ ע״ש במכילתא. פי׳ השבת משייר קדושה. וצריכין בג׳ ימים דבתר שבתא לשמור הארת הקדושה הנשארת. וזוכין אח״כ בג׳ ימים דקמי שבתא לזכור ולהשתוקק להכין אל השבת. ואז השבת העתיד מסייע גם לפניו. ומי שישנו בשמירה ישנו בזכירה.

According to the *Mechilta,* the term *Zachor* refers to the preparations that are done prior to Shabbos, while *Shamor* refers to the ambiance of Shabbos that is felt for days afterwards. By stating that whoever participates in *Shamor* also participates in *Zachor, Chazal* seem to be emphasizing that the *Shamor* phase must occur first, followed by *Zachor.* In this context, by insisting that the *Shamor* aspect of Shabbos come first, the Torah is relating to us that we must ensure that the period immediately following Shabbos – generally assumed by *Chazal* to be the first three days of the week – be an environment in which we retain (*Shamor*) and preserve the sacred ambiance of Shabbos. In the merit of retaining the *kedushah* of the previous Shabbos during the first three days of the week, we are able to properly prepare for Shabbos in the remaining three days that immediately precede the following Shabbos (in the spirit of *Zachor*). In fact, the final three days of the week benefit from *both* the days that immediately preceded them, as well as from the *kedushah* of the following Shabbos.

The essential role played by the three days before and after Shabbos is alluded to in the structure of the *Menorah,* which consisted of three branches emanating from each side of the *Menorah's* central stem (cf. *Shemos* 25:32). We suggest that these branches symbolize the three days of the week preceding and succeeding Shabbos. It is significant that there was a knob (*kaftor*) on the central stem of the *Menorah* placed between each of the branches that emanated from the *Menorah.* Assuming that the central stem represents Shabbos (the focal point of the week), the knob, which suggests a fusing together of disparate ideas to form a united whole, may represent the dual aspects of Shabbos, which together comprise the unified theme of *Zachor* and *Shamor* that were said simultaneously. (Please refer to our chapter on *Shalosh Seudos* for further discussion of the role played by the days before and after Shabbos.)

(*Vayakhel* 5651)

☙ *Shamor* During the Week / *Zachor* On Shabbos

ובזה נראה לפרש מ״ש ז״ל אלו משמרין ב׳ שבתות מיד נגאלין ופירש מו״ז ז״ל בשם הרב ר׳ שמעלקא ז״ל כי ע״י שבת אחד ששת ימי החול כראוי ועי״ז שבת הב׳ כראוי כו׳. ולהנ״ל מובן בפשיטות דכתיב זכור ושמור. ובזכור נאמר כי ששת ימים כו׳ וינח ביום השביעי כו׳ ובשמור כתיב הוציאך ה׳ ממצרים ע״כ צוך כו׳. ופי׳ שמירה הוא בימות החול לשמור עצמו שלא לקבל עול ושעבוד לדבר אחר שנק׳ ע״ז עבודה שהיא זרה לך כו׳.

Whereas in the previous *dvar Torah* we suggested that *Shamor* and *Zachor* both refer to the period immediately before and after Shabbos, here we suggest that *Shamor* alludes to our role during the week preparing for Shabbos, while *Zachor* pertains to our conduct on Shabbos itself.

To explain our assertion, we cite the renowned *Chazal* (*Shabbos* 118b) stating that if *Klal Yisrael* would merely observe two Shabbosos they would be immediately redeemed. According to R' Shmelke of Nikolsburg (cited by the *Chiddushei HaRim*, the *Sfas Emes'* grandfather), the expression "two Shabbosos" refers to an entire week that is observed in a proper environment of Torah and fear of Hashem. To achieve such a lofty objective, the previous Shabbos must have been observed properly. By now observing the six weekdays that follow in the same spirit as Shabbos had been observed, one ensures that the following Shabbos will be enhanced as well. Thus, when *Chazal* are referring to "two Shabbosos" they are alluding to the interplay between the two Shabbosos and the week between them.

Elaborating upon this theme, we suggest that the *Shamor* aspect of Shabbos is ideally attained during the six weekdays, while the spirit of *Zachor* is reached on Shabbos itself. To appreciate the distinct roles of *Zachor* and *Shamor* and how each is best realized in its proper time context, we recall that when the Torah discusses *Shamor* it relates Shabbos to *Yetzias Mitzrayim.* By liberating us from Mitzrayim, Hashem demonstrated that He is capable of shattering any force (such as Pharaoh) that seeks to subjugate *Klal Yisrael.* Our sacred task during the week is to take to heart the message of *Shamor* and guard ourselves against any force that compromises our loyalty to Hashem. If we ever doubt our capacity to prevail over those forces that would disturb our *avodas Hashem,* we recall *Yetzias Mitzrayim* and how Hashem was able to remove the shackles of Egyptian slavery.

On Shabbos, however, our task is to accentuate the *Zachor* aspect — accepting Hashem's sovereignty which He demonstrated when creating heaven and earth. Thus, when discussing the *mitzvah* of *Zachor,* the Torah focuses on Creation (rather than *Yetzias Mitzrayim*).

Having clarified the distinct aspects of *Zachor* and *Shamor,* we now return to the intricate association between the weekdays and Shabbos. As we indicated previously, there is a close relationship between the manner in which Shabbos is observed and the spiritual level achieved during the weekdays that lie ahead. Moreover, by observing the week properly, we ensure that the following Shabbos will be appreciated to a much greater extent. Specifically, by accepting Hashem's sovereignty during the first Shabbos, we are better poised to reject any forces that would compromise our relationship with Him during the week ahead. In turn, by taking care during the week to summarily reject any force that would deflect us from our relationship with Hashem, we will be better able to accept Hashem's sovereignty during the following Shabbos. This ongoing relationship between these two Shabbosos and the week between them, in which *Klal Yisrael* rejects non-Torah values and is continuously accepting Hashem's sovereignty, will have the effect of hastening the Final Redemption. (*Shabbos HaGadol* 5632)

☙ A Source of *Berachos*

והוא בחי שלום ונותן ברכה לכל זמן

Perhaps the dual nature of Shabbos', *Zachor* and *Shamor,* symbolizes the fact that Shabbos is not only a blessed day but also, as *Chazal* state, "A vehicle that contains *berachah*" (cf. *Uktzin* 3:12). In fact, this relationship between being blessed and blessing others can be found in the realm of *Makom* (sacred places), as well as *Zeman* (sacred occasions). Thus, the *Beis HaMikdash* not only occupies one of the most blessed sites on earth but is also, in turn, a source of blessing for the entire universe. It is no coincidence that so many aspects of Shabbos are stated as pairs — the Double Bread; the double expression introducing the Psalm that discusses Shabbos, *Mizmor Shir;* and *Zachor* and *Shamor*.[1]

(*Pekudei* 5660)

❧ Parallels Between *Zachor* and *Shamor* of Shabbos and Pesach

בשבת זכור ושמור. ואיתא בזוה״ק שהוא כולל כל התורה מצות עשה ומצות ל״ת. וכמו כן ביציאת מצרים כתיב זכור כו׳ היום הזה וכתיב למען הזכור כו׳ יום צאתך. וכתיב בי׳ ג״כ שמור כו׳ חודש האביב. ושמרתם את המצות. כי יצ״מ ג״כ כולל כל התורה. לכן כתיב אשר הוצאתיך מארץ מצרים.

It is significant that the same dual relationship that exists between *Zachor* and *Shamor* in reference to Shabbos also exists for the *Yom Tov* of Pesach. When discussing *Yetzias Mitzrayim,* the Torah writes, זָכוֹר אֶת הַיּוֹם הַזֶּה אֲשֶׁר יְצָאתֶם מִמִּצְרַיִם, *Remember the day on which you departed from Egypt* (*Shemos* 13:3). Similarly, the Torah states, לְמַעַן תִּזְכֹּר אֶת יוֹם צֵאתְךָ מֵאֶרֶץ מִצְרַיִם כֹּל יְמֵי חַיֶּיךָ, *So that you will remember the day of your departure from the land of Egypt all the days of your life* (*Devarim* 16:3).

The Torah also uses the term *Shamor* in reference to Pesach, שָׁמוֹר אֶת חֹדֶשׁ הָאָבִיב, *You shall observe the month of springtime* (Nissan in which Pesach occurs) (ibid. 16:1). Also, וּשְׁמַרְתֶּם אֶת הַמַּצּוֹת, *You shall safeguard the matzos* (from rising) (*Shemos* 12:17).

If we assume (as we have in many of our *divrei Torah* in this chapter) that *Zachor* and *Shamor* pertain not only to Shabbos but actually represent

1. According to the *Sfas Emes* one has to earn the distinction of becoming a source of *berachos* to others. In particular, those whose *neshamah* on earth is linked to its heavenly roots merit not only to be blessed but also to bless others. Thus, Moshe *Rabbeinu* is described by *Chazal* (*Yalkut Shemos* 414) as אִישׁ אֱמוּנוֹת רַב בְּרָכוֹת, *The man of trust and the source of blessings* (*Mishlei* 28:20). Since his presence on earth is rooted in so trustworty a source in heaven, he can generously dispense *berachos.*

all of the positive and negative commandments of the Torah, we can appreciate why the Torah utilizes *Zachor* (*Shemos* 13:3) and *Shamor* (*Devarim* 16:1) in the context of *Yetzias Mitzrayim,* as well as Shabbos. *Yetzias Mitzrayim,* which is the foundation of the entire Torah (our observance is based on the underlying premise that Hashem not only created heaven and earth but also liberated us from Egypt), should be expressed in the form of *Zachor* and *Shamor* which represents all of the *mitzvos* of the Torah.

(*Shabbos HaGadol* 5648)

יום טוב של פסח נק׳ בתורה שבת כדכ׳ ממחרת השבת. כי פסח דומה לשבת כמ״ש בשבת זכור ושמור כמו כן בפסח והי׳ היום הזה. לכם לזכרון. וכ׳ למען תזכור. וכ׳ שמור כו׳ חודש האביב. ושמרתם את המצות. כי זכירה היא נקודה פנימית שאין בה שכחה. ולפי שבשבת מתגלה נקודה זו בנפשות בנ״י לכן צריכה שמירה שלא להתפשט נקודה פנימיות למקום שיש בו שכחה. ולכן זכור ושמור בדיבור אחד נאמרו. והוא עצמו הענין בגאולת מצרים. שבכל חג המצות נעשה איש ישראל לברי׳ חדשה כמו שהי׳ ביציאת מצרים כקטן שנולד. ומתחדש בו אותו הנקודה שנטע הקב״ה בנפשות בנ״י.

The apparently superficial resemblance between Pesach and Shabbos (that both festivals share the terms *Zachor* and *Shamor*), upon further contemplation, may be quite profound. Let us assume that the term *Zachor* alludes to the *nekudah penimis,* that inner spark of *kedushah* that surfaces every Shabbos. By using the term *Zachor,* "to remember," the Torah alludes to the enormous potential of every Jew to always remember Hashem and the Torah. Just as one can never forget certain things due to their association with our very existence (e.g., our name), so too, because of the presence of this inner spark, a Jew will never forget his *Yiddishkeit.* However, this spark must be protected against abuse or distortion. It is only by remaining loyal to the Torah that the *Shamor* aspect — safeguarding the inner spark — may be managed. Just as the inner spark emerges every Shabbos, so too, every Pesach the Jew feels a sense of renewal, almost as if he is an entirely different individual ready to begin again. Just as the inner spark of Shabbos must be protected, so too, the sense of resurgence (*Zachor*) that we enjoy every Pesach must be safeguarded.

(*Pesach* 5657)

למען תזכור כו׳. וכ׳ ושמרת כו׳ החקה כו׳ מימים ימימה. כי כל התורה תלוי׳ ביצ״מ וכלולה בזכור ושמור מ״ע ומל״ת. ויום הפסח מאיר על כל השנה בבחי׳ זכירה ושמירה. וליל שמורים נותן שמירה על הלילות לכן כתיב שמורים לשון רבים. ויום הפסח נותן זכירה על כל הימים כמ״ש זכור את היום כו׳ אשר יצאתם ממצרים. ומצות מצה רומז על השמירה. וכוסות הוא בחי׳ הזכירה זכרהו על היין.

Elaborating further on the theme of *Zachor* and *Shamor* in reference to *Yetzias Mitzrayim,* we suggest that both the *Zachor* and *Shamor* aspect of Pesach pertain not only to that *Yom Tov* but also to the entire year. Specifically, the night of the *Seder* known as לֵיל שִׁמּוּרִים (the night of watching) is a source of protection for every night of the year (as indicated by the plural form *shimurim,* "protections"), while the day of Pesach enables us to remember *Yetzias Mitzrayim* the entire year. As the Torah states, *Remember the day on which you departed from Egypt.* Even specific aspects of the *Yom Tov* simulate the *Zachor* and *Shamor* of Shabbos. For example, the four cups of wine assist in fulfilling the *mitzvah* of *Zachor,* which on Shabbos is also performed through the medium of wine when we recite *Kiddush.* On the other hand, the matzah allows us to preserve the message of *Yetzias Mitzrayim,* as the Torah states, *You shall safeguard the matzos* (*Shemos* 12:17). (*Pesach* 5653)

Remembering Hashem On Shabbos

זכור ושמור כולל כל התורה. זכור מ״ע שמור מל״ת כדאיתא בזוה״ק. ופי׳ זכור כו׳ יום השבת כמו וזכרת את ה״א דשבת שמא דקוב״ה. ה׳ זכרנו שהוא עיקר הזכירה ופנימיות.

By interpreting *Zachor* as referring to all of the positive commandments and *Shamor* as referring to all of the negative commandments, *Chazal* may be interpreting the *mitzvah* of *Zachor* and *Shamor* as a plea to remember and never forget Hashem Who gave us the Torah. According to the *Zohar,* Shabbos is a Name of *HaKadosh Baruch Hu.* Consequently, זָכוֹר אֶת יוֹם הַשַּׁבָּת should be interpreted as a plea "to remember Hashem Whose Name is Shabbos." Based on this interpretation, the *pasuk* may be alluding to the Divine Spark that Hashem implanted within us at the time of *Matan Torah*. In fact, the blessing associated with Shabbos may be derived from the fact that we remember Hashem on that day. As we read, *In any place where I permit My Name to be mentioned, I will come to you and bless you* (*Shemos* 20:21).

(*Va'eschanan* 5661)

☙ A Guide to Dealing with Materialism (*Zachor* and *Shamor* of Eating)

ד״ש זכור ושמור בכלל כל המצות. זכור הוא בחי׳ מ״ע לעורר הפנימיות וניצוצי קדושה שיש בכ״ד ע״י המ״ע. ושמור ע״י הל״ת לשמור החיצוניות וקליפות שלא יתמשכו יותר מדאי. ובב׳ אלו הם בכ״ד שבעולם. לכן כתי׳ ושבעת וברכת הוא בחי׳ זכור בפה. השמרו לכם בחי׳ שמור בלב.

Assuming that *Zachor* and *Shamor* do not only pertain to Shabbos, but rather are symbolic of all of the Torah's positive and negative commandments (as we discussed frequently throughout this chapter), we suggest that by examining these concepts closely we can acquire a useful approach to dealing with the material world.

In order to counteract the harmful effect of overindulgence in food and other material amenities, the Torah prescribes two remedies. First is the commandment to recite a *berachah* (cf. *Devarim* 8:10, וְאָכַלְתָּ וְשָׂבָעְתָּ וּבֵרַכְתָּ אֶת ה׳ אֱלֹהֶיךָ), followed by a strict warning not to forget Hashem when partaking of the pleasures of This World (הִשָּׁמֶר לְךָ פֶּן תִּשְׁכַּח אֶת ה׳ אֱלֹהֶיךָ, ibid. 8:11).

We suggest that these two *mitzvos* associated with eating and remembering Hashem while eating, parallel *Zachor* and *Shamor*. Just as the function of every positive commandment is to bring out the potential *kedushah* that the object associated with the *mitzvah* contains (or the latent *kedushah* that every *neshamah* possesses through the Spark of Holiness that Hashem implanted in us), so too, by reciting a *berachah*, we elicit the inherent sanctity of the food.[1] Similarly, by recalling while

1. In order to appreciate the approach of *Sfas Emes* to *berachos* and its relationship to *Zachor* and *Shamor*, the primary theme of this chapter, we recall the famous interpretation of the *Ari HaKadosh* to the *pasuk*, כִּי לֹא עַל הַלֶּחֶם לְבַדּוֹ יִחְיֶה הָאָדָם כִּי עַל כָּל מוֹצָא פִי ה׳ יִחְיֶה הָאָדָם, *Man does*

eating the Torah's warning not to become overly immersed in material values, we are fulfilling the function of *Shamor*, ensuring that we are not unduly affected by the materialism inherent in the food.

(*Eikev* 5649)[1]

In a previous *dvar Torah*, we suggested that *Zachor* corresponds to our ability to serve Hashem through speech (*dibbur*), while *Shamor* alludes to the role played by the heart in *avodas Hashem*. We may now extend this approach to the *Zachor* and *Shamor* aspects associated with eating. On one hand, by verbalizing a *berachah*, in the spirit of *Zachor*, we ensure that we are sustained by the spiritual component of food. On the other hand, by bearing in our heart the Torah's reminder not to be swayed by materialism, we are fulfilling the spirit of *Shamor*. (Ibid.)

◆§ Parallels Between *Zachor* and *Shamor* of Shabbos And *Zachor* and *Shamor* of Lashon Hara

וכמו שיש בשבת זכור ושמור ושמרו בזוה"ק שכל התורה כלולה בזכור ושמור כמו כן בלשון הרע ב' השמר וב' זכור. וכן כתיב מוצא שפתיך ת' דרשו חז"ל מ"ש מ"ע השמור מל"ת כו' שכל התורה תלוי בפה כנ"ל. ובאמת גם בשבת היא בחי' הפה דיש ראי' שמיעה ריחא ודיבור. וימי המעשה הם בחי' ב' עיינין [ב'] אודנין ב' נוקבין דחוטמא. והשבת הוא הפה שנק' סהדותא ושבת יעשה כולו תורה. לכן אמרו לכל יש בן זוג. אבל הפה יחיד.

It is significant that the same "duality" of *Zachor* and *Shamor* that permeates the *mitzvah* of Shabbos is also found in reference to the grave sin of *lashon hara*. In that context, the Torah writes, *Remember*

---

not live on bread alone, rather on the expression of the word of Hashem does man live (Devarim 8:3). According to the *Ari* there are two distinct components of food. On one hand, there is a *spiritual* component which is derived from "the expression of the word of Hashem" (the Divine command through which the food item was created). It is from this component that man's soul is nurtured. On the other hand, there is a *material* component which feeds our body and which has the potential to lead us astray and become overly inclined towards material values (*gashmiyus*).

1. Refer to the original text of *Sfas Emes* in which he utilizes this approach to explain the significance of discussing Torah thoughts while enjoying a meal, as well as the famous statement of *Chazal*, אִם אֵין קֶמַח אֵין תּוֹרָה, *If there is no flour, there is no Torah* (*Avos* 3:21).

(זָכוֹר) *what* H*ASHEM*, *your God, did to Miriam on the way, when you were leaving Egypt* (*Devarim* 24:9), which is interpreted by *Chazal* as a positive *mitzvah* to recall the *lashon hara* (albeit on a very miniscule level) spoken by Miriam and the punishment that she experienced as a result of speaking *lashon hara* (cf. *Ramban* on *Devarim* 24:9-10), immediately preceded by, *Beware* (הִשָּׁמֶר) *of a tzaraas affliction* (a negative commandment not to speak *lashon hara*).

It is also noteworthy that a similar relationship is found in reference to the *mitzvah* of fulfilling one's pledges to *tzedakah*.[1]

Perhaps there is an association between these three aspects of Torah that are presented to us in the form of *Zachor* and *Shamor* — they are all related to the power of speech. While it is evident that both the prohibition of *lashon hara* and the obligation to redeem one's pledges are linked to the power of speech, we will demonstrate that Shabbos is also a *mitzvah* that is closely associated with speech and the mouth.

As we know, the human body perceives its environment through various receptors, including the eyes, nose (the sense of smell), the ear, and the mouth. It is noteworthy that whereas all of the other receptors exist in pairs (two eyes, two ears, two nostrils), the mouth uniquely exists alone. We suggest that the six receptors that are used to see, smell and hear correspond to the six weekdays, while Shabbos corresponds to the mouth, which exists by itself. Whereas during the week we absorb various aspects of our environment by hearing, seeing or smelling, on Shabbos, we fulfill an entirely different function. On this most sacred day, we dedicate ourselves to testify (through our capacity of speech) to Hashem's creation of the universe and to study Torah. Perhaps, the renowned *Chazal* (*Bereishis Rabbah* 11:8) that unlike all of the other days of the week which each enjoy a pair, Shabbos exists alone, alludes to the human mouth, which exists alone — just like Shabbos. In contrast to the senses of sight, hearing, and smell which simply react to external stimuli, the gift of speech is far more profound, reflecting the inner depth and thoughts of every individual. Unlike the other receptors whose essence is shared with all of mankind, the gift of speech acquires a special dimension for *Klal Yisrael* who uses this capacity to discusss *divrei Torah*.

(*Ki Seitzei* 5646)

---

1. According to *Chazal*, the phrase מוֹצָא שְׂפָתֶיךָ, the expression of your lips (cf. *Devarim* 23:24) refers to the positive commandment to honor one's pledges to charity, while the immediately succeeding term, תִּשְׁמֹר, *You shall observe*, is a negative commandment violated when a pledge to *tzedakah* is not promptly honored.

◆§ Two Forms of *Teshuvah*

והנה יש תשובה בבחי׳ הנשמה ובבחי׳ הגוף בחי׳ זכור ושמור. תשובה מיראה על החטאים והם מצד הגוף בחי׳ סור מרע מל״ת. ותשובה (מיראה) [מאהבה] על חסרון המעשים טובים ומיעוט הארת הנשמה שעיקר האדם נברא שתשלוט הנשמה על הגוף.

Whereas in previous *divrei Torah,* we suggested that *Zachor* and *Shamor* correspond to the Torah's positive and negative commandments respectively, we now extend the analysis and propose that these two concepts correspond to two methods of repentance (*teshuvah*). Specifically, a vital first step is to return to Hashem out of fear of the retribution that will be inflicted upon us in *Gehinnom* (תְּשׁוּבָה מִיִּרְאָה). This form of repentance, which is a prerequisite to higher forms of *teshuvah,* is associated with the concept of *Shamor* – regretting the negative commandments that we violated and, in general, expressing remorse that too often we yielded to the material impulses of our body (refer to previous *divrei Torah* where we suggested that *Shamor* refers to the humbling of the body). Once this initial form of *teshuvah* has been successfully implemented, we may advance to a higher form of repentance, out of love of Hashem (תְּשׁוּבָה מֵאַהֲבָה), which corresponds to the soul. Now our primary focus is on performing more positive commandments (*Zachor*) and permitting the influence of the *neshamah* to permeate the entire body. One who performs *teshuvah* out of love of Hashem is motivated by an acute yearning to come close to Him and to develop an intimate relationship with Him, which corresponds to the theme of *Zachor.* Unlike תְּשׁוּבָה מִיִּרְאָה, which is based on fear of punishment in *Gehinnom,* this love-based repentance is more motivated by a desire for the soul to reside in *Gan Eden.* Whereas *teshuvah* based on fear may be practiced by the wicked, *teshuvah* motivated by love can only be performed by *tzaddikim* who seek an ever-closer relationship with Hashem. Shabbos, the day when we already enjoy an intimate relationship with our Creator, is a particularly propitious time for תְּשׁוּבָה מֵאַהֲבָה.[1]

(*Shabbos Shuvah* 5662)

1. For further discussion of this theme of *teshuvah* with love, refer to *Days of Awe,* pgs. 222-223 and 243-252.

Melachah

In this chapter we will discuss the significance and symbolism of the prohibition of work on Shabbos (*issur Melachah*), with particular emphasis on the statement of *Chazal* (*Rashi, Shemos* 20:9) that "once Shabbos arrives, it should seem to you as if all your work (that needs to be done) is already completed."

◆§ The Power of Believing

ובמכילתא וכי אפשר לאדם לעשות כל מלאכתו בו' ימים אלא שבות כאילו כל מלאכתך עשוי'. ד"א שבות מהירהור מלאכה. והאמת כי ע"י שביתה זו אם הוא באמת אצל האדם כאילו כל מלאכתו עשוי'. יכולה היא שתרדום. וברגע א' נגמר כל מלאכתו. כמ"ש חז"ל אילו שמרו ישראל שבת א' כהילכתו מיד הם נגאלים. אם היו שומרי שבת לשם ה' ולשכות מכל הדברים. הוי' מיד גאולה. וכן הוא בפרט כל א' כפי השביתה.

According to *Rashi*, the *pasuk* שֵׁשֶׁת יָמִים תַּעֲבֹד וְעָשִׂיתָ כָּל מְלַאכְתֶּךָ, *Six days shall you work and accomplish all of your work* (*Shemos* 20:9), is not only an implicit prohibition not to work on Shabbos, but also a plea that once Shabbos arrives, one should feel that all of the work that we require is actually completed. Commenting on this *pasuk*, the *Ohr HaChaim HaKadosh* suggests that the Torah is bestowing a *berachah* upon those who observe Shabbos. According to him, the first segment of the *pasuk, Six days shall you work,* may be interpreted as an assurance that it will be sufficient to toil for six days without jeopardizing one's livelihood.

With this approach, we gain new insight into the *Chazal* (*Shabbos* 118b) stating that if *Klal Yisrael* observed even one Shabbos, they would be redeemed. Perhaps they are referring not only to the Future Redemption that awaits the Jewish nation but also to the personal redemption from fears and worries that the Shabbos brings to all those who cherish it.

(Adapted from *Yisro* 5657)

רש״י פי׳ שיהי׳ כאלו כ״מ עשוי׳. ובאוה״ח פי׳ שהוא ברכה שבששת ימים תוכל לעשות כל מלאכתך ולא תצטרך לעבודת יום השבת ע״ש. והאמת כי זאת הברכה היא עי״ז שנעשה בעיני האדם כאילו כל מלאכתו עשוי׳. ואינו מהרהר אחר מלאכה בעבור רצון המקום ב״ה. על ידי זה נעשה מלאכתו באמת באין מחסור. וזהו בהקדמת זכור את יום השבת לקדשו. והנה הזכירה הוא בחול. כי בשבת הוא עצם היום. רק בימי המעשה צריכין לזכור יום השבת. ועי״ז ניתוסף ברכה בהמעשים. פי׳ שגם בימי המעשה שצריך לעסוק במעשים ומלאכות גשמיות. מ״מ צריך שיהי׳ השתוקקת האדם להשבת. שיהי׳ עליו לעול ולמשא מה שצריך לעסוק בזה. ומכ״ש להיות מוכן לבטל מעשהו. שיהי׳ כאילו מלאכתו עשוי׳. אם הי׳ רצון המקום שישבות ממלאכה מבטל עצמו מלהרהר אחר מלאכה. ובזוכרו זאת יש ברכת השבת במעשיו. וזה ענין כל שישנו בשמירה ישנו בזכירה. ושמירה הוא השתוקקות להשבת כמו שמר את הדבר.

It is possible that both of the foregoing approaches to this *pasuk* are closely related. Specifically, by believing that all of one's work is completed by the conclusion of the six weekdays (*Rashi's* approach) — to the extent that one does not even think about *Melachah* on Shabbos — merits the *berachah* that indeed one does not need to work on Shabbos to sustain oneself.

But how does one achieve a spiritual level so exalted to actually feel that all the work that needs to be done is completed at the commencement of Shabbos? The answer to this question lies in the previous *pasuk*: זָכוֹר אֶת יוֹם הַשַּׁבָּת לְקַדְּשׁוֹ, *Remember the Shabbos day to sanctify it* (*Shemos* 20:8), which is interpreted as referring to our obligation during the six weekdays to always remember Shabbos[1] (refer to *Rashi* and *Ramban*, ibid.). By always recalling Shabbos even in the midst of the workweek, one merits to achieve the state of mind whereby one is able to realize that no more work is required by the workweek's conclusion. This blessed attitude, in turn, is the source for the *berachah* alluded to by the *Ohr HaChaim HaKadosh* – that the six days of the week will provide enough sustenance for the entire week.

Exploring further the concept of remembering Shabbos during the week, we suggest that this worthy objective can be achieved by perceiving the *spiritual rest* of Shabbos as one's *priority*, rather than the physical work of the weekdays. We should consider the work which we are required to perform during the week as a necessary burden which Hashem expects us to pursue, rather than as our primary objective. If the work that we are required to perform on the weekdays is perceived as being nothing more than a reluctant requirement, while our true yearning is for the bliss of Shabbos (when we enjoy the opportunity to fulfill Hashem's commandment that we rest from our physical labors), it follows that it is relatively simple to feel that one's work is indeed complete at the conclusion of the six workdays. Consequently, we can benefit from the *berachah* enjoyed by those who observe Shabbos (that the work performed during the first six days will be sufficient for an entire week).

With this idea, we derive new insight into the statement of *Chazal* (*Berachos* 20b), כָּל שֶׁיֶּשְׁנוֹ בִּשְׁמִירָה יֶשְׁנוֹ בִּזְכִירָה, "Whoever is included in guarding (*Shamor* aspect) the Shabbos is also included in remembering (*Zachor* aspect) the Shabbos." (Refer to our chapter on *Zachor V'Shamor* for numerous interpretations of this *Chazal*.) In the episode relating Yosef's dreams, *Rashi* interprets the term *Shamor* as "to anticipate" (cf. *Bereishis* 37:11). We suggest that *Chazal* are teaching us that whoever anticipates the advent of Shabbos all week long will merit to perform the *mitzvah* of זָכוֹר אֶת יוֹם הַשַּׁבָּת לְקַדְּשׁוֹ, to always recall the Shabbos – even while engaged in mundane work – and to enjoy the *berachos* granted to those who long for Shabbos. (*Yisro* 5637).

1. *Chazal's* assumption that this *pasuk* refers to the obligation to remember Shabbos during the weekdays rather than on Shabbos itself may be based on the term *zachor*. On Shabbos itself, one would hardly require a reminder that we are currently observing Shabbos. It is only during the weekdays, when one might forget Shabbos because of one's preoccupation with work, that the Torah feels obliged to remind us to recall the Shabbos (cf. *Beitzah* 15b, "Remember the Shabbos when you are about to forget it").

◆§ Merit of Yearning for Shabbos

ובאמת ע״י התשוקה והרצון לקבלת השבת יוכל להיות נעשה ונגמר כל מלאכתך כמ״ש בע״ה בחילא סגי בשעתא חדא ורגעא חדא מתקנין הכל ע״ש. לכן איתא שיש רשות לאדם לרוץ ברה״ר בע״ש בה״ש. והבן זאת: והנה השבת הוא משל לעוה״ב. וכפי מה שיוכל האדם להתקרב לקדושת השבת כן יש לו שייכות לעוה״ב. לכן צריך האדם בכל שבת לעזוב כל עניני עוה״ז ולזכור עצמו שצריך להכין עצמו לשבת הגדול היינו לעוה״ב. לכן צריכין לשוב בתשובה בעש״ק כמו קודם הסתלקות האדם מעוה״ז וע״י השתוקקות אל השבת כמ״ש.

It is possible that merely by yearning all week long for Shabbos, and especially for the moment at the conclusion of the six workdays when we welcome Shabbos (*Kabbolas Shabbos*), that in this merit alone, we are assured that indeed all of our required activities necessary to earn a livelihood are already completed before Shabbos arrives. This supposition that one day of the week, Shabbos (or even yearning for Shabbos to begin), is the source of an entire week's *parnassah* (contrary to the popular wisdom that it is by laboring during the six weekdays that we are assured of our livelihood), is similar to the *Zohar* stating that at times it is possible to accomplish in one moment what otherwise may take a long time. When *Chazal* permit one to run on *erev Shabbos* (in the period immediately preceding sunset) and actually absolve one of damages that may result from running (cf. *Bava Kamma* 32a), they may be referring not only to the physical pace of our activity which, of necessity, hastens every Friday afternoon but also to the rapid spiritual surge that we all enjoy as Shabbos approaches. Likewise, the *Ohr HaChaim HaKadosh* notes that by stating, "Six days you shall work" rather than "*in* six days you shall work," the Torah is emphasizing that every Shabbos we (and the entire universe) derive enough sustenance to last us for an entire week. Once a week has passed, it is necessary to return to the source of our strength, Shabbos, so that we are nurtured for another week.

While it is true that one moment can be enough to sustain a long period, this is particularly true if this moment is spent in an atmosphere of *teshuvah*. In fact, the *Zohar* mentioned previously specifically refers to the power of a *baal teshuvah* to accomplish in one moment what it may take others a long time to achieve. By doing *teshuvah* before Shabbos arrives (and particularly by yearning for Shabbos to come), we are assured that we will enjoy the full impact of Shabbos and its ability to sustain us in the week ahead. Moreover, just as it is meritorious for an individual who is about to leave This World for *Olam Haba* to do *teshuvah*, so too, as we leave behind the workday week to enter the spiritual realm of Shabbos, it is an opportune time for *teshuvah*. (*Yisro* 5639)

◆§ You Already Have Everything (*Sheleimus*)

וכמו כן בכל פרט איש ישראל כפי כח שמירת שבת שבו שמשליך כל מחשבת מלאכת חול בביאת הש״ק. כמו כן נשלם אצלו ג״כ עבודת הבורא ית״ש. הגם שהוא חסר השלימות. השבת נותן לו שלימות. ולכן הגם שהיו זריזין במלאכת המשכן. כשבא שבת כאלו נשלם המשכן ששבת שלום משלים המלאכה כמ״ש. וז״ש למעט שבת ממלאכת המשכן.

Alternatively, by recommending that all of our *Melachah* be considered as completed at the onset of Shabbos, *Chazal* are reassuring us that nothing more needs to be done. While it is human nature to always strive to do more, in this instance, *Chazal* assure us to the contrary. In fact, the Shabbos day is called *Shalom* (refer to our chapter on this topic), a name which alludes to the *sheleimus*, completeness (perfection) inherent in this sacred day. Even if we perceive that the work that we should have accomplished has not yet been completed, the merit of Shabbos alone is sufficient to ensure that whatever we sought to do will be finished. At times, we may be concerned about any potential loss suffered as a result of not working on Shabbos. However, we know that such losses are compensated by the merit of Shabbos itself. As *Chazal* note, "The Shabbos day has mercy on those who observe its precepts and assures them that they will suffer no harm" (*Shabbos* 12b).

This same sense of completion that permeates the Shabbos explains why the construction of the *Mishkan* had to cease at the beginning of Shabbos. One can imagine how the dedicated builders of the *Mishkan* felt knowing that so much of their sacred work had yet to be done.

Nonetheless, they ceased building the *Mishkan* at the advent of Shabbos, realizing that just as Shabbos "completes" all of our physical tasks to the point that no more work is necessary, so too, their sacred form of Divine service – perhaps the highest form of physical activity ever performed – was already complete when Shabbos arrived. (*Ki Sisa* 5661)

◆§ All of Your Spiritual Work Accomplished

כמ״ש שיהיה כל מלאכתך עשויה. שבהתגלות אות השבת נשלם הכל. ולכן אין צריכין בשבת כל הבנינים והצירופים שהכל נגמר ע״י השבת. ובאמת כל מלאכת המשכן וחיבור שמים וארץ הכל בחי׳ סולם לעלות אל השורש. וכשזוכין אל עלי׳ אין צריכין הסולם.

In the previous *divrei Torah,* we assumed that when *Chazal* refer to all of our work being completed at the onset of Shabbos, they are referring to *physical* work. However, in a sense, our *spiritual* efforts for that week are also consummated when Shabbos begins.

To explain this concept, we recall that the *Mishkan* was beyond doubt the highest form of creativity ever performed by man. In fact, according to *Chazal* (*Berachos* 55a), Betzalel constructed the *Mishkan* not only on the basis of his superior *artistic* skills but because of his unique *spiritual* capacity to fuse various Names of Hashem (which had originally been used to create heaven and earth). Using these combinations of sacred Names, Betzalel was able to create the *Mishkan,* which became the dwelling place for the *Shechinah.* Yet, on Shabbos even this most rarefied form of creativity – which according to our explanation was largely spiritual – ceased. In light of our foregoing contention that on Shabbos, our spiritual efforts for that week are consummated, we can appreciate why it was not appropriate (or necessary) to construct the *Mishkan* on Shabbos. Just as when someone is already on the highest floor of a structure, he does not require a ladder to reach the top, so too, on Shabbos, one does not require the various combinations of sacred Names used by Betzalel to build the *Mishkan* to come close to Hashem. On Shabbos, our spiritual as well as our physical efforts are complete. On Shabbos, one does not require the erection of the *Mishkan* to come close to Hashem. (*Ki Sisa* 5654)

◆§ Completing Work By Not Working

כי בששת ימי בראשית נברא בכל יום ענין מיוחד לא ראי זה כראי זה. אך השבת הוא הכולל כל הימים והוא כלי מחזיק ברכה ע״י שיש בו האחדות לכן הוא קיום כל הימים כדאיתא באת שבת באת מנוחה ונגמרה המלאכה כי אם אין שלום אין כלום.

According to *Chazal*, the work of the six weekdays was not completed until Shabbos when Hashem "enhanced" the universe with the addition of *menuchah*, rest (*Rashi, Bereishis* 2:2). To explain the importance of why the concept of rest was necessary for the consummation of Hashem's (and our) work, we should recall the effect of the creations of the six weekdays. During each day of the Six Days of Creation, only specific aspects of the universe were created, rather than the universe's totality. It was only when the Six Days of Creation ended and there was the advent of harmony and peace that accompanied Shabbos that the universe could be considered totally complete. (*Korach* 5647)

ולכן נק׳ השבת שלום שהוא תכלית הבריאה. כמ״ש מה הי׳ העולם חסר מנוחה בא שבת נגמרה המלאכה. ולכן נקראו בנ״י השולמית שהם כלי לקבל אותה הנקודה.

To indicate that Creation was not complete and did not achieve harmony until the first Shabbos, *Chazal* use the term *shalom* (which is derived from *sheleimus*, harmony) to describe Shabbos. (*Beshalach* 5648)

כי בריאת העולם היה להשפיע אור וטובו של השי״ת בעוה״ז שהוא הטבע ושעל שם זה נקרא עולם על שם ההעלם כבוד ה׳ בעוה״ז כמ״ש אא״ז מו״ר זצלה״ה. אך כמו שצריך להיות הכל בטל אל המכוין אז נתגדל שמו ית׳ בעוה״ז יותר כדכתיב וירא אלהים כל אשר עשה טוב מאוד ... והוא השבת שכולל כל ימי השבוע ושבת דאתאחדת ברזא דאחד כו׳. שכל הדברים מתעלים ונעשין אחד מיוחדים להיות כלי להשי״ת לעשות בהם כרצונו. וז״ש ויכלו במד׳ שנעשה מעשה בראשית כלי והוא ע״י התכללות.

In fact, we maintain that the true purpose of Creation, that the entire universe be suffused with *Kavod Shamayim* (Glory of Hashem), was not attained until Shabbos. It was only when the entire universe was completed — as the Torah states: וַיְכֻלּוּ הַשָּׁמַיִם וְהָאָרֶץ, *Thus heaven and earth were finished* (*Bereishis* 2:1) — that the *Melachah* of the Six Days of Creation was truly consummated. (Adapted from *Bereishis* 5631)

דאיתא מלאכה שהי׳ צריך לעשות בשבת כפלו ועשאו בששי. שבששי נעשו ב׳ ברואים. ב״ח ואדם. נמצא דהי׳ ראוי להיות בריאת אדם בש״ק. והענין הוא דאדם יש בו גשמיות ורוחניות והיא חיבור ימי המעשה עם הש״ק. וז״ש חכמים למה נברא באחרונה שיכנוס לשבת מיד. פי׳ שאדם הוא מחבר כל הבריאה להתדבק ע״י כולם בעולם העליון.

Alternatively, when *Chazal* state that Hashem's *Melachah* was completed on Shabbos, they may be alluding to the unique role that man plays in Creation. In reality, man should have been created on Shabbos, just as every other aspect of Creation deserved a day in its own right. However, in order to allow man to enjoy every moment of *Shabbos Kodesh,* Hashem created man, as well as higher forms of animals, on *erev Shabbos.*[1] Thus, as soon as Shabbos began — immediately after the creation of man, who could now bask in the *kedushah* and serenity (*menuchah*) of this special day — the work of the Six Days of Creation was completed. (*Bereishis* 5638)

מכש״כ יעקב אע״ה אשר חכמים הגידו צורתו חקוקה תחת כסה״כ. פי׳ שהוא מקיים כל הבריאה. כמ״ש וירא אלקים כו׳ כל אשר עשה כו׳ טוב מאד. אדם. שראי׳ זו מקיים כל הבריאה. ומזה נעשה מנוחת שבת וגמר המלאכה. והוא אדם השלם שבעבורו נברא הכל. לכן צורתו חקוקה. וכביכול הקב״ה משגיח בו תמיד. ובזה מקיים כל הבריאה.

Expanding upon this theme, we suggest that not merely the creation

1. An additional reason why man was created on *erev Shabbos,* rather than on Shabbos, is that had he been created on Shabbos, a day that is completely spiritual, man would have consisted of a soul without a body. By creating man on *erev Shabbos,* Hashem ensured that man's body (which was created then) would be supplemented by the *neshamah yeseirah* of Shabbos, which he received almost immediately upon his creation on *erev Shabbos* (*Bereishis* 5654).

of man[1] but also the recognition that eventually there would emerge a unique individual in whose merit the entire universe would be sustained – Yaakov *Avinu* – is what led to Hashem's great satisfaction and the completion of Creation.

When *Chazal* speak of Yaakov's likeness being engraved on the Heavenly Throne (*Targum Yonasan, Bereishis* 28:12), they are alluding to the future merit of this exemplary *tzaddik*, which contributed not only to the creation of the universe but also to its ongoing existence.

(*Vayishlach* 5643)

Perhaps, when *Chazal* state that the work of the Six Days of Creation was completed with the arrival of Shabbos, they may be referring to our spiritual mission in This World. All week long, *tzaddikim* can never rest on their laurels. Instead, they are always seeking to attain higher levels of *kedushah*. It is only on Shabbos, which is a microcosm of *Olam Haba*, that they can feel a measure of satisfaction about their accomplishments. What greater *menuchah* – which is the consummation of all Hashem's *Melachah* – than a feeling of spiritual accomplishment.

(Adapted from *Bereishis* 5653)

וזה תכלית הבריאה ושבת הוא מעין עוה״ב שיורד בו הארה מן הראשית הנ״ל. ולכן נקרא שבת תכלית שמים וארץ.

When *Chazal* refer to Shabbos as the consummation of Hashem's *Melachah*, they are possibly referring to the Heavenly source of everything that has ever been created. It is well-known that everything on earth has heavenly roots. Those roots were nurtured on Shabbos, the day which we describe in our Shabbos prayers as תַּכְלִית [מַעֲשֵׂה] שָׁמַיִם וָאָרֶץ, *the conclusion of the creation of heaven and earth*. It is on Shabbos that we experience here on earth something of the spiritual roots that were first created on Shabbos.

(Adapted from *Bereishis* 5654)

1. The relationship between the creation of man and the sense of completion the world derived on the first Shabbos may be alluded to from the word מְאֹד, whose rearranged letters spell אָדָם.

חז״ש וירא אלקים כו׳ כל אשר עשה הוא הכלל. טוב מאוד. אם כי עדיין הי׳ חסר המנוחה שהיא השלימות וגמר הבנין כמ״ש באתה מנוחה ונגמרה המלאכה עכ״ז כתיב טוב מאוד זאת ההכנה ולא הי׳ חסר רק הגמר שזאת מוכרח להיות בא מלמעלה בסיוע אל ית׳ כנ״ל.

The question arises, if Creation was not completed until Shabbos when the universe achieved *sheleimus* (perfection) through the addition of the concept of *Menuchah,* why did Hashem proclaim on that first *erev Shabbos* (*before* the creation of *Menuchah*) that He was very satisfied with the world that He had created? Evidently, when Hashem proclaimed that the universe was טוֹב מְאֹד, *very good,* despite the absence of Shabbos and *Menuchah* – which is the culmination of Creation – He was praising the elaborate preparations that occurred during the Six Days of Creation and that were now complete (with the exception of the additional component of *Menuchah*).

From Hashem's lavish praise of an "unfinished universe," we learn the great importance of doing all that we can – even if our efforts can never be completed by us alone. In future generations, when mankind would utilize all that Hashem created during the six weekdays as the basis for all of its technological progress, it is important to remember that there are definite limits to our achievements. All that we can accomplish is the preparation. Having done that, we may cease our activities knowing that the final phase and completion of our efforts can only be consummated by Hashem. (*Korach* 5640)

וכן כתיב וירא אלקים כו׳ כל אשר עשה והנה טוב מאד. והסתכלות זה שהוטב בעיניו מקיים כל העולם. וזה תכלית מעשה בראשית. וזה החן הוא סוד השבת שכן כתיב והנה טוב מאד ויהי ערב כי כו׳.

Extending this approach, we suggest that the great joy that Hashem derived from His universe, as indicated by His declaration that the nearly-completed world was טוֹב מְאֹד, *very good,* in itself was enough to complete the universe.

In contemporary times as well, the sheer joy experienced by *tzaddikim* every Shabbos is enough to sustain the universe, just as Hashem's satisfaction was instrumental in the universe's consummation.

(*Ki Seitzei* 5636)

◈§ Gaining By Giving Up

ובאמת ע״י חסרון זה בגוף זוכה אל השלימות כי הגוף הוא בעל חסרון.

When *Chazal* state that the universe was completed when Hashem ceased creating, they are reaffirming a basic principle of Torah that one gains spiritually by yielding something of material value. By abstaining from *Melachah,* which on the surface appears to be a form of loss, Hashem actually perfected the universe and allowed us to enjoy the intense spiritual ambiance of *Shabbos Kodesh.* True *sheleimus* (perfection) can only occur when we forfeit material gains in favor of spirituality. As Dovid *HaMelech* writes: כִּי אֵין מַחְסוֹר לִירֵאָיו, *there is no deprivation for His reverent ones* (*Tehillim* 34:10). Whatever they give up materially, is compensated by the spiritual gains they achieve.

The *bris milah* is another example of the great gains that one can achieve by giving up something material (the *orlah*). The intimacy with Hashem that Avraham *Avinu* achieved occurred only *after* he was circumcised. (*Lech Lecha* 5636)

◈§ Creating Equilibrium

ויתכן לפרש כמו ששת ימי המעשה הם כוחות הבריאה לעשות תולדות לקיום הבריאה. כן יום השבת הנותן מנוחה לכל הבריאה ולימי המעשה. וששת ימים שם הש״י אותם כלים לעשי׳. ויום הז׳ למנוחה.

In the previous *dvar Torah,* we emphasized that the universe is sustained not only through our deeds performed during the six weekdays but also through our abstaining from creating on Shabbos. Expanding upon this theme, we suggest that both the creative phase of the six workdays and the rest of the Shabbos day are necessary for the universe's continued existence. Whereas Hashem's objective during the Six Days of Creation was not only to bring the universe into existence in the form that it was originally created, but also to enable additional forms of life to emerge from Hashem's original creations, on Shabbos, by abstaining from creating new forms of life, Hashem achieved an entirely different objective. He brought a sense of equilibrium and "rest" to a constantly dynamic world. In other words, the six weekdays are a vehicle (a concept known as *keilim)* for the continuing replenishment of the universe, and Shabbos is the weekly opportunity to appreciate the universe in its perfect harmony. This is something that is only possible when the process of constant creation is temporarily halted. By abstaining from work, we are demonstrating the necessity of both the dynamic process of continuous creation and the beautiful symmetry and harmony of the universe that can only be appreciated while the universe is at rest from creating (equilibrium). (*Yisro* 5646)

⊛ Active Rest

פי' לעשות את השבת עפ"י דברי הרמב"ן ז"ל בהאבות שבקשו אות במה אדע כו'. ופי' כי דבר שנעשה בו מעשה הוא קיים לעד והמעשה הוא חיזוק ההבטחה ע"ש. ואמר שנראה זה טעם המצות כי יש לכל מצוה שורש בשמים. וע"י מעשינו נתחזק השורש להיות קיים לעד. וכמו כן במצות שבת דכתיב לעשות. שגם הנחת המלאכה נקרא מעשה כמו חסמה בקול כו' ועי"ז מתקים השבת יותר כנ"ל ודפח"ח.

We generally assume that by not performing *Melachah* on Shabbos, we are, in effect, acting in a passive capacity. In reality, the Torah itself indicates that this is not the case by defining the prohibition of performing *Melachah* on Shabbos in *positive* terms — וְשָׁמְרוּ בְנֵי יִשְׂרָאֵל אֶת הַשַּׁבָּת לַעֲשׂוֹת אֶת הַשַּׁבָּת, *The Children of Israel shall observe the Sabbath, to make the Sabbath an eternal covenant for their generations* (*Shemos* 31:16). This means that the Jewish people should guard (observe) the Shabbos (by not performing *Melachah*) to create (לַעֲשׂוֹת) the Shabbos. By observing the Shabbos and not working, we are actually "creating" the Shabbos in an active sense.

To explain why abstaining from work, seemingly a passive act, is described by the Torah as an act of creation, we recall the renowned *Ramban* (*Bereishis* 15:7) who notes that the *Avos* always sought an affirmative act from Hashem to "confirm" His word. While they certainly never doubted the capacity of Hashem to fulfill His promises, they sought reassurance in the form of a physical symbol, so that they could be confident of the permanence of the Divine Word to them, regardless of *Klal Yisrael's* merit. Once a physical symbol was added to the verbal guarantee, the *Avos* were assured that Hashem's promise to them was irrevocable. Thus, Avraham was not content just with Hashem's promise that the Jewish people would return to *Eretz Yisrael* once they completed their exile and slavery in Egypt, rather he requested a Divine sign of the permanence of Hashem's promise (which Hashem promptly gives him, in the form of the בְּרִית בֵּין הַבְּתָרִים). The underlying reason for the *Avos'* request for a positive affirmation for the Divine promise was to fortify the heavenly roots of what they had been told would occur on earth. As we have learned, everything in This World is linked to its heavenly source (*shoresh* — refer to our chapter, "The Gift of Shabbos"). When an act is performed on earth to confirm what has been promised by Hashem, the heavenly roots of the promise are strengthened to the point that we can be assured of the Divine word's permanence.

By observing Shabbos and not performing *Melachah* (refer to *Sanhedrin* 65b where the Gemara implies that muzzling an ox merely by shouting at it that it shouldn't eat is considered to be a positive act because of its impact), we leave an impact in heaven so substantial that our passive act is considered by the Torah to be a form of *maaseh* (action). The Heavenly roots of this sacred day are thereby strengthened to the point that we may be assured that the Shabbos will remain a permanent bond between *Klal Yisrael* and *HaKadosh Baruch Hu.* As the next *pasuk* continues: בֵּינִי וּבֵין בְּנֵי יִשְׂרָאֵל אוֹת הִיא לְעֹלָם, *Between Me and the Children of Israel it is a sign forever* (*Shemos* 31:17). It is a permanent bond between Hashem and the Jewish people. (*Ki Sisa* 5635)

אם כי השבת הוא השביתה ממלאכה. אעפ״כ הוא תיקון העשיה. כי ביטולו של דבר זה קיומו. ע״י שהמעשים מתבטלים בבוא יום השבת. עי״ז הוא דבר של קיימא.

This same theme — that abstaining from *Melachah* on Shabbos is the highest form of creation — can be deduced from even a surface reading of the *pasuk* introducing the *melachos* of Shabbos to the Jewish people in the aftermath of the Golden Calf. Moshe begins his plea to observe Shabbos with these words: אֵלֶּה הַדְּבָרִים אֲשֶׁר צִוָּה ה׳ לַעֲשֹׂת אֹתָם, *These are the things* (words / the detailed Shabbos laws) *that* H*ASHEM* *commanded, to do them* (*Shemos* 35:1). It is clear from the context that the *pasuk* is referring to the restrictions on *Melachah,* rather than any of the positive aspects of Shabbos laws. If, nonetheless, the Torah insists upon referring to these prohibitions as acts of creation, it must be because of its positive impact. In accordance with the renowned Rabbinic saying (*Menachos* 99a), בטולו של דבר הוא קיומו – by refraining from doing *Melachah* this alone accomplishes as much as if had actually been performed, we suggest that by Hashem not creating during the first Shabbos, it was as effective in maintaining the universe as if He had actually continued the process of creation on Shabbos. (*Vayakhel* 5639)

וזה הבחינה שנתן הקב״ה לבנ״י בהיותם בעולם הזה הגשמיי להיות להם חלק בקדושה עליונה.

In itself, this is a great tribute to *Klal Yisrael,* indicating that despite our existence in this physical world, we leave an impact on the *entire* universe (in the spiritual realm as well as here on earth). (*Vayakhel* 5654)

◈§ A Permanent Not a Temporary Rest

וברש״י שבת שבתון מנוחת מרגוע ולא עראי. פי׳ שלא יהי׳ השביתה עייכוב המלאכה לפי שעה רק לשכוח מכל ענין המלאכה. שבאמת שבת קודש הוא הכנה לעוה״ב. כמ״ש חז״ל שהוא מעין עוה״ב. וצריך האדם להתלמד לשכוח כל המעשים בוא יום השבת. וכמו כן יזכה בנקל למנוחת עוה״ב.

While we tend to think of Shabbos' rest as a temporary cessation from *Melachah,* in reality, much more is involved. It is not enough for us not to work on Shabbos, rather it is our obligation to totally forget about the concept of *Melachah.* As *Rashi* indicates, מְנוּחַת מַרְגּוֹעַ וְלֹא מְנוּחַת עֲרָאִי, "It is a rest of relaxation (permanent rest), not a temporary / casual rest" (*Shemos* 31:15, ד״ה שבת שבתון). When one rests on Shabbos it is not enough not to perform *Melachah,* instead one should (ideally) totally forget about the concept of *Melachah.*

Chazal describe Shabbos as a microcosm of the World to Come. Just as it is necessary to remove any thoughts of *Olam Hazeh* before entering

Olam Haba, so too, to appreciate the Shabbos, it is necessary to shed any residual links to the *Melachah* of the weekdays. In that sense, Shabbos is a permanent day of rest, an entirely different universe than the *Melachah*-dominated weekday world. (*Ki Sisa* 5638)

❧ Negating Oneself to *Klal Yisrael*

פי׳ שבני ישראל באין באמת בש״ק למנוחה. ולא שיניחו מלעשות מלאכה בע״כ. רק שבבוא יום הש״ק באים בנ״י למנוחת השבת. וזה האות והעדות. אמת שאין כל יחיד זוכה לזה רק ע״י הביטול מקודם זוכה אח״כ גם לזה. אבל בכלל בנ״י מקוים כל זה.

Returning to the theme we discussed in the previous essay, when we rest on Shabbos we are not merely abstaining from work because we have no more work to perform or because we need to rest. The Shabbos and *Klal Yisrael* are natural partners. When Shabbos arrives it is perfectly normal for *Klal Yisrael* to cease *Melachah.* While it may be difficult for each individual to exist on so lofty a spiritual level that ceasing from engaging in work comes naturally at the end of the week, this phenomenon is certainly true of *Klal Yisrael,* and of every individual Jew who negates himself to *Klal Yisrael.*

(Adapted from *Ki Sisa* 5641)

❧ The Limits of Human Efforts

וע״ז כ׳ ששת ימים תעבוד כו׳ מלאכתך. יגיעת האדם. ויום השביעי כו׳ לה׳ שהוא מתנות כמ״ש מתנה טובה יש לי שהארה המתגלה בש״ק א״א להשיג בכח יגיעת האדם. רק במתנה כנ״ל. וע״ז רמזו לא עליך המלאכה לגמור. כי מאדם הוא ההתחלה. לי כחודה של מחט. הוא יגיעת האדם בימי המעשה. ואנכי אפתח לכם כפתחו של היכל ואולם הוא בש״ק כמ״ש ביום השבת יפתח.

To gain additional insight into the prohibition of *Melachah* on Shabbos, we turn to the language used by the Torah in the *Aseres HaDibros:* שֵׁשֶׁת יָמִים תַּעֲבֹד וְעָשִׂיתָ כָּל מְלַאכְתֶּךָ וְיוֹם הַשְּׁבִיעִי שַׁבָּת לַה׳ אֱלֹהֶיךָ, *Six days shall you work and accomplish all your work; but the seventh day is Sabbath to HASHEM, your God* (*Shemos* 20:9-10). Despite the critical significance of our efforts symbolized by the work that we perform during the week, it is important to remember that everything that we do is but a beginning. True success can only be achieved if our initiative is consummated with a Divine gift — the Shabbos day (refer to our chapter on "The Gift of Shabbos" where we expand upon this theme). In fact, Hashem describes the Shabbos as "a great gift that is hidden in His treasure house." Actually, the spiritual level attained by us on Shabbos would be impossible — no matter how much progress we made during the week — without the *berachah* that Hashem bestows upon us every Shabbos. By abstaining from *Melachah* on Shabbos, we are voicing our firm conviction that there are real limits to the strides that we can make on our own despite our best efforts. Our work performed during the six weekdays can only be truly successful if it is climaxed with Hashem's *berachah* on Shabbos. In this light, we may interpret the renowned saying of the *Midrash* (*Shir HaShirim Rabbah* 5:3), "Open for me an opening the size of the eye of a needle and I will create for you an opening as large as the Temple gates," as alluding to the relationship between the week and Shabbos. Our efforts all week long are little more than the "opening of a needle's eye." It is only when the "Temple gates" open on Shabbos that we can be assured that our efforts will be crowned with success.[1]

The renowned Mishnah in *Pirkei Avos* (3:21), "It is not for you to complete the work," may also be interpreted in this light. No matter how much we try, our efforts are not enough. It is only with Divine assistance that we can complete the initiatives that we have begun.

The fact that there are real limits to human efforts pertains not only to the relationship between Shabbos and the weekdays but also to the study of Torah. While it is certainly important that we exert ourselves as much as possible to study Torah, it is also important to remember that our efforts are but a beginning. As *Chazal* (*Megillah* 6b) say, יָגַעְתִּי וּמָצָאתִי תַּאֲמֵן, "If one says, 'I have made an effort to study Torah, and I have found success,' believe him." Even after all of our efforts to comprehend the Torah, any insight that we ultimately gain is considered a *metziah* — a true "find" and a Divine Gift. (*Yisro* 5648)

1. Refer to *Yechezkel* (46:1) where the prophet describes the gates of the third *Beis HaMikdash* opening on Shabbos.

◆ Negating Oneself (and One's Creativity) to Hashem

ובנ״י בנו באמת הבנין אח״כ במשכן ובביהמ״ק בכח זה האחדות רק שהי׳ כוונתם לש״ש להתבטל אליו יתברך. והרשעים של דור הפלגה מרדו בהשי״ת ונק׳ חילול שבת שכשמשיגין בחי׳ הדעת שהיא הארה העליונה בש״ק צריכין להתבטל מכל מלאכה. והם אדרבא הרבו לבנות ולעשות ושכחו בה׳ וסמכו על מעשיהם ודי למבינים.

In the previous *dvar Torah,* we noted that by abstaining from *Melachah,* we acknowledge that there are limits to what we can accomplish through our own efforts. Extending this analysis, we suggest that not only our physical ability to create but also our intellect (a concept known as דַעַת, *daas*) is subject to real constraints. By abstaining from *Melachah* on Shabbos, we negate our *daas* to Hashem, indicating that everything we enjoy (including our creative ability) stems from Hashem.

As we examine the early history of mankind and the eventual fate of two generations that rebelled against Hashem — the Generation of the Flood and the Generation of the Tower of Bavel — we realize that their most tragic flaw was their inability to negate themselves to Hashem. Whereas the Generation of the Flood had deteriorated to the point where they had severed all ties to Hashem (and consequently were totally incapable of negating themselves to Hashem), the builders of the Tower of Bavel sinned in a somewhat more sophisticated manner. From the Torah's description of their plans it seems that these individuals were aware of *HaKadosh Baruch Hu's* Presence; nonetheless, they were determined to rebel against Him. In fact, Hashem "descended" to view what they had built and to determine whether anything beneficial would result from their efforts. Concluding that though this generation was well-aware of His Presence yet was determined to rebel against Him, Hashem disrupted their plans and dispersed them throughout the universe. It was left to *Klal Yisrael,* in future generations, to build a dwelling place for the *Shechinah* (the *Mishkan,* the *Beis HaMikdash*) here on earth. If we examine the sin of the Tower Builders, we can better grasp the gravity of performing *Melachah* on Shabbos. By being aware of

Hashem's Presence (as *Klal Yisrael* certainly is) and nonetheless persisting in pursuing our own material goals in defiance of His resting from creating, we are replicating the sin of the Tower Builders — not negating ourselves to the *Shechinah*. (*Noah* 5641)

והנה באר בשדה כו' שלשה עדרי צאן כו' והאבן גדולה ע"פ הבאר ונאספו כו'. פי' שבשבת נפתח מקור מים חיים וזהו באר בשדה. וג' עדרי צאן הם מה שבנ"י מתבטלין בשבת להשי"ת בכל לבבך ונפשך ומאדך. ונק' נפש רוח נשמה שצריך האדם לבטל הכל להשי"ת.

Utilizing this approach, we derive a beautiful homiletic interpretation of a short passage describing Yaakov's first moments in Aram. The Torah relates that Yaakov came to a well which was covered by a large stone. Moreover, three flock of sheep and their shepherds were gathered around the well, and were attempting to dislodge the large stone that was blocking access to the water that they required for their flocks. Assuming that the well and its natural water symbolizes *Shabbos Kodesh*, which is a source of nurturement and sustenance for the entire week, we suggest that the three flocks of sheep congregating around the well represent the three methods through which we negate ourselves to Hashem, as we recite in *Shema*: בְּכָל לְבָבְךָ וּבְכָל נַפְשְׁךָ וּבְכָל מְאֹדֶךָ, *with all of your heart, with all of your soul, and with all of your material possessions* (*Devarim* 6:5). The act of gathering around a well is the Torah's allusion to the fact that the Shabbos (the source of all our *berachah*) sustains those who negate every aspect of their life to its *kedushah*. The episode continues with the shepherds valiantly attempting to roll the rock off the surface of the well. In light of this approach, we suggest that the stone on the mouth of the well represents the *kelipah*, the external forces — all of the material influences that too often dominate our lives during the week — that make it difficult to immediately absorb the *kedushah* of Shabbos. It is only by fusing together all of our innate capabilities — our heart, soul, and wealth — that we can roll away the "stone," those external factors that prevent us from enjoying the vibrant sustaining waters of *Shabbos Kodesh*.

(Adapted from *Vayeitzei* 5634)

◆§ Parallels Between the Splitting of the Reed Sea and Shabbos

וכן איתא במד׳ כי שביעי של פסח כמו שבת קודש ע״ש. והוא בחי׳ הקול כנ״ל. וז״ש ואתם החרישון שאין צריך ליגיעה. ה׳ ילחם כו׳.

Midrash Rabbah (*Shemos* 19:7) notes that the seventh day of Pesach, when *Kerias Yam Suf* occurred, corresponds to Shabbos. We will attempt to understand this analogy in light of the previous *dvar Torah* which attributes the prohibition of *Melachah* to an ongoing need to negate ourselves to Hashem.

Even on a surface level, the timing of the splitting of the Reed Sea and the first Shabbos are remarkably similar. Just as Shabbos occurred at the conclusion of a week of creation, on the seventh day, so too, *Kerias Yam Suf* occurred at the conclusion of a climactic week that commenced with *Yetzias Mitzrayim*. Drawing the parallel between the universe's first week and the week of *Yetzias Mitzrayim* even further, we suggest that while Creation was "perfected" through the act of *Yetzias Mitzrayim* (in which Hashem demonstrated His capacity to perform miracles on behalf of *Klal Yisrael*), the Shabbos day and its theme of abstaining from material effort were not fully appreciated until the moment of *Yetzias Mitzrayim*. On both occasions, the Torah emphasizes cessation of physical activity. Just as on the first Shabbos, Hashem ceased creating, so too, at the moment of *Kerias Yam Suf* the Jewish people were instructed by Moshe to make no effort to turn the tide in their favor, but rather to remain totally silent and negate themselves to their Creator. Moshe assures *Klal Yisrael*, "Hashem will fight for you and you will remain silent" (cf. *Shemos* 14:14).[1] (*Pesach* 5633)

◆§ Remembering Hashem

פ׳ מלאכה הוא הכח שנותן האדם באיזה דבר... אבל הוא נפרד ממנו

To appreciate why *Melachah* is prohibited on Shabbos we need to define the concept of *Melachah*. We suggest that *Melachah* refers to

1. By contrast, when departing Mitzrayim – an event which parallels Creation – *Klal Yisrael* was instructed to perform the *mitzvos* of *korban pesach* and *bris milah*.

anything that has been created but nonetheless remains distinct from its creator. For example, an individual may write letters or build a house. However, the identity of the writer or builder is not necessarily obvious to those living in the house or reading that letter.

In a similar vein, when Hashem created His universe, He arranged that it be formed in such a manner that His subjects, while benefitting from His universe, would not necessarily identify with its Creator. In fact, the term *beriah* (creation), which is used frequently in the Torah's discussion of Creation, may be interpreted as an external force. All week long, while performing *Melachah,* Hashem's subjects may experience difficulty in "connecting" with the universe's Creator. By prohibiting *Melachah* on Shabbos, we are not only negating all those material forces that may contribute to our "forgetting" our Creator but we also remember that the universe did not emerge by itself and are thereby linking everything that has been created to its Source.

It is only *Klal Yisrael,* whose roots lie in *Olam Haba* – and are able to benefit from the *neshamah yeseirah* and the other-worldly ambiance of Shabbos – who can participate in the prohibition of *Melachah* on Shabbos. It is only *Klal Yisrael* who, on *Shabbos Kodesh,* can probe beyond the surface of the material world and find its Creator.[1]

(Adapted from *Bereishis* 5654)

וז״ש במשנה אבות מלאכות מ׳ חסר אחת ולא אמרו ל״ט. רק לרמוז כי חסר אחת אותו השורש של כל המלאכות כח הפועל בנפעל. וי״ל שזה נרמז בדברי הגמ׳ והמלאכה היתה דים לאו ממנינא דשלימו להו עבידתא. פי׳ דבמלאכת המשכן הי׳ שם כח השורש של כל המלאכות והיא אחת החסר באבות מלאכות בש״ק שאינה נמצאת בשדה כנ״ל.

With this approach, we can appreciate why the Mishnah, which categorizes the *melachos* that are prohibited on Shabbos (cf. *Shabbos* 73a), states that there are "forty less one" categories of work rather than simply "thirty-nine." We suggest (homiletically) that the expression "less one" refers to Hashem, the One Whose Presence is often not perceived while we engage in our mundane pursuits. The *melachos* listed by the Mishnah, which we pursue all week, are a necessary conduit to evoke

1. For a more complete development of this concept refer to the original text of *Sfas Emes.*

the sparks of *kedushah* (נִיצוֹצֵי קְדוּשָׁה) present in the natural world; however, on Shabbos we are able to access *kedushah* without benefit of these *melachos.*

Using this theme – that the thirty-nine *melachos* are prohibited because they may lead us to "forget" Hashem – we derive new insight into an observation of the Talmud (*Shabbos* 49b), that the thirty-nine *melachos* may correspond to the 39 instances in which the Torah mentions the term *Melachah.*[1] However, the Talmud indicates that the *pasuk* וְהַמְּלָאכָה הָיְתָה דַיָּם, *But the work had been enough* (*Shemos* 36:7), demonstrates that the donations of the contributors to the *Mishkan* were sufficient for its construction. And consequently, the fact that Moshe accepted no further donations is not included as a fortieth instance where the Torah uses the term *Melachah,* since it refers to the completion rather than the construction of the *Mishkan.*

(Adapted from *Vayeishev* 5659)

Reversing *Tohu Va'vohu* (Desolate and Void): Returning to the Commencement of Creation

בקידוש היום זכרון למעשה בראשית. והענין כי בראשית ברא את השמים ואת הארץ הוא מאמר אחד הכולל כל הבריאה והוא שורש הבריאה הדבוק בראשית ואח"כ דכתיב והארץ היתה תהו התחילו ששת ימי המעשה ומאמר הראשון הוא חופף על הבריאה ומזה המאמר נמשך ברכה וקיום אל הבריאה ... וזה זכרון למעשה בראשית הוא המאמר של בראשית ויברך את יום השביעי ויקדש אותו פי' להיות קדוש ונבדל מן הזמן ...

By resting on Shabbos, Hashem is actually returning the universe to its starting point. Describing the universe at the beginning of Creation, the Torah writes, בְּרֵאשִׁית בָּרָא אֱלֹהִים אֵת הַשָּׁמַיִם וְאֵת הָאָרֶץ, *In the beginning of God's creating the heavens and the earth* (*Bereishis* 1:1). This famous *pasuk* implies that at first, before the multi-faceted universe emerged, the Presence of Hashem permeated the entire world.[2] We

1. This approach differs from the renowned reason for the 39 *melachos* which asserts that they correspond to the 39 categories of work that were performed in the *Mishkan.*

2. The suggestion of *Sfas Emes* that the first *pasuk* of the Torah – *Bereishis* – refers to the commencement of Creation, rather than merely serve as a general introduction to the story of

allude to this perfect world when we recite in *Kiddush,* זִכָּרוֹן לְמַעֲשֵׂה בְרֵאשִׁית, [*Shabbos is*] *a remembrance of Creation.* While it would seem that Shabbos is a tribute to the cessation of Creation, and not to Creation itself, by utilizing this expression, we are implying that every Shabbos we return to the state of the universe at the time of the *first* act of Creation. Every Shabbos, we return to the pure harmony and the very visible presence of the *Shechinah* that existed at the universe's beginning.

It was only once the process of Creation unfolded, and the many detailed aspects of the universe emerged, that the sense of clarity that the universe enjoyed at its onset began to yield to a far more complex world. It is in reference to this new, far more complex universe that the Torah writes, וְהָאָרֶץ הָיְתָה תֹהוּ וָבֹהוּ, *The earth was desolate and void.*[1] It is this universe that was created through the various forms of *Melachah* performed by Hashem during the Six Days of Creation, which we leave behind every Shabbos as we cease from performing *Melachah,* in favor of returning to the universe's very beginning, the true *maaseh bereishis.*

(*Bereishis* 5655)

◆§ The Opening of the Well

ולכן פי הבאר נברא בע״ש בימ״ש. הרמז כפי מה שמקבלין את השבת ומבטלין כל המלאכות. ומצפין להשפעת קדושה מלמעלה נפתח פי הבאר.

In a previous *dvar Torah* we discussed how by observing Shabbos and abstaining from *Melachah* we are indicating our belief that there are real limits to human efforts. This theme is well-stated in *Pirkei Avos* (5:8), which notes that ten things were created on *erev Shabbos,* at twilight, including the "opening of the well." We may interpret this term in the Mishnah homiletically as referring to the beautiful *berachos* that *Klal*

Creation, is supported by *Chazal's* assertion (*Megillah* 21b) that *Bereishis* is one of the Ten Statements through which Hashem created the universe. Refer also to *Sfas Emes'* commentary on *Pirkei Avos* (5:1).

1. The *Sfas Emes'* implication that the state of תהו ובהו occurred *after* the events described in the first *pasuk* (initial creation of heaven and earth) is seemingly in contradistinction to *Rashi* who maintains that the universe was desolate *before* Creation. Refer also to *Ramban* for his approach regarding the sequence of the Torah's first *pesukim.*

Yisrael receive every Shabbos, when Hashem opens His wellsprings of *berachos*, enough to sustain us for an entire week. While only Hashem can shower us with these blessings, we are capable of gaining access to these *berachos* through our conduct on Shabbos. By abstaining from work (and, in a larger sense from the material values that often dominate during the week) as Shabbos begins, we are capable of opening "the well" and meriting Hashem's bountiful *berachos* during the week.

Chazal relate that unlike a *mikveh* which requires a substantial amount of rain water to purify those who became ritually defiled, in the case of a natural source of water (*maayan/be'er*) even the slightest amount of water is sufficient. Every Shabbos — and especially at the time of *Kabbalas Shabbos* as the weekday world yields to the sacred atmosphere of Shabbos — we make the initial effort by ceasing to work. When we open "the mouth of the well" by observing Shabbos, Hashem crowns our efforts with success and fills up the entire well (symbolic of the six workdays which are a receptacle for Hashem's *berachos*, just as a well contains water) with His *berachos*. (*Chukas* 5658)

⸎ Emulating Hashem

כי מה זה הטעם כי ששת ימים עשה לכן צוה אותנו לנוח בשבת והוא באמת עדות לבנ״י כמ״ש רש״י. בפסוק אות הוא ביני בהנחילו לנו יום מנוחתו למנוחה. וחז״ל אמרו בשבת ניתנה תורה דכ׳ זכור כו׳ בעצומו של יום. משמע שבכח קבלת התורה ניתן לנו השבת. דכ׳ אנכי ה׳ אלהיך וחל אלקותו ית׳ בנפשות בנ״י לכן כיון שהקב״ה נח בשבת צריך כל איש ישראל לנוח.

In truth, the Torah itself states the reason why we abstain from *Melachah* on Shabbos: כִּי שֵׁשֶׁת יָמִים עָשָׂה ה׳ אֶת הַשָּׁמַיִם וְאֶת הָאָרֶץ ... וַיָּנַח בַּיּוֹם הַשְּׁבִיעִי, *For in six days* HASHEM *made the heavens and the earth ... and He rested on the seventh day* (*Shemos* 20:11); ... וּבַיּוֹם הַשְּׁבִיעִי שָׁבַת וַיִּנָּפַשׁ, *... and on the seventh day He rested and was refreshed* (ibid. 31:17). By abstaining from work on Shabbos we are emulating *HaKadosh Baruch Hu*, Who rested on that day.

The Torah also describes Shabbos as an אוֹת, *a sign* between Hashem and the Jewish people for all generations (כִּי אוֹת הִיא בֵּינִי וּבֵינֵיכֶם לְדֹרֹתֵיכֶם, ibid. 31:13). What better indication of the bond that exists between us and Hashem than the fact that He allowed us to rest on the same day that He rested (refer to *Rashi* on that *pasuk*).

How can *Klal Yisrael* even presume to emulate Hashem? What is the basis for us arrogating Hashem's day of rest as our own? The answer lies in the First Commandment. When Hashem said, אָנֹכִי ה׳ אֱלֹהֶיךָ, *I am HASHEM your God* (*Shemos* 20:2), He didn't merely require us to accept Him as our God but He also implanted a spark of Godliness in every Jewish soul. By virtue of that Divine Spark, we are able to adopt Hashem's day of rest as our own. (*Yisro* 5648)

ולכן סמך פ׳ לא תשא למצות שבת שכיון שיש באיש ישראל חלק אלקות לכן נאסרו במלאכה ביום השבת כי בו שבת.

We support our contention that the prohibition of *Melachah* is based on our desire to emulate Hashem, Who abstained from work on Shabbos, from the juxtaposition of the *mitzvah* of Shabbos to the prohibition of taking Hashem's Name in vain. It is because we are bearers of the *Shechinah* and because of *Klal Yisrael's* unique relationship with Hashem (enjoying a closeness that no other nation has) that we are able to observe the day that He rested as our own day of rest. (*Yisro* 5656)

◆§ Our Divine Spark Also Rests

וזהו שייחד הקב״ה שמו על בנ״י אנכי ה׳ אלקיך פי׳ שלא יש שום כח לאיש ישראל שיהי׳ נפרד מאלקותו ית״ש. וזה עדות השבת שצוה לשבות מכל מלאכה לפי שבמלאכות איש ישראל יש בו כח אלקי לכן צריך לשבות ביום השבת.

When Hashem commenced the *Aseres HaDibros* with the words, אָנֹכִי ה׳ אֱלֹהֶיךָ, *I am HASHEM your God,* Hashem was not only commanding us to accept Him as our God, but with this commandment He ensured that there is a spark of the *Shechinah* in every activity that we perform. Any success that we enjoy is made possible by the Divine Spark that has been implanted in all of us. Consequently, just as Hashem rests on Shabbos, so too, the Divine Spark that resides in all of us and participates in all that we do, also ceases to work on Shabbos.

(*Shelach* 5661)

☙ Attaining *Ruach Hakodesh*

וזה נקרא מנוחה שהיא בחי׳ נביאה ורוה״ק

To appreciate why *Melachah* is prohibited on Shabbos, we need to consider its antithesis, the concept of *menuchah*. While we generally translate *menuchah* as rest, in reality, a more profound spiritual transformation takes place. Every Shabbos, as we cease our weekday activities, we Jews attain a measure of *ruach hakodesh* (Divine Inspiration).[1] On Shabbos, a day described by *Chazal* as a microcosm of the World to Come, we approach the spiritual level that the Jewish people will enjoy in the Future World — as the Prophet describes the Future World, "Your sons and daughters will prophesy" (*Yoel* 3:1). On this most spiritual of days, imbued with the *neshamah yeseirah*, we rise to the level where, in a sense, we too can perceive Hashem in His Universe, just as the Prophets were able to discern the *Shechinah*.

During the six weekdays, *Melachah* plays an essential role. Through the various forms of *Melachah* that we undertake, we seek to infuse the universe with *kedushah*. By means of our activities all week long in finding the *Shechinah*, in what may appear (superficially) to be a mundane world, we accomplish a great deal. On Shabbos, however, having attained our objective that the universe is now a worthy receptacle for *ruach hakodesh* and prophecy, we cease performing *Melachah*. On the contrary, anyone who performs *Melachah* on Shabbos is guilty of desecrating this most sacred of days (a capital offense). By working on Shabbos, we imply that we have not yet attained the level of intimacy with Hashem (approaching *ruach hakodesh* and prophecy) that we can actually enjoy on this blessed day.

(Adapted from *Bereishis* 5662)

1. Refer to *Yirmiyahu* where Baruch ben Neriah describes his inability to prophesy as וּמְנוּחָה לֹא מָצָאתִי, *I didn't find rest* (45:3).

◆§ The Perfection of Creation

וזה האות שרצה בנו הקב"ה במה שנתן לנו השבת. לומר כי הברכה והקדושה בשבת הכל תלוי כפי הרצון שמעלין בנ"י במעשיהם. לכן אומרים בקידוש היום ורצה בנו.

By ceasing to create on Shabbos, Hashem indicated that the entire universe had achieved its ideal state. As we state in our *Maariv tefillah* every Friday night, תַּכְלִית מַעֲשֵׂה שָׁמַיִם וָאָרֶץ, [*Shabbos is*] *the conclusion of the creation of heaven and earth.* By abstaining from work on Shabbos, we are demonstrating our belief that the universe as it was created during the Six Days of Creation is complete and requires no further modification.

Immediately preceding that first Shabbos, Hashem beheld the world that He had just finished creating and He derived great satisfaction. As it says, וַיַּרְא אֱלֹהִים אֶת כָּל אֲשֶׁר עָשָׂה וְהִנֵּה טוֹב מְאֹד, *And God saw all that He had made and behold it was very good* (*Bereishis* 1:31). The same sense of Divine *nachas* is experienced every Shabbos in direct proportion to our accomplishments of the preceding weekdays. The more *nachas* Hashem derives from His universe every Shabbos, the greater the blessing of that Shabbos. In this light, we may interpret the *pasuk* in the *Aseres HaDibros* — ... כִּי שֵׁשֶׁת יָמִים עָשָׂה ה׳ אֶת הַשָּׁמַיִם וְאֶת הָאָרֶץ וַיָּנַח בַּיּוֹם הַשְּׁבִיעִי עַל כֵּן בֵּרַךְ ה׳ אֶת יוֹם הַשַּׁבָּת וַיְקַדְּשֵׁהוּ, *For in six days* H*ASHEM made the heavens and the earth ... and He rested on the seventh day; therefore,* H*ASHEM blessed the Sabbath day and sanctified it* (*Shemos* 20:11) — that after creating the universe in six days, Hashem derived pleasure (*nachas*) and therefore blessed the Shabbos day and imbued it with *kedushah.*

Upon closer analysis, we note that the *pasuk* states that Hashem rested from *all* that He had created — וַיִּשְׁבֹּת בַּיּוֹם הַשְּׁבִיעִי מִכָּל מְלַאכְתּוֹ אֲשֶׁר עָשָׂה, *He abstained on the seventh day from all His work which He had done* (*Bereishis* 2:2) — implying that He rested from creating not only the universe that was visible at the termination at the Six Days of Creation, but also from everything that would ever be created during *all* of world history. Everything that was and would ever be created was present before Him at the consummation of Creation. When Hashem pronounced His satisfaction with all that He had created, Hashem was indicating the *nachas* that He derived from *everything* that would ever emerge throughout history. While man can only witness the consummation of all that ever was created at the *conclusion* of history — the day that is described by *Chazal* (*Tamid* 33b) as the "day that is a complete Shabbos" — Hashem perceived at the *commencement* of history everything that would ever be created and expressed His satisfaction on the first Shabbos. Every Shabbos marks the consummation of another aspect of Creation, from which Hashem derives *nachas*. Moreover, Hashem will continue to derive *nachas* each Shabbos until the conclusion of all history — the day of the final Shabbos.

(*Yisro* 5654)

תשמורו כו׳. לשון רבים. כי יש בכל דבר חיות משבת קודש והיא הנקודה המשלמת הכל כמ״ש רש״י ז״ל ויכל אלקים ביום השביעי שבשבת נגמר המלאכה כו׳. הפי׳ כנ״ל ששבת משלים כל דבר. והוא הגמר והקיום של כל דבר שהוא שורש החיות. ובשבת קודש מתעורר שורש זה בכל דבר. ולכך נק׳ מנוחה שמחזיר כל דבר לשורשו.

When the Torah discusses the *mitzvah* of observing Shabbos, it utilizes the plural form *Shabbsosai,* My Sabbaths (rather than the singular form *Shabosi,* My Sabbath), as indicated in the *pasuk,* אֶת שַׁבְּתֹתַי תִּשְׁמֹרוּ, *You must observe My Sabbaths* (*Shemos* 31:13). This denotes that the sense of perfection and completion (*sheleimus*) attained on Shabbos pertains not only to the Shabbos but also to every aspect of Creation. A sense of that harmony that prevailed that first Shabbos is latent in everything that Hashem created. Moreover, this sense of perfection derived from Shabbos *Kodesh* is what allows everything to exist.

Every Shabbos that sense of perfection that marked the first Shabbos is experienced. Every Shabbos everything that exists derives a newfound sense of harmony and completion. Perhaps for that reason, we describe Shabbos as a day of *menuchah,* referring not only to *physical* rest but also to the fact that everything that exists returns to its heavenly roots, which is the essence of *Menuchah* (refer to our chapter on *Menuchah* for discussion of that concept). (Adapted from *Ki Sisa* 5633)

◆ The Perfect Day

יש לפרש ימי תמימים הם שבתות השנה וימים טובים. שהם הימים שאין בהם מלאכה גשמיות וכל מה שנעשה בהם מתקשר ומתדבק בשורש החיות לכן נקראו ימי תמימים. גם נקראו ימי תמימים שהם מיוחדים רק לתמימי דרך. והם בני ישראל שנאמר עליהם ועמך כולם צדיקים [ונחלתם לעולם תהי׳ כי מיני מתברכין כל שיתא יומין] כי שבת הוא התחדשות שמיוחד לבנ״י. לכן בנקל להתדבק בו בהשי״ת כי התחדשות כל יום הוא לכל הבריאה. לכן מתערב בה גשמיות. אבל התחדשות של שבת מיוחד לבני ישראל תמימי דרך כנ״ל.

In the previous *dvar Torah* we discussed how the universe achieved *sheleimus* on Shabbos. Utilizing a similar approach, we gain new insight into the *pasuk*, יוֹדֵעַ ה׳ יְמֵי תְמִימִם, *HASHEM knows the perfect days* (*Tehillim* 37:18). We suggest that this *pasuk* refers to Shabbos (and *Yom Tov*), occasions that are so imbued with spirituality (since we abstain from performing *Melachah*) that the days themselves have achieved perfection. Whereas all week long when we may be preoccupied with our material tasks it is difficult to link our world with its heavenly roots,[1] on Shabbos we attain a level of *kedushah* that is sufficiently great that we can "connect" these days and all of our relevant activities to their supernatural roots.

Extending our analysis even further, we suggest that Shabbos and *Yom Tov* are occasions that Hashem designated for the exclusive benefit of *Klal Yisrael*, who are known as תְמִימֵי דֶרֶךְ, "those who pursue the path of perfection."[2] The *pasuk* (*Tehillim* 37:18) which commences by describing the days of perfection continues, וְנַחֲלָתָם לְעוֹלָם תִּהְיֶה, *their inheritance* (legacy) *will remain forever*. In this context, this segment of the *pasuk* may refer to the effect of Shabbos on the rest of the week. The legacy of Shabbos lingers on and is a source of blessing for the entire week. (*Chayei Sarah* 5634)

1. The *Sfas Emes* alludes here to a theme that is explicated in numerous instances in his writings. Everything in This World is linked to its heavenly (and supernatural) roots. On certain occasions, such as Shabbos and *Yom Tov*, we are able to shed some of the material aspects that prevent us from "connecting" to those roots.

2. Refer to אַשְׁרֵי תְמִימֵי דָרֶךְ, *Praiseworthy are those whose way is perfect* (*Tehillim* 119:1) and Yeshayahu who describes *Klal Yisrael* as *tzaddikim* — וְעַמֵּךְ כֻּלָּם צַדִּיקִים, *Your people are all righteous* (*Yeshayahu* 60:21).

◆§ The Purpose of Creation

והוא בחי׳ ישבת שבו מתאחד כל הבריאה. ונק׳ שלום. וחל עליו ברכה. והוא תכלית שמים וארץ שהוא העיקר כמ״ש לעיל ולכל תכלית כו׳ חוקר.

Previously, we explained the prohibition of *Melachah* on the basis of the phrase utilized in the Friday evening *Shemoneh Esrei*: תַּכְלִית מַעֲשֵׂה שָׁמַיִם וָאָרֶץ, [*Shabbos is*] *the conclusion* (purpose) *of the creation of heaven and earth*. Whereas in that context, we understood that this phrase refers to the "perfection of creation" which the Shabbos represents, here we suggest an additional aspect of this concept and further justification for the prohibition of *Melachah* by noting that the term *tachlis* may also be defined as "purpose." Shabbos is the *purpose* of Creation. By ceasing from doing *Melachah* on Shabbos, just as Hashem "rested," we are asserting that Shabbos – rather than the six weekdays – is the true purpose of Creation. By demonstrating that Shabbos, a day imbued with such *kedushah*, is the purpose of Creation, we also dispel some of the darkness (i.e. the inability of mankind to perceive Hashem) that often seems to permeate the universe. As it says in *Iyov* (28:3), קֵץ שָׂם לַחֹשֶׁךְ וּלְכָל תַּכְלִית הוּא חוֹקֵר, *He sets a limit to the darkness, and He investigates the end of everything*. Hashem determined that there would be an end to the darkness when we search for the *tachlis*, the true purpose of Creation – Shabbos. (*Mikeitz* 5642)

◆§ Forgetting *Olam Hazeh* / Preparing for *Olam Haba*

ובאמת שבת הוא עדות שבנ״י הם בני עוה״ב. והכנת ימי המעשה לשבת כמו הכנת עוה״ז לעוה״ב. וכפי מה שאדם זוכר בעודנו בעוה״ז הכנת עוה״ב. כך זוכה לעוה״ב. כדאיתא שא״י לעלות לגן עדן עד ששוכחין כל הרהורים מעוה״ז. וכפי זכירת עוה״ב בעוה״ז. כך יכולין לשכוח עוה״ז בעת הסתלקותו מעוה״ז. וכמו כן כפי הזכירה של השבת בימי המעשה. כך יכולין לשכוח בשבת כל מחשבות עבודה. וכפי מה שזוכה האדם לשבות בשבת. כך הוא סימן על עוה״ב.

שמעי בת כו׳ ושכחי עמך כו׳ משל למי שראה בירה דולקת כו׳ הציץ עליו בעל הבירה אני הוא בעל הבירה כו׳. עיקר תיקון האדם כפי מה ששוכח הבלי עולם כמ״ש שכחי עמך ולזכור כי נשתלח בעוה״ז לעשות שליחותו וזה בחי׳ זכור ושמור מ״ע ומל״ת הוא בחי׳ זכירה ושכחה ששניהם צריכין לאדם לשכוח הבלי עולפ ואז יכול לזכור ולהתדבק בעולם העליון וזה שרמזו מי שישנו בשמירה ישנו בזכירה ובאמת בשבת שכל ישראל שובתין ממלאכה והוא בחי׳ שכחה מעוה״ז לכן זוכין לנשמה יתירה זכירה ודביקות בעוה״ב בשבת קודש שהוא מעין עוה״ב. וזה זכור ושמור בשבת. אבל באמת השבת ללמד על הכלל כולו יצא. שאיש ישראל צריך לעולם לשמור ב׳ בחי׳ הנ״ל שמעי בת. ושכחי. ואברהם הי׳ הראשון שהשליך הבלי העולם וזכה למשוך אור בעולם ועליו נאמר מי העיר ממזרח וכו׳, וזה הענין של בירה דולקת כי כל עוה״ז נברא רק כדי לשכוח ולבטל הבלי עולם.

By abstaining from *Melachah,* we are doing much more than simply resting, we are also disassociating ourselves from all of the materialism of *Olam Hazeh.* By encouraging us to not only cease from work but to even refrain from *thinking* about our *Melachah, Chazal* are teaching us that it is possible to disengage oneself from the material world on Shabbos.

The renowned statement of *Chazal,* כָּל שֶׁיֶּשְׁנוֹ בִּשְׁמִירָה יֶשְׁנוֹ בִּזְכִירָה, that whoever participates in the *Shamor* aspect of Shabbos will merit to participate in the *Zachor* aspect (which is usually interpreted that whoever is obligated to observe the negative commandments of Shabbos is also obligated to observe its positive commandments — refer to our chapter entitled, "*Zachor V'Shamor*"), may also refer to the relationship between leaving behind *Olam Hazeh* and benefitting from *Olam Haba.*

Whoever guards himself from the fleeting pleasures of This World merits to experience some aspect of the spiritual intimacy of *Olam Haba.* This is especially true on Shabbos, when by abstaining from *Melachah* we are already giving up some of our association with *Olam Hazeh.* Consequently, we can benefit from the *neshamah yeseirah* and the other-worldly ambiance of Shabbos.

By extension, just as we make every effort to leave behind *Olam Hazeh* every Shabbos by focusing on our spiritual objectives, so too, during our life span in This World we endeavor to prepare for the World to Come. This is so that when it is our time to depart from *Olam Hazeh* we may have successfully severed any lingering links with This World.

(*Yisro* 5656; *Lech Lecha* 5660)

ביאור הענין כי השי״ת במדת טובו הי׳ נותן לצדיקים כל טוב גם בעוה״ז. אבל כי עוה״ב א״א להיות רק אחר כל השלימות. לאשר הוא הטוב בכל מיני השלימות ... אכן מתנה טובה נתן השי״ת לבנ״י והוא השבת שיש בו מעין עוה״ב ע״י ביטול המלאכה נותן לבנ״י הארה משלימות שלעתיד.

Ordinarily, it would be impossible to enjoy the spiritual treasures of *Olam Haba* before completing our mission in This World. However, on Shabbos, when we leave behind many of the material concerns associated with *Melachah,* we are able to partake of at least a "taste" of *Olam Haba* while we are still living in This World. (*Eikev* 5638)

◆ Our Temporary Life Span in *Olam Hazeh*

וכן פשוט מצות מנוחת השבת לשבות מכל מלאכה ולזכור כי העיקר הנשמה וכל חיי עולם הזה רק גירות וארעי. ושבת יומא דנשמתין ולאו דגופא.

By refraining from *Melachah* on Shabbos, we demonstrate our awareness that our life span in This World and all of our accomplishments here are temporary. Just as we cease working for one day each week, so too, we will eventually be in an environment where material concerns no longer matter.

In this context, we can appreciate the renowned comment of *Chazal*

(*Sanhedrin* 58b) that a gentile who observes Shabbos has committed a capital offense.[1] The foregoing *Chazal* implies that *Klal Yisrael* is uniquely capable of living a spiritual existence, similar to what they will eventually enjoy in the World to Come, on the most spiritual of days — Shabbos. (*Haazinu* 5648)

☙ Freedom from the "Shackles" of *Olam Hazeh*

וחז״ל אמרו זו״ש בדיבור א׳ נאמרו כלומר שב׳ אלו תלוין זה בזה כפ׳ מה שנעשה אדם בן חורין ממאסר הגוף כך מאירה הנשמה.

When discussing the prohibition of *Melachah* on Shabbos (in the second rendition of the *Aseres HaDibros* beginning with the term *Shamor;* refer to our chapter on *Zachor* and *Shamor* for extensive discussion), the Torah connects our not working on Shabbos to remembering *Yetzias Mitzrayim* (see *Devarim* 5:15). Perhaps the association between our liberation from Egypt's slavery and the weekly Shabbos is as follows: Just as our forefathers were enslaved to Pharaoh, so too, we (and especially the material side of us, our bodies) risk becoming prisoners of the material world that we are involved in during the week. It is only on Shabbos, by severing our ties with *Olam Hazeh,* that we are released from the shackles of this oppressive form of slavery. (*Va'eschanan* 5651)

☙ Freedom for the *Nefesh*

והנה בש״ק עכ״פ מבטל כל איש ישראל בשביתה מכל מלאכה. ולכן מאיר הנשמה יתירה בגוף. ולכן הוא זכר ליצ״מ ולגאולה. וז״ש בירושלמי על שבת היום אם בקולו תשמעו זה הקול דודי שדופק בשבת.

In the previous *dvar Torah* we noted that on Shabbos we rest from the shackles of *Olam Hazeh* and materialism. Developing this theme further,

1. Refer to *Rambam* (*Hilchos Melachim*) who rules that while a gentile who observes Shabbos is liable as if he had committed a capital crime, he is not actually executed.

we suggest that the *nefesh*, the more material component of the soul,[1] rests on Shabbos, while the more spiritual dimension, the *neshamah*, prevails. By creating us in *Olam Hazeh* (rather than placing us immediately in *Olam Haba*), Hashem indicates that it is our obligation to perfect even our more material side (the *nefesh*, as well as the body itself) through our conduct during the six workdays. However, by abstaining from all material work on Shabbos, the *nefesh* rests from all of its material pursuits and its struggles with the *yetzer hara*.

We may draw an interesting parallel between the rest that the *nefesh* enjoys and Noach's Ark. Just as Noach rested from creating and from all of the universe's material pursuits during his period of confinement in the *teivah*, so too, the *nefesh* enjoys its respite every Shabbos.

As a result of the *nefesh's* subdued role on Shabbos, and the enhanced role that the *neshamah* enjoys, our latent inner potential known as the פְּנִימִיּוּת emerges. Yechezkel (46:1) alludes to this process when he writes, שַׁעַר הֶחָצֵר הַפְּנִימִית ... יִהְיֶה סָגוּר שֵׁשֶׁת יְמֵי הַמַּעֲשֶׂה וּבְיוֹם הַשַּׁבָּת יִפָּתֵחַ, *The gate of the inner courtyard ... shall be closed during the six days of labor, but on the Sabbath day it shall be opened.* Homiletically, this may be interpreted that the inner soul and the enormous potential that we all possess is "locked" all week. However, on Shabbos this latent quest for spiritual greatness surfaces. (*Noach* 5637)

Developing this theme further, we suggest that a corollary benefit to the *nefesh* — and especially the body (גוף) itself resting on Shabbos — is the emergence of the *neshamah yeseirah*. Rather than operate in isolation, the *neshamah yeseirah* leaves a great impact on the body as well. The *pasuk* in *Shir HaShirim* (5:2), קוֹל דּוֹדִי דוֹפֵק, *the voice of my beloved is knocking*, may refer to the inner voice of the *neshamah*. Though it may be somewhat confined all week long, on Shabbos, with the assistance of the *neshamah yeseirah*, the inner voice of every soul yearning to come close to Hashem comes to the forefront. According to the Talmud *Yerushalmi* (*Taanis* 3a), the *pasuk*, הַיּוֹם אִם בְּקֹלוֹ תִשְׁמָעוּ, *Today, if we but heed His call* (*Tehillim* 95:7), refers to Shabbos, the day when the inner Divine voice of every Jew comes to the forefront.

In this light, we may comprehend why the Torah justifies the prohibition of *Melachah* on the basis of the liberation from Mitzrayim. The

1. According to the Kabbalists and *Sifrei Machshavah* (classical philosophical writers) there are several aspects to the soul ranging from the *neshamah*, which is the most spiritual dimension, to the *nefesh*, the physical aspect, which (ideally) collaborates with the body (גוף) in harnessing the material world for the glory of Hashem.

concept of liberation may refer not only to the physical freedom that *Klal Yisrael* earned at the time of *Yetzias Mitzrayim* but also to the liberation from the rampant materialism of the body that we enjoy on Shabbos.

(*Shemos* 5664)

Only One Master

ומצד מערכת הטבע הם ת״י מצרים.
ולכן שבת זכר ליצ״מ כי א״י לזכות לשבת רק אחר יציאת מצרים לכן שבת לישראל עדות על יצ״מ. והנה כ׳ אנכי ה״א א׳ הוצאתיך מא״מ מבית עבדים. כמ״ש במ״א כי עולם הזה הטבעי נק׳ בית עבדים כי מעשה בראשית היא להיות ההנהגה בדרך השתלשלות המדרגות זה שליט על זה. ומצד זה היו ג״כ בנ״י עבדים לפרעה. אבל בשבת קודש מתגלה הנהגה עליונה ובטל כל הממשלות וכחות הטבע. וכן הי׳ ביצ״מ שנתגלה הנהגה עליונה ואפיק לבנ״י מחיובא דכוכבי ומזלי. ולכן צריך איש ישראל לשבות בשבת כמ״ש ינוח עבדך כו׳ כמוך להראות כי בטל כל ממשלות בש״ק.

By associating the prohibition of *Melachah* on Shabbos with *Yetzias Mitzrayim* (refer to our previous *dvar Torah*), the Torah is implying that on Shabbos there is only one master, *HaKadosh Baruch Hu.* Though for a designated period the Jewish people were under the sovereignty of Pharaoh, such servitude is only possible under the natural world order which prevailed prior to *Yetzias Mitzrayim* and during the weekdays. In such a world, Hashem has enabled certain individuals to rule over others. While He certainly maintains overall sovereignty over the universe that He created, Hashem has allowed certain individuals to master others for a particular time period. However, at the moment of *Yetzias Mitzrayim,* Hashem released *Klal Yisrael* from any form of bondage. When Hashem proclaim-ed, *"I am HASHEM, your God, who took you out of the land of Egypt, from the house of slavery"* (*Shemos* 20:2), He was assuring *Klal Yisrael* that (if deserving) they would never be subject to any form of human servitude again.

While it is true all week long that the Jewish people can never be permanently enslaved, this is especially true on Shabbos when Hashem rested from creating the natural world. In such an environment, the hierarchy in which Hashem empowered some mortals to rule over their peers falls by the wayside. With this approach, the relationship between *Yetzias Mitzrayim* (the justification given here for the prohibition of *Melachah* on Shabbos) and our obligation that our servants and maids rest on Shabbos becomes evident. On Shabbos, a day when we proclaim Hashem as the sole master of the universe, we demonstrate our conviction that there is no other controlling force, by relinquishing any control that we may have assumed over any other individual.

By abstaining from *Melachah* on Shabbos, we are also demonstrating that Hashem is the exclusive Sovereign of the entire universe. During the weekdays, we may be tempted to feel that we have contributed to the development of the universe by virtue of our creative effort — allowing a feeling of mastery over some small segment of the universe. However, on Shabbos, when we cease creating, any sense of initiative and mastery that we may have enjoyed gives way to our overwhelming recognition of Hashem's Mastery. (*Va'eschanan* 5656, 5657)

Earning *Olam Hazeh* in the Merit of Shabbos

עדות השבת שניתן לבנ״י יום מנוחה שזה המנוחה שלהם כשבטלים מכל מלאכה וכיון שזה עיקר אצלם ממילא אוכלין גם בעוה״ז שהוא באמת טפל ועיקר נחלתם בעוה״ב.

Whereas in the previous *dvar Torah* we suggested that on Shabbos we forsake the material values of *Olam Hazeh* in favor of the overwhelming spirituality of *Olam Haba*, it is also true that in the merit of observing Shabbos and abstaining from *Melachah*, we merit to live in This World. By demonstrating that for us the concept of *menuchah* does not just mean ceasing our relentless pursuit of material pleasures, but rather resting from This World and immersing ourselves in Hashem's Torah, we make clear that we are not adversely affected by This World. Consequently, we deserve to enjoy *Olam Hazeh* as well as *Olam Haba*. As *Pirkei Avos* (5:22) relates, the disciples of Avraham *Avinu* (*Klal Yisrael*) not only inherit the World to Come, but they also partake of This World. (*Balak* 5644)

◆§ Remembering Hashem's Presence in Nature

ע״כ נאמרו המלאכות בש״ק. כמ״ש בפ׳ בראשית מזה. שכל מלאכה היא נתינת כח נפרד בתוך אותה המלאכה וכמו שהטביע הקב״ה רוחות בטבע והם נסגרים עד יום שכולו שבת.

When Hashem created the universe, He left His Divine Imprint on everything in the natural world (known as *teva*). Every time we utilize our God-given capacities to exploit the universe that He created and to create other entities — a process accomplished through the thirty-nine forms of *Melachah* — we are, in effect, building upon a universe that Hashem began. However, to remember that the *Shechinah* is behind our efforts at building the universe — and to remember Hashem's Presence in the universe — we abstain from *Melachah* on Shabbos. While much of mankind forgot about the Creator of the universe when it succeeded in exploiting the world that He created, we didn't. By observing Shabbos and abstaining from creating on this day, we are reminded that it is Hashem's Presence that sustains the natural world and allows us to develop it. (Adapted from *Yisro* 5657)

◆§ Direct Revelation of Hashem

ועפ״י הפשוט וודאי גם בימות החול שנק׳ ימי המעשה ומלאכה. מ״מ יש בהם בחי׳ שבת בהסתר עכ״פ. [כמ״ש ששת ימי המעשה יהי׳ סגור כו׳] ולכך ת״ח נקראי׳ שבת. שאצלם גם בחול נמצאי׳ הארות הפנימיות. שזה עיקר פי׳ שבת. להיות דבוק בשורש החיים דמיני׳ מתברכין שיתא יומין. ומלאכות שהיו במשכן בודאי היו עפ״י אופן זה שהרי נעשה השראת השכינה ע״י מלאכות האלה. ושורש כל המלאכות ועבודת ימות החול הם מבחי׳ משכן. ולכך נלמד ל״ט מלאכות שהי׳ במשכן שרק הם נק׳ מלאכות. [והענין כמ״ש בזוה״ק תרומה ענין המשכן שהוא כהנהגת ימות החול ע״י המלאך שהוא בחי׳ מלאכה והמש״י]. ולזאת אומר הכתוב כי גם מלאכות המשכן אסור בשבת. כי בשבת יש התגלות הפנימיות.

The prohibition of *Melachah* on Shabbos certainly was not intended to denigrate these 39 categories of work. On the contrary, the most sacred place on earth, the *Mishkan*, was constructed through these *melachos*. In fact (as we shall elaborate in the *dvar Torah*, "Finding Hashem Through *Melachah*", p. 171), all of these forms of work, if utilized for a sacred purpose, can be a means of finding and coming close to Hashem. The term *Melachah*, as we shall discuss, is related to *malach* (emissary), since these forms of work are a means through which we approach Hashem. However, on Shabbos, the presence of Hashem — which is subsumed in these categories of *Melachah* — is more open and can be appreciated even without engaging in these *melachos*. Consequently, even the most sacred form of work, constructing the *Mishkan*, is prohibited on Shabbos. On a day of such *kedushah*, one can attain the sanctity that is "hidden" in the *melachos* employed to build the *Mishkan* without using the *Mishkan* as a conduit. In this spirit, we can also appreciate the renowned comment of the *Zohar* that a *talmid chacham* is called "Shabbos." Just as on Shabbos we can attain closeness to Hashem without the "intermediary" of *Melachah*, so too, the Torah scholar *always* (even during the six weekdays) enjoys a sense of intimacy with Hashem that we can only enjoy on Shabbos.

(*Ki Sisa* 5631)

◊ A Day of Complete Spirituality

והנה במן כתיב שבת לא יהי׳ בו ואיתא בזוה״ק מ״ט לא אשתכח בי׳ מנא דכל ברכאין בי׳ תליין. ואינם בהתגלות. והגם כי המן הי׳ מאכל שמלאכי השרת אוכלין. מ״מ נשבא לעולם ונתלבש בגשמיות לא ירד בשבת. כי ברכת השבת אינה יכולה כלל להתלבש בגשמיות.

By abstaining from work on Shabbos, we are hardly denigrating the role played by *Melachah* during the week. Rather, we are demonstrating that the *spiritual* gains that we achieved through *Melachah* during the week cannot be attained in this manner on Shabbos *Kodesh*. During the week, it is possible that the blessings of Hashem can be subsumed in a material "casing," as we shall elucidate. A classic example of a material base for the *berachos* of Hashem is the manna, which is the most spiritual form of substance known to man (cf. *Yoma* 75b stating that the manna was the food of angels), yet is somewhat material in nature. The blessings of Shabbos are so "other-worldly" that they simply can not sustain a physical base, no matter how rarefied. Any type of physical activity, including the highest forms of creativity used to build the *Mishkan*, or the *melachos* associated with gathering the manna, are out of place on Shabbos. (*Ki Sisa* 5658)

◈ A Day of Devotion and Love

ואם מקבלין זה העול בשלימות אני לדודי. ממילא ודודי לי. וזה מתקיים בש"ק שזה עדות השבת לשבות מכל מלאכה. ולזכור כי עיקר שבראנו לכבודו. רמז לדבר הרועה בשושנים גי' שבת. והו' יתירה לרמוז (על) דמיני' מתברכין כל שיתא ימי המעשה ג"כ. ולכן אומרים בש"ק מזמור ה' רועי. כי בשבת מתגלה הנהגתו ית' המיוחדת רק לבנ"י. כמ"ש ביני ובין בנ"י אות הוא.

The renowned *pasuk*, אֲנִי לְדוֹדִי וְדוֹדִי לִי, *I alone am my Beloved's and my Beloved is mine* (*Shir HaShirim* 6:3), (generally associated with the month of Elul when *Klal Yisrael* returns to Hashem), may also allude to the Shabbos when the Jewish people forsake all of their material pursuits and return to their Beloved. All week long, we are so immersed in the pursuit of various forms of *Melachah* that we may even forget the very reason for our existence, which is to perform Hashem's Will. On Shabbos, however, by leaving behind all forms of *Melachah*, we return to our Beloved (אֲנִי לְדוֹדִי) and, in turn, as the *pasuk* continues, וְדוֹדִי לִי, He returns to us. Our contention that this *pasuk* refers to Shabbos is further corroborated by the *gematria* (numerical equivalent) of a term that immediately follows this phrase — בַּשּׁוֹשַׁנִּים (*in roselike pastures*), which is almost identical to that of Shabbos. While the numerical equivalent of בַּשּׁוֹשַׁנִּים (708) is six more than that of Shabbos (702), this discrepancy suggests that all of the six weekdays are supported (related to the term הָרוֹעֶה, connoting *being sustained*) through Shabbos.[1]

The custom of reciting every Shabbos Chapter 23 of *Tehillim*, ה' רֹעִי, *HASHEM is my shepherd* (in the *Sfard* text for *Maariv* and during

1. This connotation of the word הָרוֹעֶה is utilized, for example, in הָאֱלֹהִים הָרֹעֶה אֹתִי מֵעוֹדִי עַד הַיּוֹם הַזֶּה, *God Who shepherds* (sustains) *me from my inception until this day* (*Bereishis* 48:15).

Shalosh Seudos) may be based on the intimate relationship between Hashem and us that is nurtured every Shabbos. (*Elul* 5657)

A Day Governed by Strict Justice: A Day of *Machshavah*

וזה שנאמר עלו במחשבה פי׳ בעולם המחשבה א״א לצאת מהדין כמלא נימא. וכמו כן כשמתקיים רצון בנ״י במשפט אמרו חז״ל כי בישראל הקב״ה מחשב מחשבה במעשה ... ובשבת קודש מתגלה בחי׳ המחשבה כמ״ש יומא דנשמתין איהו ולאו דגופא. לכן בש״ק נאסר המלאכה כי בשבת א״א להיות ע״פ דין ומשפט ממש. וכמו דאיתא שיתא אלפי שנין הוי עלמא וחד חרוב. פי׳ כיון שיהי׳ אז הכל בדיקדוק הדין והמשפט. לכן אין העולם מתקיים. כמו כן שבת מעין עוה״ב נאסר בו כל העבודה. ורק הרצון והמחשבה לשמים.

To gain an entirely different perspective on the reason for the prohibition of *Melachah*, we recall the renowned statement of *Chazal* (refer to *Rashi, Bereishis* 1:1) that Hashem originally intended to create the universe on the basis of strict justice (מִדַּת הַדִּין). However, realizing that mankind could not survive in such a fashion, Hashem "diluted" this attribute with mercy (מִדַּת הָרַחֲמִים). *Chazal* certainly did not mean that Hashem actually changed His "Mind"and decided to govern the universe in a different manner. On the contrary, they are indicating that while it would be impossible to insist that all of His Creations be held to the standard of strict justice, at least *Klal Yisrael* — whose creation Hashem contemplated even before He created the universe itself — could thrive in the ideal universe, one governed on the basis of justice. However, even for *Klal Yisrael* it is difficult to abide by so high a standard during the weekdays, when we are involved in our mundane day-to-day activities that we must perform while living in This World. As Shlomo writes, כִּי אָדָם אֵין צַדִּיק בָּאָרֶץ אֲשֶׁר יַעֲשֶׂה טּוֹב וְלֹא יֶחֱטָא, *For there is no man on earth that is so righteous that he always does good and never sins* (*Koheles* 7:20). On Shabbos, by abstaining from *Melachah*, we ascend to a new and loftier spiritual plane — the world that is governed on the basis of Hashem's original intentions, the world of *machshavah*

(Hashem's Thought). In such a universe, *middas hadin* may prevail. In order to benefit from so rarefied an environment, we must first abstain from performing *Melachah*, which enables us to leave behind the realm of *maaseh* (physical activity) in favor of *machshavah*.[1] (*Vaeira* 5636)

A Day that Is Lesser, Yet Greater

והנה יום ש״ק קדוש לה׳. אף כי לכאורה השביעי מדרגה אחרונה מששת ימים הקודמים. אך היא הנותנת. ששת ימים עליונים במעלה. ולכך נתלבשו בעוה״ז בלבושים ובמלאכה גשמיות ג״כ. אבל בש״ק מתגלה בו הארת יום השביעי בעצמו. ולכך צריך לשבות מכל מעשה. רק להיות בטל לשורש החיים שהיא הארה עליונה.

In virtually all of the *divrei Torah* in this chapter, we have attributed the prohibition of *Melachah* to the sacred nature of Shabbos and to its superior status over all of the weekdays. In some respects, however, Shabbos, which occurred at the completion of Creation — only after the first six days — may in some ways be "inferior" to the six weekdays. Yet, despite its comparatively "inferior" status, we abstain from *Melachah* on Shabbos rather than during the week. This seeming paradox may be explained as follows: Whereas the first six days are so sacred that we can't even approach their level of *kedushah* without a physical intermediary, such as the various forms of creative work that we perform on those days (a concept known as *levushim*, the outer "garments" through which we can relate to these hallowed days), on Shabbos we can enjoy and appreciate the day itself without any outer casing. Rather than perform work, as we must do to be able to relate to the Six Days of Creation, on Shabbos, when we are able to partake *directly* of the day's *kedushah*, we abstain from all *Melachah* and as much as possible attempt to come closer to Hashem. (*Beshalach* 5632)

1. A similar theme is voiced by the assertion of *Chazal* (*Rosh Hashanah* 31a) that the universe will exist for six millennia and then will be destroyed for a millennium. During that final millennium when Hashem will judge His universe on the basis of His original plan of strict justice, it will be impossible for the world to continue to exist in its previous physical form. Similarly, Shabbos, a day which is a microcosm of the Future World — a time when the universe is held to the standard that Hashem originally intended — we abstain from *Melachah*, thereby enabling us and the universe to be governed on the basis of Divine Justice.

◆§ Entering a Supernatural Universe – Welcoming Hashem

שער החצר כו׳ יהי׳ סגור ששת ימי המעשה בו׳. וכתיב הטעם [יחזקאל מ״ד] כי ה׳ אלקי ישראל בא בו. כי בשבת נתגלה הנהגה עליונה שלמעלה מן הטבע ולכן השבת מיוחד רק לבני ישראל שהם מיוחדים לקבל הנהגה זו. וכמו שיש פתיחת זה השער בביהמ״ק. כן בנפשות בני ישראל נפתח זו הנקודה שרשית מצד חלק אלוה ממעל. ולכן נאסר בו המלאכה לבנ״י.

To appreciate further why we abstain from *Melachah* on Shabbos, we recall the *pasuk* in *Yechezkel* (46:1) describing the gates of the future *Beis HaMikdash* that will be opened every Shabbos. It is through these gates that the *Shechinah* will enter the future *Beis HaMikdash.* Just as the gates of the *Beis HaMikdash* will be opened to permit the *Shechinah* to pass, so too, the gates of every Jewish soul are opened every Shabbos, enabling Hashem's Presence to penetrate. On Shabbos, the Divine Spark which is latent in all of us – but is subsumed all week long – is permitted to surface and influence us. In such a spiritual environment, it is most appropriate that we are not permitted to perform *Melachah.*

(*Shabbos HaGadol* 5660)

◆§ Negating the Natural World (*Teva*)

וכפי ביטול הטבע מתגלה הארה מעולם העליון ולכן בש״ק שהוא מעין עוה״ב צריכין לבטל המעשה והמלאכה כי ששת ימי המעשה מתלבש ההנהגה בהטבע ... וכן היה אברהם אבינו ע״ה בעודנו בחו״ל ששם ההנהגה נסתרת וע״י האמונה נאמר לו לך לך כו׳ אשר אראך שנתגלה לו הארה מעולם הנסתר כנ״ל.

In the previous *dvar Torah,* we attributed the prohibition of *Melachah* on Shabbos to our initiation into an entirely new and supernatural world on this most sacred of days. Expanding on this theme, we suggest that by abstaining from *Melachah* on Shabbos we are distancing ourselves from the natural world that preoccupies us during the week. In order to benefit fully from the other-worldly ambiance of Shabbos, we need to first negate the material world in which we live. There is no more effective method of accomplishing this than by not performing *Melachah*.

This relationship between the weekdays, when we attempt to attain *kedushah* through our involvement in (and sanctification of) the natural world, and Shabbos, when we leave behind This World, may be compared to the distinction between Avraham's relationship to Hashem before traveling to *Eretz Yisrael* and the far more intimate relationship that developed once he heeded the Divine Call of *"Lech Lecha"* – go and leave behind your birthplace and father's house. Whereas prior to arriving in *Eretz Yisrael* he could only perceive Hashem through the natural world (*teva*), upon arriving there he was able to penetrate beyond the natural limits of This World and benefit – while in *Olam Hazeh* – from the supernatural aura of *Olam Haba*. (*Lech Lecha* 5647)

◆§ A Day of *Penimiyus* (Inner Values) Not *Chitzoniyus* (External Values)

והנה במן כתיב שבת לא יהי׳ בו ואיתא בזוה״ק מ״ט לא אשתכח בי׳ מנא דכל ברכאין בי׳ תליין. ואינם בהתגלות. והגם כי המן הי׳ מאכל שמלאכי השרת אוכלין. מ״מ כשבא לעולם ונתלבש בגשמיות לא ירד בשבת. כי ברכת השבת אינה יכולה כלל להתלבש בגשמיות.

As we mentioned in a previous *dvar Torah*, every Shabbos the inner gates of the future *Beis HaMikdash* will open. We suggest that this concept does not only refer to the actual gates but, by extension, to the manner through which Hashem conducts His universe. Whereas all week long, Hashem permits His universe to be conducted on the basis of *chitzoniyus* (external factors) that prevail in the natural world, on Shabbos, Hashem conducts His universe on the basis of *penimiyus* – underlying spiritual factors that are not visible.[1] Consequently, we abstain from *Melachah* – which include different means of exploiting the natural world – on Shabbos,

1. The expression הַפּוֹרֵשׂ סֻכַּת שָׁלוֹם, *He spreads a canopy of peace*, recited in the *Maariv* prayers of Shabbos, may allude to the lesser role played by *chitzoniyus* on Shabbos. By spreading "a canopy," Hashem covers and veils every aspect of the outer world so that the inner world (*penimiyus*) may dominate.

the day when the universe is conducted on the basis of spiritual factors.

For this reason, the manna, despite its extraordinary sanctity (cf. *Yoma* 75b stating that the manna was originally the bread of *malachim*), did not fall on Shabbos. As spiritual as the manna may have been, it had a physical presence and thus could not appear on Shabbos, a day that is infused with *ruchniyus*. (Adapted from *Ki Sisa* 5658)

☙ Finding Hashem Through *Melachah*

כי כל ימי המעשה דכתיב ששת ימים תעבוד. תעשה מלאכה. ואעפ״כ יש קדושה גנוזה גם בעשי׳ ממש והוא בחי׳ מלאך ושליח כי כל דבר יש בו חיות מהשי״ת ונשתלח לעולם כדי לעשות רצון השי״ת שיש מצות בכל מעשה האדם. רק שנתלבש בעניני עוה״ז וצריך שמירה יותר אל תמר בו. רק לידע כי גם זה מחיות השי״ת כי שמי בקרבו כו׳ ועבדתם את ה׳ כו׳ הוא בחי׳ שבת בלי התלבשות המעשה כי שבת מעין עוה״ב ואז והסירותי מחלה מקרבך כו׳. וזה שא״צ בקשה על שום דבר בשבת.

Throughout this chapter, we have emphasized the sanctity of Shabbos over that of the weekdays. In this *dvar Torah*, we will show that we can evoke the *kedushah* of the *Shechinah* during the *Melachah* performed on the weekdays, as well. We suggest that everything that has ever been created by mankind is a *malach* (a messenger, not necessarily an angel) of Hashem. Without the existence of many elements of the material world, it would be almost impossible to perform *mitzvos* (imagine a *mezuzah* without a doorpost where it will be placed or *tzitzis* without clothing). Just as the messenger sent by a mortal perceives no greater honor than to perform the bidding of his mentor, so too, the function of the material world is to perform the Will of Hashem.

The essence of our *dvar Torah* that the entire material world functions as an emissary of Hashem, and that we must take great precautions not to confuse the messenger with the One Who empowers the messenger, is expressed in the following *pasuk*, הִנֵּה אָנֹכִי שֹׁלֵחַ מַלְאָךְ לְפָנֶיךָ ... אַל תַּמֵּר בּוֹ, *Behold! I send an angel* (messenger) *before you ... do not confuse him* (with the One that sends the messenger, *HaKadosh Baruch Hu*) (*Shemos* 23:20-21). According to this homiletical approach, this *pasuk* alludes to all of the material creations of the six weekdays which are a potent emissary and agent of the Divine Will. However, we dare not confuse these *malachim* of Hashem with the *Ribbono Shel Olam* Who empowers them, as the *pasuk* continues, כִּי שְׁמִי בְּקִרְבּוֹ, *for My Name is in their midst;* these agents are only in existence because Hashem empowers them. A few *pesukim* later it says, וַעֲבַדְתֶּם אֵת ה׳ אֱלֹהֵיכֶם וּבֵרַךְ אֶת לַחְמְךָ וְאֶת מֵימֶיךָ, *You should serve HASHEM, your God, and He will bless your bread and your water* (v. 25). On Shabbos, the Jew can serve Hashem *directly,* without necessarily resorting to the material world. Whereas during the weekday *Shemoneh Esrei* we discuss our material needs (asking Hashem for *parnassah,* health, etc.), on Shabbos we only recite seven *berachos* in *Shemoneh Esrei,* without even expressing our personal needs. As the Torah states, *HASHEM will bless your bread and your water.* Even without asking directly for material assistance, Hashem Himself will bless your fortunes. (*Mishpatim* 5631)

◆§ *Melachah* And *Malachim* (Angels)

וכל ימי החול הם ירדו בעוה״ז ונתלבשו בימי המעשה והשבת נשאר במקום גבוה ועי״ז מיני׳ מתברכין שיתא יומין ולכך בשבת לא ירד המן כי הוא גבוה מבחי׳ המאכל רק ע״י שיום זה נשאר כמו שהוא. עי״ז יכולין ימי המעשה ג״כ למשוך חיות ממקורם (והדברים מובנים מה שנק׳ ימי מלאכה שבחול ע״י מלאכים כנודע. ולכן אף כי ששת הימים במקורם גבוהים מהשבת רק ששבת נשאר כמו שהי׳ והבן מאוד)

ועפ״י הפשוט וודאי גם בימות החול שנק׳ ימי המעשה ומלאכה. מ״מ יש בהם בחי׳ שבת בהסתר עב״פ. [כמ״ש ששת ימי המעשה יהי׳ סגור כו׳] ולכך ת״ח נקראי׳ שבת. שאצלם גם בחול נמצאי׳ הארות הפנימיות. שזה עיקר פי׳ שבת. להיות דבוק בשורש החיים דמיני׳ מתברכין שיתא יומין. ומלאכות שהיו במשכן בודאי היו עפ״י אופן זה שהרי נעשה השראת השכינה ע״י מלאכות האלה. ושורש כל המלאכות ועבודת ימות החול הם מבחי׳ משכן. ולכך נלמד ל״ט מלאכות שהי׳ במשכן שרק הם נק׳ מלאכות. [והענין כמ״ש בזוה״ק תרומה ענין המשכן שהוא כהנהגת ימות החול ע״י המלאך שהוא בחי׳ מלאכה והמש״י]. ולזאת אומר הכתוב כי גם מלאכות המשכן אסור בשבת. כי בשבת יש התגלות הפנימיות.

On the basis of our assertion in the previous *dvar Torah* that during the week Hashem's *berachos* may be channeled through *malachim,* while on Shabbos He bestows His blessings directly, we may appreciate the comment of the *Zohar* that even though the manna (which is symbolic of Hashem's material blessings) did not fall on Shabbos, the *berachos* of the entire week are derived from Shabbos.

We suggest that in some respects the heavenly source of the six workdays — and of the *berachah* of *parnassah* that plays so great a role during the weekdays — may be more sacred than that of Shabbos. However, in order that these *berachos* leave an impact on the material environment of *Olam Hazeh*, Hashem found it appropriate to "clothe" these heavenly blessings in a material form, and to authorize *malachim* (a term closely related to *Melachah*) to channel His *berachos* to mankind. Similarly, on Shabbos, Hashem's *berachos* remain in their pure form and are not adapted for the needs of mankind. It is from these pure *berachos* that we derive *all* of the blessings that we enjoy the entire week.

(*Bereishis* and *Ki Sisa* 5631)

כי שבת הוא לפי עבודת ימות החול כי כתיב ששת ימים תעבוד כו׳ כל מלאכתך ויום השביעי שבת פי׳ שבת הוא עליות כל דבר וביטולו להשורש שהוא חיות השי״ת כח הפועל בנפעל. ומ״מ ע״כ גם בימות החול יש חיות מהשי״ת רק הוא בבחי׳ מלאכים כמ״ש בזוה״ק בחול ע״י מלא׳ כו׳ ע״ש פ׳ תרומה ... וז״ש בספרים כי ע״י מצוה נברא מלאך כן הוא כי בימות החול החיות ע״י מלאך הידוע. וזה תלוי בשמירת המצות. וז״ש עם לבן גרתי ותרי״ג מצות שמרתי זה הי׳ העצה נגד עשו כי יעקב בעצמו הוא בחי׳ שבת הגדול. רק עבודתו בבחי׳ מלאכה ועבודה הי׳ רק כדי לדחות ענין לבן ועשו. וז״ש וישלח מלאכים שזה ע״י עבודה ומלאכה כנ״ל.

Expanding upon the relationship between *Melachah* and *malachim*, we note that when completing His universe, Hashem enabled mankind to "continue to create" through his own contribution. Thus, *Melachah* represents the innate creativity which Hashem granted mankind. In effect, when mortals invent something new, they are consummating the process of creation commenced by Hashem during the Six Days of Creation. However, there is an inherent danger in any man-made invention. Being of mortal origin, rather than directly created by Hashem, there always remains the

1. See *Devarim* (8:17) where the Torah warns of the danger of coming to believe that our material success is derived from our own efforts: וְאָמַרְתָּ בִּלְבָבֶךָ כֹּחִי וְעֹצֶם יָדִי עָשָׂה לִי אֶת הַחַיִל הַזֶּה, *And you may say in your heart, "My strength and the might of my hand made me all this wealth!"*

risk that something so material can lead its creator away from Hashem.[1] It is only by associating man-made creations with a *mitzvah* (for example placing a *mezuzah* on the doorposts of a home, observing the laws of *shatnes* for clothing), that we can be confident that man's success will not lead him astray. *Chazal* also relate that every *mitzvah* leads to the creation of a *malach* (cf. *Avos* 4:13).

In light of the foregoing discussion, we can now appreciate the association between *Melachah* and *malachim*. It is through our creative efforts during the week (*Melachah*) that Hashem enables us to perform more *mitzvos*, which in turn lead to the creation of *malachim*. It is this potent combination of our creativity (*Melachah*) that is channeled into *mitzvos*, which in turn leads to the emergence of *malachim*, that defines our task during the weekdays. On Shabbos, however, when we abstain from *Melachah*, we enjoy a direct association with Hashem unlike anything that we can attain during the week. How appropriate that when sending *malachim* to Esav, Yaakov emphasizes that he observed all of the Torah's 613 *mitzvos*, even while in Lavan's house. Whereas Yaakov himself was on the spiritual level that we attain on Shabbos (and thus did not require the intercession of *malachim*), when dealing with his unworthy brother, he felt it necessary to remind him of the *malachim* that were created through the *mitzvos* that he had performed even in the difficult environment of Lavan's home. (*Vayishlach* 5631)

◆§ Shabbos – *Klal Yisrael* Ascends "Above" the *Malachim*

ולכן מתחדשין המלאכים בכל יום כמ״ש חדשים לבקרים כו׳. כי כשהקב״ה מחדש בכל יום מעשה בראשית ממילא מתחדשין המלאכים שהם החיות של הנבראים ... ותיקון המעשה בימות החול הוא ע״י המלאכים כמ״ש בזוה״ק כי בחול מנהיג השי״ת את העולם ע״י מלאך והוא ענין המלאכות של ימי המעשה. כי א״י להתדבק בבחי׳ עשי׳ אם לא ע״י המלאך. אבל בש״ק מעין עוה״ב כמ״ש חז״ל כעת יאמר ליעקב מה פעל אל כו׳. וכן בש״ק שעיקר הרצון של בנ״י בלי מעשה ומלאכה. והרצון יכול לבוא להשי״ת בלי אמצעי כנ״ל.

Whereas during the weekdays, days that are devoted to *Melachah*,

Hashem manages His universe through *malachim*, on Shabbos, which is a replica of *Olam Haba, Klal Yisrael* ascends to a level above that of *malachim*. As Bilaam notes, כָּעֵת יֵאָמֵר לְיַעֲקֹב וּלְיִשְׂרָאֵל מַה פָּעַל אֵל, *Even now it is said to Jacob and Israel what God has wrought* (*Bamidbar* 23:22) — the time will come when it will be said (by the *malachim*) to Yaakov and Yisrael (the Jewish people), "What did God do?" In the Future World (and even in contemporary times, on Shabbos), *Klal Yisrael* will have attained a level of such *kedushah* that even the angels will ask us about Hashem's Plans.

Extending this analysis, we note that during the weekdays when we serve Hashem through our actions (in the form of the various *melachos*), we require the intercession of *malachim*. One can not reach closeness to Hashem while engaging in the material pursuits of This World without the assistance of *malachim*. (Thus, the similarity between the terms *Melachah* and *malach*.) On the other hand, on Shabbos, when we serve Hashem simply on the basis of our intense desire to come close to Him, we do not require the assistance of *malachim* to foster our relationship with Hashem. (*Vayishlach* 5635)

◈ Shabbos: *Malachim* of Eretz Yisrael Weekdays: *Malachim* of *Chutz La'aretz* (Diaspora)

ויש מלאכי חוץ לארץ וארץ ישראל כמ״ש חז״ל ויפגעו בו מלאכי כו׳. וי״ל שימי המעשה שמותרין בעשיית מלאכה והוא להוציא ולברר החיות שנסתר ונעלם במעשים גשמיים ונק׳ מלאכי חו״ל כנ״ל. ואיתא מלאכים ממש. ואיך שלח לעשו מלאכים קדושים. א״כ י״ל שהי׳ בדרך נסתר מלאכי חו״ל כנ״ל בענין שמצינו שמלאכים מתלבשים בעוה״ז בגשמיות. וש״ק יום מנוחה הוא מלאכי א״י שמתגלה הרצון האמת בלב ישראל וע״י התלהבות יכולין להעלות הכל.

Whereas in the previous *dvar Torah* we implied that during the weekdays Hashem directs His universe through *malachim*, while on Shabbos He directly intervenes in His universe, it is also possible that on both occasions, *malachim* play a significant role. However, there exists a distinction between the *malachim* who dominate during the week and those of Shabbos, as we shall elucidate. We find that Yaakov *Avinu* was accompanied by two distinct groups of angels, those that were reserved for his sojourns in *Eretz Yisrael* and those that escorted him throughout *chutz la'aretz* (outside of *Eretz Yisrael*).[1] It is also fair to assume that he sent the angels associated with *chutz la'aretz,* rather than those of *Eretz Yisrael,* to his brother Esav.

The angels of *chutz la'aretz* – who often disguise themselves and appear to us in the form of human beings – are Hashem's messengers who implement His Will during the weekdays. On the other hand, on Shabbos, the totally spiritual *malachim* of *Eretz Yisrael* act as Hashem's messengers. These totally spiritual entities – lacking any physical form – implement the Divine Will on Shabbos. In what *zechus* do we deserve these special Divine emissaries on Shabbos? These extraordinary *malachim* are created in the merit of the inner yearning and great enthusiasm of every Jew to serve Hashem (which is accentuated every Shabbos).

(*Vayishlach* 5633)

◆§ Shabbos: An Ideal Day for *Teshuvah*

ולכך בשבת בנקל לשוב כי יש לכל הבריאה עלי' בשבת קודש. כדכ' ויכל כו' וישבות כו' אף שלא ברא ביגיעה עולמו רק כמ"ש ז"ל שבחול נעשה ע"י מלאכה בבחי' מלאכים ושלוחים וצמצום כחו ע"י כמה אמצעיות. ובש"ק מתיחדין ומתדבקין כולם בשורש העליון.

In the previous *dvar Torah,* we noted that during the six weekdays Hashem may conduct His universe through various emissaries (*malachim*) – and in accordance with the laws governing the natural world – while on Shabbos, His direct intervention is more apparent. One of the ramifications of this difference in how Hashem manages His world is that Shabbos, when Hashem is closest to us, is the most opportune time for *teshuvah.* Consequently, it is entirely appropriate that *Shabbos Teshuvah* is a focal point in the *Aseres Yemei Teshuvah* that we observe between Rosh Hashanah and Yom Kippur.[2]

1. Cf. *Rashi* on *Bereishis* 28:12.

2. For further discussion of this theme refer to *Days of Awe,* pgs. 208-225.

(*Shabbos Teshuvah* 5634)

☙ Renewing Our Vitality Every Shabbos

ולכן שבת מיוחד לתשובה ע״י שיש בשבת עלי׳ מכל מעשה ימות החול

We just discussed why Shabbos is an ideal opportunity for *teshuvah*. Additionally, we suggest that every Shabbos we experience a sense of resurgence. While this sense of renewal is experienced by all of the natural world (as the Torah states, וַיִּנָּפַשׁ, Hashem restores the soul of the entire universe on Shabbos), *Klal Yisrael* earns its rejuvenation because of its determination to leave behind its preoccupation with the material world on Shabbos and come closer to Hashem. Is this not the essence of *teshuvah?* — leaving behind one's material concerns and returning to Hashem. (*Shabbos Teshuvah* 5651)

☙ Building a "Six-Sided" Home for the *Shechinah*

ששת ימים תעשה מלאכה. כי כל הד׳ רוחות ולמעלה ולמטה הוא בחי׳ התאספות כל הכוחות והמדות להיות היכל לנקודה הפנימיות שהוא השבת. והוא בנין המשכן ממש כמ״ש אי זה בית אשר תבנו לי כו׳.

Previously, we discussed how we can "find" the *Shechinah* through our efforts at performing *Melachah* during the week. Elaborating on this theme, we suggest that the six days in which we perform *Melachah* correspond to the six directions (east, west, south, north, above and below) that often play a significant role in our *avodas Hashem* (just as they do in the waving of the Two Loaves during the times of the *Beis HaMikdash*, and even in contemporary times, waving a *lulav*). Just as our forefathers constructed a *Mishkan* during the six workdays, so too, through our weekday *Melachah* we construct — utilizing every possible direction and avenue — a home for the *Shechinah*. It is as if we create an environment in every part of the universe that is conducive to the presence of the *Shechinah*. On Shabbos, however, these efforts cease. On

Shabbos, once the proper ambiance has been created in every direction for the *Shechinah* to dwell in our midst, it is our sacred challenge to cease creating and just allow the *Shechinah* to reside among us.

The prophet Yeshayahu captures the essence of this *dvar Torah* by asking, אֵי זֶה בַיִת אֲשֶׁר תִּבְנוּ לִי, *What house can you build for Me?"* (66:1). While during the week we are preoccupied with the task of creating an appropriate environment for the *Shechinah* — in every possible "direction" — on Shabbos, we cease creating and allow the *Shechinah* to dwell among us in the "edifice" that we have created for Him.

(Adapted from *Vayakhel* 5636)

◆§ Defining *Melachah* Through the *Mishkan*

שהרי כל המלאכות היו במשכן ולא נקרא מלאכה רק מה שהי׳ במשכן שהמשכן הוא התרוממות כל העשי׳ להרוחניות. והשוה הכתוב זה למראות מרע״ה.

In the previous *dvar Torah* we discussed how all the material amenities of the material world that we create during the six workdays are actually a means of finding and coming closer to the *Shechinah*. We remarked how it is possible to consecrate the entire material world and utilize it as a way of achieving nearness to Hashem. In this *dvar Torah,* we will continue with this theme and note that we derive the definition of *Melachah* from the *Mishkan* (refer to *Bava Kamma* 2a where the Gemara states that the 39 categories of work that are prohibited on Shabbos are identical with the major activities performed during the construction of the *Mishkan*), the one place where the mundane world converged with the universe of spirituality. Where else but the *Mishkan* were material artifacts of exquisite beauty designed by expert artisans to be used in the service of Hashem? It is not mere mundane activity that is prohibited on Shabbos, but rather the highest form of creativity. It was in the construction of the *Mishkan* that materialism was raised to so high a plane that it was virtually identical with spirituality. It is through this type of creative activity used to construct the *Mishkan* that we define the parameters of *Melachah* on Shabbos.

To give some indication of the *Mishkan's* significance (and the various forms of work used to construct it), we recall that the Torah seems to equate the construction of the *Mishkan* to the many prophetic visions that Moshe enjoyed: כְּכֹל אֲשֶׁר אֲנִי מַרְאֶה אוֹתְךָ אֵת תַּבְנִית הַמִּשְׁכָּן וְאֵת תַּבְנִית כָּל כֵּלָיו וְכֵן תַּעֲשׂוּ, *Like everything that I show you, the form of the Tabernacle and the form of all its vessels; and so shall you do* (*Shemos* 25:9) – "Just as I appeared to you, so too, you design the *Mishkan* and all of its utensils." While Hashem appeared *directly* to Moshe when He spoke to him in a spiritual manner that no mortal can fathom (described by *Chazal* as אספקלרא המאירה), the *Mishkan*, where the material world was raised to the highest spiritual level, became the resting place for the *Shechinah*.

(*Terumah* 5642)

◆ The Greatest Unifying Force – *Melachah*

דהנה קודם זה החטא היו בנ״י דבקים בשורש כללות כנס״י שנאמר עליהם חלק ה׳ עמו. וע״י החטא נפלו לבחי׳ הפירוד כמ״ש אלה כו׳. ולכן הקהיל אותם מרע״ה כמ״ש ויקהל. וזה הי׳ רק לשעה בכח השבת דמתאחדין ברזא דאחד כו׳. אבל עי״ז באו אח״כ למעשה המשכן שהוא תיקון הנפרדים ג״כ.

Continuing along the line of reasoning just discussed regarding some of the positive effects of the 39 categories of work used to erect the *Mishkan*, we suggest that the process of constructing the *Mishkan* served to unify all of *Klal Yisrael*. We should bear in mind that the *Mishkan* was constructed in the aftermath of the sin of the Golden Calf, which (in addition to being a form of idolatory) caused a great deal of disunity in the ranks of *Klal Yisrael*. In fact, the builders of the *Egel* were so fragmented that they presented their creation, the Golden Calf, to the Jewish people as "your gods" (plural; cf. *Shemos* 32:4), rather than the singular, "your god" (cf. *Avodah Zarah* 53b stating that the Jewish people desired many deities).

Instead of merely suppressing the movement that led to the construction of the Golden Calf, Moshe sought to remedy the underlying causes of this colossal national tragedy. If disunity was a major contributing factor to the Golden Calf, then the *Mishkan*, which *Chazal* perceived as the antidote to the *Egel* was, of necessity – as part of the healing process – a unifying event. In fact, when Moshe transmits the procedures involved in the construction of the *Mishkan* to *Klal Yisrael*, he ensures that he speaks to *all* of *Klal Yisrael*. He actually gathers them to listen to the detailed instructions of the *Mishkan's* building – וַיַּקְהֵל מֹשֶׁה אֶת כָּל עֲדַת בְּנֵי יִשְׂרָאֵל, *Moshe assembled the entire assembly of the Children of Israel* (*Shemos* 35:1).

Utilizing this approach, we can appreciate why the *Mishkan* was not built on Shabbos. The primary theme of the *Mishkan* unifying the Jewish people, after they had been seriously divided as a result of the sin of the *Egel*, is accomplished through the Shabbos day itself which embodies *achdus*. (*Pekudei* 5638)

⸎ A Catalyst for Peace

וכן ימי המעשה שכל אחד עוסק בעבודה מיוחדת הן בגשמיות או בתורה ועבודה שיש ג״כ מחלוקת כמ״ש זו מחלוקת הלל ושמאי. וכשהיא לשם שמים סופה להתקיים פי׳ לבוא לאחדות והוא בש״ק שסוף כל מעשים הנעשים בימי המעשה לש״ש יש להם עלי׳ בש״ק כנודע.

Another beneficial corollary of not performing *Melachah* on Shabbos is the cessation of the *machlokes* (arguments and controversy) that too often marks our life during the weekdays. Frequently, our material efforts are the source for a great deal of the *machlokes* that divides us (i.e. in our quest for material success, we may compete with others who have similar aspirations). However, on Shabbos, when we rest from our self-serving material activities, we no longer have any reason to quarrel and a new-found sense of *shalom* (peace) prevails in our ranks.

(Adapted from *Korach* 5635)

⸎ Recreating the Universe Through The *Melachos* of the *Mishkan*

דאיתא במד׳ המשכן מכוון למעשה בראשית כתיב הכא ותכל וכ׳ התם ויכלו כו׳ ... וזה שאמר כי מלאכת המשכן הי׳ די לתקן כל מלאכת שמים וארץ וזה לכל המלאכה הידועה.

Even a surface reading of the *pesukim* describing the construction of the *Mishkan* reveals significant parallels between the *Mishkan's* construction and the creation of heaven and earth. Consider, in particular, the similarities between the responses of Moshe to the *Mishkan's* completion and Hashem to the completion of heaven and earth. Both derived great satisfaction when they looked at the finished product that had been created. In fact, their satisfied response was almost identical — a *berachah*. Just as Hashem blessed the completed universe, so too, Moshe blessed the builders of the *Mishkan*. Drawing the analogy even closer, we note that in both instances at the culmination of the process of creation, definite limits were set up, which caused the process to conclude. Just as Hashem stopped the process of creation at the conclusion of Six Days of Creation by pronouncing דַי, it is enough (cf. *Rashi, Bereishis* 43:14), so too, using almost identical language, Moshe declined the Jewish people's contributions to the *Mishkan* when they became excessive — וְהַמְּלָאכָה הָיְתָה דַיָּם לְכָל הַמְּלָאכָה לַעֲשׂוֹת אֹתָהּ וְהוֹתֵר, *But the work had been enough for all the work, to do it — and there was extra* (*Shemos* 36:7). This may also be interpreted, "The contributions to the *Mishkan* (וְהַמְּלָאכָה) were enough to sustain the entire creation of heaven and earth" (הַמְּלָאכָה — refer to *Bereishis* 2:3, מִכָּל מְלַאכְתּוֹ). Moreover, when discussing the completion of heaven and earth, the Torah writes, וַיְכֻלּוּ הַשָּׁמַיִם וְהָאָרֶץ (*Bereishis* 2:1). The *Mishkan's* conclusion is described in similar terms — וַתֵּכֶל כָּל עֲבֹדַת מִשְׁכַּן אֹהֶל מוֹעֵד, *All the work of the Tabernacle, the Tent of Meeting, was completed* (*Shemos* 39:32).

(*Vayakhel* 5640)

וירא ה׳ כו׳ כל אשר עשה כו׳ טוב מאוד כו׳ ויכלו כו׳ ויברך כו׳. כמו כן המשכן שהוא קיום העולם הי׳ ע״י וירא משה והוטב בעיניו ויברך אותם כו׳. כדאיתא בזוה״ק בכמה דוכתי שהקב״ה ברא העולם בכח התורה. והצדיקים מקיימים העולם בכח התורה ע״ש. וז״ש וירא משה שתיקנו כל המלאכה היינו כל הנבראים וכל העשי׳ ניתקן.

While the full extent of the analogy between the construction of the *Mishkan* and the creation of heaven and earth is beyond the scope of this essay, we suggest that the *Mishkan*, in effect, consummates what began through Creation. Just as Hashem created the universe after "consulting" with the Torah, so too, all the *tzaddikim* of *Klal Yisrael* helped uphold and maintain the universe through the process of creating the *Mishkan*, which was the resting place for the Torah.

The *Midrash* (*Tanchuma, Pekudei* 11) alludes to this approach by noting that the Torah describes Moshe's reaction to the completed *Mishkan* in the following terms: וַיַּרְא מֹשֶׁה אֶת כָּל הַמְּלָאכָה, *Moshe saw the entire work* (*Shemos* 39:43), rather than merely state than he beheld the *Melachah* of the *Mishkan*. Apparently, Moshe perceived that *Klal Yisrael* had not merely completed its own sacred undertaking but, in a sense, had consummated *all* of the work — even the *Melachah* that was required to create heaven and earth, a process that began during the Six Days of Creation, but was not completed until the *Mishkan* was erected.

(Adapted from *Vayakhel* 5637)

⤙ Working (*Melachah*) to Attain Spiritual Rest (*Menuchah*)

אבל כשאדם רוצה לעשות איזה מלאכה וטורח בה הרבה עד שנגמרת ונח אח״כ. זה מנוחת מרגוע. שכל המלאכה הי׳ כדי להשיג זאת המנוחה. וכן כביכול הכתיב מנוחה לעצמו כי ששת ימים כו׳. נמצא מנוחת הקב״ה כך הי׳. ונלמד מזה שכן צריך להיות מנוחת האדם בשבת כמ״ש ששת ימים תעבוד כו׳. מסמיך הכתוב העבודה למנוחת שבת. כלומר להיות כל עבודת ימי המעשה כדי להיות נגמר רצונו ית׳ וכבודו. להיות נעשה מזה השבת. ומעין זה איתא ג״כ כי לכל מעשה האדם בימי החול יש להם עלי׳ בשבת קודש.

Rashi helps us appreciate the relationship between *Melachah* (the work that we perform during the six weekdays) and *menuchah* (the rest that we enjoy on Shabbos) by defining the *menuchah* of Shabbos as מְנוּחַת מַרְגּוֹעַ וְלֹא מְנוּחַת עֲרָאִי, "a rest derived from a sense of completion of one's goals, not merely a pause (temporary rest) in our objectives" (cf. *Shemos* 31:15). While at times we rest simply because there is no more work to be done, that is certainly not the purpose of resting on Shabbos. Ceasing work simply because there is nothing more to be done is no better than the "temporary rest" (מְנוּחַת עֲרָאִי) that *Rashi* indicates, which is not what the Torah expects us to enjoy on Shabbos. On the contrary, our entire objective all week long when we perform various forms of *Melachah* (which in itself may be a form of *avodas Hashem*), is to complete our sacred tasks during the week so that we merit the sense of spiritual satisfaction that we enjoy on Shabbos. Just as the objective of the original Six Days of Creation was the sense of *menuchah* Hashem attained when He beheld the completed world on Shabbos, so too, for us mortals, our efforts all week long are but the prelude to the spiritual satisfaction that we attain on Shabbos. Thus, the Torah always juxtaposes the work that is performed during the six weekdays to the rest of Shabbos. Extending our analogy further, we suggest that the beautiful spiritual rest of Shabbos is derived from all the sacred tasks that we perform during the week. Every time that the Will of Hashem is enhanced and His Glory increases as a result of our weekday activity, that *nachas* that we give Hashem in itself contributes to the true objective of all our efforts – the *menuchah* of Shabbos. (*Ki Sisa* 5635)

◆§ More on the Relationship Between *Melachah* and *Menuchah*

וכן בש״ק שהוא נותן דעה באיש ישראל כמ״ש לדעת כי אני ה׳ מקדישכם. יש בו קידוש והבדלה זכור ושמור. השבתת מלאכה. ושביתה ומנוחה ודביקות אל השורש.

In the previous *dvar Torah* we discussed the relationship between performing *Melachah* during the six weekdays and the subsequent rest that we enjoy on Shabbos. Here we will focus on the connection between *not* performing *Melachah* on Shabbos and the *menuchah* that we then enjoy. On one hand, not performing work on Shabbos is essentially a passive act – abstaining from acts that we ordinarily perform. However, there are significant consequences resulting from not performing *Melachah*. By abstaining from *Melachah* and in general, all that links us to *Olam Hazeh* – we are able to return to our true roots in *Olam Haba*, which is the real meaning of *menuchah* – the return to spirituality. In fact, the term שְׁבִיתָה (related to Shabbos) implies both connotations – abstaining from work and yielding *Olam Hazeh* in favor of our true roots in *Olam Haba*.

This relationship between abstaining from the material aspects of *Olam Hazeh* and consequently returning to our spiritual roots – first a *passive* act followed by a *positive* act — is indicated by the two aspects of Shabbos — *Shamor*, the negation of whatever is inappropriate, and then *Zachor*, the positive aspects of Shabbos. Similarly, the relationship between *Havdalah*, which is essentially a passive act of separation from the mundane, and *Kiddush*, sanctifying the Shabbos in a positive fashion, is analogous to that of passive abstinence from *Melachah* and the active consequences of Shabbos — returning to one's roots.

Extending our analysis beyond the context of Shabbos to the broader parameters of Torah, we suggest that this relationship between the passive and the active phase is implied in the statement of *Chazal* (cf. *Berachos* 33a and *Yerushalmi Berachos* 39b) linking *Havdalah* — and the separation from outside influences (הַמַּבְדִּיל בֵּין יִשְׂרָאֵל לְעַמִּים) — and *deiah*, knowledge of Hashem. It is only by abstaining from what is contrary to the Torah that we can attain *daas Hashem* — true knowledge of Hashem. (Adapted from *Tazria* 5661)

☙ Children and Servants

וש״ק הוא בחי׳ בן לכן יש בו שביתה ממלאכה דהוא יומא דנשמתין. לכן יורד בו נשמה יתירה.

To appreciate a possible reason for the prohibition of *Melachah* on Shabbos, we recall the *Zohar's* (*Parashas Behar*) observation that there are two approaches to Divine Service — that of the servant loyally serving his master and that of the son at his father's side. In reality, *both* aspects of *avodas Hashem* are inherent in every Jew. Whereas the body (גוף) serves Hashem, just as a servant serves a master, the soul's relationship to Hashem is that of a son to his father. Extending this analogy, it can be said that during the week our function is to serve Hashem utilizing our body. Just as a servant performs all kinds of material functions for his master, so too, we can perform Divine service during the week through our material efforts that are reflected in many forms of *Melachah*. However, on Shabbos, when the soul dominates (especially because we are enhanced by the presence of the additional soul, *neshamah yeseirah*), we serve Hashem as children, rather than as servants. In this spiritual environment, physical work simply has no place.

(*Mishpatim* 5646)

◆§ *Naaseh V'Nishma*

נעשה ונשמע. דיבור וקול. והוא בחי׳ ימי המעשה ושבת קודש. כי בחול ע״י עשי׳ שמותר במלאכה והוא ג״כ לעבודת השי״ת כמ״ש במ״א שנקראו ימי עבודה. ובשבת זוכין לשמוע בלי יגיעה כנ״ל.

The relationship between Shabbos and the weekdays may be expressed in terms of the famous *Naaseh V'Nishma* relationship. During the week, we serve Hashem by exploiting the material world for a higher purpose. This is similar to the concept of *Naaseh,* serving Hashem by doing and creating. However, on Shabbos, we merit the spiritual level of *Nishma,* listening. Even without all of the effort of the weekdays in the form of *Melachah* (נַעֲשֶׂה), on Shabbos we are able to hear and listen to the Word of Hashem (נִשְׁמַע). *Melachah* is not required as a means of acquiring the desired proximity to Hashem. (*Pesach* 5633)

◆§ Returning to Sinai

השביתה היא ביטול הטבע שקרבנו השי״י לפני הר סיני היינו שנתעלו בנ״י להיות כמלאכים. והגם כי נאמר אבן כאדם כו׳ עב״ז נשאר הדביקות לזמנים. שיש בכח בנ״י לצאת מן הטבע. וזה אות השבת ביטול המלאכה.

When discussing the *Shemittah* (the Sabbatical Year, occurring every seven years), the Torah emphasizes that these laws were transmitted to Moshe at Sinai. It may well be that the Torah is not merely interested in teaching us that these laws were first given at *Har Sinai,* but also to demonstrate that by observing the *Shemittah* (and the weekly Shabbos), we can return to the rarefied atmosphere of Sinai. At that moment, *Klal Yisrael* rose to the spiritual level of angels. While after our flirtation with pagan values when we erected the Golden Calf, we descended to the levels of mortals, on Shabbos (and during the Sabbatical Year), we attempt to negate everything that is material by abstaining from *Melachah* and are able to return to our previous spiritual levels.

Extending our analysis further, we suggest that the function of the *Shemittah* (and to some extent, the weekly Shabbos) is to ensure that we do not become so acclimated to the natural world (*teva*) that we forget that This World is nothing more than a corridor that leads to the Great Palace of *Olam Haba* (cf. *Pirkei Avos* 4:21). By experiencing one day of intense spirituality, we are reminded of our enormous spiritual potential and of the true purpose of life. (Adapted from *Behar* 5644)

◆§ Returning to *Gan Eden*

כי באמת בזעת אפיך תאכל לחם היא הקללה לאחר החטא ומקודם הי' כל אכילת אדם מגן עדן. וכמו כן היו בנ"י מוכנים להיות בהר סיני. וכ"כ אמרתי אלהים אתם כוי'. אך גם אחר החטא נשאר לבנ"י זמנים שמתעורר להם זה הכח הראשון וכמו בש"ק שמבטלין מכל מלאכה ומוכנים רק לעבודת הש"י. לכן המזון ביום ש"ק הוא בקדושה.

As we just suggested, every Shabbos (and during the *Shemittah* year) we return to the levels that we attained at *Har Sinai.* Perhaps, we may expand the analysis and go back even further in history. Just like at Sinai, *Klal Yisrael* returned to the spiritual bliss that Adam enjoyed in *Gan Eden,* so too, every Shabbos when we abstain from *Melachah,* we leave behind the curse from which the first man (and his descendants) suffered. On Shabbos, Hashem's declaration, "By the sweat of your brow you shall eat bread" (*Bereishis* 3:19) no longer applies. In fact, Shabbos is a day of such intense *kedushah,* paralleling that of *Gan Eden,* that even the material aspects of life become infused with *kedushah* (just as everything in *Gan Eden* was sacred).

Consequently, on Shabbos even mundane activities, such as eating, are imbued with *kedushah.* (Adapted from *Behar* 5646)

וקודם החטא שם הקב"ה האדם בג"ע לעבדה ולשמרה ברמ"ח מ"ע ושס"ה מל"ת. ואחר החטא כ' וישלחו כו' מג"ע לעבוד כו' האדמה. א"כ בזמנים שיש שביתת מלאכה לבנ"י כמו בשבת וכן בשמיטין ושבתה הארץ. לעבוד האדמה. הוא אות לבנ"י שהם במדרגה הראשונה לעסוק רק ברמ"ח ושס"ה. כי האדם כלול משמים וארץ. נשמה משמים וגוף בארץ.

Extending the analogy to *Gan Eden*, we suggest that by abstaining from *Melachah, Klal Yisrael* returns to the original concept of "work." When placed in *Gan Eden*, Adam was commanded "to work it and to guard it" (*Bereishis* 2:15). However, *Chazal* says, no physical labor was actually required to maintain Eden, which was directly nurtured by Hashem. If, nonetheless, the Torah speaks of "working" in *Gan Eden*, it must be referring to the 248 *mitzvos asei* and the 365 *mitzvos lo sa'asei*. On Shabbos, we return to the original definition of work – nurturing the universe through our *mitzvos*. (*Behar* 5663)

וז״ש לא לרעתך נתתי השבת רק לטובתך שהטוב מבורר ולכן התענוג מצוה בשבת ובחול צריך שמירה ע״י שמעורב בו הרע ג״כ. אך בשבת כתיב פורס סוכת שלום. שע״י התגלות הארת השבת שהיא מעין עוה״ב. ניתן שלימות בכל הדברים. ומבדיל בין התערובות כנ״ל.

In yet another respect, every Shabbos we return to the spiritual level that was enjoyed prior to man's first sin. One of the most serious consequences of Adam's decision to partake of the fruit of the Tree of Knowledge of Good and Evil was that the concepts of good and evil would hereafter often be confused. Whereas prior to the first sin, man was able to know with confidence that a particular approach was appropriate and that another method would inevitably be displeasing to Hashem, after sinning it became difficult to discern between good and evil. However, on Shabbos, when we sever our ties to the material world, we return to the blessed moral clarity that existed before the first sin – a universe where one can readily discern between good and evil.

Utilizing this approach, we can appreciate why contrary to our usual practice of frowning upon those who indulge in material pleasures, it a *mitzvah* to enjoy the Shabbos day (refer to our chapter on "*Oneg Shabbos*"). All week long, when good and evil are blurred, one may be influenced in a negative sense by partaking of material pleasures. On Shabbos, a microcosm of the World to Come, when the distinctions between good and evil are restored, we may enjoy this most hallowed of days without jeopardizing our moral standing. (*Eikev* 5637)

◆§ Liberating the Soul from Material Constraints

ע״י מצות השבת שבטלים מכל מלאכה. מאיר הנפש ונמשך אחר מצות הבורא ית״ש. ונמצא ניתן השבת כדי להיות מנוחה אל הנפש מחשבות החמריות. ז״ש למען ינוח שורך כו׳. ובכל אשר אמרתי כו׳ תשמרו כו׳.

In an ideal environment, every one of Hashem's creations should instinctively follow its Creator. Yet, often, we defy the wishes of *HaKadosh Baruch Hu* and yield to the importunings of our body. It is only on Shabbos, a day when we abstain from physical *Melachah,* that the soul is liberated from all the material constraints imposed by the body, and is free to serve Hashem as it desires. Moreover, the increased role played by the soul impacts not only on our observance of Shabbos but on our performance of all the Torah's *mitzvos.* The essential theme of this *dvar Torah* — the dominance of the soul every Shabbos and the impact of Shabbos on all of Torah — may be homiletically derived from the juxtaposition of the following *pesukim*: שֵׁשֶׁת יָמִים תַּעֲשֶׂה מַעֲשֶׂיךָ וּבַיּוֹם הַשְּׁבִיעִי תִּשְׁבֹּת לְמַעַן יָנוּחַ שׁוֹרְךָ וַחֲמֹרֶךָ ... וּבְכֹל אֲשֶׁר אָמַרְתִּי אֲלֵיכֶם תִּשָּׁמֵרוּ, *Six days shall you accomplish your activities, and on the seventh day you shall desist, so that your ox and donkey may rest. Be careful regarding everything I said to you* (*Shemos* 23:12-13). By allowing our physical side — represented by the beasts of burden, the donkey and the ox[1] — to rest on Shabbos, we will merit to observe *all* of the Torah's *mitzvos.*

(*Mishpatim* 5657)

1. Note also the similarity between the term חֲמוֹר, *donkey,* and חָמְרִיּוּת meaning *materialism.*

Beyond Amalek's Reach

שבעשי׳ יש לו אחיזה. שכל בהפנימיות שהוא הקול יעקב אין לו שום מגע. והידים הם בחי׳ המעשים. אכן מצינו שבנ״י הקדימו נעשה לנשמע. וזה עצמו ענין הרמת הידים. כמו שיש נשיאית כפים. שהגם שהידים למטה מן הראש. מ״מ ע״י מסירת הנפש אליו ית׳. כענין שנאמר שאי אליו כפיך. יכולין לרומם הידים למעלה מהראש. וזה עצמו פי׳ הקדמת נעשה לנשמע כי אין הכוונה על הדיבור לבד שהקדימו נעשה לתיבת נשמע. רק מה שנמשכו במדבר אחר השי״ת קודם שקבלו התורה. זה עצמו הוא הקדמת נעשה לנשמע ... ולכן גם עתה בש״ק שיש לבנ״י כח הכתרים ממה שהקדימו נעשה לנשמע. ועם בש״ק עצמו שמבטלין בנ״י כל המעשים ושובתין מכל מלאכה הוא בחי׳ ירים משה ידו ולכן אין לו שום מגע בש״ק. ואז והי׳ בהניח כו׳ תמחה כו׳ זכר עמלק.

It is well-known that as long as Moshe was able to successfully lift up his hands, the Jewish people prevailed in their battle against Amalek (*Shemos* 17:11). Let us consider the significance of this move by Moshe and its association with *Shabbos Kodesh.*

Ordinarily, our hands are below our head. It took a great deal of effort on Moshe's part to maintain his hands above his head for a prolonged period. Extending the analogy, we note that hands symbolize the material world. Thus, Esav is depicted in the following terms, *The hands are those of Esav* (cf. *Bereishis* 27:22). By lifting one's hands above one's head, it indicates one's intention to elevate and consecrate the material world to the point where it is no longer dominated by Esav and his cohorts. Perhaps the very concept of *nesias kapayim* – when the *Kohanim* lift up their hands while blessing the Jewish people – reflects the same theme. Through the dedication of the *Kohanim,* who lift their hands above their heads, they are able to bless the Jewish people.[1]

When *Klal Yisrael* proclaimed *Naaseh V'Nishma,* "We will do and we will listen," they indicated their willingness to consecrate all of their material needs (described as *Naaseh,* "we will do") in the service of

1. It is significant that the *Kohanim* during the period of the *Beis HaMikdash* were not assigned a portion in the land of Israel. Their lives were intended to be based on spiritual values. As the *pasuk* states, ה׳ הוא נַחֲלָתוֹ, *HASHEM is their portion* (*Devarim* 18:2).

Hashem (*V'Nishma,* "we will listen/observe"). The entire theme of "lifting up one's hands" – elevating the material world in the service of Hashem – is expressed by Yirmiyahu, שְׂאִי אֵלָיו כַּפַּיִךְ, *lift up your palms [to Hashem]* (cf. *Eichah* 2:19). What better opportunity exists to lift up our hands to Hashem and to consecrate every aspect of the material world than *Shabbos Kodesh,* when we leave behind the material world and its thirty-nine forms of work. Every Shabbos, we replicate the spirit of Moshe who lifted up his hands and thus thwarted Amalek's deadly threat. Moreover (as stated in other segments of our commentary to *Sfas Emes*), every Shabbos the spirit of *Naaseh V'Nishma* is recreated. Every Shabbos, even the crowns that the Jewish people received when they proclaimed *Naaseh V'Nishma* (and forfeited when they worshipped the Golden Calf) are restored. Just as Moshe was able to fend off Amalek's threat as long as he could successfully lift up his hands, so too, every Shabbos when we simulate Moshe's action through our abandonment of the material world, we ensure that Amalek is unable to extend its influence. As the *pasuk* describing the *mitzvah* to eliminate Amalek insists: וְהָיָה בְּהָנִיחַ ה׳ אֱלֹהֶיךָ לְךָ מִכָּל אֹיְבֶיךָ מִסָּבִיב ... תִּמְחֶה אֶת זֵכֶר עֲמָלֵק, *It shall be that when* H*ASHEM*, *your God, gives you rest from all your enemies all around ... you shall wipe out the memory of Amalek* (*Devarim* 25:19). When Hashem will enable you to rest from the surface amenities of the material world, תִּמְחֶה אֶת זֵכֶר עֲמָלֵק, you will successfully erase any lingering memories of Amalek.

(*Parashas Zachor* 5647)

שבת יומא דזכירה. וע״י השבת זוכין בנ״י לזכירה. וכמו כן ע״י מחיית עמלק בא זכירה.

Let us reflect further on the relationship between Amalek and Shabbos, and the reason why Amalek's impact is greatly lessened on Shabbos. Remember that a major objective of Amalek is to lead *Klal Yisrael* to forget its loyalty to Torah and *mitzvos* and to cling to the material world. On Shabbos, however, a day known as an excellent opportunity to recall Torah (as the Torah describes the Shabbos day, זָכוֹר, *Remember the Shabbos day*),[1] Amalek fails in its mission to cause us to forget

1. Perhaps this can be interpreted homiletically, "Remember (זָכוֹר) the Torah through Shabbos."

Torah; as the Torah writes (ibid.), *you will erase the memory of Amalek ... you will not forget.* (Adapted from *Parashas Zachor* 5662)

✥ The Reward of Abstaining from *Melachah – Oneg Shabbos*

ואיתא לחם שמלאכי השרת אוכלין. דהמלאכים מיוחדים רק לשליחות הבורא יתברך לכן ניזונין מאתו ית׳. כי מלכותא דארעא כמלכותא דרקיע. וכמו שהמלך נותן מזונות לאנשי חילו כן בנ״י המיוחדים לתורת ה׳ כפי מה שעוסקין בו כך נמשך המזון שלהם ... ומעין זה בש״ק ששובתין בנ״י מכל מלאכה ועוסקין בתורה זוכין לעונג שבת שהוא מעין המן.

We conclude this chapter on *Melachah* by suggesting that those who abstain from *Melachah* merit to delight in the Shabbos day, a concept known as *Oneg Shabbos* (refer to our chapter on this topic). Just as a mortal king assumes responsibility for the physical needs (food, shelter) of those who are devoted to his service, so too (*l'havdil*), Hashem provided the Wilderness Generation – who were devoted full time to Divine Service – with His Sustenance, the manna. While we no longer enjoy the lofty level of those who enjoyed the manna, at least on Shabbos when we are removed from the material concerns of This World – as indicated by our abstention from *Melachah* – we partake of *Oneg Shabbos*, which resembles the manna. (*Beshalach* 5658)

Menuchah

In this chapter, we will discuss various aspects of the concept of *Menuchah,* beginning with the renowned comment of *Chazal,* מֶה הָיָה הָעוֹלָם חָסֵר? מְנוּחָה. בָּאת שַׁבָּת בָּאת מְנוּחָה. כָּלְתָה וְנִגְמְרָה הַמְּלָאכָה, *What was the universe lacking? Rest. When Shabbos came, rest came. The work was completed and finished"* (*Bereishis Rabbah* 10:9). We will endeavor to explain why the universe was not complete — despite its physical completion on the sixth day of Creation — until Hashem rested on Shabbos.

◆§ Perceiving the Universe in its Totality

כי הכלל לעולם מחובר בכח הפועל אם כי בפרט יש דברים שמתנגדים להקדושה. אבל בכלל נאמר הכל ברא לכבודו. ועל שם זה קודם שבת הי׳ עולם חסר מנוחה והוא השבת שכולל כל ימי השבוע ושבת דאתאחדת ברזא דאחד כו׳. שכל הדברים מתעלים ונעשין אחד מיוחדים להיות כלי להשי״ת לעשות בהם ברצונו. וז״ש ויכלו במד׳ שנעשה מעשה בראשית כלי.

It was only when Hashem ceased creating on the first Shabbos that one could perceive the entire universe as a complete entity. Any observer studying one aspect of Creation alone, might (ח״ו) be so impressed with the sheer magnificence of what Hashem created that he would forget about the Creator Himself. It was only when the first Shabbos arrived, and Hashem ceased to create, that one gained enough perspective to contemplate the universe in its entirety and perceive the Creator, as well as His creations. On Shabbos, the day that integrates every aspect of each of the Six Days of Creation in a unified and harmonious whole, we are able to behold the universe in its completed form, rather than merely examine any of its individual parts. As the author of the כְּגַוְנָא prayer (*Zohar, Terumah* 163:2, recited by many during the Friday evening service) writes, דְּאִתְאַחֲדַת בְּרָזָא דְאֶחָד, *(Shabbos is the day that the universe became) unified through the secret of Hashem Who is One* (refer to our chapter on *tefillos* of Shabbos). In other words, on Shabbos when Hashem ceased creating — the moment when the concept of *Menuchah* emerged — the universe reached its pinnacle and accomplished its purpose by becoming a perfect means through which mankind could find Hashem. As we recite at the beginning of the *Kiddush* every Friday evening, וַיְכֻלּוּ הַשָּׁמַיִם וְהָאָרֶץ, *Thus the heaven and earth were finished* (*Bereishis* 2:1), which may be (homiletically) interpreted that heaven and earth, once completed, became a *keli*, a receptacle and perfect vehicle for the sanctification of Hashem's Name. (Adapted from *Bereishis* 5631)

ולכן נק׳ השבת שלום שהוא תכלית הבריאה. כמ״ש מה הי׳ העולם חסר מנוחה בא שבת נגמרה המלאכה. ולכן נקראו בנ״י השולמית שהם כלי לקבל אותה הנקודה.

Utilizing this approach, we can appreciate why the Shabbos day is called *Shalom* in the *Zohar* (*Zohar, Korach* 3:176b). It was only when the first Shabbos arrived and heaven and earth were completed that the universe reached the state of *sheleimus* (perfection), a concept related to *shalom*.[1] Similarly, the Jewish people are described as *Shulamis* (cf. *Shir HaShirim* 7:1) since they are the perfect receptacle for the *berachos* that flow from the *sheleimus* of Shabbos.[2] (*Beshalach* 5648)

1. Editor's Note: שְׁלֵמוּת and שָׁלוֹם share the same *shoresh* ש-ל-ם; refer to our chapter on "*Shabbos Shalom.*"

2. Despite the lack of *sheleimus* that existed prior to the first Shabbos, the Torah nonetheless utilizes the expression טוֹב מְאֹד, *very good,* to describe the universe's status at the completion of the Six Days of Creation. This accolade may have been earned on the basis of *hachanah,* preparation. Once the material world has been completed — and only the Divine blessing of Shabbos' *Menuchah* is lacking — it is appropriate to describe the completion of Hashem's preparation for Shabbos as being "very good."

וכמו כן בשבת שמתאחדין כל הברואים שורה עליו ברכה ז״ש וינח ביום השביעי על כן ברך כו׳. פי׳ מנוחה הוא חיבור הכל להיות דבר שלם ועי״ז הוא כלי מחזיק ברכה והוא יסוד ובסיס וכן להיות שורה עליו הברכה וז״ש על כן ברך.

This approach, which suggests that when Hashem rested on Shabbos the universe could be perceived as an integrated whole rather than as fragmented parts, helps us to appreciate the juxtaposition of two seemingly dissimilar components of a *pasuk* that is recited in the *Kiddush* for Shabbos morning. The Torah states, וַיָּנַח בַּיּוֹם הַשְּׁבִיעִי עַל כֵּן בֵּרַךְ ה׳ אֶת יוֹם הַשַּׁבָּת, *He rested on the seventh day. Therefore,* H*ASHEM blessed the Sabbath day* (*Shemos* 20:11). At first sight, there seems to be no relationship between Hashem resting on Shabbos and His blessings for this day. However, one assumes that as a result of the process of Creation coming to an end on Shabbos, one can now perceive a harmonious universe in its totality. We can therefore appreciate why it was only on Shabbos that Hashem could bless His universe. It is only as a דָּבָר שָׁלֵם, a completed and unified entity, that the world deserves Hashem's *berachos.* As long as we are dealing with a fragmented part of a larger picture, it is inappropriate to receive His *berachos.* By ceasing to create on Shabbos, Hashem enabled a unified world to emerge, a world that was then blessed by Him. (Adapted from *Beha'aloscha* 5639)

A Double Creation – עשיה ומנוחה

בפסוק ששת ימים עשה כו׳ וינח ביום הז׳. לא כ׳ ונח. ויתכן לפרש כמו ששת ימי המעשה הם כוחות הבריאה לעשות תולדות לקיום הבריאה. כן יום השבת הנותן מנוחה לכל הבריאה ולימי המעשה. וששת ימים שם הש״י אותם כלים לעשי׳. ויום הז׳ למנוחה. כמ״ש רש״י בפ׳ בראשית הי׳ עולם חסר מנוחה באת שבת נגמרה המלאכה ע״ש. ושורש מנוחת ש״ק הוא התאחדות הבריאה. ועי״ז הוא כלי מחזיק ברכה. וינח ע״כ ברך ויקדשהו. הם בחי׳ יחוד קדושה וברכה וכ״כ וישבות כו׳ ויברך ויקדש.

While we generally assume that Hashem rested on Shabbos from His creation of the universe, in this *dvar Torah* we propose that the process of Creation continued on Shabbos. As *Rashi* (to *Bereishis* 2:2) notes, מֶה הָיָה הָעוֹלָם חָסֵר? מְנוּחָה, *What was the universe lacking? Rest.* בָּאת שַׁבָּת בָּאת מְנוּחָה כָּלְתָה וְנִגְמְרָה הַמְּלָאכָה, *When Shabbos came* (and Hashem rested) *rest came. The work was completed and finished* (then the process of Creation was completed). Our contention that the world was sustained and derives its sense of "equilibrium" as a result of Hashem's resting on Shabbos, as well His Creation during the Six Days of Creation, is also supported by the justification given in the Fourth Commandment for observing Shabbos: כִּי שֵׁשֶׁת יָמִים עָשָׂה ... וַיָּנַח בַּיּוֹם הַשְּׁבִיעִי, *because in six days [Hashem] created (heaven and earth) and He rested on the seventh day* (*Shemos* 20:11). Rather than say, וְנָח בַּיּוֹם הַשְּׁבִיעִי, *and rested on the seventh day* (which would be merely a historical account of what occurred immediately after Creation), the Torah writes, וַיָּנַח בַּיּוֹם הַשְּׁבִיעִי, *and He rested on the seventh day*, suggesting another reason for observing Shabbos — the creation of an entirely different entity, *Menuchah.*

We may deduce from the foregoing citations that the universe is being supported and balanced on an ongoing basis by twin pillars — by active creation (עֲשִׂיָּה) and by cessation from creation (מְנוּחָה). Just as all that man creates is derived from Hashem's active creation during the Six Days of Creation, so too, the *Menuchah* that is equally necessary to sustain the universe ensues from Hashem's resting on that first Shabbos.

(*Yisro* 5646).

☙ Thwarting *Mazikin* ("Demons") Through *Sheleimus*

אך הקב״ה הוא שלימות העולם. וזה בחי׳ ש״ק שנק׳ שלום כידוע בזוה״ק בע״ש ביה״ש נבראו מזיקין ורצו לשלוט בעולם רק שהקב״ה השפיע קדושת ש״ק ונשבתו המזיקין. והיינו שסוף ימי המעשה הוא בחסרון שחסר השלימות. וע״ז אמרו מה הי׳ העולם חסר מנוחה פי׳ השלימות ובא שבת והשלים.

In light of our assertion in the previous *dvar Torah* that the universe was lacking a sense of *sheleimus* until the advent of Shabbos' *Menuchah,* we can better appreciate the *Mishnah* (*Avos* 5:6) stating that the *mazikin* (demons) were created on *erev Shabbos.* It is only in a void, which best describes the status of the universe at the temination of the Six Days of Creation, that these forces of evil can lurk. Had Shabbos and its overwhelming sense of *Menuchah* not interrupted the progress of these evil forces, these *mazikin* would never have been checked and their capacity for harm would have wreaked great havoc. However, their proliferation was stunted by the advent of the *sheleimus* that Shabbos and its sense of *Menuchah* brought. With the creation of Shabbos, the universe returned to its roots (a theme to be explored in subsequent *divrei Torah*). Instead of finding a void in which they could have thrived, these demons perceived a universe whose beginning and end were inexorably linked, a universe of true *sheleimus*, true perfection. As a result, when the first Shabbos arrived, the *mazikin's* capacity to do harm was thwarted. (*Korach* 5636)

☙ Closure Can Only Be Attained With Hashem's Help

כי הקב״ה עושה שלום בעולם שנה נפש. שיש בכל מקום נטיעות מיוחדים לאותו מקום. וארץ ישראל בכח ביהמ״ק היתה עושה כל מינים כמ״ש לא תחסר כל בה. ובזמן כל יום כו׳ והשבת עושה שלום. ובנפשות בנ״י מקבלין השלימות. ובשבת קודש מתאספין כל הג׳ כמ״ש הפורס סוכת שלום עלינו ועל ירושלים.

We noted that previously it was only through the first Shabbos and its creation of *Menuchah* that the universe attained *sheleimus*. Elaborating upon this theme, we realize that this sense of closure and completion cannot be achieved through human effort alone. It was only when Hashem proclaimed an end to the process of Creation that the universe attained perfection. In fact, to achieve true closure, one requires a series of favorable conditions, including the ideal time, the appropriate location and the nation that is most appreciative and deserving of Hashem's intervention in the universe. It is only on Shabbos that *Klal Yisrael*, residing in Yerushalayim (under ideal circumstances), the city graced by the *Shechinah's* Presence, can enjoy *sheleimus*. As we emphasize in the Friday evening *tefillos* of Shabbos, הַפּוֹרֵשׂ סֻכַּת שָׁלוֹם עָלֵינוּ וְעַל

כָּל עַמּוֹ יִשְׂרָאֵל וְעַל יְרוּשָׁלָיִם, *He spreads the shelter of peace* (and *sheleimus*) *over us* (every Shabbos) *and over all His people Israel and over Jerusalem.* (*Korach* 5651)

☙ Resting Even Without Feeling a Sense of Closure

מנוחת אהבה ונדבה כו' אמת ואמונה כו'. כי לכל איש ישראל יש מנוחה בשבת וחירות משיעבוד היצה"ר כל ימות השבוע וזה זכר ליצ"מ בשבת. והוא חלק מעוה"ב כמ"ש ז"ל. אך מי שאינו זוכה להרגיש המנוחה צריך להיות בדרך נדבה שיתנדב כמו מלאכתו עשוי' בעבור רצון הקב"ה וז"ש וכבדתו כו'. ועי"ז זוכה להיות מנוחת אמת ואמונה שיוכל להאמין באמת שיש לו ג"כ מנוחה בש"ק. וע"י האמונה יזכה להיות נגלה אליו כמ"ש מנוחת שלום כו' שלימה שאתה רוצה.

In the previous *dvar Torah* we noted that it is possible through the *Menuchah* of Shabbos *Kodesh* to attain closure. However, at times, as Shabbos arrives, one simply does not perceive that his objectives for the past week have been fulfilled. In fact, we may feel that we are still engaged in combat against the *yetzer hara* that dominates our *avodas Hashem* of the weekdays. Despite that lack of spiritual satisfaction, we rest and desist from *melachah*. This concept — resting from the challenges and struggles of the week despite our perceived lack of apparent accomplishments — is alluded to in the *Minchah Shemoneh Esrei* of Shabbos where we describe Shabbos as a day of מְנוּחַת אַהֲבָה וּנְדָבָה, *a rest of love and magnanimity* — it is a day when we cease working out of sheer love of *HaKadosh Baruch Hu*, and as a day of "generous rest." To rest generously and to rest out of love for Hashem, even though we do not necessarily experience a true feeling of *sheleimus*, is the essence of מְנוּחַת אַהֲבָה וּנְדָבָה. In a similar vein, *Chazal* encourage us to feel that when Shabbos arrives, it is as if all of our work was performed. This too may reflect our belief that despite our personal lack of fulfillment, we nonetheless rest out a sense of devotion and love for *HaKadosh Baruch Hu*. (Refer to our chapter on *Melachah* for further discussion of this *Chazal*.) As Yeshayahu implores us, וְכִבַּדְתּוֹ מֵעֲשׂוֹת דְּרָכֶיךָ, *Honor Him by ceasing from performing your activities* (58:13). In other words, rest — despite your lack of fulfillment — out of honor for Hashem.

Such a magnanimous approach to Shabbos — resting even when we don't feel rested — is rewarded as we proceed to another phase of *avodas Hashem* when we attain the spiritual level where we finally can perceive the *sheleimus* of Shabbos. As the *Minchah tefillah* continues, מְנוּחַת אֱמֶת וֶאֱמוּנָה, *a rest of truth and faith.* Eventually, we will attain the *madreigah* (spiritual level) whereby we truly believe and know that we deserve to rest on Shabbos. Eventually, a sense of closure and *sheleimus* replaces the feeling of spiritual inadequacy that marked our initial efforts at *Menuchah.* But as the *tefillah* implies, there is yet another phase of resting on Shabbos that we are bound to enjoy — מְנוּחַת שָׁלוֹם וְשַׁלְוָה ... מְנוּחָה שְׁלֵמָה שֶׁאַתָּה רוֹצֶה בָּהּ, *a rest of peace and harmony ... a perfect rest in which You find favor.* This level of *Menuchah* is one of true *sheleimus* to the extent that Hashem accepts and derives satisfaction from our rest. Thus, the prayers of Shabbos allude to three phases of our *Menuchah*: First, נְדָבָה, resting without a feeling a sense of accomplishment. Second, מְנוּחַת אֱמֶת וֶאֱמוּנָה, coming to the level of appreciating our *Menuchah*, and finally, מְנוּחָה שְׁלֵמָה שֶׁאַתָּה רוֹצֶה בָּהּ, a feeling that Hashem appreciates and accepts our rest. (*Eikev* 5631)

◆§ Consequences of the Creation of *Menuchah:* *Achdus* (Unity) and *Shalom*

כי בששת ימי בראשית נברא בכל יום ענין מיוחד לא ראי זה כראי זה. אך השבת הוא הכולל כל הימים והוא כלי מחזיק ברכה ע"י שיש בו האחדות לכן הוא קיום כל הימים כדאיתא באת שבת באת מנוחה ונגמרה המלאכה כי אם אין שלום אין כלום.

By creating Shabbos and its environment of *Menuchah,* Hashem infused His universe with the stability to persevere. To appreciate this statement, we recall the *maamar Chazal* stating that there is no better source of *berachah* than *shalom* (*Uktzin* 3:12). It is only the completed and harmoniously unified universe (the concept of *achdus*), resulting from the creation of Shabbos *Menuchah,* that is truly imbued with the attributes of *shalom* and *sheleimus.* It was only after the first Shabbos that the universe derived the capacity to endure. (*Korach* 5647)

◆§ Coexisting With One's Antagonists

וכן הוא בפנימיות כל ימי המעשה יש לכל יום ענין
מיוחד ולכן שבת השלים העולם שהי' חסר מנוחה שהוא
בחי' אהבה בסופה ואז נעשה שלום וכתיב אח"כ אלה
תולדות השמים והארץ ע"ש.

Expanding upon the theme of *achdus* mentioned in the previous *dvar Torah,* we suggest that as a result of the *Menuchah* that the world gained with the advent of Shabbos, we also derived the ability to coexist and respect those who are our antagonists. Just as the universe was not complete until the unique characteristics of each day of Creation were merged into an intact whole that first Shabbos, so too, every individual, while entitled to advocate his own opinion, is also obligated to respect the views of his anatagonists. He also should acknowledge that they are entitled to maintain their unique perspective. As *Chazal* note, the inevitable result of a true *machlokes l'shem Shamayim* is *shalom,* genuine peace and understanding. This capacity to merge dissenting opinions into a unified whole that serves the interests of the greater community is derived from the first Shabbos. In fact, it is only after the first Shabbos that the Torah writes, אֵלֶּה תוֹלְדוֹת הַשָּׁמַיִם וְהָאָרֶץ, *These are the products (generations) of the heaven and the earth* (*Bereishis* 2:4). It was only after the universe experienced the calming and unifying effect of Shabbos that it could be assured of its future stability and endure.

(*Korach* 5651)

◆§ Returning to the Universe's Roots

ופי׳ ויכלו מלשון כלתה נפשי כי הוא הביטול שכל דבר מתבטל לנקודה חיות שיש בהם מהשי״ת. וזהו נק׳ מנוחה שהיא שביתות הכל ומקום ושורש הכל. ועל בחי׳ זו נאמר הוא מקומו של עולם וכמ״ש אל יצא איש ממקומו ביום השביעי כו׳. וזה כלתה ונגמרה המלאכה כי זה מכוון הבריאה.

אשר ברא לעשות פי׳ שנתן הש״י כח בהנבראים לפעול כ״ד. פעולתו. אש לשרוף. אילן לצמוח. וגם בב״ח להיות לו הבחירה לעשות כרצונו. ועכ״ז הי׳ המכוון שידע כל פעול כי הוא ית׳ הנותן לו הכח אף שעושה מעצמו הוא כגרזן ביד החוצב. וזה הי׳ המכוון הבריאה רק לבחי׳ שבת. וזש״כ תכלית שמים וארץ. וזש״כ רש״י ז״ל הי׳ עולם חסר מנוחה שהיא השבה וחזרת הכל לשורשו ונשלם בשבת עיקר הרצון בהבריאה ...

ובש״ק מחזיר כל הבריאה להכלל זה בזה עד הש״י שמעידין הכל על הסיבה הראשונה. וזה פי׳ ויכלו שנעשין כלי אחד לכבודו ית׳. וזש״כ מה חסר מנוחה שתכלית הפעולות הוא הביטול שאח״כ לחזור לשורשו.

Extending this concept, we suggest that the *Menuchah* that the universe attained that first Shabbos — and that is subsequently enjoyed every Shabbos — is, in actuality, a return to the universe's original roots. Just as when Hashem created the universe, it was abundantly clear that there was no entity other than Him, so too, on that first Shabbos when the completed universe emerged, it became clear again that it was Hashem who had masterminded every detail of Creation. In fact, the term וַיְכֻלּוּ (which in the first *dvar Torah* of this chapter was related to *keli,* that heaven and earth became a perfect receptacle through which mankind would discover the *Shechinah*) may also be associated with the expression כְּלוֹת הַנֶּפֶשׁ, *the soul yearns for the Shechinah.* After a week of creation, in which the individual elements of Creation emerged, the completed world yearns to negate itself to its Creator. It is this concept of *bitul* (negating itself to its Creator) that may be the basis of the *Menuchah* of Shabbos. As each aspect of the completed universe seeks to negate itself to its Creator, the universe, in turn, returns to its true roots. Utilizing this approach, we may derive new meaning from the *pasuk*, אַל יֵצֵא אִישׁ מִמְּקֹמוֹ בַּיּוֹם הַשְּׁבִיעִי, *Let no man leave his place on the seventh day* (*Shemos* 16:29), a reference not only to the prohibition of walking beyond the city limits or carrying four cubits in a public thoroughfare on Shabbos, but also to the requirement that every Shabbos we return to Hashem Who is known as הַמָּקוֹם, *"the Place"* (the Root and Sole Source) of the universe.

Expanding upon this theme, we recall that when Hashem created the universe, He enabled each of His Creations to function autonomously. For example, fire enjoys the capacity to burn, trees are able to sprout and grow, and above all, man enjoys the capacity of free will. As the Torah writes, אֲשֶׁר בָּרָא אֱלֹהִים לַעֲשׂוֹת, *which God created to make* (*Bereishis* 2:3) – Hashem created the universe in a manner so that His creations can create on their own. It would be tempting, but also a tragic mistake, to assume that because these entities are able to operate by themselves that they are no longer dependent upon their Creator for their continued existence. On Shabbos, when Hashem ceased the process of Creation, He made it clear that *all* that exists is dependent upon His Will for its continued existence. While it may appear that individual entities are able to function independently, in reality their role can be compared to an ax wielded by an individual who is chopping wood. Just as the ax only operates at the behest and direction of whoever is manipulating it, so too, the entire universe only operates at the direction and to fulfill the objectives of its Creator. This theme is reinforced every time we observe Shabbos, the day when the universe returns to its roots and its True Source and Creator. In fact, we may argue that the purpose of all of Creation is not what may be accomplished by all of Hashem's creations but rather the Shabbos, the day when all of His creations negate themselves to their Creator. As we recite every Friday evening, תַּכְלִית מַעֲשֵׂה שָׁמַיִם וָאָרֶץ – the Shabbos is the objective of the entire creation of heaven and earth.[1] (*Bereishis* 5631, 5632, 5635)

1. Just as every Shabbos the universe returns to its roots, so too, every time we perform a *mitzvah* both the individual and the object or the milieu associated with the *mitzvah* are also able to return to their spiritual core (*Shelach* 5638).

◆§ Revelation of the Universe's Inner Spirituality

וזה עצמו השבת שהוא סהדותא ובו נפתח השורש הפנימית והאמת. וזה עיקר המנוחה שבאין אל שורש הפנימיות. וז״ש ונחך ה׳ תמיד כו׳ והיית כגן רוה וכמוצא מים כו׳ ובשבת באין לזאת המנוחה ונעשין כמוצא מים אשר לא יכזבו מימיו.

Elaborating further on the theme of בָּאת שַׁבָּת בָּאת מְנוּחָה (*when Shabbos came, rest came*), we suggest that while we all possess an inner core of spirituality (פְּנִימִיּוּת), often this aspect of our personality is obscured by the sheer magnitude of the materialism that pervades This World. It is only on Shabbos, a day when *Klal Yisrael* is immersed in Torah, that this inner dimension of spirituality can emerge. What greater sense of *Menuchah* can there be than this comparative respite from the struggle against evil that we must engage in all week long. When Yeshayahu writes, ... וְנָחֲךָ ה׳ תָּמִיד וְהָיִיתָ כְּגַן רָוֶה וּכְמוֹצָא מַיִם אֲשֶׁר לֹא יְכַזְּבוּ מֵימָיו, *Then* H*ASHEM* *will guide you always and you will be like a well-watered garden and a source of water whose waters will never fail* (58:11), he may have been alluding to the inner beauty and *kedushah* that emerges on Shabbos. Every Shabbos, we are able to elicit the deepest sources of "water" and we can rest assured that this inner source of spirituality will never dry. (Adapted from *Chukas* 5650)

וזה ענין באה שבת באה מנוחה. וכמו שהי׳ בשבת בראשית כן הוא תמיד שכל מה שמתהוה בימי המעשה חסר השלימות. כי עולם הטבעי הוא חסר. וכשבא שבת חל השלימות על הכל ונעשין כלים להיות מוכן להקדושה כנ״ל.

To appreciate the full extent of the spiritual dimension that Shabbos brings, let us return to the very first Shabbos. When the universe was created during the Six Days of Creation, despite the majesty of Hashem's creations, there was still a void. True *sheleimus* (perfection) could only be attained with the advent of Shabbos. This was true for the first Shabbos of Creation and it is equally valid for every subsequent Shabbos. It is only on Shabbos that the universe, as well as *Klal Yisrael*, reaches its full potential, becoming a *keli*, a receptacle for *kedushah*. (*Emor* 5648)

Returning to One's Own Roots

פי׳ זה כי ענין המנוחה הוא במקום השורש כשאדם דבוק בשורשו ששם מקום מנוחתו אין לו שום יגיעה כי כל מה שעובר עליו הכל אחד וגם אצלו נמשך תמיד אחר יראת ה׳ א״כ יש לו מנוחה כמ״ש כל המקבל עליו ע״ת מעבירין ממנו ע״מ ועול ד״א.

Just as the universe returns to its roots, so too, the concept of *Menuchah* also implies that every individual Jew can return to his own roots (שֹׁרֶשׁ) on Shabbos. While involved in the challenges of daily life during the six weekdays, a Jew often must wage a struggle against all those forces that would prevent him from serving Hashem properly. However, on Shabbos, a day dedicated to *Menuchah*, the Jew is able to achieve peace of mind and face all these challenges with equanimity, resting assured that all that happens to him is the will of Hashem. On Shabbos, the Jew returns to his Torah-based roots.[1] Having done so, he is sure of accomplishing effortlessly what would require a great deal of effort during the week. As *Pirkei Avos* reminds us, "Anyone who accepts the yoke (commitment) of Torah, will merit that the yoke of the government (oppressive taxation and other evil decrees) and of earning a livelihood will be removed from him" (3:6). While the theme of this *mishnah* is true all week long, it is on Shabbos that we can especially appreciate a sense of relief from the world's challenges.

(Adapted from *Noach* 5631)

וז״ש איש על דגלו כו׳ יחנו בנ״י. פי׳ זאת יהי׳ עיקר המנוחה מה שמתקשרין כל אחד במקום שורשו להיות מרכבה לבוראם.

To corroborate our assertion that the ultimate *Menuchah* lies in returning to our roots, we cite the Torah's description of the Jewish people's

1. Using this approach, we gain insight into the *Zohar's* comment that Noach represented the ideal of Shabbos. Just as every Shabbos the Jew returns to his roots, so too, Noach who is described as an אִישׁ צַדִּיק, *a righteous man* (*Bereishis* 6:9) was always able to cling to his spiritual roots.

habitat in the Wilderness: אִישׁ עַל דִּגְלוֹ ... יַחֲנוּ, *every man camped by his banner* (*Bamidbar* 2:2) — the flag that was borne by each tribe attested to its history and its distinctiveness. It is only by returning to one's own banner (roots) that we can truly "camp" — and rest — secure in the knowledge that we have found our spiritual bearings. This process occurs every Shabbos as we rest and "reconnect" with our spiritual origins.

(*Bamidbar* 5638)

והוא בחי׳ שבת שנק׳ שלום בכח הנשמה יתירה שמתדבק האדם לשורשו ומקומו לכן נק׳ יום מנוחה ושמחה.
הנני נותן כו׳ בריתי שלום. כי חתימת אות ברית קודש נק׳ שלום כמו שבת שנק׳ שלום כי השלמת הבריאה הי׳ בו כמ״ש מה הי׳ העולם חסר מנוחה באת שבת כו׳.

According to the *Zohar*, Shabbos is also known as *Shalom*. There can be no greater sense of *sheleimus*, closure and inner serenity, than on Shabbos when every individual returns to his roots.

(*Pinchas* 5645, 5651)

שייך זכירה רק בדבר שכבר השיגו פעם אחת. ולכן כיון שבעת קבלת התורה הי׳ בהתגלות בחי׳ השבת צוה אותם לזכור זאת תמיד.

By returning to our roots every Shabbos, we are, in effect, returning to the Giving of the Torah as well. When Hashem said, אָנֹכִי ה׳ אֱלֹהֶיךָ, *I am HASHEM your God*, every Jew actually perceived the Divine Spark that He had implanted within *Klal Yisrael's* hearts and souls. At that extraordinary moment, every Jew felt themselves returning to their roots — to the Divine Presence in their midst. This process occurs every Shabbos when we find ourselves returning to our spiritual essence.

Utilizing this approach, we gain new insight into the *pasuk* prefacing the Fourth Commandment, זָכוֹר אֶת יוֹם הַשַּׁבָּת לְקַדְּשׁוֹ, *Remember the Shabbos day to sanctify it* (*Shemos* 20:8). (Refer to *The Three Festivals*, p. 255, for further discussion of this *pasuk*.) The term *zachor*, *remember*, implies that the Jewish people had previously experienced something similar to the sanctity of Shabbos, an allusion to *Matan Torah* when every Jew felt himself returning to his spiritual essence just as we do on Shabbos. In this commandment, Hashem is pleading with us every Shabbos to recall the day of *Matan Torah* (which also occurred on Shabbos) and to reconnect with our roots as we did then. (*Shavuos* 5638)

☙ The Roots of Everything that was Created

שבתותי תשמורו כו׳. לשון רבים. כי יש בכל דבר חיות משבת קודש והיא הנקודה המשלמת הכל כמ״ש רש״י ז״ל ויכל אלקים ביום השביעי שבשבת נגמר המלאכה כו׳. הפי׳ כנ״ל ששבת משלים כל דבר. והוא הגמר והקיום של כל דבר שהוא שורש החיות. ובשבת קודש מתעורר שורש זה בכל דבר. ולכך נק׳ מנוחה שמחזיר כל דבר לשורשו.

In the previous *divrei Torah* we suggested that the universe, as well as each individual Jew, returns to its roots on Shabbos. Exploring this concept further, we propose that not only the entire universe but also every entity created by man during the weekdays is dependent upon Shabbos' *Menuchah* for its continued viability. When Hashem rested on the first Shabbos, He not only ceased creating, but also through this very act of cessation established the universe on a firm and lasting foundation – as the *pasuk* relates, וַיְכַל אֱלֹהִים בַּיּוֹם הַשְּׁבִיעִי מְלַאכְתּוֹ אֲשֶׁר עָשָׂה, *God completed on the seventh day His work which He had done* (*Bereishis* 2:2). Similarly, all our efforts expended during the six workdays are inspired and validated when we rest on Shabbos. Extending this concept further, we note that just as the universe returned to its spiritual roots on the first Shabbos when Hashem rested from His Creation, so too, everything that we create returns to its heavenly roots – the spark of *kedushah* that it contains – on Shabbos. And it is through this Divine Imprint that the material world, including every element that man creates to "enhance" the universe, is sustained.

(Adapted from *Ki Sisa* 5633)

⸎ Roots of Everything Spiritual

וביום השבת עולין כל המעשים לפי עבודת האדם בימי המעשה. לכן שבת יום מנוחה גם בעבודת הבורא ית׳. כי כמה נפילות יש גם לצדיק כמ״ש שבע יפול צדיק וקם וע״י יום השבת שאין בו מגע נכרי כמ״ש ביני ובין בני ישראל אות הוא כדאיתא בגמרא שניתן בצנעא ונק׳ מתנה בבית גנזי. שאף שנמסר לבנ״י מ״מ הוא בדרך גניזה והסתר.

Whereas in the previous *dvar Torah* we suggested that every material entity created by man rests and returns to its spiritual roots on Shabbos, we now extend this approach and maintain that many of our spiritual acomplishments are also rooted in Shabbos. While a *tzaddik* may struggle all week long, pursued by the *yetzer hara* and every obstacle that seeks to deter him in his *avodas Hashem,* once Shabbos arrives he finds a measure of relief. As Shlomo writes, כִּי שֶׁבַע יִפּוֹל צַדִּיק וָקָם, *For though the righteous one may fall seven times, he will arise* (*Mishlei* 24:16). All of his spiritual endeavors, as difficult as they may be, reach fruition on the day of rest, *Shabbos Kodesh,* when even the *yetzer hara* ceases to torment him. On Shabbos, everything – not only our physical existence but also our spiritual initiatives – returns to its roots. Just as Hashem rested on the first Shabbos, so too, the *tzaddik,* having held firm against the importuning of the *yetzer hara* all week long, rests assured that his accomplishments are secure once Shabbos arrives. Perhaps the reason for this respite from the *yetzer hara* that the *tzaddik* enjoys every Shabbos is as follows: The Shabbos was originally given in an environment so intimate and private that it was barely perceived by the *yetzer hara* or any other force inimical to Torah. As the Torah writes, בֵּינִי וּבֵין בְּנֵי יִשְׂרָאֵל אוֹת הִיא לְעֹלָם, *Between Me and the Children of Israel it is a sign forever* (*Shemos* 31:17). Similarly, *Chazal* (*Shabbos* 10b) describe Shabbos as a gift that was granted to *Klal Yisrael* in an environment of complete privacy, so that no other nation was even aware of its full impact and the reward granted to those who observe this extraordinary day. It is when the treasured teachings of Torah are exposed to the world at large that we incur the risk of being challenged by forces that are opposed to the Torah. (Adapted from *Parah* 5639)

Returning to Our Roots in *Olam Haba*

כי השבת הוא מעין עוה״ב ... והוא נק׳ מנוחה שהוא עיקר שרשן של בנ״י.

Continuing our discussion of the relationship between *Menuchah* and returning to our spiritual roots every Shabbos, we suggest that *Klal Yisrael's* true roots lie in the World to Come. Whereas our existence in This World is purely transient and temporary, it is only on Shabbos, which is a microcosm of the World to Come (*Berachos* 57b – refer to our chapter on "*Mei'ain Olam Haba*"), that *Klal Yisrael* finds its roots and enjoys true *Menuchah*. (*Pesach* 5655)

A Day of Infinity

מצדם אשר לא יספר בחי׳ השורש והמנוחה בחינת השבת מעין עוה״ב דאיתא וייצר ב׳ יצירות. יצירה בעוה״ב ובש״ק מתגלה זאת. ויש להם ג״כ בחי׳ מספר כדי להעלות כל המספרים והטבע שהם במדה והמספר. וע״ז מיוסד כל חומש הפקודים ...

In light of the previous *divrei Torah* in which we asserted that on Shabbos, we (as well as the universe) return to our roots, we can now appreciate a renowned *pasuk*, וְהָיָה מִסְפַּר בְּנֵי יִשְׂרָאֵל כְּחוֹל הַיָּם אֲשֶׁר לֹא יִמַּד וְלֹא יִסָּפֵר, *Yet the number of the Children of Israel will be like the sand of sea which can neither be measured nor counted* (*Hosea* 2:1). There is an obvious question here – the *pasuk* first implies that *Klal Yisrael* does consist of a finite number (מִסְפָּר) of individuals which can be counted, and then immediately afterwards seemingly contradicts itself by saying that we are infinite like the sand of the sea. We suggest that the first segment of the *pasuk* is referring to the weekdays in which *Klal Yisrael* is living within the natural world (*teva*). In such an environment, our sacred task is to consecrate the natural world with all of its finite parameters and dimensions. In fact, an entire *sefer* of the Torah, *Bamidar*, also known as *Chumash HaPekudim*, the segment discussing numbers, is devoted to the count of the Jewish people. However, on Shabbos, when *Klal Yisrael* (as well as the universe) returns to its sacred roots, we leave behind This World with its finite dimensions and proceed toward the infinite *Olam Haba*. What greater source of *Menuchah* — of true spiritual respite — than yielding a finite universe for a world of boundless spiritual potential. (*Bamidbar* 5641)

◈ A Weekly Renewal of the *Menuchah* Concept

ותקנו בקידוש היום זכרון למעשה בראשית. והענין כי בראשית ברא את השמים ואת הארץ הוא מאמר אחד הכולל כל הבריאה והוא שורש הבריאה הדבוק בראשית ואח״כ דכתיב והארץ היתה תהו התחילו ששת ימי המעשה ומאמר הראשון הוא חופף על הבריאה ומזה המאמר נמשך ברכה וקיום אל הבריאה ... וזה זכרון למעשה בראשית הוא המאמר של בראשית ויברך את יום השביעי ויקדש אותו פי׳ להיות קדוש ונבדל מן הזמן ... ואיתא מחדש בטובו בכל יום מעשה בראשית ויש נוסחאות שאין אומרים ביוצר של שבת המחדש בטובו מעשה בראשית. אבל באמת יש לאמרו כי כמו שבכל יום מתחדש מעשה בראשית כן בשבת קודש מתחדש זה השורש של מעשה בראשית כמ״ש.

Every Shabbos the universe returns to its roots — to the very beginning of Creation (בְּרֵאשִׁית בָּרָא אֱלֹהִים) when Hashem's Presence was visible amidst all of the turmoil (תֹהוּ וָבֹהוּ) that prevailed before the process of Creation commenced. In this light, the expression utilized in *Kiddush*, זִכָּרוֹן לְמַעֲשֵׂה בְרֵאשִׁית, *a remembrance of Creation*, attains new meaning: Every Shabbos we return to the beginning of the Creation, to the time described by the Torah as בְּרֵאשִׁית בָּרָא אֱלֹהִים, *in the beginning of God's creating*.

According to some versions, the phrase הַמְחַדֵּשׁ בְּטוּבוֹ מַעֲשֵׂה בְרֵאשִׁית, *He Who renews in His Goodness the process*, was deleted on Shabbos since Hashem rested rather than created on this day. However, we suggest that every Shabbos, Hashem renews the concept of *Menuchah*. Just as the universe returned to its roots on the first Shabbos, so too, every Shabbos the same sense of return and renewal is experienced by us.

(*Bereishis* 5655)

◆§ The Guarantor of the Universe's Continued Existence

וביאור הענין כי באמת בשבת לא הי' שום בריאה רק שביתה. ושביתה זו היא קיום כל הברואים דכ' והחיות רצוא ושוב פי' שכל מקבל צריך להיות בטל אל הנותן ולפי דביקות שיש לו להמשפיע כמו כן קבלתו מתקיימת ולכן בשבת שנתעלו כל הנבראים לשורשם שע"י במנוחה נתברר שיש עליהם אדון מושל. שברצותו מרחיב וברצותו מקצר זה עצמו הוא גמר הבריאה ותיקונו...

While we generally assume that when Hashem rested the process of Creation ceased, it is also true that the universe's continued existence is totally contingent upon the Shabbos. When *Chazal* refer to the Shabbos rest as being the completion of the universe, they may be referring to the fact that the universe would not be able to continue to exist without the rest of Shabbos.

To elucidate this concept, we draw the analogy to a recipient of a gift, who, if he is truly appreciative develops a close relationship with his benefactor. By doing so, he ensures that he will be able to continue to benefit from this gift. So too, all of Hashem's creations ensure their continued existence through the Shabbos day when they develop an intimate relationship with *HaKadosh Baruch Hu*. On this day, when Hashem ceased creating, it became clear that the universe didn't emerge by itself, rather it only emerged through Hashem's Will. This recognition, embodied in the *Menuchah* of Shabbos, is what ensures the vitality and continued existence of the entire universe. (*Bereishis* 5636)

◆§ Creation of Spirituality

דאיתא מלאכה שהי' צריך לעשות בשבת כפלו ועשאו בששי. שבששי נעשו ב' ברואים. ב"ח ואדם. נמצא דהי' ראוי להיות בריאת אדם בש"ק. והענין הוא דאדם יש בו גשמיות ורוחניות והיא חיבור ימי המעשה עם הש"ק. וז"ש חכמים למה נברא באחרונה שיכנוס לשבת מיד. פי' שאדם הוא מחבר כל הבריאה להתדבק ע"י כולם בעולם העליון.

In reality, when Hashem rested on Shabbos, He didn't merely abstain from creating but actually laid the foundation for spirituality (*ruchniyus*).

As the *pasuk* recited in *Kiddush* emphasizes, וַיְקַדֵּשׁ אֱלֹהִים אֶת יוֹם הַשְּׁבִיעִי, *HASHEM sanctified the seventh day.* In other words, the Sabbath day became the source for everything spiritual.

In truth, assuming that beneath the outer surface of anything physical there lies a spiritual core, we may then argue that Shabbos is the source for everything that exists — material as well as spiritual.[1] The entire universe — its spiritual core as well as every physical entity — is only assured of its continued existence through the infusion of spirituality that resulted when Hashem rested on Shabbos.

With this approach, we can appreciate why man was created as the climax of Creation. In the words of *Chazal,* he emerged as the conclusion of the Six Days of Creation so that he would immediately benefit from Shabbos. In other words, even the physical aspect of man emerged as close as possible to the day that is the source of everything spiritual, *Shabbos Kodesh.* (Adapted from *Bereishis* 5638)

◈ Linking Spirituality (*Ruchniyus*) and Materialism (*Gashmiyus*)

וגם לפי הפשוט מאחר שהשבת הוא ברית א״כ הוא ממוצע בין עליונים לתחתונים ולכן נקרא שלום כי באמת עוה״ז מהופך מעולם העליון. רק בשבת יש בו התאחדות לעליונים עם התחתונים ונק׳ יום מנוחה ושלום. לכן מצוה בשבת להתענג באכילה ושתי׳. וכ׳ קודש הוא לכם. אפילו בגשמיות שורה הקדושה בשבת.

In the previous *dvar Torah,* we related the concept of *Menuchah* to the universe's spiritual genesis, which occurred when Hashem rested on the first Shabbos. In reality, by ceasing to create on Shabbos, Hashem not only initiated the universe's spiritual dimension but He also created an environment in which spirituality and materialism can coexist, as the following remarks elucidate.

The Torah describes Shabbos as אוֹת הִיא בֵּינִי וּבֵינֵיכֶם, *a sign between Myself* (Hashem) *and You* (the Jewish people). In other words, *HaKadosh Baruch Hu,* Who is the very essence of spirituality (lacking a physical

1. In the language of Jewish thought (*machshavah*), the *chomer* (material substance) of everything that exists is actually supported by its *tzurah* — its inner spiritual core.

substance), "relates" to His people, *Klal Yisrael,* through the medium of Shabbos. Similarly, the Shabbos is described as a *bris,* covenant, alluding to the covenant arranged between us and Hashem and the relationship that is forged every Shabbos between *Klal Yisrael,* with all of its material needs, and Hashem. According to the *Zohar, Shalom,* peace, is one of the names of Shabbos. In light of the theme of this *dvar Torah,* we suggest that on this extraordinary day, a unique sense of harmony emerges between the Jewish people, residing on Earth – despite all of their material tendencies – and the Heavenly Presence of the *Shechinah.* As further indication of the capacity of the weekly day of rest to synthesize spirituality and material needs, consider the *mitzvah* of *oneg Shabbos* (delighting in the Shabbos by partaking of Three Meals and other material amenities; refer to our chapters on *Oneg Shabbos* and *Shalosh Seudos*). Unlike during the week when indulging in material pleasures is discouraged, on Shabbos, the day when spiritual requirements and our material needs blend harmoniously, we allow ourselves these pleasures without concern about any harmful consequences. All of these thoughts are derived from the ambiance of *Menuchah* that Hashem instilled in His universe on the first Shabbos. (*Ki Sisa* 5648)

❧ Creating by Not Creating

וצריך להשלמת הבורא ית׳ וכל מה שאדם מחסר גופו בעבור כבוד הבורא ע״ז נאמר דורשי ה׳ לא יחסרו כל טוב ונא׳ אין מחסור ליראיו. והוא ענין באת שבת באת מנוחה כלתה ונגמרה המלאכה כמ״ש שם במקומו.

We suggest yet another approach to *Chazal's* contention that the *Menuchah* of Shabbos is the true completion of the universe. While we generally assume that creation is a positive act, at times Hashem completed His Creation by no longer creating. This "passive form of creation" set a precedent for *Klal Yisrael,* and especially Avraham *Avinu* who fulfilled the *mitzvah* of *milah* by yielding a part of himself (the *orlah*). The underlying lesson that we derive from both the *Menuchah* of Shabbos, which completed the process of Creation, and the sacrifice of Avraham *Avinu* is that we often serve Hashem by yielding something of our own. By doing so, we demonstrate our firm belief that we can not attain *sheleimus* (perfection) on our own but only with Hashem's assistance. We also learn from both Creation and the circumcision of Avraham *Avinu* that whatever we yield in order to perform Hashem's Will is not in any sense a loss, but rather a means of attaining true *sheleimus*. As we recite at the conclusion of *Birchas Hamazon*, דֹרְשֵׁי ה׳ לֹא יַחְסְרוּ כָל טוֹב, *Those who seek HASHEM will never lack anything good.*

(*Lech Lecha* 5637)

◆§ Working to Rest

אבל כשאדם רוצה לעשות איזה מלאכה וטורח בה הרבה עד שנגמרת ונח אח״כ. זה מנוחת מרגוע. שכל המלאכה הי׳ כדי להשיג זאת המנוחה. וכן כביכול הכתיב מנוחה לעצמו כי ששת ימים כו׳. נמצא מנוחת הקב״ה כך הי׳. ונלמד מזה שכן צריך להיות מנוחת האדם בשבת כמ״ש ששת ימים תעבוד כו׳. מסמיך הכתוב העבודה למנוחת שבת. כלומר להיות כל עבודת ימי המעשה כדי להיות נגמר רצונו ית׳ וכבודו. להיות נעשה מזה השבת. ומעין זה איתא ג״כ כי לכל מעשה האדם בימי החול יש להם עלי׳ בשבת קודש.

Commenting on the term שַׁבַּת שַׁבָּתוֹן, *a Sabbath of cessation* (*Shemos* 31:15), *Rashi* notes that when we rest on Shabbos it is מְנוּחַת מַרְגּוֹעַ וְלֹא מְנוּחַת עֲרָאִי, which *Sfas Emes* interprets: "a rest derived from a sense of completion of one's goals, not merely a pause in our objectives." With these words, *Rashi* is granting us a great deal of insight into the concept of *Menuchah* on Shabbos. Rather than merely resting because no more work remains (מְנוּחַת עֲרָאִי), by resting on Shabbos we are attaining the goal of all our creative efforts during the week (מְנוּחַת מַרְגּוֹעַ). Just as Hashem rested on the first Shabbos — and by doing so enabled the entire universe to reach fruition and a sense of completion — so too, when we rest on Shabbos all our efforts of the past week come closer to fruition (refer to the chapter on *Melachah* for a similar theme).[1] (*Ki Sisa* 5635)

1. Alternatively, the term מְנוּחַת מַרְגּוֹעַ utilized by *Rashi* may refer to the "perfect fit" that exists between *Klal Yisrael* and the Shabbos. Rather than rest merely because the Torah commands us to cease working on Shabbos, the Jewish people quite naturally — and on their own initiative — desire to rest on Shabbos. This alone is a tribute to *Klal Yisrael* and its relationship to Hashem. As the Torah writes, לָדַעַת כִּי אֲנִי ה׳ מְקַדִּשְׁכֶם, *to know that I am HASHEM, Who sanctifies you* (*Shemos* 31:13) — that all of mankind should know through your observance of the Shabbos that it is Hashem Who consecrates you.

Passive and Active Aspects of *Menuchah*

וכן בש"ק שהוא נותן דעה באיש ישראל כמ"ש לדעת כי אני ה' מקדישכם. יש בו קידוש והבדלה זכור ושמור. השבתת מלאכה. ושביתה ומנוחה ודביקות אל השורש.

While we generally assume that *Menuchah* is simply the absence of work, essentially a passive concept, in reality that is only one dimension of Shabbos' rest. Just as the Fourth Commandment was stated in both passive (*shamor*) and active (*zachor*) terms (refer to our chapter on *Zachor V'Shamor* for detailed discusson of this theme),[1] so too, there is an active as well as a passive dimension to the concept of *Menuchah*. On one hand, we certainly abstain from the thirty nine categories of *melachah* on Shabbos. But that is only one aspect of Shabbos *Menuchah*. As a result of not performing *melachah*, we develop an intimate relationship with *HaKadosh Baruch Hu*. These two aspects of *Menuchah* are known as הַשְׁבָּתַת מְלָאכָה, abstaining from *melachah*, and שְׁבִיתָה, attaining true rest and a relationship of *deveikus* (clinging to *HaKadosh Baruch Hu*), respectively. (*Tazria* 5661)

A Taste of *Gan Eden*

לכן דרשו ויניחהו בג"ע הוא מנוחה של שבת. שבימי החול צריך להיות העבודה ע"י הגשמיות לכן כתיב בכל יום ויהי ערב אח"כ ויהי בוקר שבא האור ע"י הערב והחושך. אבל בשבת לא כ' ערב שיש בשב"ק הארה מעין שהי' קודם החטא ...

When seeking to describe a sense of the bliss that Adam enjoyed briefly in *Gan Eden*, *Chazal* compared this fleeting moment to the

1. Similarly, there is a passive and negative aspect through which we welcome and depart from Shabbos.While we welcome Shabbos with *Kiddush* — a positive affirmation of Shabbos and its *kedushah* — we conclude this greatest of days with *Havdalah*, which is devoted to the distinction between *Klal Yisrael* and mankind, essentially a passive affirmation of the Jewish people's uniqueness (emphasizing how we are different than mankind at large rather than focusing on our inherent *kedushah*).

Menuchah of Shabbos. [In fact, virtually the identical expression is used to describe Adam's brief stay in *Gan Eden* (וַיַּנִּחֵהוּ) and the *Menuchah* of Shabbos (וַיָּנַח).] By doing so, they are not only granting us a glimpse of *Gan Eden,* but also through the analogy of Shabbos to *Gan Eden* implying that every Shabbos we enjoy some of the overwhelming spirituality of *Gan Eden.*

As further indication of Shabbos' overwhelming spirituality, we note that unlike the other days of Creation where the Torah first writes, וַיְהִי עֶרֶב, *it was evening,* and only then וַיְהִי בֹקֶר, *it was morning,* in reference to Shabbos, the Torah only speaks of the seventh *day.* During the week, it is necessary to serve Hashem and find spirituality in a world that is often engulfed in darkness. In fact, one often arrives at the light (and achieves clarity) by removing the outer facade of darkness. On Shabbos, however, a day of such consummate spirituality, one can reach the light without first confronting darkness. (*Bereishis* 5644)

כמו שהי׳ אז בשבת בראשית. ויניחהו בגן. והוא עיקר השביתה והרצון שעלה לפניו ית״ש. ובאמת בכל שב״ק יש הארה מזה. לכן יורדת נשמה יתירה מג״ע. ונק׳ מנוחה. אך אז במדבר הי׳ מתוקן לגמרי. ונק׳ שבת ראשונה.

Utilizing this approach, we can appreciate why *Chazal* (*Shabbos* 118b) insist that if the Jewish people had properly observed the first Shabbos (after they had been informed about the *mitzvah* of Shabbos), no nation would have been able to attack them. While it is true that *every* Shabbos, the Jewish people — benefiting from the presence of the *neshamah yeseirah* — enjoy an aura of the intense spirituality of *Gan Eden,* on that first Shabbos, had we not sinned, we could have genuinely returned to the spiritual level that the first man enjoyed in Eden prior to sinning. Just as Adam during his brief stay in Eden basked in an atmosphere of intense spirituality, so too, *Klal Yisrael,* prior to the first act of *chilul Shabbos,* could enjoy a taste of the intense spirituality that Adam enjoyed in Eden. (Adapted from *Beshalach* 5645)

◈ A Time for the *Neshamah* to Prevail

אבל מקרא זה בא ללמד כי הניח פתח לכנוס בג"ע מי שראוי רק יש בו שמירה ולכן ביום ש"ק דכתיב שער החצר הפנימית רמז לג"ע הפונה קדים ובגן כ' מקדם שנפתח בשבת פתח והארה מג"ע ... א"כ בשבתות ויו"ט שנאמר מלאכת העבודה הרי זה עדות שהוא זמן עבודת הנשמה כמו שהי' בג"ע וזה בחינת מנוחה כמ"ש במד' ויניחהו רמז למנוחת שבת.

In a previous *dvar Torah,* we described the rest of Shabbos as a return to the values that prevailed in *Gan Eden.* Expanding upon this theme, it follows that just as in *Gan Eden* it was the soul and not the body that was dominant, so too, every Shabbos it is the *neshamah* rather than the *guf* that prevails.

Whereas after sinning, Man was consigned to work the land from which he had been created, on Shabbos, when all forms of *melachah* are prohibited, it follows that we are prepared to return again to the spirituality of *Gan Eden.* When Adam was expelled from *Gan Eden,* Hashem never sealed the garden but merely placed sentries to block access to the undeserving. On Shabbos, the day of *Menuchah* (when we attain a spiritual status far superior to that of the weekdays), we are able to overcome any of these barriers and return to *Gan Eden* and its overwhelming spirituality. (*Bereishis* 5661)

ובחול כ' ועשית כל מלאכתך. היינו ע"י היגיעה בעוה"ז כדי להחיות כל הברואים שהוא בהשתתפות נשמה וגוף. ועשית הוא לשון כפי' שיש מלחמה בימי המעשה. אבל ש"ק נק' מנוחה. וכן בגוף הישראלי יש כח לנשמתו לגבור על הגוף יותר בש"ק. ולכן נק' נשמה יתירה בתוספות כח. דבחול כח שניהם שוה. ונלחמת הנשמה עם הגוף. ובשבת הגוף נכנע.

We may support our contention that the dominance of the soul over the body every Shabbos is an integral component of *Menuchah* by noting that the term וְעָשִׂיתָ כָּל מְלַאכְתֶּךָ, generally translated as *you shall perform all of your work* (*Shemos* 20:9), may also be interpreted, "you shall be coerced" into performing your work.[1] All week long, involved in the battle against the *yetzer hara*, we simply are unable to rest. It is only on Shabbos when the soul prevails, that we are able to enjoy a sense of *Menuchah*. Perhaps, the concept of *neshamah yeseirah* may allude to the enhanced ability of our *neshamah* to prevail on Shabbos over the importunings of the material component of man and his physical needs. (*Yisro* 5644)

☙ Opening the Wellsprings of Heaven

במדרש מעין נרפש ומקור משחת כשם שא"א למעין להרפש ולמקור להשחת כך אי אפשר לצדיק למוט לפני רשע וכשם שמעין נרפש כו' כך צדיק ממיט עצמו לפני רשע. פירוש כי שורש המעין והמקור א"א להירפש ולהשחת וכמו כן מעין הצדיק אין בו מגע נכרי. אבל התפשטות המעין להיות נחלים ונהרות נמשכין ממנו. שם יש מחלוקות ומלחמות עם הסט"א. וכ"כ גן נעול גל נעול מעין תהום. והאמת שכשזוכין לעבור זו המלחמה אז נפתח המעין.

To appreciate yet another dimension of *Menuchah*, we cite a *pasuk* in *Mishlei* (25:26), מַעְיָן נִרְפָּשׂ וּמָקוֹר מָשְׁחָת צַדִּיק מָט לִפְנֵי רָשָׁע, which the *Sfas Emes* explains: "If a well is muddy and its source is corrupted, it is because a *tzaddik* engages and subsequently flees from a *rasha*." The true source from which a *tzaddik* is nurtured, emanating directly from Hashem, is never muddied or clogged. However, while doing battle with evildoers (as Yaakov confronted Esav and Lavan, or as we contend with the *yetzer hara* all week), there exists the risk that even surface contact with the forces of evil could corrupt even the most pure. On Shabbos, having emerged unscathed from our confrontations of the week, we now can benefit again from the pure heavenly source of all *berachos*. What greater source of *Menuchah* than returning to the true source of all *berachos*. (*Vayishlach* 5649)

1. Refer to *Gittin* (88b) stating that a *get* given under duress is described as a גֵּט מְעוּשֶּׂה. Similarly, גָּדוֹל הַמְעַשֶּׂה יוֹתֵר מִן הָעוֹשֶׂה, "The one who causes the performance [of charitable deeds] is greater than the one who [actually] performs [the deed]" (*Bava Basra* 9a).

אכן בשבת שנק׳ יום מנוחה כל הסט״א ערקית מגרמה. ולכן נפתח פי הבאר והוא באמת כחו של מרע״ה שמתגלה בשבת קודש כדאיתא מזמור שיר ליום השבת ר״ת למשה. ומ״מ גם השבת תלי׳ בימי המעשה. אחרי הכותו הוא בימי המעשה. הואיל באר הוא בשבת.

Expanding further upon the relationship between conquering the forces of evil and eliciting the pure waters of Torah, we note that Moshe *Rabbeinu* is only able to relate *Sefer Devarim* to *Klal Yisrael* [a mission which is described by the Torah as בֵּאֵר אֶת הַתּוֹרָה הַזֹּאת, *explaining this Torah* (*Devarim* 1:5), interpreted homiletically, "to draw upon the deep wellsprings of the Torah] after conquering the mighty warriors (and the personification of evil), Sichon and Og. Both Sichon, who resided in Cheshbon (which homiletically may be interpreted as referring to the capacity of the forces of evil to corrupt the pure מַחְשָׁבוֹת, *thoughts*, of the Jewish people), and Og, who lived in Edrei (which homiletically is related to זְרוֹעַ, *outstretched arm*, symbolic of military might),[1] attempted to affect our capacity to perform *maasim tovim*. They had to be neutralized before Moshe *Rabbeinu* could tap the wellsprings of Torah, which we know as *Sefer Devarim*.

Every Shabbos, the day of spiritual *Menuchah*, the *yetzer hara's* capacity to disrupt our thoughts and corrupt our deeds is diminished even without us undergoing the struggles that Moshe faced and that we all are required to undergo all week long. In fact, the first letters of the opening words of the *Mizmor* devoted to Shabbos, מִזְמוֹר שִׁיר לְיוֹם הַשַּׁבָּת, spell (albeit rearranged) לְמֹשֶׁה, *to Moshe*. What Moshe accomplished through his conquest of Sichon and Og — being able to reach the deepest wellsprings of Torah — we may try to achieve every Shabbos, but only because of the initiative first launched by him.

Going even further, we suggest that the efforts of Moshe in confronting evil, and our efforts all week long in battling the *yetzer hara*, are necessary preludes to the mastery of the intricacies of Torah that we attain on Shabbos. After Moshe vanquished Sichon and Og, he was able to elicit the waters of Torah to the extent that he could teach *Sefer Devarim* to *Klal Yisrael*. Similarly, as a result of our efforts all week long in confronting the *yetzer hara*, we can successfully elicit the wellsprings of Torah every Shabbos. (*Devarim* 5652)

1. עֶדְרֶאִי is related to זְרוֹעַ based on the premise that the letters ד and ז are interchangeable.

◆§ Eliciting the Waters of the Well

וכמו כן לעולם בשבת קודש הוא יום מנוחה וחירות ונפתח הבאר. ונשאר רשימה על ימות החול שיכולין ע״י הנדיבות והרצון והשתוקקות להשבת. כמ״ש לזכור בכל יום השבת. עי״ז יכולין לעורר הרשימות גם בימי המעשה כנ״ל.

In the previous *dvar Torah,* we drew an analogy between the *Menuchah* of Shabbos and pure well water. Extending this association to the Well of Miriam, which *Klal Yisrael* enjoyed during the forty years it spent in the Wilderness, we note that the Torah describes the well in the following terms: בְּאֵר חֲפָרוּהָ שָׂרִים כָּרוּהָ נְדִיבֵי הָעָם, *Well that the princes dug, that the nobles of the people excavated* (*Bamidbar* 21:18) — which is interpreted homiletically, "[It was] the well dug by the princes and extended by those members of *Klal Yisrael* who expressed a great desire (*nadiv*) [to enjoy its waters]." While the Well was originally dug by the "princes" of *Klal Yisrael* (a term describing the status of the Jewish people before they sinned), its waters are now evoked by anyone with an intense desire to come close to Hashem. Similarly, the Shabbos day — a day in which we are liberated from the passions of This World — is compared to those princes who originally dug the Well. However, even during the week, although we lack that exalted level while we are immersed in This World, we still may elicit the waters of the Well by becoming a *nadiv* — someone with a strong desire to tap the inherent spirituality of Shabbos. (*Chukas* 5639)

◆§ In Direct Proportion to Divine Service During the Week

ובימות החול בנ״י מכינים בעבודה ביגיעות רבות שיזכו בשבת למנוחה כדאי׳ מי שטרח בע״ש כו׳ וזה לחם משנה שכפי היגיעה בחול מתרבה הברכה בשבת עבור ימי החול ג״כ.
בחול ע״י טירחא ובשבת בשובה ונחת וכפי היגיעה בחול זוכין למנוחה בש״ק

It is only through our *avodas Hashem* during the week (combating the *yetzer hara*) that we earn the *Menuchah* of Shabbos. As *Chazal* note,

מִי שֶׁטָּרַח בְּעֶרֶב שַׁבָּת יֹאכַל בַּשַּׁבָּת, *Whoever toils on erev Shabbos, will eat* (enjoy the *Menuchah* of) *on Shabbos* (*Avodah Zarah* 3a). Perhaps it is for this reason that we partake of the *lechem mishneh* (Double Bread) on Shabbos. By doing so, we are alluding not only to the Two Loaves enjoyed during the Shabbos meals but also to the two sources of *berachah* that we enjoy on Shabbos — its own merit and the efforts in *avodas Hashem* made during the week. In fact, the relationship between Shabbos and the weekdays may be compared to that of Yissachar and Zevulun. Just as Zevulun supported his brother's Torah study — and consequently is mentioned first in the Torah[1] — so too, our efforts during the weekdays which precede Shabbos, sustain the Shabbos itself.

(*Vayechi* 5634; cf. *Bo* 5635)

וכמו שיש בשבת זכור ושמור ואמרו בזוה״ק שכל התורה בלולה בזכור ושמור כמו כן בלשון הרע כ׳ השמר וכ׳ זכור. וכן כתיב מוצא שפתיך ת׳ דרשו חז״ל מ״ש מ״ע תשמור מל״ת כו׳ שכל התורה תלוי בפה כנ״ל. ובאמת גם בשבת היא בחי׳ הפה דיש ראי׳ שמיעה ריחא ודיבור. וימי המעשה הם בחי׳ ב׳ עיינין [ב׳] אודנין ב׳ נוקבין דחוטמא. והשבת הוא הפה שנק׳ סהדותא ושבת יעשה כולו תורה. לכן אמרו לכל יש בן זוג. אבל הפה יחיד.

To better appreciate the relationship between our efforts during the week and our resting on Shabbos, we need to define further the different tasks that we assume on Shabbos and during the week. The fact that there is a perfect match between the 248 positive commandments and the identical number of limbs in the human body (and, similarly, the correspondence between the 365 negative commandments and a like amount of sinews), is not coincidental. Rather, it indicates the nature of our sacred challenge during the weekdays to ensure that through our performance of *mitzvos*, our body becomes an appropriate resting place for the soul. The more effective we are at this task, the more likely that the full effect of the *neshamah yeseirah* is experienced every Shabbos. As David *HaMelech* writes, גַּם צִפּוֹר מָצְאָה בַיִת וּדְרוֹר קֵן לָהּ, *Even the bird finds its home and the swallow her nest* (*Tehillim* 84:4) — just as the bird

1. Whenever the Torah discusses the blessing enjoyed by these two brothers, the *berachos* of Zevulun are stated before those of Yissachar.

(an allusion to the soul) finds its habitat and the undomesticated fowl finds its nest, so too, the *neshamah yeseirah* finds its resting place.

(*Ki Seitzei* 5647)

אשר ע״ז אמרו חכמים אלו שמרו בנ״י ב׳ שבתות הם נגאלין ... ויש בחי׳ שבת הבא ע״י יגיעת העבודה בחול ונק׳ שבת של חול והוא מציאת המנוחה ע״י היגיעה כמ״ש יגעתי ומצאתי תאמין. שהגם שמנוחה היא למעלה מהטבע עכ״ז צריכין להאמין שע״י יגיעה בטבע זוכין להמנוחה כנ״ל.

Utilizing the foregoing approach that it is through our efforts of the week that we enjoy true *Menuchah* on Shabbos, we gain new insight into the statement of *Chazal* that if *Klal Yisrael* only observed two Shabbosos they would be immediately redeemed (*Shabbos* 118b); we can also understand the renowned expression, שַׁבָּת שֶׁל חוֹל, *the Shabbos of the weekdays.* Perhaps the reference to two Shabbosos refers to two distinct aspects of Shabbos — the efforts that we make during the week to combat the *yetzer hara,* as well as the actual observance of Shabbos, which is a Divine gift resulting from our efforts during the weekdays that lead up to Shabbos. A week which is observed in such a manner that at its conclusion merits the Divine gift of Shabbos, deserves the distinction of being called שַׁבָּת שֶׁל חוֹל, the Shabbos of the weekdays.[1] (*Vayechi* 5638)

◆§ Perceiving the *Kedushah* of Shabbos During the Week

ובימי המעשה יכולין ג״כ להרגיש קדושת השבת ע״י התשוקה והרצון לאחוז למעלה ממדריגתו בחי׳ בעלי תשובה בחילא סגי ואינו מסוגר רק כמ״ש במדרש ודגלו ודילוגו כו׳ ע״ש כל הדרשות. עוד פי׳ נרננה בישועתך כי יש לבנ״י לשמוח בהש״ת לבד שהוא מלך עוזר ומושיע תמיד.

In the previous *dvar Torah* we discussed the relationship between our efforts during the weekdays to combat the *yetzer hara* and the *Menuchah*

1. Refer to the foregoing *Sfas Emes* who draws an association between these two Shabbosos and the two Messiahs, *Mashiach ben Yosef* and *Mashiach ben David,* and to the unique roles of Yosef and Yehudah.

of Shabbos. Extending this analysis even further, we propose that it is possible to perceive, to some extent, the *kedushah* of Shabbos during the week simply on the basis of our intense desire to rise to a higher spiritual level (*madreigah*). Just as the *baal teshuvah* is blessed with the ability to attain great levels of *kedushah*, depending on his desire to grow spiritually, so too, our intense desire for a higher spiritual level, to some extent, allows us to perceive the *kedushah* of Shabbos during the week.

By granting each tribe within *Klal Yisrael* its own banner (*degel*)[1] (cf. *Bamidbar* 2:2), *HaKadosh Baruch Hu* is emphasizing that even if we haven't yet attained an ideal spiritual state, nonetheless, we can ascend (look upwards) and strive for more spirituality. In fact, the institution of *degalim* was only granted to the Jewish people after their flirtation with *avodah zarah* at the time of the sin of the Golden Calf. Instead of permitting them to remain at the low level to which they had descended, by assigning each tribe its own banner, Hashem is assuring them that they would succeed in restoring some of their previous spiritual gains by looking upwards and seeking to improve themselves. So too, by rising above our limitations and "looking forward" to the intense *kedushah* of Shabbos, we are assured that indeed, we will be able to attain some degree of holiness even during the week. (*Bamidbar* 5640)

וענין שליחות המרגלים שנפרשו מאנשי דור המדבר שהיו תחת ענן ה׳. הי׳ כמו ההפרש שבין שבת לימי המעשה. אך ע״י המצות שהם בעשי׳ יכולין לעורר בחי׳ השבת גם בימי המעשה כנ״ל. וזהו ענין שליחי מצוה כי התורה גוף האור כדכתיב תורה אור והוא בחי׳ אספקלריא המאירה בחי׳ מרע״ה.

Moreover, every time that we perform a *mitzvah* with total devotion (*sheleimus*), we experience a taste of Shabbos, even during the week. With this in mind, Moshe sought to channel the Jewish people's desire to send spies (*meraglim*) to *Eretz Yisrael* into a *dvar mitzvah* by insisting that they be appointed according to Hashem's Will (עַל פִּי ה׳). Though undoubtedly it would have been preferable if this mission had never

1. Typically, troops in battle, when sighting their nation's banner, experience a sense of enthusiasm and renewed dedication to their cause.

been launched — and in particular because the *meraglim* previously shielded by the Divine Cloud (עָנָן) were now exposed to the many risks of the outside world — by proposing that it be conducted within the Torah's guidelines, Moshe was, in effect, giving it the status of a *dvar mitzvah.* Similarly, upon leaving the confines and security of Shabbos and entering the weekdays — where we are exposed to the ongoing challenges of the outside world — we are well served by elevating (as much as possible) our mundane activities to the status of a *dvar mitzvah.* We are thereby able to evoke the spiritual *Menuchah* of Shabbos during the week.

Drawing the association between the spies' mission and the spiritual *Menuchah* of Shabbos even further, we suggest that the distinction between *Klal Yisrael's* conception of how to conquer *Eretz Yisrael* (by using spies) and Hashem's fervent wish that the Jewish people simply trust His assurance that they would enter the Land without resorting to this flawed expedition, is comparable to the distinction between Shabbos and the week. By designating their mission, however flawed, as a *dvar mitzvah,* (and by involving himself in their preparations), Moshe, the transmitter of the Torah, hoped to salvage the situation by allowing some of the spiritual *Menuchah* of Shabbos to permeate the week as well. (Adapted from *Shelach* 5638)

◆§ A Day Untainted by Evil

בשש צרות יצילך ובשבע לא יגע בך רע כו׳. כבר כתבנו כי שש צרות הוא בששת ימי המעשה. ושבת הוא יום מנוחה שאין בו תערובות רע כלל.

Previously, we suggested that the *Menuchah* of Shabbos marks a return to the pure source of Heavenly sustenance untainted by any spiritual evil that may have confronted us during the week. To corroborate this theme, we refer to the *pasuk* in *Iyov:* בְּשֵׁשׁ צָרוֹת יַצִּילֶךָּ וּבְשֶׁבַע לֹא יִגַּע בְּךָ רָע, *From six travails He will save you, and in the seventh, no evil will reach* (touch) *you* (5:19). Whereas during the six weekdays, Hashem saves us from being influenced by any evil that we may encounter, on Shabbos (the seventh), Hashem ensures us that to a great extent, we will not even have to confront evil. (*Vayishlach* 5650)

◆§ The Defeat of Evil

ויש ללמוד מזה כי בשבת קודש שנק׳ מנוחה. הכתיב מנוחה לעצמו מי שכ׳ בו לא ייעף כו׳. הפי׳ שבש״ק נגלה זה שהכל מחיות הש״י. כמ״ש ע״ה אימה שבת עליו.

ובש״ק נאמר זכר ליצ״מ ע״י שמעידין בנ״י בשבת כי כח מעשה בראשית ממנו ית׳. ומאחר שכ׳ מנוחה בשבת וינח כו׳ הוא ג״כ ע״ז שנק׳ יגיעה. כמ״ש במד׳ במה אני ייגע כו׳. שבש״ק ע״ה אימת שבת עליו. שאין כח לסט״א להגבי׳ עצמה בש״ק. ויוכל כל א׳ לעורר חיות הפנימיות של כל הבריאה. וש״ק נותן חיים על כל ישבוע. כמ״ש מיני׳ מתברכין כו׳.

ובשבת שהוא יום מנוחה היפוך היגיעה מתקיים ג״כ בב׳ בחי׳ הנ״ל דכ׳ בו שבת וינפש. שביתות המעשה דבששת ימים ברא ונח בשביעי. וינפש הוא הנייחא שהי׳ לפניו מקבלת מלכותו שקיבלו הברואים היינו אדם הראשון שאמר לכל הברואים לכו נרננה כו׳.

וכיון שזה נק׳ יגיעה ממילא השבת שנק׳ מנוחה נתבטל בו כעס אויל. לכן כל שבת הוא זכר ליצ״מ שקודם יצ״מ לא הי׳ יכול להתגלות בחי׳ השבת כנ״ל.

To appreciate yet another dimension of *Menuchah,* let us consider the antithesis of "rest." Is there anything that "tires" *HaKadosh Baroch Hu* (כביכול)? While one might imagine that the creation of heaven and earth (whose conclusion Shabbos commemorates) would be portrayed as a form of Divine effort, according to *Chazal* (*Midrash Rabbah, Parashas Bo*), Hashem did not exert Himself during Creation. Rather it is the practitioners of evil and, in particular, those who anatagonize Hashem by speaking *devarim beteilim,* idle and meaningless chatter, in His Presence that "tire" Him. It is the existence of vile individuals such as Pharaoh, who boasted that the Nile was created by him (and consequently that he was a deity in his own right) that "exert" Hashem. Not only the avowed opponents of the *Shechinah* anger Him, but even any individual whose approach to life is based upon the mistaken premise that כֹּחִי וְעֹצֶם יָדִי עָשָׂה לִי אֶת הַחַיִל הַזֶּה, *My strength and the might of my hand made me all this wealth* (*Devarim* 8:17). Those who maintain that it is through their own initiative, rather than Divine assistance, that all of their achievements have been attained are the ones who anger and "tire" Hashem.

It is on Shabbos, when heaven and earth are revealed in their complete splendor, that the totally unfounded and heretical statements of evildoers may finally be put to rest. It is only on Shabbos that those misguided individuals, who pretended that all their fame and fortune is the result of their efforts, are forced to acknowledge the true Creator of heaven and earth. *Chazal* recognize the impact of Shabbos also on those least observant members of *Klal Yisrael* by noting that even an *am ha'aretz* (an individual ignorant of the Torah's basic precepts) is awed by the *kedushah* of this day, to the extent that he is reluctant to lie (cf. *Demai* 4:1).

How appropriate that Shabbos was designated as the day of *Menuchah* for Hashem — and for us. *HaKadosh Baruch Hu* was unable to "rest" until the evildoers learned to recognize Him as the sole Creator of the universe. It is on this day, when the misguided reasoning of those who are a source of so much "exertion" to the *Shechinah* are finally subdued, that has been designated as an eternal day of rest — for *HaKadosh Baruch Hu* and *Klal Yisrael*.

Utilizing this approach, we can appreciate yet an additional reason why Shabbos is described as זֵכֶר לִיצִיאַת מִצְרָיִם, *a remembrance of the Exodus*. It was in the aftermath of the Exodus, when Pharaoh's conceited sense of self-worth and his mistaken belief that he enjoyed the status of a deity were shattered, that Shabbos earned its distinction as a day of *Menuchah*. (*Bo* 5631, 5632, 5638, 5639)

◌ A Day That Is Only Good

ונפרש עוד כי הוא ההפרש בין השפע הבא בימי המעשה שהוא ע״י צמצום בטבע וגשמיות. ומזה ניזון כל העולם. וזהו שמלכך נער ושריך בבוקר יאכלו. כי באמת בכל יום השי״ת מחדש בטובו מעשה בראשית. אך השבת כולו טוב כמ״ש טוב להודות ולכן בשבת לא כתיב ויהי ערב כו׳. לכן אשריך ארץ שמלכך בן חורים הוא יום שבת מנוחה ושריך בעת יאכלו שהוא יום שכולו טוב ועת רצון לה׳. ויום השבת מיוחד לבנ״י שהם בני חורין ויכולין להפרד מן הגשמיות.

Expanding upon the theme developed in the previous *dvar Torah*, we suggest that Shabbos is not only the day when the forces of evil are vanquished, but also the day that consists entirely of good without a residue of evil. This assertion can be deduced from the striking difference between the Torah's description of the first Shabbos and the other days of Creation. Whereas in reference to each of the Six Days of Creation, the Torah says, וַיְהִי עֶרֶב וַיְהִי בֹקֶר, *it was evening and it was morning,* in reference to Shabbos no mention is made of the evening. Rather, the Torah only speaks (*Bereishis* 2:2,3) of the seventh *day* (יוֹם הַשְּׁבִיעִי). On Shabbos there is solely light and goodness. It is only during the week, when we are exposed to the material world with all of its potential for evil, that darkness coexists along with light.

This distinction between the blurred mixture of good and evil that prevails during the week and the immense clarity associated with Shabbos is also indicative of the very different means through which *Klal Yisrael's* sustenance (*parnassah*) and that of mankind-at-large is provided. Whereas mankind is sustained by the material blessings of the Six Days of Creation, *Klal Yisrael* lives off the spirituality of *Shabbos Kodesh.* Unlike the material and finite blessings that emanate from the שֵׁשֶׁת יְמֵי הַמַּעֲשֶׂה (Six Days of Creation), days that contain darkness as well as light, the sustenance provided to *Klal Yisrael* is derived from the infinite spiritual ambiance of Shabbos.

The foregoing theme is alluded to by King Shlomo (cf. *Koheles* 10:16-17), who distinguishes between the unfortunate king who is sustained every day — an allusion to the gentile world which receives a daily infusion of material blessings from *HaKadosh Baruch Hu* — and the happy king who revels in his freedom and "eats" at a designated time. This is a reference to the unique means by which the Jewish people are sustained through the outpouring of spiritual blessings associated with *Shabbos Kodesh.* (*Shemini* 5649)

◆§ *Kedushah* and *Menuchah*: A Reciprocal Relationship

אכן בשבתות ויו״ט מעצמו מתבטל ההסתר כדאיתא כולהון ערקין. ומתגלה הקדושה. וזה יש לפרש יום מנוחה וקדושה לעמך נתת. כי בש״ק יכולין לזכות לקדושה מתוך המנוחה. מה שבימי המעשה צריכין להלחם ביגיעות רבות. ומו״ז ז״ל אמר יום מנוחה וקדושה שעיקר מנוחה ונייחא של בנ״י בהתגלות הקדושה. לכן ש״ק יום מנוחתנו ע״י שנמצא בו הקדושה.

בש״ק דמתאחדין ברזא דאחד לכן סט״א ערקית ויורד הקדושה לבנ״י. יום מנוחה וקדושה לעמך נתת. מנוחה בחי׳ שמור גדר ערוה וקדושה בחי׳ זכור להמשיך קדושת שבת בפה בקידוש היום.

In the *Minchah Shemoneh Esrei* of Shabbos, we describe the Shabbos as יוֹם מְנוּחָה וּקְדֻשָּׁה, *a day of contentment* (rest) *and holiness*. In this *dvar Torah*, we will explore the relationship between these different concepts. We propose that there is a symbiotic assocation between *kedushah* and *Menuchah*. On one hand, the *Menuchah* of Shabbos implies not merely physical rest, but also a respite from the struggle against the *yetzer hara* that dominates much of the week. As a result, on Shabbos we attain, even without acrimony, levels of sanctity that during the weekdays could only be achieved through confronting the *yetzer hara*. On Shabbos, *kedushah* can be achieved through *Menuchah* — rather than confrontation with the forces of evil. On the other hand, as the *Chiddushei Harim* (the *Sfas Emes'* grandfather) noted, true *Menuchah* is not only the catalyst for *kedushah* but also its result. What greater sense of spiritual rest and comfort than basking in the sacred atmosphere of *Shabbos Kodesh*. (*Kedoshim* 5646)

Alternatively, the relationship between *Menuchah* and *kedushah* may be similar to that of *Zachor* and *Shamor* (refer to our chapter on that topic). By abstaining from *melachah* and resting (*Menuchah*), we are fulfilling the spirit of *Shamor* — guarding the spirit of Shabbos by not performing *melachah*. On the other hand, by partaking of Shabbos' intense *kedushah* — and by proclaiming Shabbos' holiness by reciting *Kiddush* — we are bringing to fruition the *Zachor* aspect of Shabbos, which refers to a positive affirmation of this day's *kedushah*.

In fact, this relationship between *Menuchah* and *kedushah*, as well as

Zachor V'Shamor, pertains not only to Shabbos but to the daunting task of achieving *kedushah* in our lives. It is only through a dual process — first abstaining from sinning (in the spirit of *Shamor* and *Menuchah*) and then performing positive acts that lead to an enhanced state of *kedushah* (such as *mitzvos asei*) — that this objective can be accomplished.

(*Kedoshim* 5664).

☙ The Impact of *Menuchah* and *Kedushah*

הפי׳ דכתי׳ כי קדוש אני ה״א. פי׳ כמו שהקב״י למעלה קדוש ונבדל מכל השרים ומנהיגים. כמו כן בנ״י עם ה׳ צריכין להיות למטה קדוש ונבדל מכל התחתונים. יכול כמוני שנוכל להיות כ״כ קדוש ונבדל מן העמים כמו שהקב״ה קדוש ונבדל למעלה ת״ל כו׳ שאין כח בנו להיות נבדל לגמרי מהם. אך בש״ק דכתי׳ ביני ובין בנ״י אות היא כח השבת מסייע לנו להיות נבדל מהם. וכן איתא האל הקדוש שאין כמוהו המנחיל מנוחה כו׳ שבש״ק דכתי׳ אני ה׳ מקדישכם יכולין להיבדל לגמרי מן העמים כמ״ש המבדיל בין קודש לחול בין ישראל לעמים.

In the previous *dvar Torah* we discussed the relationship between two aspects of Shabbos, *kedushah* and *Menuchah*. Extending this theme, let us consider the impact of both Shabbos' sense of *kedushah* as well as its environment of *Menuchah*. As a result of the convergence of both of these factors on Shabbos, *Klal Yisrael* is able to attain a level of intimacy with Hashem that it cannot reach during the week.

The Torah calls upon us, קְדֹשִׁים תִּהְיוּ, *You should be holy* (*Vayikra* 19:2). Moreover, it specifies כִּי קָדוֹשׁ אֲנִי ה׳ אֱלֹהֵיכֶם, *Because I,* H*ASHEM*, *your God, am holy.* While no mortal can attain the level of *kedushah* of the *Shechinah,* the *pasuk* is implying that just as Hashem in His celestial sphere is infinitely more sacred than any of the heavenly beings (angels) that He has created, so too, we — residing on earth — should distinguish ourselves in every sense from mankind at large. However, under ordinary circumstances — residing in the material world during the six weekdays — even this goal is seemingly beyond our reach. It is only on *Shabbos Kodesh,* when we enjoy unprecedented levels of *kedushah* and bask in an environment of true *Menuchah,* that we successfully attempt to be as unique in our world as Hashem is in His sphere.

This thought is voiced in the בְּרָכָה מֵעֵין שֶׁבַע, *The seven-faceted blessing* (an abbreviated version of the *Shemoneh Esrei* recited every Friday night immediately after the congregation recites *Shemoneh Esrei* silently), where we describe Hashem as הָאֵל הַקָּדוֹשׁ שֶׁאֵין כָּמוֹהוּ הַמֵּנִיחַ לְעַמּוֹ בְּיוֹם שַׁבַּת קָדְשׁוֹ, *the Holy God Who is unequalled, Who grants rest to His people on His holy Shabbos day*. It is because the *kedushah* which *Klal Yisrael* derives from Hashem is enhanced by the spirit of *Menuchah* permeating every Shabbos, that we ascend to the spiritual level where we are as unique in our environment as Hashem is in His Universe. Just as He is sacred in a manner that is incomparable to any form of *kedushah* attained by any other entity, so too on Shabbos — the day that Hashem has granted to us for *Menuchah* — we attain a uniqueness somewhat similar to His. On Shabbos, the day that the Torah describes as אוֹת הִיא בֵּינִי וּבֵינֵיכֶם, *a sign between Me and you* (*Shemos* 31:13), *Klal Yisrael* attains a level of unparalleled intimacy with Hashem. Thus, we can truly say that we have achieved a level of *kedushah* in our sphere similar to *HaKadosh Boruch Hu* in His.

This theme, that on Shabbos we gain the ability to distinguish ourselves from our environment just as Hashem maintains His distinctiveness from His Heavenly Servitors, is borne out by the *Havdalah* service in which we recite, הַמַּבְדִּיל בֵּין קֹדֶשׁ לְחוֹל ... בֵּין יִשְׂרָאֵל לָעַמִּים, [*Hashem*] *has created a separation between the sacred and the secular ... between Israel and the nations*. On this day, when we enjoy the capacity to separate from whatever is mundane and reinforce our sense of *kedushah*, we are best able to distinguish ourselves from the gentile world.

(*Kedoshim* 5662)

◆§ More on *Menuchah* and *Kedushah*

וזאת אות השבת קודש שהנחילו השי״ת הוא עדות שבנ״י נפשותיהם ורצונם אל הקדושה וזה מנוחתם.

Expanding upon the theme discussed in the previous *divrei Torah* on the association between *kedushah* and *Menuchah*, we suggest quite simply that for *Klal Yisrael*, *Menuchah* is virtually identical with *kedushah*. For us, rest is synonomous with the increased levels of sanctity that we enjoy on Shabbos. In fact, when the Torah refers to the Shabbos as an אוֹת, *a sign* (of the relationship between *Klal Yisrael* and Hashem), it may be referring to the reason why Hashem granted us Shabbos with all of its spirituality as our day of rest. Undoubtedly, this Divine Gift is a testament to the purity of *Klal Yisrael*. It demonstrates that our sole desire is to seek increasing levels of sanctity rather than merely rest in a physical sense. (*Bamidbar* 5664)

◆§ The Day of Yosef *HaTzaddik*

ולפי שנגע בכף ירכו לכן בשש צרות צריכין הצלה. אבל יום שבת מנוחה הוא בחי׳ יוסף הצדיק שאע״ג שגם הוא תולדות יעקב.

Returning to the *pasuk* that we cited in a previous *dvar Torah* ("A Day Untainted By Evil", p. ???), בְּשֵׁשׁ צָרוֹת יַצִּילֶךָּ וּבְשֶׁבַע לֹא יִגַּע בְּךָ רָע, *From six travails He will save you, and in the seventh, no evil will reach* (touch) *you* (*Iyov* 5:19), we suggest that the reference to the six periods of suffering refers to the many crises undergone by Yaakov *Avinu* and his children, the *shevatim*. Just as we contend with evil during the six weekdays, so too, did they battle Esav and Lavan. The concluding segment of the *pasuk*, referring to the seventh period when you will be shielded from any contact with evil, alludes to the level of Yosef *HaTzaddik* who is called נְזִיר אֶחָיו, *the one who was separated from his brothers* (*Devarim* 33:16). While Yaakov's thigh was temporarily wounded by Esav's angel, Yosef himself (as a result of his successful triumph over the wife of Potiphar) reached the level that henceforth he was shielded from contact with evil. On Shabbos, we achieve a spiritual level similar to that enjoyed by Yosef *HaTzaddik* — to be insulated from outside compromising influences that prevent us from attaining our spiritual potential. As the *pasuk* concludes, *on the seventh* (day of the week) *no evil* (harm) *will reach* (touch) *you*. What greater respite, what greater sense of *Menuchah*, than to be shielded from even the minutest contact with evil. (Adapted from *Vayishlach* 5659)

◆§ Becoming a Receptacle (*Keli*) for Hashem's *Berachos* and for *Kedushah*

דכתיב וישבות ביום השביעי אח"כ ויברך ויקדש השביתה הוא הכנת הכלי להיות העולם מוכן לקבל ברכה וקדושה והוא בחי' מנוחה.

We can gain further insight into the concept of *Menuchah* by recalling one of the first instances in which the Torah mentions that Hashem rested (*Bereishis* 2:1-3). In the portion known as וַיְכֻלּוּ (recited as part of *Kiddush,* as well as during the Friday evening *Shemoneh Esrei*) we read, וַיִּשְׁבֹּת בַּיּוֹם הַשְּׁבִיעִי, [*Hashem*] *rested* (abstained) *on the seventh day.* Subsequently, we read, וַיְבָרֶךְ אֱלֹהִים אֶת יוֹם הַשְּׁבִיעִי וַיְקַדֵּשׁ אֹתוֹ, *God blessed the seventh day and He sanctified it.* From the sequence of this *pasuk* we may deduce that *Menuchah* is a prerequisite for *kedushah* and the *berachos* of *Shabbos Kodesh.* It is only through *Menuchah* that the universe becomes a *keli,* a suitable receptacle to receive the *kedushah* and blessings of Shabbos. (*Vayigash* 5657)

◆§ Asserting *Klal Yisrael's* Uniqueness

והיא בחי' השבת דכ' ביני ובין בנ"י אות הוא. ולכן מתיחדין בשבת ברזא דא'. ונפרשין מן האומות. ואז חל עליהם שם שמים ... שנק' שבת יום מנוחה במה שנבדלין מהתערובות ומקבלין הנשמה יתירה ...

Just as the Shabbos is portrayed as a day of *Menuchah* and as a permanent legacy for *Klal Yisrael,* so too, the *Beis HaMikdash* is described in such terms. Thus, the Torah describes the permanent resting place of the *Shechinah* as מְנוּחָה and נַחֲלָה, a *resting place* and *heritage* (cf. *Devarim* 12:9).

Exploring the association between Shabbos and the *Beis HaMikdash* further, we note that in both instances the Jewish people are able to reassert their unique relationship with Hashem. Whereas all week long,

Klal Yisrael must serve Hashem while sharing the material world along with all of mankind, on Shabbos, we develop a unique relationship with Hashem. As the Torah writes, אוֹת הִיא בֵּינִי וּבֵינֵיכֶם, *it is a sign between Me and you.* So too, in the *Beis HaMikdash, Klal Yisrael* is able to separate itself from mankind at large and develop a unique relationship with Hashem. In this insulated atmosphere, we are able to put aside our differences and develop true *achdus* within the ranks of *Klal Yisrael.*[1]

(*Re'eh* 5645)

☙ The Soul Rests

אכן בשבת קודש כמו שהכתיב הקב״ה מנוחה לעצמו בשבת קודש. כן נפשות בני ישראל יש להם מנוחה בשבת. ולכן המלאכות אסורים בשבת קודש כי אז הנשמה בעצמה מקבלת אור אלקות וזהו פי׳ נשמה יתירה בשבת קודש. והאור שמקבלת הנשמה בש״ק בזה יש לה כח בימי המעשה שאח״כ להאיר ולהנהיג את הגוף. ולכן שבת יומא דנשמתין שהנשמה מקבלת בו אור וחיות. והוא בחי׳ משה רבינו ע״ה אספקלריא המאירה. ולכן שבת יעשה (בו) כולו תורה. והוא מעין יום שכולו שבת שלעתיד יהי׳ הגוף מתוקן והנשמה מקבלת אור חדש תמיד.

To appreciate yet another dimension of Shabbos' *Menuchah,* we cite the *Gemara* (*Berachos* 10a) which compares the soul's relationship to the body to Hashem's relationship with His universe. Just as Hashem supports and sustains His universe, so too, the soul nurtures the body. In particular, the soul motivates the body to enrich itself spiritually by participating in *mitzvos* which can only be fulfilled through its active involvement.[2]

1. Utilizing this approach regarding the unique capacity of the *Beis HaMikdash* to insulate *Klal Yisrael* from the outside world and to develop a sense of harmony within our ranks as well, we suggest a novel approach to the following *pasuk*: לֹא תַעֲשׂוּן כְּכֹל אֲשֶׁר אֲנַחְנוּ עֹשִׂים פֹּה הַיּוֹם אִישׁ כָּל הַיָּשָׁר בְּעֵינָיו, *You shall not do everything that we do here today, [rather] each person what is proper in his eyes* (*Devarim* 12:8): Whereas during the period prior to the building of the *Beis HaMikdash,* or during the weekdays, we can possibly accomplish things on the basis of our individual merits, on Shabbos (and when the *Beis HaMikdash* stood), in an environment of *Menuchah* and *nachalah,* we can no longer exist alone. On Shabbos, our efforts are no longer contingent only upon our own merits, rather as a united *Klal* we are now materially assisted by the *Shechinah.*

2. For example, one hasn't fulfilled the *mitzvah* of *tefillin* merely by studying its significance and symbolic meaning. It is only by performing the *mitzvah* and actually donning the *tefillin* that one has discharged one's obligation.

To continue the analogy between the soul and *HaKadosh Baruch Hu*, we suggest that just as Hashem rested on Shabbos, so too, the soul rests on Shabbos from its mission of actively directing the body. On this sacred day, when all *melachah* is prohibited and the material world is yielded in favor of a more spiritual ambiance, the soul may actually rest from its week long task of keeping the body in check. On Shabbos, the day known for its *neshamah yeseirah*, the soul "nurtures itself," receiving sufficient Divine inspiration to enable it to sustain the body in the following week. It is in this sense that *Chazal* describe Shabbos as a day that is completely immersed in Torah and as microcosm of *Olam Haba* (cf. *Berachos* 57b). On this day, the soul, relieved of its weekday role of controlling the body, is able to focus on its own spiritual development. Just as in *Olam Haba*, the body will have attained the level of perfection so that the soul no longer needs to monitor its development — and the soul is able to bask in the Presence of Hashem — so too, on Shabbos. Freed from its obligation to tend to the body, the soul is able to immerse itself in Torah as it receives continued inspiration from Hashem and renews its strength for its weekday mission of channeling the body's spiritual development. (Adapted from *Beha'aloscha* 5661)

◆§ Body and Soul Rest

פי׳ שבשבת יש מנוחה בכל הענינים הן בגשמיות הן בעבודת השי״ת לכן צוה הקב״ה להיות נוחין בה גם ממלאכת עבודה כדי שיהי׳ ניכר המנוחה בכל דבר. והטעם שמתגלה בשבת רצון השי״ת שיש לו נייחא בשבת מהבריאה ע״י שומרי שבת. וכשמתגלה רצון השי״ת נמצא מנוחה בכל הנבראים כי כולם נבראו ממנו ית׳ שהוא שלימות הכל. וז״ש שאתה רוצה בה ועי״ז היא מנוחה שלימה בכל.

While we generally assume that on Shabbos we rest from the many forms of physical exertion utilized during the week, we demonstrated in the previous *dvar Torah* that on Shabbos our soul also participates in the *Menuchah* of Shabbos. In this *dvar Torah*, we suggest that every Shabbos *both* the body and the soul rest from their weekday activities. As we pray every Shabbos afternoon, מְנוּחָה שְׁלֵמָה שֶׁאַתָּה רוֹצֶה בָּהּ, *a complete rest that You desire.* By utilizing the term "a complete rest" we are emphasizing that *every* aspect of our personality – body and soul – partakes of Shabbos' *Menuchah*.

With this approach – that Shabbos is a day of total *Menuchah* – we can appreciate why the soul as well as the body rests from its travails on Shabbos. It is only by allowing every aspect of our personality to rest on Shabbos – the body from its physical exertion and the soul from its struggles with the *yetzer hara* – that both the physical and spiritual dimensions of the *Menuchah* that we enjoy on Shabbos become clear.

(*Pinchas* 5634)

Resting for the Right Reasons

אבל המבוקש מבנ״י להתדבק בעיקר המנוחה. יכירו וידעו כו׳. ואא״ז מו״ר ז״ל אמר הגמ׳ המענג השבת נותנין לו משאלות לבו וצריך האדם להכין לו רצון אמת להיות משאלות לבו להש״ית ולעבודתו כו׳. וזה המשאלות לב הוא כל ימי השבוע.

As discussed in previous *divrei Torah*, every aspect of our personality, body as well as soul, rests on Shabbos. In fact, not only *Klal Yisrael* but all of Hashem's creations achieve a certain degree of equilibrium and *Menuchah* on Shabbos. However, it is imperative that we rest for the appropriate reasons. It should not simply be a pause from our physical activities, but rather a time to come closer and to cling to Hashem (a concept known as *deveikus*). We emphasize the critical importance of resting for the right reasons in our *Minchah* services by saying, יַכִּירוּ בָנֶיךָ וְיֵדְעוּ כִּי מֵאִתְּךָ הִיא מְנוּחָתָם, *Your children should recognize and acknowledge that their rest is derived from You.*

In a similar vein, *Chazal* (*Shabbos* 118b) note that one who delights in the Shabbos will be granted the (fondest) wishes of his heart. It is important that we express the loftiest wishes every Shabbos and that we seek to be rewarded by coming closer to Hashem, rather than through mere gratification of our physical needs. (*Pinchas* 5634)

◆§ Mortals Approaching the Level of Hashem's Heavenly Servitors

שהתחתונים מתרעמין למה העליונים נזונין מטמיון והתחתונים אם אינם יגיעים אין אוכלין. תו העליונים קרובים אל המלך והתחתונים נדחו ע״ש. והנה בשבת הוא יום מנוחה ונק׳ מתנה טובה וא״צ יגיעה והתחתונים מתקרבין ויש להם עלי׳ ולכן הוא שלום שעליונים ותחתונים נעשין אחד ביום השבת.

To appreciate another dimension of the concept of *Menuchah*, we recall the *Midrash* (*Yalkut Bereishis* 4) that distinguishes between Hashem's creations on earth (especially man), who must strive to attain *kedushah* and to come close to Hashem, and those heavenly servitors of Hashem, who attain closeness to Him without such efforts. However, on Shabbos, a day of *Menuchah*, even Hashem's servants on earth (*Klal Yisrael*) have the potential to acquire the spiritual level that is generally enjoyed by *malachim* (and other spiritual entities) in heaven. It is in this sense that we may also understand *Chazal's* description of Shabbos as a Divine gift (refer to our chapter on this topic). What greater gift than to enjoy the potential to approach Hashem in a manner well beyond that which we possess during the week.

Utilizing this approach, we may interpret the *Zohar* (cf. *Bereishis* 48a) that suggests that the Shabbos day is also called *Shalom*, a time of peace (refer to our chapter on this topic). Whatever "acrimony" may have been fostered between us here on earth and Hashem's servitors in heaven — by Hashem's decision to require mortals to strive for *kedushah* while Hashem's servitors attain exalted levels of sanctity without such efforts — is remedied on the Shabbos. An atmosphere of peace prevails on Shabbos between Hashem's mortal servants on earth and those who serve Him in heaven. Even mortals may rest from their strenuous efforts on Shabbos and with comparative ease attain a level of *kedushah* resembling that of *malachim*. (*Bereishis* 5653)

◈ A Taste of *Olam Haba* (Yaakov and Yisrael)

פי׳ כי בעוה״ז האדם נק׳ מהלך ממדרגה למדרגה כענין שאמרו הצדיקים אין להם מנוחה ילכו מחיל אל חיל וכשהאדם מתקן כל מעשיו מסתלק מעוה״ז נמצא אין להם מנוחה רק בבא יום השבת שהוא מתנה מן השמים שיהי׳ יום מנוחה וכמ״ש ז״ל שיהי׳ כאילו כל מלאכתך עשוי׳ שבכל מקום שאדם עומד בבא יום השבת חל עליו השלימות ויש עלי׳ לכל המעשים שעשה עד עתה כאילו כל מלאכתו עשוי׳ ולכן נק׳ יום מנוחה בעוה״ז מעין עוה״ב.

During our lifespan on this earth, it is difficult to achieve perfection or even to enjoy the opportunity to bask in one's previous spiritual accomplishments. In fact, during our entire existence in *Olam Hazeh* we are considered to be a *mehalech*, a traveler who is constantly seeking new dimensions and greater levels of *kedushah*. Indeed, it is only when we have completed the spiritual journey that is expected of us that we then depart from This World. However, on Shabbos, a day of rest that *Chazal* describe as a time when all of our work (that we are capable of doing at that time) has been completed, we can rest from our constant spiritual striving and reflect on what has been accomplished thus far. Regardless of the spiritual progress we have made, with the advent of Shabbos, we perceive a sense of *sheleimus* at that level. (*Bereishis* 5653)

וכתב במדרש ויבוא יעקב שלם וכו׳ ויחן את פני העיר שנכנס בע״ש כו׳. כי אחר תיקון כל השלימות נמשך הארה מעולם העליון והוא שבת מנוחה מעין עוה״ב. וזה הי׳ שינוי שמו של יעקב שיש גם לכל איש ישראל ב׳ שמות בעוה״ז ובעוה״ב. והנה יעקב זכה להמשיך שם עליון לעצמו בהיותו בעוה״ז.

To attain a taste of *Olam Haba* every Shabbos, one must have earned this distinction through his efforts during the six weekdays preceding Shabbos. *Chazal* (*Yalkut Bereishis* 340) relate that Yaakov *Avinu* entered Shechem immediately before the onset of Shabbos. Perhaps they are indicating that he exploited every moment of the week, until he achieved spiritual perfection at the week's close. As the *pasuk* states, וַיָּבֹא יַעֲקֹב

שָׁלֵם עִיר שְׁכֶם, *Yaakov arrived intact at the city of Shechem* (*Bereishis* 33:18) — when he was complete (שָׁלֵם) having attained as much spiritual perfection as it is possible while still in *Olam Hazeh*. Once he completed this process, Yaakov received a taste of *Olam Haba*, as the *pasuk* continues, וַיִּחַן אֶת פְּנֵי הָעִיר, *and he encamped before the city*, which can also be interpreted — "he was graced (related to חֵן) as he entered the city," with Hashem's blessing from above.

In this vein, we may justify the additional name, Yisrael, that Yaakov received. Having completed his mission, Yaakov was now entitled to another name. Whereas every Jew enjoys one name in This World and another in the World to Come, this *tzaddik* having completed his mission in *Olam Hazeh* was prepared to receive his "other-worldly" name while still living in This World. (Adapted from *Vayishlach* 5639)

וז"ש מה טובו אהליך יעקב משכנותיך ישראל. הם ב' הבחי'. יעקב הוא העבודה בעוה"ז בין האומות. וישראל הוא שורש בנ"י למעלה ושם מקום המנוחה בחי' מנוחת שבת דכתיב ביני ובין בנ"י אות הוא ואין שם מגע נכרי ושם שוכן ישראל במנוחה וזהו משכנותיך ישראל. ולמטה צריכין מכסה והגנה וז"ש אוהליך יעקב.

וב' בחי' יש בישראל. והם ב' שמות יעקב וישראל. שבעוד שהי' נלחם עם עשו ולבן נק' יעקב כמו עבודת ימי המעשה. ואח"כ נק' ישראל שהוא ע"ש החירות שרית עם אלקים כו'. והוא בחי' הש"ק. ועל ב' אלו כתיב טובו אהליך יעקב. משכנותיך הוא השבת מנוחה ושם לא יש מגע נכרי וזהו לבדד ישכון כדכ' ה' בדד ינחנו כו'.

In fact, the two names Yaakov and Yisrael may represent the Jewish people's status during the weekdays and Shabbos respectively. Just as Yaakov *Avinu* was forced to confront enemies such as Lavan and Esav with tactics that may have appeared to be deceptive — as the name Yaakov (related to וַיַּעְקְבֵנִי זֶה פַעֲמַיִם, *he deceived me twice*; *Bereishis* 27:36) implies — so too, during the weekdays, *Klal Yisrael* is locked in constant battle against the ideals of non-Torah influences. However, on Shabbos, a day when, to some extent, we prevail over the *yetzer hara*, we utilize the name Yisrael given the Patriarch to celebrate his triumph against his adversaries. Bilaam alludes to this distinction by proclaiming, מַה טֹּבוּ אֹהָלֶיךָ יַעֲקֹב מִשְׁכְּנֹתֶיךָ יִשְׂרָאֵל, *How goodly are your tents, O Yaakov, your dwelling places, Yisrael* (*Bamidbar* 24:5). Whereas on Shabbos, the day of *Menuchah,* we rest comfortably in our dwelling places, during the weekdays we require the protection offered by our "tents" (against the often hostile external environment). (*Balak* 5640, 5644)

ובמדרש בשש צרות יצילך ובשבע לא יגע בך רע. כי ששת ימי המעשה הכנה לשבת ונקראים ימי עבודה שצריך אדם לעבוד בהם הן בגשמיות וברוחניות עבודה שבלב הכל הכנה לשבת להיות נכנס לקבל השבת במנוחה וכמו כן ימי עוה"ז הכנה לעוה"ב. וכמו כן יציאת אבינו לחו"ל הי' הכנה לחזור לא"י במנוחה.

In fact, our entire lifespan in *Olam Hazeh* may be compared to the six weekdays. Just as we prepare during the week for Shabbos, while we are alive in This World we are preparing for the World to Come. Moreover, the decades that Yaakov was compelled to spend in *chutz la'aretz* (outside Israel) may also be perceived as a time of preparation for his return to *Eretz Yisrael,* which is reminiscent of *Olam Haba.* The enhanced spirituality of *Eretz Yisrael,* in turn, evokes the *ruchniyus* of *Olam Haba.* How fitting it is that Yaakov returns to Shechem and to *Eretz Yisrael* at the onset of Shabbos. Perhaps, Hashem granted us the sublime spirituality of Shabbos in the merit that the *Avos* loved *Eretz Yisrael.*

(*Vayishlach* 5640)

רק כפי מה שפורש עצמו מעוה"ז כך זוכה לטעום טעם עוה"ב. וכמאמר חז"ל מי שטרח עצמו בערב שבת. פי' התערובות שנתערב תאוות האדם לחיצוניות עוה"ז ... ובנ"י שומרי שבת פי' ששומרים הרצון שלא להתערב בדברי הבל. וע"ז נאמר מי שטרח בע"ש כו'. כי בימות החול הוא הבירור מלהתגאל בהבלי עולם ועי"ז זוכה לטעום בשבת טעם עוה"ב כי שבת מעין עוה"ב.

Continuing this analogy between Shabbos and *Olam Haba,* we gain additional insight into *Chazal's* statement, מִי שֶׁטָּרַח בְּעֶרֶב שַׁבָּת יֹאכַל בְּשַׁבָּת, *Whoever toils on erev Shabbos will eat* [enjoy the pleasures of] *on Shabbos* (*Avodah Zarah* 3a). Based on the foregoing analogy between Shabbos and *Olam Haba, Chazal* are suggesting that whoever makes an effort in This World, described as *erev Shabbos* — because of the mixture (*eruv*) of sensual pleasures along with spirituality — will merit to enjoy the spiritual bliss of *Olam Haba*, the world that is truly Shabbos. In general, there is a direct relationship between the extent that we abstain from the material pleasures of This World and our eventual enjoyment of the spiritual bliss of *Olam Haba*.

Using this approach, we gain additional understanding of the concept of being *shomrei Shabbos*. Just as the concept of Shabbos alludes to the spiritual pleasures of *Olam Haba*, those who are *shomrei Shabbos* guard themselves from the superficial allure of the worldly pleasures of This World in favor of the true pleasures to be enjoyed in the World to Come. Great significance can be attached to what a person desires — the sensual pleasures of *Olam Hazeh* or the spirituality of *Olam Haba*.

(*Chukas* 5636)

◈§ Attaining *Ruach Hakodesh*

וזה בחי׳ מנוחה שהיא בחי׳ נבואה ורוה״ק כמ״ש ונחה עליו רוח ה׳ וכן דרשו חז״ל מנוחה לא מצאתי על הנבואה וזה בחי׳ נשמה יתירה מעין עוה״ב שיהי׳ כל עם ה׳ נביאים כמ״ש ונבאו בניכם ובנותיכם. ולכן בשבת נאסר המלאכה לבנ״י כי תכלית המלאכה והמעשה להיות כלי שיחול הקדושה ורוה״ק על הבריאה וכל ימי המעשה הכנה לשבת וע״י המלאכה היא הסתלקות רוה״ק ונקרא חילול שבת.

To appreciate yet another dimension of the concept of *Menuchah*, we recall various *pesukim* which imply that the concept of *Menuchah* is virtually synonomous with *Ruach Hakodesh* (the Divine Spirit). For example, Yeshayahu, when describing *Mashiach*, writes, וְנָחָה עָלָיו רוּחַ ה׳, *The spirit of Hashem will rest on him* (11:2), a clear reference to the *Ruach Hakodesh* that will imbue *Klal Yisrael's* future leader. Similarly, the comment of Baruch ben Neriah, וּמְנוּחָה לֹא מָצָאתִי, *and I have found no rest* (*Yirmiyahu* 45:3), is understood by *Chazal* as a reference to *Ruach Hakodesh*. We suggest that just as in the Future World every Jew will merit to attain the level of prophecy (refer to *Yoel* 3:1 — וְנִבְּאוּ בְּנֵיכֶם וּבְנוֹתֵיכֶם, *your sons and daughters will prophesy*), so too, on Shabbos, which is a microcosm of *Olam Haba* (and a day when we benefit from the additional dimension of the *neshamah yeseirah*), we attain a level of closeness to

Hashem that resembles *Ruach Hakodesh* (refer to our chapter on *Melachah* for discussion of the relationship between the *Ruach Hakodesh* that we attain every Shabbos and the prohibition of *Melachah*).

(*Bereishis* 5662)

◈ The Divine Spark Within Us Rests

ולכן סמך פ׳ לא תשא למצות שבת שכיון שיש באיש ישראל חלק אלקית לכן נאסרו במלאכה ביום השבת

When we rest on Shabbos, it is not only our body (*guf*) that rests but also the very Presence of the *Shechinah* that is contained within all of us. When Hashem proclaimed, אָנֹכִי ה׳ אֱלֹהֶיךָ, *I am Hashem your God,* He ensured that every Jewish soul was imbued with a spark of the *Shechinah*. Just as He rested on Shabbos, so too, we – and specifically the Divine Presence that every Jewish *neshamah* possesses – rest as well.

Utilizing this approach, we gain new insight into the *pasuk* which implies that we must rest on Shabbos because Hashem created the universe in six days and then rested on Shabbos. What is the relationship between Hashem's abstinence from creating on Shabbos and our obligation to rest on Shabbos? In light of the foregoing approach, we suggest that the Torah is drawing an association between Hashem resting on the first Shabbos and His Presence within us that partakes of the *Menuchah* that every Shabbos brings. (*Yisro* 5648)

This idea linking the obligation to observe Shabbos to the Divine Presence within every Jew is supported by the juxtaposition of the commandment of לֹא תִשָּׂא אֶת שֵׁם ה׳ אֱלֹהֶיךָ לַשָּׁוְא, *You shall not take the Name of Hashem, your God, in vain* (*Shemos* 20:7), which alludes to the Divine Presence that lies within every one of us (a theme discussed in *The Three Festivals,* pg. 255), to the *mitzvah* of Shabbos. If the obligation of resting on Shabbos was merely based on the historical fact that Hashem once rested on Shabbos, then all mankind – not only *Klal Yisrael* – should be obligated to emulate its Creator by resting on Shabbos. However, in light of the above approach that it is primarily the Divine Spark that every Jew possesses that rests on Shabbos, we can appreciate the uniqueness of this *mitzvah* for the Jewish people.

(Adapted from *Yisro* 5656)

◆§ Attracting Sparks of *Kedushah*

וזה ענין שביתת שבת שנק' יום מנוחה כי כל המלאכות בימי המעשה הכל להוציא הני"ק שבתוך העשי'. וכשאדם עוסק בהם מתדבקין בו. ויש להם עלי' והוא בדרך יגיעה. אבל בשבת כ' אל יצא איש ממקומו. ממילא משמע דבימי המעשה צריך לצאת ממקומו לעסוק במלאכות. ובשבת יום מנוחה שאדם במקומו וממילא מתקרבין הני"ק השייכים אליו.

Yet an additional insight into the impact of the *Menuchah* of Shabbos may be derived from the observation of the *Ohr HaChaim*, that the Jewish people have been charged with the mission of attracting sparks of *kedushah* that may have been intermingled with the world at large. Throughout the *galus*, wherever we migrated, we enjoyed the capacity to elicit *nitzotzei kedushah* (sparks of holiness) even in the most inhospitable environment. In fact, this objective — finding sparks of *kedushah* in a world saturated by non-Torah values — may well be a primary mission during our stay in *galus*. However, if *Klal Yisrael* fulfills its historic mission of being immersed in Torah, it is able to attain the same objective (attracting sparks of *kedushah*) without even leaving the sacred environment of *Eretz Yisrael*.

Following the approach of the *Ohr HaChaim HaKadosh*, we suggest that all week long as the Jew leaves his sheltered environment and performs various forms of *melachah* to exploit the universe that Hashem created, he is also fulfilling his mission of elicting sparks of *kedushah* through his conduct in the material world. (Of course, this mission is accomplished at all times through *limud Torah*.) Similarly, every Shabbos, though we don't leave our immediate environment (cf. *Shemos* 16:29, *Let no man leave his place on the seventh day*), we are able to accomplish our objective of attracting sparks of *kedushah* simply by partaking of Shabbos' *Menuchah*. (*Yisro* 5658)

◆ The Relationship Between Noach and the Concept of *Menuchah*

בזוה׳ק כ׳ נח בחי׳ שבת כו׳ ע״ש. ברש״י עיקר תולדותיהם של צדיקים מצות ומעש״ט. כל הנבראים צריכין לעשות תולדות פי׳ כי השי׳ת נתן נקודה קדושה בכלל הבריאה.
וז׳ש הפ׳ אלה תולדות נח בחי׳ מנוחה וישוב הדעת לחזור כ״א לשרשו ולהבין כי אין לו חיות מעצמו כלל ועי״ז עושה תולדות והתפשטות עכ״ז עיקר התולדות תלוין בזה.
בזוה״ק כ׳ נח הוא בחי׳ שבת כו׳ ע״ש. ברש״י עיקר תולדותיהם של צדיקים מצות ומעש״ט. כל הנבראים צריכין לעשות תולדות פי׳ כי השי״ת נתן נקודה קדושה בכלל הבריאה ... וז״ש הפ׳ אלה תולדות נח בחי׳ מנוחה וישוב הדעת לחזור כ״א לשרשו ולהבין כי אין לו חיות מעצמו כלל ועי״ז עושה תולדות אף כי בחי׳ זו היפוך התולדות והתפשטות עכ״ז עיקר התולדות תלוין בזה ... שבשבת כל הברואים מתבטלים לשורשן וזה כבודו ית׳ כי כל מה שברא הקב״ה בעולמו לכבודו ברא. ולכן כפי מה שיודע האדם שכל כח התולדות הוא ממנו ית׳. ומבטל עצמו אליו ית׳ קודם כל דבר. עי״ז יש קיום והתפשטות למעשיו ויכול לעשות תולדות כנ״ל [ונראה כי לכך ת״ח מזדווגין משבת לשבת לברר כי התולדות הם רק ע״י הביטול אליו ית׳ ובשבת הם עיקר התולדות כנ״ל].

According to the *Zohar* (cf. *Bereishis* 118), Noach personified the concept of Shabbos. In addition to the obvious similarity between the *Menuchah* of Shabbos and Noach's name (the term *noach* resembles that of *Menuchah*, and they both may connote a sense of rest), a more profound relationship may be manifest between this *tzaddik* and the day of rest.

Just as on Shabbos every Jew returns to his roots (refer to many of our previous *divrei Torah* on this theme that resonates throughout the *Sfas Emes'* writings), so too, a *tzaddik* such as Noach is always able to cling to his roots despite any association he may have with the secular world. The *Zohar* notes further similarities between Noach and the Shabbos, stating that they both were able to produce "fruits" — *toldos*, to bring another generation into fruition. While this characterization seems appropriate for Noach who bore three children, it would seem that the Shabbos day — the one occasion when Hashem rested from creating — should not be described in such terms. Evidently, it is not the actual creation of the universe during the six weekdays, but rather the return of the universe to its sacred roots on Shabbos that is the true source of the ongoing existence of This World. While on the surface it may appear that the creations of the six days are the source of everything that exists, the only permanent "fruit" that the universe bears is made possible through Hashem's cessation from creating on Shabbos.

In fact, just as the permanent impact of Shabbos is felt because of the capacity of the universe to return to its sacred roots on this day, so too, the generations reared by Noach were made possible because of his capacity to negate himself to the Source of his life (his true *shoresh*), Hashem, as we shall elucidate. While it is certainly true that Hashem endowed every one of His creations, and especially mankind, with the capacity to bear future generations, to be fully effective — and enjoy worthy children — it is necessary to replicate the pattern followed by Hashem when He created the first human beings. Just as Hashem implanted His Divine Spark in the first man that He created, so too, when mortals bring into fruition future generations, they also need to realize that whatever generations they produce are only possible because we negate ourselves to the *Shechinah*. It is only by understanding that it is *HaKadosh Baruch Hu* rather than ourselves that enables us to have children that we merit to bring future generations into This World. As the first *pasuk* in *Parashas Noach* may be interpreted, אֵלֶּה תּוֹלְדֹת נֹחַ, "these are the generations that were made possible by following the spirit of Noach" — returning to one's roots.

Drawing upon our foregoing remarks that success in bearing future generations is contingent upon realizing that it is *HaKadosh Baruch Hu* Who actually brings future generations into fruition, we suggest that it is perhaps for this reason that Torah scholars generally observe their *leil onah* on Friday night (cf. *Kesuvos* 62b). What better occasion to appreciate that our capacity to bear children depends upon our ability to negate ourselves to the true Source of Life, Hashem, than Shabbos when the entire universe returns to its heavenly roots.

(*Noach* 5635)

וש״ק כמו תיבת נח שבימות החול טרוד כ״א בעסקי עוה״ז ובש״ק יש מקום לבני ישראל לברוח ולהניח כ״ז להסתופף תחת צל כנפי השכינה והיא פריסת סוכת שלום כמו שהי׳ נסתר נח בתיבה והוא הביטול לשורש החיות שכל העולם חרב והי׳ צריך לקבל חיות חדש משורש החיים וכן בכל ש״ק כנ״ל.

We may also draw a beautiful analogy between the Shabbos day and Noach's *teivah,* ark (as well as Noach himself). All week long, we are so immersed in worldly matters that we seldom have time to come close to Hashem. On Shabbos, however, we depart from This World that is so defined by materialism and prefer to seek shelter under the protective embrace of Hashem — as we recite in the *Maariv* service every Friday evening, הַפּוֹרֵשׂ סֻכַּת שָׁלוֹם עָלֵינוּ, [*Hashem,*] *Who spreads the canopy of peace over us* (*Klal Yisrael*). In effect, every Shabbos we are replicating Noach's behavior. Just as Noach fled from a universe that had spiritually deteriorated, by seeking shelter in his ark, so too, *Klal Yisrael* escapes the mundane secular world of the six days in favor of the Heavenly canopy of peace that shields us every Shabbos.[1]

(*Noach* 5633)

1. Whereas Noach was compared to Shabbos, the *Avos* attained the spiritual level of *Yom Tov.* To appreciate this analogy consider the following distinction between Shabbos and *Yom Tov.* Whereas *Klal Yisrael* played no role in Creation, the event leading up to the first Shabbos, we participated in *Yetzias Mitzrayim, Matan Torah,* and the Divine Cloud — the seminal events commemorated by the *Yamim Tovim* of Pesach, Shavuos and Succos respectively. Even the precise date when the Festival is observed is determined by the *Sanhedrin* when it proclaims the New Moon, while the timing of Shabbos is always constant. Similarly, Noach was only able to attain his lofty spiritual level with Hashem's assistance, while Avraham, Yitzchak and Yaakov were not only great individuals but also through their own initiative were able to bring the *Shechinah* down to This World (*Noach* 5641).

While it may appear that the *Avos* achieved a higher spiritual level than Noach, it is important to recall that Noach's approach to *avodas Hashem* — depending upon Hashem's assistance — was a necessary prerequisite for the level attained by the *Avos.* As David *HaMelech* writes, *Lift up my soul from confinement to acknowledge Your Name* (*Tehillim* 142:8). Once Noach was lifted from his spiritual incarceration, it was possible for the *Avos* to truly praise Hashem. A similar relationship exists between Shabbos and *Yom Tov.* Every Shabbos, assisted by the *neshamah yeseirah,* the soul reaches a new relationship with Hashem, enabling the righteous to coronote Hashem. On *Yom Tov, tzaddikim* have attained a level so lofty that they are able on their own initiative to sanctify Hashem's Name (adapted from *Noach* 5646).

דאיתא בזוה"ק נח הוא בחי' שבת ונקרא נח ע"ש המנוחה כי הגם שגם נח הוכיח את דורו כדאיתא במדרש אך בעבור כי לא קבלו ממנו הי' ירא לנפשו פן יחטיאו גם אותו וביקש להציל א"ע ובמדה זו נהג עמו הקב"ה והסתירו בתיבה.

Drawing the parallel between the *teivah* and the spiritual protection afforded by *Shabbos Kodesh* even further, we suggest that Noach was genuinely concerned that despite his efforts at admonishing his peers regarding their grave sins, that he would be influenced by them and eventually emulate them. To protect him from the unsavory influence of his contemporaries, Hashem shielded him in the protective environment of the *teivah*. Similarly, every Shabbos, the day of *Menuchah*, we are sheltered from all harmful outside influences that may affect our spiritual growth. (Adapted from *Noach* 5661)

☙ A Day of *Chein* (Divine Favor)

ולכן נח מצא חן בעיני ה' שעל הצורה הפנימית חל החן. וכמו כן הוא בזמן בש"ק שהוא יום מנוחה דכתיב וינח. יש בו החן והוא הנחמה כמ"ש ששם נח על זה ינחמנו. ולכן שבת זכר למעשה בראשית דכ' וירא אלקים וכו' טוב מאוד ואיתא במד' שאמר הקב"ה עולמי עולמי הלואי שתהי' מעלת חן לפני כשעה זו ע"ש. ובכל ש"ק יש מציאות חן הזה לכן הוא זכרון למעשה בראשית והוא ג"כ ללמד על הכלל כולו על כל הזמנים וכמו כן מילה בנפשות בנ"י.

As we contemplate the parallel between Noach and the *Menuchah* of Shabbos (refer to the previous *dvar Torah*), it is important to remember that Noach was graced with the gift of *chein* (cf. *Bereishis* 6:8 — וְנֹחַ מָצָא חֵן בְּעֵינֵי ה'). To appreciate the concept of *chein* and to draw parallels between Noach's *chein* and the *Menuchah* of Shabbos, we recall that according to *Chazal* (*Zohar Bereishis* 59b), Noach was already circumcised at birth (and thus didn't require a *bris milah*). Whereas for most individuals the foreskin (known as the *orlah*) symbolizes an outer layer of materialism that must be removed through the sacred ritual of *bris milah*, by which a Jew can attain his true spiritual potential, in Noach's case, his potential for spirituality was manifest already at birth. When the Torah describes Noach's *chein,* it is alluding to his inner purity which was self-evident. The same sense of *chein* is present every Shabbos. According to *Chazal* (*Yalkut Bereishis* 16), when Hashem created the universe, He voiced His fervent wish that the universe continue to find as much favor in His eyes as it did at the time of its infinitely perfect creation. Despite any flaws that may result from our sins during the weekdays, on Shabbos the universe returns to the pure state that it enjoyed during Creation.[1] Consequently, the Shabbos day of rest is a time of Divine favor. This day merits to enjoy Hashem's *chein,* just as Noach found favor in Hashem's eyes. (*Noach* 5662).

והנה שבת מתעלה האדם בשורשו וחל עליו החן וזה שנק׳ שבת מנוחה ויש בו נשמה יתירה שהוא התגלות ציור הפנימי לכן שקול שבת בכל המצות.

In a similar vein, we suggest that not only the universe but also every individual returns to his sacred roots on Shabbos. This is evidenced by the introduction of the *neshamah yeseirah,* which allows us the opportunity to evoke our true inner potential. What greater source of *Menuchah,* of spiritual rest and comfort, than the *chein* that the universe finds every Shabbos in Hashem's eyes and all the indications of this new-found *chein* — the return of each Jew to his roots, the return of the universe to its roots, and the presence of the *neshamah yeseirah.*

(Adapted from *Ki Seitzei* 5655)

1. We refer to this concept during the Shabbos *Shemoneh Esrei* where we describe the Shabbos as זֵכֶר לְמַעֲשֵׂה בְרֵאשִׁית. While this phrase is usually translated, "a remembrance of the Creation," a literal translation of the term מַעֲשֵׂה בְרֵאשִׁית suggests that Shabbos is a reminder of the very inception of Creation — בְּרֵאשִׁית, the beginning of the universe.

⸎ Parallels Between the Wilderness Generation and the *Menuchah* of Shabbos

וזכו לזה בענין הדגלים שהם כמו מלאכי השרת שגופם מזוכך רק לעשות רצון קונם. וכמו כן יש מזה גם עתה כפי השתוקקות האדם ליישר כל מעשיו זוכה אל המנוחה דכ׳ ימצאהו בארץ מדבר כו׳ ולא הי׳ להם רק הרצון. וסובבנהו בענני הכבוד. יבוננהו בארון תוך הדגלים שהוא השראת אורו ית׳ מלבר ומלגאו. וכמו כן נמצא מזה בכל עת ע״י העבודה בימי המעשה מתקיים בשבת הארות אלו שנק׳ יום מנוחה כמ״ש על דגלו יחנו. יסובבנהו כמ״ש פורס סוכת שלום יבוננהו הוא הדעת וההשגה שניתוסף לבנ״י בשבת כמ״ש נשמה יתירה ניתוסף לאדם.

To appreciate the magnitude of the benefits accruing from the atmosphere of *Menuchah* that permeates Shabbos, we turn to an entire generation, the דוֹר הַמִּדְבָּר (Wilderness Generation). While traveling through the Wilderness enroute to *Eretz Yisrael,* they merited to be sheltered by the Divine Cloud and to live in close proximity to the *Mishkan* and, in particular, the *Aron* (ark containing the Tablets). Moreover, every tribe enjoyed its unique *degel* (banner), which besides its immediate significance for that tribe alluded to the exalted spiritual level that the Jewish people then enjoyed. According to *Chazal,* under ordinary circumstances, only angels merit the spiritual level to have banners of their own. The Jewish people in the Wilderness rose to a level similar to that of *malachim.* Consequently, they enjoyed these symbols of their distinctiveness and greatness.

In what merit did *Klal Yisrael* deserve to bask under the Divine Cloud and to enjoy these constant reminders of the *Shechinah*? — the *Aron* and the *degalim.* It appears that it was on the basis of their intense desire to fulfill the Divine Will and to follow Hashem no matter where He took them. As Moshe recalls in the Song of *Haazinu,* ... יִמְצָאֵהוּ בְּאֶרֶץ מִדְבָּר יְסֹבְבֶנְהוּ יְבוֹנְנֵהוּ, *He discovered him in the wilderness land ... He surrounded him* (with the Divine Cloud), *He granted him discernment* (*Devarim* 32:10). This discernment is achieved through the enhanced understanding of Hashem that arises from the presence of the Ark as well as the tribal banners.

So too, every Shabbos – simply on the basis of our sheer desire that we demonstrate all week long (through our *mitzvah* observance) to bask in the spiritual serenity and *Menuchah* of *Shabbos Kodesh* – we enjoy an environment similar to that enjoyed by our forefathers in the Wilderness. Just as they were sheltered by the Divine Cloud, so too, every Shabbos, Hashem spreads His canopy of peace over the Jewish people, sheltering them from any harm that may befall them. As we read in the Friday evening *tefillah*, הַפּוֹרֵשׂ סֻכַּת שָׁלוֹם עָלֵינוּ, *He spreads the canopy of peace over us* (refer to our chapter on *Tefillos* Shabbos). Similarly, every Shabbos, inspired by the presence of the *neshamah yeseirah*, we gain enhanced understanding of *HaKadosh Baruch Hu* just as our forefathers, assisted by the tribal banners and the Ark, came close to Hashem.

(*Bamidbar* 5638)

◆§ A Safe Habitat (a haven from materialism)

והוא עיקר ומתגלה בש״ק כדאיתא פורס סוכת שלום עלינו א״כ מתעלין בנ״י להיות בצילו ית׳. וגם זה בכלל שהוא ביתך. וכ׳ אל יצא איש ממקומו ביום בשביעי א״כ יש לכל איש ישראל מקום מיוחד בש״ק שקונה בו שביתה ולכן כתיב לעשות את השבת לדורותם שנשחגה דירות בנ״י בש״ק. ובני ישראל הם דומין לבוראם כמ״ש מקום אתי דרשו חז״ל הוא מקומו של עולם ואין עולמו מקומו כן איש ישראל אינו משועבד למקום אבל בכחו למצוא לו מקום שביתה.

When discussing the manna that was enjoyed by *Klal Yisrael* during the years that it spent in the wilderness, the Torah writes, אַל יֵצֵא אִישׁ מִמְּקֹמוֹ בְּיוֹם הַשְּׁבִיעִי, *Let no individual leave his place on the seventh day* [to gather the manna] (*Shemos* 16:29). By using the phrase "his place" in the context of Shabbos, the Torah is implying that an integral component of the rest that we enjoy on Shabbos is the ability of every Jew to find a safe haven on that blessed day and a place that is secure from the material temptations of the natural world. We evoke a similar sentiment in the *Maariv tefillah* of Shabbos by saying, הַפּוֹרֵשׂ סֻכַּת שָׁלוֹם עָלֵינוּ, [*Hashem*], *Who spreads the canopy of peace over us* and consequently protects us from the outside world. When David *HaMelech* expresses his gratitude for being admitted into Hashem's Home through His abundant kindness (cf. *Tehillim* 5:8, וַאֲנִי בְּרֹב חַסְדְּךָ אָבוֹא בֵיתֶךָ), he may be referring to the haven that every Jew enjoys on Shabbos. In fact, in this regard a parallel may be drawn between *Klal Yisrael* and Hashem (כביכול). Just as we know that He is מְקוֹמוֹ שֶׁל עוֹלָם וְאֵין הָעוֹלָם מְקוֹמוֹ, *the Place of the universe* (He is Omnipresent) *rather than the universe being the place where He is located* (even the entire world can't contain Him), so too, rather than being bound to the world in which we live, *Klal Yisrael* enjoys the capacity, especially on Shabbos, to find a spiritually secure place for itself. (*Noach* 5650)

Negating Materialism – Attaining the *Neshamah Yeseirah*

ובזוהר איתא בפסוק נותן נשמה לעם עלי׳ ורוח להולכים בה פירוש המתהלכים בארץ הגשמיי אין להם רק רוח. ואותן שהם עלי׳ ושולטים על הארץ. להם יש נשמה ע״ש. וכמו כן בשבת שמבטלים כל המעשים אליו ית׳ וזה החירות והמנוחה שהאדם שולט על המעשים לבטלם בעבורו ית׳. אז זוכין לנשמה יתירה.

The *Menuchah* of Shabbos refers not only to the safe habitat that we enjoy (as discussed in the previous *dvar Torah*), but also to our efforts to negate everything material in favor of the spirituality of Shabbos.

To appreciate how we benefit from negating the material world every Shabbos, we quote from Yeshayahu: נֹתֵן נְשָׁמָה לָעָם עָלֶיהָ וְרוּחַ לַהֹלְכִים בָּהּ, *Who gave a soul to the people upon it, and a spirit to those who walk on it* (42:5) – Hashem grants a *neshamah* to those who are "above" the earth and a "*ruach*" to those who walk on it (the earth). This *pasuk* may suggest that a lesser form of spirituality, known as *ruach*, may be enjoyed even by those who walk on and partake of this earth. The term *neshamah* seems to imply a more advanced spiritual state, that may only be attained by those who are above the earth and transcend all of the material pleasures of this earth in favor of true spirituality. Every Shabbos – when in the spirit of *Menuchah* we negate everything material – we earn the distinction of enjoying the *neshamah yeseirah*.

(*Vayishlach* 5644)

☙ A Day When We Can Safely Enjoy the Material World Without Harm

ומה"ט ג"כ בשבת שהוא יום מנוחה וחירות מצוה להתענג כי אין התענוגים מזיקין לנפש. וגם זה תלוי כפי היגיעה בימי המעשה.

One would imagine that on this day of *Menuchah,* enhanced by the presence of the *neshamah yeseirah,* we would be obligated to abstain from the material world. On the contrary, on Shabbos, when we are finally free from the ill effects of the *yetzer hara* – and after having engaged the forces of evil for an entire week – we are now capable of enjoying some of the pleasures of This World (תַּעֲנוּגִים) without any adverse effect. While during the week material pleasures affect our soul's quest for spiritual growth, on Shabbos, a day of such rest and freedom from the *yetzer hara,* we can safely absorb the pleasures and comforts of This World without such harm. (*Re'eh* 5649)

☙ A Day of "Dual Freedom"

שגם במצרים שמרו השבת והוא יום מנוחה לכל מיני עבודות. ובשבת נעשה בן חורין ויכול לקבל עליו עול מלכות שמים. ויש שבת גדול מזה למי שכל ימיו תחת עול מלכות שמים. אז בשבת קודש יש לו מנוחה לעבדו ית' באהבה וברחבות לב. ואין צריך ליגיעה כמו בחול. ואז לשיצאו בנ"י ממצרים וכשהבטיח להם משה רבינו ע"ה שיצאו במכה זו האחרונה נעשו בני חורין ויצאו מעבדות פרעה ולכן השבת נק' שבת הגדול.

It is well-known that already in Egypt, the Jewish people observed the Shabbos as a day of *physical* respite from Pharaoh's slavery (refer to *Shemos Rabbah* 28 stating that at Moshe's urging Pharaoh granted his Jewish slaves a day of rest on Shabbos). For them, Shabbos was not only a welcome relief from Pharaoh's oppression but also an opportunity to recommit themselves to Hashem (a concept known as קַבָּלַת עוֹל מַלְכוּת שָׁמַיִם) at least once a week.

In later generations, when *Klal Yisrael* no longer faced the physical persecution of Pharaoh, the *Menuchah* of Shabbos assumed new meaning. Instead of being a welcome break from the slavery of the week past and a rare opportunity to come closer to Hashem, the Shabbos became a day of rest from many of the *spiritual* challenges of the week. For the Jew who has already accepted the challenge of Torah and *mitzvos* (עוֹל מַלְכוּת שָׁמַיִם), the six weekdays are often a time of intense conflict, contending with the *yetzer hara's* numerous attempts to tempt him to sin. For him, Shabbos is an opportunity to rest from such struggles and to serve Hashem with love and in an environment of comparative freedom from the importunings of the *yetzer hara*, a concept known as רַחֲבַת לֵב.

Utilizing this approach, we gain additional insight as to why the Shabbos before Pesach is known as *Shabbos HaGadol*, the great Shabbos. Whereas Shabbos had previously been observed (in Mitzrayim) as a time of *physical* relief from Egyptian slavery, once *Klal Yisrael* had been assured that their redemption from Egypt was imminent — and that Shabbos would no longer be needed as a day of respite from persecution — this greatest of days assumed an entirely different dimension. Now it became the day when the loyal Jew can rest from his *spiritual* struggles. Hence the term *Shabbos HaGadol*, the great Shabbos, the occasion when Shabbos attained its spiritual dimension. (*Shabbos HaGadol* 5634)

◆§ Freedom from the *Yetzer Hara*

וכ״ז נעשה בעצת הרשע ערום שע״י החטא מעה״ד מקדים היצה״ר באדם. ולכן קשה להיצ״ט לגבור עליו. והיה רצון השי״ת שיאכל אדם מקודם מעה״ח ולא הי׳ מזיק לו אח״כ עה״ד וע״י החטא הקדים היצה״ר. אכן איתא במד׳ כי הנשמה קודמת לבוא בעודו בבטן אמו לכן הנשמה מסייע ליצ״ט לגבור על יצה״ר ולכן שבת נקרא מנוחה שיש בו הארת הנשמה יתירה.

What greater sense of *Menuchah* than a respite from the *yetzer hara*, which is constantly tempting us to sin. On Shabbos, reinforced with the presence of the *neshamah yeseirah*, we are able to cope and contend with the Evil Impulse.

Had the First Man partaken of the fruit of the Tree of Life before enjoying the fruit of the Tree of Knowledge of Good and Evil, he would never have sinned and, in fact, would have remained in *Gan Eden*. To prevent us from repeating Adam's error and succumbing to our *yetzer hara,* Hashem implants the *yetzer hatov* already at the time of conception, while the *yetzer hara* emerges at birth. By reversing the sequence of Adam, who exposed himself to evil first, we are confident that we may prevail in the battle against the importuning of the *yetzer hara.* Our capacity to contend with evil is enhanced every Shabbos, the day of *Menuchah* when we benefit from the additional presence of the *neshamah yeseirah.* (*Noach* 5656)

ודבר זה נוהג בכל אדם כי מקודם צריכין ללחום עם היצה״ר ולפרוש עצמו ממנו. ולגבור נגד כל המחשבות והרצונות אשר לא לה׳ המה. ואז נעשה בן חורין והוא בן עוה״ב. כי מי שהוא בן חורין מיצה״ר ואינו משועבד לסט״א. הוא בן עוה״ב. והוא בחי׳ שבת. מנוחה בלי מלחמה ועבודה.

When Shabbos is compared to *Olam Haba* (*Berachos* 57b), it may be for this reason. Just as someone who is a true *ben Olam Haba* (having successfully overcome his *yetzer hara*), even while living in *Olam Hazeh,* is no longer tormented by the *yetzer hara,* so too, every Shabbos we may enjoy this respite (*Menuchah*).[1] (*Vayeishev* 5635)

ובש״ק א״צ עבודה בשום דבר אף במלחמת היצה״ר. דכ׳ ששת ימים תעבוד. ואם היינו מקיימין העבודה כראוי. אז ויום השביעי כו׳ לה׳. ומה שאין מרגישין המנוחה כראוי בשבת. הוא ע״י חסרון עבודה בחול. כמ״ש מי שטרח בע״ש כו׳. אעפ״כ כשבא שבת ורואין עצמם מרוחקין מקדושת השבת. ועי״ז שבין בתשובה מאהבה לבוא לקבל הארת השבת. ועי״ז איתא בע״ת בשעתא חדא וברגעא חדא. מתקנין הכל. וע״י אותו התשוקה לשבת נגמרין כל המעשים. לכן נא׳ ועשית כל מלאכתך. שיש בכח התדבקות אל השבת להשלים כח חסרון עבודה בחול כנ״ל.

Under ideal circumstances, we would feel a palpable sense of relief from the *yetzer hara* every Shabbos. The renowned *pasuk,* שֵׁשֶׁת יָמִים תַּעֲבֹד וְעָשִׂיתָ כָּל מְלַאכְתֶּךָ וְיוֹם הַשְּׁבִיעִי שַׁבָּת לַה׳ אֱלֹהֶיךָ, *Six days you shall*

1. The *tzaddik,* however, is not content to attain the already exalted level of being a *ben Olam Haba.* Once this status has been achieved, he now seeks to rectify his entire past. Using the context of Shabbos and the six weekdays, we suggest that the mission of the *tzaddik* is to consecrate the entire week (and his entire past) so that it will enjoy the same *kedushah* as Shabbos.

work and accomplish all of your work, and on the seventh day it is Sabbath to H*ASHEM*, *your God* (*Shemos* 20:9-10), may be interpreted as referring to the struggle against the *yetzer hara*. By working intently all week long to defeat the *yetzer hara*, all of your work — spiritual as well as material — will be completed by Shabbos.

If, in fact, we don't necessarily perceive a feeling of spiritual bliss and *Menuchah* as Shabbos arrives, it may be because we have been deficient in the intensity of our struggle against the *yetzer hara* during the previous weekdays. As *Chazal* relate, "Whoever exerts himself on *erev Shabbos* by challenging the *yetzer hara* will 'eat' (enjoy the *Menuchah* of) on Shabbos" (cf. *Avodah Zarah* 3a). Moreover, even those of us who haven't invested sufficient effort in the struggle against evil during the week, may still benefit from the *Menuchah* of Shabbos. This can be done by merely realizing when Shabbos arrives how distant we are from the *kedushah* of Shabbos and how insufficient our attempts at combatting evil all week long have been. When we come to this realization, we repent not merely out of fear of the consequences of not being prepared for the coming of Shabbos, but rather out of love (תְּשׁוּבָה מֵאַהֲבָה) as we enthusiastically seek to bask in the *kedushah* of Shabbos. By virtue of these feelings alone — despite our inadequate preparation all week long — we merit to enjoy the *Menuchah* and spiritual bliss of Shabbos. As the *Zohar* relates, the *baal teshuvah* can accomplish in one moment spiritual levels that it may take others a much longer period to achieve. As the foregoing *pasuk* implies, וְעָשִׂיתָ כָּל מְלַאכְתֶּךָ, *and perform/accomplish all of your work* – all your work will be done merely by yearning to develop an association with Shabbos. Despite our previous lack of preparation, we are able to return to Hashem with such love and enthusiasm that we can truly partake of Shabbos' *Menuchah*. (*Yisro* 5636)

כי ששת ימי המעשה הוא בבחי' מלחמה ז"ש תאכל מצות וביום השביעי יום מנוחה ומתגלה בו הארת התורה והוא ג"כ יום השירה דכתיב טוב להודות וכתיב ויום השביעי משבח ואומר כו'.

Utilizing this approach, we may be able to gain new insight into a seemingly difficult *pasuk* that apparently discusses the relationship between the first days of Pesach and the seventh day of this *Yom Tov*. The Torah says, שֵׁשֶׁת יָמִים תֹּאכַל מַצּוֹת וּבַיּוֹם הַשְּׁבִיעִי עֲצֶרֶת לַה׳ אֱלֹהֶיךָ, *Six days you shall eat matzos and on the seventh day there shall be an assembly for*

Hashem your God (*Devarim* 16:8). Responding to the obvious difficulty that one is only required to partake of matzah on the first evening of Pesach, not for six days, we suggest (homiletically) that the *pasuk* is alluding to the struggle against the *yetzer hara*, which we face for six days of the week: For six days you shall be engaged in combat, fighting the Evil Inclination,[1] and on the seventh day – Shabbos – basking in the environment of the Torah (which was given on Shabbos, refer to *Shabbos* 86b), you may rest assured that you will no longer be tormented by evil.

In fact, this theme stating that after six days of intense struggle against the *yetzer hara* we rest secure in the knowledge that we will no longer need to contend with evil, may pertain to the simple context of the foregoing *pasuk* that is referring to the seventh day of Pesach. After contending with the residue of Mitzrayim's evil environment for the six days immediately following liberation, *Klal Yisrael* finally finds itself free to convene a sacred assembly (*atzeres*) dedicated to Divine Service (especially by singing the שִׁירַת הַיָּם as we do on the seventh day of Pesach). Just as we recite in the Shabbos services that the seventh day is such an opportune time to sing Hashem's praises, so too, the day itself praises Hashem (וְיוֹם הַשְּׁבִיעִי מְשַׁבֵּחַ וְאוֹמֵר, *the seventh praises [Hashem] and says*). Similarly, on the seventh day of Pesach, the Jewish people after having prevailed against the *yetzer hara* are now able to sing Hashem's praises.[2] (*Pesach* 5654)

כי הנה כל המסעות היו להלחם עם הסט"א כמ"ש ויהי בנסוע כו' קומה כו' ויפוצו אויבך והוא בחי' ימי המעשה. ובנוחה הוא בחי' שבת. ובחי' יעקב הוא המלחמות שכל ימיו הי' לו מלחמות עם עשו ולבן. ואח"כ כשבא לבחי' ישראל הוא בחי' סתים ומנוחה בחי' שבת קודש. ובימי המעשה הוא בחי' גליא והוא ימי מלחמה להלחם עם הסט"א שהטבע מסתיר ומעלים בקדושה אבל איש ישראל צריך להלחם ולברר ולהעיד כי כל הטבע הכל מאתו ית"ש בלבד. וזהו בנסוע הארון. כמו שרמזו בנסוע גי' יעקב. והוא בחי' ימי המעשה.

With this approach – that we rest on Shabbos from our ongoing struggle against the *yetzer hara* – we gain new insight into the association between two *pesukim* that according to *Chazal* (*Shabbos* 116a) are a distinct

1. According to this approach, the term מַצָּה is related to וְכִי יִנָּצוּ אֲנָשִׁים, *If men shall fight* (*Shemos* 21:22).

2. For further elaboration on the association between Shabbos and the seventh day of Pesach refer to *The Three Festivals*, pages 107-111.

Book of the Torah — וַיְהִי בִּנְסֹעַ הָאָרֹן, *When the Ark would journey;* and וּבְנֻחֹה יֹאמַר, *And when it rested, he would say* (*Bamidbar* 10:35-36). These seminal *pesukim* may represent our challenges during the weekdays and Shabbos respectively. Whereas for six days we actively engage the *yetzer hara,* as the *pasuk* implies, קוּמָה ה׳ וְיָפֻצוּ אֹיְבֶיךָ, *Arise,* H*ASHEM*, *and scatter Your foes* (10:35), on Shabbos, the day of וּבְנֻחֹה (when we rest), we can prevail over the force of evil without a headlong confrontation.

A parallel may be drawn between the very different methods by which we cope with spiritual adversity on Shabbos and during the week and the names that characterize each phase of Yaakov's *Avinu's* life and struggle against evil. Just as Yaakov for much of his life was forced to openly contend with Esav and Lavan, so too, during the weekdays we openly engage the *yetzer hara.* That phase of his life is indicated by the name Yaakov, which alludes to his many struggles with Esav beginning at birth when he grabbed hold of Esav's heel (עָקֵב). However, just as Yaakov ultimately triumphed over Esav's angel and acquired the name Yisrael, which refers to vindication and victory over the forces of evil, so too, on Shabbos we rest from our incessant struggle against evil.[1]

(*Beha'aloscha* 5647, 5660)

ואח״כ לשכנו תדרשו כי הנה במקדש כ׳ מנוחה ונחלה דכמו דיש בשבת מנוחה שהיא הקדושה המתגלה בזמן ומתעברין מיני׳ כל חשכות הזמן לכן נק׳ מנוחה. כמו כן יש בעולם מקום בהמ״ק דהוא מנוחה שסט״א אין לה שליטה בשם. וכמו כן בנפשות רוה״ק נק׳ מנוחה כמ״ש גבי ברוך ומנוחה לא מצאתי ע״ש. והאדם צריך לדרוש לאותו המקומות והזמנים והנפשות שהקדושה מתגלה בהם וזה לשכנו תדרשו.

It is significant that both Shabbos and the *Beis HaMikdash* are described in terms of *Menuchah* — the first as a day of rest and the second

1. In this context, the *Sfas Emes* offers a beautiful definition of the *yetzer hara's* avowed purpose and our mission in deflecting and defeating the forces of evil. We present first a partial Hebrew text and a free translation of the *Sfas Emes'* insights: מי שונא לבורא עולם רק שהסט״א מסתיר ומעלים שלא לראות חסדי ה׳ וטובו אשר הם מלאים בכל העולם ... ובימי המעשה ... ימי מלחמה להלחם עם הסט״א שהטבע מסתיר ומעלים הקדושה אבל איש ישראל צריך להלחם ולברר ולהעיד כי כל הטבע הכל מאתו ית״ש בלבד, "Who hates the Creator of the universe? None other than the *sitra achara* (the force of evil) who makes every effort to hide and conceal so we don't see the kindnesses of Hashem and His good deeds that fill the universe ... during the weekdays, every Jew has to combat the *yetzer hara* who tries to conceal Hashem's kindnesses and who tries to attribute everything to natural causes ... Our function is to testify that everything in the entire natural world is directly attributable to Hashem alone" (*Beha'aloscha* 5660).

as a resting place for the *Shechinah.* Just as we elaborated in previous *divrei Torah* that on Shabbos we enjoy a respite from the importunings of the *yetzer hara,* so too, in the *Beis HaMikdash* we enjoyed a similar respite. In fact, in each of the three realms of *kedushah* – *olam* (universe), *shanah* (realm of time), and *nefesh* (soul) – we find a site that is immune from the forces of evil. Whereas the *Beis HaMikdash,* in the realm of *olam,* served as a safe haven from evil and Shabbos serves a similar purpose in the realm of time, so too, the gift of *Ruach Hakodesh,* the Divine Spirit (realm of *nefesh*), is enjoyed by those who prevail over the *yetzer hara* (refer to our earlier essay, "Attaining *Ruach Hakodesh*"). It is our sacred challenge to seek out those sacred "sites" and conditions which allow us to serve Hashem without the distracting influence of evil, as the Torah writes, לְשִׁכְנוֹ תִדְרְשׁוּ, *shall you seek out His Presence* (*Devarim* 12:5) – seek out those venues in which His *Shechinah* prevails.

(*Re'eh* 5648)

⁂ Unique to *Klal Yisrael*

בחי׳ שבת קודש יעשה כולו תורה ומיוחד רק לבנ״י ושם אין מגע נכרי ונק׳ יום מנוחה.

In the previous *dvar Torah* we noted that on Shabbos, the day of rest, we take a pause in our struggle against the *yetzer hara.* Shabbos is a day when we are immune to the importunings and blandishments of the *yetzer hara.* Similarly, Shabbos, a day in which the Covenant between *Klal Yisrael* and Hashem is reasserted (refer to *Vayikra* 24:8 where the Shabbos is described as *bris olam,* an eternal convenant), is an opportunity to immerse oneself in Torah and thus enjoy an intimate relationship with our Creator – a relationship shared by none of Hashem's other creations. (*Beha'aloscha* 5660)

◆§ A Day in Which We Can Listen to Hashem's Voice

ומאחר דכ׳ ולא שמעו מקוצר כו׳. א״כ בשבת קודש שיש בו נשמה יתירה ויום מנוחה. והוא היפוך מקוצר רוח ועבודה קשה. לכן כ׳ היום אם בקולו תשמעו על שבת קודש כמ״ש בירושלמי.

We may deduce from the fact that the Torah attributes the Jewish people's inability to listen to Moshe's assurances that they would be liberated from Egypt to מִקֹּצֶר רוּחַ וּמֵעֲבֹדָה קָשָׁה, *because of shortness of breath and hard work* (*Shemos* 6:9), to mean they suffered from a lack of spirituality and from hard labor. Shabbos, the day graced by the presence of the *neshamah yeseirah*, additional spirituality, and *Menuchah* (which is the antithesis of the conditions suffered by our forefathers in Egypt), is a particularly opportune time to listen to Hashem's Voice. As we say in *Kabbalas Shabbos*, הַיּוֹם אִם בְּקֹלוֹ תִשְׁמָעוּ, *today, if we but heed His call*, which *Chazal* say refers to Shabbos. (*Vaeira* 5650)

◆§ A Day of *Nishma* (Listening)

וזהו עצמו ענין הקדמת נעשה לנשמע שבנ״י נעשו ערבים לתקן העשי׳ כמ״ש עושי דברו. אח״כ לשמוע בקול דברו הוא לעתיד כמ״ש בעת יאמר ליעקב כו׳. וזה ג״כ נרמז בפסוק היום לעשותם כו׳ עקב תשמעון כי בעוה״ז נעשה ובעקב יהי׳ השמיעה.

In the previous *dvar Torah*, we stated that Shabbos is the ideal time and opportuntity to listen to Hashem's Voice. Expanding upon this theme, we note that by prefacing נַעֲשֶׂה, *we will do*, to נִשְׁמַע, *we will obey* (*Shemos* 24:7), *Klal Yisrael* was indicating that a certain sequence should be followed in our *avodas Hashem*. First in This World is נַעֲשֶׂה, loyally following the Divine Will without even obtaining a complete understanding of His wishes. Eventually, in the World to Come we will be privileged to not only understand the Divine Will but to actually perceive that we are hearing His Voice (נִשְׁמַע). This relationship can be deduced from the juxtaposition of the conclusion of *Parashas Va'eschanan* (*Devarim* 7:11) where the Torah writes הַיּוֹם לַעֲשׂוֹתָם, *today, to perform them,* meaning today (in This World) one must perform *mitzvos,* and the beginning of *Parashas Eikev* (7:12), וְהָיָה עֵקֶב תִּשְׁמְעוּן, which can be translated, *in the end you will will be able to listen.*

However, on Shabbos, which is a microcosm of the World to Come, even while we are in This World, we can listen to Hashem's Voice and obtain a more profound insight into His Will. On this day, when we rest from all מַעֲשֶׂה, acts of creation, we can focus on the נִשְׁמַע, listening and comprehending Hashem's Voice. (*Eikev* 5643)

⸎ A Day of Spiritual Reward

והשבת היא הנקודה כללית שצריך להיות התכלית שבאין ע״י כל המדות בפרט אל השלימות לכוון הלב להבורא ית׳. וזו המנוחה היא רק בעוה״ב לכן שכר מצוה בהאי עלמא ליכא כמ״ש עקב תשמעון. אכן בש״ק שהוא מעין עוה״ב מתנה טובה זוכין להארה כללית הנ״ל.

While we generally assume that שְׂכַר מִצְוָה בְּהַאי עַלְמָא לֵיכָּא, *we are not rewarded for our performance of mitzvos as long as we live in This World* (cf. *Chullin* 142a), to some extent that is not the case on Shabbos, which is a microcosm of *Olam Haba.* On Shabbos, a day of *Menuchah* when we enjoy a sense of spiritual "closure" and *sheleimus,* we benefit from an enhanced understanding of Hashem's attributes. As a result of this greater comprehension of His ways, we can serve Him with all of our capacities. Whereas during the week, we perceive various aspects of *avodas Hashem* (such as *yiras Hashem, simchah,* and *ahavas Hashem*) as being virtually distinct forms of Divine service, on Shabbos we enjoy the capacity to view these traits as part of a distinct whole. What greater reward in This World than this enhanced comprehension of how we can best serve Hashem.

(Adapted from *Eikev* 5647)

◆§ Our Sole Request on Shabbos

וכמו בש״ק דכתיב ממצוא חפצך כו׳ ע״י שמתגלה בש״ק הארה יתירה צריך האדם לשכוח עניני גופו וניתקן רק בקשה למנוחה וטהר לבנו כו׳ רק ממילא בודאי האדם שנזכר לפני השי״ת ממילא כ׳ אין מחסור ליראיו וממילא מי שיש לו חולה מתרפא ע״י תפלת שבת ג״כ אף שאיננו מתפלל עליו וזהו ענין לבקר את החולה . . .

The theme of *Menuchah* permeates and defines every aspect of Shabbos, including our *tefillos*. Whereas the weekday *Shemoneh Esrei* is replete with references to our *physical* needs (health, *parnassah*), on Shabbos we forgo all of these personal requests in favor of a simple plea for more enhanced *spirituality*. As we plead every Shabbos morning, וְטַהֵר לִבֵּנוּ לְעָבְדְּךָ בֶּאֱמֶת, *purify our hearts to serve You sincerely* (in truth). Just as we refrain from discussing our mundane personal and commercial needs on Shabbos, so too, we even avoid any reference to these matters in our *tefillah*. These needs are negated in favor of a simple plea for true *Menuchah* — a respite from the materialism of the week and a return to true *kedushah*.

Despite our reticence to specifically mention even pressing personal matters (such as an individual who urgently requires a *refuah sheleimah*) in our Shabbos *Shemoneh Esrei*, we may be assured that our unarticulated requests are heard by Hashem on Shabbos. As we recite at the conclusion of *Birchas Hamazon*, כִּי אֵין מַחְסוֹר לִירֵאָיו, *for there is no deprivation for His reverent ones* — those who fear Hashem never lack anything. By demonstrating our fear of Hashem through our staunch *shemiras Shabbos*, as reflected in our *tefillos* as well as in our overall behavior, we are assured that Hashem listens to both our unstated requests and our more explicit requests that we formulate during the weekday prayers. Specifically, whoever is pleading on behalf of a gravely ill individual may be assured that his *tefillos* on behalf of spirituality every Shabbos will assist the *choleh's* speedy and complete recovery.

(*Vayeira* 5634)

◆§ Attaining *Parnassah* Without a Struggle

ושבת נק׳ מנוחה שבשבת זוכין ללחם זה שלא ע״י ענוי ובירור. דאין בו פסולת.

Just as the *Menuchah* of Shabbos makes it unnecessary to specifically request a *refuah sheleimah* for those who are ill (refer to the previous *dvar Torah*), so too, we are assured that on Shabbos our material needs and our *parnassah* will be attained without all of the effort that is often required during the week. Just as *Klal Yisrael*, during the long period of slavery that they endured in Mitzrayim, were only able to obtain their bread through a great deal of suffering (hence the concept of *lechem oni*, the bread of poverty), so too, during the week we are required at times to struggle for our livelihood.[1] On Shabbos, however, a day of *Menuchah*, we may be able to earn our bread without those intensive eforts. (Refer to our chapter on *Lechem Mishneh* for further development of this theme.) (*Vayechi* 5656)

וכתי׳ והיתה שבת הארץ לכם לאכלה. פי׳ אכילת השמיטה לא יהי׳ ע״י הכנת האדם רק ע״י המנוחה והוא בחי׳ עונג שבת.

There is a precedent for our contention that *Klal Yisrael*, if proven worthy, can be sustained on the basis of *Menuchah* rather than through physical toil and exertion. In reference to the *Shemittah* (Sabbatical year), the Torah writes, וְהָיְתָה שַׁבַּת הָאָרֶץ לָכֶם לְאָכְלָה, *The Sabbath produce of the land shall be yours to eat* (*Vayikra* 25:6) — the cessation of work will be a source of your livelihood. You will be sustained during the *Shemittah* not by working the land, but rather by resting from work. Similarly, it is by participating in the *mitzvah* of *oneg Shabbos* that one will merit to benefit from Hashem's material blessings. Only those who rest from *melachah* are privileged to enjoy that sense of support and sustenance that Shabbos inevitably brings. (Adapted from *Behar* 5646)

1. This may refer either to the physical exertion involved during the process of earning our livelihood or to the constant struggle against the *yetzer hara* which dominates our lives during the weekdays.

❧ Two Ways of Winning Battles

ה׳ שמו הוא בהתגלות ביום השבת שנקרא יום מנוחה וז״ש שמע ישראל כו׳.

In previous *divrei Torah,* we have suggested that on Shabbos the entire natural world changes. Consequently, our objectives that are ordinarily accomplished at least partially through natural means, such as *parnassah* and good health, are realized supernaturally on Shabbos. In a similar vein, we suggest that Hashem helps us achieve victory against our foes on Shabbos through different means than during the week. Whereas during the week we attain success through what may appear to be natural means, on Shabbos, the day of *Menuchah,* we rest from this ongoing struggle against our foes. On this day, we prevail against all natural odds. On Shabbos, the mere mention of Hashem's Name is enough to ensure victory. On this sacred day, the overwhelming *kedushah* is enough to motivate our foes not even to attack. We allude to these distinct methods of waging battle whenever we recite the *Shiras HaYam,* ה׳ אִישׁ מִלְחָמָה ה׳ שְׁמוֹ, *HASHEM is Master of war, HASHEM is His Name* (*Shemos* 15:3). Whereas during the weekdays Hashem guides our fortunes in battle, acting as "Master of War,[1] on Shabbos the mere mention of His Name is enough to thwart any potential foe.

(Adapted from *Shoftim* 5650)

Extending our discussion of these two approaches to battle, we suggest that in each instance we are amply rewarded for our efforts. While we generally associate the concept of *neshamah yeseirah* with Shabbos, the day that we rest from battle, in reality, one can merit the presence of this "extra dimension of the soul" even during the week, by waging those battles that need to be fought (against our foes or against their spiritual equivalent, the *yetzer hara*), as we shall demonstrate.

1. According to *Sfas Emes,* at times Hashem may initiate the battle (motivate our foes to attack) in the interests of granting us a well-deserved triumph. As the *pasuk* implies, ה׳ יִלָּחֵם לָכֶם, *HASHEM shall do battle for you* (*Shemos* 14:14) — Hashem will cause the battle to occur for your benefit (לָכֶם).

בסוכה שחל ש״ש על הסוכה. ומעין זה בכל ש״ק פורס סוכת שלומו עלינו לכן נק׳ יום מנוחה.

As further proof that on Shabbos we can accomplish through peaceful means those objectives that we can only achieve all week long through a protracted struggle, we cite the *tefillah* recited specifically at *Maariv* of Shabbos, הַפּוֹרֵשׂ סֻכַּת שָׁלוֹם עָלֵינוּ, *Who spreads the canopy of peace over us.* Perhaps for this reason, Shabbos is known as a day of *Menuchah.* What greater respite than residing under Hashem's canopy of peace.

(*Succos* 5654)

בפסוק כ״ת מחנה כו׳ ה״א מתהלך בקרב מחנך ... וכמו שזוכין בשבת לבחי׳ נשמה יתירה ע״י המנוחה כמו כן בימי המעשה ע״י המלחמה לשם שמים.

When describing the preparation of Jewish armies for battle, the Torah writes, כִּי ה׳ אֱלֹהֶיךָ מִתְהַלֵּךְ בְּקֶרֶב מַחֲנֶךָ, *Because* H*ASHEM*, *your God, walks in the midst of your camp* (*Devarim* 23:15). We suggest that this refers to the presence of the *Shechinah* in each of us (our own individual "camp"). By fighting battles for Hashem's sake, we merit that the Divine Spark innate in each of us becomes the dominant force governing our lives, just as the *neshamah yeseirah* graces us every Shabbos. (*Ki Seitzei* 5660)

◆ Why We Don't Require the *Shofar* on Shabbos Rosh Hashanah

גם בבחי׳ הגוף. ובזה נלחם יעקב עם עשו ולבן. ובזה צריכין שופר כמ״ש וכי תבואו מלחמה כו׳ על הצר הצורר כו׳ והרעותם בחצוצרות. וכמ״ש זה בזוה״ק על תרועת ר״ה. אבל בשבת מתגלה בחי׳ ישראל. נחלה בלי מצרים. זה נחלת יעקב פי׳ מה שזכה יעקב אח״כ לשם ישראל הוא נחלה בלי מצרים. והוא יום מנוחה. ומה שנתגלה ע״י השופר כח הפנימית כמ״ש באור פניך יהלכון כן מהגלה בשבת בעצם היום.

Utilizing an approach similar to the theme of the previous *divrei Torah,* we may be able to understand with greater clarity why the *shofar* is not sounded on Shabbos Rosh Hashanah. It is only when Rosh Hashanah occurs on a weekday, when our primary mission is to combat the *yetzer hara* and every force that thwarts our efforts to serve Hashem, that we require the assistance of the *shofar*. Just as when we battle our physical foes the Torah requires us to sound the חֲצֹצְרֹת, *trumpets* (refer to *Bamidbar* 10:9), so too, when engaging the *yetzer hara* we turn to the *shofar*. On Shabbos, however, a day of peace not only in our relationship with our tormentors but in our struggle against the forces of evil, we can prevail even without the *shofar's* assistance.

This relationship between those times when Rosh Hashanah occurs on Shabbos — when we do not require the *shofar's* active intervention — and the more common occurrence of Rosh Hashanah during the week when we sound the *shofar*, may be compared to the names given to Yaakov *Avinu*. First, he is called Yaakov, indicative of the many battles that he endured against Esav and Lavan. Later, he is named Yisrael, representing the time when he triumphed over the forces of evil. Similarly, the *shofar* symbolizes Yaakov's constant struggles against those forces that thwart our *avodas Hashem*. Just as Yaakov attained the name Yisrael when he finally vanquished the last remnants of evil, so too, on Shabbos Rosh Hashanah we can accomplish through *Menuchah* and even without benefit of the *shofar* what otherwise would have required an intense struggle. (Refer to *Days of Awe* for further discussion as to why the *shofar* is not sounded on Shabbos.)

(Adapted from *Rosh Hashanah* 5662)

Why We Don't *Bentch Esrog* on Shabbos Succos

ומינים צלולך הם סימני דנצחון קרבא. לכן יש בהם ד׳ מינים בנ״ל עם חסיד כו׳. וסוכה היא המנוחה [ואפשר לכך אין נוטלין לולב בשבת כי הוא יום מנוחה לישראל. והמלחמה ליעקב בימי המעשה בלבד]

Following an approach similar to the previous *dvar Torah*, we can appreciate why we don't *bentch esrog* when Succos coincides with Shabbos. Just as the *shofar* represents the battle which we wage all week long against the forces of evil, so too, the *lulav* is identified by the *Zohar* as being מאני דקרבא, *tools of battle.* Just as we take weapons in our hands, so too, the Torah insists that we take the *lulav* and its other species in our hands. To combat the יָדַיִם יְדֵי עֵשָׂו, *the hands of Esav,* we respond with the spiritual armor of the Four Species held in our hands. On Shabbos, however, a day when we are not required to directly challenge the forces of evil, we triumph over our foes, physical and spiritual, even without the potent addition of the *arba minim.* Just as Yaakov eventually rests from his battle against "the hands of Esav," so too, on Shabbos we rest from these struggles and no longer require the Four Species. (*Succos* 5650)

לכן בשבת אין צריכין לולב שהיא יומא דנשמתין ולאו דגופא והיא יום מנוחה.

In a similar vein, we note that a primary purpose of the *arba minim* is to help our *guf* reach its full potential for Divine Service without being thwarted by the *yetzer hara* (cf. *Yalkut Vayikra* 652, which identifies various organs of the human body that correspond to each of the Four Species). However, on Shabbos, a day of *Menuchah,* the values of the *neshamah* so dominate that we no longer require the *arba minim.*

(*Succos* 5649)

☙ Accomplishment Without Controversy (*Machlokes*)

בענין הבארות עשק שטנה הוא עבודת ימי המעשה ורחובות הוא בשבת. כי בחול משיגין אלה הבארות ע״י המחלוקות ומריבות עם היצה״ר. ובשבת בא ע״י מנוחה מעצמו. ולכן נק׳ רחובות כי הרחיב ה׳ לנו. כי כשבא ע״י מעשה האדם א״י להתפשט הרבה שמביא לידי חסרונות. אבל בש״ק שבא ע״י השי״ת בלבד יש בו ברכה ומתרחבין הדברים וז״ש כי הרחיב ה׳ לנו ופרינו בארץ.

To appreciate another aspect of Shabbos' *Menuchah,* we recall the three wells that were dug by Yitzchak's shepherds and, in particular, the names that were given to them by Yitzchak (cf. *Bereishis* 26:19-22). Whereas the first two names (*Esek* and *Sitnah,* terms alluding to controversy) allude to the controversy that Yitzchak faced, the third, *Rechovos* (derived from rachav, *wide / broad*), indicates the wide acceptance that Yitzchak eventually attained. So too, our efforts during the weekdays often involve numerous confrontations with the *yetzer hara.* On Shabbos, basking in the atmosphere of *Menuchah,* we can accomplish our spiritual objectives without controversy.

Even the name which was given to the third well, *Rechovos* (connoting expansion) alludes to the spirit of Shabbos. Whereas anything accomplished during the weekdays of necessity involves considerable controversy and may be limited in scope, whatever is attained on Shabbos through a Divine gift is not subject to such limitations. As the *pasuk* in *Toldos* continues regarding the name *Rechovos,* כִּי עַתָּה הִרְחִיב ה׳ לָנוּ וּפָרִינוּ בָאָרֶץ, *Now HASHEM has granted us ample space, and we can be fruitful in the land* (26:22). (*Toldos* 5637).

ימי המעשה בחי׳ עשק ושטנה. ורחובות הוא ש״ק. יום מנוחה. והוא בחי׳ יעקב אבינו דכתיב בי׳ נחלה בלי מצרים ופרצת ימה כו׳ ע״ש במדרש. והרמז שא״י לבוא לבחי׳ זו עד שעוברין מקודם בחי׳ עשק ושטנה.

Expanding upon this theme, we suggest that the third well, *Rechovos,* corresponds to Yaakov *Avinu,* the third of of the *Avos.* Just as Yaakov was blessed with the *berachah* (*Bereishis* 28:13-15) that there would be no limits to his impact on the universe (וּפָרַצְתָּ יָמָּה וָקֵדְמָה וְצָפֹנָה וָנֶגְבָּה), so too, the impact of *maasim tovim* that *Klal Yisrael* performs on Shabbos is not subject to the same restraints that we face during the week.

On the other hand, we should not minimize the significance of the first two wells dug by Yitzchak's servants. It is virtually impossible to reach the level of *Rechovos* without first experiencing the preliminary difficulties that they faced. It is only through the efforts of the weekdays that one can achieve the gains of *Shabbos Kodesh.*[1] [2] (*Toldos* 5644)

1. Utilizing this approach distinguishing between wells that are dug in an environment of controversy (such as *Esek* and *Sitnah*) and the waters of *Rechovos* achieved without strife, we can appreciate why Moshe was unable to calm the Jewish people's fears when they despaired of finding waters at a site later named *Merivah,* strife. Moshe, who was on a *madreigah* (spiritual level) that was far removed from *machlokes,* simply could not "relate" to the approach of coming closer to Hashem through dissension and struggle. Every Shabbos we leave behind the approach of *mei merivah* in favor of *mei Menuchah,* the calm stability that was typical of Moshe *Rabbeinu* (*Chukas* 5656).

2. Refer to the previous footnote. To elaborate on this theme, and to appreciate why Moshe

דרשו את והב בסופה אהבה בסופה. כי בכל מלחמות ה׳ שהאדם לוחם עם הסט״א לשם שמים זוכה אח״כ למנוחה. והוא ענין מנוחת השבת אחר ימי המעשה שהם בחי׳ עבודה ומלחמה לברר האמת מתערובות הסט״א ובשבת אהבה בסופה.

When *Chazal* (*Yalkut Bamidbar* 764) note that antagonists who quarrel — if their arguments are *l'shem Shamayim* (in the interests of attaining greater comprehension of Torah rather than to enhance their own glory) — will eventually become close friends, they may be alluding to our struggles against the *yetzer hara* during the week. By being vigilant all week long, we eventually enjoy a measure of respite on Shabbos.

(*Chukas* 5648)

במדרש שלוחי מצוה דוחה השבת. הרמז כי באמת שבת הוא המנוחה והחזרת הנפש לשורשו כמ״ש שבו איש תחתיו ומעין שהי׳ הנשמה קודם השתלחותה בעוה״ז. אבל האדם נשתלח בעוה״ז וזה השליחות לעשות רצון הבורא ית׳ דוחה את השבת וכמ״ש נוח לאדם שלא נברא משנברא אעפ״כ הלא האדם עיקר חפצו ותשוקתו צריך להיות לעשות רצון בוראו וזה דוחה הכל וע״ז אמרו יפה שעה אחת בעוה״ז בתשובה ומעש״ט מכל חיי עוה״ב. וזהו הי׳ חטא המרגלים.

On the other hand, it is important to also appreciate the role of *machlokes l'shem Shamayim*. While it is certainly easier for us to enjoy the *Menuchah* and spiritual bliss of Shabbos, the controversy and challenges of the weekdays are equally critical. Just as the soul is reluctant to leave the spiritual tranquility that it enjoys before its emergence into the world — but does so nonetheless because this is the Will of Hashem — so too, while preferring the world without struggle that Shabbos epitomizes, we are prepared to follow Hashem's bidding and plunge into the challenges that the weekdays present. In a sense, the *Menuchah* of Shabbos

---

was commanded to speak to the rock (rather than strike it), we suggest that as the exemplar of reaching his objectives without *machlokes*, it would have been inappropriate for him to use force in obtaining water. On the contrary, it would have been appropriate for Moshe to speak to the rock, utilizing the approach of *mei menuchos*. Every Shabbos, a day which is dedicated to Torah and a day in which we evoke the spirit of Moshe, we return to this sacred level and achieve our objectives through the voice of Torah rather than through struggle against the *yetzer hara* (*Chukas* 5661).

is derived, to an extent, from successfully coping with the challenges of the week. In fact, the *neshamah* only reaches its full potential through its confrontation with evil in This World rather than in *Olam Haba.* It is purely in the Future World that we will enjoy יוֹם שֶׁכֻּלּוֹ שַׁבָּת, *a day* (or week) *that is totally imbued with the spirit of Shabbos.*

Unfortunately the *meraglim* (spies sent by Moshe who maligned *Eretz Yisrael*) erred in this respect. They were all too reluctant to leave the sheltered environment that they enjoyed in the wilderness in favor of the many challenges — spiritual as well as physical — that they would face living in *Eretz Yisrael.* They should have realized that fulfilling Hashem's Will rather than satiating oneself (even spiritually) is the purpose of our existence in This World.

Chazal (cf. *Yalkut Bamidbar* 13) allude to the relationship between the *meraglim's* fallacy and Shabbos by their pithy statement, שְׁלוּחֵי מִצְוָה דּוֹחֶה אֶת הַשַּׁבָּת, *Those who are sent on a mission that is a mitzvah may perform this mitzvah even at the expense of Shabbos.*[1] While we may prefer the rarefied ambiance of Shabbos — when the soul returns to its spiritual roots — to the struggles of the week, as designated emissaries of Hashem (*sheluchei mitzvah*), we are required to fulfill this function even at the expense of the Shabbos-like environment that we crave.

(*Shelach* 5657)

הוא המלחמה עם הסט״א כמו שהיו ימי יעקב בתחלתו להלחם עם עשו ולבן ואח״כ זכה לשם ישראל שהיא המנוחה בחי׳ שבת ... וע״ז נקרא שמו יעקב ע״ש וידו אוחזת בעקב עשו כי שם בעקב יש אחיזה לעשו וכמ״ש ויגע בכף ירכו. וזו היו״ד הנלחמת עם עשו וסט״א.

The significance of the struggles of the weekdays as well as Shabbos' rest is also borne out by the life of Yaakov *Avinu* and, in particular, by his names. Just as the Patriarch was destined to first undergo epic confrontations with Esav and Lavan, as the name Yaakov indicates (reminding us of the struggle against evil already at the pre-natal stage when he clutched his brother's heel), so too, we need to endure the

1. In this *dvar Torah,* the *Sfas Emes* is not discussing the halachic implications of the *Midrash* but rather its *aggadic* (homiletical) significance.

processs of combatting evil during the week. His struggle against evil eventually concluded with the triumph over Esav's angel and the acquisition of a new name, Yisrael, which represents the ultimate victory of good over the forces of evil. Similarly, after combatting the *yetzer hara* during the week, we rest assured on Shabbos knowing that our efforts have been successful. (*Shelach* 5660)

◆§ *Machlokes* During the Week Leads to *Menuchah* on Shabbos

והיא מחלוקת לש״ש וסופה להתקיים שע״י המחלוקת בא אח״כ למנוחה. וזה עצמו ענין ימי ימעשה ואח״כ בשבת קודש יום מנוחה כמ״ש לעיל בפ׳ קרח מזה. והוא ענין אומרם ז״ל לעולם ירגיז אדם יצ״ט על יצה״ר נצחו מוטב וא״ל יקרא ק״ש. פי׳ אף שאינו גובר לגמרי. מ״מ ע״י המחלוקת זוכה אח״כ בעת שבא זמן מנוחה ודביקות שאין לך אדם שאין לו שעה ואז נזכר לו זכות המחלוקת כנ״ל.

In the previous *divrei Torah,* we have emphasised the centrality of both the sense of *Menuchah* and *shalom* that permeates the Shabbos, as well as the challenges of engaging the *yetzer hara* during the week.

Expanding upon this theme, we suggest that the *machlokes* that we often are required to engage in during the week leads directly to the *Menuchah* of Shabbos. As *Pirkei Avos* relates, כָּל מַחֲלֹקֶת שֶׁהִיא לְשֵׁם שָׁמַיִם סוֹפָהּ לְהִתְקַיֵּם, *Every controversy that is intended for Heaven's sake will eventually be realized* (5:20). By engaging the *yetzer hara* during the week, we are assured that the objective of attaining a peaceful environment enabling us to serve Hashem will be achieved.[1] (*Pinchas* 5635)

1. Utilizing this approach, we can better appreciate the Gemara (*Berachos* 5a) which suggests that ideally one should, with the assistance of the *yetzer hatov,* confront the *yetzer hara.* However, if that approach does not succeed, then one should recite the *Shema Yisrael,* which is conducive to battling the temptation to sin. Apparently, the mere struggle and confrontation with evil — even if not totally successful — is a worthy first step enabling the individual to proceed to other more efficacious methods of engaging the *yetzer hara.* In fact, even when the individual has finally attained a measure of tranquility and is no longer beset by the *yetzer hara,* his previous confrontation against evil will still be considered meritorious (*Pinchas* 5635).

◆ Creating Conditions for Rebuilding the *Beis HaMikdash*

כי זה בכלל לשכנו תדרשו ע״י התכללות באחדות. כיון שע״י שנאת חנם נחרב. כ״ש שע״י אהבת ישראל יהי׳ נבנה בעזה״י. ושבת מוכן לזה. כמ״ש מו״ז ז״ל דכתי׳ כי לא באתם ע״ע אל המנוחה כו׳ הנחלה וש״ק יום מנוחה ונחלה כו׳. וביאור הדברים כי בהמ״ק וא״י הביא אחדות לבנ״י ולכן מקודם שלא הי׳ להם זה האחדות. הבמות מותרין. ובש״ק מתעורר האחדות.

As we indicated in the previous *divrei Torah*, on Shabbos we are able to accomplish without controversy many of the objectives that during the week are difficult to achieve without *machlokes*. The Torah (*Devarim* 12:9) may be alluding to the capacity of Shabbos to generate *achdus*, unity, by noting that the *Beis HaMikdash* can only be completed in an environment of מְנוּחָה וְנַחֲלָה, *a sense of peace and a true inheritance*. On Shabbos, a day of *ahavas Yisrael* (love of one's fellow Jews) and of unity, we are able to create these conditions that are conducive to the rebuilding of the *Beis HaMikdash*. Just as baseless hatred (שִׂנְאַת חִנָּם) contributed to the destruction of the *Beis HaMikdash*, so too, *ahavas Yisrael* and *achdus* will lead to its rebuilding. There can be no more favorable opportunity to create these prerequisites for *binyan Beis HaMikdash* than the day of Shabbos, a time of *Menuchah* from all of the *machlokes* of the week. (*Re'eh* 5641)

◆ Every Week a New Challenge: Every Shabbos Renewed Respite

ויש מחלוקת לש״ש וכניסי׳ לשם שמים. והם ימי המעשה ויום השבת. וכן כ׳ ויסעו ויחנו ויסעו ויחנו. וכמו הנ׳ שבתות השנה שבודאי בכל שבוע צריך להיות מלחמה חדשה ואח״כ בשבת קודש מנוחה וכניס׳ לש״ש כמ״ש ובנוחה יאמר שובה ה׳ רבבות אלפי ישראל שהוא הכניסי׳ של בנ״י. וכן לעולם הצדיקים אין להם מנוחה כדכ׳ ילכו מחיל אל חיל דרשו חז״ל מבהמ״ד לביהכ״נ.

In the previous *dvar Torah*, we emphasized the central role played by both the *machlokes* and struggles of the weekdays as well as the respite of Shabbos. This constant duality is alluded to by *Pirkei Avos* which emphasizes both the need for מַחֲלֹקֶת לְשֵׁם שָׁמַיִם, *controversy for Heaven's sake* (5:20), which is typical of our behavior during the weekdays when we engage the *yetzer hara*, and of כְּנֵסִיָּה לְשֵׁם שָׁמַיִם, *a unified gathering for Heaven's sake* (4:14), which accurately portrays the harmony of Shabbos.

Just as in the Wilderness, our forefathers first traveled – and in the process combated the enemies of *Klal Yisrael*, as well as the *yetzer hara* – and then rested (cf. *Bamidbar* 33:1-49 where the Torah presents a detailed itinerary of the journeys and rest stops during the Jewish people's sojourn in the Wilderness), so too, we first experience the challenges of the weekdays and then enjoy the respite of Shabbos. Just as our forefathers were never simply content with the objectives that they achieved during the first stages of their long journey through the wilderness but continually sought new challenges, so too, having experienced the respite of Shabbos, we seek new challenges as we embark upon the following week. As *Chazal* relate (*Berachos* 64a), צַדִּיקִים אֵין לָהֶם מְנוּחָה, *the righteous never rest*, but instead seek new challenges as they successfully combat the importunings of the *yetzer hara* and determine not to be absorbed in the material pleasures of This World. In general, we don't rest on our previous gains, rather we pursue new spiritual quests. This process of challenge followed by rest and then by further challenges continues as long as we live in This World.

(*Masei* 5645)

⁂ A Day that Is Free of Internal *Machlokes*

וזה המחלוקת באדם עצמו שמדה זו ממשיכו לכאן וזה לכאן. ובש״ק שזוכין לסייעתא דשמיא שורש העליון בהארת נשמה יתירה נק׳ יום מנוחה שבו מתאחדין כל המדות להיות אחד.

While we generally assume that *machlokes* refers to our struggle against an external foe, in reality, we all experience a certain degree of internal *machlokes* during the weekdays. Our various *middos* (character traits) each attempt to dominate our entire approach to life, but on

Shabbos, the day of *Menuchah,* they coalesce and we are not subject to this ongoing sense of internal dissension. On this day, blessed by the presence of the *neshamah yeseirah,* we attain a level of *achdus* (internal unity and harmony) unlike anything that could be achieved during the week. Thus, *middos* that at times may conflict during the week coexist harmoniously on Shabbos.[1] (*Korach* 5649)

◆§ A Day that Is Free from Controversy

ולכן אמר לא תבערו אש כו' ביום השבת. כי בחי' אש הוא זו המחלוקת שבאדם לשם שמים שזה בית יעקב אש להלחם עם עשו ועמלק. אבל שבת בחי' אור הבא מלמעלה בחי' שם ישראל והוא יום מנוחה לכן לא הבערו אש.

In the previous *dvar Torah,* we learned that the term *Menuchah* may refer to the cessation of *machlokes.* In this light, we may gain new insight into the renowned *pasuk,* לֹא תְבַעֲרוּ אֵשׁ בְּכֹל מֹשְׁבֹתֵיכֶם בְּיוֹם הַשַּׁבָּת, *You shall not kindle a fire in any of your dwelling places on the Sabbath day* (*Shemos* 35:3), which may be homiletically interpreted, "Do not kindle the fire of *machlokes* on Shabbos." Whereas all week long, it is often necessary to engage in protracted struggle against the forces of evil — just as Yaakov *Avinu* struggled against Esav — on Shabbos, the name Yisrael that the Patriarch gained when he prevailed against Esav is paramount (cf. *Bereishis* 32:29, *because you have striven with the Divine and with man and have overcome*). On Shabbos, represented by the name Yisrael, we no longer need to engage in such combat.

(*Vayakhel* 5657)

1. This thought is similar to the *Rambam's* observation that while love and fear are generally conflicting emotions, in the service of Hashem they both interact harmoniously.

◆§ Children and Servants

ואיתא בזוה"ק כי כל איש ישראל צריך לעבוד השי"ת בבחי' עבד לקיים פקודת המלך ובבחי' בן לחפשא בגנזין דמלכא. והם בחי' הדברות והמשפטים כנ"ל. והוא עבודת ימי החול. ושבת בחי' בן שאנו זוכין בשבת להתגלות דעת האדם שיסכים השכל לקיים רצון אבינו שבשמים בלי מלחמות. וזהו שנק' שבת שלום כי משפטי ה' אמת ובשמים הכל מעידין על צדקת הבורא וכ' ה' עוז לעמו יתן כו' יברך כו' בשלום. פי' ע"י שגוברין בכח התורה על היצה"ר זוכין אח"כ לשבת בחי' שלום.

All week long, our relationship to Hashem is that of servants of the King, whose function is to wage the King's battles and specifically to fight for the truthful teachings of the Torah in This World, which is so dominated by falsehood (a concept known as עלמא דשקרא). On Shabbos, we assume an entirely different function — we act as Hashem's children. What greater *Menuchah* than to assume the role of children "gathered around their Father's table," immersed in the spirituality of Shabbos. We are free of the controversy and deceit so typical of This World that we must contend with during the week.

Whereas a servant must often be coerced to fulfill the wishes of his master — and even we often perform *mitzvos* out a sense of obligation during the week — on Shabbos, as children of Hashem who are privy to the most profound thoughts of His Torah, we merit to reach the point where we desire on our own to fulfill the Divine Will. It follows that what is accomplished only through great effort during the weekdays, is attained without difficulty on Shabbos. (Adapted from *Mishpatim* 5636)

והענין הוא כי בנ"י שיצאו מא"מ להיות צבא מלחמה להלחם עם אויבי ה' כמ"ש יצאו כל צבאות ה'. וכתי' וחמשים עלו מזוינים זה הכח נטלו בנ"י ביצ"מ שנק' עבדי ה' ללחום מלחמות ה'. אך בקבלת התורה זכו בנ"י לבחי' בנים ובזה הכח יכולין לקרב מן האומות הראוים לזה וזה כח התורה עוז לעמו יתן יברך א"ע בשלום.

To appreciate further why on Shabbos we enjoy the status of becoming Hashem's children while during the week we remain His servants, we recall the time when each of these distinctions was first earned. While we became servants of Hashem at the time of *yetzias Mitzrayim*, it was not until the Giving of the Torah that we earned the distinction of becoming His children. As servants of Hashem, our primary function was to wage His battles, as evidenced by the Torah's assertion, וַחֲמֻשִׁים עָלוּ בְנֵי יִשְׂרָאֵל מֵאֶרֶץ מִצְרָיִם, *The Children of Israel were armed when they went up from Egypt* (*Shemos* 13:18). As children, however, our function is, wherever possible, to bring the rest of mankind to a greater appreciation of Hashem. This capacity to reach out to mankind and bring them closer to the Torah originated at the time of *Matan Torah*. As *Tehillim* states, ה׳ עֹז לְעַמּוֹ יִתֵּן ה׳ יְבָרֵךְ אֶת עַמּוֹ בַשָּׁלוֹם, *HASHEM will give might to His nation, HASHEM will bless His nation with peace* (*Tehillim* 29:11) – when Hashem gave His people "strength" (the Torah), He blessed them with peace and the ability to reach out peacefully to mankind.

On Shabbos (refer to our chapter on "Shabbos *Shalom*"), the day which is synonomous with peace, we assume the role of *banim*, children, which we first earned at *Matan Torah*. Thus, we are able to engage our spiritual foes through peaceful means rather than confrontation. However, during the week, maintaining our status as servants of Hashem, we focus on our more traditional role of battling the *yetzer hara*. (*Shoftim* 5660)

☙ Travels and Rest Stops (*Kohanim* and *Leviim*)

והענין הוא כדאיתא אין מלחמה נאה אלא לבחור לכן נדמה הקב״ה וב״ש בים כבחור איש מלחמה ובמתן תורה כזקן מלא רחמים ע״ש. והלוים הם אנשי מלחמה שקדים מרים ולכן רק קטנים כשרים ... וכמו שיש זמנים שבקדושה והפנימיות מתגלה בהם כמו כן יש צדיקים שעל ידיהם מעשה השלימות בעולם. והלוים היו בחינת הנהגה של ימי המעשה בקטנות.

Expanding upon the relationship between Shabbos and the weekdays and, in particular, how it pertains to the concept of *Menuchah*, we note that the sacred artifacts of the *Mishkan* (e.g. the *Aron*, *Menorah*, and the *Shulchan*) were borne by the *Leviim* while they were in transit and were administered by the *Kohanim* while they were at rest. By considering the distinct roles played by each of these descendants of Levi, we can appreciate why each group was suitable for its unique function. The *Leviim* were those who took a stand and battled for the integrity of Torah (we recall their courageous stand in the aftermath of the *Egel*). When the *Aron* and the other artifacts traveled through the treacherous Wilderness, replete with dedicated enemies of the Jewish people and numerous obstacles, *Klal Yisrael* required the guidance of the *Leviim*. On the other hand, while at rest and ensconced in the *Mishkan*, the ideal guardians were the *Kohanim*, whose primary function (emulating Aharon) was to infuse an environment of *shalom* into *Klal Yisrael*. This same distinction, first contending with struggles (as symbolized by the *Leviim*) followed by unity and a sense of serenity and harmony (symbolized by the *Kohanim*), characterize the relationship between Shabbos' *Menuchah* and the weekdays. (Adapted from *Korach* 5652)

◈ Resting While Traveling

על פי ה׳ יחנו ועל פי ה׳ יסעו היינו שגם בבחי׳ המסעות ובריחות שהיו בורחין ממקום למקום עכ״ז הי׳ אצלם המנוחה ולא הוצרכו לחלל השבת וכדאיתא בגמ׳ כיון דכ׳ על פי ה׳ כו׳ כסותר ע״מ לבנות במקומו דמי ע״ש. כי כל מסע היא שינוי מקום וביטול המנוחה והשביתה. אבל במסעות שלהם היו ג״כ אצל המנוחה.

We generally assume that "resting" is the antithesis of traveling. In order to enjoy a complete rest, we presume that we must remain in a stationary position. However, the journeys of *Klal Yisrael* in the Wilderness, in which our forefathers rested even while they were journeying, are the perfect counterexample to this notion. *Chazal* (*Bamidbar Rabbah* 23) go to great lengths to demonstrate that throughout their many journeys, our forefathers were never in flight. On the contrary, Hashem protected them at all times from the forbidding wilderness environment and from all of their foes. For *Klal Yisrael*, their various journeys while in the Wilderness were simply means of reaching their destinations. The Torah repeatedly describes their journeys as וַיִּסְעוּ וַיַּחֲנוּ, *they traveled and they camped*. Rather than being in flight, *Klal Yisrael* was simply traveling between each of their resting places. In the words of the Gemara (*Shabbos* 31b), כֵּיוָן דִּכְתִיב "עַל פִּי ה׳ יַחֲנוּ" כְּסוֹתֵר עַל מְנָת לִבְנוֹת בִּמְקוֹמוֹ דָּמֵי, *Since it is written* in the Torah: "*By the word of God they would encamp,*" their dismantling of the Tabernacle *was tantamount to dismantling it for the purpose of building* it again *in that very same place* (*Shabbos* 31b). This gemara (which has implications for *hilchos Shabbos* and, in particular, *hilchos boneh* and *sosair*) may be interpreted homiletically as follows: If we have an objective in mind, even while we are traveling towards that objective it is considered as if we are already at rest and have achieved our goal.

Nevertheless, by distinguishing between the journeys of the Jewish people and their rest stops, the Torah is indicating that the rest stops symbolized a higher *madreigah* (spiritual level) than their journeys to these destinations. This concept is somewhat similar to the association between the Shabbos and the weekdays in our lives, as we shall elaborate.

For us, too, the weekdays are not days of flight (ח"ו), but rather a means of achieving the ultimate *Menuchah* that every Shabbos brings. Just as our forefathers "rested" even while they traveled, so too, we partake of Shabbos' rest even during the week while we are en route to the next objective — the following Shabbos. In much the same way that our forefathers grew spiritually as they traveled from rest place to rest place, so too, each of the weekdays brings us closer to the following Shabbos, and each Shabbos, in turn, enables us to grow and ascend to even a higher plane. In fact, there is a numerical parallel (approximate) between the number of Shabbosos in the calendar year (approximately fifty) and the number of rest stops enjoyed by *Klal Yisrael* in the Wilderness (also fifty).[1] To draw the parallel even further between our forefathers in the Wilderness and the contemporary Jew, we conclude that just as they grew as they traveled from place to place and then rested, so too, we advance spiritually from week to week. (*Masei* 5643)

Attaining Enhanced Understanding of the Divine Will

וע"י היגיעה בחושך שהוא עבודת ימי המעשה זוכין בשבת להשגת הדעת שהוא נק' מנוחה מה שאדם מבין בשכלו ומשיג שורש הדברים לאמיתותן.

The relationship between Shabbos and the weekdays resembles the association that exists between the concepts of *emunah* (faith) and *emes* (truth). Just as we faithfully believe in Hashem's teachings (*emunah*) even prior to comprehending His Will (*emes*), so too, during the weekdays

1. This calculation is based on the assumption that *Klal Yisrael* experienced the 42 *masa'os* (travels) cited in the Torah, as well as the eight stops when they retreated after the passing of Aharon (refer to *Rashi, Devarim* 10:6). Similarly, the *Sfas Emes* assumes that there are approximately fifty Shabbosos during the year.

we serve Hashem even though we comprehend very little of His Divine Word. In the merit of the *emunah* that we display all week long in observing *mitzvos* and endeavoring to understand Hashem's Torah, we attain an enhanced understanding of Hashem's Word every Shabbos.

What greater sense of *Menuchah* than to better comprehend a more complete meaning of Hashem's Will. (*Mishpatim* 5639)

◊ Nothing but the Divine Will (*Ratzon Hashem*)

ובשבת מתבטלין בפועל כל המעשים והוא רצון בלי מעשה. וכן גם עתה כפי הביטול בשבת מתחדש רצון חדש לימי המעשה שאח"כ.

In the previous *dvar Torah,* we discussed our enhanced understanding of Hashem's Will that results from the *Menuchah* of Shabbos. Based on this approach, we can appreciate another aspect of the relationship between the Six Days of Creation and Shabbos. While undoubtedly everything that was created during the שֵׁשֶׁת יְמֵי הַמַּעֲשֶׂה (Six Days of Creation) was created according to Hashem's blueprint, it may appear that His imprint is obscured by His very creation (a concept known as *tzimtzum*). It may be difficult to perceive the *Shechinah* because of the magnificent universe that He created according to His Will. However, on Shabbos, a day when Hashem rested from creating, the material aspects recede to the extent that we can now perceive His Will without any obstruction or interference from the universe itself. (*Naso* 5634)

◊ Loyally Following Hashem (the *Chukah* Concept)

ולכן כתיב כי פרוע הוא שנפרשו מן אחדות האמת שהי' להם. ולכן אחר התיקון כתיב ויקהל משה שחזרו אל האחדות. ובכח השבת שהוא ג"כ בענין החוקה מתנה טובה יש לי. ואינו תלוי בעבודת האדם. ולכן כל בנ"י מתאחדין בשבת. ואז יש להם דביקות בעץ החיים ... כמ"ש ומצאן מנוחה אשה בית אישה. כי עיקר מנוחת האשה להיות סומכת ונמשכת אחר אישה. וזה הי' תחילת בחירת הקב"ה באברהם אבינו ע"ה לך לך מארצך כו' אל הארץ אשר אראך.

To appreciate another dimension of the *Menuchah* concept, we turn to *Megillas Rus* where Naomi wishes Rus and Orpah that they should attain מְנוּחָה אִשָּׁה בֵּית אִישָׁהּ, *rest, each woman in the home of her husband* (1:9). There can be no greater sense of rest and security for a woman than to place her confidence in her husband and to loyally follow his wishes. So too, every Shabbos, *Klal Yisrael* reinforces its innate capacity to loyally obey Hashem's Will. This trait is derived from Avraham who forsook his ancestral home and birthplace to follow the Divine command of לֶךְ לְךָ מֵאַרְצְךָ ... אֶל הָאָרֶץ אֲשֶׁר אַרְאֶךָּ, *Go for yourself from your land to the land that I will show you* (*Bereishis* 12:1).

Perhaps the capacity of Shabbos to evoke our latent ability to loyally obey Hashem's Will is derived from the very origin of this special day. According to *Chazal* (cf. *Shabbos* 10b), Shabbos is an unrequited gift granted by Hashem to *Klal Yisrael* (*matanah tovah*). Just as a gift could be granted by its donor without consideration as to the merit of its recipient but simply out of blind love (refer to our chapter, "The Gift of Shabbos"), so too, every Shabbos, we may attain the enhanced capacity to loyally fulfill the wishes of Hashem — regardless of our own perceived interests. While there are many aspects of *mitzvos* (e.g. עֵדוּת, מִשְׁפָּטִים), it is the חֻקִּים, *chukim* (statutes), those commandments for which there is no apparent reason, that require the greatest degree of subordination on our part. Every Shabbos, the day when we benefit from Hashem's unrequited gift, we are particularly inspired to loyally follow Hashem's Will.

One of the benefits that result from our renewed capacity to staunchly follow the Divine Will every Shabbos, is a renewed sense of *achdus* among the members of *Klal Yisrael*. To appreciate the relationship between *achdus* and observing Hashem's statutes (*chukim*), we turn to the two trees in the Garden of Eden. While the first man defied Hashem's Will and partook of the Fruit of the Tree of Knowledge, which led to the inevitable conflict between Good and Evil that has plagued every individual since the first sin, he could have chosen another and better alternative — to partake of the Tree of Life. Instead of being tormented by his constant quest to comprehend reasons for the Divine Will, which resulted from his eating the fruit of the Tree of Knowledge, Adam (and his descendants) would have been able to unwaveringly follow Hashem's bidding had he only partaken of the Tree of Life first. A similar error was repeated by the Jewish people at the time of the sin of the Golden Calf. Rather than simply trust Hashem, they sought to logically understand His Wishes and rebelled against Him (by erecting the *Egel*) at the first moment when they could no longer rationally grasp His Will.

In the aftermath of the *Egel*, *Klal Yisrael* was divided into many feuding factions — each with its own (incorrect) version of the Divine Will. As *Chazal* (*Avodah Zarah* 53b) note, the Jewish people reacted to the emergence of the Golden Calf by saying, אֵלֶּה אֱלֹהֶיךָ יִשְׂרָאֵל, *This is your god, O Israel* (cf. *Shemos* 32:4). Every faction of *Klal Yisrael* sought its own deity. The Torah describes the completion of the *Mishkan*, which was a rectification (*tikkun*) of the sin of the Golden Calf, in these words, וַיַּקְהֵל מֹשֶׁה אֶת כָּל עֲדַת בְּנֵי יִשְׂרָאֵל, *Moshe gathered* (and united) *the entire assembly of the Children of Israel* (*Shemos* 35:1). Similarly, every Shabbos — a day when we set aside our natural desire for an intellectual understanding of the reasons for *mitzvos* and instead follow Hashem loyally (in the spirit of *chukim*) — we too benefit from a renewed sense of Jewish unity.[1] (Adapted from *Parah* 5656)

☙ Attributing All Our Possessions to Hashem

ובימי המעשה שהוא על ידי כח האדם הגם כי הכל בעזר העליון. מ״מ אינו מבורר שהוא מן השמים. ובשבת קודש שמניחין כל המעשים בעבור השבת מתברר שהכל מהקב״ה. וכן שמעתי מפי מו״ז ז״ל שע״ז אומרין בתפילת שבת יכירו בניך וידעו כי מאתך היא מנוחתם. ולכן אין על זה מריבות. ונק׳ רחובות כי הרחיב ה׳ לנו דייקא. וי״ל כי כל המריבות הי׳ רק ע״ז. כמ״ש לאמר לנו המים. כי הגם שמיחס הכ׳ לרועי גרר. מסתמא נמצא מריבות אלו בלב כל איש. שנמשך פניות העבודת האדם כל שאינו מתברר כראוי ונגרר אחר המעשים תערובות רע.

Recalling the theme discussed in previous *divrei Torah* (see "Accomplishment Without Controversy," pgs. 264-268) that the well of Rechovos, which was dug without controversy, represents the *Menuchah* of Shabbos, while the first two wells named Esek and Sitnah attest to the constant struggle that we face all week long as we contend with the

1. As additional corroboration of the relationship between loyally following Hashem and engendering a sense of unity in *Klal Yisrael*, we recite the renowned *pasuk*, זָכַרְתִּי לָךְ חֶסֶד נְעוּרַיִךְ אַהֲבַת כְּלוּלֹתָיִךְ לֶכְתֵּךְ אַחֲרַי בַּמִּדְבָּר בְּאֶרֶץ לֹא זְרוּעָה, *I remember for you the kindness of your youth, the love of your united nation, [when] they followed Me in the wilderness, a land that was not sown* (*Yirmiyahu* 2:2). It was by following Hashem into the uncharted wilderness that we merited to earn the distinction of becoming *Klal Yisrael*.

yetzer hara, there is yet another dimension of Shabbos' *Menuchah*. It is the enhanced awareness that all that we possess is a Divine Gift, rather than the product of our efforts and hard work. Whereas the shepherds of Gerar, who were contesting Yitzchak's sovereignty over the first two wells, insisted that לָנוּ הַמָּיִם, *The water is ours* (*Bereishis* 26:20), no one doubted that it was Hashem Who enabled Yitzchak's shepherds to find the third well. It is not enough to rest on Shabbos, but rather it is also critical that we attribute our ability to rest (and take a pause from the material world around us) to *HaKadosh Baruch Hu*. All week long when we often make a strenuous effort to sustain ourselves, it is sometimes too difficult to appreciate that all that we possesss is a Divine gift. On Shabbos, however, when we cease all of these efforts, it is easier to realize that everything that we have is derived from Hashem. As we recite during the Shabbos *Minchah Shemoneh Esrei*, יַכִּירוּ בָנֶיךָ וְיֵדְעוּ כִּי מֵאִתְּךָ הִיא מְנוּחָתָם, *Your children recognize and acknowledge that their rest* (and the cessation from materialism that the *Menuchah* of Shabbos implies) *comes from You*. (*Toldos* 5645)

ואיתא אין טיפה שיורדת מלמעלה שאין טפחיים עולות כנגדה. ואלה הטפחיים הם עשק ושטנה. וע״ז רמז טוב מלא כף נחת שהוא בחי׳ שבת קודש. מנוחה מתת אלקים. ממלא חפנים שהם טפחיים העולות מלמטה שהם ע״י עמל ורעות רוח.

While it is certainly true that we generally only merit the Divine gift that we enjoy on Shabbos after the intensive efforts of the week (just as Yitzchak was only able to enjoy the waters of Rechovos after his strenuous efforts to dig the first two wells), it is important that we recognize that our efforts are nothing more than a beginning, which can only be consummated with Hashem's help. When *Chazal* (*Taanis* 25b) state, "Every drop of rainwater that comes from heaven is met by two drops of water coming from the earth," they may be alluding to the relationship between our efforts all week long and Hashem's blessing on Shabbos. Just as the first two of Yitzchak's wells symbolize our efforts all week long, so too, those "two drops of water coming from earth" allude to our efforts during that period. However, these two drops would be insignificant without the "single rain drop" (corresponding to the third well of Yitzchak) that emanated from Heaven. *Koheles* (4:6) alludes to the relationship between the two drops coming from earth and the single drop coming from heaven (the Divine blessing of Shabbos) by writing, טוֹב מְלֹא כַף נָחַת מִמְּלֹא חָפְנַיִם עָמָל וּרְעוּת רוּחַ, *Better is one handful of pleasantness* (emanating from Hashem on Shabbos) *than two fistfuls of hard work and vexation of spirit* — the result of our efforts during the week. (*Toldos* 5651)

◆§ Negating Oneself to Hashem

והנה ביטול באמת אין נמצא בעולם רק בבנ״י כמ״ש בפסוק אתם המעט ממעיטין עצמכם כי יש בעצם לבות בני ישראל דביקות וביטול לה׳ אחד. וזה אות השבת קודש שהוא עדות על בנ״י כי הביטול מכל המעשים הוא יום מנוחה להם שכל מגמתם להניח ממעשיהם ולהתבטל אליו ית׳. [וז״ש ישמחו במלכותך שומרי וקוראי עונג.]

Previously, we suggested that by resting on Shabbos, we demonstrate our loyalty to Hashem and emphasize that all of our material possessions are, in reality, His. It follows then that by ceasing to work every Shabbos, *Klal Yisrael* sets aside all of its material concerns and negates itself to Hashem.[1]

In fact, this is the very reason why *Klal Yisrael* was chosen as Hashem's Nation (*am segulah*) from all of mankind. As the Torah says, כִּי אַתֶּם הַמְעַט מִכָּל הָעַמִּים, *for you are the fewest of all the peoples* (*Devarim* 7:7) — because you are the nation that minimizes itself (i.e. negates itself) more than any other nation (see *Rashi* ibid.). This trait was demonstrated throughout Jewish history, and, in particular, by the Wilderness Generation which loyally followed Hashem wherever He took them. This *middah* is particularly manifested every Shabbos when we yield all of our material pursuits in favor of basking in His ambiance. Moreover, when we negate ourselves to Him, this is not merely out of a sense of obligation,

1. Our contention that there exists a relationship between *Menuchah* and negation to Hashem is demonstrated by the way the Torah describes the moment when *Klal Yisrael* entered the Sinai Wilderness: וַיָּבֹאוּ מִדְבַּר סִינַי וַיַּחֲנוּ בַּמִּדְבָּר, *They arrived at the Sinai wilderness and they rested in the Wilderness* (*Shemos* 19:2). What more apt description of the moment that *Klal Yisrael* began the process of *Kabbalas HaTorah* than "rest" — a sense of complete self-negation to Hashem.

but rather with great delight and joy. As we pray during *Musaf,* יִשְׂמְחוּ בְמַלְכוּתְךָ שׁוֹמְרֵי שַׁבָּת וְקוֹרְאֵי עֹנֶג שַׁבָּת, *They shall rejoice in Your kingship – those who observe the Sabbath and call it a delight.* This means that happy is the nation that coronates You (every Shabbos) and proclaims its great delight so that it negates itself to You. (*Bamidbar* 5644)

והוא מנוחה של בנ״י להראות כי כל התכלית ביטול המעשים. וכל המעשים ובקשת פרנסה וקיום הבריאות רק כדי לבוא להמנוחה כמו חול מכין לשבת. ולכן כיון שכל רצונם האחדות ממילא לא שייך כלל להאומות להתדמות אליהם ... וכיון שכל עוה״ז טפל אצלם לכך אינו בחשבון. כלשון המשנה אוכלין בעוה״ז ונוחלין לעוה״ב שהיא עיקר נחלתם. וכמ״ש תורתן קבע ומלאכתן עראי זה וזה נתקיים.

Utilizing this approach, we can appreciate Bilaam's reluctant acknowledgment that *Klal Yisrael* enjoys an extraordinary fortune. He exclaims, הֶן עָם לְבָדָד יִשְׁכֹּן וּבַגּוֹיִם לֹא יִתְחַשָּׁב, *Behold, it is a nation that will dwell alone* (it often enjoys uniquely good fortune) *and not considered among the nations* – when other nations celebrate their good fortune, it also enjoys their fate. (*Bamidbar* 23:9, cf. *Rashi*).

We attribute *Klal Yisrael's* good fortune to the fact that its sole purpose is to negate itself to Hashem, as indicated by its abstention from *melachah* every Shabbos. Even its mundane requests, such as *parnassah* and good health, are only means to achieve its sole objective of negating itself to Hashem. Any nation motivated by such noble ideals deserves extraordinary fortune. (*Balak* 5643)

וזה עדות השבת שניתן לבנ״י יום מנוחה שזה המנוחה שלהם כשבטלים מכל מלאכה וכיון שזה עיקר אצלם ממילא אוכלין גם בעוה״ז שהוא באמת טפל ועיקר נחלתם בעוה״ב.

This same theme is voiced by the Mishnah (*Avos* 5:19) stating that Avraham's disciples enjoy both This World (without any corresponding diminution of their ultimate reward) and *Olam Haba*. By negating themselves to Hashem and by ceasing all of their material pursuits every

Shabbos, *Klal Yisrael* is demonstrating that all of the pleasures of This World are trivial compared to the eternal reward of *Olam Haba*. Consequently, they deserve to reap the peripheral benefits of This World without being deprived of the true reward that lies ahead in *Olam Haba*.

(*Balak* 5644)

◆§ Derived from Hashem's *Nachas*

פי׳ שבשבת יש מנוחה בכל הענינים הן בגשמיות הן בעבודת השי״ת לכן צוה הקב״ה להיות נוחין בה גם ממלאכת עבודה כדי שיהי׳ ניכר המנוחה בכל דבר. והטעם שמתגלה בשבת רצון השי״ת שיש לו נייחא בשבת מהבריאה ע״י שומרי שבת. וכשמתגלה רצון השי״ת נמצא מנוחה בכל הנבראים כי כולם נבראו ממנו ית׳ שהוא שלימות הכל. וז״ש שאתה רוצה בה ועי״ז היא מנוחה שלימה בכל.

In previous *divrei Torah*, we demonstrated that both fulfilling as well as negating oneself to Hashem's Will are important aspects of Shabbos' *Menuchah*. We now suggest that, to a certain degree, a sense of rest and equilibrium is created from the fact that Hashem's Will has been realized. Perceiving that *Klal Yisrael* rests on Shabbos just as He did when He completed His creation, Hashem derives great *nachas* from the universe. This sense of *nachas* alone is enough to provide the universe that He created with a sense of rest and stability (*Menuchah*).

We voice this theme in *Minchah* every Shabbos afternoon by describing Shabbos rest as מְנוּחָה שְׁלֵמָה שֶׁאַתָּה רוֹצֶה בָּהּ, *a perfect rest in which You find favor* — a day of perfect (complete) rest that results from the satisfaction (רָצוֹן) that You, the perfect Creator, derived from all of Your creations.

(*Pinchas* 5634)

◈ Reciprocating Hashem's Attention

אך בשבת שהוא מעין עוה״ב הם נפרשין לגמרי מן האומות דכ׳ ביני ובין בנ״י אות הוא כו׳ כי ששת ימים כו׳ וינפש. פי׳ כמ״ש ופניתי אליכם פונה אני מכל עסקי כו׳ וזה בעוה״ב. ובש״ק מעין עוה״ב כביכול הקב״ה פונה מכל עשיות ששת ימים אל בנ״י. ולכן יש לנו ג״כ לשבות ביום ש״ק ולהניח הכל לפנות רק לעבודת השי״ת בלבד וזהו המנוחה.

Previously, we noted that by resting from *melachah* on Shabbos, *Klal Yisrael* is negating all of its material desires to Hashem. In a sense, Hashem acts in a similar manner every Shabbos. As we read in the *Kiddush* of Shabbos morning and in the Shabbos *Shacharis Shemoneh Esrei*, בֵּינִי וּבֵין בְּנֵי יִשְׂרָאֵל אוֹת הִיא לְעֹלָם, *between Myself and the Jewish people it* (Shabbos) *is a sign forever* ... וַיִּנָּפַשׁ, that *Sfas Emes* interprets, "He focused His 'Soul' on *Klal Yisrael*." Just as Hashem "focuses" His attention on *Klal Yisrael* and consecrates this day as a sign of His extraordinary relationship with them, so too, we "reciprocate" and abstain from all forms of *melachah* and instead devote our attention to His Torah and Divine Service. (*Balak* 5649)

◈ A Time to Appreciate Hashem's Wonders

ובאמת השבת ניתן ע״י להיות יום מנוחה להתבונן במעשה הבורא ית׳. שע״ז הוסד המזמור ליום השבת מה גדלו מעשיך כו׳.

There is no better time to appreciate the many wonders of Hashem than on Shabbos, when we rest from our material concerns. In fact, the Psalm (92) that is designated to be said on Shabbos, מִזְמוֹר שִׁיר לְיוֹם הַשַּׁבָּת, is primarily devoted to extolling the many wonders of Hashem — מַה גָּדְלוּ מַעֲשֶׂיךָ ה׳, *How great are Your wondrous creations, Hashem.* (*Shabbos HaGadol* 5647)

A Day of *Kabbalas HaTorah* (Without *Yesurim*)

והיא בחי׳ עבודת ימי המעשה שנק׳ ימי מלחמה. ובש״ק יום מנוחה יום שנתנה בו תורה.

On Shabbos, the day when the Torah was granted to *Klal Yisrael,* we enjoy a measure of *Menuchah* that we are unable to attain during the week. During the week (and during the period before *Klal Yisrael* received the Torah), the primary emphasis is placed on observance of specific *mitzvos.* While it is certainly possible to attain *kedushah* using this approach, doing so successfully inevitably leads to many battles with the *yetzer hara.*

In fact, the six days of the week are known as יְמֵי מִלְחָמָה, days that are devoted to battling the forces of evil. On Shabbos, however, enjoying an atmosphere dominated by Torah, we can rest, immune from the importunings of the *yetzer hara.* (*Bo* 5648)

כי גלות מצרים הי׳ הכנה למתן תורה שהוא מהג׳ מתנות שזוכין ע״י יסורים. אכן בזכירת יצ״מ יכולין לבוא לתורה בלי יסורים. וכמו כן בש״ק שהוא זכר ליצ״מ הוא יום מנוחה שזוכין לתורה בלי יסורים.

Utilizing this approach, we can better appreciate why Shabbos is described as זֵכֶר לִיצִיאַת מִצְרָיִם, *a remembrance of the Exodus from Egypt. Chazal* (*Berachos* 5a) relate that Torah is one of three entities that can only be obtained through suffering (*yesurim*). However, once *Yetzias Mitzrayim* occurred, relating the story of the Exodus is, in a sense, as effective as suffering is in enabling us to achieve knowledge of Torah. So too, on Shabbos, which is an eternal remembrance of *Yetzias Mitzrayim,* one can achieve greatness in Torah without experiencing suffering. Thus we derive another dimension of *Menuchah* – the weekly opportunity to attain great strides in Torah without experiencing *yesurim.*

(*Bo* 5657)

וזה הוא באנשים גדולים ומעין זה בכל איש ישראל כפי מה שמבטל ומכתת גופו כך זוכה לתורה. וכ״ז נעשה בדור הראשון שאחר כל היסורים זכו כמ״ש לב לדעת עינים ואזנים כו׳ היינו שנתהפך כל גופם תורה. אכן יש עוד פי׳ הסכת עשו כתות והוא דרך המנוחה שיכולין ג״כ לזכות לתורה ע״י כח כללות בנ״י. וכך הי׳ מוכן קודם החטא. ועי״ז הוכיח מרע״ה את בנ״י ... והיא בחי׳ מחלוקת לש״ש וכנסי׳ לש״ש. והם בחי׳ ימי המעשה בבירור תיקון הגוף שצריך כתיתה. ויום שבת מנוחה היא כנסי׳ לש״ש.

We demonstrate our assertion that, in some respects, one can acquire Torah with fewer prerequisites and less suffering on Shabbos than during the week from the two approaches offered by the Gemara (*Berachos* 63b) to explain the term הַסְכֵּת (used in *Devarim* 27:9). On one hand, it means כַּתְּתוּ עַצְמְכֶם עַל דִּבְרֵי תוֹרָה, *grind yourselves down over the words of Torah* (i.e. exert yourselves). On the other hand, it can mean עֲשׂוּ כִּתּוֹת וְעִסְקוּ בַּתּוֹרָה, *form study groups and engage in Torah study.* Whereas during the week, the former approach takes precedence – since it is only by depriving oneself of material amenities that one can integrate the Torah into his personality – on Shabbos, the latter approach pertains. By uniting oneself with all of *Klal Yisrael* and recommitting oneself to Torah, despite all of the material pleasures which accompany the Shabbos (in the form of *oneg Shabbos*), one can absorb *divrei Torah* more readily.

Chazal emphasize the significance of both מַחֲלֹקֶת לְשֵׁם שָׁמַיִם, *controversy for Hashem's sake,* and כְּנֵסִיָּה לְשֵׁם שָׁמַיִם, *a gathering for Hashem's sake* (cf. *Pirkei Avos* 5:20, 4:14). Based on the foregoing discussion, we may assume that during the week we achieve our Torah-related objectives through the means of *machlokes* – a direct confrontation with every material force that prevents us from reaching our true potential. On Shabbos, however, we are able to achieve our spiritual objectives without resorting to outright *machlokes.* Instead, by becoming an integral part of *Klal Yisrael,* the nation that received the Torah, we strengthen our own commitment and knowledge of Torah.

In fact, prior to the sin of the Golden Calf, *Klal Yisrael* had reached a spiritual level so great that it could absorb the Torah's teachings without first experiencing self-deprivation. It was only after that sin that *Klal Yisrael* had to experience all of the trials of the forty years that they spent in the Wilderness before they were prepared to truly master Torah. Every Shabbos, when we enjoy an atmosphere of *Menuchah,* we return to our former status where *yesurim* are no longer a prerequisite for Torah. (*Ki Savo* 5651)

שעיקר נתינת יום המנוחה כדי לעסוק בתורה כמ״ש שבת יעשה כולו תורה. ובשבת ניתנה תורה. והטעם שיש בכח יותר לבוא להשגת הדעת בש״ק. לכן קבעו הש״י יום מנוחה לישראל. וכמו בקבלת התורה קיבלה העולם בחי׳ נשמה כנ״ל. כן בש״ק יש נשמה יתירה.

Extending our analysis, we suggest that not only does the sense of *Menuchah* that we enjoy on Shabbos allow us to study Torah in a totally different frame of mind than during the week, it is also the very reason why Shabbos was designated as the יוֹם מְנוּחָה, *the day of rest* – so that we can enjoy the opportunity to study Torah. Just as the Torah was given on Shabbos, a day that is most opportune for mortals to achieve some insight into Hashem's teachings, so too, every Shabbos, taking advantage of the unprecedented opportunity for *Menuchah* that we enjoy, we draw closer to Hashem and attain further insight into His Torah. In fact, the *neshamah yeseirah* of Shabbos may be derived from the Torah-saturated environment of Shabbos. Just as the universe's "soul" (its spirituality) originated at the time of *Kabbalas HaTorah* (refer to *The Three Festivals*, pg. 195 for discussion of this concept), so too, on Shabbos, the day of enhanced spirituality, we enjoy the presence of an additional dimension of *ruchniyus*, the *neshamah yeseirah*. (*Yisro* 5642)

☙ A Day Permeated With Torah – Even for the סוחר

וכמו כן בעול דרך ארץ. הגם מי שצריך לעבוד על פרנסתו מ״מ נתן לנו השי״ת מצות השבת שהוא יום מנוחה. וכדאיתא שבת יעשה כולו תורה. וכל סוחר צריך להיות מקבל עול תורה ביום השבת ובכח זה מעבירין ממנו עול דרך ארץ בימי המעשה.

On a very simple level, we suggest yet another dimension of Shabbos' *Menuchah*: This day is an invaluable weekly opportunity for *everyone* to immerse themselves in Torah, even those who are absorbed in their material pursuits and quest to earn a livelihood all week long. The true significance of the *Menuchah* that we enjoy on Shabbos is the increased opportunity to study Torah that results from our forsaking all of our material pursuits. As *Chazal* (*Tanna d'Bei Eliyahu*) say, שַׁבָּת יַעֲשֶׂה כּוּלּוֹ תּוֹרָה, *make the Shabbos into a day that is exclusively devoted to Torah study.*

Utilizing this approach – that Shabbos affords even the סוֹחֵר (businessman) the possibility of being totally immersed in Torah – we derive new insight into a renowned mishnah (*Avos* 3:6), assuring us that כָּל הַמְקַבֵּל עָלָיו עֹל תּוֹרָה מַעֲבִירִין מִמֶּנּוּ ... עֹל דֶּרֶךְ אֶרֶץ, *anyone who takes upon himself the yoke of Torah ... the yoke of worldly responsibilities are removed from him.* Every businessman who commits himself especially on Shabbos to intensive Torah study, merits that the overwhelming burden of earning a livelihood during the week may be eased.

(*Toldos* 5648)

וכי ח"ו אין לדורות אלו חלק בתורה. ולכן נאמר שבש"ק זוכין בנ"י להיות בכלל אוכלי המן. וגם לפי הפשוט כן הוא שניתנה תורה לאוכלי המן שיש להם מנוח לעסוק בתורה ואין טרודין בפרנסה. ומה"ט ניתן השבת למנוחה לבנ"י לעסוק בתורה כמ"ש ז"ל שבת יעשה כולו תורה.

Just as the Torah was given originally to the generation that was nurtured by the manna – so that the Jewish people not be preoccupied with the pursuit of *parnassah* – so too, every Shabbos when we enjoy a respite from our material concerns, Hashem enables us to immerse ourselves in Torah. In fact, the reason why *Klal Yisrael* are required to rest on Shabbos may be to allow themselves the weekly opportunity to be immersed in Torah. (*Beshalach* 5647)

ואף שהשבת ניתן קודם התורה. מ"מ הי' בכח בתורה שמוכן לבנ"י. רק בקבלת בתורה נגמר בפרטות ובפועל ממש.

We suggest further, that not only is Shabbos the most opportune time to study Torah, but that the entire institution of Shabbos was granted to *Klal Yisrael* in the merit of *Kabbalas HaTorah.* While it is true that *Klal Yisrael* was already informed about Shabbos *prior* to *Kabbalas HaTorah* (at Marah; cf. *Rashi, Shemos* 15:25, שָׁם שָׂם לוֹ), nonetheless, it was only in the merit of *Klal Yisrael's* future acceptance of the Torah that we were given the Shabbos. (*Yisro* 5648)

Returning to Sinai

דהנה בראשונים כתיב חרות על הלוחות דרשו חז"ל חירות. דכתיב והלוחות מעשה אלקים המה שהיו דבוקים באלקותו ית"ש כמו שהיו מוכנים בנ"י בשעת מתן תורה להיות כמלאכים כמ"ש אמרתי אלקים אתם ... וכפי החירות שנמצא בנפשות בני ישראל כך מתקיים חרות על הלוחות. ולכן בש"ק שנק' יום מנוחה וחירות יש התגלות בתורה וזה קריאה התורה בשבת.

In the foregoing *divrei Torah,* we noted that as a result of the spirit of *Menuchah* that permeates the Shabbos, we are able to immerse ourselves in Torah study. Even the businessman, who all week long is preoccupied with his business, is able to exploit this opportunity for increased *limud haTorah.*

Furthermore, on Shabbos, we are even able to transcend the limits to our understanding of Torah that were imposed in the aftermath of the sin of the Golden Calf and ascend to new levels of comprehension, as we shall elaborate.

Prior to erecting the Golden Calf, *Klal Yisrael* was able to perceive the Divine Will simply by studying the *Aseres HaDibros.* As the Torah writes, וְהַלֻּחֹת מַעֲשֵׂה אֱלֹהִים הֵמָּה, *The Tablets were God's handiwork* (*Shemos* 32:16). This implies that through the *Luchos* which Hashem transmitted to Moshe (with the intention of presenting them to the Jewish people), *Klal Yisrael* would be able to develop an extraordinarily intimate relationship with Hashem — so close that by merely studying their content, the Jewish people could deduce the Will of Hashem. When *Chazal* (*Avos* 6:2) discuss the sense of freedom that was associated with the first *Luchos,* אַל תִּקְרָא חָרוּת אֶלָּא חֵרוּת, *Do not read "charus"* [that Hashem's Word was engraved on the *Luchos*] *but "cheirus"* (freedom), it may be alluding to the unusual intimacy that the *Luchos* were able to precipitate between Hashem and *Klal Yisrael* prior to the sin of the *Egel.* However, after sinning, the Jewish people, relegated to a less lofty spiritual level, were introduced to the vast body of *halachos* and *midrashim* which we now require to comprehend the Divine Will.[1]

1. Refer to the full text of *Sfas Emes* for a beautiful rendition of this theme. In particular there is a discussion of the unusual intimacy between *Klal Yisrael* and Hashem that we enjoyed at that time as reflected in the concept of *cheirus.*

Yet every Shabbos — a day that is permeated with an aura of *Menuchah* and freedom from the material world — we are, to some extent, able to retrieve the spiritual level that we attained at Sinai and enjoyed until the sin of the *Egel*. On Shabbos, we feel close enough to the Torah itself (as well as to the many teachings of *Chazal* that we utilize during the week to understand what Hashem expects of us) that we are given the opportunity to read the Torah itself (*krias haTorah*) at greater length than at any other time (in contrast to Mondays and Thursdays).

(*Ki Sisa* 5656)

◆§ Parallels Between the *Menuchah* of Sinai and Shabbos

וכמו שמנוחת השבת מאיר לאדם לימי המעשה כמו כן המנוחה שהי׳ לבנ״י במדבר סיני נאמר להם רב לכם הרבה זכות יש לכם כו׳ והי׳ בכוחם לירש את הארץ. שבת כמו שבת יום מנוחה כן הי׳ מקום המנוחה להם בהר הזה.

An interesting parallel may be drawn between the *Menuchah* that we enjoy every Shabbos and the Jewish people's stay (for almost a year) at *Har Sinai*. The Torah alludes to the similarities between both occasions by writing, רַב לָכֶם שֶׁבֶת בָּהָר הַזֶּה, *Enough of your dwelling by this mountain* (*Devarim* 1:6). By utilizing the term שֶׁבֶת (*dwelling/rest*), which is similar to Shabbos, the Torah implies that the time that *Klal Yisrael* spent on Sinai was a source of spiritual strength to them, just as Shabbos is for us. In the same manner that the *Menuchah* of Shabbos inspires us during the week ahead, so too, the time experienced by *Klal Yisrael* at *Har Sinai* would have enabled us to successfully conquer *Eretz Yisrael*. It was only because of their subsequent errors (i.e. the sin of the *meraglim*), that a forty-year stay in the Wilderness was necessary to supplement the time that they had spent at *Har Sinai*.

(*Devarim* 5661)

☙ A Day of *Penimiyus* (Inner Spirituality)

ועתה התחיל לבוא לפנימיות שלו בחי׳ שם ישראל כנ״ל. וכל איש ישראל יש בו ב׳ בחינות אלו. ויש בש״ק התגלות הפנימיות לכן נקרא יום מנוחה ויש בו הארה מבחי׳ תורה כמ״ש שבת יעשה כולו תורה.

Just as Yaakov *Avinu* enjoyed two names — the name Yaakov reflecting an *outer* (though highly significant) *dimension* that involved struggles with Esav and Lavan, and Yisrael, reflecting his *inner spirituality* that came to the forefront once Yaakov had prevailed over all of his foes — so too, all of us enjoy both dimensions: Our surface aspect predominates during the week, while our true inner side emerges every Shabbos. What greater *Menuchah* than spending the Shabbos day immersed in Torah, which, in turn, allows our inner spirituality to emerge.

(*Vayishlach* 5648)

וחז״ל רמזו חד אמר מטבע תיקן להם וחד אמר מרחצאות תיקן להם. והוא כנ״ל כי צורתו של יעקב חקוקה תחת כסה״כ והוא הצורה שרצה הקב״ה לברוא בעולם והוא מתגלה בשבת קדש ולכן מבקשין ישדר לן שופריה והוא שופרא דיעקב ודאדם. ויעקב לימד דרך להוציא צורה זו. וגם מרחצאות תיקן להם האיך להעביר הסט״א לרחוץ עצמו מלכלוך הגשמיות.

We may corroborate our contention that the inner *neshamah* of every individual emerges on Shabbos from the Torah's description of the Shabbos that Yaakov observed in Shechem. Having arrived there just prior to Shabbos (cf. *Yalkut Bereishis* 134) — and having designated the *techumim*, outer limits of the city (to determine how far one may travel on Shabbos) — Yaakov is graced with the blessing, וַיִּחַן אֶת פְּנֵי הָעִיר, *and he encamped before the city* (*Bereishis* 33:18). This may be interpreted homiletically, that he received the attribute of חֵן (Divine Grace) in sufficient measure that his פְּנִימִיּוּת, his inner spirituality (related to פני) emerged.

Chazal (ibid.) relate that when entering Shechem, Yaakov erected bathhouses, or (according to another version in the *Midrash*) instituted a currency system. We may homiletically interpret these comments of our Sages as being different suggestions how to attain *penimiyus* – reaching one's internal nature. We may either "wash away" previous sins (through a process of *teshuvah*), or evoke and bring to the forefront our true inner *penimiyus* (our true "currency" – our טֶבַע, *nature*), rather than the *chitzoniyus* (surface behavior) that often dominates during the week.

(Adapted from *Vayishlach* 5653)

◆§ Becoming A Witness

וזהו עיקר המנוחה דכתי׳ וינח דכת׳ וינח ביום השביעי. וינח גי׳ עד שהכל לכבודו ברא. מכ״ש בנ״י שנבראו להעיד על הבורא ית׳ כמ״ש עם זו יצרתי כו׳ תהלתי יספרו. והטבע מסתיר. וזהו המלחמה בעוה״ז שהסט״א עומד לבטל זה העדות. ובשבת וינח כמו והנחה למדינות עשה. וסהדותא איקרי שבשבת יכולין להעיד על הבורא וזה תכלית המנוחה.

A primary function of *Klal Yisrael* is to testify through their sterling conduct about the existence of *HaKadosh Baruch Hu*, as Yeshayahu (43:21) states, עַם זוּ יָצַרְתִּי לִי תְּהִלָּתִי יְסַפֵּרוּ, *I created this nation for Me so that they might declare My praises.* During the week when we struggle against the pervasive materialism of This World, it is difficult to completely perform this function. However, on Shabbos, a day of *Menuchah* from the natural constraints and the materialism of This World, we are able to elicit our inner desire for *ruchniyus*. Consequently, once we lead a more spiritual life, we may be in a far better position to accomplish our primary mission – bearing witness to Hashem.

When the Torah relates the *mitzvah* of resting on Shabbos to *yetzias Mitzrayim*, it may be for the purpose of assuring us of the success of our mission to testify about Hashem – at least on Shabbos. Just as at the moment of the Exodus, *Klal Yisrael* was able to extricate itself from the spiritual (as well as physical) slavery that we experienced in the depraved environment of Egypt, so too, every Shabbos, we gain the capacity to remove the "shackles of materialism" that prevent us from serving as witnesses to Hashem. In fact, the term וַיָּנַח בַּיּוֹם הַשְּׁבִיעִי, traditionally translated that *He rested on the seventh day*, may be interpreted that

Hashem eased the spiritual burdens of *Klal Yisrael* on that day.[1]

To support our contention that a primary function of the *Menuchah* of Shabbos that we enjoy is the ability, at least for one day, to testify about Hashem, we note that the *gematria* (numerical equivalent) of וַיָּנַח (74) is identical to that of עֵד, *a witness*. (*Va'eschanan* 5661)

◆§ In Direct Proportion to Our Efforts

ואין מובן הלשון מבקש ליתנה והלא נתן לנו את השבת. רק הפי׳ שזה עצמו כח השבת שבני ישראל הם כלים לקבל המתנה טובה זו שא״י להתגלות רק בשבת קודש. ובכל שבת ושבת הוא מתנה חדשה ... לכן מבקשין בכל שבת והנחילנו כו׳ שבת קדשך. כי הגם שבכלל נתן לנו השבת. אבל יש שבת פרטי בכל שבת ושבת וצריכין לקנות שביתה זו בכניסת היום והוא ענין קבלת שבת.

While we frequently perceive *Menuchah* as being a passive concept (a sense of rest initiated by Hashem), in reality, the degree of *Menuchah* that we enjoy is in direct proportion to our efforts at *shemiras Shabbos*. As stated elsewhere ("A Day of *Penimiyus*"), *Chazal* teach us that Yaakov entered Shechem immediately prior to the arrival of Shabbos. Rather than merely wait for the inception of Shabbos, in the last minutes of *erev Shabbos*, Yaakov demarcates the *techumim* (the city limits) of Shechem for the purpose of determining how far one would be permitted to walk. In the merit of his initiative in observing the laws of Shabbos, Yaakov was not only blessed with the gift of enjoying *Menuchah* on Shabbos, but also actually merited the ability to precipitate and create the *Menuchah* of Shabbos. As the *pasuk* reads, וַיִּחַן אֶת פְּנֵי הָעִיר, *and he encamped before the city* (*Bereishis* 33:18), Yaakov made it possible to rest (according to this homiletic approach, וַיִּחַן is related to וַיַּחֲנוּ, which means to camp) in one place rather than travel further, because of his previous initiative in the closing minutes of *erev Shabbos*.

The very concept of *techumim*, and especially the *halachah* of *eruv techumim* wherein one can extend the area that one may walk on Shabbos

1. According to this approach, the term וַיָּנַח is similar to וַהֲנָחָה לַמְּדִינוֹת, *amnesty for the provinces* (*Megillas Esther* 2:18), which refers to the easing of the tax burden on the occasion of Esther becoming queen.

by locating oneself at a certain site at the commencement of Shabbos and then measuring two thousand cubits from there (rather than from one's primary residence), all are indicative of the importance of taking the initiative in ushering in the *Menuchah* of Shabbos. *Chazal* (cf. *Eruvin* 45b) emphasize the significance of קוֹנֶה שְׁבִיתָה, *acquiring a resting place* (a location from which to measure the distance that we may walk on Shabbos). This signifies that we must take the initiative and precipitate the *Menuchah* of Shabbos, rather than wait for the spiritual serenity of Shabbos to greet us. While this is not a simple task, we are assured of Hashem's assistance in this regard. As we pray during the *Shacharis Shemoneh Esrei*, ... וְהַנְחִילֵנוּ שַׁבַּת קָדְשֶׁךָ, *grant us Your holy Sabbath as a heritage.* While we generally don't position ourselves at the city limits at the beginning of Shabbos, the ceremony of *Kabbalas Shabbos* whereby we recite additional prayers in honor of the forthcoming Shabbos reflects the same theme — that we are actively seeking the *kedushah* and *Menuchah* of Shabbos. (*Vayishlach* 5648)

וע״ז נאמר יגעתי ומצאתי והוא יגיעת האדם בימי המעשה. עי״ז זוכה אח״כ בשבת יום מנוחה. מתנה טובה כו׳.

The renowned expression, יָגַעְתִּי וּמָצָאתִי (cf. *Megillah* 6b), which generally refers to the effort that is a prerequisite for Torah study, may also allude to the relationship between Shabbos and the weekdays. All of our efforts during the week (יָגַעְתִּי) are rewarded in the form of Shabbos' *Menuchah* (מָצָאתִי). In this spirit, *Chazal* (*Shabbos* 10b) describe Shabbos as a Divine gift (מַתָּנָה טוֹבָה — refer to our chapter on the "Gift of Shabbos"). (*Vayeishev* 5638)

⁂ A Barometer of One's Future Portion in *Olam Haba*

וכן בש״ק מעין עוה״ב שנק׳ יום מנוחה. ומנוחה הוא רק אחר היגיעה. וכפי היגיעה בימי במעשה ובעוה״ז. כן המנוחה בש״ק ובעוה״ב. והאמת כי מנוחת הצדיק בשבת היא אות ועדות למנוחתו בעוה״ב. וע״ז הענין אמרו יגעתי ומצאתי. יגעתי בחול ומצאתי בשבת.

Just as we demonstrated in the prevous *dvar Torah* that our sense of *Menuchah* on Shabbos is directly proportional to our efforts during the week, so too, our reward in the World to Come is commensurate with our efforts in This World. The famous observation of *Chazal* (cited previously) that we give great credence to anyone who says יָגַעְתִּי וּמָצָאתִי, *I have exerted myself and I have found satisfaction,* may refer to the two parallel relationships that we have developed in these *divrei Torah.* By toiling during the week we enjoy the fruits of our labor on Shabbos. Similarly, by exerting ourselves and successfully engaging the *yetzer hara* in This World, we merit the peace and final reward of *Olam Haba.*

Furthermore, we suggest that we can gauge a *tzaddik's* reward and spiritual peace in *Olam Haba* from his *Menuchah* every Shabbos in *Olam Hazeh.* (*Re'eh* 5637)

◆§ A Divine Gift

וכל אלה הג׳ מדריגות ישנם בכל איש ישראל שלפעמים צריכין לכוף עצמם בע״כ. והוא בחי׳ ימי המעשה ועשית כל מלאכתך. ועשי׳ הוא לשון כפיה בקטטות ומריבות. וכן כתיב במעשה המשכן ועשו לי משכן בע״כ ... ושבת הוא בחי׳ מתנה כמ״ש ז״ל מתנה טובה יש לי כו׳ לכן הוא יום מנוחה. אכן בהי׳ הראשונה בלקיחה זה הי׳ באמת למעלה מהטבע כמ״ש רז שמלאכי השרת משתמשין.

While it is certainly true that the *Menuchah* of Shabbos is earned in direct proportion to our efforts at *avodas Hashem* during the week, in another sense, it is also a Divine gift (refer to our chapter, "The Gift of Shabbos").

To appreciate the relationship between our efforts at spiritual growth during the week and the gift of *Menuchah* on Shabbos, we recall that a similar relationship exists in reference to *Kabbalas HaTorah.* In fact, there are three different stages that *Klal Yisrael* experienced at the time of *Kabbalas HaTorah.* First, the Torah was acquired through their own initiative. It was when the Jewish people proclaimed, נַעֲשֶׂה וְנִשְׁמַע, *We will do and we will obey* (*Shemos* 24:7), that they merited to receive the Torah. This initial phase is described by *Chazal* (cf. *Shemos Rabbah* 28:1) as לְקִיחָה – the time when *Klal Yisrael* "took'" the Torah as its prized possession through its own outstanding efforts. This preliminary phase leading up to the *Aseres HaDibros* was followed by the Divine gift of Torah, in which Hashem presented to *Klal Yisrael* the many *mitzvos* of the Torah. The third and more tragic phase occurred after the calamitous sin of the Golden Calf when the Torah is considered to be in "captivity." (Refer to *Tehillim* 68:19 where each of these stages is alluded to in the following words: עָלִיתָ לַמָּרוֹם שָׁבִיתָ שֶּׁבִי לָקַחְתָּ מַתָּנוֹת בָּאָדָם, *You ascended to heaven, You took captives, You took gifts of man.*) Despite the amount of spiritual damage that occurred as a result of the sin of the *Egel*, we are nonetheless obligated to follow the Torah's dictates. Although we may feel a certain lack of readiness to fulfill the *dvar Hashem*, we must do so in the same manner that a captive must always obey his captor's commands.

During the weekly cycle, we follow the same sequence of events that *Klal Yisrael* experienced as it prepared for *Kabbalas HaTorah*. It is not enough to take the initiative during the Shabbos when we desire to follow Hashem. We must still do more and observe Torah and *mitzvos* during the weekdays, even when we may be sorely tempted to do otherwise — just as a captive unfailingly follows his captors' commands even against his natural instincts to do as he pleases. In fact, the term וְעָשִׂיתָ כָּל מְלַאכְתֶּךָ, *and accomplish all your work* (*Shemos* 20:9), used in the context of the work performed by us during the six workdays, may also be translated as "*you will be coerced* to perform your Divine Service." In the merit of fulfilling the Divine Will during the six weekdays, despite the many difficulties that we may encounter, we deserve the enviable gift provided by Hashem — *Menuchah* every Shabbos.

(Adapted from *Terumah* 5652)

A Day of Unrequited Love

בימי המעשה היא בחי' תלוי' בדבר. ובשבת שנק' מהנה טובה היא שאינה תלויה בדבר. ונק' יום מנוחה.

Expanding upon the theme discussed in the previous *dvar Torah* in which we related the *Menuchah* of Shabbos to a Divine gift, we suggest that Hashem's love towards us assumes two distinct forms. During the weekdays it is based upon our behavior and performance of *mitzvos* and *maasim tovim*, as it says in *Pirkei Avos* (5:19), Hashem's affection for the Jewish people during the week may be described as אַהֲבָה שֶׁהִיא תְלוּיָה בְדָבָר, *love that depends on a specific cause* — our spiritual conduct. However, on Shabbos, the day of *Menuchah,* the innate love of Hashem for *Klal Yisrael* comes to the forefront. This love is no longer contingent upon our spiritual conduct, but as the Mishnah states, it is a אַהֲבָה שֶׁאֵינָה תְלוּיָה בְדָבָר, *love that is not contingent upon any factor.* On this day of rest, Hashem's love for us reaches the point that despite any shortcomings in our Divine Service, He nonetheless showers us with His love. (*Rosh Hashanah* 5657)

"Angels of Rest" for a Day of Rest

וכן בבחי׳ הזמן יש מלאכי שבת ומלאכי חול. פעם א׳ כתיב מלאכיו יצוה לך ופ״א כ׳ חונה מלאך ה׳ סביב כמ״ש מזה בזוה״ק ר״פ וישלח. מלאכיו יצוה מלאכי חול. לכן כתיב לשמרך בכל דרכיך. וחונה מלאך ה׳ על יום המנוחה דכתיב בי׳ אל יצא איש ממקומו ... ולכן אומרים בש״ק שלום עליכם מלה״ש. ויתכן לפרש צאתכם לשלום על מלאכי חול שעולין למעלה. ומקדימים בואכם לשלום. הגם דכאן כתיב עולים ואח״כ יורדים.

The concept of *Menuchah* even affects the type of Heavenly protection that is afforded to us on Shabbos. We find that David *HaMelech* describes two different functions that are served by *malachim* who protect us. On one hand, he says, כִּי מַלְאָכָיו יְצַוֶּה לָּךְ לִשְׁמָרְךָ בְּכָל דְּרָכֶיךָ, *He will designate His angels for you, to protect you in all your ways* (*Tehillim* 91:11). This refers to the angels that escort us all week long as we go out in search of our *parnassah.* On the other hand, he also says, חֹנֶה מַלְאַךְ ה׳ סָבִיב לִירֵאָיו, *The angel of Hashem encamps around His reverent ones* (ibid. 34:8), referring to those angels who guard us on Shabbos, a day when we heed the Torah's commandment that אַל יֵצֵא אִישׁ מִמְּקֹמוֹ בַּיּוֹם הַשְּׁבִיעִי, *let no man leave his place on the seventh day* (*Shemos* 16:29). On this day (Shabbos), when we do not travel on the road, Hashem's angels surround (and protect) us, as we remain in place.

With our assumption that Shabbos is endowed with its unique *malachim* we can appreciate the closing stanza of the *Shalom Aleichem* that is chanted every Friday night. While it seems presumptuous that we bid farewell (by saying צֵאתְכֶם לְשָׁלוֹם) to the angels that we had just greeted with the words שָׁלוֹם עֲלֵיכֶם (*peace unto you*), in reality we are not parting from the same angels that we just welcomed. On the contrary, it is the angels of Shabbos that we welcome and those of the week to whom we bid farewell. In fact, we are never left alone – without the protection of *malachim*. It is only after welcoming the *malachim* of the Shabbos with the words שָׁלוֹם עֲלֵיכֶם that we take leave of the weekday *malachim*. (*Vayetzei* 5661)

ויש מלאכי חוץ לארץ וארץ ישראל כמ״ש חז״ל ויפגעו בו מלאכי כו׳. וי״ל שימי המעשה שמותרין בעשיית מלאכה והוא להוציא ולברר החיות שנסתר ונעלם במעשים גשמיים ונק׳ מלאכי חו״ל כנ״ל. ואיתא מלאכים ממש. ואיך שלח לעשו מלאכים קדושים. א״כ י״ל שהי׳ בדרך נסתר מלאכי חו״ל כנ״ל כענין שמצינו שמלאכים מתלבשים בעוה״ז בגשמיות. וש״ק יום מנוחה הוא מלאכי א״י שמתגלה הרצון האמת בלב ישראל וע״י התלהבות יכולין להעלות הכל.

We extend this analysis further and draw a parallel between the angels of Shabbos and the weekdays and the angels of *Eretz Yisrael* and *chutz la'aretz* (the Diaspora) that accompanied Yaakov *Avinu*. Just as the angels that protect us during the week help us elicit sparks of *kedushah* amidst the material world, so too, the angels that escorted Yaakov in his travels through *chutz la'aretz* helped him find *kedushah* even in those areas that may have seemed remote from holiness. On the other hand, the *malachim* of *Eretz Yisrael* are able to tap the latent *kedushah* that every Jew feels, without having to pierce the outer layers of materialism that we must contend with during the week. In this sense, they resemble the *malachim* of *Shabbos Kodesh*.

The question is raised, was it appropriate for Yaakov to send sacred angels to greet his brother Esav? In response, we suggest that it was those angels whose role it is to protect us as we travel through the material world – the angels of *chutz la'aretz* and of the weekdays – that were sent to Esav. (*Vayishlach* 5633)

◆§ A Day of *Sheleimus* (Perfection) – Becoming a *Malach*

ד״ש. מלאכיו יצוה הוא בימי המעשה לכן כתיב בכל דרכיך כי האדם נק׳ מהלך. אבל בש״ק דכתיב אל יצא איש ממקומו והוא כמלאך שנק׳ עומד ... אך בשבת ניתן מתנה לבנ״י להיות להם השלימות כנ״ל ואז חונה מלאך ה׳ שהוא יום מנוחה והרמז דכתיב ויחלצם ז״ש בשב״ק והחליצנו ...

Elaborating upon the theme that we introduced in the previous *dvar Torah* – where we stated that the *malachim* of Shabbos protect us as we rest (while those of the week shield us during our worldly journeys) – we suggest that on Shabbos we approach the level of angels. Just as an angel is described as an עוֹמֵד, *one who remains standing* (cf. *Zechariah* 1:8-10), because he is incapable of ascending (and does not have to) from one level of *kedushah* to another, so too, on Shabbos, having successfully combatted evil during the week,[1] we have now attained, in a sense, the spiritual level of perfection (*sheleimus*). Just as angels do not ascend from one level of *kedushah* to another, so too on Shabbos, having attained the level of *malachim*, we are commanded, *Do not leave your place on the seventh day* (*Shemos* 16:29). Can there be any greater *Menuchah* than having attained *sheleimus*?

We allude to this aspect of Shabbos' *Menuchah* – the ability to rest from our struggles with evil and remain at a constant spiritual level – by commencing the special segment of the *Birchas HaMazon* dedicated to Shabbos with the words רְצֵה וְהַחֲלִיצֵנוּ. This may be translated, "Grace us and shield us from evil," an allusion to our enhanced status on Shabbos. Every Shabbos, instead of confronting evil, we ascend to a spiritual level whereby we are comfortably shielded from evil. Only the *malach* of Shabbos is given the following mission (as indicated in a previous *dvar Torah*): חֹנֶה מַלְאַךְ ה׳ סָבִיב לִירֵאָיו וַיְחַלְּצֵם, *The angel of* HASHEM *encamps around His reverent ones and He releases them* (*Tehillim* 34:8) – He spares them from evil. So too, *Klal Yisrael*, having achieved a status similar to that of *malachim*, rests comfortably on Shabbos knowing that they are spared from any confrontation with evil. (*Vayishlach* 5650)

1. During the week the Jew is described as a *mehaleich*, one who travels from one level to another level, whereas on Shabbos we attain the status of *omeid*, being able to remain comfortably at rest on the level that we have just attained.

◆§ Also Enjoying *Menuchah* During the Weekdaysl

בחי׳ יו״ט של חנוכה היינו הארה הנמצאת גם בימות החול. כי באמת יש לכל הדברים אחיזה בשורש השבת כנ״ל שנק׳ תכלית שמים וארץ.

By relegating all of our accomplishments during the week to the Shabbos, which is described as תַּכְלִית מַעֲשֵׂה שָׁמַיִם וָאָרֶץ, *the true purpose* (conclusion) *of the creation of heaven and earth,* we ensure that some aspect of the *Menuchah* associated with Shabbos is also enjoyed during the week.[1] Moreover, the existence of *Yamim Tovim* that celebrate the theme of *Menuchah,* such as Chanukah [which is composed of the words חָנוּ כ״ה, *they rested on the 25th day* (of Kislev)] and Purim [which is celebrated on the day when the Jewish people rested from waging war against Amalek, not the day of their triumph], also validates our contention that the concept of *Menuchah* (spiritual rest) exists during the week as well. (*Mikeitz* 5642)

להתיישב מנוחת השבת בלב על כל ימי המעשה. וזהו נק׳ שבתון מנוחת מרגוע ... כי השבת יצא מהכלל ללמד על הכלל כולו. שכך הוא גם לפי הפשוט שניתן יום מנוחה לבנ״י שינוחו מכל המעשים וישוב לבו לעבודת הבורא. ומכל שבת צריך להישאר זכירה גם בימי החול לזכור שלא לעשות מלאכתו קבע בזוכרו מה שעבר על לבו ביום השבת.

Our premise that the spirit of *Menuchah* is by no means confined to Shabbos itself but, on the contrary, permeates the six weekdays as well, is alluded to by *Rashi.* He interprets the expression שַׁבַּת שַׁבָּתוֹן, *a day of complete rest* (*Shemos* 31:15) as meaning, מְנוּחַת מַרְגּוֹעַ וְלֹא מְנוּחַת עֲרַאי, *a permanent rest not a temporary rest.* In other words, *Rashi* is

1. Just as the *Menuchah* of Shabbos permeates the entire week, so too, the joy of the *Yamim Tovim* allows us to rejoice during the entire year. In fact, the renowned *pasuk,* וְשָׂמַחְתָּ בְּחַגֶּךָ, *You shall rejoice on your festival* (*Devarim* 16:14), may be interpreted in the following manner: Rejoice all year long in the knowledge that Hashem has granted us the Three Festivals. Refer to *Pesach* 5655 for further discussion of the relationship between Shabbos' *Menuchah* and the *simchah* associated with *Yom Tov.*

emphasizing that the spirit of resting from our material pursuits on Shabbos should also affect every aspect of our behavior during the forthcoming week.

To appreciate this concept even more, we recall one of the Thirteen Principles through which the Torah is interpreted: כָּל דָּבָר שֶׁהָיָה בִּכְלָל וְיָצָא מִן הַכְּלָל לְלַמֵּד, לֹא לְלַמֵּד עַל עַצְמוֹ יָצָא, אֶלָּא לְלַמֵּד עַל הַכְּלָל כֻּלּוֹ יָצָא, *A concept that was included in a general principle and was then singled out as an exception to this principle – [this exemption] comes not only to teach about itself but also to teach us something about the entire generality.* By imbuing the Shabbos day with a sense of *Menuchah* (seemingly an exception to the norm of constant creativity) and by enabling us on this day to take a respite from the material world, Hashem is demonstrating that, to some extent, one can lead such a lifestyle during the week as well. Torah should be our fixed practice, as *Pirkei Avos* (1:15) implores us, עֲשֵׂה תוֹרָתְךָ קֶבַע, *let your study of Torah be your permanent preoccupation,* while your own work should be just a temporary pursuit.

(*Ki Sisa* 5652)

פי׳ שלא יהי׳ המנוחה במקרה ולשעה. רק שיעשה באדם רשימה נשאר לעד. ורמז שבתון שיהי׳ כל האדם נמשך אחר השבת שיהי׳ בו בעצמו בחי׳ השבת ושבתון פועל יוצא. שהשבת נותן שביתה ומנוחה לנפשות בנ״י. ועל זה כ׳ ה׳ נותן לכם השבת כו׳ שבו איש תחתיו. פי׳ תחתיו של השבת.

Utilizing this approach, we gain new insight into the expression שַׁבַּת שַׁבָּתוֹן (*Shemos* 31:15), which the Torah uses to describe Shabbos. We suggest that שַׁבָּתוֹן is, in effect, a state of being – a "*Shabbosdikke Yid*" – not only on Shabbos itself but on all occasions.

When informing *Klal Yisrael* that the manna would not fall on Shabbos, Moshe tells them, רְאוּ כִּי ה׳ נָתַן לָכֶם הַשַּׁבָּת, *See that HASHEM has given you the Sabbath* (*Shemos* 16:29). In this context, we propose that the *pasuk* is alluding to the beneficial effect of Shabbos on the Jew. Shabbos is a day when we are transformed into an entirely different person – as we integrate a sense of *Menuchah* (spiritual rest) that lasts an entire week. Again while discussing the manna, the Torah writes, שְׁבוּ אִישׁ תַּחְתָּיו, *Let every man remain in his place* (ibid.), which literally means, "every man stay under him." Interpreted homiletically, this may reinforce the theme of this *dvar Torah* – whatever you do, remain *under* (תַּחַת) the sheltering confines of the Shabbos. By doing so, you can be assured that the *kedushah* of Shabbos will permeate every aspect of your life. (*Ki Sisa* 5657)

כי מקדושת השבת צריכין להמשיך קדושה לכל ימי המעשה. וע״ז מתפללין והנחילנו כו׳ באהבה כו׳ ש״ק וינוחו בו כו׳. וקשה הלא אומרים וש״ק באהבה וברצון הנחילנו א״כ מה בקשה זו. הגם כי באמת השבת אין לו שיעור כמ״ש במ״א בפי׳ שבתותי לשון רבים. ולעולם מבקשין לשבת עליון. אך יתכן לפרש שהיא בקשה להתדבק בהארת השבת כי נקרא נחלה שאין לה הפסק ומבקשין שנקבל הארה מקדושת השבת על כל השבוע וינוחו בו. שע״י זו ההארה יהי׳ לנו מנוח בימי המעשה. כי ש״ק מעצמו הוא יום מנוחה. א״כ בקשת וינוחו בו היא על ימי מלחמה כנ״ל.

This idea offers new insight into a prayer which we recite in each of the Shabbos *tefillos*. וְהַנְחִילֵנוּ ה׳ אֱלֹהֵינוּ בְּאַהֲבָה וּבְרָצוֹן שַׁבַּת קָדְשֶׁךָ וְיָנוּחוּ בוֹ יִשְׂרָאֵל מְקַדְּשֵׁי שְׁמֶךָ, *O* HASHEM, *our God, with love and favor grant us Your holy Sabbath as a heritage, and may Israel, (the nation) that sanctifies Your Name, rest on it.* While the simple interpretation of this *tefillah* is a fervent plea to be able to enjoy the restful atmosphere of Shabbos, this seems to be redundant since we already requested that Hashem grant us Shabbos as a day of *Menuchah* (as it states earlier in this prayer, רְצֵה בִמְנוּחָתֵנוּ, *accept our rest*). If Shabbos is already designated by Hashem as a day of *Menuchah,* why is it necessary for us to request that we be able to rest on this day? While it is certainly true that there are different levels of *kedushah* and *Menuchah* to which *Klal Yisrael* may aspire – and we may request to enjoy an even higher level than we would ordinarily merit[1] – it is also possible that by *requesting* that Hashem grant us Shabbos as a legacy (וְהַנְחִילֵנוּ), we may be implying a plea that the ambiance of *Menuchah* which permeates Shabbos should penetrate the week as well. In fact, the term נַחֲלָה, *a legacy/ heritage,* implies that the atmosphere of Shabbos never ceases and continues throughout the week. (Adapted from *Kedoshim* 5646)

---

1. This approach is supported by the Torah's use of the term שַׁבְּתֹתַי, *My Sabbaths* (*Shemos* 31:13), in the plural sense, indicating that there are many levels of *kedushah* and *Menuchah* associated with Shabbos.

◆§ Setting the Tone for the Entire Week

ויתכן ללמוד מזה כי השבת שנק׳ יום המנוחה הוא המנהיג לכל ימי המעשה. וי״ל ולא נחם ד״א פלשתים הוא שלא הי׳ הנהגה שלהם ע״פ הטבע ובחי׳ ימי המעשה. רק הי׳ בחי׳ שבת בלבד.

Rashi (*Shemos* 13:17) interprets the phrase וְלֹא נָחָם אֱלֹהִים דֶּרֶךְ אֶרֶץ פְּלִשְׁתִּים to mean that Hashem did not lead (translating נָחָם as נְהָגָם, *lead them*) the Jewish people through the land of the Pelishtim. Extrapolating from *Rashi* that the term *Menuchah* may mean to "lead" as well as "to rest," we may deduce yet another nuance of the *Menuchah* of Shabbos. Shabbos is the day that *leads*, that sets the tone and direction for the entire week. By not leading the Jewish people through the land of the Philistines, which is descibed as דֶּרֶךְ אֶרֶץ (the natural route), Hashem is indicating that *Klal Yisrael's* destiny is to be led *directly* by Hashem and His constant intervention, rather than be subjected to the natural order (*teva*). In fact, not only after the Exodus but throughout their travels in the Wilderness, *Klal Yisrael* was led supernaturally; whereby Hashem directed us in the spirit of Shabbos rather than the more natural course (*derech eretz*) associated with the weekdays.

(*Beshalach* 5647)

Some Parallels Between the Menuchah of Shabbos and of Chanukah

◆§ Attaining *Menuchah* Under Challenging Circumstances

כי מנוחת שבתות ויו״ט זכו בני ישראל בעת היותם במקומם הראוי. אבל חנוכה ופורים הם יו״ט שזכו בני ישראל בימי גלותם ואינו מנוחה ברורה וזה החילוק בין זה הדבר לכה. ונקרא חנוכה שהרגישו בחי׳ מנוחת שבת באספקלריא שאינה מאירה כנ״ל. ובאמת זה עדות נאמנה לבנ״י להודיע שגם בגלות לא ניתקו ח״ו ממקומם הראשון והוא מחזק ידינו בגלות.

There are numerous parallels between the *Menuchah*, the sense of rest and relief, *Klal Yisrael* enjoys on Chanukah and that associated with Shabbos. Firstly, the very name of the *Yom Tov*, Chanukah, is derived from the words חָנוּ כ״ה, *they rested on the 25th* [of Kislev]. Just as on Shabbos we commemorate the moment when Hashem rested from creating (rather than Creation itself), so too, on Chanukah, we commemorate our respite from our foes rather than the military victory itself.

In a sense, the *Menuchah* of Chanukah is even a greater feat than that of Shabbos. Whereas *Klal Yisrael* attained the *Menuchah* of Shabbos under ideal circumstances — when they enjoyed a great deal of access to *HaKadosh Baruch Hu* through *neviim* and when they were in the Wilderness poised to enter *Eretz Yisrael* — the *Menuchah* of Chanukah (and Purim, which also celebrates the day when the Jewish people rested from their foes rather than the time of their military triumph) was attained under less than ideal circumstances. It was a time when *Klal Yisrael* was in *galus* (as in the case of Purim) or in *Eretz Yisrael* (at the time of the Chanukah miracle), but without the intimacy with Hashem that they had previously enjoyed.

We can draw a parallel between the *Menuchah* of Shabbos and Chanukah on one hand, and the prophecy of Moshe *Rabbeinu* and that of all the other prophets. *Chazal* (*Yevamos* 49b) note that Moshe *Rabbeinu* perceived Hashem from the perspective of אַסְפַּקְלַרְיָא הַמְּאִירָה (*a clear light,* alluding to his intimate relationship with Hashem), while all other prophets perceived Him from the perspective of אַסְפַּקְלַרְיָה שֶׁאֵינָה הַמְּאִירָה (*an unclear light,* lacking the intimacy that Moshe enjoyed). Likewise, the *Menuchah* of Shabbos given to *Klal Yisrael* under ideal circumstances is compared to a clear light and that of Chanukah and Purim to an unclear luminary. This thought is alluded to by the second segment of the term Chanukah (כה) which can be interpreted not only as representing the letters כ and ה, referring to the the 25th day of Kislev, but also as כֹּה (*so, thus*), the term used by virtually all of the prophets (other than Moshe) to transmit their prophecy to *Klal Yisrael.*[1]

(*Chanukah* 5635)

ובנ"י ע"י גזירת יון הרשעה נחלש אצלם כח הקדושה ורק נקודה אחת נשאר בהם. ולכן אחר יגיעות מלחמות הגדולות עם מלכות יון. לא הי' כח לבני ישראל לעמוד על השלימות ועזר להם הבורא ית' בדרך נס שנתברך זאת הנקודה ובאו ברגע אחת לכל השלימות. וע"ז קראו שם חנוכה שזכו לבוא מיד אל המנוחה כי השלימות נקרא מנוחה שזוכין לבוא להשורש כמ"ש במ"א.

Extending the parallel between Chanukah and Shabbos' *Menuchah* even further, we recall that in a previous *dvar Torah* we defined *Menuchah* as a form of *sheleimus* – reaching a level of perfection unattainable during the workweek. As great as the *sheleimus* that we attain every Shabbos is, we suggest that the ability of *Klal Yisrael* to achieve a sense of *sheleimus* and *Menuchah* at the time of the Chanukah miracle was an even greater accomplishment. After the military struggles and the spiritual battles against Greek and Hellenistic domination, *Klal Yisrael* lacked the capacity to attain *sheleimus.* It was only with Hashem's assistance that the Jewish people were swiftly transformed from a nation that was weary of its battles against Greek culture to a state of perfection worthy

1. Refer to *Rashi* (*Bamidbar* 30:2) stating that whereas Moshe utilized the phrase זֶה הַדָּבָר, *this is the Divine Word,* to communicate his prophecies, all other *neviim* lacking this intimate perspective that Moshe enjoyed, used the phrase כֹּה אָמַר ה', *so said Hashem.*

of the name *Menuchah*. While there was always a *pintele yid*, a spark of purity in every Jewish soul, it was only through Hashem's intervention that this latent source of *kedushah* that remained intact throughout the period of Hellenistic oppression was transformed into the source of *Klal Yisrael's sheleimus*. (*Chanukah* 5639)

◆§ The Relationship Between the *Menuchah* of Shabbos and Amalek's Extinction (*Mechiyas Amalek*)

וזה מחיית עמלק. וכתיב והי׳ בהניח נכלל עם שבת בזה שהוא יום מנוחה והוא התדבקות בשורשו שהוא ענין מנוחת שבת. כמ״ש במ״א. וכמ״ש אל יצא איש ממקומו והוא בחי׳ זכור כנ״ל. ולכן בשבת יכולין למחות עמלק יותר ולהתדבק בבחי׳ זכרון שלא לעשות דרך עראי כנ״ל.

ועמלק אין לו שורש כלל והוא כולו שקר היפוך הצדיק יסוד עולם. והוא שורש האיבוד וההפסד שנמצא בעולם. לכן כתיב קרך. וכן אשר קרהו. שאינו רק במקרה ועראי. לכן הוא היפוך השבת שהוא המנוחה והעלאת כל דבר לשורשו. והוא אין לו שורש רק ברפידים לשיש קצת פירוד מן השורש אז הוא בא למלחמה. ולכן בש״ק שבאין לדביקות השורש יש לזכור למחות אותו כדכתיב והי׳ בהניח.

By insisting that the *mitzvah* of liquidating Amalek not be performed until *Klal Yisrael* enjoyed a sense of respite from all of its foes (וְהָיָה בְּהָנִיחַ ה׳ אֱלֹהֶיךָ לְךָ מִכָּל אֹיְבֶיךָ, *It shall be that when* HASHEM, *your God, gives you rest from all your enemies*; cf. *Devarim* 25:19), and, moreover, by utilizing the term וְהָיָה בְּהָנִיחַ connoting rest, the Torah is drawing a relationship between these two critical objectives: resting on Shabbos and eliminating Amalek.

We suggest that the most opportune time to obliterate Amalek is Shabbos,[1] the day when every Jew is able to return to his spiritual roots

1. The *Sfas Emes* frequently cites a *Midrash* (cf. *Yalkut Devarim* 938) which notes that both the *mitzvah* of observing Shabbos as well as that of liquidating Amalek commences with the term *zachor*. Whereas in the case of *Klal Yisrael* observing Shabbos, they are assured eternal life, for Amalek the term *zachor* initiates a process leading to extinction. The relationship between the term *zachor* of Shabbos and that of *mechiyas Amalek* may be as follows: It is only by clinging

(*shoreshh*). As the Torah says, אַל יֵצֵא אִישׁ מִמְּקֹמוֹ בַּיּוֹם הַשְּׁבִיעִי, *let no man leave his place* (his spiritual essence and roots) *on the seventh day* (*Shemos* 16:29). It is only by returning to our enormous latent spiritual potential, especially on *Shabbos Kodesh*, that we can successfully vanquish Amalek. In fact, the term *Menuchah*, used both in reference to Shabbos' rest and the respite necessary before our attempted annihilation of Amalek, alludes to much more than mere physical rest from labor. On the contrary, that term connotes a sense a true relief from all of the material passions that so often engulf us. This relief can only be attained by returning to our spiritual essence as we do every Shabbos and in preparation for Amalek's destruction. The term *zachor, remember*, which the Torah uses to exhort us to eliminate Amalek is also an implied plea to discover our own inner spiritual essence (שֹׁרֶשׁ). It is only in reference to matters that are truly essential — and that can never be forgotten — that the term *zachor* pertains. To successfully eliminate Amalek, we muster all of our latent potential and never forget even for a moment the lethal nature of our most dedicated foe. It is on Shabbos, the day of *Menuchah*, when we return to our roots — and through the welcome respite from all of our foes — that we can successfully implement the spirit of *zachor*.

To reinforce our contention that it is the *Menuchah* of Shabbos and the return to our spiritual roots that it engenders that allows us to successfully combat Amalek, consider the stark contrast between the Torah's characterization of Amalek and the essence of Shabbos. The rogue nation of Amalek is described as a fleeting, rootless phenomenon (refer to *Devarim* 25:18, אֲשֶׁר קָרְךָ בַּדֶּרֶךְ, *that happened upon you on the way*) — the nation that happened to attack you while you were on the road. Similarly, Haman, Amalek's descendant, is characterized as קָרָהוּ, *happened to him* — the individual to whom events occur by chance (see *Esther* 4:7). By contrast, the Shabbos day when *Klal Yisrael* returns to its roots is the essence of spiritual stability and permanence. It is no coincidence that Amalek could only successfully challenge *Klal Yisrael* when our forefathers began to question their relationship to *HaKadosh Baruch Hu*. It was only in Rephidim, when the Jewish people questioned whether Hashem was in their midst (cf. *Shemos* 17:7, הֲיֵשׁ ה׳ בְּקִרְבֵּנוּ אִם אָיִן), that Amalek was able to pose a viable threat to *Klal Yisrael*. (*Zachor* 5632, 5645)

---

to and remembering the Divine spark within us that we can successfully vanquish Amalek. There is no more opportune time to recall and evoke that inner spark than every Shabbos.

ובשבת קודש יש הארה לבני ישראל מהקדמת נעשה לנשמע. כמו שהי׳ קודם החטא. לכן נאמר והיה בהניח. שהוא שבת יום מנוחה. שבאין למקומם שהוא הקול קול יעקב. וכולין למחות שם עמלק.

Developing this theme further, we suggest that every Shabbos when we return to our historical roots, we are invoking some of *Klal Yisrael's* greatest sources of merit: The merit of our forefathers pledging נַעֲשֶׂה וְנִשְׁמַע, *we will do and* (only then) *we will hear* (understand the reasons for *mitzvos*), comes to the forefront every Shabbos, a day of spiritual respite when we may cast off our material burdens and return to our true origins. Moreover, when we evoke our roots and recall the spirit of נַעֲשֶׂה וְנִשְׁמַע, we also benefit from the assurance that Yitzchak gave to future generations of *Klal Yisrael* — הַקֹּל קוֹל יַעֲקֹב, *The voice is the voice of Yaakov* (*Bereishis* 27:22). It is through the "voice of Yaakov" — the sound of Torah and *tefillah* — that we will prevail over Amalek.

(Adapted from *Zachor* 5635)

פי׳ שע״י השבת יום מנוחה שמתדבקין בני ישראל בנקודה הפנימיות שהוא ענין העלאת הנרות כו׳.
ע״ז והיה בהניח כו׳. כי בנ״י היו ראוין בעת יצ״מ להיות כל הנהגתם למעלה מהטבע כמו שיהי׳ לעתיד. רק ע״י זה הרשע עמלק ימ״ש שעירבב אותנו קודם גמר התיקון כמ״ש בדרך. לכן צריכין כל אלו היגיעות וגליות המרים. ולכן בש״ק שמתעורר הנהגת ישראל שלמעלה מהטבע. כמ״ש שהוא מעין עוה״ב. ע״ז מתעורר בשבת שנאת עמלק. ובכל שבת יש קצת מחיית עמלק כפי שמירת שבת שבישראל.

Whenever Klal *Yisrael* returns to its natural roots, as we do every Shabbos, we can be assured that all of Amalek's efforts at corrupting us will come to naught. As the Torah writes, וְהָיָה בְּהָנִיחַ ה׳ אֱלֹהֶיךָ ... תִּמְחֶה אֶת זֵכֶר עֲמָלֵק, *It shall be when* H*ASHEM*, *your God, gives you rest ... you shall wipe out the memory of Amalek* (*Devarim* 25:19) — when Hashem will enable you to rest and you will return to your natural roots, you will surely wipe out any vestige of Amalek.

It is only appropriate that it is on Shabbos, the day when every Jew discovers the supernatural Divine spark that was embedded in him and the day that is the microcosm of *Olam Haba*, that we read the *parashah* discussing Amalek's elimination. By becoming fully cognizant every

Shabbos of the spiritual devastation caused by Amalek (שִׂנְאַת עֲמָלֵק), we are, in effect, voicing our fervent plea that he be totally annihilated. Prior to that challenging and difficult encounter with the embodiment of evil, the universe was governed on a supernatural basis. Just as *yetzias Mitzrayim* was accomplished in defiance of all natural law, so too, the entire lifestyle of *Klal Yisrael* would have continued to exist on a supernatural basis in a manner reminiscent of Adam in *Gan Eden* – and similar to *Klal Yisrael* in the future world – were it not for our lethal encounter with Amalek. On Shabbos, the weekly opportunity for the Jew to connect with the supernatural presence of Hashem embedded in him (a concept known as the נְקוּדָה הַפְּנִימִיּוּת), we seek to return the universe to its former blessed state by annihilating Amalek. (*Zachor* 5636)

ושבת הוא רמז ליום שכולו שבת ומנוחה לחיי העולמים. הרמז דכתיב מלחמה לה׳ בעמלק מדור דור ולעתיד כשימחה שמו. מנוחה כביכול לחי עולמים. לכן יש בשבת מחיית עמלק.

The Torah emphasizes that the battle waged by Hashem against Amalek is eternal, as it says, מִלְחָמָה לַה׳ בַּעֲמָלֵק מִדֹּר דֹּר, *The battle of* Hashem *against Amalek is from generation to generation* (*Shemos* 17:16). Not until the final generation of *Mashiach* will the goal of Amalek's annihilation be accomplished. In fact, it is only then that Hashem Himself will "rest" from His climactic battle against Amalek. However, on Shabbos, the day of *Menuchah,* which to some extent resembles the peace and harmony of the Messianic Era (cf. *Tamid* 33b stating that the song sung by the *Leviim* on Shabbos was dedicated to the theme of the Final Sabbath of *Mashiach*), the impact of Amalek may be blunted. Consequently, it is on Shabbos, the most opportune time to negate Amalek's evil effects, that we read about Amalek's destruction.

(Adapted from *Zachor* 5649)

וכשיהי׳ יום מנוחה אז יתבטל השקר. וז״ש והי׳ בהניח כו׳ תמחה כו׳ זכר עמלק. ומעין זה בכל שבת. יום מנוחה. מעין עוה״ב. יום שכולו שבת. ושבת סהדותא אקרי לכן הוא זמן מחיית עמלק.

It is only in This World, which to some extent (at least on the surface) is dominated by values that are false and totally opposed to the Torah, that Amalek may prevail.[1] When *Klal Yisrael* finally succeeds in vanquishing all of its foes [as the Torah writes, וְהָיָה בְּהָנִיחַ ה׳ אֱלֹהֶיךָ לְךָ מִכָּל אֹיְבֶיךָ, *It shall be that when HASHEM, your God, gives you rest from all your enemies* (*Devarim* 25:19)], and when falsehood (perpetuated by the very foes that we destroyed) ceases, then it is possible that any last vestige of Amalek will be successfully destroyed. Every Shabbos replicates, to an extent, the ideal conditions for the extinction of Amalek. On this day, by virtue of our abstaining from all *melachah*, we bear true testimony to the creation of heaven and earth. On this day, described as a microcosm of the World to Come (*Berachos* 57b), we are best able to succeed in the mission of wiping out Amalek. (*Zachor* 5657)

לכן ביום המנוחה הוסיפו שנאה עליו. ואז מחו את שורשו בכח השנאה. והוא עיקר היו״ט. כמ״ש ונוח מאויביהם׳ ״. וכ״כ והי׳ בהניח כו׳ תמחה. ולכן ביקשה אסתר לקיים הנקמה גם ביום י״ד שהי׳ זמן המנוחה כנ״ל.

It is significant that one of the greatest moments of מְחִיַּת עֲמָלֵק ever experienced in This World was the destruction of Haman at the time of the Purim miracle. It is no coincidence that *Klal Yisrael* celebrates that notable triumph on the day that we *rested* (וְנוֹחַ מֵאֹיְבֵיהֶם) from battle — the 14th of *Adar* — rather than on the previous day when we actually prevailed in the battlefield. (For further discussion of the relationship between resting from the battle against Amalek and Purim refer to the following citations: Purim 5641, 5646, 5647, 5659)

Why Pesach is Called Shabbos

ולכן שם נפש מלשון מנוחה כמ״ש וינפש שעיקר זמן חרותנו הוא בנפש להיות לו מנוח ממאסר הגוף. ולכן נק׳ חג הפסח שבת ע״ש המנוחה כנ״ל.

If we assume that the concept of *Menuchah* refers to spiritual as well as physical respite, we can appreciate why the *Yom Tov* of Pesach is

1. In fact, *Olam Hazeh* is often called עָלְמָא דְשִׁקְרָא, *the world of falsehoods,* because of the tendency for false values to be widely accepted.

described as being a Shabbos (see *Vayikra* 23:15). Just as every Shabbos we attain a degree of spiritual freedom — as the soul is released from the powerful grip of the body — so too, on Pesach, זְמַן חֵרוּתֵנוּ, the *Yom Tov* which celebrates our freedom, we commemorate not only our physical liberation from Egypt but also our spirtual redemption.[1] (*Pesach* 5647)

◆§ Relationship Between the Concept of *Menuchah* and *Sefiras HaOmer*

רק שבת הוא מנוחה ותכלית ימי השבוע. וצריך לברר כל מדה בשלימות ואז הוא שבת ומנוחה למדה ההיא וכ״ה בכל הז׳ שבתות עכ״ד ז״ל. וביאור הדברים כי בכל מדה יש כמה מדרגות שפעמים מתעלה ע״י המדה ופעמים היא בקטנות ויש עליות וירידות בכל מדה. ואח״כ נעשה השלימות והיא שבת ומנוחה בתיקון כל פרטי המדה כנ״ל.

It is significant that the Torah describes the seven-week period of counting the *Omer*, beginning on the second day of Pesach and culminating just before Shavuos (a period known as the *Sefirah*), as שֶׁבַע שַׁבָּתוֹת, literally translated, *seven Sabbaths* (cf. *Vayikra* 23:15). To appreciate the relationship between Shabbos and the *Sefirah*, we recall that during each week of the *Sefirah* we undertake תִּקּוּן הַמִּדּוֹת, *rectification and improve-ment of our character traits.*[2] Just as creation of the universe was not completed until the *Menuchah* of Shabbos, so too, the weekly task that we engage in during the *Sefirah* — pursuing perfection — is not completed until we attain a sense of *Menuchah*, the sense of perfection and completion, similar to what every Shabbos brings. As anyone who has attemp-ted to perfect his character traits has learned, the process of self-improvement does not always lead to consistent results. There are days in which much progress is made and other days in which we seem to be making no progress. It is only when attaining the same sense of *sheleimus* and *Menuchah* that Shabbos brings that we can finally achieve our objective — to develop and perfect our *middos*. (Adapted from *Emor* 5653)

1. We can corroborate that a primary aspect of *yetzias Mitzrayim* was the liberation of the soul from the spiritual depravity of Egypt by noting that the *gematria* (numerical equivalent) of נֶפֶשׁ, *soul*, is 430, which corresponds to the 430 years spent by the Jewish people in Mitzrayim.

2. *Tikkun hamiddos* is included in several *tefillos* recited by many people after they count the *Omer*.

◆§ Some Parallels Between Shabbos and the Day of *Matan Torah* (Shavuos)

כי במה שהי׳ במקרה ביום שבת לא שייך לומר זכור בעצומו של יום. והענין הוא עפ״י מ״ש ז״ל בפסוק יום הששי למה הוסיף ה׳ תנאי התנה הקב״ה אם מקבלין ישראל התורה כו׳. וכ׳ מקודם וירא אלקים כו׳ כל אשר עשה כו׳ טוב מאוד וזה החן קיים כל העולם ומזה נעשה השבת שהוא הנייחא שיש להקב״ה ובו״ש מהבריאה במה שראה שעתידין בנ״י לקבל התורה שנקרא טוב. נמצא כמ״ש בשבת הטעם כי בו שבת וזה הי׳ השלמת העולם כמ״ש רש״י מה הי׳ עולם חסר מנוחה באת שבת נגמרה המלאכה. כן הי׳ ביום מתן תורה שזה השלמת העולם ממש והוא עיקר המנוחה והנייחא לפניו ית׳ וזה גמר הבריאה. וכמו כן מצד התחתונים יום השבת הוא קיום ומנוחה של בנ״י שהוא החזרת הדברים לשורשם וזה עיקר הנייחא. וזה הטעם השני של השבת דכתיב וזכרת כי עבד היית כו׳ פי׳ שהוציאנו לחירות להיות במקום מנוחה ושורשו זה הוא השבת שיש ממנוחה וחירות זה חלק בש״ק לכל איש ישראל לכן הוא מעין עוה״ב. ועיקר מנוחה זו ג״כ נתקיים ביום מתן תורה שאז הי׳ התדבקות כל נפש ישראל בשורש השייך לו וזה עיקר המנוחה כמ״ש אנכי ה׳ אלקיך אשר הוצאתיך כו׳.

Chazal (*Shabbos* 86b) emphasize that the Torah was given on Shabbos. In their words, the Fourth Commandment, זָכוֹר אֶת יוֹם הַשַּׁבָּת, *Remember the Sabbath day* (*Shemos* 20:8), was presented to *Klal Yisrael* בְּעִצּוּמוֹ שֶׁל יוֹם, *on the very day of Shabbos.* By using this expression, they are indicating that it was no coincidence that the Torah was given on Shabbos. To some extent, there is an innate association between Shabbos and the Giving of the Torah, as we shall explore.

The first Shabbos was preceded by Hashem expressing great satisfaction with the universe that He had just created. As the Torah states, וַיַּרְא אֱלֹהִים אֶת כָּל אֲשֶׁר עָשָׂה וְהִנֵּה טוֹב מְאֹד, *And God saw all that He had created and behold it was very good* (*Bereishis* 1:31). This sense of Divine satisfaction was not only Hashem's response to the universe that had just been consummated but also, in itself, was the bedrock and foundation of the continued existence of the universe. While the world was created in the שֵׁשֶׁת יְמֵי הַמַּעֲשֶׂה, *the Six Days of Creation,* its continued vitality is derived from the נַחַת (*nachas*), sheer pleasure that Hashem obtained from the completed universe. Moreover, the *nachas* that Hashem derived from His completed universe — in particular *Klal Yisrael* who would accept the Torah — was the catalyst which made Shabbos possible. Such an intense spiritual experience could only emerge from the *nachas ruach* that Hashem gained from His universe.

So, too, *Matan Torah.* When else could *HaKadosh Baruch Hu* derive such intense satisfaction from His universe than when *Klal Yisrael* received the Torah? How appropriate that *Matan Torah,* a moment of intense Divine satisfaction, occurred on the same day that Hashem first expressed His intense satisfaction with His universe — Shabbos.

Drawing the analogy between Shabbos and *Kabbalas HaTorah* even closer, we recall the statement of *Chazal,* בָּאת שַׁבָּת בָּאת מְנוּחָה, *Sabbath came, rest came* (cf. *Rashi, Bereishis* 2:2) — when Shabbos came, a sense of *Menuchah* also emerged. (Refer to our *divrei Torah* on this theme earlier in this chapter.) By these words *Chazal* are expressing their contention that the universe's true consummation only occurred with the advent of the first Shabbos. It was then that the concept of *Menuchah,* ceasing all material efforts, became a reality. Only then could it truly be said that the universe was complete.

But the sense of "closure" and completion present at the first Shabbos was contingent upon another such great moment — the acceptance of the Torah by *Klal Yisrael* many generations later. As *Rashi* (*Bereishis* 1:31) notes, by writing יוֹם הַשִּׁשִּׁי, *the sixth day* (of Creation) with the definite article ה (*the*), the Torah is alluding that the continued vitality of the universe that was about to be completed was contingent upon another "sixth day" — the sixth of Sivan when *Klal Yisrael* accepted the Torah.

Drawing the parallel between the *Menuchah* of Shabbos and *Matan Torah* even further, we note (as we have discussed at length in many *divrei Torah*) that an integral part of the *Menuchah* of Shabbos is the return of every Jew to his *shoresh,* his Divinely inspired roots. This process commencing with the first Shabbos (when the universe returned to its indigenous roots) was most pronounced at *Matan Torah.* When *Klal Yisrael* heard the opening words of the *Aseres HaDibros,* אָנֹכִי ה' אֱלֹהֶיךָ, *I am HASHEM, your God,* every Jew was able to discard all of the material "shackles" that confined him to This World and evoke his inner spirituality to draw closer to Hashem.

Using this approach, we may derive new meaning in the association that the Torah draws (in the second rendition of the *Aseres HaDibros*) between *yetzias Mitzrayim* and observing Shabbos. Just as we were released from material bondage when we left Egypt, so too, every Shabbos all of the material factors that prevent us from finding our true spiritual roots give way to the *kedushah* of Shabbos. When *Chazal* describe Shabbos as being מֵעֵין עוֹלָם הַבָּא, *a semblance of the World to Come* (*Berachos* 57b), they are alluding to the ability of every Jew on Shabbos to discard all of the material trappings of This World and, in some fashion, attain some of the spirituality ordinarily associated with the World to Come.

(Adapted from *Shavuos* 5644)

◆§ A Day Without Limits (Some Thoughts on Shabbos During the *Bein Ha'metzarim*)

והוא בחי׳ מנוחת השבת שכתי׳ והאכלתיך נחלת יעקב נחלה בלי מצרים. שזה הכח הבא מלמעלה הוא בלי גבול וע״ז נאמר יוסף עליכם כו׳. לכן גם בימים בללו שנקראו בין המצרים מ״מ בש״ק ע״י הביטול להשורש זוכין למנוחה.

While we designate the period between the 17th of Tammuz and Tishah B'Av as בֵּין הַמְּצָרִים, a time when *Klal Yisrael* is confined to definite limits,[1] on Shabbos, a day when we enjoy נַחֲלָה בְּלִי מְצָרִים, *a limitless legacy* (*Shabbos* 118a), we are able to transcend those limitations. By negating ourselves to Hashem, we enjoy the *Menuchah* of Shabbos (refer to our *divrei Torah* on the association between negation to Hashem and *Menuchah*) which knows no limits.

To corroborate our contention that it is only those *berachos* granted by mortals that are subject to limits, while the blessings of Hashem are never subject to any constraints, we recall that after blessing *Klal Yisrael*

1. This term is derived from the *pasuk*, כָּל רֹדְפֶיהָ הִשִּׂיגוּהָ בֵּין הַמְּצָרִים, *all those who pursued her* (the Jewish people) *overtook her in narrow straits* (*Eichah* 1:3). While the simple meaning of this *pasuk* refers to the inability of the Jewish people at the time of the destruction of the *Beis HaMikdash* to find any sanctuary from their foes, homiletically this expression may indicate that this period is a time of definite limits to our capacity for growth.

with his own *berachos* (stating that Hashem should increase their numbers a thousandfold), Moshe *Rabbeinu* invokes the blessings of *HaKadosh Baruch Hu* which are limitless (see *Devarim* 1:11).

(*Devarim* 5641)

❧ A Day of Unity (*Achdus*)

ובשבת קודש הוא מעין זה ונקרא שלום כמ״ש יעקב ובניו ינוחו בו. ובו מתאחדין כל הדעות. ולכן בתפלת מנחת שבת חשיב י״ב מנוחות מנוחה וקדושה כו׳ אהבה נדבה כו׳ שלום כו׳. והוא כלל כל הי״ב שבטים. שנעשין אחד.

Another aspect of Shabbos's *Menuchah* is the ability of individuals of different "persuasions" to put aside their differences and unite. According to the *Zohar, Shalom* (peace) is one of the names of *Shabbos Kodesh.* This indicates that the very essence of the day brings together different factions within *Klal Yisrael.* This aspect of *Menuchah* is emphasized in the *Minchah Shemoneh Esrei* where we recite, יַעֲקֹב וּבָנָיו יָנוּחוּ בוֹ, *Jacob and his children would rest on it* — despite the differences among the *shevatim,* Yaakov's children are able to come together every Shabbos. In fact, during this *tefillah* we allude to twelve different forms of *Menuchah* (מְנוּחָה וּקְדֻשָּׁה לְעַמְּךָ נָתָתָּ ... מְנוּחַת אַהֲבָה וּנְדָבָה מְנוּחַת אֱמֶת וֶאֱמוּנָה מְנוּחַת שָׁלוֹם וְשַׁלְוָה וְהַשְׁקֵט וָבֶטַח מְנוּחָה שְׁלֵמָה שֶׁאַתָּה רוֹצֶה בָּהּ), corresponding to the twelve children of Yaakov (*shevatim*) who are able to come together on Shabbos. This theme is reinforced in the opening words of the Shabbos *Minchah Shemoneh Esrei,* וּמִי כְּעַמְּךָ יִשְׂרָאֵל גּוֹי אֶחָד בָּאָרֶץ, *and who is like your nation, Yisrael, one (unified) nation on earth.*

(*Vayigash* 5647)

◈§ Unity of Heart (*Lev*) and Mind (*Moach*)

וזה הי׳ בחי׳ יהודה בכלל ישראל. מלך במלחמה בחי׳ הלב. ויוסף הוא בחי׳ המוח בחי׳ גאולה. כי עיקר הגאולה בנפש. כשהנשמן והמוחין מאירין לאדם ואז שקטה מלחמת הלב ונעשה לב אחד. וע״ז כ׳ בשמחתו לא יתערב זר לשנתמלא בשמחת הנפש מתבטל לב כסיל. לכן בשבת קודש דיש נשמה יתירה המאירה לנפש האדם. סט״א ערקית. ושבת הוא יום שמחה כמ״ש חז״ל ביום שמחתכם אלו השבתות לפי שהנשמה מאירה באדם ... ועיקר האחדות לב ומוח בש״ק יום החירות ומנוחה והארת הנשמה. לכן זכור ושמור בדבור אחד נאמרו. זכור במוח שמירה בלב.

Whereas in the previous *dvar Torah,* we emphasized that the *Menuchah* of Shabbos helps unite different factions within *Klal Yisrael,* we now suggest that on this day of *Menuchah* the different aspects of each individual are also able to coalesce. Generally, the heart (*lev*) and the mind (*moach*) are employed in different ways to serve Hashem.[1] On Shabbos, the environment of *Menuchah* allows the mind and soul to jointly serve Hashem. (Refer to our chapter on *Zachor V'Shamor* where we suggested that *Zachor,* the capacity to recall Shabbos, is associated with the mind, while *Shamor,* guarding Shabbos, is related to the heart.)

(*Vayigash* 5660)

◈§ The Association Between *Menuchah* and the *Mishkan Shiloh*

וזה מנוחה ונחלה דרשו חז״ל מנוחה זו שילה נחלה ירושלים. כי ירושלים היא בחי׳ יהודה ודהע״ה שהיא בנין קבוע כמ״ש ירושלים בין הגוים שמתי׳. והיא חומה המבדלת בין ישראל לעמים. אכן בחי׳ משכן שילה הוא מקום שאין התנגדות האומות מגיע שם כלל וזהו בחי׳ השבת שנקרא מנוחה.

It is significant that the term *Menuchah* is used by the Torah not only in the context of Shabbos but also to depict the *Mishkan Shiloh* (the

1. Refer to the full text of *Sfas Emes* for a discussion of the unique role played by the heart and soul.

Tabernacle which served as the resting place of the *Shechinah* during the period of the Judges; also refer to *Devarim* 12:9, *Rashi* ibid.). Let us consider some of the similarities between Shabbos' *Menuchah* and the *Mishkan Shiloh*. Firstly, we note that they both were temporary in nature. Just as the *Mishkan Shiloh* was only the temporary residence of the *Shechinah* (eventually yielding to the more permanent abode of Yerushalayim and the *Beis HaMikdash*), so too, the infinite, rarefied spiritual level of Shabbos cannot be totally sustained all week; it is temporary in nature. Moreover, we note that unlike Yerushalayim which was surrounded by a wall (which defined its outer perimeter), Shiloh had no walls. In fact, there were no physical boundaries to its reach. Instead, one was permitted to partake of *korbanos* at any location from where one could see the *Mishkan Shiloh* (cf. *Megillah* 9b). This distinction between the walls of Yerushalayim and the open borders of Shiloh resembles the relationship between Shabbos and the week. Whereas during the weekdays we are protected by a "wall"[1] that separates us from the gentile world, on Shabbos we attain so exalted a level that we require no such protection. On Shabbos, the Jew is on such a high spiritual level that he is consequently less affected by opposition to his ideals and beliefs.[2] (*Vayechi* 5647)

למעלה מן הטבע. ובשבת מתגלה הארה זו. לכן נק׳ מנוחה. נחלה בלי מצרים. אכן באמת בנ״י נבראו בעוה״ז לברר מלכותו ית׳ גם בעולם הטבע. וזה הי׳ בנין בהמ״ק ולכן הי׳ צריך מחיצה והבדל להיות השראת השכינה אפי׳ בוע״הז.

Drawing the association between the *Menuchah* of Shabbos and the *Mishkan Shiloh* even further, we note that just as there was no wall surrounding Shiloh, so too, there are no limits to the supernatural *kedushah* of Shabbos. Thus, *Chazal* (*Shabbos* 118a) describe the reward due those who meticulously observe Shabbos as נַחֲלָה בְּלִי מְצָרִים, *an inheritance without boundaries*. On the other hand, by insisting that Yerushalayim, the permanent resting place of the *Shechinah*, be surrounded by a wall, the Torah is confirming that even the natural world enjoys *kedushah* as

---

1. This allusion to a wall may refer to the Torah and *mitzvos* which distinguish us from mankind, or simply to the protection that Hashem affords us.

2. Perhaps, it is for this reason that in the Friday Evening Service we delete the usual closing *berachah* of שׁוֹמֵר עַמּוֹ יִשְׂרָאֵל לָעַד, *[Hashem] eternally guards His people.*

long as we remain within the parameters (walls) that separate us from the rest of mankind.[1] (*Vayechi* 5648)

◆§ A Feeling of Liberation

איתא במד׳ בפסוק לא תאספון כו׳ תכבד העבודה שלא הי׳ מניח להם לנוח בשבת ע״פ המדרש שמשה רבינו תיקן להם השבת ע״ש ... לכן הצדיקים כמו האבות ומשה רבינו ע״ה הרגישו בקדושת השבת והוציאו מכח אל הפועל אפי׳ קודם שניתן כמ״ש במ״א כי המתנות הקדושות שנתן לנו הקב״ה נותנין ברכה וקדושה לפניהם ולאחריהם. ולא זו [אלא] שאפי׳ אותו הרשע פרעה הבין שיש להם הארת הגאולה בכח המנוחה ביום השבת. וזה הרמז לא תאסיפון על השבת שיש בו תוספת נשמה יתירה מלמעלה ... וז״ש ל״ת לתת תבן שלא להוסיף להם תבונה מלמעלה. הם ילכו וקוששו הוא בחי׳ ימי המעשה שצריכין לעבוד בל״ט מלאכות כנ״ל.

Yet another aspect of the *Menuchah* of Shabbos is a sense of liberation (*geulah*). Even in the darkest moments of *Klal Yisrael's* history, such as in the *galus* of Mitzrayim, when our forefathers were brutally enslaved, they nonetheless enjoyed a measure of relief on Shabbos. Even if their bodies remained enslaved to Pharaoh, their souls, particularly on Shabbos, were never shackled to Pharaoh's chains. When we describe Shabbos as being זֵכֶר לִיצִיאַת מִצְרָיִם, *a memorial of the Exodus from Egypt,* we may be alluding to the sense of freedom that the Jewish soul enjoys every Shabbos.[2] If in Egypt – prior to the time when *Klal Yisrael* received the *mitzvah* of Shabbos – our forefathers enjoyed a sense of liberation on Shabbos, certainly we, fortified with the *mitzvah* of Shabbos, can benefit from the sense of redemption that occurs every Shabbos.

Utilizing this idea, we may derive a new (and homiletical) approach to Pharaoh's abrupt reaction to Moshe's and Aharon's first plea that the

1. Refer to text of *Sfas Emes* where he elaborates on the theme that during the period of *Mishkan Shiloh* our relationship with Hashem was that of *banim*, children, while when the *Beis HaMikdash* stood, we assumed the role of *avadim*, servants of Hashem.

2. Alternatively, by constantly recalling that Shabbos is זֵכֶר לִיצִיאַת מִצְרָיִם, *a memorial of the Exodus from Egypt,* we are emphasizing that whatever sense of *Menuchah* we enjoy on this hallowed day can be directly attributed to the Exodus – rather than as a reward for our efforts all week long. Had Hashem not redeemed us from Egypt, we would have been physically and spiritually enslaved to Pharaoh. As we recite at the *Seder,* וְאִלּוּ לֹא הוֹצִיא הַקָּדוֹשׁ בָּרוּךְ הוּא אֶת אֲבוֹתֵינוּ מִמִּצְרַיִם ... מְשֻׁעְבָּדִים הָיִינוּ לְפַרְעֹה בְּמִצְרָיִם, *If the Holy One, Blessed is He, had not taken our forefathers out of Egypt ... we would still be enslaved to Pharaoh in Egypt.*

Jewish people be given their freedom. Rather than acquiesce to their request, he insists that their regimen be made even more difficult. Instead of being given straw from which to form bricks, now they would be required to wander through Egypt in search of the raw materials needed to produce bricks. Specifically, Pharaoh responds to their request in the following terms, לֹא תֹאסִפוּן לָתֵת תֶּבֶן לָעָם ... הֵם יֵלְכוּ וְקֹשְׁשׁוּ לָהֶם תֶּבֶן, *You shall no longer give straw to the people ... let them go and gather straw for themselves* (*Shemos* 5:7). This may be homiletically interpreted as follows – do not allow the Jewish people to enjoy the *neshamah yeseirah* (the "additional soul," related to תֹאסִפוּן, *to add*) which graces every Shabbos. Similarly, the term תֶּבֶן, *straw*, may be related to תְּבוּנָה, *additional insight*, which Shabbos and the *neshamah yeseirah* provide. Instead, let them continue "to gather straw" and pursue all thirty-nine forms of *melachah* as they would during the weekdays. (Adapted from *Shemos* 5652)

◆§ *Menuchah* in the Future World

ששת ימים כו׳ למען ינוח שורך וחמורך כו׳. כי שבת הוא עצה לקרב כל מעשה בראשית להשי״ת ע״י שמירת שבת שהוא עדות שהשי״ת ברא מעשה בראשית. וזהו למען ינוח כו׳ כמ״ש במ״א באורך. ולמען ינוח הוא טעם על ששת ימים תעשה מעשיך כי מהראוי היה שבנ״י יהיו בחי׳ עולם שכולו שבת. רק שנשתלחו נשמות ישראל בעוה״ז כדי לתקן בחי׳ נפש הבהמיות וכדי שיתוספו עליהם גרים. לכן יש ימי המעשה. ופי׳ למען ינוח וינפש כו׳ הוא לעתיד יהי׳ שייכות שורך כו׳ והגר ג״כ להמנוחה. השבת כמ״ש ששת ימים תעשה מעשיך כו׳ השביעי תשבות למען ינוח שורך כו׳. פרשנו כנ״ל ע״י ביטול הימי מעשה להשבת כמ״ש לזכור בכל יום. השבת. וכן בבוא ש״ק ומניחין כל המלאכות עי״ז יש המשכת קדושה השבת גם בעשי׳. ועי״ז ינוח שורך וחמורך שהוא תיקון החומריות ונפש הבהמיות וכל העשי׳ כמ״ש. גם פי׳ למען ינוח הבטחה על העתיד שע״י ביטול החומר אף שאינו יכול להכניעו ולתקנו בשלימות. אבל כפי היגיעה בעוה״ז מי שטרח בע״ש יאכל בשבת. ולעתיד ליום שכולו שבת ינוח ממש שורך וחמורך בשלימות. שאז יהי׳ גמר התיקון לכ״א כפי העבודה בעוה״ז. ומעין זה קצת בכל ש״ק שהוא מעין עוה״ב.

While in This World the *Menuchah* of Shabbos can only be appreciated and enjoyed by *Klal Yisrael*, in the Future World, all of mankind will, in some measure, benefit from the ambiance of Shabbos. This thought may be derived from a *pasuk* which offers a seemingly novel reason for the *mitzvah* of Shabbos: שֵׁשֶׁת יָמִים תַּעֲשֶׂה מַעֲשֶׂיךָ וּבַיּוֹם הַשְּׁבִיעִי תִּשְׁבֹּת לְמַעַן יָנוּחַ שׁוֹרְךָ וַחֲמֹרֶךָ וְיִנָּפֵשׁ בֶּן אֲמָתְךָ וְהַגֵּר, *Six days shall you perform your deeds, and on the seventh day you shall desist, in order that your ox and donkey should rest and your maidservant's son and the convert should rest* (*Shemos* 23:12). This *pasuk* which justifies the *Menuchah* of Shabbos on the basis of the impact it leaves on the animal world, as well as on your domestic help and the convert to Judaism, may refer to the eventual impact of Shabbos on all of mankind. In effect, the *pasuk* is saying, observe Shabbos in This World – with all of its material constraints with which we struggle during the six weekdays – so that even your נֶפֶשׁ הַבְּהֵמִית (the material aspect of your personality) shall be affected by the *kedushah* of Shabbos, and the non-Jewish world, being duly impressed by the *kedushah* of Shabbos, will join the ranks of *Klal Yisrael*. This approach may be supported by the Torah's emphasis on the future using the term לְמַעַן (*in order that*), implying that by observing Shabbos even in This World, we are confident that eventually the spirit of Shabbos will be shared by all of mankind. (*Mishpatim* 5632, 5641)

◆§ Where Are We Headed?

והנה בעוה״ז תחת השמש יש לכל הברואים שינוים. ולכן העליונים נק׳ עומדים ותחתונים מהלכים. כי הכל הי׳ מן העפר והכל שב אל העפר. ומדומם נולד צומח ומצומח ניזון החי ומחי מדבר והכל למיתה הולכין ובעבור המיתה אין עמידה בעולם כידוע שאין כל שעה שלא יהי׳ שינוי והתחלפות בכל הברואים מטעם הנ״ל. אבל הדברים שמתחברין לשורש אין בהם שינוי. לכן כמו שנסדר הלחם נשאר כך בלי שינוי. וזה הי׳ עדות להנ״י שהגם שהלחם כבר נעשה בו כמה שינוים עד שנעשה לחם. מ״מ בכח איש ישראל להעלות הכל אל השורש ונפשט מכל בשינוים. וזה ענין מנוחת השבת. כדכתי׳ אל יצא איש ממקומו. ולכן נאסרו המלאכות בשבת שכל המלאכות הם בחי׳ השינוים. והשבת הוא יום מנוחה ולכן הוא מעין עוה״ב.

To appreciate yet another dimension of Shabbos, we recall that every mortal is living a life of constant change. Each day of our life is one day closer to the inevitable end of our physical existence when the body expires. Thus, unlike angels who live an eternal, unchanging existence (and for that reason are called עוֹמְדִים, *standing*, cf. *Zechariah* 3:7), man is a מְהַלֵּךְ – constantly in a state of motion and flux. This downward drift is halted on Shabbos.[1] As the Torah states, אַל יֵצֵא אִישׁ מִמְּקֹמוֹ בַּיּוֹם הַשְּׁבִיעִי, *Let no man leave his place on the seventh day* (*Shemos* 16:29). It is only in the material world – where we may have put some distance between ourselves and our Creator – that there is the sense of constant change and motion which ultimately culminates in death. However, in the world of spirituality, and especially on Shabbos when the Jew connects to his roots, this transitory process comes to an end. From this perspective, we gain new insight into the justification for the prohibition of *melachah* on Shabbos. By performing *melachah,* we are participating and actively contributing to (and enhancing) the material world, which is dominated by constant change and a sense of complete drift. On the other hand, by abstaining from *melachah* and enjoying Shabbos' *Menuchah,* we are indicating that at least on this hallowed day, our lives are dominated by the values of *Olam Haba* – a world of permanent and constant spirituality. In such an ambiance, we attain the status of עוֹמְדִים. Just as *malachim* do, we devote ourselves permanently to Divine Service without experiencing the sense of downward drift that is so much a part of This World.

From this perspective, we can appreciate why the Showbread (לֶחֶם הַפָּנִים), placed on the *Beis HaMikdash's* Table on Shabbos and removed the following Shabbos, always remained fresh. Whereas bread and anything material ultimately deteriorates, the Bread of Shabbos, placed in so hallowed a location in the Presence of the *Shechinah,* was exempt from the downward drift and decay that permeated anything material.

(Adapted from *Emor* 5656)

1. Of course, this process is somewhat halted during the weekdays by immersion in Torah study.

◆§ Accelerating the Pace of Our Spiritual Growth

והאדם נקרא מהלך ע״י שצריך להשיג השלימות מעט מעט ואח״כ בשמתקן עצמו כראוי הולך לעולם העליון. אך בנ״י נתאוו אל השלימות. וזכו לזה במתנה. וכמו כן יש זמנים שזוכין התחתונים לזה וכן בש״ק שנק׳ מתנה טובה כו׳. אך צריכין לראות שזאת הוא במתנה ולידע להכיר את מקומו להלוך למצוא השלימות מצד עצמו. וכשהאדם מכיר זאת אין הקב״ה מונע ממנו זאת המתנה. וזהו הרמז איש על מחנהו. אעפ״י שהוא על דגלו. וזהו ימלא כל משאלותיך. וכ״כ בשבת המענג את השבת נותנין לו משאלות לבו.

Whereas in the previous *dvar Torah,* we noted that one aspect of *Menuchah* is that the sense of drift that is so much a part of *Olam Hazeh* is halted on Shabbos, here we go further and suggest that our pace of spiritual growth is actually accelerated on Shabbos.

To appreciate this theme, we recall a fundamental distinction between a mortal and an angel. Whereas angels have already attained their full potential necessary to fulfill their personal mission, human beings generally need to proceed incrementally in their quest for spiritual growth. This significant distinction can be deduced from the fact that *malachim* are described as being עוֹמְדִים, standing and going at a steady pace, while mortals are known as מְהַלְּכִים, *travelers,* as they journey from one dimension of *ruchniyus* to another.

However, there are occasions in which mortals can transcend their limitations and rise from one spiritual plane to another at an accelerated pace. Certainly the Wilderness Generation, because of their intense desire for spiritual growth, merited to ascend rapidly to levels of *ruchniyus* that are ordinarily unattainable. When *Chazal* (*Bamidbar Rabbah* 2:3) note that the banners that every tribe held aloft emulated the level of *kedushah* attained by *malachim,* they may have been referring to their ability to rise rapidly to unimagined levels of *kedushah,* similar to an angel who has already reached the pinnacle of *kedushah.* Likewise, every Shabbos, a time when the universe itself ascends to a loftier level, *Klal Yisrael* is able to trancend all of its limitations and reach undreamt of levels of spirituality.[1]

---

1. This relationship between the rapid spiritual growth associated with Shabbos and that enjoyed by *Klal Yisrael* in the Wilderness may be alluded to when *Chazal* (cf. *Rashi, Bamidbar* 2:2)

To ensure that we can achieve these unimagined spiritual gains every Shabbos, it is critical that we always recall that our ability to grow at so rapid a pace is a Divine gift, rather than a result of our own effort. Just as Shabbos itself is a Divine gift (refer to our chapter "The Gift of Shabbos"), so too, our ability to surmount all of the obstacles to our growth is also a gift from Hashem. As we read in the Torah's description of the banners that every tribe possessed (and chant in the Shabbos *zemiros*), אִישׁ עַל מַחֲנֵהוּ וְאִישׁ עַל דִּגְלוֹ, *every man at his camp and every man at his banner* (cf. *Bamidbar* 1:52). It is only with our feet planted firmly on the ground, realizing our true current spiritual level (our "camp"), that we can enjoy our "banners" — the level that we aspire to and attain every Shabbos.

When *Chazal* (*Shabbos* 118b) assure us that whoever delights in the Shabbos (refer to our chapter on *Oneg Shabbos*) will be granted the desires of his heart, they may be referring to the sense of dynamic spiritual growth that we experience every Shabbos. What greater wish can every Jew have! (*Bamidbar* 5646)

Enabling Us to Observe the Entire Torah

בפסוק ששת ימים תעשה מעשיך וביום השביעי תשבות למען ינוח כו׳ ובכל אשר אמרתי אליכם תשמרו. רמז שהמקיים השבת כאלו קיים כל התורה ומצות. ובאוה״ח פי׳ כי כל מצוה מתקן אבר מיוחד לכן צריכין לקיים כל המצות כדי להיות נשמרים כל האברים. ז״ש ובכל אשר אמרתי אליכם תשמרו וכמו כן בשמירת שבת כיון ששקול ככל המצות נשמר כל האדם. וכן אמר מו״ז ז״ל כי המצות שאמרו חכמים ששקולין ככל המצות היינו שמתקנים כל האדם. ובאמת על ידי השבת זוכין לקיים כל המצות.

Whereas in previous *divrei Torah* we spoke of the eventual effect of Shabbos on the material world, we now suggest that even in This World we gain a measure of relief from materialism by abstaining from

note that the tribes were camped no further than 2000 cubits from the Ark, enabling them to walk there on Shabbos. Just as every Shabbos we bask in the spiritual environment of this sacred day, so too, *Klal Yisrael* in the Wilderness enjoyed so lofty a level that they were always proximate to the Ark.

melachah on Shabbos, thus allowing the soul to prevail. In turn, the enhanced spirituality of Shabbos not only benefits us on that day to observe Shabbos itself but also enables us to observe more effectively all of the Torah's *mitzvos.* As the *pasuk* reads, וּבְכֹל אֲשֶׁר אָמַרְתִּי אֲלֵיכֶם תִּשָּׁמֵרוּ, *Be careful regarding everything I have said to you* (*Shemos* 23:13). Homiletically, this may be interpreted: In the merit of resting on Shabbos from materialism (as stated in the previous *pasuk*), you will merit to perform all of the *mitzvos.* (*Mishpatim* 5657)

The Three Meals of Shabbos – Shalosh Seudos

וַיֹּאמֶר מֹשֶׁה אִכְלֻהוּ הַיּוֹם כִּי שַׁבָּת הַיּוֹם לַה׳ הַיּוֹם לֹא תִמְצָאֻהוּ בַּשָּׂדֶה

Moshe said, "Eat it today, for today is a Sabbath for HASHEM*; today you shall not find it in the field"* (*Shemos* 16:25)

The Gemara derives from the three-fold repetition of the term הַיּוֹם, *today*, that we are obligated to partake of three meals on Shabbos, a concept known as *Shalosh Seudos*. In the following section, we will explore the impact of this *mitzvah* and in particular the significance of three (rather than two or four) meals.

◆§ The Power of *Shalosh Seudos*

כל הברכה ופרנסה בימי השבוע היא רק בכח השבת

Contrary to the popular perception that we earn our livelihood during the week and then rest from our labors on Shabbos, in reality, our *parnassah* all week long is made possible by the *mitzvah* of *oneg Shabbos* (enjoying the Shabbos), and especially the three meals that we partake of on Shabbos, known as שָׁלֹשׁ סְעוּדוֹת, *Shalosh Seudos*. This thought is stated explicitly by *Chazal* (*Shabbos* 118a), הַמְעַנֵּג אֶת הַשַּׁבָּת נוֹתְנִין לוֹ נַחֲלָה בְּלִי מְצָרִים, *One who delights in the Shabbos receives an inheritance without limits* (i.e. boundless reward). [The term נַחֲלָה connotes a means of support, an adequate livelihood.] In fact, the term שָׁלֹשׁ סְעוּדוֹת – translated literally as the "Three Supports" (related to סַעַד, *assistance*) – reinforces our contention that our livelihood all week long is sustained by the Three Meals of Shabbos. As further corroboration of how dependent we are on the *Shalosh Seudos*, we should remember that the *mitzvah* of partaking of three meals on Shabbos is derived from the manna (cf. *Shabbos* 117a where the Gemara notes that the three-fold mention of the term הַיּוֹם, *today*, in reference to the cessation of the manna on Shabbos alludes to the three meals of Shabbos). Just as *Klal Yisrael* were dependent upon the manna for their daily sustenance, so too, are the Three Meals of Shabbos necessary for them to survive.

(Adapted from *Bereishis* 5645; refer also to *Naso* 5635)

◆§ Food for the *Neshamah Yeseirah* (Extra Dimension of Shabbos)

גם הנשמה יתירה נזונות מסעודת שבת

An analogy may be drawn between the sanctity of the Three Meals of Shabbos and the meal that Avraham served the angels who visited his home. As *Chazal* state (*Yalkut Bereishis* 82), פתא סעדתא דלבא, *Bread satiates the heart*. While ordinary food primarily satiates the body, and only after a process of refinement the soul, the bread of Avraham *Avinu* was so sacred that it could immediately nurture the *heart* of angels.[1] (Refer to *Rashi*, *Bereishis* 18:5, who notes that angels lack an evil impulse. Thus, their essence is entirely pure and only consists of a *yetzer hatov*.)

Similarly, the meals of Shabbos are so pure (as we sing in *zemiros*, סְעוּדָתָא דִמְהֵימְנוּתָא, *the meal of pure faith*) that they can sustain the *neshamah yeseirah* – that extra spiritual dimension that we all enjoy on Shabbos.

(Adapted from *Vayeira* 5653)

1. For further discussion of this process of refinement, the reader is referred to *Eikev* 5652.

⁂ Sustaining Our *Emunah* (Faith) for an Entire Week

כי המה סועדים האמונה והוא הכנה לימי המעשה

The Three Meals of Shabbos are so sacred that they sustain our *emunah, faith,* for the entire week. It is well-known that just as there are periods of relative clarity in which we enjoy some insight into Hashem's ways, there are periods of darkness in which we are sustained by our *emunah* alone. As we recite every night in *Maariv,* גּוֹלֵל אוֹר מִפְּנֵי חֹשֶׁךְ, *removing light before darkness* — Hashem removes the light in favor of darkness. While enjoying the light of Shabbos, it is imperative that we prepare for the comparative darkness of the week. By partaking of the Shabbos meals, known as סְעוּדָתָא דִמְהֵימְנוּתָא, the meals of *emunah,* we ensure that our faith in Hashem will persevere even during the weekdays.

(*Chayei Sarah* 5652)

⁂ A Meal for Two Days

כל סעודה סעוד לב׳ ימים

Whereas in the foregoing *divrei Torah* we asserted that the Three Meals provide sustenance for the week *ahead,* we propose in this *dvar Torah* that *Shalosh Seudos* may even leave an impact on the *previous* week. To appreciate this perspective, we recall the comment of *Mechilta* that while the *mitzvah* of זָכוֹר אֶת יוֹם הַשַּׁבָּת, *Remember the Shabbos day* (*Shemos* 20:8), obliges us to *look forward* and prepare for Shabbos before it arrives, the commandment of שָׁמוֹר אֶת יוֹם הַשַּׁבָּת, *safeguard the Shabbos day* (*Devarim* 5:12), motivates us to *look back* at the previous Shabbos and preserve, as much as possible, the *kedushah* we attained then. In fact, these two *mitzvos* — looking forward to the forthcoming Shabbos and looking back at the previous Shabbos — may be tasks that engage the devoted Shabbos observer for an entire week. Specifically, the three weekdays preceding Shabbos (Wednesday, Thursday, Friday) are dominated by a sense of anticipation of the forthcoming Shabbos. On the other hand, the three weekdays immediately succeeding Shabbos (Sunday, Monday, Tuesday) are an excellent opportunity to preserve the gains achieved during the previous Shabbos. In fact, these two components of the week may interact. By striving during the days following Shabbos to preserve the strides we achieved the previous Shabbos, we merit to develop the proper sense of anticipation of the coming Shabbos. Moreover, by longing for Shabbos during the three days prior to its advent, we benefit from the impact of the future Shabbos even before it arrives.

How does one develop the capacity during the weekdays to both preserve the gains made during the previous Shabbos and to look forward to the following Shabbos? We propose that each of the Three Meals leaves a significant impact on two of the weekdays (refer to our first *dvar Torah* entitled, "The Power of *Shalosh Seudos,*" in which we suggested that the *Shalosh Seudos* provides sustenance for the entire week ahead). Specifically, one of the Shabbos meals enables us on Sunday to preserve the gains of the previous Shabbos and, simultaneously, to look ahead on Friday to the Shabbos that is about to arrive. Similarly, the second meal leaves an impact on both Monday and Thursday, while the third meal has the same effect on us on Tuesday and Wednesday.

Drawing the analogy even further between the three Shabbos meals and each of the three weekdays preceding and succeeding Shabbos, we propose that the *Shalosh Seudos* correspond to the three components of the soul known as *nefesh, ruach,* and *neshamah.* According to the sainted mystical thinker, the *Ari,* the days of the week also correspond to these aspects of the soul. Specifically, the three days preceding Shabbos — Wednesday, Thursday, and Friday — correspond to *nefesh, ruach,* and *neshamah* respectively. The days following Shabbos — Sunday, Monday, and Tuesday — correspond to *neshamah, ruach,* and *nefesh* respectively. It follows then that each of the Shabbos meals, corresponding to one aspect of the soul, leaves a significant impact on those two weekdays that represent the same component. (*Vayakhel* 5651)

☙ Why Three Meals? Past, Present, Future

ויברך היא סעודה ג׳ שנותן ברכה על שבוע הבאה

To appreciate the significance of enjoying three meals on Shabbos, we refer to the first description of Shabbos in the Torah (*Bereishis* 2:1-3) in the passage beginning וַיְכֻלּוּ הַשָּׁמַיִם וְהָאָרֶץ, *The heaven and the earth were finished* (recited in the *Kiddush*, as well as in the *Maariv* of Friday evening). It is significant that the term יוֹם הַשְּׁבִיעִי (*the seventh day*) is utilized three times (ibid., vs. 2, 3) in this brief *parashah*. Just as *Chazal* derive the *mitzvah* of partaking of three meals from the three-fold reference to the term הַיּוֹם in *Parashas Beshalach* (in the context of the manna), so too, if we examine carefully each context in which the term יוֹם הַשְּׁבִיעִי is used in this *parashah*, we may derive the distinct function of each of these meals.

In the first instance the Torah writes, וַיְכַל אֱלֹהִים בַּיּוֹם הַשְּׁבִיעִי מְלַאכְתּוֹ אֲשֶׁר עָשָׂה, *God completed on the seventh day all the work that He had performed* (ibid. 2:2). The multi-faceted universe that Hashem assembled during the Six Days of Creation was not considered to be complete until the advent of the first Shabbos. In a similar fashion, by partaking of the Shabbos meal on Friday night and going from the workweek into Shabbos, we are consecrating all of our mundane activities during the previous week by associating them with Shabbos.

The Torah then notes that Hashem *ceased* working on Shabbos (וַיִּשְׁבֹּת בַּיּוֹם הַשְּׁבִיעִי). The elaborate tapestry that Hashem created during the week – and completed on Shabbos – yielded to the overwhelming spirituality of *Shabbos Kodesh*. The entire universe, with all of its material splendor created by Hashem, gave way to the splendid sanctity of *Shabbos Kodesh*. Every Shabbos morning, by partaking of the second meal, we link the entire material world to its spiritual source (a concept known as התעלות אל השורש) – Hashem.

Finally, the Torah speaks of the *berachah* that Hashem bestowed upon the Shabbos: וַיְבָרֶךְ אֱלֹהִים אֶת יוֹם הַשְּׁבִיעִי, *God blessed the seventh day* (ibid. 2:3) – alluding to the blessings of the entire week that are derived from Shabbos. By partaking of the third Shabbos meal, its residual blessing impacts on the week that follows.

(Adapted from *Bereishis* 5645)

◆§ Experiencing the Primeval Light of Creation

בשב״ק יש הארה מג׳ ראשונת

It is significant that the Torah alludes to the Three Meals by utilizing the term הַיּוֹם (*today*) three times in the same *pasuk* (refer to *Shemos*

16:25). It is also noteworthy that unlike every other day of Creation where the term יוֹם is used only once (e.g. וַיְהִי עֶרֶב וַיְהִי בֹקֶר יוֹם אֶחָד), when referring to Shabbos (in the *parashah* of וַיְכֻלּוּ), the Torah utilizes the term יוֹם three times. What is the significance of the three-fold repetition of this word?

Perhaps, the answer to this question lies in the Torah's description of the first day of Creation — וַיִּקְרָא אֱלֹהִים לָאוֹר יוֹם, *God called the light* (that had just been created) *"Day"* (cf. *Bereishis* 1:5). Just as the Torah equates light and day in this first reference to the concept of יוֹם, so too, every other reference to יוֹם may also be understood in this context. Consequently, when repeating the term יוֹם three times in the context of Shabbos (and especially *Shalosh Seudos*), the Torah is alluding to an infinitely potent spiritual source of light that we enjoy every Shabbos. While the great Light of Creation was eventually hidden from public view (and reserved for the righteous in the World to Come; cf. *Rashi, Bereishis* 1:4), it did serve as the sole luminary for the universe for the first three days of Creation. It was only on the fourth day, when Hashem created the sun and moon, that this spiritually dazzling light was hidden.

To emphasize that every Shabbos — a day which is a replica of the World to Come — we enjoy some small measure of the great Light of Creation (which had been the sole source of light for the first *three* days of Creation), we partake of *three* meals, which are alluded to by the term יוֹם (which we have defined as referring to light as well as day). Whereas the universe is generally subject to the finite parameters of the natural world created in seven days (refer to the previous *dvar Torah* asserting that the universe was not completed until Shabbos), on Shabbos, we transcend those natural limitations and bask in a scintilla of the great Light of Creation, a theme reinforced by the Three Meals.

(*Bereishis* 5648)

❧ Thought, Speech, Deed (מחשבה, דבור, מעשה)

מלאכתו היא בעשי׳ ויברך בדיבור ויקדש הוא במחשבה

By partaking of three meals on Shabbos, we may be alluding to the three-fold manner in which Hashem "rested" on Shabbos. Hashem created the universe by utilizing three distinct "processes": מַחֲשָׁבָה,

thought (refer to *Rashi, Bereishis* 1:1, stating that Hashem *intended* to create the universe with the attribute of strict justice); דִּבּוּר, *speech,* indicated by the frequent references to וַיֹּאמֶר אֱלֹהִים, *God said;* and, of course, מַעֲשֶׂה, *deeds.* So too, on Shabbos, He ceased from utilizing each of these forms of creativity.

The three-fold nature of the first Shabbos is demonstrated by the three different expressions used to describe Hashem's cessation of Creation (see *Bereishis* 2:1-3). Firstly, וַיִּשְׁבֹּת – Hashem *rested* from all that He had created (realm of deeds). Then וַיְבָרֶךְ, He *blessed* (verbally) the Sabbath Day (realm of speech). Finally, וַיְקַדֵּשׁ, He *sanctified it,* is an allusion to Hashem "resting" from the realm of thought (and the spiritual world He created, which may eventually be realized in the Messianic Era – יוֹם שֶׁכֻּלּוֹ שַׁבָּת).

Not only do we partake of three meals which correspond to the three-fold manner in which Hashem "rested," but many other aspects of Shabbos observance also are closely associated with the number three. For example, Yeshayahu (58:13) urges the Jewish people to rest every Shabbos from *doing* one's weekday activities (וְכִבַּדְתּוֹ מֵעֲשׂוֹת דְּרָכֶיךָ), from *speaking* in the same manner as during the week (וְדַבֵּר דָּבָר), and (under certain circumstances) from even *thinking* about our daily mundane activities (מִמְּצוֹא חֶפְצְךָ). The three distinct *tefillos* of Shabbos (unlike *Yom Tov* in which virtually the identical *Shemoneh Esrei* is recited for *Maariv, Shacharis* and *Minchah,* on Shabbos each *tefillah* is unique) also reflect these three aspects of Shabbos observance. Specifically, the *Maariv tefillah* recited on Friday night emphasizes that on Shabbos, Hashem *rested* from creating heaven and earth (deed). On Shabbos morning (*Shacharis*), the focus shifts to the Ten Commandments (in which Shabbos is prominently featured) which were *spoken* to *Klal Yisrael* on Shabbos (speech). Finally, the *tefillah* of Shabbos afternoon, *Minchah,* revolves around the theme of the Future Shabbos of the Messianic Era (יוֹם שֶׁכֻּלּוֹ שַׁבָּת), which at this time is a dream that has yet to be fulfilled (thought). (*Bereishis* 5649)

With this approach – emphasizing that we celebrate Shabbos by "resting" not only from our weekday activities but also by changing our speech and thought patterns – we can appreciate why the *mitzvah* of Shabbos was given sequentially (rather than all at once) to *Klal Yisrael.* When the concept of Shabbos was first mentioned, primary emphasis was placed on ceasing from prohibited activities. As the Torah states, שְׁבוּ אִישׁ תַּחְתָּיו, *let every man remain in his place* (*Shemos* 16:29), and refrain from his usual weekday activity. It was only at Sinai, when the

Jewish people listened as Hashem *spoke* to them the *mitzvah* of Shabbos, that we gained the capacity to modify our speech on Shabbos. The ultimate dream, that the spirit of Shabbos will permeate our thoughts as well as our deeds and words, awaits *Mashiach's* arrival — the era described by *Chazal* as being יוֹם שֶׁכֻּלּוֹ שַׁבָּת, a day (and era) that is dominated by the spiritual ambiance of Shabbos.

Even the reward granted to those who observe Shabbos reflects this three-fold theme of מַעֲשֶׂה, *deeds;* דִּבּוּר, *speech;* and מַחֲשָׁבָה, *thoughts.* Yeshayahu continues his discourse on Shabbos and its reward (58:14): אָז תִּתְעַנַּג עַל ה׳, *Then* (if you observe the Shabbos through your deeds, speech, and thoughts) *you will delight in* HASHEM. This is a reference to the enhanced understanding of Hashem's Ways that will be enjoyed by those who observe Shabbos properly. וְהִרְכַּבְתִּיךָ עַל בָּמֳתֵי אָרֶץ, *I will lift you to the highest places on earth,* is a reference to the prosperity and success awaiting those who observe Shabbos. He concludes, וְהַאֲכַלְתִּיךָ נַחֲלַת יַעֲקֹב אָבִיךָ, *I will present you with the heritage of Yaakov, your father,* alluding to the enhanced ability to speak and study Torah (which was spoken to *Klal Yisrael*) enjoyed by those who observe Shabbos. This is in contrast to Esav who prides himself on his physical prowess (symbolized by his hands), while Yaakov is renowned for his voice, which is used to articulate Torah thoughts. (*Yisro* 5655)

◆§ Creation, *Yetzias Mitzrayim,* a Day of Intense *Kedushah*

ומתעוררין בשב״ק בח׳ מ״ב ויצ״מ והקדושה

By analyzing carefully the text of *Kiddush,* we may deduce three distinct aspects of Shabbos. First, Shabbos commemorates Hashem's creation of heaven and earth (זִכָּרוֹן לְמַעֲשֵׂה בְרֵאשִׁית). In addition, by observing Shabbos we acknowledge that Hashem liberated us from Egypt (זֵכֶר לִיצִיאַת מִצְרָיִם). Finally, we observe Shabbos simply because it is a day of intense *kedushah,* as we recite at the conclusion of *Kiddush* — וְשַׁבַּת קָדְשְׁךָ בְּאַהֲבָה וּבְרָצוֹן הִנְחַלְתָּנוּ, *Your holy Shabbos,with love and favor did You give us as a heritage.*

While the three meals of Shabbos represent these three distinct themes, there remains another aspect of Shabbos — the dream of the Future Shabbos and of *Mashiach*. Since this aspect of Shabbos is unrealized as yet, we do not dedicate one of the Shabbos meals explicitly to it. Instead, the post-Shabbos, *Melaveh Malkah* is dedicated *to David HaMelech* whose descendant Mashiach will lead *Klal Yisrael* in that era. As we sing every *Motzaei Shabbos*, דָא הִיא סְעוּדָתָא דְדָוִד מַלְכָּא מְשִׁיחָא, *This is the meal of David the king* [*whose descendant will be*] *Mashiach.*

(*Bereishis* 5651)

◆§ A Triple Renewal

התחדשות א׳ הבריאה ... הב׳ יצ״מ ... הג׳ קבלת התורה

Using a somewhat different approach, we suggest that the Three Meals correspond to three seminal events of world and Jewish history — Creation, *Yetzias Mitzrayim*, and the Giving of the Torah. While each of these events represent a different phase in the development of *Klal Yisrael*, they share something in common — a sense of newness or renewal, a concept known as הִתְחַדְּשׁוּת. Of course, creation of the universe from the chaos and void that had previously existed was the ultimate act of הִתְחַדְּשׁוּת — a highly developed universe emerged from a total void. Similarly, by liberating the Jewish people from the Egyptian tyranny — against all odds — Hashem reminded a skeptical universe not only of His Presence, but also that He had created heaven and earth and enjoyed the capacity to overwhelm any tyrant that sought to defy Him. When the world at large became newly aware of Hashem's Presence and capacity to hold them accountable for their actions, this undoubtedly catalyzed a renewal of their belief in Him. Finally, when *Klal Yisrael* received the Torah at Sinai, the universe itself was reinvigorated and given renewed strength. [Refer to *Shabbos* 88a where *Chazal* state that the universe's very existence was in jeopardy until the Jewish people agreed to accept the Torah. Also refer to our essay entitled "*Eretz Yarah Ve'Shakatah* — The Earth Feared and Then Grew Calm" (*The Three Festivals*, p.285) for further discussion of this concept.] This theme, and in particular our contention that *Matan Torah* was the third event associated with the universe's renewal, may be alluded to in the first words used to describe *Matan Torah* — בַּחֹדֶשׁ הַשְּׁלִישִׁי, *in the third month* (*Shemos* 19:1), which may be homiletically interpreted to mean "the third renewal" (בְּחִידוּשׁ הַשְּׁלִישִׁי).

By observing Shabbos, we acknowledge each of these three great moments of renewal – Creation, *Yetzias Mitzrayim* [as we read in the text of the *Aseres HaDibros* found in *Sefer Devarim* (5:15), וְזָכַרְתָּ כִּי עֶבֶד הָיִיתָ בְּאֶרֶץ מִצְרַיִם, *and you shall remember that you were a slave in the land of Egypt*), and *Matan Torah*. What better opportunity to recall *Matan Torah* than on Shabbos, the day that the Torah was originally given to *Klal Yisrael*. Each of the Three Meals, derived from the three-fold repetition of the term הַיּוֹם (*today*), also represents another aspect of the three-fold renewal occurring every Shabbos. (*Yisro* 5642)

◈ Birth, Receiving the Torah, Praising Hashem

יצירתו ... תורתו ... קילוסו ... וגם בכל שבת הג' סעודות

Midrash (*Parashas Tazria*) notes three phases in the development of every individual – יְצִירָתוֹ, his creation; תּוֹרָתוֹ, when he is ready to study Torah; and finally קִילוּסוֹ, when he has matured sufficiently to praise Hashem. Using this *Midrash*, we can develop a link between the Three Festivals, which seemingly commemorate unrelated events. Whereas Pesach celebrates the birth of the Jewish Nation and, in a sense, the rebirth of the entire universe, and Shavuos the acceptance of the Torah by *Klal Yisrael*, Succos, the Time of our Rejoicing (coming after the atonement achieved during Rosh Hashanah and Yom Kippur), is a time to praise Hashem as we bask in the *succah* which reminds us of His protection. Not only the Three Festivals, but also every Shabbos (which is a day comprised of three distinct time periods – Friday evening, Shabbos morning and *Minchah*, each with its own unique *Shemoneh Esrei*) incorporates each of these dimensions. For example, the *tefillos* of Friday evening focus on the creation of heaven and earth (תַּכְלִית מַעֲשֵׂה שָׁמַיִם וָאָרֶץ), while those of Shabbos morning revolve around the theme of *Matan Torah* (יִשְׂמַח מֹשֶׁה בְּמַתְּנַת חֶלְקוֹ). It is only on Shabbos afternoon, during the *Minchah* service, after we have achieved a level of closeness to Hashem, that we permit ourselves to sing Hashem's Praises. As we note during *Shemoneh Esrei*, אַתָּה אֶחָד וְשִׁמְךָ אֶחָד וּמִי כְּעַמְּךָ יִשְׂרָאֵל גּוֹי אֶחָד בָּאָרֶץ, *You are One, and Your Name is One and who is like Your Nation, Israel, one nation on earth*. At a moment of such intimacy between Israel and its Creator, it is fitting that we sing His praises. As the *Shemoneh Esrei* continues, אַבְרָהָם יָגֵל יִצְחָק יְרַנֵּן, *Avraham rejoices, Yitzchak sings.*

Just as the three *tefillos* of Shabbos parallel the various phases of our development — Creation, Receiving the Torah, and attaining the capacity to sing Hashem's praises — so too, the Three Meals reflect this multifaceted theme. [Author's note: While the *Sfas Emes* does not explicate exactly how each meal corresponds to a specific phase of *Klal Yisrael's* development, we suggest — in light of the overall context of this *dvar Torah* — that the meal on Friday evening commemorates the universe's creation; the Shabbos morning meal, the Giving of the Torah; and Shabbos afternoon, having reached so intimate a relationship with Hashem (כביכול), we feel free to praise Him. Perhaps for that reason, the *Seudah Shelishis* meal is uniquely renowned for its emphasis on singing *zemiros*. In this piece the *Sfas Emes* implies parallels between the Three Meals and the concepts of מַעֲשֶׂה(deeds), דִּבּוּר(speech) and מַחֲשָׁבָה (thoughts), and also between the Three Meals and the three aspects of the soul — *nefesh, ruach,* and *neshamah*. It appears that *Seudah Shelishis,* the most rarefied time of Shabbos, is when the *neshamah,* the most sublime component of the soul, is dominant and when our most esoteric and beautiful thoughts allow us to achieve an intimacy with Hashem unattainable at any other time.] (*Tzaria* 5648)

Three Phases of Listening

וה״ג סעודות של שבת מסייעין לאלה ג׳ השמיעות

According to the *Talmud Yerushalmi* (*Taanis* 3b), if the Jewish people would observe properly even one Shabbos, they would immediately be liberated from the *galus*. This is derived from the *pasuk* (*Tehillim* 95:7) recited during *Kabbolas Shabbos*, הַיּוֹם אִם בְּקֹלוֹ תִשְׁמָעוּ, *Today* (*Mashiach* will arrive) *if you will listen to His voice.* While the term הַיּוֹם, *today,* could refer to any day, we derive an analogy from the three references to הַיּוֹם in the *pasuk* from which the Three Meals of Shabbos are derived, to conclude that in the merit of Shabbos, *Mashiach* is likely to come.

Upon closer examination of this insight of *Chazal,* it seems that *Mashiach's* arrival is contingent not merely upon observing Shabbos but also listening closely to the voice of Hashem on Shabbos. As the *pasuk* reads, הַיּוֹם אִם בְּקֹלוֹ תִשְׁמָעוּ, *Today* (*Mashiach* will arrive) *if you will listen to His voice.* By relating this *pasuk* containing the term הַיּוֹם once to the *pasuk* (from which we derive the Three Meals of Shabbos) in which the term הַיּוֹם appears three times, *Chazal* seem to be implying that a three-phased listening process is necessary for the Final Redemption to occur.

To appreciate the dimensions of this process, we turn to the introduction to Yaakov's blessings in which he urges his children, הֵאָסְפוּ וְאַגִּידָה לָכֶם ... הִקָּבְצוּ וְשִׁמְעוּ בְּנֵי יַעֲקֹב וְשִׁמְעוּ אֶל יִשְׂרָאֵל אֲבִיכֶם, *Assemble yourselves and I will tell you ... Gather yourselves and listen, O sons of Jacob, and listen to Israel, your father* (*Bereishis* 49:1-2). The first phase of the three-phased process simply involves gathering together for a common purpose. *Achdus*, unity, among Jews facilitates our ability to heed Hashem's voice. There is no more opportune moment for *achdus* among Jews than Shabbos. As we recite in the כְּגַוְנָא prayer (immediately before *Borchu* on Friday night), דְאִתְאַחֲדַת בְּרָזָא דְאֶחָד, (Shabbos is the day the universe became) *unified through the secret of Hashem Who is One.* Once we resolved to unite to listen to Hashem's call, two more phases follow. First, a preliminary listening to the Word of Hashem, followed by a more profound form of learning, in which the listener attempts to fully grasp, without any distraction, the message of Hashem. As the Torah says (*Devarim* 11:13), שָׁמֹעַ תִּשְׁמְעוּ, *if you continually hearken* – your first attempts at listening will be succeeded by a more intensive form of listening, and it will enable you to successfully grasp the Word of Hashem. The Three Meals of Shabbos (derived from the three references to הַיּוֹם) assist us in proceeding with the three-phased listening process – in which we learn to heed the voice of Hashem and thus precipitate the Final Redemption. (*Vayechi* 5648)

Soul, Time, Place,

אכלוהו היום הוא בירור הנפשות שבת היום בח׳ הזמן היום ל״ת בשדה בח׳ המקום

From the *pasuk* (*Shemos* 16:25) which is the source of the three Shabbos meals, we also derive some indication of the impact of *Shalosh*

Seudos. Frequently, the entire universe is analyzed from the perspective of עוֹלָם (the various places in the universe), שָׁנָה (the year and, in a larger sense, the role time plays in the universe) and נֶפֶשׁ (the soul). Each of these dimensions is alluded to in *Shemos* (16:25): אִכְלֻהוּ הַיּוֹם, *Eat it today* — you, *Klal Yisrael*, by eating the three meals on Shabbos will leave a beneficial impact on all of mankind. שַׁבָּת הַיּוֹם לַה׳, *for today is a Sabbath for HASHEM* — partake of the Three Meals on *this day*, Shabbos, and this will accrue to your benefit during the week. הַיּוֹם לֹא תִמְצָאֻהוּ בַּשָּׂדֶה, *today you will not find it* (the manna) *in the field* — this is a reference to the sacred nature of the Shabbos-observant home, far removed from "the field" of the outside environment. On Shabbos, we partake of three meals trusting that their impact will benefit every person (נֶפֶשׁ), every time of the year (שָׁנָה) and every place on earth (עוֹלָם).

(*Beshalach* 5650)

◈ Three Divine Gifts

מן באר ענני הכבוד והם ג׳ סעודות בשבת

The Three Meals may also correspond to the three gifts that Hashem granted *Klal Yisrael* during their sojourn in the Wilderness: the Well of Miriam, the manna (which we enjoyed in Moshe's merit) and the Divine Cloud which protected the Jewish people (in Aharon's merit). Specifically, the Friday meal, described in the introductory paragraph to the *Arizal's Zemiros* (based on the *Zohar HaKodosh*) as being סְעוּדָתָא דַּחֲקַל תַּפּוּחִין קַדִּישִׁין, *The meal of the sacred apple field*, corresponds to Miriam's Well (refer to *Bereishis* 29:2 in which the Torah discusses a well placed in a field), which was created on *erev* Shabbos at twilight (Avos 5:8). The Shabbos morning meal reminds us of the manna, which we enjoyed in Moshe's merit. This association between Shabbos morning and Moshe *Rabbeinu* is already reflected in the Shabbos morning *Shemoneh Esrei* which commences with the words יִשְׂמַח מֹשֶׁה בְּמַתְּנַת חֶלְקוֹ, *Moshe rejoiced in the gift of his portion*. Finally, the Shabbos afternoon meal reminds us of the Divine Cloud. Moreover, through the three Divine gifts, Hashem extends His protection to *Klal Yisrael* from every direction — above, below, and from all sides. (*Chukas* 5648)

⁂ Three Blessings: Life, Children, and *Parnassah*

בני חיי ומזוני שע״ז ניתקן ה״ג׳ סעודות

By juxtaposing the portion of the Torah dealing with the sacred artifacts of the *Mishkan* (*Shemos* 31:1-12), including the Table (שֻׁלְחָן) and the *Menorah,* to the portion dealing with the Shabbos and Festivals (*Shemos* 31:12-17), the Torah seems to be drawing a relationship between the blessing associated with those sacred vessels and the *Yamim Tovim*. Specifically, the Table and its twelve Showbreads served as a conduit to bring the *berachah* of *parnassah* to *Klal Yisrael* (refer to *Ramban, Shemos* 25:24). The *Mizbeiach HaKetores* (the Altar located inside the Temple on which incense was offered every morning and afternoon, and especially the incense itself) was particularly effective in prolonging life. This was amply demonstrated when Aharon utilized the *ketores* to prevent the plague that occurred after Korach's insurrection from taking even more lives (cf. *Bamidbar* 17:12-13). And finally, the *Menorah* (and its Western Lamp which was never extinguished) reminded *Klal Yisrael* of the *Shechinah's* Presence in their lives (cf. *Shabbos* 22b). There could be no better indication of *Klal Yisrael's* supernatural existence than the *Menorah* whose light was miraculously never extinguished. Just as the *Menorah* remained lit by an act of Divine intervention, so too, every time a Jewish child is born we witness a direct manifestation of Hashem's Presence in our lives (cf. *Taanis* 2a, stating that the process of childbirth is never delegated to any of Hashem's emissaries, but rather is always conducted by Hashem Himself).

These three blessings – children (בָּנֵי), life itself (חַיֵּי) and *parnassah* (מְזוֹנֵי) – are not only symbolized (and effectively delivered to *Klal Yisrael*) by these three vessels of the *Mishkan* – the Table, the *Menorah,* and *Mizbeiach* – but are also represented by the Three Festivals, which are juxtaposed to the vessels of the *Mishkan*. Moreover, the Shabbos itself, consisting of three distinct phases (Friday evening, Shabbos morning, and *Minchah*), each with its unique *Shemoneh Esrei,* may allude to each of the three blessings of children, life itself, and sustenance. By partaking of three meals on Shabbos, we acknowledge the three-fold nature of this extraordinary day, as demonstrated by its three blessings. (Refer to this citation in *Sfas Emes* that also relates three Names of Hashem to these three *berachos*.) (Adapted from *Emor* 5647)

◆§ Three *Kedushos* (Sacred Entities): Hashem, Torah, *Klal Yisrael*

אתה קדוש ושמך קדוש וקדושים ... ועליהם נרמזין הג׳ סעודות בשבת

To appreciate the Three Meals of Shabbos, we refer to the following passage in *Shemoneh Esrei,* which acknowledges the existence of three sacred entities (קְדוּשׁוֹת): אַתָּה קָדוֹשׁ וְשִׁמְךָ קָדוֹשׁ וּקְדוֹשִׁים בְּכָל יוֹם יְהַלְלוּךָ סֶּלָה, *You are holy and Your Name is holy, and holy ones praise You every day, forever.* It appears that three distinct levels of *kedushah* are indicated in this *tefillah.* Firstly, the supreme *kedushah* of Hashem (אַתָּה קָדוֹשׁ), which is totally incomprehensible to mortals. However, Hashem, Who desires to impart some of His sanctity to *Klal Yisrael,* has provided us with the ideal medium to appreciate His *kedushah* — the Torah. In His infinite love for *Klal Yisrael,* Hashem has contained His limitless sanctity within the finite parameters of the Torah. We allude to this process, and the extraordinary role played by the Torah as the conduit for Hashem's *kedushah* to be enjoyed by *Klal Yisrael,* by saying וְשִׁמְךָ קָדוֹשׁ. The Torah, which is comprised of many variations of Hashem's Name (refer to *Ramban* in his introduction to Torah who writes, כָּל הַתּוֹרָה כּוּלָּה שֵׁמוֹתָיו שֶׁל הַקָּדוֹשׁ בָּרוּךְ הוּא, *The entire Torah consists of Hashem's Names*) is sacred. As a result of our exposure to Torah, we are able to appreciate, to some extent, Hashem's *kedushah,* and pay homage to Him. As we conclude, וּקְדוֹשִׁים בְּכָל יוֹם יְהַלְלוּךָ סֶּלָה, The Jewish people (as well as the sacred angels on high), profoundly affected by their exposure to the sacred Torah, are now able to acknowledge Hashem's *kedushah.*

These three levels of *kedushah* — the infinite and inscrutable *kedushah* of Hashem brought down to earth through the *kedushah* of Torah and appreciated by His sacred nation — are reflected in the Three Meals of Shabbos. The *pasuk* from *Yeshaya* 58:14 (often cited in this section as referring to *Shalosh Seudos*) alludes to the relationship between the Three Meals and the three levels of *kedushah* in these words: אָז תִּתְעַנַּג עַל ה׳, "You will delight in the infinite *kedushah* of Hashem"; וְהַאֲכַלְתִּיךָ נַחֲלַת יַעֲקֹב אָבִיךָ, "I will present you with the heritage of Yaakov" — the Torah; and finally, וְהִרְכַּבְתִּיךָ עַל בָּמֳתֵי אָרֶץ, "I will elevate you — despite your mortality — to enjoy the *kedushah* that is present on earth." (*Emor* 5655)

◆§ Reflections on the Shabbos Meals

ג׳ שבתות יש ... שבת דמעשה בראשית ודיצ״מ ודקבלת התורה והגם ג׳ סעודות דשבת

Please refer to our previous *dvar Torah,* "A Triple Renewal" (p. 333) in which we suggested that the Three Meals correspond to Creation (which is commemorated by the Friday night meal), *Yetzias Mitzrayim,* and *Matan Torah,* respectively. According to this approach, it follows that the meal of Shabbos morning corresponds to *Yetzias Mitzrayim.* Appropriately, the *Zohar* (which we allude to in the paragraph introducing *Arizal's zemiros,* with the words, אַתְקִינוּ סְעוּדָתָא דִמְהֵימְנוּתָא) refers to this meal as the סְעוּדָתָא דְעַתִּיקָא קַדִּישָׁא, *The meal of the Ancient Holy One (HaKadosh Baruch Hu).* At no point was the enormous power of Hashem to trounce tyrants better demonstrated than at the time of *Yetzias Mitzrayim.* Pharaoh, who had questioned Hashem's existence, was forced to yield to the Infinite Strength of the Ancient Holy One. In truth, the term עַתִּיקָא קַדִּישָׁא, reflecting Hashem's enormous capacity, refers most appropriately to the other future Shabbos when miracles even greater than those of *Yetzias Mitzrayim* will occur. However, we also use this term to refer to *Yetzias Mitzrayim* since at that hallowed moment, we enjoyed an event that, to some extent, simulated the miracles that *Klal Yisrael* will eventually enjoy.

It follows then that the Third Meal, described as the סְעוּדָתָא דִזְעֵיר אַנְפִּין, *The meal of the lesser way,* corresponds to the Giving of the Torah. The sequence of these meals and the historical events that they commemorate illustrates one of Hashem's greatest kindnesses — allowing *Yetzias Mitzrayim* to occur before *Matan Torah.* Under ordinary circumstances, the Jewish people should have been required to earn their liberation by first accepting the Torah. However, *Klal Yisrael,* spiritually enfeebled by years of *Galus Mitzrayim* and its assimilationist pressures, was simply incapable of accepting the Torah until they had first been exposed to the miracles of *Yetzias Mitzrayim* and the Splitting of the Sea. The Torah's assertion that we left Mitzrayim in haste (בְּחִפָּזוֹן) may refer not only to the swiftness of our departure from the land of Egypt but also to the fact that Hashem accelerated the usual sequence, enabling us to depart Mitzrayim before we were spiritually prepared.

It is also possible that, to some extent, the Jewish people did merit to participate in *Yetzias Mitzrayim* even before they had received the Torah — simply by virtue of the *mitzvos* associated with the *Korban Pesach* (Paschal Lamb) on the Shabbos before they left Mitzrayim. In the merit of observing some *mitzvos* even *before* they received the Torah, the Jewish people earned the right to be liberated before the Torah was given to them. In fact, the renowned affirmation of *Klal Yisrael*, נַעֲשֶׂה וְנִשְׁמַע, *We will do and we will listen*, may refer to our forefathers' acceptance of specific *mitzvos* while still in Mitzrayim, before they received the Torah. (*Shabbos HaGadol* 5655)

The Double Bread – Lechem Mishneh

In this chapter we will discuss the significance of utilizing *lechem mishneh,* two loaves during every Shabbos meal. This practice was instituted by *Chazal* (*Shabbos* 117b), to commemorate the double portion of manna which the Jewish people enjoyed every *erev Shabbos,* for almost forty years, while they traveled through the Wilderness.

◆§ Linking Two Worlds (*Olam Hazeh* and *Olam Haba*)

ולכן בשבת לחם משנה לרמוז כי בו מתחברין ב׳ העולמות ...
הוא כלי שמחזיק ברכה.

Chazal (*Yalkut Bereishis* 2) offer two reasons why the Torah begins with the letter *beis.* Firstly, because this letter connotes (and is the first letter of the term) *berachah,* Hashem's blessings. Moreover, by commencing with a *beis* (which is equivalent to the number two), the Torah indicates at the very outset the linkage between the two worlds that a Jew enjoys, *Olam Hazeh* (This World) and *Olam Haba* (the World to Come).

By utilizing two loaves at every Shabbos meal, we are not only recalling the *berachah* of Shabbos experienced by our forefathers in the form of the double portion of the manna, but also indicating the reason for Shabbos' abundant blessings – it is the day when both universes, This World and the World to Come, converge. As we discuss extensively in the chapter devoted to this topic, Shabbos is a microcosm of the World to Come (*mei'ein Olam Haba*). It is the weekly opportunity for all of us to enjoy a taste of the World to Come while still in This World.

(*Bereishis* 5657)

Linking Body and Soul

כי האבות הן המרכבה והם בחי׳ נשמה בלי גוף כדאיתא שלשה לא שלטה בהם יצה״ר. ויוסף מרכבת המשנה התקשרות הנשמה בגוף מרכבת הנשמה כי הלא הקב״ה הרכיב הנפש בגוף א״כ הוא כלי מוכן לקבל ציור הנשמה כמ״ש אין צור כאלקינו. צייר. שצר צורה תוך צורה וזה מדת הצדיק לקשר הגוף בנשמה ... וכן בחי׳ השבת לחם משנה ומקשר גם הגוף אל הנשמה וזה כפי הכנת האדם בימי המעשה. והנה נר שבת הוא הארת הנשמה שנק׳ נר ה׳ נשמת אדם.

Whereas in the previous *dvar Torah* we suggested that the *lechem mishneh* symbolizes the interaction and linkage of *Olam Hazeh* and *Olam Haba*, this relationship between the spiritual and material exists within every individual as well. Every individual faces the potential dichotomy of body and soul. It is no mean feat to be able to attend to both the material needs and desires of the body, as well as the spiritual yearnings of the soul. In the earliest phases of the Jewish people's existence, we were led by the *Avos*, spiritual giants whom *Chazal* perceive as being individuals who were spared this constant struggle between body and soul. As the Gemara (*Bava Basra* 17a) states, Avraham, Yitzchak, and Yaakov were completely spared from the evil influences of the *yetzer hara*.

The *Avos* were succeeded by Yosef *HaTzaddik*, who (though constantly exposed to the moral void of Egypt) successfully overcame the importunings of Potiphar's wife. Yosef, by his sterling moral conduct, represented the capacity of the committed Jew to be dominated by the *neshamah,* even in an environment that on the surface is permeated with rampant materialism. Pharaoh, upon appointing Yosef to his prominent position as Egypt's viceroy, insisted that this *tzaddik* ride in the *mirkeves hamishneh* (literally, in the second chariot, which immediately followed Pharaoh), the double chariot, which alludes to the capacity of this *tzaddik* to fuse two entirely disparate elements, body and soul. By maintaining such a sacred lifestyle amidst the spiritual depravity of Egypt, Yosef demonstrated that body and soul can coexist.

Every Shabbos, the day that is simultaneously graced by the spiritual presence of the *neshamah yeseirah* as well as the *mitzvah* of *oneg Shabbos,* by partaking of the Double Bread *(lechem mishneh)* we likewise demonstrate that body and soul can coexist. Of course, one can only achieve such an exalted status on Shabbos through intensive preparation during the previous week. It is only by allowing the spiritual values of the soul to dominate during the week, even as we appear to be preoccupied with material matters, that every Shabbos we enjoy the harmonious blend of body and soul symbolized by the *lechem mishneh.*

(Adapted from *Mikeitz* 5662)

ובש״ק מאיר הנשמה בתוספות גם בגוף לפי שהוא מעין עוה״ב. שבעוה״ב גם הגופות יהיו מזוככים. וזה בחי׳ משנה לחם. לכן מצוה לענג גם הגוף בשבת קודש.

Based on our previous assertion that the body as well as the soul attains sanctity on Shabbos, we can understand the rationale for the *mitzvah* of *oneg Shabbos* — allowing the body as well as the soul to delight in the Shabbos day (refer to our chapter on this topic).

To further appreciate the extraordinary *kedushah* that even the body can attain on Shabbos, we recall the renowned *Chazal* (*Berachos* 57b) stating that Shabbos is a replica of the World to Come (*mei'ein Olam Haba*). Just as in the Future World the body will attain a state of purity equivalent to the soul, so too, every Shabbos, our material nature as well as our spiritual core, the *neshamah,* attains *kedushah.* As stated previously, by enjoying the Double Bread we are emphasizing the dual aspect of Shabbos' *kedushah* — the sanctity of the body as well as the soul.

(*Shemini* 5664)

◆§ Linking the Soul to Its Heavenly Roots

ולכן כל דבריו של שבת כפולין כדאיתא במדרש לחם משנה כו' פי' שבשבת עולה ומתקשר החלק שלמטה בהשורש וזה השלימות.

Just as *Olam Hazeh* and *Olam Haba* converge every Shabbos (refer to our previous *dvar Torah*), so too, the two dimensions of every soul meet on *Shabbos Kodesh*. According to the *Zohar Hakadosh* (*Parashas Noach*), there are two dimensions to every Jewish *neshamah* — the surface dimension that operates in This World and the roots of every soul that remain in heaven. *Tzaddikim*, by virtue of their extraordinary righteousness, are privileged that there is no chasm between the lofty levels maintained by the *neshamah* that resides in its heavenly abode and its counterpart in This World. When Avraham met the supreme challenge of the *Akeidah*, prepared to sacrifice the son that he loved in order to fulfill the Divine Will, he was greeted with a "double" Divine call "Avraham, Avraham" (cf. *Bereishis* 22:11). This indicated that he had attained the spiritual level whereby his *neshamah* on earth was equivalent to its heavenly counterpart.

Every Shabbos, to some extent, we replicate the lofty level attained by *tzaddikim* in which their *neshamah's* physical presence on earth — integrated with the human body — is able to match the rarefied spiritual level enjoyed by the soul in its pristine form in heaven. To indicate the "merging" of both components of the human soul — that the two elements of the *neshamah* become one — we partake of the Double Bread. [The parallel between the levels generally attained by *tzaddikim* and the achievements of every Jew on Shabbos illustrates the relationship between the *kedushah* that permeates sacred occasions (קְדוּשַׁת הַזְּמַן) and the sanctity that *tzaddikim* enjoy every day (קְדוּשַׁת הַנֶּפֶשׁ).]

(Adapted from *Vayeira* 5652)

ובשבת קודש מתנה מבית גנזי יש הארה מחלק הנסתר. ולכן יש בו נשמה יתירה. ולכן כל מעשיו כפולים כמ״ש חז״ל זכור ושמור. לחם משנה. מזמור שיר. רמוז לב׳ בחי׳ הנ״ל.
כי החלק שלמטה אינו שלום רק בהתדבקות לחלק שלמעלה ...
וזה הי׳ תכלית כל המשכן להיות כלי מחזיק ברכה לכל העולם.
וכמו כן שבת בזמן שכל מעשי׳ כפולים. לחם משנה. מזמור שיר. זכור ושמור.

The foregoing theme, that every Shabbos we are able to derive inspiration from our soul's heavenly roots, may be corroborated from the renowned *Chazal* (*Shabbos* 10b) stating that Hashem grants us a gift from His treasure house — the Shabbos (refer to our chapter "The Gift of Shabbos"). By utilizing this expression, *Chazal* are alluding to the heavenly component of the soul. While it is difficult to find those roots while we dwell in this material world, on Shabbos, having set aside all material concerns, we are able to surmount any barrier that prevents us from connecting to our spiritual roots in heaven.

It is significant that several aspects of Shabbos are described as "pairs." For example, the positive and negative commandments of *Zachor* and *Shamor;* the introduction to the Psalm of Shabbos (*Tehillim* 92), which is described as not being merely a song but rather מִזְמוֹר שִׁיר (*a psalm, a song*); and, of course, the Double Bread (*lechem mishneh*). In all of these instances, by observing the *mitzvah* with dual components, we are emphasizing the extraordinary links between our physical presence in This World and our soul's heavenly roots which predominate on Shabbos. (*Terumah* 5655; *Pekudei* 5660)

וזו היא מטבע של אש שהראה הקב״ה למרע״ה לומר שיש חלק לבנ״י בצורה זו דאש. מחצית הצורה מלמעלה ומחצית מלמטה. ובבית המקדש שהי׳ מוכן לאש מן השמים הי׳ המצוה לערוך ג״כ אש שלמטה. וכן בזמן בשבת שיורדת נשמה יתירה והיא מיוחד לבנ״י בחי׳ לחם משנה מן השמים ומן הארץ.

Contemplate some other parallels to the concept that *all* of our actions here on earth are directly linked to their heavenly source. For example, by insisting that we contribute a half-shekel coin — rather than a complete shekel — the Torah is indicating that our efforts in This World are but a beginning, which can only be consummated with Hashem's assistance. In fact, when Moshe *Rabbeinu* experienced difficulty in comprehending the exact nature of the half-shekel coin, Hashem showed him a fiery half-shekel, which Moshe used as a model for the coins to be contributed by the Jewish people. The function of this Divine-inspired replica of the half-shekel was to emphasize that our efforts at consecrating the *Mishkan* could only reach fruition with the active blessing of Hashem Who enables us to exploit the heavenly roots of our *neshamah.* Similarly, *Klal Yisrael* was commanded to kindle the Altar, even though the *Mizbeiach* was always lit by a fire descending from heaven. By insisting that the Altar be lit by a flame contributed by *Klal Yisrael,* as well as the fire emanating from heaven, the Torah is emphasizing that our efforts below — critical as they are — can only be realized with Divine assistance from above. (*Tzav* 5660)

וזהו רמז ז׳ כפולות כדאיתא במד׳ כל מעשה שבת כפולים זכור ושמור משנה לחם שני כבשים כו׳. וזה עצמו ענין לחם משנה דכתיב בשבת שהחלק שלמטה מתאחד בשורש שלמעלה. לכן נקרא שבת שלום שמחבר עליונים לתחתונים ויש עליות נשמות למעלה וירידת נשמה יתירה למטה.

With this insight, we can better understand why Shabbos is described as the day of *shalom* (refer to our chapter on this topic). The term *shalom* is derived from *sheleimus,* a sense of completeness that can only be attained on Shabbos, a day of such immense *kedushah* that our soul here on earth is able to link with its heavenly roots. In fact, a symbiotic and bilateral relationship is developed every Shabbos. On one hand, our soul is linked to its heavenly counterpart. On the other hand, the *neshamah yeseirah* "descends" to join us here on earth. (*Beha'aloscha* 5651)

ולפימ״ש א״ש דחוט תכלת שמחציתו לבן יום א׳ הוא והוא באמת יום הז׳ דקי״ס שהי׳ מכוון ליום השבת כדאיתא במד׳ בא.

In this vein, we can also appreciate the symbolic meaning of the two different forms of *tzitzis* threads that are inserted into the corners of all four-cornered garments, the sky-blue *techeiles* and the white threads, known as *lavan*. According to the *Rambam* (*Hilchos Tzitzis* 1:6), there was no single *tzitzis* thread that consisted entirely of *techeiles*. On the contrary, the three white threads (symbolizing the three days of the week that relate to the previous Shabbos and those that are associated with the forthcoming Shabbos — refer to our chapter on *Shalosh Seudos* for further discussion of this concept) are joined by one thread that is dyed in equal proportions with the colors of *techeiles* and plain white (*lavan*). Assuming that *techeiles* reminds us of Hashem's Heavenly Throne (*Kisei HaKavod*, cf. *Menachos* 43b), we may deduce that by dyeing a thread with equal amounts of *techeiles* and white, we are alluding to the intimate connection between the soul on earth and its heavenly roots, a process which occurs every Shabbos. (*Shelach* 5651)

◆§ The Heavenly Roots of "Time"

דהנה כל הדברים יש להם שורש בשמים. הן בחי׳ עולם שנה ונפש לכולם יש שורש בשמים. וז״ש יום ליום יביע אומר. יום שלמעלה ליום שלמטה. והצדיקים צריכים לחבר הכל אל השורש. וזה עיקר שם צדיק כמ״ש ז״ל דאחיד בשמיא וארעא ... וכמו כן בזמן ושנה. שבת שלום. ולכן כל מעשי שבת כפולים. לחם משנה. זכור ליום כו׳ שבו מתעלה הזמן אל השורש.

Refer to the previous *dvar Torah* in which we suggested that by partaking of the Double Bread, we allude to the link forged every Shabbos between that dimension of the soul appearing on earth and its sacred roots in heaven. Extending this theme, we propose that not only the soul but also the concept of time exists on two levels — the visible and surface aspect of time that exists on earth (in the form of days and nights) and the spiritual roots of the dimension of time (*z'man*) as it exists in heaven. When King David sings, יוֹם לְיוֹם יַבִּיעַ אֹמֶר, *Day speaks to day* (*Tehillim* 19:3), he is alluding to the association that exists between the dimension of time as it appears on earth and the roots of *z'man* in heaven. When we describe *HaKadosh Baruch Hu* as הַמְחַדֵּשׁ בְּטוּבוֹ בְּכָל יוֹם תָּמִיד מַעֲשֵׂה בְרֵאשִׁית, *He who renews, in His goodness, Creation every day*, we may be alluding to the ties that bind the concept of *z'man* — the days and nights that we experience on earth and its heavenly *shoresh*. Every day, Hashem is infusing our existence on earth and its physical dimension of time with renewed spirituality stemming from the Heavenly source of time. On Shabbos — a day known as *mei'ein Olam Haba* — when every Jew samples a taste of the spirituality of the World to Come, the gap closes between the temporal dimension of time as it exists on earth and the true Heavenly source. To emphasize the convergence of the earthly dimension of time with its Heavenly root, we partake of the Double Bread. (Adapted from *Chayei Sarah* 5654)

והשבת הוא לחם משנה כל מעשיו כפולין ולכן מחצה לבן מחצה תכלת. כי תכלת דומה לכסא הכבוד והוא השורש שלמעלה. והשבת מחבר חלק שלמטה עם חלק שלמעלה כמש״ל בפ׳ בהעלתך פי׳ לחם משנה... ועליו כתיב ויושע ה׳ ביום ההוא לשון נסתר. פי׳ שהי׳ בו התקשרות הזמן דלתתא בשורש שלמעלה. והוא כפול לחם משנה כמ״ש.

In the preceding *dvar Torah,* we explored the significance of the *tzitzis* thread, which was dyed both sky blue and plain white, and its association with the three *tzitzis* threads that were only dyed white. Perhaps, we may extend the analogy even further by suggesting that those six threads represent the six days that the Jewish people spent together prior to the Splitting of the Sea. The seventh day, when *Keriyas Yam Suf* occurred, is symbolized by the thread that is dyed both blue and white. On that day, the very concept of time — with all of its natural limitations — was linked to its Heavenly supernatural roots. How appropriate that this process occurred while the Jewish people were crossing the sea. *Techeiles* itself is compared not only to Hashem's throne — the supernatural root of everything on earth — but also to the sea which *Klal Yisrael* was now crossing. The Torah alludes to the day of *Keriyas Yam Suf* as being a time in which the universe and its sense of time was superseded by a supernatural, timeless world — based on Hashem's direct intervention in the universe that He created — by saying, וַיּוֹשַׁע ה׳ בַּיּוֹם הַהוּא אֶת יִשְׂרָאֵל, *HASHEM saved Israel on that distinct day,* rather than בַּיּוֹם הַזֶּה, *this day* (cf. *Shemos* 14:30). As stated earlier in this *dvar Torah,* the *lechem mishneh* restates our belief that there is a supernatural dimension of time rooted in heaven that is intimately connected to the concept of time as practiced on earth. By partaking of the Double Bread, we are demonstrating the extraordinary linkage between these two dimensions of time. (*Shelach* 5651)

◆§ "Heavenly Bread" / Bread of Mortals

הרמז הוא כי זכו ונזדככו נפשות בנ״י להיות ניזונין מלחם שמלאכי השרת ניזונים בו בזכות אברהם שנזדכך כ״כ שהכין לחם למלאכים. כמ״ש והוא עומד עליהם כו׳ ויאכלו. שכל כך היו מעשי האבות הקדושה והשכינה שורה במעשי ידיהם. לכן אכלו המלאכים הלחם שלו. וכ׳ לכו לחמו בלחמי שיש לחם מן הארץ הם בתיקונים שצדיקים מתקנים בעוה״ז. ויש להם עלי׳ למעלה. וכמו כן הלחם יורד מן השמים. ולכן בשבת לחם משנה רומז על לחם. כדאיתא בזוה״ק ביני ובין בנ״י שסעודות שבת מתענגים בו עליונים ותחתונים ע״ש פ׳ ויקהל.

To appreciate another dimension of the *lechem mishneh,* we recall that the Torah speaks of both bread that descends from heaven — such as the manna (cf. *Shemos* 16:4) — and the bread that is extracted from the soil of *Eretz Yisrael,* which is described as the "bread from the earth" (*Bamidbar* 15:19).

This distinction between Heavenly Bread and the bread of the earth is cited in the *Zohar* (cf. 1:246a). A similar theme is also voiced in the *Midrash* (*Yalkut Bereishis* 82) that attributes the manna enjoyed by *Klal Yisrael* to the bread prepared by Avraham *Avinu* on behalf of the angels. While *malachim* generally do not partake of food prepared by mortals, they could enjoy Avraham's meal since he (as well as the other *Avos*) was on so lofty a level that one could perceive Hashem's Presence even in his mundane activities. When eating Avraham's bread, the *malachim* were (כביכול) partaking of a meal in the *Shechinah's* Presence.

The concept of לֶחֶם מִן הָאָרֶץ, *bread from the earth,* best describes the sacred food prepared by Avraham for the angels. In the merit of Avraham whose material activities were so graced with *kedushah* that he was able to share his bread with angels, his descendants, the Jewish people, reached such an exalted a level that they could partake of Heavenly Bread, the manna.

Reflecting on the linkage between the bread of mortals and Heavenly Bread, the *Zohar* (cf. 2:204b) states that the meals of Shabbos are not only enjoyed by the Jewish people on earth, but also bring a great deal of satisfaction to the Heavenly source of our *neshamos.* (Refer to our *dvar Torah,* "Linking the Soul to Its Heavenly Roots", p. 346; and to our commentary on *Shalosh Seudos.*) (Adapted from *Beshalach* 5662)

◆§ Yosef and His Brothers

והי׳ צריך להיות נפרש יוסף מהם ואז יוציאו הם מדריגותיהם מכח אל הפועל. ואיתא דיש לחם מן השמים ולחם מן הארץ. הוא בחי׳ יוסף עם השבטים. כי יוסף מעלה לחם מן הארץ ללחם מן השמים כמ״ש במ״א בענין משנה לחם. וי״ב חלות שהי׳ במקדש הוא בחי׳ י״ב שבטים. ולבונה זכה לאזכרה הוא בחי׳ יוסף בחי׳ זכירה.

The distinction between living a supernatural existence ("Heavenly Bread") and living a natural life on earth based on the Torah's precepts ("bread from the earth") is also reflected in the dispute that arose between Yosef and his brothers. Whereas Yosef[1] was on a spiritual level far removed from his peers and the material world (and thus was particularly well-suited to cope with the many challenges of Egypt's sensual society), his brothers' challenge was to live in This World and infuse it with the spirit of the Torah. The enforced decade-long separation of Yosef and his brothers may have been necessary in order for each of these approaches to *avodas Hashem* to develop autonomously. While Yosef's lifestyle of abstaining totally from the material pleasures of This World may have been ideal, his brothers maintained that their approach was equally valid and absolutely essential for *Klal Yisrael's* future survival; especially when it would be faced with less than ideal circumstances for the observance of Torah and *mitzvos.* By demonstrating that it is possible to remain loyal to Torah even while being involved in *Olam Hazeh,* Yosef's brothers enabled Jews who were surrounded by an alien, often materially inclined, environment to remain loyal to Torah.

By partaking of the Double Bread, we are manifesting our belief that both the approach of Yosef and that of his brothers in contending with the material world are equally valid. While there are times when we are able to shun any association with the material world — an approach that

1. Yosef is described by Yaakov *Avinu* and Moshe *Rabbeinu* as נְזִיר אֶחָיו, *the brother who was distinguished above all of his brethren* (*Bereishis* 49:26 and *Devarim* 33:16).

served Yosef *HaTzaddik* well — at other occasions, the Torah-true Jew's challenge is be an active part of This World and by participating in *Olam Hazeh* sanctify Hashem's Name.

Not only the Double Bread but also the *Lechem HaPanim,* the Show-Bread placed on the Table of the *Mishkan* every Shabbos, reflected the validity of both the approach of Yosef and that of his brothers: The twelve breads that were placed on the Table correspond to the twelve tribes, who consecrated every material aspect of This World through their sterling behavior. The minuscule amount of pure incense which was separated from the twelve loaves and offered on the Altar remind us of Yosef's approach — to reject all of the material amenities of This World in favor of complete dedication to *avodas Hashem.*

(Adapted from *Vayeishev* 5658)

☙ The Bread We Earn / The Bread We Receive as a Divine Gift

ובימות החול בנ״י מכינים בעבודה ביגיעות רבות שיזכו בשבת למנוחה כדאי׳ מי שטרח בע״ש כו׳ וזה לחם משנה שכפי היגיעה בחול מתרבה הברכה בשבת עבור ימי החול ג״כ. ונק׳ לחם משנה שבשבת נמשך שפע ברכה מצד עצם היום. ולבד זה מצד היגיעה בחול והוא ב׳ לחם הנ״ל. והוא כדמיון יששכר וזבולון שהקדים זבולון בתורה שנתן לפיו של יששכר. כן המיגע בחול לש״ש מתחבר עם בחי׳ שבת כנ״ל.

By partaking of *lechem mishneh,* the "Double Bread," we are alluding to the well-known tradition that our *parnassah* (our material sustenance) is derived from two distinct sources: Firstly, our own efforts at earning a livelihood. However, our efforts all week long are merely a beginning. It is only through Hashem's generous assistance and His outpouring of kindness that our sustenance is assured. It is on Shabbos, the day when all of our efforts at eking out a material existence yield to intense spirituality, that we are direct beneficiaries of Hashem's assistance in deriving our *parnassah.*

Yaakov *Avinu* alludes to the dual source of our *parnassah* when blessing his children Yissachar and Zevulun with a unique partnership, whereby Zevulun through his material success as a merchant is able to support Yissachar's immersion in Torah study. Just as Zevulun's efforts are a critical prerequisite for Yissachar's growth in Torah, so too, the efforts invested by all of us during the week (both materially and, in a spiritual sense, the battles that we wage successfully against the *yetzer hara*) prove to have been worthwhile every Shabbos when we enjoy respite from the ongoing struggles of the week. *Chazal* allude to this relationship between the many challenges of the week and the harmony of Shabbos by noting, "Whoever exerts himself on *erev Shabbos* will eat (i.e., will enjoy the fruits of his efforts) on Shabbos" (*Avodah Zarah* 3a).

In a previous *dvar Torah* (entitled "Yosef and His Brothers", pg. 336) we cited the *Zohar's* distinction between "bread from heaven" and "bread from the earth." Based on our earlier remarks associating our efforts all week long with the unparalleled bliss of Shabbos, we suggest that the term *lechem min ha'shamayim* (Heavenly Bread) refers to the generous outpouring of blessings every Jew enjoys on Shabbos as a result of his efforts during the week (which the *Zohar* describes as *lechem min ha'aretz,* "bread from the earth"). In fact, the term *lechem mishneh,* "Double Bread," may refer not only to the relationship between the sustenance that we derive from our efforts during the week and those of Shabbos, but also to the dual source of Shabbos' *berachos.* Every Shabbos we are sustained not only by the blessings that are inherent in that sacred day itself, but also through the efforts of the entire week that we enjoy on *Shabbos Kodesh.* (*Vayechi* 5634)

◆§ Feeding the Body / Feeding the Soul

אכן המן הי׳ בחי׳ לחם מן השמים ונראה שהוא סועד המוח והוא היפך מזון הגשמיי שבא דרך כבד ולב אל המוח. והמן אדרבא סועד המוח ונמשך ממוח ללב ולכבד מלמעלה למטה שהוא לחם מן השמים. ורמז לדבר דכתי׳ עומר לגלגולת... והנה בסעודת שבת פי׳ בזה״ק משנה לחם שבחי׳ לחם מן השמים ומן הארץ נעשין א׳ ע״ש פ׳ ויחי. כי בשבת יש נשמה יתירה והוא התחזקות המוח ויש בו ג״כ מצות אכילת לחם מן הארץ.

Whereas most foods sustain the body first and only then the soul, the manna sustains the soul first and then the body. Thus, when describing how the Jewish people were nurtured by the manna, the Torah writes, וַיְעַנְּךָ, *He afflicted you* (*Devarim* 8:3).[1] Just as on a fast day, when the body is not nurtured, the soul predominates, so too, the spiritual substance of manna, which sustained the soul before nourishing the body, was described as a form of affliction and deprivation. In fact, the Torah (*Shemos* 16:16) alludes to the manna's capacity to feed the mind and soul by insisting that the people gather עוֹמֶר לַגֻּלְגֹּלֶת, *an omer per person* (lit., *skull*) — only an *omer's* worth of manna is sufficient to nurture every person.

Thus, the generation that was poised to enter *Eretz Yisrael* — and consequently was somewhat more materialistic than those who departed Egypt — were unable to benefit from the manna's special nature and, in fact, complained about the manna (*Bamidbar* 21:5).

Every Shabbos, by eating the Double Bread, we replicate the process through which *Klal Yisrael* was nurtured in the wilderness. We not only sustain the body through the Three Meals, we also sustain the extra dimension, the spiritual aspect of Shabbos known as the *neshamah yeseirah.*

(*Eikev* 5652)

◆§ Bread of Poverty / Bread of Luxury

בזוה"ק בפסוק מאשר שמנה לחמו לחם משנה בשבת דאית לחם עוני ולחם פנג כו׳ ע"ש כל הענין. משנה גימ׳ השמים והוא בכח הנשמה. כי האדם כולל נשמה מן השמים והגוף מן הארץ. ושבת יומא דנשמתין ולאו דגופא. ויורד הנשמה יתירה שהיא החלק מן השמים וז"ש ביני ובין בנ"י אות היא כו׳ ששת ימים עשה כו׳ השמים כו׳.

The *Zohar* (1:246a) distinguishes between two forms of bread: the bread of poverty, known as *lechem oni*, and the bread of luxury which it describes as *lechem panag*. When Yaakov blesses his son Asher that his bread will have richness (מֵאָשֵׁר שְׁמֵנָה לַחְמוֹ, *From Asher – his bread will have richness; Bereishis* 49:20), he was alluding to a *parnassah* that is enjoyed in an atmosphere of tranquility and complete spiritual satisfaction ("bread of luxury"). It is on Shabbos that this blessed state of

1. For further elaboration, refer to *Ramban, Devarim* 8:3, that וַיְעַנְּךָ refers to the manna.

affairs exists. The Jew rests from the struggles of the entire week ("the bread of poverty"), and assisted by the *neshamah yeseirah* (that extra dimension of spirituality that we enjoy on Shabbos), he is able to partake of the bread of luxury.

The *Zohar* continues by noting that the term *lechem mishneh* may be alluding to the ability of the Jew on Shabbos, infused with the *neshamah yeseirah,* to add an additional dimension to the bread that he enjoys all week. Instead of merely partaking of the hard-earned bread of poverty, he now participates in the additional aspect of Shabbos – the ability to enjoy the bread of luxury. There is no greater luxury and source of satisfaction than to partake of the material blessings of Hashem (which all week long are achieved through great effort, "the bread of poverty") in an environment that is spiritually conducive.

(Adapted from *Vayechi* 5650)

◆§ The Written Law / The Oral Law

ונ״ל שזה רמזו חז״ל מענגי׳ לעולם כבוד ינחלו ... ולפי הנ״ל פי׳ מענגי׳ לעולם. שאפי׳ בעת צר לו מניח הכל ומענג השבת. ולכן כבוד ינחלו בלי מצרים. ויתכן עוד לפרש לעולם ממש כי השבת צריך להיות נשאר באדם אפי׳ בימי המעשה שהוא ברית עולם. וכשאדם נזכר מן השבת צריך להיות מלא עונג ושמחה כמ״ש שש אנכי על אמרתך.

משנה תורה והוא כמו משנה לחם בשבת שהוא התחברות תורה שבכתב לתורה שבע״פ.

וכן בענין רמ״ח ושס״ה שהם ב׳ מדרגות אברים וגידים כמ״ש שם בזוהר. אבל בשבת זכור ושמור בדיבור א׳ נאמרו. כי בשבת מ״ע ומל״ת באחדות ושולט בו שם ישראל.

משנה תורה כמו משנה לחם בשבת. והם בחי׳ תורה שבכתב ותורה שבע״פ ואין לחם אלא תורה. והוא בחי׳ התחברות בנ״י לאביהן שבשמים.

The *Zohar* cited in the foregoing *dvar Torah* also distinguishes between Heavenly Bread and bread derived from the earth. It notes that every Shabbos the distinction that normally exists between these two is obscured and a link is drawn between the bread of heaven and that of earth.

In order to appreciate the *Zohar's* meaning, we suggest that the terms Heavenly Bread and the Bread of the Earth are allusions to the sources from which we derive Hashem's Torah – the Written Law (תּוֹרָה שֶׁבִּכְתָב) emanating from Heaven and the Oral Law (תּוֹרָה שֶׁבְּעַל פֶּה) which is deduced from the teachings of *Chazal* here on earth. While Torah study is essential *all* week, no time is more conducive for learning than Shabbos. Thus, the Torah, which to some extent is in heaven – the source of the Written Law – during the week, is fully appreciated by *Klal Yisrael* on Shabbos. (Perhaps, for that reason, it is obligatory to read the Torah every Shabbos.) Whereas during the week, it may be difficult for *Klal Yisrael* to fully appreciate the Torah's manifold insights, on Shabbos (assisted by the *neshamah yeseirah*), we are able to attain an enhanced comprehension of the Torah's teachings. The contributions of the Jewish people through their interpretations of the Oral Law is fused with the Written Law every Shabbos. By partaking of the *lechem mishneh,* we are alluding to the association between both forms of spiritual sustenance that we enjoy every Shabbos – the Written and Oral Laws.

This linkage between the Written and Oral Law is reflected in Moshe who served in the dual role of bringing the Written Law, in the form of the *Aseres HaDibros*, to *Klal Yisrael* and who then went even further and taught the Jewish people the myriad details of the Oral Law.

To corroborate our assertion that the *lechem mishneh* refers to the linkage of the Written and Oral Laws occurring every Shabbos, we note that the final book of the Torah, *Devarim*, is also known as *Mishneh Torah*. In *Sefer Devarim*, Moshe elaborates orally on the Written Law that he had previously taught *Klal Yisrael*.

(Adapted from *Vayechi* 5652; refer also to *Devarim* 5652, 5654, 5661)

הגם שאין זה בחי׳ פנים בפנים. ובאמת יום השבת עצמו ג״כ מעורר בנו זה הרצון כמ״ש במרע״ה אנכי עומד בין ה׳ וביניכם כו׳. כמו בשבת כ׳ אות הוא ביני ובין בנ״י. וזה בחי׳ לחם משנה בשבת חיבור תורה שבכתב ושבעל פה פנים בפנים.

To appreciate why on Shabbos we fuse the Written Law with the teachings of *Chazal* in the Oral Law, we recall the intimacy that existed between the Jewish people and Hashem at the time of the Giving of the

Torah. As Moshe *Rabbeinu* relates, פָּנִים בְּפָנִים דִּבֶּר ה׳ עִמָּכֶם, *HASHEM spoke to you face to face* (*Devarim* 5:4). At that time, the Jewish people benefitted by receiving both the Written Law directly from Hashem and the Oral Law, which was transmitted by Moshe on the basis of Hashem's teachings. That same intimacy through which *Klal Yisrael* first received both the Written Law and the Oral Law is regained every Shabbos. The ambiance of a face-to-face encounter with Hashem that we enjoyed at *Matan Torah* is replicated to some extent every Shabbos, a time of such *kedushah* that it is described as אוֹת הִיא בֵּינִי וּבֵינֵיכֶם, *A sign [of the intimacy] between Myself and you.* When such ideal conditions exist, it is possible to create again the environment in which the Written and Oral Laws converge as they did at Sinai. (*Ki Sisa* 5662)

◆§ Opening the Gates of Heaven and the Gates of Our Heart

לכן שבת מיוחד ביותר לתשובה כי בו נפתח שער בתורה ונפתחים לבות בנ״י לקבל התורה. לכן בשבת לחם משנה רמז לתורה שבכתב ושבע״פ שנתגלה בו טעמי תורה. ונפתח בו לב איש ישראל לקבל דברי תורה.

In the same vein that the Double Bread symbolizes the linkage between the Written and Oral Law, so too, it represents the processes which occur both in heaven and on earth which enable us to fuse the Written and Oral Law. Every Shabbos, the gates of heaven open and Hashem grants us the intuition and wisdom to study Torah. Simultaneously, the gates of *Klal Yisrael's* hearts on earth (which all week long are often absorbed with material concerns) open, allowing the teachings of Torah to penetrate. It is no coincidence that the Torah was given on Shabbos. There is no more opportune time to absorb and integrate the teachings of Torah than Shabbos. (*Shabbos Shuvah* 5660)

◆§ The Ten Divine Statements (*Asarah Maamoros*) and the Ten Commandments

ואיתא כי בשבת יש לחם משנה לחם מן השמים ולחם מן הארץ. והוא כנ"ל לחם מן הארץ הוא מ"ב. ולחם מה"ש הוא התורה. והנה שבת יש בו כח עשרה מאמרות שפרשת ויכלו הוא גמר מעשה בראשית. ויש בו כח בתורה שפרשת זכור את יום השבת הוא חלק לחם מן השמים בשבת מתעלה הטבע ומתקשר ע"מ בעשרת הדיברות כנ"ל.

By partaking of the *lechem mishneh* on Shabbos, we are also alluding to two aspects of Shabbos — the Creation of the universe, which was consummated on Shabbos and the Giving of the Torah, which also occurred on Shabbos. (Refer to *Shabbos* 86b stating that the Torah was given on Shabbos.)

Extending the analysis between Creation and the Giving of the Torah further, we note that both the universe itself and the Torah were initiated through a series of Divine edicts. Whereas the universe was created through Ten Divine Statements (*Asarah Maamoros*), the Torah was presented to *Klal Yisrael* in the form of the Ten Commandments (*Aseres HaDibros*). Despite the apparent similarity of the Ten Statements and the Ten Commandments, there is an important distinction between them, as well. The universe, which emanated from the Ten Statements, is generally bound by the laws of nature that Hashem initiated. These laws are generally immutable. The natural world rarely changes. On the other hand, the Torah, transmitted to *Klal Yisrael* through the *Aseres HaDibros*, is dynamic, always lending itself to new insights deduced by *talmidei chachamim* of every generation. This distinction between the static natural world and the ever-dynamic Torah is voiced by Shlomo *HaMelech* in *Mishlei*: ה׳ בְּחָכְמָה יָסַד אָרֶץ כּוֹנֵן שָׁמַיִם בִּתְבוּנָה, *Hashem in His wisdom created the earth; He establishes the heavens with His insight* (3:19). Unlike the earth (defined by the natural laws that Hashem set into place) which was created (utilizing the past tense), the heavens (the spiritual realm dominated by the Torah) are constantly being (re)established, as new Torah thoughts are being discovered. In fact, the ordinarily static natural world may be "renewed" as a result of the *limud Torah* of its scholars. (Consequently, Hashem frequently performs miracles and alters the natural balance of the universe as a result of the pleas of those who are immersed in Torah study.) This thought is voiced by the Mishnah stating that "*Tzaddikim* sustain the universe which was created through the Ten Statements" (*Avos* 5:1). The Torah scholar totally dedicated to Torah study is constantly infusing new life into the "static" universe, which emerged from Hashem's Ten Statements.

As stated previously, the *lechem mishneh* alludes to both aspects of Shabbos — the natural world which began at Creation's conclusion, as well as the Torah given to *Klal Yisrael* on Shabbos which is constantly reinvigorating the universe.

In previous *divrei Torah,* we cited the *Zohar* which interprets the Double Bread as the linkage between the Bread from Heaven and the bread of the earth. Based on the foregoing remarks, we attain new understanding of the *Zohar's* insight. Every Shabbos, the natural world — the universe with its well-established natural principles through which Hashem governs the earth — is linked with the heavens, the supernatural world which is not necessarily subject to the unyielding natural laws. There is no occasion that is more auspicious for this interaction between heaven and earth than Shabbos. Shabbos simultaneously commemorates the Torah and its supernatural content given from Heaven (through the Ten Commandments) and the creation of the natural world (accomplished through the Ten Statements). (*Yisro* 5653)

Fear and Love of Hashem

כמ״ש בספרים כי בימי המעשה עיקר ביראה ובש״ק באהבה ע״ש. וע״י היראה בימי במעשה זוכין בש״ק לאהבה. וכמו כן ע״י אהבה שבשבת יש להוסיף היראה בימי במעשה כענין שאמרו יראתי מתוך שמחתי ושמחתי מתוך יראתי. [רמז להנ״ל כי השבת כל מעשיו כפולין כדאיתא במד׳ קרבנו כפול. עומר. לחם משנה ע״ש. והוא כמ״ש ז״ל העובד מיראה לאלף דור ומאהבה לאלפים. הרי אהבה כפול מיראה.]

By partaking of the *lechem mishneh,* we are also alluding to the relationship between love of Hashem (*ahavas Hashem*) and fear of Hashem (*yiras Hashem*). While the ability to love Hashem is in large part a

Divine gift, this is only granted on the basis of our own *yiras Hashem.* To merit the gift of *ahavas Hashem* on Shabbos (refer to *Kiddush,* וְשַׁבַּת קָדְשְׁךָ בְּאַהֲבָה וּבְרָצוֹן הִנְחַלְתָּנוּ, *Your sacred Shabbos, with love and grace did You give us as a heritage*), we need to develop a sense of *yiras Hashem* during the week. In turn, the love of Hashem which we derive every Shabbos, contributes to enhanced fear of Him during the week that lies ahead. This relationship between fear of Hashem and love of Him is reflected in the famous statement (*Sefer Ikarim*), "My fear of Hashem is derived from my joy and my joy is derived from my fear."

(*Va'eschanan* 5648)

◆§ Exodus and the Giving of the Torah

ושבת נק׳ מנוחה שבשבת זוכין ללחם זה שלא ע״י עינוי ובירור. דאין בו פסולת.

Returning to the theme of Heavenly Bread and bread from the earth, as well as our previous remarks about the distinction between the bread attained through poverty and that easily achieved (the bread of luxury), we propose that the Double Bread alludes to seminal events of Jewish history, such as the Exodus (*yetzias Mitzrayim*) and the receiving of the Torah (*Kabbalas HaTorah*). Just as the Jewish people developed initially through the painful but ultimately rewarding experience of the Egyptian slavery and the eventual Exodus, so too, all week long our bread is derived through a great deal of effort (of course, blessed by Hashem). The struggles of the week against the *yetzer hara* and all those forces that could affect us adversely in our struggle for *parnassah* resemble the suffering in Mitzrayim. They are aptly described as both the "bread of poverty," as well as "the bread from the earth." However, on Shabbos our *parnassah* is achieved effortlessly. The sustenance we enjoy on Shabbos is reminiscent of the Giving of the Torah — a Divine gift from Heaven to the Jewish people. The bread of Shabbos is appropriately described as the "bread of luxury," as well as the "Bread of Heaven." By eating the Double Bread on Shabbos, we recall two events that are intimately associated with Shabbos — *Yetzias Mitzrayim,* which we recall every Shabbos (as we recite in *Kiddush,* זֵכֶר לִיצִיאַת מִצְרָיִם), as well as the Giving of the Torah which occurred on Shabbos. (*Vayechi* 5656)

◆§ Sustaining the Entire Week

ומעין זה הוא ימי המעשה שהם הכנה לשבת לכן יש בשבת לחם משנה וכל מעשי שבת כפולין שהשבת מקבל ברכה גם לימי המעשה.

By partaking of the Double Bread on Shabbos, we are alluding to the extraordinary capacity of Shabbos to give material support to the entire week. Despite the fact that every form of material work is prohibited on Shabbos, it is nonetheless the source of support for our material activities of the entire week. The blessings of Shabbos are not only enjoyed on that day but are also the source of sustenance for the entire week. Just as bread sustains and gives strength, so too, the blessings of Shabbos uphold *Klal Yisrael*. By partaking of two breads at every meal, we are alluding to the foregoing capacity of Shabbos to sustain not only itself but also the entire week.

An analogy may be drawn between Shabbos' extraordinary capacity to sustain the entire week as well as itself and the renowned relationship between two of Yaakov's children, Yissachar and Zevulun. As is well known, Zevulun, the seafaring merchant, supported Yissachar's Torah study. However, the relationship between these two brothers was not unrequited. On the contrary, Yissachar was blessed with a double measure of Divine reward for his learning — one portion for himself and an equal measure for his brother who had labored so strenuously to support him. (The name יששכר, *Yissachar is* derived from the term שָׂכָר, *reward*. By utilizing a double שׂ, the Torah implies that Yissachar receives a double reward, enough for himself and for his brother and sponsor, Zevulun.) So too, the Shabbos day is such an abundant source of Divine blessings that there is sufficient reward not only to sustain us on Shabbos but also to sustain the entire week, which is the prelude to and preparation for Shabbos. Without the preparatory efforts of the days leading up to Shabbos, we would not be able to fully benefit from the *berachos* of Shabbos. (*Vayechi* 5653)

The "Extra" Supernatural Dimension of Shabbos

ותוכן התשובה כי השבת הוא מעין עוה"ב. ואיך יוכל בעוה"ז לקבל הארות עוה"ב. לכן הוא בא בדרך תוספות ... וכמו כל ימי עוה"ז בכלות ימי האדם ועומד לקבל הארת העוה"ב מסתלק מעוה"ז. כ"כ ימי המעשה והשבת.

To appreciate better the nature and effect of the Double Bread on all of us, let us recall the first instance where the Torah describes explicitly the function of the Double Bread. When Moshe explains to *Klal Yisrael* why they received a double portion of manna on *erev Shabbos,* he recommended that they prepare (cook and bake as they pleased) the first portion for their personal use on that day. However, the "extra portion" (described by the Torah as הָעֹדֵף, *Shemos* 16:23) should be reserved for Shabbos. Evidently, the concept of a double portion is significant in a *qualitative* as well as a quantitative sense. The Jewish people not only enjoy a double portion of manna every *erev Shabbos* but also on Shabbos itself, when they participate in a spiritual experience that is "extradimensional" beyond anything that we can fathom in This World. As we know (refer to our chapter "Shabbos – a Microcosm of the World to Come"), Shabbos is a microcosm of the World to Come (*mei'ein Olam Haba*). From a purely rational perspective, it is incomprehensible how mortals living in This World could indeed begin to sample even a scintilla of the World to Come. It is only through the extra dimension of Shabbos symbolized by the Double Bread – and especially the "extra portion" designated for Shabbos – as well as the *neshamah yeseirah* that we possibly can sample *Olam Haba* while living in *Olam Hazeh.*

Let us extend the concept of the "extra dimension" of Shabbos' bread somewhat further, by suggesting that not only the Shabbos day's supernatural spirtuality, but also the entire week is sustained by this "extra dimension." Just as Moshe intimates that the "extra provisions" should be preserved (לְמִשְׁמֶרֶת), so too, we suggest that the extraordinary spirituality of Shabbos preserves *Klal Yisrael* during the week ahead. (This theme is similar to the *Zohar* that we have frequently cited that the blessings of Shabbos are the material support of the entire week.)

Going beyond the weekly Shabbos, we derive implications that pertain to our life span in This World and beyond, in *Olam Haba.* Just as the generations of *Klal Yisrael* who had toiled spiritually all week long enjoyed an extra other-worldly portion of manna on Shabbos, so too, if we strive to attain our spiritual potential in This World, at the conclusion of our allotted life span in This World, we will be prepared for the boundless ("extra") spiritual dimension of *Olam Haba.* In fact, the timing of our departure from This World may be related to the degree of preparation attained in This World. Once we have achieved sufficient merit (through our efforts while in *Olam Hazeh*) to be able to partake of *Olam Haba's* "extra dimension," our soul will ascend to its just reward.

(*Beshalach* 5639)

Oneg Shabbos

כָּל הַמְעַנֵּג אֶת הַשַּׁבָּת נוֹתְנִין לוֹ נַחֲלָה בְּלִי מְצָרִים ... כְּיַעֲקֹב שֶׁכָּתוּב בּוֹ ״וּפָרַצְתָּ יָמָּה וָקֵדְמָה וְצָפֹנָה וָנֶגְבָּה״,
Anyone who delights in the Shabbos will receive an inheritance without limits... Similar to that of Yaakov of whom it says, "You will spread to the west, to the east, to the north, and to the south (*Shabbos* 118a-b).

כָּל הַמְעַנֵּג אֶת הַשַּׁבָּת נוֹתְנִין לוֹ מִשְׁאֲלוֹת לִבּוֹ,
Anyone who delights in the Shabbos will be granted the wishes of his heart (*Shabbos* 118b).

כָּל הַמְשַׁמֵּר שַׁבָּת כְּהִלְכָתוֹ ... מוֹחֲלִין לוֹ,
Anyone who observes Shabbos, in accordance with Halachah, will merit that his sins are forgiven (*Shabbos* 118b).

◆§ Enjoying Shabbos' Arrival – Nullifying Our Problems

איתא המענג את השבת כו׳ פי׳ מוזז״ל שלא אמרו המענג עצמו בשבת רק המענג את השבת שיהי׳ לו תענוג בבוא יום השבת שבו שבת אל מכל מלאכתו ומתוך שמחה זו שוכח כל צערו וכל טרדותיו כו׳.
וזה ענין המענג את השבת כשבא שבת שהוא יום מנוח ושמחה לפניו במרום. צריך האדם לשכוח כל הצער שיש לו.
רק כפי מה שפורש עצמו מעוה״ז כך זוכה לטעום טעם עוה״ב. וכמאמר חז״ל מי שטרח עצמו בערב שבת. פי׳ התערובות שנתערב תאוות האדם לחיצוניות עוה״ז.
וז״ש ז״ל המענג שבת נותנין לו משאלות לבו ואמר אא״ז ז״ל לראות עכ״פ להיות משאלות הלב לטוב ולשמים. ואפשר לומר שגם זה הפי׳ שנותנין לכל אדם מישראל רצון ומשאלות לב לטובה. אמת גם ע״ז שייך משאלות לב לבקש רצון אמת.

The *mitzvah* of *oneg Shabbos* is often misconstrued to mean that one should enjoy *oneself* on Shabbos. If that were the case, *Chazal* (*Shabbos* 118a, cited in the introduction to this chapter) should have written, "One who enjoys *himself* on Shabbos will receive an inheritance without limits." By stating מְעַנֵּג אֶת הַשַּׁבָּת, *who delights in the Shabbos, Chazal* are extolling those individuals whose greatest delight is the arrival of Shabbos. Contemplating the imminent arrival of Shabbos, the day when Hashem rested from all of His labors, the Jew sets aside all of his worries – no matter how troublesome – and delights in the Shabbos. (*Vayeira* 5633)

Utilizing this approach to the *mitzvah* of *oneg Shabbos*, we can derive new insight into the Gemara cited in the introduction to this chapter: כָּל הַמְעַנֵּג אֶת הַשַּׁבָּת נוֹתְנִין לוֹ נַחֲלָה בְּלִי מְצָרִים ... כְּיַעֲקֹב שֶׁכָּתוּב בּוֹ "וּפָרַצְתָּ יָמָּה וָקֵדְמָה וְצָפֹנָה וָנֶגְבָּה", *Anyone who delights in the Shabbos will receive an inheritance without limits... Similar to that of Yaakov of whom it says, "You will spread to the west, to the east, to the north, and to the south.* Just as Yaakov *Avinu*, despite his numerous troubles (such as being pursued by Esav), ignored all of his personal crises and simply prayed that Hashem's Name should be great and His Will be fulfilled (a concept known as *davening l'shem Shamayim*), so too, upon the arrival of Shabbos, the true Shabbos observer forgets all of his personal problems and rejoices. This thought is voiced in the *zemiros* chanted every Friday evening (prior to *Kiddush*): צְוָחִין אַף עַקְתִין. בְּטֵילִין וּשְׁבִיתִין, *screaming and anguished, nullified and suspended* — If we put aside (nullify) our manifold problems in favor of the overwhelming joy of *Shabbos Kodesh*, then indeed our *tzoros* will be suspended. (*Vayetzei* 5654)

Utilizing this approach, we derive additional insight into the phrase recited in the *Mussaf* services: מְעַנְּגֶיהָ לְעוֹלָם כָּבוֹד יִנְחָלוּ, *Those who always* (forever) *delight in it* (Shabbos) *will inherit honor*. The apparently superfluous term *always* may refer to those who honor Shabbos even in times of personal distress. Despite their numerous afflictions, these individuals derive so much pleasure from the arrival of Shabbos that they successfully put aside all their problems when Shabbos arrives. As a result of this excellent frame of mind, they receive the limitless reward associated with *oneg Shabbos*. As the *tefillah* says, כָּבוֹד יִנְחָלוּ, *they will inherit honor* — the infinite honor promised by Hashem to Yaakov *Avinu* and to all of his descendants whose delight is the Shabbos day.

The mere fact that *Klal Yisrael* derives its pleasure from (and anticipates the arrival of) Shabbos — rather than from the many material pleasures available all week long — testifies that they are uniquely deserving of the Divine gift of Shabbos. The renowned Rabbinic saying, מִי שֶׁטָּרַח בְּעֶרֶב שַׁבָּת יֹאכַל בְּשַׁבָּת, *Those who exerted themselves on the eve of Shabbos will eat on Shabbos* (*Avodah Zarah* 3a), may also allude to the Jewish people's resolve not to yield to the many temptations of This World, which can be described as an עֶרֶב, *mixture* (related to the term תַּעֲרוֹבֶת) of many material pleasures. By resisting the temptations to succumb to such passions, we will enjoy the infinitely more valuable pleasures of *Shabbos Kodesh* and of the World to Come (of which Shabbos is a microcosm; cf. *Berachos* 57b). The term שׁוֹמֵר שַׁבָּת may refer not only to our observance of Shabbos but to our determination not to dilute the true *oneg* of Shabbos with the superficial material pleasures of the week. Those who are שׁוֹמֵר שַׁבָּת *watch* themselves and ensure that their sole aspiration is to delight in the Shabbos.

It is essential to always recall the significance of possessing the appropriate aspirations. Those who are able to withstand successfully the temptations of This World, and consistently aspire for spiritual treasures rather than material amenities, will ultimately enjoy the true pleasures of the World to Come. (*Chukas* 5636)

Just as it is essential that all week long we look forward to the spiritual delight of Shabbos rather than other superficial pleasures, it is also true that if we participate in the *mitzvah* of *oneg Shabbos,* we will merit to seek the proper objectives. The Rabbinic saying, כָּל הַמְעַנֵּג אֶת הַשַּׁבָּת נוֹתְנִין לוֹ מִשְׁאֲלוֹת לִבּוֹ, *Anyone who delights in the Shabbos will be granted the wishes of his heart,* does not necessarily mean that *all* of his desires — no matter how inappropriate — will be fulfilled. Instead, *Chazal* are assuring us that anyone who delights in the Shabbos will merit that all of his objectives (in every aspect of life) will be proper. The expression נוֹתְנִין לוֹ מִשְׁאֲלוֹת לִבּוֹ, *will be granted the wishes of his heart,* may be interpreted in a similar light — that Hashem will grant him the desire to seek what is truly appropriate. (*Eikev* 5632)

Eating for the Sake of a *Mitzvah*

בפסוק אכלוהו היום כי שבת היום לה׳. וקשה בלא״ה היו אוכלין בו ביומו כדכ׳ אל יותר ממנו כו׳. וי״ל הרמז שאכילת שבת צריך להיות לשמו ית׳ לשם עונג שבת. וז״ש אכלוהו היום. מטעם כי שבת היום. על כוונה זו תהי׳ האכילה כנ״ל.

In the previous *dvar Torah,* we emphasized that the *mitzvah* of *oneg Shabbos* should not be construed as an opportunity to satiate all our physical passions on Shabbos. Rather than indulge ourselves on Shabbos, we make every effort to delight and rejoice in the advent of Shabbos, to the extent that we are able to set aside all of our other concerns in favor of *kedushas Shabbos.*

One of the ramifications of this conception of *oneg Shabbos* is an entirely different approach that we adopt on Shabbos to the often mundane activities of eating and drinking. Realizing that our primary focus should be to delight in the Shabbos, rather than merely enjoy ourselves on Shabbos, we undertake to eat *l'shem Shamayim* (literally, for Hashem's sake). This theme is reflected in Moshe's charge to the Jewish people: אִכְלֻהוּ הַיּוֹם כִּי שַׁבָּת הַיּוֹם לַה׳, *Eat it* (the manna) *today, because today is Shabbos for* H*ASHEM* (*Shemos* 16:25). It seems unlikely that Moshe merely intended to instruct the Jewish people to eat all of the manna on Shabbos. The prohibition of leaving over manna for another day had already been told to the Jewish people (refer to *Shemos* 16:19, אִישׁ אַל יוֹתֵר מִמֶּנּוּ עַד בֹּקֶר, *No man may leave over from it until morning*). Evidently, Moshe meant to emphasize the manner and approach that should be assumed while eating the

Shabbos meals. He insists, "Eat today (אִכְלֻהוּ הַיּוֹם) because (and only because) today is Shabbos (כִּי שַׁבָּת הַיּוֹם)." (*Beshalach* 5651)

◆ *Oneg Shabbos* During the Weekdays

ויתכן עוד לפרש לעולם ממש כי השבת צריך להיות נשאר באדם שפי׳ בימי המעשה שהוא ברית עולם. וכשאדם נזכר מן השבת צריך להיות מלא עונג ושמחה כמ״ש שש אנכי על אמרתך.

In a previous *dvar Torah* we offered a novel interpretation of the phrase recited during the *Mussaf* service, מְעַנְּגֶיהָ לְעוֹלָם כָּבוֹד יִנְחָלוּ, *Those who always delight in the Shabbos will inherit honor.* It is also possible that the term לְעוֹלָם, *always,* refers to those who delight in the Shabbos even during the weekdays. Since Shabbos is described as a בְּרִית עוֹלָם, *eternal covenant* (*Vayikra* 24:8), we may assume that its impact may be felt even during the weekdays. Ideally, the mere thought of Shabbos – and of the unique opportunity that we as members of *Klal Yisrael* enjoy to testify every Shabbos that Hashem created heaven and earth – should be a source of great joy even in the midst of the week. (*Vayechi* 5651)

◆ Negating Oneself to Hashem

וזה אות השבת קודש שהוא עדות על בנ״י כי הביטול מכל המעשים הוא יום מנוחה להם שכל מגמתם להניח ממעשיהם ולהתבטל אליו ית׳. [ווז״ש ישמחו במלכותך שומרי שבת וקוראי עונג.]

While the concept of *oneg Shabbos* is generally associated with eating and drinking, albeit for Hashem's sake (*l'shem Shamayim*), there is an additional aspect to this *mitzvah* – completely negating oneself to Hashem. There is no nation that is capable of such self-sublimation to its creator as the Jewish people. As the Torah writes, כִּי אַתֶּם הַמְעַט מִכָּל הָעַמִּים, *for you are the fewest of all the peoples* (*Devarim* 7:7) – "You are the nation that more than any other nation diminishes itself (in favor of Hashem)." Every Jew possesses an inner spark of *kedushah* that seeks to cling to Hashem. Moreover, *Klal Yisrael* not only negates itself in favor of its Creator but also does so with such great joy. This trait of self-negation enabled our forefathers to loyally follow Hashem into the treacherous wilderness. It is by virtue of this admirable trait that *Klal Yisrael* is uniquely equipped to appreciate the Shabbos. What other nation could delight in the one day when all of its physical creativity ceases? Only the Jewish people whose primary objective is to negate its accomplishments to the source of its success, Hashem, can truly appreciate the Shabbos. All of these thoughts – negation to Hashem expressed through *shemiras Shabbos* as well as the sheer delight that we experience in negating ourselves – are expressed in the *Mussaf tefillah* of Shabbos: יִשְׂמְחוּ בְמַלְכוּתְךָ שׁוֹמְרֵי שַׁבָּת וְקוֹרְאֵי עֹנֶג, *They* [the Jewish people] *rejoice when accepting Your Kingdom, because they guard the Shabbos and delight* [in negating themselves to Your Sovereignty]. (*Bamidbar* 5644)

◆§ Finding the Divine Spark in Every Aspect of Life

אך פי׳ המענג את השבת הוא שכל תענוגיו הם רק לזאת הנקודה הפנימיות שנק׳ שבת באמת שהוא מנוחת הכל. ולאשר יודע שהוא העיקר נתברך בזה. ונק׳ תאות גבעות עולם שכל הנבראים מתאוין לידבק בזאת הנקודה כי היא מחי׳ כולם.

In the previous *dvar Torah,* we discussed the concept of "delighting in the Shabbos" and explained the distinction between *oneg Shabbos* as perceived by *Chazal* and simply indulging in physical pleasures on Shabbos. We may extend this concept further by suggesting that the term Shabbos refers to the Divine Spark embedded in every Jew (known as the נְקוּדָה הַפְּנִימִית, *inner spark*). Where else does one find the perfect harmony (שְׁלֵמוּת) and the inner peace that the universe enjoyed upon its completion that first Shabbos, than in the pure soul implanted by Hashem in all of us? Utilizing this approach, we suggest that the expression "one who delights the Shabbos" refers to those individuals who are motivated by one objective – to delight and bring *nachas* to the Divine Spark in their midst which is known as Shabbos. As we become increasingly aware of the "Shabbos" – Hashem's Presence in every aspect of our life – we draw closer to Him to the extent that we attain the *middah* (attribute) of *deveikus* (clinging to Him). (Refer to *Devarim* 10:20 and 11:22, stating that Hashem desires that we perfect ourselves to the extent that we ultimately reach the *madreigah* (spiritual level) of *deveikus*.

With this approach, we gain new insight into the *Chazal* cited in the introduction to this chapter, כָּל הַמְעַנֵּג אֶת הַשַּׁבָּת נוֹתְנִין לוֹ נַחֲלָה בְּלִי מְצָרִים, *Anyone who delights in the Shabbos will receive an inheritance without limits.* Just as Hashem and the Divine Soul contained within all of us is not confined to any finite limits, so too, those who are preoccupied with the task of delighting in the Shabbos — the Divine Spark that we enjoy — are infinitely rewarded.

Yaakov *Avinu* alludes to the infinite potential played by the Divine Spark and the reward enjoyed by those who exploit this potential by blessing Yosef with these words: בִּרְכֹת אָבִיךָ גָּבְרוּ עַל בִּרְכֹת הוֹרַי עַד תַּאֲוַת עוֹלָם, *The blessings of your father* (Yaakov) *are greater than the blessings of my parents* (Avraham and Yitzchak), *they extend until the furthest dimensions ever sought by man* (cf. *Bereishis* 49:26). What greater blessing than to live a life that is dominated by the Shabbos, the inner Divine Spark!

(Adapted from *Vayechi* 5632)

◆§ Shabbos Is the Source of the Entire Week's Parnassah

כי מצות עונג שבת הוא לברר כי כל הברכה ופרנסה בימי השבוע הוא רק בכח השבת וזה הג׳ סעודות של שבת וחז״ל דרשו מג״פ היום בפ׳ המן. וגם בפ׳ זו כ׳ ויכל ביום השביעי וישבות ביום השביעי ויברך את יום השביעי ... א״כ מלאכת ימי המעשה מתקשר אז להשבת וזה סעודת ליל שבת. וישבות הוא יום השבת וסעודת שחרית שהיא התעלות הכל אל השורש לכן נאמר בו שביתה ויברך הוא סעודה ג׳ שנותן ברכה על שבת הבאה. ונק׳ סעודות שהם סועדין ומפרנסין לכל הימים.

לכן כתיב שבת שבתון שיהי׳ השביתה לשם השבת עצמו. ולא בעבור ברכת השבת לעובדין דחול.

וכתי׳ והיתה שבת הארץ להם לאכלה. פי׳ אכילת השמיטה לא יהי׳ ע״י הכנת האדם רק ע״י המנוחה והוא בחי׳ עונג שבת.

Perhaps the simplest reason for the *mitzvah* of *oneg Shabbos* is to demonstrate that all of our blessings — and especially the *berachah* of *parnassah* (enjoying an adequate livelihood) — are enjoyed in the merit of Shabbos. Similarly, the three meals of Shabbos (*Shalosh Seudos)* are called סְעוּדוֹת, related to סַעַד, *support*, because they sustain us for an entire week. As *Chazal* state, כָּל הַמְעַנֵּג אֶת הַשַּׁבָּת נוֹתְנִין לוֹ נַחֲלָה בְּלִי מְצָרִים, *Anyone who delights* (derives pleasure) *in the Shabbos will receive an inheritance without limits.*

This concept that the workweek is sustained by the spirituality of Shabbos, rather than the converse, is not entirely without precedent. By writing, וְהָיְתָה שַׁבַּת הָאָרֶץ לָכֶם לְאָכְלָה, *The Sabbath of the land will be your source of food* (*Vayikra* 25:6), the Torah is implying that the entire prosperity of the six years of the seven-year *Shemittah* cycle is made possible because of the cessation of work during the seventh year. Similarly, it is through the cessation of all physical efforts at obtaining our livelihood, in favor of the spiritual bliss and *oneg* that we enjoy every Shabbos, that we are able to sustain ourselves all week.

Despite the abundant reward assured those who delight in the Shabbos, the Torah encourages us to observe Shabbos for its own sake (to commemorate the creation of heaven and earth) and not because of any potential reward that we might enjoy during the forthcoming week. This is indicated by the repeated expression of כִּי שַׁבָּת הַיּוֹם לַה׳, *for today is a Shabbos for HASHEM* (*Shemos* 16:25), implying that Shabbos should be observed because it is Hashem's day of rest, rather than because of any potential benefits that we may accrue during the week ahead.

(*Bereishis* 5645; *Ki Sisa* 5645; *Behar* 5646)

◆§ Finding the Path to Eden

וזה ענ"ג שבת שכתבו שהוא בחי' נהר יוצא מעדן להשקות הגן עד"ן נה"ר ג"ן שיש לכל איש ישראל בבחי' אלו בכח המילה.

By placing the First Man in *Gan Eden*, Hashem demonstrated that *every* individual is capable of living there. Despite our mortality, we are blessed with a soul that can ascend to such great levels that we can simulate (through Torah which is compared to the Tree of Life) the great *kedushah* of the Tree of Life that stood in the center of the Garden. While the soul's capacity to reach such rarefied heights was impeded when Adam was expelled from Eden, every Shabbos we are able to find the path back to *Gan Eden*. Yechezkel alludes to this by writing, שַׁעַר הֶחָצֵר הַפְּנִימִית הַפֹּנֶה קָדִים יִהְיֶה סָגוּר שֵׁשֶׁת יְמֵי הַמַּעֲשֶׂה וּבְיוֹם הַשַּׁבָּת יִפָּתֵחַ, *The gate of the innermost courtyard facing to the east* (reminding us of *Gan Eden* which was located in the east) *will be closed during the six work-days and it will be opened every Shabbos* (46:1). When describing the path that led out of Eden, the Torah writes: וְנָהָר יֹצֵא מֵעֵדֶן לְהַשְׁקוֹת אֶת הַגָּן, *A river issues forth from Eden to water the garden* (*Bereishis* 2:10). Each of the three "markers" used by the Torah to describe Eden's location are contained in the term עֹנֶג. The ע corresponds to עֵדֶן, the נ to נָהָר, and the ג to גָּן.

When we participate in the *mitzvah* of *oneg Shabbos*, we are commencing a great undertaking which will ultimately lead us back to Eden.

(Adapted from *Lech Lecha* 5657)

◆§ Achieving Forgiveness Through *Oneg Shabbos*

אך את שבתותי תשמורו. וכן כתיב ביוה״כ אך בעשור. לומר כמו שיוה״כ מכפר לפני ה׳ תטהרו. כן שבת דרשו חז״ל שומר שבת מחללו מחול לו. וביוה״כ הוא ע״י ועניתם ובשבת ע״י עונג שבת. וכמו שדרשו התם אך מכפר הוא לשבים ואינו מכפר לשאינם שבים כן בשבת מ״ש חז״ל מוחלין לו הוא ע״י תשובה. רק השבת מוחל הפגמים שנעשו ע״י העונות.

One would never contemplate that the joy and delight of Shabbos is comparable in any manner to the fasting and denial of material pleasures that we experience on Yom Kippur. Yet, *Chazal* teach us that just as our sins are forgiven on Yom Kippur, so too, they are forgiven every Shabbos (refer to *Shabbos* 118b where the expression מְחַלְלוֹ is interpreted as מָחוּל לוֹ, *his sins are forgiven*). Whereas on Yom Kippur we attain forgiveness by fasting and abstinence from material amenities, on Shabbos this objective is achieved through *oneg Shabbos* (refer to *Shabbos* 118b, mentioned at the beginning of this chapter, כָּל הַמְשַׁמֵּר שַׁבָּת כְּהִלְכָתוֹ ... מוֹחֲלִין לוֹ, *Anyone who observes Shabbos, in accordance with Halachah, will merit that his sins are forgiven*).

Drawing the analogy between Yom Kippur and Shabbos further, we suggest that in the same manner that one can not attain forgiveness on Yom Kippur merely by fasting, but rather through heartfelt repentance, so too, the mitzvah of *oneg Shabbos* enables us to attain forgiveness along with *teshuvah*. While our sins are forgiven by repenting sincerely every Shabbos, it is only through *oneg Shabbos* that any lingering stain on our *neshamah* remaining from the sins that we committed is expunged. It is through *oneg Shabbos* that the Jewish soul is returned to its former (and natural) pristine state. (*Ki Sisa* 5661)

◆§ Eliciting One's Hidden Potential

וכן איתא המענג את השבת נותנין לו משאלות לבו שיוכל להוציא מכח אל הפועל התשוקה הגנוזה בו. כמ״ש והמתענג על ה׳ ויתן לך משאלות לבך. זהו עונג שבת על ה׳ שהוא בח׳ השבועה כמ״ש. ויתכן עוד לומר שבכח שבועה זו נתן הקב״ה התורה לבנ״י שכל אחד נשבע ועומד בהר סיני שיצאה נשמתן במתן תורה ונחקק בנפשותם דביקות הבורא כמ״ש וחיי עולם נטע שלא יוכל להיות נכבה לעולם. ובשבת ניתנה תורה ומתעורר זה הכח והשבועה. וזה קריאת התורה בשבת. והבן הדברים.

וכמו דכתי׳ שער כו׳ סגור יהי׳ כו׳ כי ה׳ אלקי ישראל בא בו. וביום השבת יפתח. כן הוא באיש ישראל נקודה מסוגרת שהיא חלק אלקי ממעל. וביום השבת יפתח כו׳. והוא בחי׳ נשמה יתירה וענג שבת כמ״ש.

Chazal state, כָּל הַמְעַנֵּג אֶת הַשַּׁבָּת נוֹתְנִין לוֹ מִשְׁאֲלוֹת לִבּוֹ, *Anyone who delights in the Shabbos will be granted the wishes of his heart* (*Shabbos* 118b). It is fair to assume that our Rabbis are not referring to the mundane desires that we may harbor at any time. Instead they are suggesting that those who delight in the Shabbos will be able to achieve their full spiritual potential. By using the expression מִשְׁאֲלוֹת לִבּוֹ, *the wishes of his heart, Chazal* seem to be alluding to the dynamic inner potential that is embedded in the recesses of every Jewish heart. In the merit of *oneg Shabbos,* this inner force comes to the forefront. The *pasuk* cited by the Gemara, אָז תִּתְעַנַּג עַל ה׳, *You will then delight in Hashem,* seems to corroborate our contention that the reward for *oneg Shabbos* is the realization of one's inner potential — enabling us to draw closer to Hashem — rather than physical amenities.

The Gemara (*Shabbos* 10b) relates that the Shabbos is an invaluable gift granted by Hashem to the Jewish people and emanates from Hashem's treasure house (refer to our chapter entitled "The Gift of Shabbos" for an in-depth discussion of this concept). We may draw an analogy between the source of the Shabbos day and the reward granted to those who observe *oneg Shabbos*. Just as the Shabbos itself is rooted in the innermost recesses of the supernatural world (that only Hashem can fathom), so too, those who delight in the Shabbos day are able to elicit their own hidden inner potential. Drawing the analogy even further, we reason that in the same manner that the Shabbos day originating from this esoteric hidden source is granted to *Klal Yisrael*, so too, on Shabbos we are able to benefit from the original light of Creation which was hidden from This World (and reserved for the righteous in the World to Come). Similarly, the prophet Yechezkel (46:1) notes that a certain gate in the future *Beis HaMikdash* will open every Shabbos. While the full impact of his prophecy will not be realized until the rebuilding of the *Beis HaMikdash*, we suggest that the gates of our heart that are somewhat closed during the week open every Shabbos, when we enjoy the *neshamah yeseirah* and participate in the *mitzvah* of *oneg Shabbos*.

To further substantiate our contention that on Shabbos we are able to evoke our unrealized potential, we recall that the Torah was given on Shabbos (refer to *Shabbos* 86b). *Chazal* relate that at the time of the Giving of the Torah, Hashem infused the Jewish people with a "new soul" (refer to our essay in *The Three Festivals* entitled, "After *Matan Torah*," pg. 269, elaborating on this concept). As a result of this "Divine Implant" the Jewish people are permanently and inexorably linked to their Creator. The inexorable bond between Hashem and *Klal Yisrael* achieved through Torah study is expressed in the blessing which one recites after being called to the Torah — וְחַיֵּי עוֹלָם נָטַע בְּתוֹכֵנוּ, *He has implanted within us eternal life* (the capacity to cling to Hashem under all circumstances). Just as the Torah was originally granted to us on Shabbos, so too, every Shabbos in the merit of *oneg Shabbos*, we evoke the inner capacity for spiritual greatness that we first received at the time of *Matan Torah*. (*Vayeira* 5661, *Metzora* 5654)

◆§ Yaakov's Heritage – Reconnecting With Hashem

ולכן אמרו חז"ל המענג השבת זוכה לנחלת יעקב והאכלתיך נחלת יעקב אביך. זה מעליו איש טוב. צדיקים אלהיהם מתקיים עליהם והוא בחי' השבת.

Chazal (*Shabbos* 118a) relate that those who delight in the Shabbos will enjoy the heritage of Yaakov. To appreciate this particular metaphor, let us turn to the *berachos* that Yaakov received from his father, Yitzchak. Unlike Esav who was blessed that his *material* aspirations should be realized (refer to *Bereishis* 27:39-40 – where Esav is blessed with abundant fertility, military success and potential domination of his brother Yaakov if the Jewish people stray from Torah), Yaakov's *berachos* are focused on always retaining his relationship with Hashem. Yitzchak emphasizes the Divine Source of all of Yaakov's (and by extension, of all of Yaakov's descendants, the Jewish people) blessings by saying, וְיִתֶּן לְךָ הָאֱלֹהִים מִטַּל הַשָּׁמַיִם וּמִשְׁמַנֵּי הָאָרֶץ, *May* H*ASHEM* *give you from the dew of the heaven and the fat of the earth* (*Bereishis* 27:28; refer to *Rashi* who notes that the term וְיִתֶּן, *"and" Hashem should give*, implies that Hashem is constantly renewing Yaakov's *berachos*).

Similarly, those who delight in the Shabbos enjoy a blessing far more significant than material abundance. They are assured that despite the material ambiance in which we live while in This World, we will never lose our extraordinary relationship with Hashem.

The renowned comment of the *Zohar* that Shabbos is the source of the blessings of the entire week may be similarly appreciated. By renewing our relationship with Hashem – Who is the Source of all Blessings – every Shabbos, we ensure that all the material blessing that we hope to enjoy in the forthcoming week will serve to enhance our relationship with Him (rather than draw us further into the material world so devoid of Torah). (*Toldos* 5653)

וכמו כן בשבת ההנהגה ע״י הקב״ה בעצמו למעלה מהטבע והזמן. וזה רמז היום לא תמצאוהו בשדה.

In fact, the *pasuk* cited by *Chazal* as the Biblical source for the manifold rewards enjoyed by those who participate in *oneg Shabbos*, אָז תִּתְעַנַּג עַל ה׳, *You will then delight in* H*ASHEM* (*Yeshayahu* 58:14), corroborates our contention that one of the most significant benefits enjoyed by those who participate in this *mitzvah* is an intimate relationship with Hashem. Whereas those blessings that are channeled through the laws of nature (and implemented through *malachim*, cf. *Ramban, Vayikra* 18:25) are subject to dilution by the material ambiance of This World, the blessings accruing to those who participate in the *mitzvah* of *oneg Shabbos*, emanating directly from Hashem, remain pure. (*Re'eh* 5652)

Leading to Spiritual Growth

דכמו שבאותן המינים טמאים מתטמטם נפש האוכלם ולכן נק׳ מאכלות אסורות שנאסר בהם הנפש וגם כח החיות שבו וניצוץ הק׳ נאסר בהם וא״י להתגלות. כמו כן יש אכילה דקדושה שהיא בחי׳ חירות ומתרחב נפש האוכלם וכתי׳ בהם ואכלת לפני ה״א וכן הוא בעונג שבת. ואיתא במשנה שלשה שאכלו על שלחן א׳ ואמרו עליו ד״ת כאלו אכלו משלחנו של מקום שנאמר זה השלחן אשר לפני ה׳.

While we generally perceive eating as a mundane activity, in truth certain forms of eating can be a form of Divine Service. For example, eating *maaser sheni* (the tithe that is brought to Yerushalayim) is described as eating "in the Presence of Hashem." Similarly, by discussing Torah thoughts while eating, we enhance our meal to the point that the table that we are utilizing is described as Hashem's table (refer to *Avos* 3:4). So too, through the *mitzvah* of *oneg Shabbos*, food and drink which often retard our spiritual growth, are transformed into powerful vehicles for our advancement.

To explore this concept further, it is useful to recall that prohibited food is frequently described as מַאֲכָלוֹת אֲסוּרוֹת, which translated literally means "food that ties us." Just as non-kosher food actually stifles our spiritual growth, so too, eating in the context of a *mitzvah* (e.g., *oneg Shabbos*) actually allows us to advance in our service of Hashem.

(*Re'eh* 5661)

A World Without Limits — The World of the Soul

לכן אכילת שבת מצוה כי הוא מתקן הגוף ובא לנחלה בלי מצרים כנ״ל.

Chazal (*Shabbos* 118a) relate that those who delight in the Shabbos will enjoy נַחֲלָה בְּלִי מְצָרִים, *an inheritance without limits.* This promise is based on the *pasuk*, וְהַאֲכַלְתִּיךָ, *I will provide you* (literally, "I will feed you"), נַחֲלַת יַעֲקֹב אָבִיךָ, *with the heritage of Yaakov, your father* (*Yeshayahu* 58:14). Just as Yaakov was promised, וּפָרַצְתָּ יָמָּה וָקֵדְמָה וְצָפֹנָה וָנֶגְבָּה, *You will spread to the west, to the east, to the north, and to the south* (*Bereishis* 28:14), so too, those who participate in the *mitzvah* of *oneg Shabbos* will enjoy a boundless reward.

To appreciate the concept of "reward without boundaries" and its association with Yaakov, we recall that Hashem only imposed finite limits on His infinite universe because of the presence of the wicked. In fact, the Divine Name ש-די is derived from the need to impose strict limits on a universe that otherwise would have infinitely expanded. Just as Hashem hid the First Light of Creation from the "gaze" of the wicked, so too, He set finite limits to an otherwise infinite world, because of His concern regarding the impact of the wicked on an ever-expanding universe. For the righteous, however, these limits do not apply. Just as a Jewish king is authorized to break down any existing fences (on private property) to expand his dominion (cf. *Sanhedrin* 20b), so too, there are no limits to the sovereignty and impact of the *tzaddik*. The extraordinary ability of the *tzaddik* to transcend all temporal limits is demonstrated by the fact that the entire land of Israel was "folded up" so that it fit snugly under Yaakov's head as he slept at Mount Moriah (cf. *Rashi, Bereishis* 28:13).

On Shabbos, the day in which the material aspect of every Jew yields to the soul, we are able to overcome the limits imposed on our universe all week long. Our ability to transcend the "boundaries" imposed on our capacity for growth during the week is enhanced by the *mitzvah* of *oneg Shabbos*. By partaking of food and drink — not to satiate our material cravings, but rather to bring an aura of sanctity even to those material aspects of our life such as eating and drinking — we merit that even our body is influenced by the soul. In an atmosphere of such overwhelming sanctity, where the material side of man attains the trappings of *kedushah*, all constraints are lifted. The relationship between partaking of the Sabbath meals and attaining the boundless reward enjoyed by *tzaddikim* may be alluded in the *pasuk* cited by the Gemara, וְהַאֲכַלְתִּיךָ נַחֲלַת יַעֲקֹב אָבִיךָ, "I will grant you the capacity to eat (as a means of attaining your objectives) and consequently you will enjoy the legacy of Yaakov, your father" (cf. *Yeshayahu* 58:14).

(*Vayetzei* 5636)

◆§ Protection from the Foe

איתא כי מרע"ה תיקן לבנ"י שבת במצרים. אף כי עדיין לא ניתן להם השבת. רק בעבור כי בנ"י שובתין בשבת קודש אין מקום שישלטו עליהם האומות עובדי אלילים בשבת כי כל שליטתן ע"י המלאכות ועובדין דחול שבנ"י עושין. עי"ז ניתן להם כח לשלוט להם. ובשבת אין להם שליטה. וכמ"ש המענג את השבת נותנין לו נחלה בלי מצרים כו'. ועי"י שבת זכו לגאולה כמ"ש ז"ל שנתאספו בש"ק ונתעוררו בתשובה ... ולכן בשבת נק' חירות שאין עליהם עול הגלות כמ"ש המקבל עול תורה מעבירין ממנו עול גליות וד"א ועי"ז נזכה לגאולה במהרה בימינו אמן.

One of the most beneficial consequences of *oneg Shabbos* is a sense of increased security and protection from all our foes. All those forces that oppress *Klal Yisrael* are only able to have an impact during the weekdays — in which we, along with the rest of mankind, are preoccupied with work. On Shabbos, when we rest not only from the thirty-nine categories of work that were utilized to construct the *Mishkan* but also from all forms of secular activity that are inappropriate for Shabbos (a concept known as עוּבְדָא דְחוֹל), the Jewish people attain a sense of protection unlike anything that they enjoy during the week.

Utilizing this approach, we suggest another interpretation of the *Chazal* stating that one who delights in Shabbos will enjoy "an inheritance without limits." What greater reward than to be released every Shabbos from the shackles and constraints imposed upon us by our foes. This renewed sense of freedom that a Jew enjoys every Shabbos, a day which is devoted to Torah study, is alluded to by the Mishnah (*Avos* 3:6) stating, כָּל הַמְקַבֵּל עָלָיו עֹל תּוֹרָה מַעֲבִירִין מִמֶּנּוּ עֹל מַלְכוּת וְעֹל דֶּרֶךְ אֶרֶץ, *Anyone who accepts the yoke of Torah will be freed from the yoke of the government and the yoke of worldly responsibilities.* On Shabbos, when we are immersed in Torah study, the Jew feels no other yoke. Both the specter of deadly foes determined to annihilate *Klal Yisrael* and the crushing burden — felt all week long — of providing a livelihood will dissipate, with the newly-found sense of freedom and security gained every Shabbos.

Perhaps, it was for this reason that Moshe introduced the concept of Shabbos while our forefathers were still enslaved in Egypt, well before the *mitzvah* of Shabbos was formally transmitted to the Jewish people. By insisting that they observe Shabbos even while they suffered under the oppressive yoke of their Egyptian taskmasters, Moshe ensured that *Klal Yisrael* would experience a measure of protection and security unattainable during the week. In fact, the comparative respite that the Jewish people enjoyed on Shabbos enabled them to set aside their burdens long enough to contemplate how they had strayed from Hashem and eventually to repent.

Even today in the contemporary *galus*, we enjoy a measure of security on Shabbos, unlike anything that we experience during the week. We pray that just as in Egypt the first taste of freedom enjoyed on Shabbos was followed by redemption, so too, the secure environment that we enjoy in our contemporary *galus* every Shabbos, should be the harbinger of the Final Redemption. (*Shemos* 5634)

◆§ From *Nega* to *Oneg* Via *Gan Eden*

ענג. נהר יוצא מעדן להשקות כו׳. ושמירה שלא יתפשט ביותר במקום הנפרד לד׳ ראשים. כי משם יש המשכה לד׳ מלכיות. והם ד׳ מראות נגעים. ואיתא בזוה״ק כי נגע היפוך ענג כמ״ש אין למעלה מענג ואין למטה מנגע. ואמר שם כי המבטל עונג שבת מתהפך ענג לנגע. וכמו כן נאמר כי צרעת היפוך עצרת כי ביו״ט כ׳ עצרת כנופיא היפוך הפירוד.

ולכן איתא כי נגע היפוך ענג שבת דהיא בחי׳ ״עדן ״נהר ״גן שבשבת נפתח הפתח והיא נחלה בלי מצרים. שמכל אלה יש רמז בנפש האדם ולכן הושם בגן.

איתא בזוה״ק מאן דיכיל לענג השבת ולא עביד איתהפך לי׳ ענג לנגע. ממילא מדה טובה המרובה ע״י ענג שבת מתהפך הנגע לענג.

According to the *Zohar* (3:273), if one is able to participate in the *mitzvah* of *oneg Shabbos* and deliberately chooses not to avail himself of this opportunity, then his *oneg* (joy) will be transmuted into *nega* (plague and suffering, usually associated with *tzaraas*). (According to *Sefer Yetzirah*, an ancient *kabbalistic* text, *oneg* and *nega* represent diametrically opposed situations. Nothing could be better than *oneg* or worse than *nega.*) In these remarks, we will consider the relationship between עֹנֶג and נֶגַע, other than the obvious similarity in the spelling of both words. Refer to our foregoing *dvar Torah* ("Finding the Path to Eden", pg. 372) in which we suggested that by participating in the *mitzvah* of *oneg Shabbos,* the Jew undertakes the long journey which eventually will lead to man's return to Eden. It follows, then, that one who deliberately negates this *mitzvah* loses the opportunity to embark on this great odyssey. Moreover, as we stated previously, the term עֹנֶג alludes to עֵדֶן, נָהָר and גַּן, the three "markers" used by the Torah to describe the site of *Gan Eden,* as well as the four rivers that flowed from Eden. Every Shabbos, the gates of Eden open. (Perhaps, this is the true intention of the Rabbinic saying that in the merit of *oneg Shabbos* one receives "an inheritance without limits.") By participating in the *mitzvah* of *oneg Shabbos,* which corresponds to the various indicators of *Gan Eden's* location, we facilitate our return to Paradise. Moreover, by partaking of the Three Meals of Shabbos, we may merit to enjoy each of the three aspects of Eden described in the *pasuk,* referring to עֵדֶן, נָהָר and גַּן (refer to our chapter on *Shalosh Seudos,* the Three Meals). Conversely, by forfeiting this priceless opportunity, we remain outside of Eden.

Extending the analogy between עֹנֶג and נֶגַע further — with particular emphasis on understanding the consequences of not observing *oneg Shabbos* — we recall that according to the *Midrash* (*Vayikra Rabbah* 15), the four different forms of *tzaraas* correspond to the Four Kingdoms (generally assumed to be Babylonia, Persia, Greece, and Rome) that have oppressed the Jewish people throughout their long *galus.*

Similarly, *Chazal* (cf. *Yalkut Bereishis* 22) suggest that the four rivers flowing from Eden correspond to the Four Kingdoms. Those who participate in the *mitzvah* of *oneg Shabbos* merit to return to the state of the First Man who was ensconced in the Garden of Eden itself. Consequently, they are protected from the evil effects of the Four Kingdoms symbolized by the Four Rivers. By not exploiting this opportunity, one remains outside of Eden, in the domain delineated by the Four Rivers, which correspond to the Four Kingdoms — just as the four forms of *tzaraas* correspond to those four tyrannical regimes.

In summation, we are faced with the critical decision every Shabbos to either participate in *oneg Shabbos,* which allows to return to the sheltered confines of Eden, or to forfeit this opportunity which would leave us exposed to an entirely different environment, dominated by the four plagues of *tzaraas* or their contemporary equivalent, the Four Kingdoms.

To conclude on a more hopeful note — if neglect of *oneg Shabbos* leads to negative consequences, it is reasonable to assume that by participating in *oneg Shabbos*, our נֶגַע, plagues and other *tzaros*, will be transmuted into עֹנֶג, sources of joy. (*Tazria* 5658, 5661; *Metzora* 5654)

⊸§ Re-Experiencing the Exodos

כי בשבת מתעורר בח' יצ"מ כמ"ש המענג שבת נותנין לו נחלה בלי מצרים.

In a foregoing *dvar Torah,* we discussed the relationship between *yetzias Mitzrayim* and Shabbos and demonstrated that *Klal Yisrael* appreciated the significance of Shabbos even while they were enslaved in Egypt. Extending the association between the Exodous and Shabbos even further, we suggest that every Shabbos we experience a sense of liberation similar to that enjoyed by our forefathers at the time of *yetzias Mitzrayim.* Just as our forefathers were liberated from the oppressive yoke of Egyptian slavery, so too, we are granted relief every Shabbos from many of the problems that beset us in the contemporary *galus.* In particular, those individuals who diligently observe the *mitzvah* of *oneg Shabbos,* merit to feel every week as if they are experiencing the Exodus again. When *Chazal* state, כָּל הַמְעַנֵּג אֶת הַשַּׁבָּת נוֹתְנִין לוֹ נַחֲלָה בְּלִי מְצָרִים, *Anyone who delights in the Shabbos will receive an inheritance without limits,* they are alluding to the sense of relief from oppression that the Jewish people enjoyed at the time of *yetzias Mitzrayim* and that we all enjoy, in the merit of this *mitzvah* every Shabbos. In fact, the spelling of the terms מְצָרִים, *boundaries,* and מִצְרַיִם, *Egypt,* are virtually identical. By liberating *Klal Yisrael* from Mitzrayim, Hashem ensured that the Jewish people, if deserving, would be able to find relief whenever they found themselves in difficult straits. (*Yisro* 5634)

◆§ A Taste of the Manna

וכי ח״ו אין לדורות אלו חלק בתורה. ולכן נאמר שבש״ק זוכין בנ״י להיות בכלל אוכלי המן. וגם לפי הפשוט כן הוא שניתנה תורה לאוכלי המן שיש להם מנוח לעסוק בתורה ואין טרודין בפרנסה. ומה״ט ניתן השבת למנוחה לבנ״י לעסוק בתורה כמ״ש ז״ל שבת יעשה כולו תורה.

וז״ש ואנוהו שיהי׳ עיקר הנוי שלי מאתו ית׳. כמ״ש ויהי נועם ה׳ עלינו.

By participating in the *mitzvah* of *oneg Shabbos,* we not only reap many benefits (as discussed in previous *divrei Torah*) but we are also able to "connect" with the Heavenly Bread, the manna that our forefathers enjoyed while they were in the Wilderness. *Chazal* comment that the Torah could only be given to (and subsequently exploited by) those who eat the manna. While the surface interpretation of this Rabbinic saying indicates that the same generation that benefited from the manna in the Wilderness also received the Torah, *Chazal* may also have been alluding to the renewed taste of the manna enjoyed by the contemporary Jew participating in the *mitzvah* of *oneg Shabbos.* In fact, we simulate the environment that was conducive for the manna to first appear. Just as the manna was first enjoyed by Jews who were immersed in Torah, so too, every Shabbos, by setting aside all of our temporal concerns in favor of increased Torah study, we merit to enjoy again the taste of the manna.

Extending the analogy between *oneg Shabbos* and the manna even further, we recall that the manna was originally the food that sustained angels (refer to *Yoma* 75b). By proclaiming (cf. *Shemos* 15:2), זֶה אֵלִי וְאַנְוֵהוּ, *This is my God and this is my source of beauty* (the term אַנְוֵהוּ being derived from נָאֶה, *beauty*), the Jewish people voiced their fervent plea that for them the concept of beauty should always be associated with spiritual values and the *Shechinah,* rather than be related to physical beauty. In the *zechus* of stating such great ideals, our forefathers merited to be nurtured by the manna, that spiritual sustenance previously enjoyed only by angels. Every Shabbos, enjoying the rarefied presence of the *neshamah yeseirah,* the extra dimension of spirituality that graces all of us — and especially when we participate in the *mitzvah* of *oneg Shabbos* — we too are able to benefit from the spiritual nurturement of the manna.

It is well-known that the miracles enjoyed by our forefathers in the Wilderness were not only intended for their benefit but also, to some extent, for future generations of Jews. In fact, we benefit from a certain aspect of these miracles even in contemporary times. For example, the *succah* reminds us of the Divine Cloud protecting our forefathers. This is particularly true of the manna, which is described by the Torah as a מִשְׁמֶרֶת, *permanent reminder* (*Shemos* 16:32). We may assume that every Shabbos while we participate in *oneg Shabbos*, assisted greatly by the *neshamah yeseirah*, we — though far removed from the spiritual levels achieved by angels or even that of our forefathers in the Wilderness — nonetheless enjoy a taste of the manna. (*Beshalach* 5647, 5650)

◆§ Feeding the King's Army

ואיתא לחם שמלאכי השרת אוכלין. דהמלאכים מיוחדים רק לשליחות הבורא יתברך לכן ניזונין מאתו ית׳. כי מלכותא דארעא כמלכותא דרקיע. וכמו שהמלך נותן מזונות לאנשי חילו כן בנ״י המיוחדים לתורת ה׳ כפי מה שעוסקין בו כך נמשך המזון שלהם.

To appreciate the analogy between the manna and *oneg Shabbos* (a theme which we discussed in the previous *dvar Torah*) even more, let us contemplate the primary function of the manna. Just as a mortal king is morally obligated to feed his full-time dedicated servants, whose sole function is to assist him, so too, Hashem undertakes to sustain those who are completely dedicated to His service. Nothing could be more suitable to nurture Hashem's servants than the most spiritual of foods, the manna. Consider those who actually benefited from this rarefied form of sustenance — the angels on high (refer to *Yoma* 75b stating that the manna was first enjoyed by *malachim*) and subsequently, the Jewish people on earth, whose immersion in Torah study resembled the angels' dedication to Divine Service. Every Shabbos, the Jewish people forsake all their material pursuilts and immerse themselves in Torah. It is entirely appropriate that we, too, are sustained by the spiritually potent substance enjoyed by Hashem's full-time servitors — the manna or its contemporary equivalent, *oneg Shabbos*. (*Beshalach* 5658)

◆§ The *Shechinah* "Participates" in *Oneg Shabbos*

שיש לחם מן הארץ הם התיקונים שצדיקים מתקנים בעוה"ז. ויש להם עלי' למעלה. וכמו כן הלחם יורד מן השמים. ולכן בשבת לחם משנה רומז על ב' לחם. כדאיתא בזוה"ק ביני ובין בנ"י שסעודת שבת מתענגים בו עליונים ותחתונים ע"ש פ' ויקהל.

To appreciate yet an additional dimension of the *mitzvah* of *oneg Shabbos* we cite a renowned *Chazal* (*Yalkut Bereishis* 82) stating that the Jewish people enjoyed the manna in the merit of Avraham feeding bread to the angels who visited his home. Apparently, our Rabbis are alluding to the intimate relationship existing between *Klal Yisrael* on earth and the angels in heaven. Just as Avraham attained a spiritual level so exalted that even the angels could partake of his bread, so too, (and in his merit) his descendants, the Jewish people, could benefit from the manna, which was originally the sustenance of angels.

Every Shabbos when we partake of *lechem mishneh* (the two loaves of bread eaten during every meal which, translated literally, means "the double bread" – refer to our chapter on this topic for extensive discussion of this theme), we are also alluding to the "symbiotic" and unusually close relationship that exists between the Jewish people, who delight in Shabbos and partake of its meals, and the angels, who also derive pleasure from our *oneg Shabbos*. (*Beshalach* 5662-5663)

בפסוק אך את שבתותי. מדקדקין מאי אך. ויש לומר פי' שבתותי שלמעלה בשמים. ובני ישראל יש להם חלק בזה כמ"ש פורס סוכת שלום עלינו. פרס הוא חלק. וכמ"ש בזוה"ק כי בשבת יש השתתפות ברוחא דנחתא מלעילא ומתענג בתענוגי שבת ע"ש בפ' ויקהל. וכדכתיב ביני וביניכם. וזהו לשון אך חלק.

Not only the angels but even the *Shechinah* Itself derives "pleasure" from our *oneg Shabbos*. Our contention that our sense of *oneg* that we enjoy every Shabbos in our temporal residence on earth is also experienced in Heaven is alluded in the *pasuk* stating, אַךְ אֶת שַׁבְּתֹתַי תִּשְׁמֹרוּ, *However, you should observe My Sabbaths* (*Shemos* 31:13). The Torah is implying that in reality, it is Hashem's Shabbos that we are observing.

The word אַךְ, *however*, is generally intended to qualify or to indicate the active participation of another partner (refer to *Pesachim* 5a where the term אַךְ should be interpreted as חֵלֶק, *portion*). In this instance, by prefacing the *mitzvah* with the term אַךְ, the Torah is implying that while we are participants in the *mitzvah*, our joy is shared by – and is derived from – the *Shechinah*. (Adapted from *Ki Sisa* 5645)

וזה בחי׳ המענג את השבת. אותו ההארה שנחית בשבת. ועי״ז רומז הכתוב אכלוהו היום. פי׳ להאכיל היום בעונג שבת. והיא חבה יתירה לבנ״י כמ״ש ורצה בנו וש״ק כו׳ הנחילו.

If we assume that the *Shechinah* "participates" and derives *nachas* from our *oneg Shabbos*, we derive new insight into the Rabbinic saying, כָּל הַמְעַנֵּג אֶת הַשַּׁבָּת נוֹתְנִין לוֹ נַחֲלָה בְּלִי מְצָרִים, *Anyone who delights in the Shabbos will receive an inheritance without limits.* As already noted (refer to our *dvar Torah* entitled, "Enjoying Shabbos' Arrival", pg. 366), *Chazal* are not extolling those who enjoy themselves on Shabbos, but rather those who "delight the Shabbos" – the individual who derives so much pleasure from the arrival of Shabbos that he is able to forget all his other preoccupations and worries. In light of our previous remarks, perhaps the expression "delighting the Shabbos" refers to the *Shechinah* that permeates our home every Shabbos (to the extent that we can perceive Hashem's Presence on Shabbos). Those who are aware of the great pleasure that Hashem derives from our Shabbos meals (and behave accordingly) will enjoy boundless reward. (*Ki Sisa* 5664)

Sanctifying the Body

וכת׳ תן חלק לשבעה שבעת ימי בראשית וזה בכח השבת שהוא כח המסייע בבחי׳ ז׳ ימי הבנין. ולכן עונג שבת גם בגוף יש בו קדושה. ולכן נקרא שבת שלום. וגם לשמנה זו מילה בחי׳ עוה״ב כנ״ל.

With the words, תֶּן חֵלֶק לְשִׁבְעָה וְגַם לִשְׁמוֹנָה, *Distribute portions to seven, or even to eight* (*Koheles* 11:2), Shlomo *HaMelech* draws an analogy between the *bris milah* observed on the eighth day after the child's birth and the Shabbos, the seventh day of the week. Extending the analogy between these two concepts further, we suggest that just as circumcision has the effect of sanctifying the body as well as the soul, so too, on Shabbos, the body as well as the soul of a Jew is imbued with *kedushah*. The *mitzvah* of *oneg Shabbos* may be understood in this light. By participating in activities (eating and drinking) that bring pleasure to the body, we are demonstrating our conviction that on Shabbos, a Jew's body as well as his soul attain *kedushah*. (*Tazria* 5657)

☙ An Ancient *Mitzvah*

ויתכן כבוד ינחלו מה לעולם שקיים השבת קודם שניתנה וזכה לכבוד הנ"ל. כי זה סימן שמענג השבת שמימי בראשית נודע כי בו שבת הקב"ה ממלאכתו. ולכן הקדושים קיימו לכבד ולענג את השבת מסברא קודם שצוה הקב"ה לבנ"י שמירת השבת.

Although the *mitzvah* of *oneg Shabbos* had not yet been formally commanded, nonetheless, Yosef *HaTzaddik* insisted upon honoring the Shabbos even while in Egypt (cf. *Yalkut Bereishis* 149 stating that Yosef prepared a feast in honor of Shabbos). We allude to Yosef's extraordinary dedication to this *mitzvah* by reciting in the *Mussaf* prayer, מְעַנְּגֶיהָ לְעוֹלָם כָּבוֹד יִנְחָלוּ, *Those who delighted in it* (Shabbos) *forever, will inherit honor*. The term לְעוֹלָם, *forever*, implying that the *mitzvah* of *oneg Shabbos* had been observed a long time ago, alludes to Yosef's insistence upon honoring the Shabbos even while in Egypt. As a result of his diligence, he was rewarded with the unique honor that his descendant (the prince of the tribe of Ephraim) was permitted to offer his personal sacrifice on Shabbos. Contrary to the usual principle that only communal offerings may be brought on Shabbos, the sacrifice offered by Elishamah the son of Amihud, the leader of the tribe of Ephraim, dedicated at the time of the *Mishkan's* consecration, was brought on Shabbos. (*Mikeitz* 5652)

The Shabbos Lights and Friday Night Tefillos

The Shabbos Lights (הַדְלָקַת נֵר שַׁבָּת)

In this chapter we will present some of the insights of the *Sfas Emes* regarding the *mitzvah* of kindling the Shabbos lights.

◆§ Evoking the First Light of Creation

ולכן הדלקת נר בשבת לרמוז על התגלות האור בשב״ק ובנ״י שמצפים לאור הגנוז ומרגישין בחשכת עוה״ז כענין שנא׳ כי בחושך ה׳ אור לי ... בשב״ק יש הארה מ״ג ראשונות. לכן כ׳ ג״פ יום.

It is well-known that the primeval light (אוֹר הַגָּנוּז) of Creation — which emerged on the first day of the *sheshesh yemei ha'maaseh* when Hashem said, יְהִי אוֹר, *let there be light* (*Bereishis* 1:3) — was deemed to be too rarefied to be enjoyed by mankind in This World. Instead, this awesome spiritual light was hidden from us — after serving as the universe's luminary for the first three days of Creation — and reserved for the exclusive benefit of the *tzaddikim* in *Olam Haba* (cf. *Bereishis Rabbah* 1:3).

While it may appear that we will never enjoy this first light of Creation during our lifespan in This World, in reality, some aspect of this dazzling spiritual force may be perceived by us every Shabbos. To indicate our awareness of this phenomenon, we kindle the *neiros Shabbos* (Shabbos lights/candles) as Shabbos is about to begin. In fact, all week long, despite our residing in the comparative darkness of *Olam Hazeh*, we long for the onset of Shabbos when we will bask again in the spiritual radiance of the first light of Creation. As Michah says, כִּי אֵשֵׁב בַּחֹשֶׁךְ ה' אוֹר לִי, *Though I sit in darkness, HASHEM is light to me*, which may be interpreted homiletically: "*Even when I dwell in darkness* (during the six weekdays) I long for the moment, every Shabbos, *when Hashem will be my light*" (cf. *Michah* 7:8).

Expanding upon this theme, we suggest that when we speak of the revelation of the hidden light, which may be the rationale for kindling the Shabbos *licht*, we are referring to a larger phenomenon as well — the emergence of the *penimiyus* (*the inner dimension*) of every aspect of Creation on Shabbos. In a similar vein, *Chazal* (*Bereishis Rabbah* 11:2) note that a person's countenance on Shabbos is different from that of the week, alluding to the emergence of our inner spiritual personality on Shabbos. The very existence of the *neshamah yeseirah* (*extra soul*) on Shabbos also alludes to the existence of this additional facet of ourselves on Shabbos, an inner dynamic that is recessed all week long but now comes to the forefront.

It is significant that whereas the term יוֹם, *day*, is utilized only once in the context of each of the Six Days of Creation (for example when discussing the first day the Torah writes, יוֹם אֶחָד, *the first day*), in reference to Shabbos , it says יוֹם three times — וַיְכַל אֱלֹהִים בַּיּוֹם הַשְּׁבִיעִי, *God completed on the seventh day;* וַיִּשְׁבֹּת בַּיּוֹם הַשְּׁבִיעִי, *and He rested on the seventh day;* וַיְבָרֶךְ אֱלֹהִים אֶת יוֹם הַשְּׁבִיעִי, *and God blessed the seventh day* (*Bereishis* 2:2,3) — which may be an allusion to the first three days of Creation when the אוֹר הַגָּנוּז lit up the universe.[1] (*Bereishis* 5648)

1. Similarly, in *Parashas Beshalach*, the Torah alludes to the Three Meals of Shabbos by using the term הַיּוֹם three times.

◆ Purging Oneself of This World's Vanities (*Havlei Olam Hazeh*)

עיקר תיקון האדם כפי מה ששוכח הבלי עולם כמ״ש שכחי עמך ולזכור כי נשתלח בעוה״ז לעשות שליחותו ... וזה רמז אור להמשיך אורה לכל המקומות, וכן בשבת קודש יוצא אור ותורה לכל הימים, לכן מצות נר שבת ג״כ.

The expression הַדְלָקַת נֵר שַׁבָּת not only connotes *kindling the Shabbos lights,* but also a process of burning and purging oneself at the onset of Shabbos of the material vanities of This World. Just as fire has two properties – producing light (*ohr ha'meir*) and acting as a destructive agent (*ohr ha'soreif*) – so, too, the *mitzvah* of *hadlakas ner Shabbos* (*kindling the Shabbos lights*) is associated with the destruction of excessive materialism (which impedes our service of Hashem),[1] as well as the more positive connotation of lighting up our homes on Shabbos.[2]

Inasmuch as This World is nothing more than the corridor (פְּרוֹזְדוֹר) that inevitably leads to the palace (טְרַקְלִין) of the World to Come, we must take great precautions not to become immersed in the fleeting pleasures that may tempt us during our temporary stay in *Olam Hazeh.* Indeed, the very rationale for the continued existence of This World – with all of its material pleasures – is to afford us the opportunity to renounce these temptations in favor of the great spiritual joy associated with *Olam Haba.* This worthy objective is enhanced by *hadlakas ner Shabbos* – the *mitzvah* associated with destruction of all that is contrary to our spiritual growth. (*Lech Lecha* 5660)

1. For a similar use of the term *hadlakah* refer to the *Midrash* (*Bereishis Rabbah* 39:1) where it describes a בִּירָה דוֹלֶקֶת, *a burning palace.*

2. Consider the parallel between these two aspects of *hadlakas ner Shabbos* and *Zachor* and *Shamor*, the "positive" and "negative" aspects of Shabbos, respectively. Also refer to our chapter on that topic.

◆§ Dissipating Evil

בפסוק (בראשית יז, א) התהלך לפני והיה תמים, דהנה ע״י הערלה אין הנשמה מאירה באדם ועי״ז איתא גולל אור מפני חושך ובהסרת הערלה הנשמה מאירה באדם וגולל חושך מפני אור ואז נקרא תמים ושלם וכמו כן שבת נקרא שלום דסט״א אתעברית בשבת ומאיר הנשמה, וזה מצות הדלקת נר בשבת שלום בית.

With the advent of Shabbos, the darkness (and impurity) that may be associated with the weekdays gives way to the sanctity of this holiest of days. As we *daven*, גּוֹלֵל ... וְחֹשֶׁךְ מִפְּנֵי אוֹר, [*Hashem*] *removes the darkness* (of weekdays) *in favor of the light* (of Shabbos).

Specifically, the concept of *shalom bayis* (*domestic harmony*), that is frequently associated with the Shabbos lights, may allude to the internal harmony (*sheleimus*) that we may enjoy once the impact of the *sitra acharah* (*forces of evil*) is diminished upon the arrival of Shabbos (as symbolized by the light of the Shabbos candles). (*Lech Lechah* 5662)

◆§ Bringing Body and Soul Together

שהגוף ברמ״ח אברים הוא מלבוש אל רמ״ח בחי׳ שיש בנפש שהוא ציור האדם הפנימי ועי״י המצות מתקן האבר להיות דומה ונמשך אחר הנפש והנשמה ואז חל עליו חן וחסד ... וזה ענין נר שבת משום שלום בית (שבת כג:) שהגוף הוא בית לנשמה ועי״י השבת שהוא לוית חן הנ״ל ונעשה שלום בית.

Expanding upon the concept of *shalom bayis* discussed in the foregoing *dvar Torah*, we suggest that the body is the *bayis* (receptacle) for the soul. Just as there are 248 limbs that comprise the *guf* (*body*) so, too, the 248 positive commandments (*mitzvos asei*) nurture the soul. By faithfully observing those commandments, we ensure that each component of the body follows the dictates of the soul, rather than vice versa. No more opportune time exists for this collaboration between body and soul than Shabbos, the day when, assisted by the presence of the *neshamah yeseirah*, our inner spiritual dimension prevails. (*Ki Seitzei* 5655)

We reinforce this objective of bringing body and soul together by kindling two lights, one for the *guf* and another for the *neshamah.* On Shabbos we enjoy an unusual degree of harmony between body and soul, because the body and its material needs yield to the spiritual objectives of the soul. (*Likutei Yehudah*)

◆§ Kindling A Heavenly Flame

להדליק נר של שבת, וכן להדליק נר חנוכה. ולא אמרו נר בחנוכה, רק שזה הנר חנוכה צריך איש ישראל להדליק, וכן נר שבת, הנרות הם למעלה ואותנו צוה להדליקם שבמעשה האדם למטה מאירין הנרות למעלה.

It is significant that we recite the *berachah* of לְהַדְלִיק נֵר שֶׁל שַׁבָּת, *to kindle the light* ***of*** *Shabbos* (rather than לְהַדְלִיק נֵר בְּשַׁבָּת, *to kindle a light* ***on*** *Shabbos*).[1] It is well-known that our *mitzvos* on earth are significant not only in their own right but also because of the great impact that they leave in heaven. By kindling the Shabbos *licht* here on earth, we are able to evoke and "kindle" the heavenly source of these lights. (*Chanukah* 5659)

◆§ Lighting Up the Entire Week

כי מביהמ״ק האור יוצא לכל העולם, וכן אור תורה כמ״ש (שם ב, ג) מציון תצא תורה, ולכן צריכים בנ״י להכין הנרות לקבל האור היוצא להמשיך אורה לכל המקומות, וכן בשבת קודש יוצא אור ותורה לכל הימים, לכן מצות נר שבת ג״כ.

Just as the *Menorah* that was kindled in the *Beis HaMikdash* was a source of (spiritual) light for the entire universe,[2] so, too, the Shabbos

1. Similarly, we recite, לְהַדְלִיק נֵר חֲנוּכָּה (or של חנוכה) *to kindle the light (of) Chanukah,* rather than לְהַדְלִיק נֵר בַּחֲנוּכָּה, *to kindle a light on Chanukah.* Refer to *Days of Joy,* pgs 114-115 for further discussion.

2. Cf. *Yeshayahu* כִּי מִצִּיּוֹן תֵּצֵא תוֹרָה, *The Torah will go forth from Zion* (2:3).

licht bring light to the entire week. To draw the analogy even further, we suggest that the soul of a *tzaddik* illuminates many other *neshamos*. As we have demonstrated, in every realm — *olam* (*the universe*), *zeman* (*time*), and *nefesh* (*soul*) — the impact of *ruchniyus* (*spirituality*) penetrates well beyond its original source. (*Beha'aloscha* 5660)

ולכן מצות נר בשבת ויו"ט חובה, כי א"א להיות האור בעולם רק ע"י זמני קודש אלו.

Perhaps for this reason, the *mitzvah* of kindling the Shabbos lights enjoys the virtually unique status of being a חוֹבָה, *obligation* (cf. *Shabbos* 25b).[1] Inasmuch as the luminescence and outpouring (שֶׁפַע) of the Divine Blessings of the entire week is derived from these lights, it would be inconceivable to be negligent in any manner in performing this great *mitzvah*. (Adapted from *Emor* 5654)

☙ Rectifying Chavah's Sin

ואיתא (רש"י שבת לב, מבר"ר ספי"ז) כי האשה מדלקת נר שבת שהיא כבתה נרו של עולם, פי' שקודם החטא הי' הנשמה בקביעות באדם, ואחר החטא נסתלקה רק בזמני קודש ומקום המקודש מתגלית, וצריכין להדליק הנר להמשיך אור הנשמה, דכתי' (משלי כ, כז) נר ה' נשמת אדם.

According to *Chazal* (cited by *Rashi* in *Shabbos* 32a, s.v. הריני), the *mitzvah* of kindling the Shabbos *licht* primarily devolves upon the woman. This is because the first woman, Chavah, "extinguished the light of the universe" (an allusion to the soul) by eating — and enticing her husband to eat — from the fruit of the Tree of Knowledge. Consequently, by kindling the Shabbos candles, the Jewish woman helps to rectify Chavah's sin.

By utilizing the expression, "she extinguished the light of the universe,"

1. Cf. *Rambam Hilchos Berachos* (11:2) defining חוֹבָה as מִצְוֹת ... שֶׁאָדָם חַיָּיב לְהִשְׁתַּדֵּל וְלִרְדּוֹף עַד שֶׁיַּעֲשֶׂה אוֹתָהּ, *those mitzvos for which an individual is obligated to make every effort and to pursue until he accomplishes it.*

Chazal are not implying that (ח"ו) mankind's capacity for spirituality (associated with the soul) was negated as a result of Chavah's sin. Rather, they are motivating us to strive harder to attain the *ruchniyus* that was so readily available prior to the first sin. The spiritual growth that could be easily achieved before Adam's and Chavah's sin, can still be attained, but only with the active assistance of certain *mitzvos* and especially at certain propitious times. In particular, through the *mitzvah* of kindling the Shabbos *licht* [cf. *Mishlei,* נֵר ה׳ נִשְׁמַת אָדָם, *the lamp of* HASHEM *is the soul of man* (20:27); also נֵר מִצְוָה (ibid. 6:23)] which is compared to the soul, and on Shabbos, the day that we enjoy the *neshamah yeseirah,* we are able to evoke, to some extent, the spiritual levels and the prevailing role that the *neshamah* played before the first sin. (*Emor* 5660)

◆§ ***Kabbalas Shabbos***

In this section we will present excerpts from the *Sfas Emes'* commentary on *Tehillim* (and on the Torah) that help elucidate passages recited during the *Kabbalas Shabbos* service (which consist largely of selected chapters of *Tehillim*).

[**AUTHOR'S NOTE:** Please note that in this chapter, where there is no specific reference to the *Sfas Emes'* commentary on Torah, the *Divrei Torah* are based on his *Tehillim* commentary.]

Why We Recite Lechu Neranenah During the Kabbalas Shabbos Service

לְכוּ נְרַנְּנָה לַה׳
Come! Let us sing to HASHEM *(Tehillim 95)*

בֹּאוּ נִשְׁתַּחֲוֶה וְנִכְרָעָה נִבְרְכָה לִפְנֵי ה׳ עֹשֵׂנוּ
Come! Let us prostrate ourselves and bow,
let us kneel before HASHEM*, our Maker.*

◆§ Following the First Man's Lead

ואיתא במדרש כי אדם הראשון אמר לכל הבריאה בקבלת שבת לכו נרננה כי מרע״ה נותן זה הכח לבני ישראל בכל שבת כדאיתא (שבת י:) לך והודיעם עכ״ד צ״ל וכ״כ (ישעי׳ מג, כא) עם זו יצרתי כו׳ תהלתי יספרו, כי לא כל מי שרוצה בואו נשתחוה נכרעה כו׳ והיינו שהוא הי׳ כולל כל הברואים ובהכנעת עצמו נכנעו כולם, אך אחר החטא שנתערב טוב ורע נבחרו בני ישראל, ותיקן מרע״ה זאת לבנ״י, ולכן אומרים בקבלת שבת לכו נרננה.

By commencing the *Kabbalas Shabbos* with the call of ... לְכוּ נְרַנְּנָה לַה׳ בֹּאוּ נִשְׁתַּחֲוֶה וְנִכְרָעָה נִבְרְכָה לִפְנֵי ה׳ עֹשֵׂנוּ, *Come! Let us sing to Hashem ... Come! Let us prostrate ourselves and bow, let us kneel before* H*ASHEM*, *our Maker*, we are following the lead of Adam *HaRishon.* Immediately at the close of Creation on the first *erev Shabbos*, in his role as the elite of Hashem's creations, he called upon all those who were created by Hashem to pay homage to their Creator: "Let us sing the praises of Hashem. Let us us bow down and bend our knee to Hashem our Creator" (cf. *Pirkei d'Rabbi Eliezer* 11). While the first man originally motivated all of Hashem's creations to sing the praises of their Creator, after partaking from the fruit of the Tree of Knowledge (a sin which resulted in the blurring of good and evil) the task of singing Hashem's praises was assumed by *Klal Yisrael*. As Yeshayahu proclaims: עַם זוּ יָצַרְתִּי לִי תְּהִלָּתִי יְסַפֵּרוּ, *I have created this nation for Me to sing My praises* (43:21). This daunting task is best performed on Shabbos, a day when we bear witness to Hashem's creation of heaven and earth.

(*Chanukah* 5648)

☙ Giving Hashem *Nachas*

וינפש הוא הנייחא שהי׳ לפניו מקבלת מלכותו שקיבלו הברואים היינו אדם הראשון שאמר לכל הברואים לכו נרננה ...

By commencing the *Kabbalas Shabbos Tefillah* with לְכוּ נְרַנְּנָה לַה׳, *Come! Let us sing [praises] to HASHEM*, we are reminded of the great *nachas* (spiritual satisfaction) that He derived from that first *erev Shabbos*. Not only was it from the universe's completion but also from the unanimous acceptance of His sovereignty by all of His creations. When Adam proclaimed, לְכוּ נְרַנְּנָה לַה׳, he was doing so not just on his own behalf but also as a representative of all of Hashem's creations, indicating their acceptance of His rule. In fact, the term used in the Shabbos morning *Kiddush*, שָׁבַת וַיִּנָּפַשׁ, *His soul "rested"* from creating, may also be understood in this light. Whereas שָׁבַת connotes Hashem's "resting" from creation, וַיִּנָּפַשׁ alludes to the great personal satisfaction (נַחַת) that Hashem derived at that time from His completed universe.

Even today, every *shomer Shabbos*, who by his actions confirms his belief that Hashem created heaven and earth, is a great source of *nachas* to Him.

(Adapted from *Bo* 5638)

☙ Three Phases of Divine Service

וזה רמז ג׳ הלשונות נשתחוה ונכרעה נברכה, כי בבוקר השתחואה להיות עכ״פ מודה בטובת הבורא ית׳ ענין ברכת השחר, ובמנחה כריעה היא הרגשה ביותר להכניע ולהכריע עצמו אליו ית״ש עד שבערב נתבטל לגמרי אל השורש, וזה תפלת ערבית השבת הנפש אליו ית״ש וזה נברכה להיות נרכב ונברך אל השורש, וכן הוא בכלל ימי האדם בימי הנעורים להכניע עצמו עכ״פ להודות ולהכיר חסדו ית״ש וכשבא בימים מבין ומכריע עצמו להיות רוב מעשיו בעבודת הבורא, וכשבאים לימי זקנה נתבטלין לגמרי אליו ית״ש, וזה זקן שקנה חכמה (קדושין לב:) פי׳ שעושה עיקר מן החכמה ויודע כי הכל הבל רק לעשות רצונו ית״ש בעולם, ואלה הג׳ בחינות הם בחי׳ נר״נ, כי האדם כלול מתלת עלמין כמ״ש בזוה״ק שלח והנפש שהיא נטבע בגוף בחי׳ עולם העשי׳ שרובו רע צריך עכ״פ להכניע עצמו, ובחי׳ הרוח הכרעה לעבור הטוב על הרע, ובחי׳ הנשמה להיבטל לגמרי אליו ית״ש, לכן צריך כל אדם להיות לו ג׳ בחי׳ הנ״ל נשתחוה ונכרעה נברכה.

"Isn't bending one's knee, (i.e., kneeling), included in the category of bowing down? ... Moshe, forseeing that the *Beis HaMikdash* would soon be destroyed and that the *Bikkurim* ceremony would no longer exist, instituted three prayers to be recited every day"

(*Midrash Tanchuma, Ki Savo*).

According to the foregoing *midrash,* the three expressions utilized in this *pasuk* by which we pay homage to Hashem — נִשְׁתַּחֲוֶה וְנִכְרָעָה נִבְרְכָה — allude to the three prayer services that are recited every day. Whereas when the *Beis HaMikdash* stood we were able to negate ourselves to Hashem (and return to our spiritual roots), especially during the *Bikkurim* ceremony, now, to some extent, we accomplish the same objective through prayer. By specifying three different expressions of homage — נִשְׁתַּחֲוֶה וְנִכְרָעָה נִבְרְכָה— the Psalmist may be alluding to the three daily prayer services of *Shacharis, Minchah,* and *Maariv,* during which we render homage to our Creator [as the *pasuk* concludes, לִפְנֵי ה׳ עֹשֵׂנוּ, *before* (in the presence of) *HASHEM our Maker/Creator*].

Expanding upon this theme, we suggest that each of these expressions represent a different part of the day. Firstly, נִשְׁתַּחֲוֶה, *we prostrate ourselves* – every morning we commence our daily *avodas Hashem* by reciting the

Birchas HaShachar (*morning blessings*) in which we acknowledge our gratitude to Him for being able to perform so many physical functions. By midday, at *tefillas Minchah,* we have reached the point where we can do more than merely acknowledge Him. This time, in the spirit of וְנִכְרָעָה, [homiletically translated,] "we determine that our lives are primarily dedicated to *avodas Hashem*" (related to לְהַכְרִיעַ, *to decide*). Consequently, we bend our knees, indicating a greater form of tribute than נִשְׁתַּחֲוֶה. Finally, at *Maariv* time, we fulfill the spirit of the third expression of fealty to Hashem, נִבְרְכָה. This may be translated, *we "graft" ourselves*[1] – we integrate ourselves with Hashem, implying a far more thorough form of negation to our Creator. Just as the First Fruits provided a sense of vitality and freshness in our *avodas Hashem* in the times of the *Beis HaMikdash,* so, too, each *tefillah* gives us renewed strength for that part of the day.

Extending the analogy even further, we suggest that these three expressions of homage to Hashem may be used to describe three critical (and inevitable) stages of our own lives. At first, during our youth, נִשְׁתַּחֲוֶה, we should undertake to at least humble ourselves and to acknowledge our Creator. By the time that we have reached our middle years, it is appropriate that we devote most of our time (and effort) in service of Hashem, as וְנִכְרָעָה, *let us determine* (that our lives be devoted to Divine Service) implies. Finally, as older individuals, we negate ourselves totally to Him, which the term נִבְרְכָה, *let us "integrate" ourselves,* indicates. In fact, *Chazal* (*Kiddushin* 32b) describe an elderly person as זֶה שֶׁקָּנָה חָכְמָה, *one who has acquired wisdom,* one who has realized that his sole purpose on this earth in his remaining years is to do the will of Hashem.

Moreover, we suggest that these three expressions of homage may also refer to the three distinct components of our soul: *nefesh* (the most material aspect); *ruach* (where both the material and spiritual aspect of man are found); and finally the most spiritual component of the soul, *neshamah.*[2] The unique function of each of the soul's components is alluded to in these three expressions of submission to Hashem. Whereas the *nefesh,* often immersed in the material world, should at least humble itself and pay homage to its Creator (נִשְׁתַּחֲוֶה), in the case of the *ruach,* the forces motivating us to do good should prevail over the forces of evil (נִכְרָעָה). Finally, in the realm of the *neshamah,* often described as the חֵלֶק אֱלֹקַ׳ מִמַּעַל, *the Divine Portion in all of us,* נִבְרְכָה לִפְנֵי ה׳ עֹשֵׂנוּ, *we will*

1. Cf. *Kilayim* 7:1 for a similar usage of the term נִבְרָכָה as "graft": הַמַּבְרִיךְ, *one who grafts vines.*
2. Refer to the *Zohar, Parashas Shelach* describing these three components of the soul.

"integrate" ourselves (כביכול) *in the presence of* H*ASHEM our Creator.* Returning to the theme of the *midrash* cited previously, we suggest that the three *tefillos* that we pray every day may leave their impact on the *nefesh, ruach* and *neshamah* respectively.

The immediate following *pasuk* may also allude to each component of our soul: כִּי הוּא אֱלֹהֵינוּ, *for He is our God,* is an allusion to the *neshamah* which is the Divine Presence in our midst. וַאֲנַחְנוּ עַם מַרְעִיתוֹ *we are the flock* (people) *of His pasture,* is a reference to the *ruach.* Finally, וְצֹאן יָדוֹ, *the sheep of His Hand,* alludes to the *nefesh.* Each aspect of the Jewish soul, even the most material, can reach its potential for Divine Service provided the condition stipulated at the *pasuk's* conclusion is met — אִם בְּקֹלוֹ תִשְׁמָעוּ, *if you but listen to His voice.* The voice of Hashem is best evoked through our immersion in Torah and through earnest prayer. (*Ki Savo* 5655)

שִׁירוּ לַה׳

***Let us sing to* H*ASHEM* (*Tehillim* 96)**

יַעֲלֹז שָׂדַי ... יְרַנְּנוּ כָּל עֲצֵי יָעַר ... כִּי בָא כִּי בָא לִשְׁפֹּט הָאָרֶץ

The field will exult ... all the trees of the forest will rejoice ... for He has come, He has come to judge the earth.

Rejoicing in Judgment

במדרש לשפוט הארץ בר״ה ויוכ״פ ע״ש פ׳ אמור, כי בנ״י מבינים כי במה שכל באי עולם עוברים לפניו במשפט הוא כדי לזכות אותנו, ולכן יש לשמוח במה שנזכרין לפניו במשפט, ולעתיד עתידין כל באי עולם לשמוח בזה, ז״ש כי בא כי בא לשפוט, ב׳ פעמים כי בא, פי׳ שמרננים על כי בא ה׳, והגם כי בא לשפוט מ״מ שמחים בביאת ה׳ שמבינים כי באור פני מלך חיים אעפ״י שבא לשפוט, ועצי היער הם האומות שעתידין כולם לשמוח בזה.

While the concepts of מִשְׁפָּט, *judgment,* and שִׂמְחָה, *joy,* seem to be dichotomous (we fear the *yom ha'din* rather than joyously look forward to it), nonetheless, *Klal Yisrael* rejoices every Rosh Hashanah and Yom Kippur. It feels assured that (whatever its shortcomings) it will be vindicated and its unique role as the *am Hashem,* a nation that is distinct from all of mankind, will be perpetuated. Ultimately, not only the Jewish people but even mankind-at-large (symbolized by the trees of the forest who, while presently barren, will ultimately bear fruit) rejoice.

This theme of rejoicing in judgment may be the justification for the apparently redundant expression כִּי בָא כִּי בָא, *He has come, He has come.* While the first term expresses our great joy that Hashem judges us, in the second instance the term כִּי בָא may be interpreted as *despite.* Well aware of the awe prevailing on the Day of Judgment and mindful of the consequences, we nonetheless rejoice in the belief that the mere presence of the *Shechinah* is a source of life to all of us (cf. *Mishlei* 16:15, בְּאוֹר פְּנֵי מֶלֶךְ חַיִּים, *in the light of the King's Presence there is life*).

The joy that we experience during the *yamim noraim* is reflected most intensely on Succos (*zeman simchaseinu, the time of our rejoicing*). By describing the *arba minim* (Four Species) as potent symbols of *Klal Yisrael's* vindication, *Chazal* (cf. *Yalkut Vayikra* 651) may have been referring to the great joy with which we perform these *mitzvos.* It is only a nation that has prevailed — and been vindicated in judgment — that can proceed from the awesome environment of the *yamim noraim* to the joy of Succos.

אָז יְרַנְּנוּ כָּל עֲצֵי יָעַר
Then all the trees of the forest will rejoice.

Man Inspires Nature

בפסוק (ויקרא לג, ד) ועץ השדה יתן פריו, דרשו (ח״ב שם) חז״ל אילני סרק עתידין לעשות פירות נראה כי הכל תלוי בעבודת האדם כי האדם נק׳ עולם קטן ויש בו מכל פרטי הבריאה, וכפי התעוררות האדם בכל קומה שלימה שלו לעבודת השי״ת, כך מעורר כל הברואים, וכמו שיש בעולם אילנות מפירות ויש אילני סרק, כן נמצא כזה האדם אברים שהחיות מתרבה בהם, ויש שהחיות מועט בהם, וכשהאדם מתקן הכל וזה כענין החוקים שאין האדם מרגיש הטעם, אעפ״כ נמשך אחר גזירת המלך, ובזה מתקן אותן המקומות שאין החיות מתגלה בהם, וזהו אילני סרק שעתידין לעשות פירות הלא מצינו (תענית יא.) אבן מקיר וכפים מעץ יעננה, מכל שכן הצדיק במעשים טובים בוודאי משמיע קולו כאשר למרחוק לעורר ישנים, ומכש״כ בכללות ישראל כאשר יתקנו הכל אז ירננו כ״ע היער.

To explain the term אָז, *then,* which implies that there is a particular catalyst that motivates the trees (and all of nature) to burst forth in song, we suggest that it is man (and, in particular *Klal Yisrael*) through his Divine Service that inspires all of Hashem's creations to sing His praises. If we dedicate every component of our body to *avodas Hashem,* this, in turn, enables the natural world to evoke its full potential for Divine Service as well. Just as man is comprised of organs that are clearly suited for sacred purposes (such as his lips and tongue) and others that are less obvious vehicles for Divine Service, so, too, the natural world consists not only of fruit-bearing trees but also of trees that are barren. When man consecrates every fiber of his body, even those that are not particularly well-suited, to *avodas Hashem,* then all of nature in turn — even those trees that are barren — in their own fashion pay tribute to Hashem.

ה׳ מָלָךְ תָּגֵל הָאָרֶץ
When HASHEM will reign,
***the world will rejoice* (*Tehillim* 97)**

אוֹר זָרֻעַ לַצַּדִּיק
A light that is firmly planted
(is merited) by the righteous.

◆§ The *Tzaddik's* Mission: Nurturing Other *Tzaddikim*

כמו שיש באילנות מזריע זרע, כן יש הצדיקים שבכחם להמשיך נפשות לזרוע צדיקים בארץ, ופי׳ איש יהודי שעושה יהודים בעולם, וע״ז כתיב אור זרוע לצדיק, שהצדיק יש בו אור להכריע ולהוליד פרי עץ חיים, והנה סיום הפסוק ולישרי לב שמחה זה בחי׳ בעלי תשובה שצריכים ליישר העקמומיות.

Just as when we plant seeds we have the expectation that a tree (or any form of vegetation) will eventually emerge, so, too, the *tzaddik* enjoys the capacity to plant "seeds" of his own. By his sterling eaxmple, he inspires other to follow his ways. The analogy to planting a tree is particularly appropriate if we recall the Torah's description of a person as עֵץ הַשָּׂדֶה, *a tree of the field* (*Devarim* 20:19). A prime example of a *tzaddik* who implants his righteousness in others is Mordechai, described as being מִזֶּרַע הַיְּהוּדִים, *of Jewish descent* (*Esther* 6:13), which may be homiletically interpreted as a Jew who "plants" (זרע) other Jews. Mordechai himself is called an אִישׁ יְהוּדִי (*Jewish man;* ibid. 2:5), which also may refer to a man who "makes Jews" — he enables other Jews to return to their heritage. The *pasuk* continues, וּלְיִשְׁרֵי לֵב שִׂמְחָה (*the upright merit joy*), which homiletically refers to the *baal teshuvah* whose primary focus is to redress past iniquities (i.e., "straighten out" the heart — יִשְׁרֵי לֵב).

אוֹר זָרֻעַ לַצַּדִּיק וּלְיִשְׁרֵי לֵב שִׂמְחָה
A light that is firmly planted (is merited by)
the righteous (while) *those who are upright* (merit) *joy.*

◆§ The Upright (*Yashar*) and the Righteous (*Tzaddik*)

ונראה כי ישר הוא כמו שהי׳ קודם החטא דכ׳ (קהלת ז, כט) עשה את האדם ישר, ואחר החטא שנעשה תערובות טוב ורע אז נעשה בחי׳ צדיק ורשע כי צדיק הוא ברובו כמ״ש (קידושין מ:) כל שזכיותיו מרובין ה״ז צדיק, אבל בחי׳ ישר הוא שלא יהי׳ שום התנגדות, לכן כתיב בנח איש צדיק, ואברהם אבינו התחיל לתקן כל שורש החטא והוא הדרך שזכו בנ״י בכח התורה, כדכ׳ (משלי יב, ו) יצפון לישרים תושי׳ וזה א״א להיות הדרך בטבע, רק האבות המשיכו זה הדרך לעולם, וע״ז כ׳ ולישרי לב שמחה כי שמחה הוא כשאין הערובות סט״א כלל, וכמו שהי׳ קודם החטא, כשמחך יצירך בג״ע מקדם (וכו׳). ומ״מ הוכרח נח לתקן מקודם בחי׳ צדיק ואח״כ באו באבות בבחי׳ ישרים שכ״כ אור זרוע לצדיק אח״כ לישרי לב שמחה.

The Gemara (*Taanis* 15a) notes the discrepancy between the rewards accruing to the *tzaddik* who benefits from the Divine gift of light (*orah*), while the *yashar* enjoys the even greater blessing of joy (*simchah*). To appreciate the distinction between the *simchah* enjoyed by the *yishrei leiv* and the *orah* that the *tzaddik* receives, we need to distinguish between the outstanding personalities who are endowed with these traits.

It appears that the *yashar* adopts a lifestyle that is reminiscent of the first man's original habitat, *Gan Eden.* To merit this pristine environment, one had to be a true *yashar, perfectly upright,* without even a scintilla of sin. While this is undoubtedly a formidable challenge, we should recall that man was originally created in this fashion. As *Koheles* writes, אֲשֶׁר עָשָׂה הָאֱלֹהִים אֶת הָאָדָם יָשָׁר, *God created man to be upright* (7:29). It was only after the first sin, when Adam partook of the fruit of the Tree of Knowledge of Good and Evil, that it became virtually impossible to live a life totally devoid of sin. Thus Noach, despite his many worthy attributes, is described as a *tzaddik, righteous individual,* but not as a *yashar.* While one can attain the status of *tzaddik* on the basis of having performed more *mitzvos* than *aveiros,*[1] it is only those who are virtually without sin who deserve the tribute of being called *yashar.* Consequently, it was only Avraham *Avinu,* followed ultimately by his children and grandchildren, the *Avos* and *shevatim* of *Klal Yisrael,* who began the process of returning the universe to the purity and sin-free environment that it enjoyed before the first sin. They were the true *yishrei leiv,* individuals possessing upright hearts. It was they who deserved the title of *yesharim,*[2] and it is those individuals who emulate their lifestyle that deserve the Divine gift of *simchah.*[3]

However, one should not conclude on the basis of our foregoing discussion extolling the virtues of the *Avos* and their attribute of *yashrus* that Noach, who personified the *middah* of *tziddkus,* played an insignificant role in bringing the universe back to the status it enjoyed before Adam's sin. On the contrary, it was by demonstrating that it was possible to remain a *tzaddik* in a universe corrupted by his contemporaries that Noach enabled the *Avos* to eventually return the universe to its original status of *yashrus.* In other words, the *tzaddik,* while receiving the "comparatively inferior" gift of *orah,* is a necessary prerequisite for the eventual emergence of the *yashar,* who experiences Divine joy. This sequence can be deduced from this *pasuk* which commences, אוֹר זָרֻעַ לַצַּדִּיק, *the righteous enjoys a light that is firmly implanted;* and concludes, וּלְיִשְׁרֵי לֵב שִׂמְחָה, *and those who are upright enjoy joy.*

1. Refer to *Rambam, Hilchos Teshuvah* (3:1) stating that anyone whose merits exceed his sins is considered to be a *tzaddik.*

2. Refer to *Avodah Zarah* 25a where *Sefer Bereishis* is called *Sefer HaYashar* because it details the life of the *Avos.*

3. When we wish a newly wed couple שַׂמֵּחַ תְּשַׂמַּח רֵעִים הָאֲהוּבִים (*Gladden the beloved companions*), that they should rejoice as Adam and Chavah did in *Gan Eden,* we are voicing our fervent hope that their years together be as free of sin so they will deserve the joy that Adam enjoyed during his short-lived stay in Eden. The *yesharim* benefit from this even today.

ה׳ מָלָךְ יִרְגְּזוּ עַמִּים
When Hashem will reign nations will tremble (Tehillim 99)

אַתָּה כּוֹנַנְתָּ מֵישָׁרִים — *You have established justice.*

◆§ Hashem: The Source of All Rational Laws (*Mishpatim*)

והוא ענין הקדמת נעשה לנשמע כו׳, גם ברש״י ז״ל מה הראשונים מסיני כו׳, ופרשנו עפ״י דברי מו״ז (החי׳ הרי״מ) ז״ל שגם משפטי ה׳ אף שיש בהם טעמים, עכ״ז כל הטעמים ע״י רצונו ית׳ והוא העיקר, והטעמים נמשכים אחר רצונו, וז״ש שהם מסיני, אף שהשכל מבין שכך צריך להיות עכ״ז הכל ע״י שכך גזרה חכמתו ית׳, וז״ש אתה כוננת מישרים פי׳ שע״י רצונו יתברך נעשו משפטיו ישרים וכל העולם מודים ומבינם שישר משפטיו שכל הדעת נמשך אחר רצון השי״ת כנ״ל, וכן צריך להיות ציווי השי״ת קודם לשכל האדם וזהו לפניהם כנ״ל, וכו׳.

With these few words, David *HaMelech* is defining the relationship between rationality (and especially those *mitzvos* such as *mishpatim* that appear to have a rational basis) and the source of all rational thinking, *Hakadosh Baruch Hu.* While it may be tempting to assume that some aspects of the Torah are based on pure logic, in this *pasuk* we are told that, on the contrary, אַתָּה כּוֹנַנְתָּ מֵישָׁרִים, which is translated by *Sfas Emes, You have established* (those laws that appear to be) *justice.* The fact that we perceive many of the Torah's statutes as rational and just, is because You, Hashem, have ordained these laws.

This theme — emphasizing the Divine origin of even the most apparently rational aspects of Torah — is already expressed in the first comment of *Rashi* in *Parashas Mishpatim,* מָה הָרִאשׁוֹנִים מִסִּינַי אַף אֵלּוּ מִסִּינַי, *Just as those stated previously* (the *Aseres HaDibros*) *clearly originated from Sinai, so, too, these* (*the mishpatim*) *originate from Sinai* (*Shemos* 21:1). We reiterate this theme in our daily *tefillos:* מַגִּיד דְּבָרָיו לְיַעֲקֹב חֻקָּיו וּמִשְׁפָּטָיו לְיִשְׂרָאֵל, *He relates His Word to Yaakov, His statutes and judgments to Yisrael* (*Tehillim* 147:19). It is only by accepting the Torah (דְּבָרָיו, *Hashem's*

Word) and Hashem's Stewardship of the universe[1] that we can appreciate the reasoning behind His *mishpatim* and even His *chukim* (aspects of the Torah whose reason is generally not understood).

Most fundamentally, when the Jewish people proclaimed *Naaseh V'Nishma, we will do and we will listen* (comprehend), they indicated their appreciation of the relationship between understanding the logic of the Torah (and the justice of its *mitzvos*) and accepting the Torah itself. It is through *naaseh,* first *unconditionally accepting* the Divine Will that we may merit *nishma, understanding* the reasons for His *mitzvos.*

מִשְׁפָּט וּצְדָקָה בְּיַעֲקֹב אַתָּה עָשִׂיתָ
The justice and charity of Yaakov, You have made.

◆§ Uniqueness Of *Klal Yisrael's* Compassion And Justice

כי בשני הדברים אלו מצינו שנבחרו בנ"י שהאומות מה דעבדין לגרמייהו עבדין לכן חסד לאומים חטאת. ובבנ"י כתיב צדקה תרומם גוי. ולכן אין מקבלין שקלים מהאומות כדכ׳ ולכם אין כו׳ וזכרון כו׳. וכמו כן המשפט שהוא עפ"י דעת השופט ואעפ"כ צריך להתבטל ולידע כי הכל שלו ואין זה באפשרות בטבע רק בנ"י הם כלים לדברים אלו.

While it may appear that justice (מִשְׁפָּט) and charity (צְדָקָה) are universal traits, we may infer from this *pasuk* that these admirable *middos* are unique, to some extent, to *Klal Yisrael.* Thus, *Chazal* discourage us from accepting charity or donations from idolaters for building the *Beis HaMikdash,*[2] perceiving that only *tzedakah* contributed by *Klal Yisrael* is given for truly altruistic reasons.

Similarly, the attribute of justice while apparently universal assumes unique dimensions when practiced by *Klal Yisrael's* judges (*dayanim*). While our judges seemingly utilize their rational judgment in rendering a verdict, at the same time they realize that their decisions are inspired by Hashem. This capacity to render an erudite decision and simultaneously

1. The term דְּבָרָיו may be related to יַדְבֵּר עַמִּים, *He will lead nations* (*Tehillim* 47:4).

2. Refer to *Bava Basra* 10b, חֶסֶד לְאוּמִּים חַטָּאת. Also *Ezra,* לֹא לָכֶם וָלָנוּ לִבְנוֹת בַּיִת לֵאלֹקֵינוּ, *it is not for us and you to build the house of God* (4:3).

accept that the verdict that they had issued is not based on their own wisdom may be unique to *Klal Yisrael.* To the Torah-true *dayan,* the verdict that he issues so brilliantly is nothing but a Divine gift. As this *pasuk* reads, מִשְׁפָּט וּצְדָקָה בְּיַעֲקֹב אַתָּה עָשִׂיתָ, *our capacity for charity and justice You created.*[1] [2]

Traits That Are Embedded In *Klal Yisrael's Neshamah*

כי באמת גם בני נח מצווין על הדינין (סנהדרין נו.) אבל כתיב חקיו ומשפטיו לישראל היינו שבנ״י מכוונים אל המשפט האמת דכתיב (דברים א, יז) המשפט לאלקים הוא ובנ״י המה רק כלים שהקב״ה מנהיג העולם על ידיהם ונגמרים משפטי ה׳ ע״י סנהדרין שבישראל, וז״ש אתה עשית כי עשיית בנ״י הוא בכח סיוע משמים, והם הארות שגנוזים בנשמות בנ״י, דהנשמות נק׳ מעשי ידיו של הקב״ה כמ״ש בזוה״ק, וכדכתיב (ישעי׳ נז, טז) ונשמות אני עשיתי, וז״ש משפט וצדקה כו׳ אתה עשית שאין המשפט על פי שכל פשוט, רק שיש דעת בחכמי ישראל לברר משפטי ה׳, והכל בכוחות שגנוזי׳ בנשמתם, כמ״ש (הושע יד, ט) ממני פריך נמצא, וכן בצדקה ונדבה שנמצא בלבות בנ״י הם הכל כחות הבורא ית׳ וז״ש (משלי יד, לד) צדקה תרומם גוי וחסד לאומים חטאת ואמרו חז״ל (עי׳ ב״ב י:) מה דעבדין לגרמייהו עבדין, פי׳ שאין למעשיהם דביקות בשורש אבל מעשה בנ״י המה בדביקות נשמתם, ונק׳ הכל מעשה ה׳ ממש, רק שהמה כלים להוציא הדברים מכח אל הפועל.

By utilizing the expression אַתָּה עָשִׂיתָ, *You have created,* the *pasuk* is implying that when Hashem created the Jewish people, He embedded in their very *neshamos* the capacity to render justice and be truly compassionate. As Hosea writes, מִמֶּנִּי פֶּרְיְךָ נִמְצָא, *from Me* (My presence in your soul) *your fruits* (accomplishments) *are found* (14:9).

While it is certainly true that the concept of justice is not confined to the

1. In fact, *Klal Yisrael's* unique capacity for rendering judgment — and the fact that it enjoys the Presence of the *Shechinah* in its *batei dinim* (courts) — may be directly related to its great humility. It is precisely because we realize that our accomplishments are nothing more than a Divine gift that we merit the Presence of the *Shechinah* as an integral part of our legal process.

2. The Biblical prohibition of accepting bribes may also be based on this premise. Once a judge has compromised himself by taking something from either party — even if his judgment is not directly affected — he has forfeited his direct relationship to Hashem Who generally graces his *beis din.*

Jewish people (in fact, gentiles are obligated to establish a court system as an integral part of the Seven Noachide Laws), it is also true that *Klal Yisrael* enjoys a unique capacity to derive by its own reasoning a correct assessment of the Divine Will and to render judgment in accordance with Hashem's wishes. This uncanny ability to arrive through one's own logic at the correct interpretation of the *retzon Hashem* is based on our capacity to evoke the Divine Presence that is deeply rooted in our *neshamos*.[1]

מִזְמוֹר לְדָוִד

A Psalm of David (Tehillim 29)

ה׳ עֹז לְעַמּוֹ יִתֵּן ה׳ יְבָרֵךְ אֶת עַמּוֹ בַשָּׁלוֹם

HASHEM will give strength to His nation,
HASHEM will bless His nation with peace.

Written and Oral Law

ה׳ עוז לעמו יתן. זה תורה שבכתב. שאף שנעלמה מעיני כל חי אעפ״כ היא עוז ועץ חיים למחזיקים בה. ה׳ יברך כו׳ עמו בשלום היא תורה שבע״פ שהוא מצד השגת בנ״י מעצמותם כמ״ש וחיי עולם נטע בתוכנו והוא השלימות שנק׳ בנ״י השולמית ע״ש שהם גומרין השלימות. אם כי השלימות רק מהקב״ה שהוא שלומו של עולם שהשלום שלו. אבל בעוה״ז נמשך השלימות ע״י בנ״י. לכן נקראו בנ״י תמכין דאורייתא שנאמר עליהם ותומכי׳ מאושר שהם הרגלים והיסוד שהתורה תהיה נגלית בעוה״ז על ידיהם כנ״ל. ובאמת התורה מתנה בנפשות בנ״י אבל כפי תיקון האדם כך מתחדש לו אור התורה. וע״ז אומרים כי היא לנו עוז ואורה. עוז בעצם. ואורה בהתפשטות התורה כפי מה שיגעים בה כך מתחדש להם בכל עת כמ״ש דדי׳ ירוך כו׳. ולכן כתיב עוז לעמו יתן. ואח״כ כתיב יברך את עמו בשלום. והברכה היא תוספות בהתחדשות התורה בכל עת. כדאיתא היושב והוגה בתורה הקב״ה יושב ושונה כנגדו.

By utilizing two different expressions to indicate Hashem's intimate relationship with *Klal Yisrael* (granting strength and the blessing of

1. Note the similarity between the term עָשִׂיתָ in this *pasuk* and its use in the *pasuk*, וּנְשָׁמוֹת אֲנִי עָשִׂיתִי, *and I made* [*their*] *souls* (*Yeshayahu* 57:16) describing the creation of the soul.

peace), David *HaMelech* is alluding to two distinct means by which we comprehend the Divine Will. On one hand, this is achieved through the Written Law (תּוֹרָה שֶׁבִּכְתָב), which in itself is a great source of strength. As *Mishlei* states: עֵץ חַיִּים הִיא לַמַּחֲזִיקִים בָּהּ, *It* (the Torah) *is a tree of life for those who hold on to it* (3:18). On the other hand, we have the Oral Law (תּוֹרָה שֶׁבְּעַל פֶּה), which is not only studied by the Jewish people but is also the source of our *sheleimus (perfection)*, a concept related to *shalom* (which in this context is translated as complete). Every time that we delve into the תּוֹרָה שֶׁבְּעַל פֶּה and derive new insights (*chiddushei Torah*), we further perfect ourselves. Moreover, we are hardly alone as we study the Oral Law. *Chazal* relate that anyone who immerses himself in Torah is joined by *HaKadosh Baruch Hu*, who is also "studying" Torah along with us. It is this sense of arriving at new Torah insights whenever we learn – and the perception that the *Shechinah* materially assists us in our pursuit of Torah knowledge – that, in reality, is the greatest blessing that Hashem can bestow upon His people.

We reflect this theme by chanting on Simchas Torah, כִּי הִיא לָנוּ עֹז וְאוֹרָה, *for it* (the Torah) *is our source of strength and light*. While, as indicated previously, the Written Law is our source of strength, it is only through immersing ourselves in the Oral Law that the light of Torah can penetrate every fiber of our body. It is through the Oral Torah that we can achieve true *sheleimus*.

While the original source of *sheleimus* (perfection/completion), of course, is *HaKadosh Baruch Hu*, it is only through *Klal Yisrael's* immersion in the תּוֹרָה שֶׁבְּעַל פֶּה that a sense of *sheleimus* can be attained in This World. Thus, we find that the Jewish people are described as being תּוֹמְכִים דְּאוֹרַייתָא, *the support of Torah*. It is only through their immersion in Torah that there exists a basis (support) for Torah – whose origins are in heaven – to be revealed on earth. Consequently, it is entirely appropriate that the beautiful *berachah* enjoyed by the supporters of Torah rebound to our advantage. As *Mishlei* teaches us, וְתֹמְכֶיהָ מְאֻשָּׁר, *those who support it* (the Torah) *will be blessed with happiness* (3:18).

◆§ A Dual Covenant

והם ב׳ הבריתות ברית הלשון וברית המעור. והם ב׳ האותות תפילין למען תהי׳ תורת ה׳ בפיך. ואין עוז אלא תורה ואין עוז אלא תפילין. יברך את עמו בשלום הוא ברית המעור שמחבר ומקשר כל הרמ״ח אברים ובפנימיות הרמ״ח מ״ע. ושס״ה גידין ול״ת. והשי״ת חקק באיש ישראל הכח בפה ולשון להמשיך אור התורה. ובברית לקשר כל הקומה אחר אור התורה. וזהו נק׳ שלום כדאיתא במדרש התהלך לפני והי׳ תמים ע״י המילה עמ״ש שם. והוא המקום ששורה בו הברכה כמו בגשמיות שעושה פירות וברי׳ חדשה כן הוא בפנימיות. ושורש הברכה בעולם ביהמ״ק כדכ׳ שם צוה ה׳ את הברכה. ובנפש המילה. ובזמן השבת והכל אחד.

Alternatively, the two expressions connoting Hashem's extraordinary relationship with *Klal Yisrael* — עֹז, *strength,* and שָׁלוֹם, *peace/ harmony* may reflect the dual covenant that Hashem has established with His people. First we have the בְּרִית הַלָּשׁוֹן, *the covenant of the tongue (speech),* which is exemplified whenever we articulate *divrei Torah,* and through the *mitzvah* of *tefillin* whose observance helps assure that the words of Torah will always be on our lips, לְמַעַן תִּהְיֶה תּוֹרַת ה׳ בְּפִיךָ, *so that the Torah of HASHEM be on your mouth* (cf. *Shemos* 13:9). Moreover, both Torah and *tefillin* are depicted as being עֹז, *strength* (cf. *Berachos* 6a).

At the same time, it is through meticulous observance of the בְּרִית הַמָּעוֹר, *the covenant of morality,* that we are assured of the blessing of *shalom.* While we generally perceive the 248 positive commandments (*ramach mitzvos asei*) and the like number of limbs of the human body as being two entirely distinct entities (which by coincidence are equivalent), for the individual who leads a life of *kedushah* and morality, the two are identical. What greater gift of *shalom* (internal harmony) than the blessed individual whose 248 limbs clearly derive their nurturement from the like number of positive *mitzvos* that they perform.

While the gift of עֹז and the covenant of speech enables us to disseminate the teachings of the Torah, it is only by observing the *bris ha'maor* and by living an appropriately moral lifestyle, that our entire personality — our body as well as our soul — can be motivated to follow the path of Torah.

Overview of Mizmor Shir L'Yom Ha'Shabbos

◆§ Perceiving Our Heavenly Roots On Earth

פי׳ שהתגלות קדושתו ית׳ בעוה״ז תלוי בעבודת האדם. ומ״מ חלק ה׳ עמו ויש להם דבקות בשורשם למעלה בהקב״ה לעולם. אך אם זוכין מתגלה כח השורש גם למטה. וע״ז הוסד כל המזמור ליום השבת. להגיד בבוקר חסדך ואמונתך בלילות. דכ׳ גולל אור מפני חושך ולכן כשאין הקדושה מאירה בעולם צריכין בנ״י להאמין בו ית׳ עד כי יבא בקר. וכן הוא בקדושה המתגלה בשבת היא אות ועדות על הקב״ה גם על כל ימי המעשה. ולכן כשבא השבת ומאירה הקדושה טוב להודות פי׳. וזה החילוק בין הרשעים וכל השורש שלהם שיש להם קצבה מיוחדת ולכן כשהם יורדין יורדין הם עם השורש. וזהו בפרוח רשעים כו׳ להשמדם עד׳ עד. וזה אויביך ה׳ הוא למעלה המקטרגים על בנ״י והם מסטרא דשמאלא. אויביך יאבדו הדבקים בהם מלמטה. כמ״ש בפי׳ סוס ורוכבו רמה כו׳ ע״ש. ואתה מרום לעולם. שאפי׳ בזמן הגלות וחושך הקב״ה למעלה שומר חלקן של בנ״י. ואדרבה חסד הוא שאין האור מתגלה בשעה שהחושך שולט גולל אור מפני חושך. והחושך מתגבר עד תכליתו ואז יאבדו ויתפרדו כו׳. ואח״כ ותרם כראם קרני כו׳. וזה החילוק בין הרשעים וכל בשורש שלהם שיש להם קצבה מיוחדת ולכן כשהם יורדין יורדין הם עם השורש. וזהו בפרוח רשעים וכ׳ להשמדם עדי עד. וזה אויביך ה׳ הוא למעלה המקטרגים על בנ״י והם מסטרא דשמאלא. אויביך יאבדו הדבקים בהם מלמטה. כמ״ש בפי׳ סוס ורוכבו רמה כו׳ ע״ש. ואתה מרום לעולם. שאפי׳ בזמן הגלות וחושך הקב״ה למעלה שומר חלקן של בנ״י. ואדרבה חסד הוא שאין האור מתגלה בשעה שהחושך שולט גולל אור מפני חושך. והחושך מתגבר עד תכליתו וז״ש יאבדו ויתפרדו כו׳. ואח״כ ותרם כראם קרני כו׳.

To appreciate a primary theme of this Psalm, we recall the *midrash* (*Toras Kohanim*) stating that if the Jewish people adhere to a high standard of *kedushah*, it is considered as if they had sanctified Hashem (כביכול).

While *HaKadosh Baruch Hu's* inherent sanctity is in no way dependent upon our personal behavior, this *midrash* may be alluding to the *visible* presence of the *Shechinah* on earth. While *Klal Yisrael's* roots in heaven are always secure — regardless of their behavior — nonetheless, when they are found deserving they merit to perceive Hashem's *kedushah* even here on earth.

With this basic premise in mind — the relationship between our deportment and the manifestation of the *Shechinah* on earth — we gain new insight into this entire chapter of *Tehillim* (and *tefillah* which is recited repeatedly on Shabbos), as we shall elucidate.

לְהַגִּיד בַּבֹּקֶר חַסְדֶּךָ וֶאֱמוּנָתְךָ בַּלֵּילוֹת
To relate Your kindness in the morning and Your trust in the nights.

Not only in the bright light of morning — in times when the kindness of Hashem is manifest — but even in the dark night (of *galus)* when, because of our failings, Hashem's Presence may not be as apparent, we still maintain our trust in Him.

In a similar vein, while we may merit to perceive Hashem's kindness on Shabbos, our *emunah* remains intact even in the comparative darkness of the weekdays.[1]

Consequently, טוֹב לְהֹדוֹת לַה׳, *it is good to express our gratitude and to acknowledge Hashem.* We rejoice and express our gratitude to Hashem upon the arrival of Shabbos, knowing full well that even in the weekdays (and throughout the dark night of *galus)* the *Shechinah* is with us.

בִּפְרֹחַ רְשָׁעִים ... לְהִשָּׁמְדָם עֲדֵי עַד
When the wicked flourish ... they are destroyed forever.

While our roots in heaven always remain secure, when evildoers face judgment, not only their physical presence here on earth but also their very roots in heaven are affected. Not a trace remains of them, as the *pasuk* indicates: לְהִשָּׁמְדָם עֲדֵי עַד, *they are destroyed forever.*

כִּי הִנֵּה אֹיְבֶיךָ ה׳ כִּי הִנֵּה אֹיְבֶיךָ יֹאבֵדוּ
For behold! Your enemies, HASHEM,
for behold! Your enemies shall perish.

Our enemies are not content to merely oppose us here on earth but they

1. A similar theme is voiced in the *Maariv tefillah,* גּוֹלֵל אוֹר מִפְּנֵי חֹשֶׁךְ, *He removes the light in favor of darkness.* At times, Hashem conceals His light because of the moral void and darkness that may permeate the universe.

also challenge us in heaven (seeking to condemn *Klal Yisrael* in the presence of the Heavenly tribunal). This duality is indicated by the repetition of the term אֹיְבֶיךָ, *Your enemies.* At first they are described as אֹיְבֶיךָ ה׳, *Your enemies, Hashem* – forces in heaven that seek to jeopardize Hashem's unique relationship with the Jewish people. Subsequently, they are characterized as אֹיְבֶיךָ, *your enemies* – *Klal Yisrael's* opponents here on earth.[1]

וְאַתָּה מָרוֹם לְעֹלָם ה׳
But You, HASHEM, remained exalted forever.

Even in the darkest days of the *galus,* when the *Shechinah's* Presence on earth may have been veiled, nonetheless, Hashem remained eternally vigilant, safeguarding from heaven *Klal Yisrael's* unique role.

◆§ Invoking the Spirit of Moshe

נסמך פסוק ויתן אל משה לפרשת השבת כמ״ש בשבת יעשה כולו תורה שכן כתיב וביום השביעי שבת וינפש ויתן אל משה. כי בששת ימי המעשה עשה השמים וארץ וביום השבת מיוחד אל התורה ובכל (השבת) [שבת] מתחדש נתינה זו. וכמו כן מרע״ה נותן התורה לבנ״י בכל שבת. כמ״ש מזמור שיר ליום השבת ר״ת למש״ה. וכתיב ואתה דבר אל בני ישראל כו׳ אך את שבתותי תשמורו. כי משה רע״ה נטע בבנ״י הארת השבת. וכחו של מרע״ה מתעורר בכלל ישראל ביום השבת. והוא הנשמה יתירה היורדת בשבת קודש.

It is noteworthy that the first letters (rearranged) of each of the words in the first *pasuk* of this chapter of *Tehillim,* מִזְמוֹר שִׁיר לְיוֹם הַשַּׁבָּת, *A psalm, a song for the Sabbath day,* spell לְמֹשֶׁה, *to Moshe,* implying a link between Moshe *Rabbeinu,* who transmitted the Torah to *Klal Yisrael,* and Shabbos. This relationship is further exemplified by the juxtaposition of שֵׁשֶׁת יָמִים עָשָׂה ה׳ אֶת הַשָּׁמַיִם וְאֶת הָאָרֶץ וּבַיּוֹם הַשְּׁבִיעִי שָׁבַת וַיִּנָּפַשׁ, *in a six day period HASHEM made heaven and earth, and on the seventh day He rested and was refreshed* (*Shemos* 31:17); and (the following *pasuk*) וַיִּתֵּן אֶל מֹשֶׁה, *and He gave to Moshe* (the *Luchos*). Whereas during the six weekdays Hashem created heaven and earth and the entire universe, He

1. The renowned *pasuk,* סוּס וְרֹכְבוֹ רָמָה בַיָּם, *horse and its rider were cast into the sea* (*Shemos* 15:1), may be interpreted in a similar manner. Not only the horse but also its rider – the heavenly force that motivates it to do harm – were toppled at the time of *Kerias Yam Suf.*

designated Shabbos for spiritual growth through immersion in Torah. In the words of the renowned *Midrash* (*Tanna D'bei Eliyahu* 1), שַׁבָּת יַעֲשֶׂה כֻּלּוֹ תּוֹרָה, *Shabbos should be observed entirely as a day of Torah study.*

Just as our bond with the Torah is renewed every Shabbos, so too, our relationship with Moshe *Rabbeinu,* the transmitter of the Torah, is reinforced every Shabbos. On Shabbos we may perceive that Moshe *Rabbeinu* is again transmitting the Torah to us. In fact, one of the Torah's portions that discusses the Shabbos most elaborately commences with the words, וְאַתָּה דַּבֵּר אֶל בְּנֵי יִשְׂרָאֵל, *and you* (Moshe) *should speak to the Children of Israel* (*Shemos* 31:13).

It is well-known that on Shabbos, we benefit from the presence of the *neshamah yeseirah* (additional soul). We may attribute this phenomenon to the spirit of Moshe *Rabbeinu,* which we successfully evoke every Shabbos.

עֲלֵי עָשׂוֹר
On a ten-stringed instrument.

Why A Ten-Stringed Lyre?

כי השירה תליא בזמן. ולכן בכל יום יש שיר אחר כי ההתחדשות שיש בכל יום נותן בשירה כמ״ש ז״ל כי השמש אומרת שירה וזורחת ע״ש בפסוק שמש בגבעון דום. כי בכל יום יש הארה אחרת כדאיתא בשם האר״י ז״ל כי אין כל יום דומה לחבירו מבריאת עולם. ובמדרש קח את הלוים כמה נימין הי׳ בכנור שבע ולימות המשיח ח׳ ולעתיד עשרה בנבל עשור כו׳. ונראה דהלוים מיוחדים לבחי׳ הזמן דיש רק בחי׳ עולם שנה נפש. דצריך כל אדם בפרט ומכש״כ כלל ישראל לתקן המקום והזמן שמיוחד לו בתיקון נפשו. ובנ״י תקנו המקום בכח ארץ ישראל ולכן נתחלק להם הארץ ולשבט לוי לא הי׳ חלק. והלוים מוכנים לתקן בחי׳ שנה לכן הלוים נפסלים בשנה ולא במומים. כמ״ש במשנה כשר בכהנים פסול בלוים. והכהן מיוחד לבחי׳ נפש לכן צריך שלא יהי׳ בו מום. ואין נפסל בשנים. ולכן תליא השיר בבחי׳ הזמן. ולימות המשיח וכן לעתיד יהי׳ שינוי בזמן וישתנה השיר. וכמו כן שבת מעין עוה״ב לכן מזמור שיר ליום השבת כתיב בי׳ עלי עשור.ושבת הוא בחי׳ שיר השירים שכולל כל השירים של ימי המעשה.

To appreciate why this *mizmor* dedicated to the Shabbos day calls upon us to praise Hashem with a ten-stringed instrument rather than the seven-stringed instrument used in the *Beis HaMikdash*, we recall *Chazal's* (*Arachin* 13b) observation that in the Future World the lyre of the *Beis HaMikdash* will indeed have ten strings. On Shabbos, which is a microcosm of the World to Come (refer to our chapter on this topic), it is appropriate that we praise Hashem with a lyre consisting of ten strings.

To expand on this theme, we recall the observation of the *Ari HaKadosh* that since Creation, every day in the history of the universe has been a unique and distinct experience. No day has been identical to any other day. There is no better reason to sing the praises of Hashem than the vitality and renewal that each truly distinct day brings. There are no better emissaries to sing Hashem's praises and play the lyre of the Temple than the *Leviim*, whose mission is confined to a certain period of their lives. (Levites are only permitted to perform their Divine Service between the ages of twenty-five and fifty.)

Inasmuch as the song of the *Leviim* is inspired by the sense of renewal that every day brings, it is entirely appropriate that during periods of significant change — such as the Messianic Age and the Future World — that we adapt the instrument used to convey our songs to reflect those changing times.

מַה גָּדְלוּ מַעֲשֶׂיךָ ה׳ מְאֹד עָמְקוּ מַחְשְׁבֹתֶיךָ
How great are Your deeds/creations,
HASHEM, how profound are Your thoughts.

Thought and Deed (Shabbos and *Sheishes Yemei HaMaaseh*)

והוא ג״כ בחי׳ ימי המעשה ושבת דכתיב מה גדלו מעשיך ה׳ בחי׳ ימי המעשה מאוד עמקו מחשבותיך הוא בחי׳ השבת שניתן רק לבנ״י. וז״ש ביני ובין בני ישראל אות הוא. שהשבת מעיד על בני ישראל כי ששת ימים עשה כו׳. ומצד עשי׳ יש לכל הברואים אחיזה. וביום השבת שבת והוא בחי׳ הרצון והמחשבה ושמה לא יש דביקות רק לבני ישראל. וע״י התבוננות כח הבורא ית׳ במעשה בראשית. נלמד מכ״ש מה מאוד עמקו מחשבותיו כי לעולם המחשבה עמוקה מהמעשה.

We suggest that מַה גָּדְלוּ מַעֲשֶׂיךָ ה׳, *how great are Your deeds/creations,* HASHEM, refers to the Six Days of Creation (*sheishes yemei hamaaseh,* when He created the universe in all of its splendor), while the concluding phrase of this verse, מְאֹד עָמְקוּ מַחְשְׁבֹתֶיךָ, *how profound are Your thoughts*, alludes to Shabbos, a day devoted to *ratzon* (Hashem deriving *nachas* from His completed universe) and *machshavah* (thoughts). It is on Shabbos, the day when Hashem ceased creating and all *maaseh* comes to end, that we can begin to appreciate *HaKadosh Baruch Hu* in the realm of thought as well as deed.

In fact, by juxtaposing deed and thought, the Psalmist may be implying a *kal vachomer* (a conclusion inferred from a lenient law to a strict one, and vice versa). If His deeds are so magnificent, how much more so are His thoughts so profound!

◆§ Qualitative and Quantitative Aspects of Hashem's Majesty

מאוד עמקו מחשבותיך. דיש בחי׳ כמות ואיכות. חצוניות העולם וחכמת הטבע. ועי״ז נאמר מה גדלו כדכ׳ גדולים מעשי ה׳ דרושים לכל חפציהם. אבל איכות הפנימיות הוא רב מאוד ועי״ז נאמר מאוד עמקו מחשבותיך בער לא ידע הוא דור המבול שפשעו בבחי׳ הכמות וחטאו בגופם כסיל לא יבין הוא דור הפלגה שהי׳ להם דעת אבל חטאו בחכמתם שלא לשם שמים. לכן לא השיגו עומק הפנימיות. וחטאם הי׳ בחכמה. ולא זה וזה יש בהם רוח חיים. בפרוח רשעים וכו׳ להשמדם עדי עד כמו שהי׳ בדור המבול. כי הנה אויביך יאבדו דור המבול. יתפרדו הוא דור הפלגה. ולבנ״י מתן הקב״ה תורה ומצות לעמוד על ב׳ הבחי׳. תורה היא הפנימיות. ומצות במעשה להבין כח מעשיו.

From the entire context and somewhat similar themes of *How great are Your deeds HASHEM, how profound are Your thoughts*, we may deduce that the Psalmist is referring to two distinct aspects of Hashem's Majesty. On one hand is the sheer grandeur of the natural world created by Him. About this phenomenon the Psalmist rhapsodizes, מַה גָּדְלוּ מַעֲשֶׂיךָ ה׳, *How great are Your deeds/creations, HASHEM*. Despite the sheer magnificence of the natural world (*teva*) set into motion by Hashem, it pales in comparison to the spiritual realm whose profundity knows no limits. Evidently, with these words the Psalmist is extolling both the *quantitative* aspects of the immense universe created by Hashem (כַּמוּת), as well as its *qualitative* aspects (איכות).

We now continue by enumerating entire generations of mankind that failed to appreciate either the quantitative or qualitative aspects of Hashem's grandeur:

אִישׁ בַּעַר לֹא יֵדָע
The immoral man does not know.

This refers to the Generation of the Flood who could not even appreciate the sheer magnitude (כַּמוּת) of the universe that Hashem created — and consequently sinned.

וּכְסִיל לֹא יָבִין אֶת זאת
A fool does not comprehend this.

This is an allusion to the generation of the Tower of Bavel (*dor haflagah*), who despite their apparent sophistication failed to appreciate the full *spiritual* dimensions (איכות) of the universe created by Hashem. Consequently, they challenged Him by erecting the Tower of Bavel.

כִּי הִנֵּה אֹיְבֶיךָ ה׳ ... יֹאבֵדוּ
Behold! Your enemies, HASHEM ... will be destroyed.

This is a reference to the ignominious and total destruction of the Generation of the Flood.

יִתְפָּרְדוּ כָּל פֹּעֲלֵי אָוֶן
All those who do evil will be dispersed.

This is a clear reference to the dispersion of the Builders of the Tower of Bavel.

While mankind failed to appreciate both the external aspects of the universe (*chitzoniyus*) and its enormous depth, fortunately *Klal Yisrael* has been equipped with the tools which enable it to appreciate both the external splendor of the universe and the sheer profundity of Hashem's creations. On one hand, the *mitzvos* that we perform involving creative action on our part help us appreciate the splendid *physical* universe that He created. On the other hand, it is through (in-depth) study of Torah that we learn to appreciate the *spiritual* dimensions of Hashem's creation.

וְאַתָּה מָרוֹם לְעֹלָם ה׳
But You remain exalted forever, Hashem.

◈ Exalted Above All – Dimensions Of *Kedushah*

כי הקדושה אינו פרישה בלבד אך הש״י הוא מרומם ונבדל מכל נברא כמ״ש ואתה מרום לעולם. פי׳ הגם שהוא בורא הכל ומחי׳ הכל אף ע״פ כן הוא מרומם ונבדל וזה עדות על עצם קדושתו.

By praising Hashem as being מָרוֹם, *exalted,* we are introducing an additional dimension of *kedushah.* While we generally define *kedushah* as *perishah,* abstinence from immorality and other transgressions, there is another (though related) aspect of this critical concept – a sense of being exalted. As the source of all *kedushah,* Hashem remains far more exalted and above any of His creations.

◈ Exalted Even In This World

דאיתא בשם האר״י ז״ל ביציאת מצרים דכתיב אני ולא מלאך כי מרוב טומאת מצרים לא הי׳ יכול מלאך לכנוס בתוכו והקב״ה לפי עצם קדושתו הוא נבדל ומרומם בכל מקום וזה מרום לעולם ה׳ רוממות אתה כו׳ בעולמך.

Chazal (*Yalkut Tehillim* 843) comment, רוֹמְמוֹת אַתָּה בְּעוֹלָמֶךָ, *You are exalted* (even while You are) *in Your world.* Unlike most mortals whose attempts at living a sacred life is often compromised by the necessity of living in *Olam Hazeh,* Hashem – despite being the Source of every living being in This World – remains distinct from His universe. As the *Ari HaKadosh* noted, no *malach* – no matter how exalted – could have survived the rampant *tumah* of Mitzrayim. Consequently, it remained for Hashem, Who is exalted above any *malach,* to liberate *Klal Yisrael* from Mitzrayim, as it says in the *Haggadah,* אֲנִי וְלֹא מַלְאָךְ, "*I (Hashem) and not an angel.*"

◆§ The "*Vov*" *Tzaddikim* Also Attain *Kedushah*

וכתיב ואתה ו' מוסיף. לומר שהצדיקים הדבקים בו ית' גם המה מתרוממין וזוכין לבחי' הקדושה. ומעלה זו יש בישראל על המלאכים שהרי בנ"י ירדו למצרים ומ"מ נשארו בקדושה. וזה הרמז שב' במד' כי למלאכים קדושה א' ולבנ"י שני קדושות. דקדושת המלאך מה שהוא נפרש ונבדל מגשמיות אבל יש עוד קדושה שניתן לישראל שהגם שהם בגשמיות ובלבוש גשמיי אעפ"כ יכולין להישאר בקדושה.

The letter *vov* (in וְאַתָּה) connoting *and* implies that not only Hashem but also another entity (כביכול), the *tzaddikim* who cling to Him, are able, to some extent, to attain exalted levels of *kedushah*. Just as Hashem (rather than an angel) was able to "withstand" the moral abyss of Egypt, so, too, the Jewish people were able to retain their inherent sanctity despite their prolonged stay in Mitzrayim.

Utilizing this approach — emphasizing the virtually unsurpassed *kedushah* of *Klal Yisrael* — we gain new insight into the assertion of *Chazal* (cf. *Yalkut Vayikra* 203) that mortals are graced with a "double *kedushah*", while angels enjoy a single *kedushah*. Although we may share with *malachim* the capacity to abstain from the material pleasures of *Olam Hazeh*, only humans enjoy that other dimension of holiness — to retain their *kedushah* even in a material environment replete with *tumah*.

צַדִּיק כַּתָּמָר יִפְרָח
A righteous individual will flourish like a palm tree.

◆ Evoking Hashem's "*Taavah*"

במדרש מה תמרה יש לה תאוה כן הצדיקים כו' ומייתי עובדא דדקל תמרה ע"ש. ויפלא הלא הרשעים מלאים תאוות. ומפרש בעזה"י כי הצדיקים מעוררים האהבה למעלה בתאותם כענין שנאמר רוצה את יריאיו כו' המיחלים לחסדו. כי הם מתאוים לדבוק בשורשם למעלה כעובדא דאותו דקל שהתאוה אל מקום שורשו וע"ז נאמר נפשי אויתיך בלילה ודקדק בס' הזוה"ק דהול"ל אותך כי אויתיך הוא פועל יוצא. ויתכן לפרש שהם מביאים כביכול התאוה אל הבורא ית'. וזה שבח הצדיקים שהרצון והתאוה בשמים הוא בידם ואחז"ל הקב"ה התאווה להיות לו דירה בתחתונים. וכמו כן בנ"י התאוו לדגלים ואז נגמר מכח אל הפועל.

On this *pasuk, Chazal* (*Yalkut Tehillim* 845) comment, מַה תָּמָר וָאֶרֶז יֵשׁ לָהֶם תַּאֲוָה כַּךְ צַדִּיקִים יֵשׁ לָהֶם תַּאֲוָה, *Just as the date and cedar tree have a sense of desire* (to be productive), *so, too, tzaddikim are motivated by desire.* One wonders about the usage of the term *taavah* – it would appear that *reshaim* rather than *tzaddikim* are possessed by a sense of sensual desire (תַּאֲוָה). If despite this obvious question, the *Midrash* associates the righteous with the attribute of *taavah,* it must be referring to an entirely different form of desire — the capacity of *tzaddikim* to evoke Hashem's "*taavah*" to become even closer to His people. As the Psalmist writes, רוֹצֶה ה' אֶת יְרֵאָיו אֶת הַמְיַחֲלִים לְחַסְדּוֹ, HASHEM *desires* [*to become close to*] *to those who fear Him, to those who seek His kindness* (147:11).

To better appreciate this insight, we recall the *midrash* describing a palm tree that had been planted in a town called Chamsan. Despite the best efforts of all concerned, the tree remained unproductive until a passer-by suggested that the tree's true roots lie in Yericho. Indeed, when the struggling palm tree was grafted with (branches from) its counterpart from Yericho, it bore fruit. Just as the palm tree seeks its true roots, so, too, *tzaddikim* desire an ever-closer relationship with Hashem. Moreover, the righteous not only seek intimacy with Hashem, but they are also able to evoke Hashem's desire for a more intimate relationship with *Klal Yisrael.*

שְׁתוּלִים בְּבֵית ה׳ בְּחַצְרוֹת אֱלֹהֵינוּ יַפְרִיחוּ

Those who are firmly planted in the house of H*ASHEM,*
in the courtyards of our God they will flourish.

עוֹד יְנוּבוּן בְּשֵׂיבָה דְּשֵׁנִים וְרַעֲנַנִּים יִהְיוּ

They will again give forth fruit in old age,
they will be vibrant and fresh.

☙ Beyond Time

[עפי׳] הפסוק ברזל ונחושת מנעליך וכימיך דבאך. פרש״י כימים שהם טובים לך כך ימי זקנתך. ואמר אמוז״ל כי ז״ש מקודם ברזל ונחושת מנעליך. לומר לפי מה ששומרים בימי הנעורים הכחות והמדות במנעל ברזל ונחושת שלא להתפשט לחוץ כך נשאר הנח לימי הזקנה ודפח״ח ... [וז״ש] שתולים בבית ה׳ כו׳ עוד ינובון בשיבה. והנה באמת כימיך דבאך הוא לבנ״י שהם למעלה מן הזמן כי ... הכתוב קורא ימי הבחרות ימים כימיך שמצד הזמן הבחרות עיקר הכח. אבל אם זוכין לצאת מן הטבע והזמן אז כימיך דבאך כמ״ש עוד ינובון. ועוד לשון תוספות הוא.

To appreciate the primary theme of these *pesukim,* we refer to one of Moshe *Rabbeinu's* final *berachos* (*Devarim* 33:25), בַּרְזֶל וּנְחֹשֶׁת מִנְעָלֶךָ וּכְיָמֶיךָ דָּבְאֶךָ, which may be interpreted homiletically, "to the extent that you lock in (guard and exploit well your potential) *with an iron and copper lock during your days* (of youth), *so too* you will retain your strength *during the days of your flow* (i.e., when your strength would generally ebb)." By utilizing our youth to its utmost, and taking great pains to "lock in" (as מִנְעָלֶךָ implies) and preserve all that we have accomplished then, we may be assured that even our older years, when we would generally lose some of our vitality, will be truly vibrant.[1]

How does one achieve this elusive goal of enjoying senior years that are as fruitful as one's youth? The answer lies in the *pasuk,* שְׁתוּלִים בְּבֵית ה׳, by being *firmly planted in the house of Hashem* (during one's

1. This same theme is voiced by Shlomo *HaMelech,* וּזְכֹר אֶת בּוֹרְאֶיךָ בִּימֵי בְּחוּרֹתֶיךָ עַד אֲשֶׁר לֹא יָבֹאוּ יְמֵי הָרָעָה וְהִגִּיעוּ שָׁנִים אֲשֶׁר תֹּאמַר אֵין לִי בָהֶם חֵפֶץ, *Remember your Creator during the days of your youth before the evil days come* (i.e., one's older years), *and those years arrive of which you will say, "I have no pleasure in them"* (*Koheles* 12:1).

younger years), one may be assured that עוֹד יְנוּבוּן בְּשֵׂיבָה, *that he will always remain fruitful* (even during his older years). Only those who live a primarily material life based on nature (טֶבַע) alone will experience the full effect of aging. Those, however, who determine to live a spiritual life that is לְמַעְלָה מִן הַטֶּבַע, *supernatural,* may not be affected to the same extent by the ravages of aging. For them, it is possible to remain vibrant even as they grow older.

In fact, the *tzaddik* — whose roots are firmly embedded in Torah and *mitzvos* during his youth — not only continues to remain vibrant in old age, but actually may strive for and achieve even higher levels of *kedushah.* This thought is indicated by the term עוֹד, which according to *Rashi* (*Bereishis* 46:29) connotes *more* (as well as the traditional interpretation of this term, *again*).

לְהַגִּיד כִּי יָשָׁר ה׳ צוּרִי וְלֹא עַוְלָתָה בּוֹ
To declare that HASHEM is just,
my Rock in Whom there is no wrong.

Returning to the Universe's Pure Beginnings

והיינו כדכ׳ במזמור שיר ליום השבת להגיד כי ישר ה׳ צורי. פי׳ להראות כי באמת שמים וארץ הכל אחד. רק הפסולת ותערובת טו״ר שנעשה ע״י החטא מעבב. לכן הוצרך למטה כל התקונים וכ׳ בכל יום ויהי ערב ובוקר. והשבת לא שלטא סט״א כדכ׳ ויציצו כו׳ להשמדם עדי עד. ונק׳ שבת ששבת ממזיקין כדאיתא במדרשים. ובהסתלקות הסוגים מתגלה הטוב הצפון. וזה עדות כי ישר כו׳ ולא עולתה בו.

By speaking of the need to validate that Hashem is *yashar* (just / upright) and that there is no corruption in Him, we are not referring to *HaKadosh Baruch Hu* Himself, of course,[1] but rather to the universe and, in particular, to the earth that He created.

While no one doubts the innate purity of heaven, we may wonder about the earth. Ever since the first man partook of the fruit of the Tree

1. Refer to *Devarim* 32:4 for a *pasuk* that is very similar to this one: הַצּוּר תָּמִים פָּעֳלוֹ כִּי כָל דְּרָכָיו מִשְׁפָּט אֵל אֱמוּנָה וְאֵין עָוֶל צַדִּיק וְיָשָׁר הוּא, *The Rock, His work is perfect, because all of His Ways are just, [He is] a God of faith, and there is no corruption, He is righteous and upright.*

of Knowledge, the earth became a confusing mixture of good and evil (תַּעֲרוֹבֶת טוֹב וָרָע). However on Shabbos, when we perceive more acutely the destruction of evil (as indicated in the previous *pesukim*), we can attest that even on earth there is only good and no evil.

As confirmation of this approach, we note that in reference to Shabbos, the Torah does not utilize the phrase וַיְהִי עֶרֶב וַיְהִי בֹקֶר, *it was evening and it was morning.* The very concept of *erev* [related to תַּעֲרוֹבֶת, *a mixture* (of good and evil)] does not pertain to Shabbos, a day when the capacity of the forces of evil to cause harm is mitigated. In fact, *Chazal* note that this day is called Shabbos to allude to the cessation (שָׁבַת) of the power of the *mazikin* (demons) to cause harm. As a result of the mitigation of the *koach hara* (forces of evil), the inherent goodness of Hashem's creations emerges on Shabbos.

ה׳ מָלָךְ
HASHEM reigns (Tehillim 93)

ה׳ מָלָךְ גֵּאוּת לָבֵשׁ
HASHEM reigns, He "clothes" Himself in exaltation.

◈ Above Exaltation

גיאות הוא התרוממות. ובוודאי הקב״ה רם ונשא ומתגאה על כל. אבל כמו גודל התנשאות הקב״ה על כל. כמו כן מתרומם ומתנשא על כל בחי׳ הגיאות. שכל התרוממות על הנבראים אין בזה שייכות כלל לעצם כבודו א״כ הוא גאה ורם וגבוה על בחי׳ הגיאות. שכל הגיאות דבר שפל וכלא לגבי רוממותו ית״ש. ולכן כתיב גאות לבש שצימצם הקב״ה עצמו בהתלבשות שיוכל לקבל הגיאות על העולם. ובאמת הוא בעבור בנ״י כמ״ש על ישראל גאותו. ובשביל ישראל צימצם הקב״ה עצמו לברוא העולמות. ולהיות כביכול מקבל גיאות והתנשאות מן הנבראים. ובאמת האדם צריך לידע ב׳ הבחי׳ שהקב״ה הוא רם ונשא ונבדל מכל בחי׳ הגיאות הזה. וצריך ג״כ לידע שאחר כל זה הקב״ה מנהיג ומשגיח על כל. ומקבל גיאות מן העליונים ותחתונים כמ״ש שהוא רחוק מכל רחוק וקרוב מכל קרוב.

To appreciate the primary theme of the opening *pasuk* of this Psalm (and, by extension, of the entire *mizmor),* we need to focus on the term לָבֵשׁ, *He clothed Himself*. Just as clothing ordinarily serves as an external layer to protect and even enhance an individual – but should never be mistaken with the person himself – so, too (כביכול), Hashem adopts the outer raiment of גֵאוּת, *exaltation* for the purpose of governing His universe and especially for the benefit of His people, *Klal Yisrael*.[1]

To expand upon this theme, we know that the very concept of exaltation – in human terms – is unimaginable when speaking of *HaKadosh Baruch Hu*. As we read in the *Shirah*, גָאֹה גָּאָה, *(Hashem) is exalted above all exaltation* (refer to *The Three Festivals*, pgs. 164-166 for expansion of this theme). If despite being above the very notion of haughtiness in human proportions, Hashem still reigns over His universe with great grandeur and majesty, it is on behalf of mankind and especially the Jewish people. It is for the benefit of His subjects that Hashem has been *metzamtzem* Himself (allowed His Infinite Self to be portrayed in finite and almost human terms), so that we mortals can accept His Sovereignty and acknowledge and pay homage to Him.

We may derive two distinct lessons from this phenomenon of גֵאוּת לָבֵשׁ, Hashem's adapting the attribute of גֵאוּת, *exaltation*, to meet the requirements of mortals. On one hand, Hashem is exalted above and beyond any other entity. In this vein, He is described as רָחוֹק מִכָּל רָחוֹק, *distant more than anything distant*. There are simply no words to describe Hashem's Majesty. But, He is also depicted as being קָרוֹב מִכָּל קָרוֹב, *closer than anything close*. Despite His extraordinary stature, Hashem "confines" Himself and "wears" the mantle of exaltation in such a fashion that even mortals can benefit from His גֵאוּת and learn to fear Him (גֵאוּת לָבֵשׁ).

1. As we read, עַל יִשְׂרָאֵל גַּאֲוָתוֹ, *on* [*behalf of*] *Israel* [*is*] *His exaltation* (cf. *Tehillim* 68:35).

לָבֵשׁ ה׳ עֹז הִתְאַזָּר
HASHEM clothes Himself in strength,
He girds Himself.

◈§ Sharing His Strength With Us

ובמדרש וארא שהקב״ה נק׳ מלך הכבוד. מלך ב״ו אין לובשין לבושו והקב״ה לבש עוז התאזר. ונתן לבנ״י זה הלבוש. עוז לעמו יתן ע״ש. רמזו חז״ל כאשר הקב״ה וב״ש צימצם כביכול אלקותו להתלבש בתורה ותרי״ג מצות. התאז״ר גי׳ תרי״ג כן זיכה את בנ״י בתרי״ג מצות התורה שיוכלו להתלבש בחלוקא דרבנן ע״י המצות. וע״ז איתא קוב״ה ואורייתא וישראל כולא חד. ויש אדם לבטל עצמו לצאת מן הטבע להתלבש כולו באור המצות. וליקח ק״ו ממה שצימצם הקב״ה אלקותו בשביל בנ״י.

The *gematria* (numerical equivalent) of the term הִתְאַזָּר corresponds to תרי״ג, *taryag,* 613, which is an allusion to the *taryag mitzvos* that were transmitted at Sinai. Just as Hashem "confined" (a concept known as *tzimtzum*) His indescribable Majesty and His exalted status in a manner that mortals can learn to venerate Him (refer to the previous *dvar Torah*), so, too, He provided us with the ideal vehicles to appreciate His Attribute of Strength — Torah and *mitzvos.*

Drawing the analogy between *tzimtzum HaShechinah* and the Torah even further — we note that just as Hashem enabled us to perceive Him through His Torah and mitzvos, so too, by observing *mitzvos* and studying Torah, we merit our own garments of glory described as *chalukah d'rabbanon* (the garments of *talmidei chachamim*),[1] and the *ohr ha'mitzvos,* the spiritual light that graces those who perform *mitzvos.*

This theme — sharing His Attribute of Strength with *Klal Yisrael* — is also reflected in the Psalm (29) recited immediately before *Lechah Dodi,* which ends with the words: ה׳ עֹז לְעַמּוֹ יִתֵּן, *HASHEM grants His people strength* (in the form of Torah and *mitzvos*).[2]

1. This may refer not only to the distinctive garb adopted by Torah scholars but also to the overall aura and luminescence that is often radiated by them.

2. The renowned saying of the *Zohar* (cf. *Acharei Mos* 73a), הקב״ה וְאוֹרַיְיתָא וְיִשְׂרָאֵל כֻּלּוֹ חַד, *the Holy One Blessed is He and His Torah and the Jewish people are one,* may also allude to the capacity of *Klal Yisrael* to "emulate" Hashem's attribute of Strength by delving into Torah.

There is a lesson to be derived from the very notion that Hashem shares His Attribute of Strength with us. Consider the following *kal vachomer:* If Hashem confines (*metzamtzem*) His Infinite strength in the form of Torah and *mitzvos,* then certainly we should negate our material pursuits and our excess concern with the natural order of things (*teva*) in favor of "clothing" ourselves in the "bright light" of *mitzvos* (*ohr ha'mitzvos*).

Friday Night Maariv

כְּגַוְנָא דְאִינּוּן מִתְיַחֲדִין לְעֵלָּא בְּאֶחָד אוּף
הָכִי אִיהִי אִתְיַחֲדַת לְתַתָּא בְּרָזָא דְאֶחָד

In the same manner that they (Hashem's heavenly servitors)
unite and proclaim Him to be One on high,
so, too, they proclaim the secret of His Unity on earth.

◈ The Secret of His Unity – *Baruch Shem Kevod Malchuso*

כגוונא דאינון מתייחדין לעילא באחד וכו' לתתא ברזא דאחד. פירוש הענין שנקרא רזא דאחד, כי ה' אחד ושמו אחד, פי' ה' אחד הוא יחודא דלעילא שה' אחד ממש נגלה כי אין עוד מלבדו ולעילא השמים אין הסתר וכולם רואים שהוא אחד, ולתתא נקרא רזא דאחד כי היחוד נכסה כי הטבע מכסה להיות נדמה לדבר נפרד ח"ו, ולכך לעתיד נאמר (פסחים נ.) שיהי' ה' שלם ושמו אחד כו' ועתה צריכין בנ"י עבודות רבות לעורר ולמצוא הנקודה הפנימיות שהוא יחוד שמו כנ"ל, וזה יחודא עילאה ית' שהוא שמע ישראל כו' שנכתב בתורה כי במקום תורה שבכתב שם נגלה אחדותו ית', ויחודא תתאי שהוא בשכמל"ו בחי' ושמו אחד אינו מפורש בתורה רק יעקב אמרו לבניו כמ"ש חז"ל (שם נו.) לומר בחשאי כו' שזה תלוי בעבודתנו לברר זאת.

The paragraph of כְּגַוְנָא, *Kegavnah,* originating in the *Zohar* (*Terumah* 134:1), and recited by those who *daven Nusach Sefard* (at the beginning of Friday night *Maariv*), commences by distinguishing between the (public) manner through which Hashem's heavenly servitors proclaim His Unity and the "secret" method through which *Klal Yisrael* performs the same mission here on earth. The reason for the distinction appears to be as follows: Whereas in heaven there are no barriers that prevent His Servitors from perceiving the *Shechinah*, on earth, where it may appear that events follow a natural course, it may at first be difficult to detect the Presence of Hashem. Here on earth, it is very tempting to attribute whatever occurs as a separate phenomenon and to ignore that it is Hashem Who harmoniously orchestrates all that happens. *Achdus* (unity) is indeed a secret which can only be "deciphered" through our assiduous and persistent efforts at *avodas Hashem.*

It is only by appreciating Hashem's Name — His many great deeds and His wondrous universe — that we on earth can pierce through the "veil of nature" that frequently hides the Presence of the *Shechinah.* We emphasize the distinctions that exist between the approach taken by Hashem's Servitors in perceiving Him and that assumed by *Klal Yisrael* from the different emphasis of the first two passages of the *Kerias Shema.* We commence by proclaiming loudly, שְׁמַע יִשְׂרָאֵל ה׳ אֱלֹהֵינוּ ה׳ אֶחָד, *Hear, O Israel,* HASHEM *is our God,* HASHEM *the One and Only,* implying that one can clearly perceive Hashem's Oneness — an exalted level reserved for *malachim.* Immediately, we continue in an undertone with, בָּרוּךְ שֵׁם כְּבוֹד מַלְכוּתוֹ לְעוֹלָם וָעֶד, *Blessed is the Name of the glory of His Kingdom for all eternity* — placing the emphasis on Hashem's Name. This quiet proclamation alludes to the somewhat veiled presence of the *Shechinah,* which can be brought to the forefront through our *avodas Hashem.* In This World, we can only begin to perceive our Creator by relating to His Name — the manifestations of His Presence in the natural world.

To corroborate our contention that the term רָזָא דְאֶחָד, *the secret of His Oneness,* may allude to בָּרוּךְ שֵׁם כְּבוֹד מַלְכוּתוֹ, we recall the origins of that prayer. According to *Chazal* (*Pesachim* 56a), when Yaakov *Avinu* wondered whether there was (ח״ו) another Yishmael or Esav lurking in his family, his children, arrayed around his deathbed, proudly stated, "שְׁמַע יִשְׂרָאֵל ה׳ אֱלֹהֵינוּ ה׳ אֶחָד, *Hear* (our father) *Israel* (Yaakov), HASHEM *is our God,* HASHEM *is the One and Only.*" Upon hearing such wonderful tidings, Yaakov responded by proclaiming, "בָּרוּךְ שֵׁם כְּבוֹד מַלְכוּתוֹ, *Blessed is the Name of the glory of His Kingdom.*" While *Chazal* felt that both the response of Yaakov's children (*Shema Yisrael*) as well as his own reaction (*Baruch Shem*) should be included in the *Shema,* they noted that the Torah only preserves the *pasuk* of *Shema Yisrael.* Rather than omit entirely Yaakov *Avinu's* heartfelt response to his children's unanimous ringing proclamation of their solidarity with the faith of their fathers, *Chazal* ruled that *Baruch Shem* should be recited silently. It is this silent and subdued declaration of *kavod Shamayim* that is *Klal Yisrael's* secret method of attesting to Hashem's *achdus.*

(Adapted from *Likutei Sfas Emes, Vayishlach*)

While one might think that *Klal Yisrael's* method of proclaiming Hashem's Oneness is inferior to that of the *malachim,* we may deduce from the following phrase, לְמֶהֱוֵי אֶחָד בְּאֶחָד, *to be one* (our attempt at proclaiming Hashem's Unity) *with One* (the *malachim's* perception of *yichud Hashem*) that this is not the case. In other words, the Jewish people's road towards recognizing *achdus ha'Borei* (Oneness of the Creator) by His many wonders is in no way inferior to the dazzling clarity through which the angels on high can appreciate their Creator.

(*Likutei Sfas Emes, Vayishlach*)

◆§ Single-Minded Devotion to Hashem

איתא בת״כ (ויקרא ט,ו) זה הדבר אשר צוה ה׳ תעשו אותו היצה״ר העבירו ותהיו כולכם בלב א׳ ועצה אחת לשרת לפניו כמו שהוא יחידי בעולם כן תהי׳ עבודתכם מיוחדת לפניו, עשיתם כן וירא אליכם כבוד ה׳, והוא מתקיים בש״ק שמניחין כל המלאכות להיות מיוחד לעבודת השי״ת, והוא ממש הלשון שכתוב בזוה״ק כגוונא דמתיחדין לעילא באחד שצריכין לבוא אל האחדות מיוחד אליו.

To appreciate another dimension of *Klal Yisrael's yichud* of Hashem, we recall the renowned *midrash* (*Toras Kohanim, Vayikra* 9:6) stating in part, וְתִהְיוּ כֻּלְּכֶם בְּלֵב אֶחָד וְעֵצָה אַחַת לְשָׁרֵת לְפָנָיו כְּמוֹ שֶׁהוּא יְחִידִי בָּעוֹלָם כֵּן תְּהִיֶה עֲבוֹדַתְכֶם מְיוּחֶדֶת לְפָנָיו, *And you should all serve Hashem with one heart and with the same unified objective. Just as He is One in the universe, so, too, your Divine service should be with single-minded devotion.* Leaving behind all of our weekday pursuits (that often divide us) in favor of a united and single-minded resolve to serve Hashem, every Shabbos may be the state of affairs described by the words, כְּגַוְנָא דְאִינּוּן מִתְיַחֲדִין לְעֵלָּא בְּאֶחָד, *in the manner with which we unite* (as one) *to serve Hashem* (every Shabbos).

(*Shemini* 5654)

◆§ Bringing Yehudah and Yosef Together

במדרש (בר״ר צג, ב) אחד באחד יגשו (איוב מא, ח) זה יהודה ויוסף כו׳, כי יהודה ויוסף אינם אנשים פרטיים אבל כל אחד הוא כלל המאחד נפשות בני ישראל, ולכן בהתיחדם כאחד נעשה כל תיקון הצריך כמ״ש בזוה״ק (ח״א רו.) ויגש אליו תקרובתא דעלמא בעלמא, וביאור ב׳ מיני האחדות עפ״י מ״ש בזוה״ק תרומה כגוונא דמתיחדין לעילא כו׳ קוב״ה לא יתיב על כורסיא עד דאתעבידת ברזא דאחד, דיש יחוד בשורש הנשמות למעלה וכמו כן בנפשות בנ״י למטה, ויוסף הוא אחד לעילא ויהודה לתתא, לכן איתא שיהי׳ משיח בן יוסף ובן דוד יהי׳ לבסוף, כי יהי׳ גאולה מקודם בשורש למעלה, ואח״כ יגאלו נפשות וגופות למטה.

Alternatively, the contrasting concepts of יִחוּד לְעֵילָא (*proclaiming Hashem's Oneness above*) and יִחוּד לְתַתָּא (*proclaiming His Oneness below*) may allude to two outstanding personalities, Yosef and Yehudah, who though exemplifying different aspects of *avodas Hashem* join forces. Commenting on the confrontation — and later reconciliation — of the brothers, the *Zohar* (I 206a) notes, תקרובתא דעלמא בעלמא, [*It was a*] *rapprochement of one world with another world.*

Consider the contrasting approaches in *avodas Hashem* between Yosef and Yehudah. Yosef's mission was to be totally separate from his immediate environment,[1] which can aptly be described as יִחוּד לְעֵילָא, *proclaiming Hashem's Oneness above* — from his perspective of being isolated from the world.[2] Yehudah, on the other hand, was *mekadesh shem Shamayim* through his involvement in the secular world, a concept somewhat analogous to יִחוּד לְתַתָּא, *proclaiming His Oneness below.*[3]

1. Elsewhere, the *Sfas Emes* emphasizes the role of Yosef as נְזִיר אֶחָיו, *the one who was separated from his brothers*, a reference to his existence on an entirely different (spiritual) plane than his exalted brothers. Moreover, the Torah (*Bereishis* 39:12) describes his encounter with Potiphar's wife with the words, וַיֵּצֵא הַחוּצָה, which may be translated homiletically, *he was taken outside* in that he was totally removed from the impact of his surroundings.

2. While it is certainly true that for most of Yosef's career, he was employed in a secular capacity, first as Potiphar's aide and then as the Viceroy of Egypt, nonetheless, this *tzaddik* enjoyed the capacity of remaining totally distinct and above his immediate surroundings — even while seemingly interacting with the world at large.

3. Cf. *Sotah* 36b noting that while Yosef sanctified Hashem's Name in private (i.e. while he was essentialy removed from true interaction with his immediate surroundings), Yehudah did so publicly (by exonerating Tamar), which may allude to his capacity for *kiddush Hashem* while involved in worldly matters.

What greater proclamation of *kavod Shamayim* than the fusing of both aspects of *yichud Hashem*. As the *Kegavnah tefillah* continues, קוּדְשָׁא בְּרִיךְ הוּא ... לְעֵילָא לָא יָתִיב עַל כּוּרְסַיָּא דִיקָרֵיה עַד דְאִתְעֲבִידַת אִיהִי בְּרָזָא דְאֶחָד, *the Holy One Blessed is He does not sit on His Throne of Glory until it is done* (the proclamation of His Name) *with the secret of His Oneness*. It is only when those who function primarily in This World (following the example of Yehudah) proclaim His Oneness that Hashem sits on His Throne of Glory (i.e., publicly affirms His Sovereignty).

Just as Yehudah and Yosef jointly affirm *yichud Hashem*, so, too, the two *mashichim* (messiahs), who will emerge from their descendants, exemplify each of these traits. First is *Mashiach ben Yosef*, who will unite the souls (which are rooted in heaven, יִחוּד לְעֵילָא) of *Klal Yisrael*, followed by *Mashiach ben David*, who will bring our bodies together as well (יִחוּד לְתַתָּא). This represents a two-fold redemption, first of our *neshamos* and then of our bodies (*gufim*). (*Vayigash* 5647)

קֻדְשָׁא בְּרִיךְ הוּא ... לָא יָתִיב עַל כּוּרְסַיָּא דִיקָרֵיהּ,
עַד דְּאִתְעֲבִידַת אִיהִי בְּרָזָא דְאֶחָד
The Holy One, Blessed is He does not sit on His
Throne of Glory until it is done with the secret of His Oneness.

Eliciting the Inner Divine Spark

והוא בשבת שכל הנבראים עולים ונכללים בנקודה זאת שנק׳ רזא דאחד שהוא חיות פנימי שבכל הנבראים ובשורש הכל רק נקודה א׳ ונק׳ רזא דאחד, ופי׳ דאתעבידת שנמשך האחדות תוך המעשה וימי העבודה ומלאכה, וכמ״ש לעשות את השבת למשוך הארת השבת לימי המעשה כמ״ש במ״א.

The term רָזָא דְאֶחָד, *the secret of His Oneness*, may allude to the inner Divine Spark that we all share. It is this Presence of the *Shechinah* that links all of Hashem's creation — no matter how different we may appear to be externally. While during the weekdays the distinct and unique aspect of each one of us may prevail, on Shabbos we all return to the Divine Spark that unites us. It is only when we return to this common bond — the Presence of the *Shechinah* in us — that Hashem, in turn, resides on His Throne of Glory. By returning to this inner spark, that the liturgist describes as the רָזָא דְאֶחָד, *the secret of His Oneness,* we may be assured that the following words of the *Kegavnah tefillah* will be realized, וְכָל דִינִין מִתְעַבְּרִין מִנָּה, *and all* [*harsh*] *judgments will be removed from him.*

But it is not enough for this sense of *achdus* to dominate on Shabbos. As the *tefillah* continues, דְאִתְעֲבִידַת אִיהִי בְּרָזָא דְאֶחָד, *only when it is done* (performed) *with the secret of His Oneness,* an allusion to the weekdays, days of *avodah* (*melachah,* work). It is critical that even then, the unity which is fostered on Shabbos remain. As we read in the *Kiddush* of Shabbos morning, לַעֲשׂוֹת אֶת הַשַּׁבָּת, *to perform* (*do*) *the Shabbos,* that the spirit of *achdus* that prevailed on Shabbos should linger on into the *yemei ha'maaseh* (days of "creating"). (*Korach* 5631)

◆§ Negating Oneself To *Klal Yisrael*

ויש ללמוד מק"ו דלא יתיב כו' מכש"כ ששום אחד מישראל לא יוכל לקרב עצמו בלי ביטול לכללות ישראל שעי"ז יוכל להבטל ולהכלל בשורש חיות הכל כנ"ל.

In the foregoing *dvar Torah* we noted that Hashem does not "mount" His Heavenly Throne until *Klal Yisrael* finds the Divine Spark that each of its members shares. From here we may deduce an important *kal vachomer* (*reasoning from less stringent to more stringent*): If Hashem does not sit on His Throne of Glory until the Jewish people elicit the inner Divine Spark that we all have in common, then certainly we can't get close to Him unless we negate our own individual interests to those of *Klal Yisrael.* (Ibid.)

◆§ The Relationship Between *Achdus* and *Kedushah*

דאתאחדת ברזא דאחד. כתוב (שמות לא, יד) ושמרתם את השבת כי קודש הוא לכם, פי׳ קדש הוא לכם לכללות ישראל, ״קדש ״הוא ״לכם ר״ת קה״ל, כי עיקר החטאים גורמים שאין יכולין להתאחד באחדות האמת, והשבת נותן האחדות כמ״ש דמתאחדין ברזא דאחד, ואז הקדושה מתגלה בקהל ישראל, ובאמת צריך כל איש ישראל להאמין כי נמצא בו הקדושה השבת קודש, הן רב הן מעט, כי קדש הוא לכם קאי שאפילו למי שאינו מרגיש הקדושה, כי המרגיש יודע בעצמו, והתורה מעידה קדש הוא לכם לכל איש ישראל, וכפי׳ רוב האמונה שאדם מאמין בקדושת שבת ששורה בו, כך מתגלה לו שיוכל להרגיש הקדושה ג״כ.

Wherein lies the source of the *achdus* that *Klal Yisrael* enjoys every Shabbos? We suggest that there is a direct relationship between the levels of *kedushah* that we attain every Shabbos and the resulting unity that permeates the ranks of *Klal Yisrael.* If the differences that arise within *Klal Yisrael* may well be attributed to our sins, on Shabbos when we are blessed with an infusion of *kedushah,* we are also able to come together. In fact, the first letters of the phrase קֹדֶשׁ הִיא לָכֶם, *it is sacred for you* (*Shemos* 31:14), spell the word קָהָל, *congregation.* On Shabbos, the day when we enjoy an extraordinary degree of sanctity, we can indeed become a unified congregation.

While we may not immediately perceive the enhanced *kedushah* that Shabbos brings, it is critical that we believe that this phenomenon occurs. When the Torah writes, כִּי קֹדֶשׁ הִיא לָכֶם, *because it* (the Shabbos) *is sacred for you,* it is not primarily addressing the individual who already perceives the *kedushah* of Shabbos. Heretofore, such an individual is aware of the special status that he enjoys on Shabbos. On the contrary, it is to the individual who is as yet unaware of the potential of Shabbos to elicit his potential *kedushah* that the Torah speaks and assures him that he, too, may attain unprecedented levels of sanctity on Shabbos. Moreover, there is a direct correspondence between a person's belief (*emunah*) that he enjoys greater levels of sanctity on Shabbos and his ability to eventually perceive his new-found *kedushah.* (*Ki Sisa* 5648)

◆ An All-Inclusive *Mitzvah*

במד׳ (ויק״ר כא, ה) בזאת יבא כו׳ בתחבולות תעשה לך מלחמה כו׳ חבילות של מצות כו׳, אהרן הכהן נכנס בכמה מצות כו׳ שבת (ישעי׳ נו,ב) אשרי אנוש יעשה זאת כו׳. והלא שנינו (ברכות ה:) א׳ המרבה וא׳ הממעיט, ומה ענין חבילות של מצות, אבל הענין שיש מצות כלליות ונק׳ חבילות, כענין השבת שנאמר יעשה זאת בפרט שהיא כוללת כל המצות וכל המעשים מתיחדים בזו המצוה כמ״ש דאתאחדת ברזא דאחד. וכן המילה שנק׳ ברית כידוע, ואלה המצות נאמר עליהם בתחבולות תעשה כו׳ מלחמה.

The expression דְּאִתְאַחֲדַת בְּרָזָא דְאֶחָד may also be translated in the following manner: *They integrate* (all of the *mitzvos*) *through this one mitzvah.* While, of course, all of the 613 commandments are equally significant, some of the *mitzvos* are described by *Chazal* as being *chavilos, bundles,* all-inclusive in nature. For example, the *bris milah,* which is a covenant between the Jewish people and Hashem is such a seminal *mitzvah.* Similarly, the Shabbos (the very foundation of our *emunah* in Hashem's creation of heaven and earth) may also be classified as such a *chavilah, bundle.* (*Acharei* 5638)

◆ Removing the "Veil" from Evil

כולהו ערקין ומתעברין מינה. בפסוק (במדבר כא, א) וישמע הכנעני כו׳ שמע שמת אהרן כו׳ אל תקרי ויראו אלא וייראו כו׳ (ר״ה ג.). כי אהרן תיקן את אשר כתי׳ פרעה שאהרן לשמצה בקמיהם לכן חזר וכיסה אותם בענני כבוד, ופי׳ זה כי ודאי פנימיות בני ישראל לעולם במקומו עומד, אבל ע״י החטא נפגם בחי׳ החיצוניות שלהם והיו צריכין מכסה, ואיתא הוא עמלק ולבש עצמו לבושי כמעני דכ׳ ולאום מלאום יאמץ, ולכן ע״י שנחסר מבנ״י אותו המלבוש ופריסות ענני הכבוד להסתר בהם מע״ר של האומות וסט״א, כן לעומת זה הרויחו הרשעים התלבשות להסתיר עצמם בכח טומאה שלהם עד שביקשו להסתר מפני בנ״י, אך מרע״ה בתפלתו החזיר לבנ״י בעננים כמ״ש בזוהר, וכמו כן בש״ק שיש בו פריסת סוכת שלום הנ״ל, נשארה הסט״א בלי לבוש, ולכך כולהו ערקין ומתעברין מינה כו׳.

To obtain additional insight as to why the forces of evil flee upon the advent of Shabbos, we recall the significant role played by Aharon in shielding the Jewish people from the pernicious effects of the outside world. As *Chazal* relate, the Divine Cloud that *Klal Yisrael* enjoyed in the Wilderness was granted to them in the merit of Aharon. After his passing, this particularly effective form of insulation from the world at large was taken away, allowing the Amalekites, disguised as Cannanites, to attack the Jewish people (cf. *Bamidbar* 20:29–21:1 and *Rashi* thereon). In fact, the ability to disguise oneself, originally enjoyed by *Klal Yisrael*, was now usurped by the gentile world, allowing the nation of Amalek to hide its true identity when attacking the Jewish people.

According to the *Zohar*, Moshe prayed successfully that the Divine Cloud return. In a similar vein, every Shabbos, a day when Hashem shields us with His canopy of peace (הַפּוֹרֵשׂ סֻכַּת שָׁלוֹם עָלֵינוּ), we enjoy His protection again. Just as we retrieve our capacity to bask in the protective confines of the *Shechinah* every Shabbos, so, too, as Shabbos arrives, the forces of evil – which often seek to oppose our efforts at *avodas Hashem* – lose their ability to disguise themselves. Losing their "cover," and consequently their capacity to inflict damage by disguising themselves, the forces of evil naturally depart at the commencement of Shabbos. (*Chukas* 5639)

◆§ The First Two Commandments

הענין הוא דבעשרת הדברות כשאמר הקב״ה אנכי ה״א חל אלקותו ית׳ על נפשות בנ״י ונחקקו הדברים בלב כל איש ישראל כמ״ש ז״ל (שבת קה.) אנכי אנא נפשאי כו׳, וע״ז נאמר לא יהי׳ לך אלהים אחרים על פני, פי׳ על זה האלקות ששוכן בכל איש ישראל, וזה אמת והבטחה ג״כ כי על צורה זו לא יוכל לחול שום דבר אחר רק שצריך כל א׳ להתעורר בכח תורה ומצות למצוא זו הנקודה בלבו, ובאמת בש״ק מתגלה זאת בלבות בנ״י, והיא עצמו הנשמה יתירה וחזרת הכתרים שמחזיר מרע״ה לבנ״י כמ״ש במ״א בפסוק דיבר ה׳ אל כל קהלכם, א״כ בש״ק דמתאחדין ברזא דאחד חל דבר ה׳ אנכי, ולכן בשבת לית שולטנא אחרא כמ״ש לא יהי׳ לך א״א.

As we conclude our discussion of the כְּגַוְנָא prayer, we suggest that there is a common thread between the beginning of this *tefillah* and its conclusion. To appreciate this relationship, we recall that when Hashem proclaimed, אָנֹכִי ה׳ אֱלֹהֶיךָ, *I am* HASHEM *your God,* these hallowed words left an indelible imprint on the *neshamah* of every Jew. In fact, the impression left by the First Commandment was so significant that it became virtually impossible for anyone who ever heard, אָנֹכִי ה׳ אֱלֹהֶיךָ to accept any other deity as his god, as the Second Commandment indicates, לֹא יִהְיֶה לְךָ אֱלֹהִים אֲחֵרִים, *you will never have* (accept) *other gods.* By immersing ourselves in Torah and *mitzvos,*we can be assured that the spark of Hashem that became embedded in all of us when we heard the First Commandment, will never allow any pagan belief to compete for our allegiance.

We allude to both of these phenomena — the permanent Divine Imprint that resulted from the First Commandment, as well as the assurance contained in the Second Commandment that we will never adopt any other deity — in the *Kegavnah* prayer. Firstly, דְּאִתְאַחֲדַת בְּרָזָא דְאֶחָד, we return to the secret of Hashem's Oneness, the permanent imprint of the *Shechinah* that became an integral part of us when we heard אָנֹכִי ה׳ אֱלֹהֶיךָ. As a result of this initial step, we rest assured that no other force will ever cause us any harm. As we continue, וְלֵית שׁוּלְטָנָא עִלָּאָה אָחֳרָא בְּכֻלְּהוּ עָלְמִין, *there will be no other sovereign force in any universe.*

(*Va'eschanan* 5647)

הַפּוֹרֵשׂ סֻכַּת שָׁלוֹם
He Spreads the Canopy of Peace

◆§ Safeguarding the Shabbos

ופרוס עלינו סוכת שלומך. בפסוק (שמות טז, לט) ראו כי ה׳ נתן לכם השבת כו׳, דכ׳ ושמרו בנ״י את השבת, פי׳ שהתגלות הקדושה בש״ק הוא בעבור ישראל, לכן צריכין לשמור הארת השבת, והוא פריסת סוכת שלום עלינו, פי׳ שבנ״י נכנסין תחת זאת הפריסה, והם עצמם המחיצה להבדיל בין הקודש כו׳, כמ״ש במד׳ גוי ששבת חייב מיתה, וכמ״ש במ״א פי׳ בנ״י יהי׳ בן זוגך שהם מיוחדים לקבל השפעות קדושת השבת שלא תתפשט החוצה.

The term פּוֹרֵשׂ may be derived from פְּרִיסָה, a *curtain* (or *veil*; cf. *Shemos* 26:36). The immense *kedushah* of Shabbos pertains exclusively to

Klal Yisrael.[1] As Moshe relates to *Klal Yisrael*, רְאוּ כִּי ה׳ נָתַן לָכֶם הַשַּׁבָּת, *See that Hashem has granted you the Shabbos* (*Shemos* 16:29). The expression וְשָׁמְרוּ בְנֵי יִשְׂרָאֵל אֶת הַשַּׁבָּת, *The Children of Israel shall observe the Sabbath* (ibid. 31:16) may be interpreted in the following manner: *The Jewish people should guard the Shabbos* (ensuring that they alone partake of the immense *kedushah* of this day). Similarly, *Chazal* relate that while each day of the week enjoyed a partner of its own (for example Sunday and Monday), the natural partner of Shabbos is the Jewish people.

Every Shabbos, by serving as a *perisah* (פְּרִיסָה) between the sacred values which we embody and the secular world at large (as we pray, הַפּוֹרֵשׂ סֻכַּת שָׁלוֹם עָלֵינוּ), the Jewish people are ensuring the integrity and purity of the Shabbos. (Adapted from *Beshalach* 5636)

◈ A Replica of the *Teivah* (Noach's Ark)

ש״ק כמו תיבת נח שבימות החול טרוד כ״א בעסקי עוה״ז ובש״ק יש מקום לבני ישראל לברוח ולהניח כ״ז להסתופף תחת צל כנפי השכינה והיא פריסת סוכת כמו שהי׳ נסתר נח בתיבה והוא הביטול לשורש החיות שכל העולם חרב והי׳ צריך לקבל חיות חדש משורש החיים וכן בכל ש״ק כנ״ל.

Just as Noach's *teivah* insulated this *tzaddik* from a decadent world, so, too, every Shabbos the Jew yields his place in the material world for the opportunity to shelter under the protective confines of the *Shechinah* ("canopy of peace"). In much the same way that Noach received a fresh start upon completing his tenure in the Ark, so every Shabbos we are also rejuvenated. (*Noach* 5633)

1. Cf. *Sanhedrin* 58b, עכו״ם ששבת חייב מיתה.

◆§ Protecting Us in the Darkest Moments

בפסוק (דברים לב, ט-י) כי חלק ה׳ עמו כו׳ ימצאהו בארץ מדבר כו׳ יסובבנהו יבוננהו כו׳ יש בכל איש ישראל אלו ההסתרות שהם מכוחות כל האומות ואיש הישראלי צריך לתקנם, ימצאהו בארץ מדבר כו׳ יסובבנהו יבוננהו כו׳, אף שכתוב שבחר בבנ״י מימי קדם חלק ה׳ עמו כו׳, אבל עיקר המציאה הוא בעת צר והסתר מקום חושך אשר איש הישראלי מצפה להתגלות הקדושה בעולם הזה השפל, וזה נקרא ארץ מדבר שאין לו רק הרצון, וכן הוא עבודת האדם בחול וכשבא שבת קודש יסובבנהו בפריסת סוכת שלום, יבוננהו בנשמה יתירה שנתוסף דעת לאדם בשבת קודש וכו׳.

It is in the bleakest moments of our lives (or in the darkest eras of Jewish history) that we particularly crave Divine protection. It is this comforting assurance that we indeed can rely upon Hashem's protection during those difficult junctures of our lives (individually or communally), that we may be alluding to by the words הַפּוֹרֵשׂ סֻכַּת שָׁלוֹם, *He spreads the canopy of peace.*

This same thought is reflected in the Torah's description of the Heavenly protection accorded to us during our journey through the barren and harsh wilderness: יִמְצָאֵהוּ בְּאֶרֶץ מִדְבָּר וּבְתֹהוּ ... יְסֹבְבֶנְהוּ יְבוֹנְנֵהוּ, which may be interpreted, *he will find Him in the wilderness land, in desolation. .. He will surround him and He will grant him insight* (cf. *Devarim* 32:10). In the wilderness (or in the dark moments of our own lives), when it may appear that no hope remains, Hashem will allow us to find Him amidst all the adversity that engulfs us. He then — especially on Shabbos — will surround us with His Heavenly Cloud (סֻכַּת שָׁלוֹם) and grant us insight (יְבוֹנְנֵהוּ) in the form of the *neshamah yeseirah.* (*Haazinu* 5637)

◆§ Protecting Our New-Found Gains

וכמו כן בש״ק, פורס סוכת שלום עלינו, ע״י שיש בו עלי׳ להשורש צריכין להסתיר מפני הרשעים והסט״א, וכמו כן ענין הסוכה בתחלת השנה כשצריכין למשוך התחדשות לעולם צריך הסתר והגנה, וכו׳. אמנם, יש עוד לידע, כי אחר שזוכין קצת לגבור [על היצה״ר, אז צריכין שמירה ביותר, כי הכח שהי׳ בסט״א בא אל האדם והוא בא ממקום טמא שהי׳ בשבי׳ עד עתה, ולכן צריך האדם שמירה, וכן י״ל בשבת ג״כ שכתב בזוה״ק שצריך שמירה, כמ״ש פורס סוכת שלום כו׳, שג״כ הטעם כנ״ל, שכל הדברים יש להן עלי׳ בשבת לכן צריך שמירה, והעצה ע״י תשובה.

The analogy to the *succah* that we employ in this *tefillah* is of great significance. Just as we leave our homes and enter the protective confines of the *succah* almost immediately after Yom Kippur, so, too, every Shabbos we are sheltered by Hashem's canopy of peace. To help us preserve that sense of *hischadshus* (rejuvenation) that we enjoy after the *yamim noraim* on Succos, every Shabbos, as we ascend to higher levels of *kedushah*, we preserve those gains by hovering in the protective canopy provided by Hashem. (Adapted from *Noach* 5642; *Ki Seitzei* 5636)

◆§ The Universe Attains Perfection

הפסוק (בראשית ב,ב) ויכל ביום השביעי, איתא המדרש (בר״ר י,ט) משל לטבעת שחסר בה חותם ע״ש, דאיתא (בר״ר יא, ו) מכל מלאכתו אשר ברא אלקים לעשות, שכל מה שנברא בששת ימי המעשה צריך תיקון, אבל השבת הוא בחי׳ השלום, כמ״ש פורס סוכת שלום עלינו, וזה חותם המלך שאין השלימות נמצא במעשה בראשית, רק השבת משלים הבריאה ונותן בה שלימות, וזה החותם והעדות על המלך שהשלום שלו והוא פנימיות העולם והצורה של הבריאה.

The term *shalom* (traditionally translated as *peace*) may also be related to *sheleimus, perfection.* While each of the creations of the Six Days of Creation may be "perfected" by man (through his assiduous efforts at nurturing the universe created by Hashem — as the Torah states, אֲשֶׁר בָּרָא אֱלֹהִים לַעֲשׂוֹת, *which God created to make* [for us to perfect]), the Shabbos day is already perfect. In that vein, we find that *Chazal* (*Bereishis Rabbah* 10:9) describe this day as the *chosam*, signet ring of the king, the Divine stamp of approval on His creation. It is through the Shabbos day that the universe attains a measure of perfection. (*Bereishis* 5660)

◈ Attaining the Status of a *Malach*

והנה יעקב אע״ה כאשר נלחם עם המלאך וגבר אותו, זה סימן שבא לבחי׳ עומד כמלאך, היינו שתיקן כל השלימות בשלימות, לפי שתיקן חטאו של אדה״ר, כדאיתא (ב״מ פד.) שופרי׳ דיעקב מעין שופרי׳ דאדם, והי׳ צריך להסתלק מן העולם, אבל נתן לו הקב״ה שישראל שנמסר לו שליחות ועבודה חדשה בעולם, והרי הוא למעלה מבחי׳ מלאך, שאין מלאך אחד עושה שתי שליחות (בר״ר נ, ב) והוא עשה ב׳ שליחות בעולם, וזה שרמזו חז״ל (תענית ה:) יעקב אבינו לא מת, הגם דבשם ישראל מצינו מיתה, אבל שם יעקב שתיקנו בשלימות בעוה״ז ונשאר בחיים א״כ יעקב אבינו לא מת, והנה אמרו חז״ל (שבת נח, יד) והאכלתיך נחלת יעקב אביך, כי בשבת כתיב (שמות טז, כט) אל יצא איש ממקומו נמצא שזוכין בשבת לבחי׳ עומדין, והוא בכח הנשמה יתירה הבאה מלמעלה, והיא פריסת סוכת שלם, שבעוה״ז חסר השלימות כנ״ל, שתחתונים אינם יכולים לעמוד בתפקידיו בשלימות, אבל בשבת מתנה טובה לישראל (שבת י,) ויש להם חלק בבחי׳ השלום, נחלת יעקב שלא מת וגמר בעוה״ז שליחותו כנ״ל. (ובמ״א כתב ע״ז) ומעין זה השלימות יש הארה בכל שבת לכן יש בו שביתה, וכ׳ (ישעי׳ שם) אם תשיב משבת רגלך כו׳, אל יצא איש ממקומו, וע״ז אומרין פורס סוכת שלום עלינו.

Whereas in the previous *dvar Torah,* we proposed that the universe attains perfection on Shabbos, we now suggest that each one of us may reach unprecedented levels of *kedushah* on Shabbos, to the extent that we virtually attain the exalted status of an angel.

To support our thesis that we simulate *malachim* on Shabbos, we recall the statement of *Chazal* (cf. *Shabbos* 118a) that any individual who participates in the *mitzvah* of *oneg Shabbos,* merits to enjoy the inheritance of Yaakov *Avinu*. We suggest that the selection of this particular Patriarch is hardly coincidental. When Yaakov prevailed over Esav's angel, he didn't merely secure a historic victory for the forces of good over those of evil — he also attained the status of his arch-enemy (Esav's *malach*). This mortal (Yaakov) became an "angel." Just as an angel is depicted as an *omeid* (one who stands), since he has already attained his full potential – so, too, Yaakov accomplished his sacred mission when he triumphed over the angel of Esav. (It was only by receiving the new name Yisrael – indicative of a new mission – that this *tzaddik* could embark upon the many sacred challenges for the balance of his life.)

We too, in some respect, emulate Yaakov *Avinu* every Shabbos when we reach a personal *sheleimus* unattainable during the week. This theme – that we have scaled unimaginable heights every Shabbos – is also alluded to by the Torah's admonition, אַל יֵצֵא אִישׁ מִמְּקֹמוֹ בַּיּוֹם הַשְּׁבִיעִי, *no man shall leave his place* (i.e., the high level he has attained) *on the seventh day* (*Shemos* 16:29). Likewise, Yeshayahu writes (58:13), אִם תָּשִׁיב מִשַּׁבָּת רַגְלֶךָ, *If you hold back on Shabbos your feet* (i.e., you consolidate your already great gains). Inasmuch as this sense of personal *sheleimus* is virtually unattainable in This World, Hashem graces us every Shabbos with the Divine gift of the *neshamah yeseirah,* which allows us to soar above the limitations of *Olam Hazeh.*

It is this exposure to the perfect ambiance (*sheleimus*) of *Olam Haba* amidst the very imperfect environment of *Olam Hazeh* that we allude to when we *daven* הַפּוֹרֵשׂ סֻכַּת שָׁלוֹם, *He spreads His canopy of perfection.*

(*Vayishlach* 5659; *Yisro* 5652)

An Entirely Different Form of Protection

הקב״ה הכביד לב פרעה כדי שעי״ז יהי׳ הכרח לגאול את בנ״י אף שאינם ראוין לגאולה כדי שלא יאמרו ידינו רמה, וזה ג״כ נצרך לכל איש ישראל לידע כי כל התגברות היצה״ר עליו, הכל לטובה, שע״י שיאמרו (דברים לב, כז) ידינו רמה ולא ה׳ פעל כו׳, עי״ז נגאל האדם מיצה״ר כנ״ל, ואפשר כי לכך איתא שבש״ק צריכין בנ״י יותר שמירה שע״ז נאמר פורס סוכת שלום, כי בש״ק הכל מתבטלין להש״י, כדאיתא (ירושלמי דמאי פ״ד ה״א) ע״ה אימת שבת עליו, לכך לא יש עצה הנ״ל שאין מי שיאמר ידינו רמה, ולכך יש הגנה מסטרא דקדושה סוכת שלום, כי בחול צריך להיות ההגנה ע״י היצה״ר עצמו כדלעיל, וכן הי׳ בגלות מצרים, אבל בשבת זמן גאולה, בא ההגנה מסטרא דקדושה וזה סוכת שלום כנ״ל (בא תרצ״ו, וע״ע חוקת תרמ״ט)

In this *dvar Torah,* we propose that at times we are protected from the adverse effects of our *aveiros* simply because of the grave consequences of any punishment meted out to us. In effect, the sins that we commit and their likely consequences insulate us from immediate punishment. We will propose as well that while this form of protection is also enjoyed by *Klal Yisrael* during the weekdays, on Shabbos, we benefit from an entirely different form of protection, as we shall elucidate.

To illustrate our contention that sometimes we are spared the full consequences of our sins because of the impact that Divine retribution might have, we recall that at some point — when the Jewish people might have been liquidated on the basis of our deviation from Torah and *mitzvos* — we nonetheless were spared, because of the *chillul Hashem* that would inevitably have occurred had that terrible scenario happened. As we read in the *Shiras Haazinu*, פֶּן יֹאמְרוּ יָדֵנוּ רָמָה וְלֹא ה׳ פָּעַל כָּל זֹאת, *Lest they* (the foes of the Jewish people) *say, "Our hand was mighty and it wasn't* HASHEM *Who caused all of this"* (*Devarim* 32:27).

During the weekdays, we may be spared much punishment simply because of the probability that Hashem's catalysts to mete out punishment, would attribute their success to their own prowess, rather than the Divine Will. However, on Shabbos, a day when all of mankind, perceiving the *kedushah* of the day, is less likely to gloat about their success, we can not rely upon the potential for *chillul Hashem*, as a reason to spare us punishment. On this sacred day, it is the *kedushah* of the moment, rather than any possible negative consequences, that shields us from any misfortune. It is the *succas shalom*, the Divine canopy of peace, rather than the grave consequences of our destruction, that protects us on Shabbos. (*Bo* 5636; *Chukas* 5649)

◆§ A Day Without Strife

עשק ושטנה בחי׳ עבודת ימי המעשה, ואח״כ זוכין בשבת לרחובות, והיא מתנה מן השמים, כדאיתא על שבת (שבת י.) מתנה טובה יש לי כו׳, ונראה שלכך אין עליו מריבה וערעורים, הואיל ובא בכח עליון, וז״ש (בראשית כו, כב) כי עתה הרחיב ה׳ לנו, וכ״כ על שבת, פורס סוכת שלום עלינו, ואין מגע נכרי בשבת, והיא בחי׳ הנשמה יתירה שבא בשבת סיוע משורש הנשמה וכו׳.

Perhaps, most simply, when we *daven* these words, we are voicing our firm belief that Shabbos is a day when we can set aside much of the controversy that may often pursue us during the week.

To appreciate the significance of the entirely different ambiance that we enjoy on Shabbos, as well as the reason for the cessation of the *machlokes* that too often permeates our ranks during the week, we recall the classic confrontation between Yitzchak *Avinu* and the shepherds of Gerar (see *Bereishis* 26:19-22). It is clear from the Torah's description of the events surrounding the first two wells that the Patriarch dug (Esek and Sitnah, respectively), that the mere presence of antagonistic individuals thwarted Yitzchak's attempts at finding water. It also follows that his success at finally avoiding controversy while digging the third well, Rechovos, was based on the overt presence of the *Shechinah* — rather than any human effort on his part. As the *pasuk* reads, כִּי עַתָּה הִרְחִיב ה׳ לָנוּ, *Because now HASHEM has expanded* (*our dimensions*) *for us* (*Bereishis* 26:22).

Whereas during the weekdays, we often encounter a great deal of antagonism when dealing with human beings, on Shabbos, the day when Hashem spreads His canopy of peace and when His gift of the *neshamah yeseirah* permeates our very lives, we may rest assured of a more peaceful outcome to our efforts. (Adapted from *Toldos* 5645)

Casting Aside the Limitations of the Natural World (*Teva*)

כי בעוה״ז נסתר הנהגת הבורא יתברך ונתלבש בטבע, אבל המאמין בו יתברך ומשליך את הטבע זוכה להתגלות לו הארה מעולם הבא כדאיתא (זה״ק ח״ג קסט.) שעוה״ב הוא היפוך מעוה״ז וכפי ביטול הטבע מתגלה הארה מעולם העליון ולכן בש״ק שהוא מעין עוה״ב צריכין לבטל מעשה והמלאכה כי ששת ימי המעשה מתלבש ההנהגה בהטבע.

While living in This World, it is generally difficult to perceive the presence of the *Shechinah* and, in particular, His active management of the universe. However, those individuals who are determined to cast off the constraints set by the natural world, may merit to appreciate a scintilla of the World to Come while still alive in This World.

What better opportunity to yield some of This World's material pleasures in favor of the intense spirituality of *Olam Haba* than *Shabbos kodesh.* This feeling of intense closeness to Hashem that we experience every Shabbos is stated so well by the *pasuk,* שְׁבוּ אִישׁ תַּחְתָּיו, *Let every man stay in his place* (*Shemos* 16:29). Rather than go out and confront the many challenges of the natural world, on Shabbos we are perfectly content to remain where we are and rest securely under the canopy of peace unfurled by Hashem. If we determine to pursue such a path, we may be assured that we will be able to overcome the limitations of This World and perceive a taste of the World to Come, on Shabbos, which itself is known as מֵעֵין עוֹלָם הַבָּא, a microcosm of the World to Come.

(*Lech Lecha* 5647)

☙ A Product of Our Aspirations

כי הארה עוה״ב א״א לקבל בעוה״ז ומ״מ יש הארה גם בעוה״ז לצדיקים שחופף עליהם כמ״ש (בראשית כח,יג) נצב עליו, וכ״כ ויהי נועם ה׳ עלינו, וכן בש״ק פורס סוכת שלום עלינו כענין שאומרים עושה שלום במרומיו הוא יעשה שלום עלינו, כי למעלה יכולין לקבל השלימות ובתחתונים נאמר עלינו, שצריך האדם לתקן עצמו כפי כחו שיתקרב להיות הארה עליונה חופפת עליו.

To appreciate yet another dimension of the canopy of peace that pervades the Shabbos, we focus on the term עָלֵינוּ, which quite literally means, *over us* (הַפּוֹרֵשׂ סֻכַּת שָׁלוֹם עָלֵינוּ). The rarefied ambiance of Shabbos and the *sheleimus* and *shalom* which we enjoy on that extraordinary day, in reality, are well beyond anything that we could justifiably anticipate. On the contrary, these attributes are much more indicative of the milieu of the angels on high, than of mortals here on earth. Yet, by aspiring to levels of *kedushah* ordinarily well out of our reach, we may be blessed that some aspect of the world of intense spirituality that the *malachim* enjoy may be experienced by us as well. As we conclude the *Kaddish,* עֹשֶׂה שָׁלוֹם בִּמְרוֹמָיו הוּא יַעֲשֶׂה שָׁלוֹם עָלֵינוּ, *He who creates peace in His Heights, may He make peace over us.*

Similarly, by aspiring to come close to Hashem all week long — to reach the perfection and *shalom* which ordinarily is the lot of Hashem's celestial servitors — we merit that on Shabbos, Hashem spreads His canopy of peace *over us,* allowing us to pursue spiritual levels unimaginable during the week.

(*Vayeitzei* 5647)

◆§ Parallels Between Yosef and *Klal Yisrael*

בפסוק (בראשית לז, ג) וישראל אהב את יוסף כו׳ בזוה״ק (ח״א קפב:) דורש על הקב״ה שבחר בנו ולכן נתקנאו בנו האומות ע״ש, ויש לפרש לפ״ז סיום הפסוק כי בן זקונים, היינו שישראל עלו במחשבה מיומין עתיקין קודם שנברא העולם, כמ״ש חז״ל בראשית בשביל ישראל שנקראו ראשית, ועשה לו כתונת פסים הוא מה שהקב״ה פורס סוכת שלום עלינו.

We may draw a parallel between the canopy of peace that Hashem extends every Shabbos and the *kesones pasim* (the silk coat) that Yaakov prepared for Yosef. Just as Yosef is depicted as being a *ben zekunim,* allegorically translated, *an oldest child* (referring to his position of being first and foremost in his father's thoughts), so, too, the Jewish people — whose emergence was already planned before the Six Days of Creation — may be depicted as the eldest child of Hashem. Pursuing the analogy between Yosef and *Klal Yisrael* even further, we suggest that just as the *kesones pasim* served to distinguish Yosef from his brethren, so does the canopy of peace that we enjoy every Shabbos distinguishe us from mankind at large. (Adapted from *Likutim Vayeishev*)

והם ב׳ מיני עבודות, השבטים הכינו עצות להיות חומות מפסיקין, ויוסף הכין מקום לסמות עיניהם של הרשעים שלא יוכלו להסתכל ולמנוע האור מן הצדיקים, והשבת מתקיים מעין ברכת יוסף שהקב״ה פורס סוכת שלום עלינו.

Continuing on a similar theme, we note the unique capacity of Yosef *HaTzaddik* to deflect any of the harm that frequently is associated with an *ayin hara.* Whereas Yosef's brothers, the *shevatim,* were actively engaged in seeking methods to conceal their *kedushah* from the outside world, Yosef, on the other hand, enjoyed the extraordinary propensity of being virtually immune from the glare and scrutiny of mankind. In Yaakov's words, בֵּן פֹּרָת עֲלֵי עָיִן, which may be interpreted, [*Yosef*] *is a fruitful son who is above* (shielded from) *the* [*evil*] *eye* (cf. *Bereishis* 49:22). It is this attribute of Yosef that is shared by the Jewish people every Shabbos — being protected from mankind's enmity and potential jealousy — and that we allude to when we refer to the סֻכַּת שָׁלוֹם, *canopy of peace*, that we enjoy every Shabbos. (*Vayechi* 5646)

◆§ Returning to Torah

כ׳ (שמות כ, יא) ששת ימים עשה ה׳ כו׳ וביום השביעי שבת כו׳, ואיתא באוה״ח הקדוש כי הקב״ה נתן כח הבריאה על ששה ימים, ובש״ק חוזר הארה חדשה על קיום ששה ימים אחרים, ע״ש פרשת בראשית, והן הדברים אשר דברנו כי קיום הנבראים הם ע״פ משפטי התורה, וסדר המיוחד לכל הדברים בשורש העליון והוא בחי׳ השבת, לכן בשבת ניתנה תורה לישראל (שבת פו:) פי׳ שהתנהגות כל העולם במשפטי התורה, הוא ענין השבת, ובימי המעשה עבודת האדם לקבל עול מלכותו ית׳, וכפי הכנה זו זוכה בשבת לתורה, והוא ענין פריסת סוכת שלום, שהקב״ה פורס עלינו בשבת, כי שלום הוא במקום שאין מחלוקת, כמו שמתגלה בשמים כבוד מלכותו ית׳ בלי סטרא אחרא כלל, כדאיתא (זה״ק ח״ב קלה:) ולית שולטנא אחרא בכ״ע.

To appreciate yet another dimension of the *succas shalom* that we benefit from on Shabbos, we recall the renowned observation of the *Ohr HaChaim HaKadosh*: The Torah always describes Creation as a process that lasted for six days (שֵׁשֶׁת יָמִים) and then had to be renewed on Shabbos, rather than something that occurred *in* six days (בְּשֵׁשֶׁת יָמִים). In other words, the Torah is implying that each Shabbos — upon the completion of a six-day cycle — Hashem rests and renews the universe for another six days.

How does this rejuvenation of heaven and earth occur? Undoubtedly, through Torah. Just as the Torah was originally given on Shabbos, so, too, every Shabbos, upon the conclusion of a week dedicated to *avodas Hashem,* we return to the ambiance of *Kabbalas HaTorah.* At Sinai, it was made abundantly clear to all of mankind that there is no power on earth or in heaven that can challenge *HaKadosh Baruch Hu.* Likewise, every Shabbos, we again affirm our belief in the Omnipotence of Hashem by describing the *succas shalom, canopy of peace* that He provides for us. It is this ambiance of complete peace and serenity, in which no force dares to challenge the *Shechinah,* that we enjoy every Shabbos. (*Yisro* 5636)

◆§ Being a Part of the Heavenly Shabbos

אך את שבתותי, מדקדקין מאי אך, ויש לומר פי׳ שבתותי שלמעלה בשמים, ובני ישראל יש להם חלק בזה כמ״ש פורס סוכת שלום עלינו, פרס הוא חלק, וכמ״ש בזוה״ק כי בשבת יש השתתפות ברוחא דנחתא מלעילא ומתענג בתענוגי שבת ע״ש בפ׳ ויקהל, וכדכתיב ביני וביניכם, וזהו לשון אך חלק.

When introducing one of the most elaborate descriptions of Shabbos, the Torah writes, אַךְ אֶת שַׁבְּתֹתַי תִּשְׁמֹרוּ, *However, you should observe My Sabbaths* (*Shemos* 31:13). By utilizing the term אַךְ, which is frequently interpreted by *Chazal* to mean חֵלֶק, *a part of* (cf. *Pesachim* 5a), the Torah is implying that despite our status as mortals residing here on earth, we nonetheless are able to enjoy a portion of Hashem's Sabbath. According to this interpretation, the *pasuk* reads, *observe a portion of My Sabbaths* (as mortals we will merit to keep a portion of Hashem's Shabbos).

The expression הַפּוֹרֵשׂ סֻכַּת שָׁלוֹם עָלֵינוּ may also allude to our participation in Hashem's Shabbos. Assuming that פּוֹרֵשׂ is related to פְּרָס, *a portion* (as in פְּרוּסָה, *a piece*), we are acknowledging (and expressing our gratitude) that Hashem has allowed us to partake, in some fashion, in His Shabbos.

Just as we participate in שַׁבְּתֹתַי, the Shabbos of Hashem, so does He also derive great *nachas* from our efforts at observing and honoring the Shabbos. According to the *Zohar*, (*Parashas Vayakhel* 204b), *Hakadosh Boruch Hu* takes delight as we perform the *mitzvah* of *oneg Shabbos, delighting the Shabbos.*

This "symbiotic" relationship, whereby we participate in His Shabbos and He, in turn, "takes part" in our *oneg Shabbos*, may be alluded to by the Torah's description of Shabbos as אוֹת הִיא בֵּינִי וּבֵינֵיכֶם, *a sign between Myself and you* (*Shemos* 31:13). What greater indication of the extraordinary relationship that exists between the Jewish people and *HaKadosh Baruch Hu* than the capacity of each of the partners to share in each other's celebration of Shabbos.

(*Ki Sisa* 5645; *Korach* 5654)

בפסוק (שמות לא, יג) אך את שבתותי תשמורו כו׳, חז״ל אמרו (פסחים ה.) אך חלק, דכתיב (שם) אות היא ביני וביניכם, א״כ השבת הוא ממוצע, ויש בו חלק ברוחניות ובגשמיות, כמ״ש בזוה״ק ויקהל בפסוק ושמרו בני ישראל את השבת ההוא רוחא אתפשטותא דההוא נקודה כו׳ אתענג מעילא ומתתא ע״ש ד׳ ר״ד ע״ב באורך, א״כ א״ש אך חלק, שזה החלק שלמטה צריך שמירה, וכן אומרים בתפלה פורס סוכת שלום עלינו, מלשון פרס וחלק שיש לנו בסוכת שלום, וגם לפי הפשוט מאחר שהשבת הוא ברית א״כ הוא ממוצע בין עליונים לתחתונים ולכן נקרא שלום כי באמת עוה״ז מהופך מעולם העליון, רק בשבת יש בו התאחדות לעליונים עם התחתונים ונק׳ יום מנוחה ושלום, לכן מצוה בשבת להתענג באכילה ושתי׳.

In this light, we may derive additional insight into the Torah's description of Shabbos as a *bris*. By linking the *Shechinah* and *Klal Yisrael*, the Shabbos is in effect serving as a true covenant. Likewise, we can now better appreciate why the protective canopy provided by Hashem is depicted as a *succas shalom*. What more effective means of ensuring an environment of peace than bringing together heaven and earth, as the Shabbos does.

Moreover, with this approach, we can understand why the Torah insists that we *guard* the Shabbos, as the expression אַךְ אֶת שַׁבְּתֹתַי תִּשְׁמֹרוּ literally means. It is this Presence of the *Shechinah* here on earth that we enjoy on Shabbos that must be cherished, treasured and truly guarded.

(Adapted from *Ki Sisa* 5648, 5645, 5650)

The "Tools" Which Enable Us to Absorb the Gift of Shabbos

במדרש (במד״ר רפכ״א) גדול השלום שניתן לפינחס שאין עולם מתקיים רק בשלום כלי מחזיק ברכה כו׳, כי בשבת השי״ת פורס סוכת שלום עלינו דאיתא (שבת י:) מתנה טובה יש לי כו׳ לך והודיעם, כי לבד מתנה גנוזה השבת שנתן לנו הבורא ית׳ נותן לנו ג״כ הכנה שנוכל לקבל הארת השבת והוא פריסת סוכת שלום הנ״ל, כי אין עוה״ז מוכן לקבל הארה עליונה רק ע״י הנקודה שלימות שנתן לנו השי״ת והוא הנשמה יתירה שע״ז אמר לך והודיעם הוא התקשרות ודביקות הדעת להיות מוכן לקבל הארת השבת.

To appreciate yet another dimension of the canopy of peace which Hashem spreads every Shabbos, we recall the renowned *Chazal* describing

Shabbos as a heavenly gift which Hashem grants to *Klal Yisrael* (refer to our chapter on "The Gift of Shabbos"). But Hashem didn't merely provide us with the gift of Shabbos. He also gave us the "tools", in the form of the *neshamah yeseirah,* and prepared us thoroughly to be able to utilize such a gift to full advantage.

The pithy expression הַפּוֹרֵשׂ סֻכַּת שָׁלוֹם, which (in this context) may be translated as *He spread His canopy of perfection* (*sheleimus*), alludes to the perfect Divine Spark (*neshamah yeseirah*) that Hashem grants us every Shabbos along with the gift of Shabbos itself.

(*Pinchas* 5639)

◈ An Unearned Gift (as Implied in the Term *Yerushalayim*)

במדרש כי הכהונה הי' עתיד להיות משם ואח"כ ניתן לאברהם אע"ה, עוד שם כי שם קרא לירושלים שלם ואברהם יראה כמ"ש ויקרא כו' המקום כו' ה' יראה כו' ע"ש פ' לך לך, כי שם לא זכה ע"י מעשיו רק שהי' נבחר לכהונה, וזה בחי' שלום שהקב"ה שמו שלם שהוא שלימות הכל, והכלל כי הנקודה ממנו ית' שמחי' כל נק' שלום, ולכך כלי מחזיק ברכה הוא להיות בנקודה זו והיא נק' שבת ולכך ויברך כו' כי מחזיק ברכה כנ"ל, וזה פורס סוכת שלום כי בשבת יש הארה מהשי"ת במתנה בלי עבודה כמ"ש מתנה גנוזה כו', ואברהם אע"ה חידש זה לזכות ע"י עבודה וז"ש שנק' יראה שע"י היראה יזכה אדם לבחי' אהבה הבא במתנה כנ"ל.

By examining closely the term *Yerushalayim* (which is the final term in the *berachah*, הַפּוֹרֵשׂ סֻכַּת שָׁלוֹם עָלֵינוּ וְעַל כָּל עַמּוֹ יִשְׂרָאֵל וְעַל יְרוּשָׁלָיִם, *He spreads His canopy of peace over us, and over all of His people Israel and over Jerusalem*), we notice that it is comprised of two distinct terms, *yeru* (related to *yirah, fear of Hashem*) and *shalem (perfection).* This in turn alludes to two *tzaddikim,* Avraham and Shem (the son of Noach), who named the city Yireh (related to *yirah,* fear) and Shalem, respectively. Whereas Avraham deserved by virtue of his fear of Hashem all that Hashem granted him (and thus appropriately described the Holy City as ה' יִרְאֶה), Shem, though righteous in his own right, characteristically called the city Shalem, that sacred site which is graced by a Divine gift of perfection (*sheleimus*).

It is this Divine gift of *sheleimus* that we enjoy every Shabbos and that we describe as פּוֹרֵשׂ סֻכַּת שָׁלוֹם, *He* (Who is the Source of all Perfection) *spreads a canopy of perfection*. However, to benefit from this Divine gift on Shabbos, we must adhere closely to the message of the other component of the term Yerushalayim, *yirah*. It is through the fear of Hashem that we demonstrate during the week that we merit the gift of Shabbos. (*Pinchas* 5631)

◌§ Loving Us Despite Our Failings

וזהו ג״כ בש״ק, פורס סוכת שלום, שג״כ מתנה לישראל כמ״ש (שבת י.) מתנה טובה בבית גנזי כו׳ שמתגלה בשבת אהבתו ית׳ לבנ״י, כמ״ש ורצה בנו ושבת קדשו באהבה וברצון הנחילנו כו׳, וזה הוא מתנה לבנ״י.

Assuming (as we have in the preceding *divrei Torah*) that this expression (הַפּוֹרֵשׂ סֻכַּת) alludes to the Divine grant of *sheleimus* (perfection) that we all enjoy every Shabbos, we gain new appreciation of the nature of the gift of Shabbos. In reality, despite our best efforts at preparation for the advent of Shabbos, as Shabbos arrives we are far from perfect. If, nonetheless, despite our shortcomings, Hashem grants us some aspect of His Perfection on Shabbos, this is a testament to His undiluted and eternal love for *Klal Yisrael*, which is not affected even by our gravest sins.

This theme is reiterated twice in the Friday evening *Kiddush*. Firstly, when we say, וְרָצָה בָנוּ, *He graced us*, and subsequently, וְשַׁבַּת קָדְשׁוֹ בְּאַהֲבָה וּבְרָצוֹן הִנְחִילָנוּ, *and He bequeathed us His Holy Shabbos, with love and grace*. (*Pinchas* 5634)

◆§ The Perfect Day, the Perfect People, the Perfect City and Land

כי הקב״ה עושה שלום בעולם שנה נפש, שיש בכל מקום נטיעות מיוחדים לאותו מקום, וארץ ישראל בכח ביהמ״ק היתה עושה כל מינים כמ״ש לא תחסר כל בה, ובזמן כל יום כו׳ (סוטה מט.) והשבת עושה שלום, ובנפשות בנ״י מקבלין השלימות, ובשבת קודש מתאספין כל הג׳ כמ״ש הפורס סוכת שלום עלינו ועל ירושלים.

By juxtaposing the three concepts of Shabbos (the only occasion when this *berachah* is recited), *Klal Yisrael* (עַמּוֹ יִשְׂרָאֵל) and Yerushalayim, we are alluding to the best sources of perfection (to the extent that it can exist in This World), as we shall elucidate.

If there is a land that embodies perfection, it is *Eretz Yisrael*, which the Torah describes in the following words, לֹא תֶחְסַר כֹּל בָּהּ, (*a land*) *in which you will lack nothing* (*Devarim* 8:9). [The Torah's description of *Eretz Yisrael* is particularly true for Yerushalayim which is the spiritual core of *Eretz Yisrael.*] Similarly, no nation better represents the ideal of *sheleimus* than *Klal Yisrael.* This is especially so on Shabbos, which is frequently depicted as a day of *shalom* and *sheleimus.* (*Korach* 5651)

◆§ A Taste of the World to Come's Infinite Reward

כו׳, ביאור הענין, כי השי״ת במדת טובו הי׳ נותן לצדיקים כל טוב גם בעוה״ז, אבל כי עוה״ב א״א להיות רק אחר כל השלימות, לאשר הוא הטוב בכל מיני השלימות, ועבודת האדם בעוה״ז לסדר הפרקים, ובשלימות המנורה אז מאיר אור העליון, ולכן השכר בעקב אחר כל תיקון השלם, אכן מתנה טובה נתן השי״ת לבנ״י (שבת י.) והוא השבת, שיש בו מעין עוה״ב, ע״י ביטול המלאכה נותן לבנ״י הארה משלימות שלעתיד וע״ז נאמר פורס סוכת שלום.

It is well-known that we are generally not rewarded for the *mitzvos* that we have performed in This World (cf. *Chulin* 142a). Perhaps the justification for this principle is that almost intrinsically, the abundant reward of *Olam Haba* (which far surpasses anything that we could benefit from in This World) can only be attained after a lifetime that is well spent in *Olam Hazeh.* As the Torah prefaces its description of the many blessings which await those who faithfully obey the Torah, וְהָיָה עֵקֶב תִּשְׁמְעוּן, translated in this context: *the end result of your listening* (*and observing*) will be these *berachos* that will be enjoyed at the end of a lifetime of *avodas Hashem.*

However, on Shabbos, which is described as מֵעֵין עוֹלָם הַבָּא, *a microcosm of the World to Come* (*Berachos* 57a, refer to our chapter on this topic), we are permitted a taste of the infinite reward that awaits us in the future. It is this sampling of *Olam Haba's* treasures that is described as הַפּוֹרֵשׂ סֻכַּת שָׁלוֹם, *spreads the canopy of perfection,* that in some small measure Hashem shares with us on Shabbos. (*Eikev* 5638)

◆§ From Hashem's "Mouth"

וע״ז כ׳ (משלי ב, ו) ה׳ יתן חכמה, אבל מפיו דעת ותבונה היא בחי׳ התורה שנק׳ שמים, והיא הנהגה פנימיות שלא נתגלה בעולם רק לבנ״י, וכמ״ש במד׳ המשל בא בנו ונתן לו פרוסה מתוך פיו, והיא אות השבת שנתן לנו השי״ת כי בימי המעשה ההנהגה ע״פ התלבשות הטבע כמו שהי׳ בכל יום מעשה חדשה, והגם שהי׳ במאמרו ית׳ רק שנתלבש במעשה, לכן כ׳ והארץ נתן בתוספת ו׳ כי וודאי יש בארץ ג״כ המשכה כמ״ש ה׳ בחכמה יסד ארץ אבל בשבת לא הי׳ רק ויברך ויקדש, ולכן אומרים פורס סוכת שלום עלינו והיא ממש כמאמרם ז״ל פרוסה מתוך פיו כביכול.

Taken most literally (and with an appropriate sense of awe and reverence), the term פּוֹרֵשׂ most closely resembles the word פְּרוּסָה, *a piece* (of bread) that has been plucked from an individual's mouth (and has already been chewed). כביכול (*if one were permitted to say*), when we recite הַפּוֹרֵשׂ סֻכַּת שָׁלוֹם, we are stating that Shabbos is a gift emanating from Hashem's "Mouth"! This sense of rare intimacy — and of complete detachment from anything in the natural world — is primarily used to describe the manner through which Hashem gave us the Torah. As we read in *Mishlei* (2:6), כִּי ה׳ יִתֵּן חָכְמָה מִפִּיו דַּעַת וּתְבוּנָה, (*while*) *HASHEM grants wisdom, it is from His mouth that knowledge and understanding are derived.* Whereas the entire natural world was created by Hashem in the Six Days of Creation, *HaKadosh Baruch Hu,* in His infinite wisdom, decreed that the universe be generally governed by natural principles that He instituted at that time. However, on Shabbos, a day which benefits from Hashem's *direct* blessings (as it says, וַיְבָרֶךְ אֱלֹהִים אֶת יוֹם הַשְּׁבִיעִי, *God blessed the seventh day*), we enjoy an intimacy with Him unlike anything that we possibly could benefit from during the week. In the same manner that through Torah we may transcend many of the parameters and limitations of the natural world, so too, on Shabbos, the day that we partake of the "piece of bread from Hashem's Mouth." We may overcome any of these natural barriers and enjoy an intimacy with Him unlike anything that we could possibly strive for during the week.

This theme which is alluded to by the words הַפּוֹרֵשׂ סֻכַּת שָׁלוֹם is more explicitly stated in the following *pasuk,* יִפְתַּח ה׳ לְךָ אֶת אוֹצָרוֹ הַטּוֹב אֶת הַשָּׁמַיִם, *HASHEM will open for you His treasure house of goodness, the heavens ...* (*Devarim* 28:12). It is this sense that our blessings flow *directly* (פְּנִימִיּוֹת) from heaven and from Hashem's treasure house — rather than being channeled through the natural constraints of earth — that we enjoy on Shabbos. (*Ki Savo* 5649)

⤛§ Repenting With Love (תְּשׁוּבָה מֵאַהֲבָה)

בפסוק (איכה ה, כא) השיבנו ה׳ אליך ונשובה, והם ב׳ מיני תשובה, מיראה ואהבה, ובהיות האדם מלוכלך בחטא, א״א לשוב מתוך אהבה רק מיראה, וכו׳, וענין ב׳ התשובות, כמו שמתחילה יש סור מרע ועשה טוב, כן תשובה מיראה בחי׳ סור מרע שמבקש להתנקות מלכלוך העונות, אבל מאהבה הוא בחי׳ עשה טוב, ועל ידי שהעונות מעכבים האדם מלהתדבק בו ית׳, לכן מבקש התשובה כדי שיוכל לחזור לבחי׳ עשה טוב, וז״ש חדש ימינו כקדם, הוא דביקות השורש שיש לבנ״י בו ית׳, כדכ׳ (דברים לב, ט) חלק ה׳ עמו, ולכן בשבת קודש בנקל לשוב יותר, כי מתעורר השורש של בנ״י, כמ״ש (יחזקאל מו, א) וביום השבת נפתח, וכמ״ש במ״א, וזה ענין נשמה יתירה שיש לבנ״י בשבת, שהוא כח השורש שאינו תלוי בעבודת האדם, לכן נקראת יתירה, שהיא יותר מכפי זכות ועבודת האדם, וזה הכח אינו נאבד ע״י החטא, לכן יכולין לשוב בשבת קודש, וכתיב (שם לא, יז) ישובו יושבי בצלו, הוא רמז על שבת, דאיתא פורס סוכת שלום עלינו כו׳.

By portraying an image of *Klal Yisrael* residing under a protective canopy that is spread out by Hashem, we are alluding to our extraordinary capacity to repent in a loving atmosphere every Shabbos, as we shall elucidate.

The renowned *pasuk* הֲשִׁיבֵנוּ ה׳ אֵלֶיךָ וְנָשׁוּבָה, *Return us,* H*ASHEM*, *to You and we will return* (*Eichah* 5:21), implies that there are two distinct forms of *teshuvah*. While initially we repent out of *fear* of the consequences of our sins (תְּשׁוּבָה מִיִּרְאָה), this is only a first step. Once we progress beyond this preliminary attempt at doing *teshuvah*, we endeavor to "reconnect" with *HaKadosh Baruch Hu* by repenting with great love, a concept known as תְּשׁוּבָה מֵאַהֲבָה. The first phase of *teshuvah* serves to cleanse us from the stains on our *neshamah* that our transgressions invariably leave. However, it is not until we repent in an environment of love, that we can be assured that the Divine Spark that is imbedded in us is once again inseparably linked to Hashem. As the foregoing *pasuk* continues, חַדֵּשׁ יָמֵינוּ כְּקֶדֶם, *renew our days as of old* (as they were previously).

There is no better opportunity for us to return to Hashem — and do so in an atmosphere of love — than on *Shabbos Kodesh*, the day that we are graced with the presence of the *neshamah yeseirah*. As the term *yeseirah*, *extra*, implies, every Shabbos we enjoy the capacity to return to Hashem in a manner that is well beyond anything that we would deserve on the basis of our own merit. It is this extraordinary capacity to do תְּשׁוּבָה מֵאַהֲבָה that allows us to reach unprecedented heights on Shabbos.

This process is succinctly stated by Hosea, יָשֻׁבוּ יֹשְׁבֵי בְצִלּוֹ, *those who reside under His shade will be able to repent* (14:8). And, in fact, every Shabbos, when we are privileged to "bask" under the canopy of peace spread by Hashem, our efforts at returning to Hashem are crowned with success. (*Shabbos Teshuvah* 5641)

Making a Half into a Whole

הפורס פריסה לשון פרס וחלק, כמ״ש (דברים לב, ט) חלק ה׳ עמו, שבחר לו השי״ת חלק מהנבראים, [כמ״ש בתנא דב״א (פ״א) עשיר ושמח בחלקו ע״ש ובפי׳ ישועות יעקב] והשי״ת לו השלימות, ולמה בחר לו חצי דבר, אך כתיב (ישעי׳ נז, טו) אשכון את דכא כו׳, וכ׳ בזוה״ק כי זה השלימות מה שאדם נשבר לבו, ע״ש פרשת אמור, ואדרבא זה שבחו ית׳ כי בכל מקום שהוא שורה הוא שלימות והוא עושה מחצי דבר דבר שלם, וזה הפורס סוכת שלום, כי באמת הנקודה פנימיות שבכל מקום, הוא השלימות, וכן בנ״י מתוך כל הנבראים.

By carefully examining the text of this *tefillah*, we may deduce that an extraordinary process of transformation took place when Hashem selected us from all other nations. In effect, He arranged that a nation that is most humble and contrite — perceiving itself to be no more than a mere "half" (a *perusah*) — would be considered in His "Eyes" to be *shaleim*, a complete (and significant) entity. In fact, it is precisely because we (as individuals and a nation among other nations) deem ourselves to be little more than a half — a small component of Hashem's infinite universe — that we merit the presence of the *Shechinah*, the greatest source of *sheleimus*. (*Succos* 5634)

מֵעֵין עוֹלָם הַבָּא, A Microcosm of the World To Come

*C*hazal (cf. *Berachos* 57b) relate that Shabbos resembles the World to Come. In fact, the expression מֵעֵין עוֹלָם הַבָּא, *a microcosm of the World to Come,* is often used (most notably in the *zemiros)* to describe the association between Shabbos and *Olam Haba.* In this chapter we will explore the many aspects of this relationship.

A Taste of the World to Come

ובנ״י שומרי שבת פי׳ ששומרים הרצון שלא להתערב בדברי הבל. ועי״ז נאמר מי שטרח בע״ש כו׳. כי בימות החול הוא הבירור מלהתגאל בהבלי עולם ועי״ז זוכה לטעום בשבת טעם עוה״ב כי שבת מעין עוה״ב.

When *Chazal* describe Shabbos as being a microcosm of the World to Come, they may be suggesting that even during our life span in This World, it may be possible to sample something of the indescribable spiritual pleasures that await the deserving in the World to Come. In fact, the concept of *oneg Shabbos* may refer not only to the three Shabbos meals and other physical pleasures that we are encouraged to partake of on Shabbos, but also to the "taste" of *Olam Haba* that we may merit then. Likewise, when Shabbos is described as being a day of *Menuchah* (refer to the chapter on this theme), rather than referring merely to physical rest, *Chazal* may be alluding to the taste of the World to Come that we enjoy on this day. However, to merit even a sampling of the Future World while yet alive in This World, we must meet a critical prerequisite — abstaining as much as possible from the material pleasures of This World. As *Chazal* relate (*Avodah Zarah* 3a), מִי שֶׁטָּרַח בְּעֶרֶב שַׁבָּת יֹאכַל בְּשַׁבָּת, [*only*] *those who exerted themselves on the eve of Shabbos will eat* (enjoy the pleasures of) *on Shabbos.* In this context, the term בְּעֶרֶב שַׁבָּת may refer not only to the eve of Shabbos but also to the turbulent atmosphere of This World, in which we are sorely tempted to immerse ourselves in material pleasures.[1] Only those who exerted themselves during the week to resist the temptations of This World merit to partake of the taste of *Olam Haba* every Shabbos. In fact, the term *shomrei Shabbos* may refer to those who safeguard (*shomer*) and control their passions for material pleasures all week long, thereby meriting on Shabbos to "taste" the World to Come. (*Chukas* 5636)

A Hint of Our Glorious Future

ולפי שא״י בעוה״ז להתקדש לגמרי כמו בעוה״ב נתן לנו מצות לאחוז בהם בדרך הקודש. וכן שבת שהיא מעין עוה״ב. ובזוה״ק דיש לכל איש ישראל אות ברית מילה ושבת.

Shabbos is not only a taste of the World to Come but also a powerful indication to *Klal Yisrael* that it will enjoy *Olam Haba. Pirkei Avos* commences, כָּל יִשְׂרָאֵל יֵשׁ לָהֶם חֵלֶק לָעוֹלָם הַבָּא, *Every member of the Jewish people has a share in the World to Come.* While it may be impossible for us to reach anything approaching the levels of *kedushah* that we will attain in the World to Come, Hashem grants us *mitzvos* such as Shabbos, which is מֵעֵין עוֹלָם הַבָּא (and *bris milah* and *tefillin),* that help us at least to take the initial strides towards such exalted levels of sanctity.

1. According to this approach, the term עֶרֶב may be derived from תַּעֲרוֹבֶת, the confusion and mixture of good and evil that often prevails in This World. It may also be related to the expression found in *Birchas HaTorah,* וְהַעֲרֶב נָא, *may (the Words of the Torah) be sweet.* In this context, those who resisted the sweetness and fleeting pleasures of This World during the week merit to taste the World to Come on Shabbos.

The privilege of observing these *mitzvos* is an indication that we may merit the exalted atmosphere of *Olam Haba*. (Adapted from *Re'eh* 5654)

◆§ Retrieving Our Original Design

כי בוודאי הקב״ה שהכין גן עדן בשביל האדם הוא מוכן לזה לעולם אך אחר החטא כ׳ משנה פניו יצירה בעוה״ב. ושבת מעין עוה״ב. ז״ש ברכו בעטיפה וצריכין לשנות מלבושי שבת לרמז הנ״ל ולכן ע״י התורה ומצוות רמ״ח ושס״ה זוכין להמשיך הארה מצורה הפנימיות רוחניות. לזכות לג״ע. ובשב״ק יש הארה לאדם מצורה הפנימיות שהיא נשמה יתירה היורדת מגן עדן לבנ״י שהוא יומא דנשמתין ולאו דגופין כדכ׳ בזוה״ק.

When describing the creation of man, the Torah writes, וַיִּיצֶר ה׳ אֱלֹהִים אֶת הָאָדָם, *and* HASHEM *God formed man* [*and placed him in Eden*] (*Bereishis* 2:7). By spelling וַיִּיצֶר with two *"yuds,"* the Torah is implying that Hashem simultaneously created two profiles (צוּרָה) of man — a *physical* presence, which exists on earth and a distinctly different *spiritual* form, which primarily surfaces in the World to Come.

However, this possible dichotomy between our spiritual persona and our physical presence only occurred after Adam partook of the fruit of the Tree of Knowledge. Prior to sinning, the first man's profile (while he lived in *Gan Eden*) was identical to that which he would assume (after his passing) in the hereafter.

On Shabbos, we retrieve some aspect of man's original profile, resuming the spiritual existence that Adam enjoyed while in *Gan Eden*. On this day when the *neshamah yeseirah* (which itself emanates from *Gan Eden)* prevails, we are able to gain a measure of the spirituality with which we will identify in *Olam Haba*. To indicate the change in our essence that occurs every Shabbos — and to demonstrate that our very personalities are transformed each Shabbos — we doff our weekday clothing in favor of specially designated Shabbos garments.[1]

(Adapted from *Bereishis* 5650)

1. Even during the weekdays, such a transformation is possible (through immersion in Torah and *mitzvos*). In fact, the 248 limbs and the 365 sinews of the body correspond to an identical number of positive and negative commandments, respectively. This demonstrates that our physical presence is only the exterior casing for the spirituality which in fact invigorates us.

◆§ Evoking Memories of Our Great Beginnings

כי הקבלה שקבלו בנ"י מצוה הראשונה בכל לבם נחשב יותר בשמים מקיום המצוה במעשה. כי בודאי במעשה קשה להיות בלי שום חסרון. אבל הקבלה והלקיחה הי' בלב שלם לגמרי. ולאשר כי הי' אז בשבת. ושבת הוא יום שביתה שאין בו מעשה ובשבת אין צריך למעשה רק הרצון בלבד ולכן נחשב הקבלה כאלו גמרו כל המעשה בטוב. והנה עדיין לא נגמר המכוון שהי' להקב"ה בהוציאנו ממצרים להיות שמו הגדול מקודש על ידינו כמו שיהי' לעתיד. כי עמלק הרשע בלבל אותנו כמאמר אשר קרך בדרך ... כי הכלל כל מעשה שאדם עושה בלב שלם אף שבמעשה אינו נגמר כראוי בטוח הוא שיהי' לו עוד תיקון ואחרית לטובה. ולכן בשבת שהוא מעין עוה"ב יום שכולו שבת יכולין לעורר הרצון שהיה לנו בתחילת קבלת מלכותו כמאמר זכרתי לך חסד נעוריך כו'.

Every Shabbos we evoke memories of the Shabbos immediately prior to *yetzias Mitzrayim* (now known as *Shabbos HaGadol*). It was then that Hashem commanded us, מִשְׁכוּ וּקְחוּ לָכֶם, which is translated here as, *separate and take for yourselves* (the Paschal Lamb) (*Shemos* 12:21). This stirring phrase is interpreted by *Chazal* (*Yalkut Shimoni*, *Shemos* 206) in the following manner: מִשְׁכוּ יְדֵיכֶם מֵעֲבוֹדָה זָרָה, *separate from idolatory* (and then designate the Paschal Lamb). This Divine charge was wholeheartedly embraced by our forefathers. Without delay, they proceeded to rid themselves of any remaining idols and then they enthusiastically selected the *korban pesach*.

Unfortunately, much of this enthusiastic initial embrace of the Divine Will was later dissipated, largely as a result of our forefather's brush with Amalek shortly after the Exodus. However, despite any backsliding that occurred, the initial dream of being fully committed to Hashem and His Torah was never totally forgotten. In fact, any effort that is commenced with wholehearted enthusiasm, even if (often due to circumstances beyond our control) it is not fully consummated, nevertheless, we can be assured that eventually the dream and ideals that we voiced at the beginning will be realized. During the weekdays, a time which is primarily devoted to *maaseh hamitzvos* (actual performance of *mitzvos)*, our initial commitment may appear somewhat tarnished when compared to our later behavior. However, on Shabbos, a day when we abstain from all forms of *Melachah* (מַעֲשֶׂה) and focus instead on our great desire to serve

Hashem, we can evoke the great enthusiasm and desire to serve Hashem that we demonstrated just before *yetzias Mitzrayim*. This is particularly true since Shabbos is a microcosm of the World to Come, a time when all material activity ceases. Thus, every Shabbos our initial commitment to serve Hashem is fondly recalled, as we see in the words of the *navi* Yirmiyahu, זָכַרְתִּי לָךְ חֶסֶד נְעוּרַיִךְ, *I will recall the kindness of your youth* (*Yirmiyahu* 2:2) (*Shabbos HaGadol* 5635)

◈ Fulfilling One's Life Mission (*Sheleimus*)

פי׳ כי בעוה״ז האדם נק׳ מהלך ממדרגה למדרגה כענין שאמרו הצדיקים אין להם מנוחה ילכו מחיל אל חיל וכשהאדם מתקן כל מעשיו מסתלק מעוה״ז נמצא אין להם מנוחה רק בבא יום השבת שהוא מתנה מן השמים שיהי׳ יום מנוחה וכמ״ש ז״ל שיהי׳ כאילו כל מלאכתם עשוי׳ שבכל מקום שאדם עומד בבֹא יום השבת חל עליו השלימות ויש עלי׳ לכל המעשים שעשה עד עתה כאילו כל מלאכתו עשוי׳ ולכן נק׳ יום מנוחה בעוה״ז מעין עוה״ב.

As long as we are alive, our challenge is to constantly reach new levels of *avodas Hashem*. As *Chazal* note, צַדִּיקִים אֵין לָהֶם מְנוּחָה בְּעוֹלָם הַזֶּה, *the righteous do not enjoy peace in This World* (*Berachos* 64a). Indeed, when *tzaddikim* have successfully consummated all of the challenges for which they were created, they prepare to leave This World and enter *Olam Haba*.

However, upon the advent of Shabbos there is a sense of *sheleimus* – a feeling that all of our designated tasks are considered as if they have already been completed (for further discussion of these themes refer to the chapter on *Melachah*, as well as the segment of the chapter on *Shalom* discussing *sheleimus*). On Shabbos, a microcosm of the World to Come, we can feel a sense of accomplishment and completion even during our life span in This World. (*Bereishis* 5653)

ולכן שבת צריך הכנה. וזהו הודעה שקודם המהנה להיות מוכן לקבל הארה שלמעלה מעוה״ז. וז״ש לכן אמור הנני נותן כוי׳.

Utilizing this approach, we can appreciate why Hashem insisted that Moshe inform *Klal Yisrael* in advance that He was granting them the gift of Shabbos (refer to *Shabbos* 10b and to the chapter "The Gift of Shabbos"). It is difficult, if not impossible, to attain *sheleimus* in This World. It is only by anticipating the arrival of Shabbos and then preparing oneself during the week for this extraordinary day that one can achieve some measure of *sheleimus* on Shabbos, which is a microcosm of the World to Come. By informing *Klal Yisrael* of the gift of Shabbos, Moshe was affording them the opportunity to prepare for the *sheleimus* of Shabbos. (*Pinchas* 5646)

☙ Returning Creation to Its Heavenly Roots

והענין הוא כי כל מעשה בראשית הוא רמזים על שרשים העליונים וזה עצמו פירוש בראשית ברא. שיהי׳ לכל הבריאה שורש ודביקות בראשית וכן כל הדברים שדרשו חז״ל שנקראו ראשית הפי׳ שע״י אלו הדברים מעלין הדברים לשורש הראשית. ורמזו חז״ל עוה״ז דומה לפרוזדור בפני עוה״ב התקן עצמך בפרוזדור. פי׳ כפי הכנה בעוה״ז לתקן כל המעשים ונעשין האברים והגידים והחושים כלים להיות מוכן בעוה״ב לקבל הארות המיוחדים לאלה הכלים.

To appreciate another dimension of the *Olam Haba* that is inherent in every Shabbos, we suggest a profound interpretation of the first words of the Torah, בְּרֵאשִׁית בָּרָא. While this phrase is usually translated, *in the beginning* [*Hashem*] *created,* in reality, the term רֵאשִׁית may also allude to the heavenly roots and source of everything here on earth. When Hashem created the universe, He arranged that all of His creations retain a link with their original roots (*shoresh*) in heaven. In fact, the various interpretations of the term רֵאשִׁית offered by *Chazal* (refer to the *midrash* cited in *Rashi, Bereishis* 1:1 suggesting that the universe was created in the merit of the Jewish people, the *mitzvos of challah* and *bikkurim* and many other concepts of the term רֵאשִׁית), suggest that in the merit of these *mitzvos* we are able to connect with our heavenly roots even while in This World. We may interpret in a similar vein the renowned *mishnah,* הָעוֹלָם הַזֶּה דּוֹמֶה לִפְרוֹזְדוֹר בִּפְנֵי הָעוֹלָם הַבָּא, הַתְקֵן עַצְמְךָ בַּפְּרוֹזְדוֹר, *This World is like a corridor before the World to Come; prepare yourself in the corridor* (4:21): By performing *mitzvos* and *maasim tovim* in This World, we are preparing our very essence and our personality to connect to our heavenly roots in the World to Come.

There is no better occasion to "reconnect" with our roots than *Shabbos Kodesh*, which is a microcosm of the World to Come.

(Adapted from *Bereishis* 5654)

וז"ש שיושבין בשלוה כמ"ש וישב. והוא בחי' שבת מעין עוה"ב שהאדם מתדבק בשורשו. אבל הם רוצין לישב בשלוה גם בעוה"ז כנ"ל.

In this context, we may appreciate better *Chazal's* assertion that Yaakov desired to live in tranquility (*shalvah*) during his life span in This World, a dream that was shattered by the tragedy of Yosef's sale (*Rashi, Bereishis* 37:2). Rather than assume that this *tzaddik* sought to enjoy the material pleasures of *Olam Hazeh*, we suggest that the term *shalvah* refers to the inner calm and tranquility that is obtained whenever we set aside all of the material concerns of This World in favor of the spirituality that defines the World to Come. Every Shabbos we enjoy a sense of this *menuchas shalvah* as we return to our spiritual core. It was this spiritual tranquility that Yaakov sought. (*Vayeishev* 5631)

The Sacred Roots of Time

במד' בז' קני מנורה שבעה עיני ה' המשוטטים כו' ... א"כ יש ז' דרכים איך להתקשר בתורה בעוה"ז. והן הז' נימין. ולכן הלוים היו אומרים בכל יום שיר מיוחד והמשיכו דביקות בעוה"ז להשורש בכל יום באופן מיוחד. וכמו כן הכהן בז' קני המנורה ... ונר מערבי הוא שבת בזמן. שמעלה כל הימים לשורש השלשה ראשים כי שבת מעין עוה"ב שהוא כנור של עשור ... ובשבת שהוא מעין עוה"ב יש בו מעין שיר על השמינית. וכ' במד' בשבת שירו כפול מזמור שיר ליום השבת שהשבת הוא א' מהז' נימין וז' קני המנורה. אכן הוא מעלה כל הז' עד מדריגה השמינית ויש בו מעוה"ז ומעוה"ב.

Chazal (*Arachin* 13b) relate that the harp utilized by the *Leviim* in the *Beis HaMikdash* consisted of seven strings. Similarly, the *Menorah* in the *Beis HaMikdash* consisted of seven lamps. Both of these artifacts may correspond to the prophet's description of Hashem's stewardship of the universe. As *Zechariah* writes, שִׁבְעָה אֵלֶּה עֵינֵי ה׳ הֵמָּה מְשׁוֹטְטִים בְּכָל הָאָרֶץ, *these seven (lamps of the Menorah) represent the Eyes of* HASHEM *that observe the entire earth* (4:10). There is no better vehicle to "connect" with *HaKadosh Baruch Hu* and with His Torah (through which He guides His universe) than by kindling the seven lights of the *Menorah* and by playing the harp which consisted of seven strings. These sacred artifacts employed by Hashem's servitors, the *Kohanim* and *Leviim* respectively, were the perfect link between *Klal Yisrael* and Hashem and His Torah.

In this process of linking the Jewish people and Hashem, symbolized by the seven harp strings and the seven lamps of the *Menorah*, Shabbos plays an extraordinary role. This day corresponds to the extra dimension that existed in both the *Menorah* and the harps of the *Leviim*. In the *Menorah's* case, the Shabbos day represented the Western Lamp (נֵר מַעֲרָבִי) to which all of the wicks turned. While each of the *Menorah's* lamps linked one of the days of the week to its heavenly roots, it was the Western Lamp to which each wick of the *Menorah* turned, that symbolized the universe's potential to be raised to an even higher level. Similarly, every Shabbos, the day that is a microcosm of the World to Come, the universe is raised to an even higher level than is possible during the week.

Likewise, the harp strings of the *Leviim* associated with Shabbos were also different. Whereas every day the *Leviim* sang to the accompaniment of a seven-stringed harp, on Shabbos there was an additional element of song. In a sense, one could say that the harp of Shabbos represented an even higher eighth level (refer to *Tehillim* 6:1, לַמְנַצֵּחַ בִּנְגִינוֹת עַל הַשְּׁמִינִית, which may be interpreted, *to the conductor who plays on an eight-stringed harp*). Thus, the song dedicated to the Shabbos day opens with a double appeal to sing: מִזְמוֹר שִׁיר לְיוֹם הַשַּׁבָּת, *a psalm, a song for the Sabbath day* (*Tehillim* 92), alluding to the eighth (and even loftier) level of song that is associated with Shabbos.

(Adapted from *Beha'aloscha* 5656)

⁂ The Heavenly Roots of Shabbos

משכו יומין עלאין לתתאין כו׳ בפ׳ פנחס ע״ש. כי יש שבת עליון כמ״ש מעין עוה״ב יום שכולו שבת. וע״י מצות שבת מתדבקין שומרי שבת בשורש השבת.

Whereas in a previous *dvar Torah,* we discussed how all of Creation returns to its spiritual roots on Shabbos, here we suggest that the Shabbos day itself (as well as all those who diligently observe Shabbos) returns to its heavenly roots. According to the *Zohar* (*Parashas Pinchas*) the expression, מִשְׁכוּ וּקְחוּ לָכֶם, *draw out and take for yourselves* (*Shemos* 12:21 – generally assumed to be referring to the *korban pesach*) may also allude to the association between the concept of time on earth and the heavenly roots of every unit of time. Consistent with that approach, these words of the Torah are calling upon us to draw forth (מִשְׁכוּ) the heavenly roots of Shabbos. On Shabbos, a day which evokes the *kedushah* of the World to Come, we "connect" this day as it is observed on earth with its heavenly roots. (*Shabbos HaGadol* 5631)

⁂ A Reward Beyond Description (A Secret Reward)

היינו שבאמת השבת מיוחד לנשמות בנ״י שעולין בשבת קודש לג״ע עליון. אכן גם בעוה״ז נתן השי״ת לנו השבת להיות לנו ידיעה ודביקות בשבת העליון. וז״ש ושבת קדשו הנחילנו הלשון נסתר שהוא סוד ה׳ ואח״כ שבת קדשך הנחלתנו שיהי׳ לנו בועה״ז ג״כ חלק בהארה זו כדאיתא שבת הוא מעין עוה״ב וכן רמזו חז״ל מתן שכרו לא עבידי לגלויי ע״ש.

By describing Shabbos as a day that is a microcosm of the World to Come, *Chazal* may be alluding to the indescribable (and hidden) reward that this sacred day brings. When informing Moshe that He would present the Jewish people with the Shabbos, Hashem refers to this day as a valuable gift "from My treasure house" (*Shabbos* 10b – for extensive discussion of this theme refer to the chapter entitled, "The Gift of Shabbos"). By characterizing the Shabbos as a valued treasure, something that is ordinarily closely guarded, *Chazal* are granting us a glimpse of the limitless reward associated with observance of this hallowed day. In the same context,

Chazal note that the infinite reward of Shabbos is beyond description.[1]

Every Shabbos the souls of *Klal Yisrael* that reside in *Gan Eden* ascend to an even loftier level of spirituality (described as גַּן עֵדֶן הָעֶלְיוֹן, *a loftier level within Gan Eden*) where they partake of the sublime and indescribable reward of Shabbos. However, even during our life span on earth, on Shabbos we are able to obtain a sampling of the limitless (and hidden) reward associated with Shabbos. When reciting the *Kiddush* of Friday night, we seemingly repeat two very similar expressions — and in very close succession. First, we express our gratitude to Hashem by saying, וְשַׁבַּת קָדְשׁוֹ בְּאַהֲבָה וּבְרָצוֹן הִנְחִילָנוּ, *and with love and favor He gave us His holy Shabbos as a heritage,* followed by וְשַׁבַּת קָדְשְׁךָ בְּאַהֲבָה וּבְרָצוֹן הִנְחַלְתָּנוּ, *Your sacred Shabbos, with love and favor did You give us as a heritage.* By commencing with the comparatively "distant" third person (*He gave us His holy Shabbos*), and then speaking more directly to Hashem in the second person (*Your sacred Shabbos ... did You give us*), we are first alluding to the indescribable reward enjoyed by the souls of the deceased who ascend to a loftier niche in *Gan Eden* on Shabbos. Then by resorting to the more direct means of communication with Hashem in the second person, we are implying that even while we are residing on earth, we benefit from at least a small measure of the boundless reward of Shabbos, the day which is מֵעֵין עוֹלָם הַבָּא. (*Vayeira* 5648)

◆§ Bearing Testimony to Hashem

ונאמר עוד החיים לידון בחי׳ יצחק מדה״ד הוא הדין הגדול אחר התחי׳. לידע להודיע להוודע זה תכלית האחרון בחי׳ יעקב וישראל וישורון שאז יתברר דעת שלימה כמ״ש ומלאה הארץ דעה והוא תיקון השלם נחלה בלי מצרים שיהי׳ לעתיד לבוא ... והנה שבת הוא מעין עוה״ב נחלת יעקב וסהדותא אקרי בחי׳ לידע להודיע. וכ׳ בי׳ לדעת כי אני ה׳ מקדישכם. כמו שנמצא הדעת בנפשות הצדיקים. לפי שהם בני עוה״ב מתנוצץ בהם הארה גם בעוה״ז. כמו כן בזמן בשבת שהוא מעין עוה״ב.

By depicting Shabbos as a microcosm of the World to Come, *Chazal* may have been referring to the atmosphere of *Olam Haba* and especially the דַּעַת ה׳, *knowledge of Hashem,* that will permeate the Future World

1. מַתַּן שְׂכָרָהּ לֹא עֲבִידָא לְאִגַּלוּיֵי, *the reward of Shabbos will not be revealed* (Beitzah 16a).

and that we sense every Shabbos. Just as in the World to Come all men will recognize and acknowledge their Creator, so too, Shabbos, a day whose primary purpose is לָדַעַת כִּי אֲנִי ה׳ מְקַדִּשְׁכֶם, *to know that I am Hashem, Who makes you holy* (*Shemos* 31:13) – to attest that Hashem has consecrated the Jewish people — is a particularly opportune time for us to acknowledge Hashem. In fact the Shabbos is frequently described as סַהֲדוּתָא, *bearing witness* about Hashem's Creation.

Utilizing this approach, we derive new insight into a *mishnah* (*Pirkei Avos* 4:29) where we read about the ultimate destiny of all Hashem's creations. We suggest that this *mishnah* alludes to various phases in Jewish history and to the Shabbos: הַיִּלוֹדִים לָמוּת, *those who were born are destined to die* (alluding to the consequences of Adam's sin which condemned future generations to die); וְהַמֵּתִים לְחְיוֹת, *the deceased are destined to be resurrected,* in the merit of Avraham and Sarah; וְהַחַיִּים לִדּוֹן, *the living will be judged* (a reference to the Final Judgment, which all mankind will experience before resurrection). The *mishnah* continues: לֵידַע לְהוֹדִיעַ וּלְהִוָּדַע, *to know, to inform, and so it be known* (about Hashem and that He will ultimately judge all of His creations). This last segment may refer to the Shabbos when we may develop an intimate knowledge of Hashem, somewhat similar to the closeness to Him that we will enjoy in the Future World. (*Chayei Sarah* 5661)

◆§ Unparalleled Intimacy Between Us and Hashem

דהנה בקבלת התורה כתיב פנים בפנים דיבר ה׳ עמכם פי׳ פנים כמ״ש ופניתי אליכם אמרו חז״ל פונה אני מכל עסקי ועוסק בכם. וכמו כן צריך איש ישראל להיות נפנה מכל עסקים בלתי לה׳ לבדו. וכן הי׳ במעמד הר סיני דכ׳ והייתם נכונים ליום השלישי. אבל לא זכינו לעמוד במדריגה זו. ונאמר עלינו כי פנו אלי עורף ולא פנים זה כשאין מוכנים בכל הנפש אל הקדושה. וזה בושת הפנים שלנו. ומרע״ה נשאר במדריגה זו כמ״ש ודיבר ה׳ אל משה פנים אל פנים. ובשבת קודש שמניחין כל המעשים להפנות אל הקדושה זוכין לבחי׳ הנ״ל כל אחד לפי הכנתו ומ״מ יש לכל איש ישראל חלק בשבת שמבטל כל מלאכתו בשביל קדושת היום. ולכן אות הוא ביני וביניכם. פי׳ הנהגת הטבע הוא בימי המעשה. ובש״ק שהוא מעין עוה״ב שמיוחד רק לבנ״י כמ״ש ופניתי אליכם כו׳. זה מתקיים בכל שבת שכביכול פונה מכל עסקים אל בנ״י.

In truth, the Torah explicates at least one aspect of the association between Shabbos and the World to Come by describing this day as

בֵּינִי וּבֵין בְּנֵי יִשְׂרָאֵל אוֹת הִוא לְעֹלָם, *Between Me and the Children of Israel it is a sign forever* (*Shemos* 31:17). To appreciate the full significance of the foregoing description of Shabbos – and of the intimate bond between us and Hashem which seemingly reaches its full potential every Shabbos – we recall one of the most beautiful moments in the history of *Klal Yisrael* – *Matan Torah*. When Hashem granted the Torah to the Jewish people, He (כִּבְיָכוֹל) "set aside all of His other concerns" and focused entirely upon *Klal Yisrael* who were about to receive the Torah (*Rashi, Vayikra* 26:9, ופניתי). Likewise, *Klal Yisrael* in the preparatory period immediately prior to the Giving of the Torah, devoted itself totally to the formidable task of coming closer to Hashem.

Unfortunately, the Jewish people (especially after the sin of the Golden Calf) were not able to sustain the steadfast attention to its relationship with Hashem that it had nurtured at Sinai.[1] (Correspondingly, the *Shechinah* departed from our ranks, to some extent, as a result of our transgressions.) However, we will again resume this unparalleled intimacy between us and Hashem in the World to Come. Even in This World on Shabbos, which is a microcosm of the World to Come, we enjoy a scintilla of the closeness and intimacy that we once enjoyed and will (בע"ה) benefit from again. On Shabbos, we may perceive that Hashem yields all of His other "concerns" in favor of complete devotion to *Klal Yisrael*. Whereras during the weekdays, Hashem may manage His universe on the basis of natural laws (*teva*) which He instituted, on Shabbos when the intimacy between us and Hashem is restored, the universe is no longer bound by such constraints. (*Ki Sisa* 5658)

1. The only exception was Moshe *Rabbeinu* who maintained the same intimacy with Hashem – even after *Matan Torah* – that the Jewish people enjoyed at the Giving of the Torah. In fact, identical language is utilized to describe Moshe's ongoing relationship with Hashem and the Jewish people's status at the time of *Matan Torah* – פָּנִים בְּפָנִים דִּבֶּר ה׳ עִמָּכֶם, *face to face did Hashem speak with you* (*Devarim* 5:4) describes the Revelation at Sinai. Regarding Moshe's relationship with Hashem, the *pasuk* says, וְדִבֶּר ה׳ אֶל מֹשֶׁה פָּנִים אֶל פָּנִים, *Hashem would speak to Moshe face to face* (*Shemos* 33:11).

◆§ Greater Than Angels

כי כתיב שש כנפים ובכל יום החיות אומרות שירה בכנף אחד ושבת אין להם עוד כנף אומר הקב״ה יש לי כנף אחד בארץ הוא כנס״י ע״ש בתוס׳ סנהדרין ל״ז. ושמעתי מפי מו״ז ז״ל מה ענין שירה בכנף לחיות הקודש. רק שע״י השירה מהעלין כמו העוף בכנפיו. וכ״כ דאר״י ז״ל שכל עלי׳ ע״י שירה ע״ש. א״כ בני ישראל בשבת יש להם עלי׳ בכח העדות. והוא למעלה מצנא מרום. כי שבת הוא מעין עוה״ב. ולעתיד כתיב כעת יאמר ליעקב כו׳ מה פעל אל. שיהי׳ מחיצתן לפנים ממלאכי השרת.

The analogy drawn between Shabbos and the World to Come may allude to the unprecedented levels of intimacy with Hashem that the Jewish people will enjoy in *Olam Haba* and, to some extent, enjoy every Shabbos — a level even greater than that of the *malachim.* As Bilaam prophesies, כָּעֵת יֵאָמֵר לְיַעֲקֹב וּלְיִשְׂרָאֵל מַה פָּעַל אֵל, which is interpreted by the *Sfas Emes*: *"There will be a time when it will be said* (by the angels to *Klal Yisrael*), *'What is God doing?'* " (cf. *Bamidbar* 23:23). In other words, in the Future World, *Klal Yisrael* will have ascended to so exalted a spiritual level that the *malachim* will be compelled to turn to us to ascertain Hashem's intentions. In a sense, we rise to this level of intimacy every Shabbos, the day when by resting from *Melachah* we confirm and validate Hashem's creation of heaven and earth.

Utilizing this approach, we gain additional insight into a particularly intriguing assertion of *Tosafos* (*Sanhedrin* 37b, s.v. מכנף) that whereas the angels sing Hashem's praises during the week — and consequently *malachim* have six wings, corresponding to each of the six weekdays — on Shabbos, *Klal Yisrael* assumes the angels' role and sings *shirah.*[1] How appropriate that on Shabbos, when we may enjoy an intimacy with Hashem even greater than the *malachim,* we assume their role of singing *shirah.*[2]

(*Vayikra* 5647)

1. Refer to the complete text of *Sfas Emes* in which he cites a beautiful *vort* of the *Ari HaKadosh* regarding the association between wings and singing Hashem's praises. He asserts that it is through the power of song (*shirah*) that one can be uplifted to a loftier spiritual level in the same manner that a bird flies with its wings. In fact, the *Ari* writes, כָּל עֲלִיָּה עַל יְדֵי שִׁירָה, *every spiritual uplift occurs through song.*

2. The *Tosafos* cited in the body of this work preserves an interesting custom based on the fact that *Klal Yisrael* assumes the angels' role of singing *shirah* on Shabbos. Specifically, it was

☙ "Hashem Is One and His Name Is One"

אבל יש מדריגה למעלה מזו אשרי אדם עוז לו בך שדור המדבר היו בעצם תורה כמ״ש קוב״ה ואורייתא וישראל כולהו חד. ועתה ירדו מזו מהדריגה והוצרכו להשגב במגדל עוז שם ה׳. וכן הוא בחי׳ הקרבנות להקריב ולהעלות העולמות והשמות כדאיתא זוה״ק. וכ׳ עולת תמיד העשוי׳ בהר סיני שאז הי׳ נתקן העולם וע״י התמידין בכל יום נתקן העולם. אבל בקרבן שבת כתיב על עולת התמיד. שהוא בחי׳ נשמה יתירה והתחדשות. ולכן בכל יום כבש בבוקר וכבש בין הערבים ובמוסף שבת שני הכבשים קרבן א׳ מעין עוה״ב דכ׳ יהי׳ ה׳ אחד ושמו אחד.

Yet another aspect of the relationship between Shabbos and the World to Come may be deduced from the distinctive nature of Shabbos' *korbanos.* Whereas the daily sacrifice (*korban tamid*) consisted of one lamb in the morning and another in the afternoon, the Shabbos sacrifice (which was brought in addition to the daily *tamid*) was comprised of two lambs that were offered simultaneously.

To appreciate why on Shabbos we are able to fuse together these two seemingly disparate sacrifices while on a weekday those two lambs must be offered at different times, we recall that there are two distinct methods of perceiving Hashem. In some instances we come closer to Him by recognizing and acknowledging His accomplishments. As stated in *Mishlei* (18:10), מִגְדַּל עֹז שֵׁם ה׳ בּוֹ יָרוּץ צַדִּיק וְנִשְׂגָּב, *The Name of HASHEM is a tower of strength, in it the righteous and the mighty run* (there they derive shelter). While it may be difficult for us to perceive Hashem, especially in *galus,* we nonetheless can appreciate His Name, through His many wonders that we experience. However, under ideal circumstances (such as when the Jewish people perceived Hashem at Sinai, or for the Wilderness Generation that witnessed so many of His miracles), it may be possible (כִּבְיָכוֹל) to perceive Hashem Himself. This laudable objective can also be achieved by immersing ourselves in His Torah. As the

---

customary in *Eretz Yisrael* to only recite *Kedushah* (which is based largely on the theme that the Jewish people sing Hashem's praises here on earth just as angels do in heaven) on Shabbos.

Perhaps we may add the following observation: While in contemporary times, *Kedushah* is recited every day of the week, nonetheless it is significant that Shabbos' *Kedushah* is far more elaborate than that of the week. Moreover, it is only on Shabbos that *Kedushah* is sung rather than merely recited.

Ramban notes, the entire Torah consists of names of Hashem. Dovid praises those individuals who are fortunate enough to perceive Hashem Himself — אַשְׁרֵי אָדָם עוֹז לוֹ בָךְ, *Happy is the person who derives strength from You* (rather than through Your Name) (*Tehillim* 84:6). However, in *galus* we generally are unable to directly perceive Hashem Himself, even when studying Torah. Thus, we recognize Hashem by acknowledging His Name (His many miracles and kindnesses), as Yeshayahu (26:13) writes when alluding to *Klal Yisrael's* fate in *galus*: לְבַד בְּךָ נַזְכִּיר שְׁמֶךָ, *we will only recognize You through Your name.*

On Shabbos, a microcosm of the World to Come (and assisted by the presence of the *neshamah yeseirah*), we regain the capacity to perceive Hashem as well as His Name. On this blessed day, the dream of the prophet is realized, ה׳ אֶחָד וּשְׁמוֹ אֶחָד, *HASHEM is One and His Name is One* (*Zechariah* 14:9). To demonstrate our increased closeness to Hashem (allowing us to discover Hashem through His Torah), we offer both lambs on Shabbos morning rather than on two different occasions. This indicates that both aspects of our recognition of Hashem — His Name and Hashem Himself — are attainable (and become as one). (*Pinchas* 5663)

◆§ A Day of Complete Unity

ולכן אומרים ישמחו במלכותך שומרי שבת כי בשבת היא בחי׳ מלכות שמים ואין בו הרכבה כמ״ש אני ה׳ לא שניתי.ולכן שבת א״צ בירור כי אין בו שום תערובת [והמשכיל יבין דברים אלו ביותר]. והוא מעין עוה״ב שיהי׳ ה׳ אחד ושמו אחד יום שכולו שבת. וזה עיקר שכרן של עובדי ה׳ לזכות לזה השבת.

Whereas during the weekdays, we acquire our understanding of Hashem by studying (and emulating) His Attributes (*middos*), on Shabbos we can (כִּבְיָכוֹל) come close to Him. To appreciate this distinction, we recall that while during the week Hashem authorizes *malachim* to administer the natural world, on Shabbos He governs His universe entirely by Himself. When we speak of Hashem's *middos*, we are referring to attributes which may be implemented by heavenly angels. Thus, our challenge during the six weekdays is to adopt as our own those attributes which He has entrusted to His servitors. Just as He entrusted *malachim* to implement the attribute of compassion (*middas harachamim*), so too, it is our sacred challenge to become more compassionate. On Shabbos, however, we go beyond the strides that we have achieved during the week and come closer to Hashem (rather than merely His attributes).

Unlike His attributes which are manifold, Hashem Himself, of course, is the epitome of Unity and Oneness. It is particularly on Shabbos, a day described as a microcosm of the World to Come, that we can more greatly appreciate the unity of Hashem. Just as in the Future World there will be no distinction between Hashem (Who we know is the essence of *achdus*) and His attributes — as Zechariah states (14:9), בַּיּוֹם הַהוּא יִהְיֶה ה׳ אֶחָד וּשְׁמוֹ אֶחָד, *on that day HASHEM will be one and His Name* (attributes) *will also be one* — so too, every Shabbos we can appreciate how the seemingly disparate *middos* of Hashem are all an integral part of His Oneness.

As we read in the *Mussaf Shemoneh Esrei*, יִשְׂמְחוּ בְמַלְכוּתְךָ שׁוֹמְרֵי שַׁבָּת, *Let those who observe Shabbos rejoice in Your kingdom.* Whereas Hashem's many attributes celebrate various aspects of His stewardship of the universe, on Shabbos His kingdom and His authority attest to His Oneness and complete mastery of the universe. It is on Shabbos that we can appreciate and rejoice in the knowledge of Hashem's *achdus*, as we celebrate His sovereignty. (*Eikev* 5653)

◈ A Bond Between Two Worlds

הענין כי שבת הוא מעין עוה״ב. יום שכולו שבת. והשי״ת שנתן לנו המצות נתן לנו הכלים וההכנות שנוכל לקבל המצות. והשבת הוא הידיעה והתקשרות להכין להשגת עוה״ב יום שכולו שבת. כי אני ה׳ מקדישכם מתקיים לעתיד לבוא באמת. ובשבת יש קצת מעין זה. וזהו לדעת כו׳ ע״י השבת כי אני ה׳ מקדישכם. לדעת כי אני ה׳ מקדישכם. פי׳ עתיד להקדישכם בעוה״ב. וכעין זה נדרש בתו״כ בפ׳ אני ה׳ מקדישכם לעוה״ב ע״ש. ועוה״ב הוא נעלם מלהשיגה בעוה״ז. אך השבת הוא הדרך שיכולין להשיג מעין עוה״ב.

From a *pasuk* cited in a previous *dvar Torah*, לָדַעַת כִּי אֲנִי ה׳ מְקַדִּשְׁכֶם, *to know that I am HASHEM Who makes you holy* (*Shemos* 31:13), *Chazal* derive that הַנּוֹתֵן מַתָּנָה לַחֲבֵירוֹ צָרִיךְ לְהוֹדִיעוֹ, *One who gives a gift to a peer must inform him* (*Shabbos* 10b). (Refer to the chapter on the "Gift of Shabbos" for a thorough discussion of this *Chazal*.) We suggest in this *dvar Torah* that the term לְהוֹדִיעוֹ may also be interpreted "to form an (emotional) bond."[1] The bond between the Future World, which is so much beyond our comprehension (and is described as "day that is entirely Shabbos," *Tamid* 7:4), and This World is Shabbos. By appreciating the Shabbos, we can begin to grapple with the immense *kedushah* of the World to Come.

According to this approach (maintaining that Shabbos acts an indicator in This World of the great reward that lies ahead in the Future World), we may interpret the foregoing *pasuk* in the following manner: לָדַעַת כִּי אֲנִי ה׳ מְקַדִּשְׁכֶם, "that you should know through the medium of Shabbos, that Hashem will sanctify you in the totally spiritual Future World." In a similar vein, the *pasuk* קֹדֶשׁ הִוא לָכֶם is interpreted by *Sfas Emes*: "because it (the Shabbos) is sacred for your benefit" [לְצָרְכֵכֶם][2] (cf. *Shemos* 31:14). This alludes to the great benefit that we receive from the Shabbos, which serves as the road that we can take even while we live in This World, in order to begin to grasp the rarefied ambiance of the World to Come. (Adapted from *Ki Sisa* 5642, 5646)

◆§ An Attainable Objective

וזהו הרמז שבת מעין עוה״ב שכמו כן כל יגיעת עוה״ז הוא כדי להשיג אח״כ בעוה״ב בעזר אלקים. וכמו כן מתקיים בשבת. וזה הרמז נשמה יתירה כלומר שאינו לפי עבודת העובד רק שבמתנה ניתן לו יותר מכפי עבודת האדם.

By stating that Shabbos is a microcosm of the World to Come, *Chazal* may be assuring us that our efforts towards spiritual growth will surely come to fruition. Just as all our efforts in This World are ultimately rewarded with the spiritual treasures of *Olam Haba*, so too, all of our efforts during the week will not come to naught, but rather (with

1. Refer to *Devarim* 34:10, אֲשֶׁר יְדָעוֹ ה׳, *whom Hashem had known*, which alludes to Moshe's intimate bond with Hashem.

2. *Sfas Emes'* interpretation of לָכֶם as meaning, לְצָרְכְּכֶם, *for your benefit*, is analogous to לְךָ (*for yourself*) being interpreted by *Rashi* (*Bereishis* 12:1) as לַהֲנָאָתְךָ וּלְטוֹבָתְךָ, *for your pleasure and for your benefit.*

the assistance of the *neshamah yeseirah*) will reach fruition on Shabbos.
(Adapted from *Ki Sisa* 5643)

וכמו כן אות השבת שנק׳ שלום שהוא התכלית של מעשה בראשית ... כן הבריאה רק הכנה לעוה״ב שהוא התכלית כמ״ש עוה״ז דומה לפרוזדור בפני עוה״ב א״כ עוה״ז רק הכנה והתכלית הוא עוה״ב.

In a similar vein, we suggest that both Shabbos and the World to Come represent the theme of *tachlis*, completion and the attainment of one's objective. Just as Shabbos is depicted as תַּכְלִית מַעֲשֵׂה שָׁמַיִם וָאָרֶץ, "the ultimate goal of the (creation of) heaven and earth," so too, the World to Come is the ultimate objective of everything that we do (Torah and *mitzvos*) in This World. As we read in *Pirkei Avos*, עוֹלָם הַזֶּה דּוֹמֶה לִפְרוֹזְדוֹר בִּפְנֵי הָעוֹלָם הַבָּא, *This World is like a corridor before the World to Come* (4:21). It is on Shabbos, the day which was the objective of Creation, that we can appreciate something of the aura of *Olam Haba*, which is the ultimate objective of everything that we do in This World. (*Pinchas* 5661)

Only Through Effort

על ידי שזוכין לה כפי היגיעה בימי המעשה כמ״ש מי שטרח בערב שבת יאכל בשבת והוא מעין עוה״ב שהוא מה שאין בכח אדם לבוא שהרי יפה שעה א׳ של קורת רוח בעוה״ב מכל חיי עוה״ז. ואעפ״כ הוא רק שכר המעשה והוא כנ״ל שע״י העבודה יזכה למתנה ומעין זה הוא השבת.
והתקדשתם הוא בימי המעשה. והייתם קדושים בשבת שיורד בו קדושה מלמעלה לבנ״י והוא הנשמה יתירה. וגם שבת הוא מעין עוה״ב מקיים בו והייתם קדושים כמ״ש רש״י ז״ל.

Just as the infinite reward of the World to Come can only be merited through one's efforts in This World to observe Torah and *mitzvos*, so too, the bliss of Shabbos can only be appreciated by those who strive to achieve their spiritual objectives during the weekdays. As *Chazal* (*Avodah Zarah* 3a) remind us, מִי שֶׁטָּרַח בְּעֶרֶב שַׁבָּת יֹאכַל בְּשַׁבָּת, (*only*) *those who exerted themselves on the eve of Shabbos will eat* (enjoy the rewards of) *on Shabbos.*

As further proof for our contention that there is a direct correspondence between our efforts during the week and the resultant reward that we earn on Shabbos, we cite the Torah's double exhortation that we lead a sacred life: וְהִתְקַדִּשְׁתֶּם וִהְיִיתֶם קְדֹשִׁים, *You shall sanctify yourselves and you shall be holy* (*Vayikra* 20:7). By sanctifying ourselves through our efforts during the weekdays, we merit that we will become holy on Shabbos. While the expression וִהְיִיתֶם קְדֹשִׁים, *and you shall be holy,* best pertains to the World to Come which is suffused with *kedushah,* it also applies every Shabbos, which is a microcosm of the World to Come.

Using this approach, we gain new insight into the *Chazal's* (*Shabbos* 10b) characterization of Shabbos as a מַתָּנָה טוֹבָה, *a good gift* (refer to the chapter entitled, "The Gift of Shabbos" for extensive discussion of this theme). Whereas an undeserved present is not necessarily in the recipient's interest, we will surely benefit from the gift of Shabbos, which is contingent upon our efforts and spiritual preparation.[1]

(*Toldos* 5649; *Shemini* 5653)

☙ Enabling Us to Survive in the Natural World of the Weekdays

ולכן שבת קודש הוא אור שבעת הימים והוא מעין עוה"ב. ונק' באר שבע. וז"ש ויצא יעקב מבאר שבע שהתקשר עצמו בבחי' שבת כנ"ל.

It is only through the other-worldly spirituality of Shabbos that we are able to endure and survive the forbidding material world of the weekdays. Just as Yaakov travels to Beer Sheva to fortify himself in a spiritual sense before embarking on his journey to Lavan, so too, it is through the Shabbos that we can persevere in the week ahead. In the same respect that Yaakov prepares himself for his arduous journey at Beer Sheva — a term related to שִׁבְעָה, *seven* — so too, it is through the

1. As a homiletic proof for the relationship between the efforts of the week and the great spiritual reward of Shabbos, the *Sfas Emes* notes that the first letters (rearranged) of the phrase שָׁמוֹעַ תִּשְׁמְעוּ בְּקֹלִי spell Shabbos. It is only by listening to My voice during the week that you will enjoy the spiritual reward of Shabbos (*Ki Savo* 5637).

Shabbos, which is the light of the seven days (אוֹר שִׁבְעַת הַיָּמִים), that we prepare ourselves for the challenges of the week ahead. (*Vayeitzei* 5637)

◆§ Freedom from the Natural World

ובאמת זה חסד הגדול שעשה הקב״ה ביום השבת שלא להיות נטבעין לגמרי תוך הטבע. ז״ש כי ששת ימים עשה כו׳ וינח ביום השביעי. והניח יום השבת שלא נעשה בו מלאכה ממעשה בראשית. כדי להיות מקים חירות שלא לטבוע תוך הטבע. וזה הוכן לבנ״י שהם בני עוה״ב ושבת מעין עוה״ב.

In the previous *dvar Torah* we discussed the capacity of the Shabbos, a day which resembles the World to Come, to ensure that that material environment of the weekdays will not greatly impede our service of Hashem. Expanding upon this theme, we note that the mere existence of a single day every week that is devoid of material demands, and even of any form of activity (*Melachah)* employed in the quest for material objectives, enables us to enjoy a more spiritual lifestyle throughout the week. As the Torah states, ... כִּי שֵׁשֶׁת יָמִים עָשָׂה ה׳ אֶת הַשָּׁמַיִם וְאֶת הָאָרֶץ וַיָּנַח בַּיּוֹם הַשְּׁבִיעִי, *For in six days* H*ASHEM created heaven and earth ... and He rested on the seventh day* (*Shemos* 20:11). This means that Hashem set aside (i.e. designated) the Shabbos as a respite from the pursuit of any form of material creation. (*Yisro* 5662)

◆§ Sanctifying the Body (*Guf*)

כי יש בו תיקון הגוף שהוא מעין עוה״ב. ולעתיד לבוא יהיו הגופות מתוקנים ממש כמו נשמות. ובש״ק יש מעין זה תיקון הגופות קצת לכל א׳ כפי הכנת מעשיו בימי המעשה זוכה בשבת לנשמה יתירה שהוא ע״ש תוקף התפשטות כחה בגוף.

While in This World we distinguish between the soul (*neshamah*), which is inherently pure and the body (*guf*), which can only achieve this blessed state through great effort on our part, in the Future

World this distinction will end. Then the body will attain the same *kedushah* as the soul.

By describing Shabbos as מֵעֵין עוֹלָם הַבָּא, a microcosm of the World to Come, *Chazal* are implying that every Shabbos, to some extent, the body acquires some of the spirituality of the soul, a concept known as *tikkun haguf*.

(*Vayishlach* 5636)

◆§ Attaining *Sheleimus*

וכתב במדרש ויבוא יעקב שלם וכו׳ ויחן את פני העיר שנכנס בע״ש כו׳. כי אחר תיקון כל השלימות נמשך הארה מעולם העליון והוא שבת מנוחה מעין עוה״ב. וזה הי׳ שינוי שמו של יעקב שיש גם לכל איש ישראל ב׳ שמות בעוה״ז ובעוה״ב. והנה יעקב זכה להמשיך שם עליון לעצמו בהיותו בעוה״ז.

While ordinarily *sheleimus* (spiritual perfection) can only be attained in the World to Come — and by virtue of a life of Torah and *mitzvos* in This World — on Shabbos, which is a microcosm of the World to Come, this objective can be realized, to some extent, during our life span in *Olam Hazeh*.

It is significant that Yaakov attains the trait of *sheleimus* at the advent of Shabbos. The Torah states, וַיָּבֹא יַעֲקֹב שָׁלֵם ... וַיִּחַן אֶת פְּנֵי הָעִיר, *Yaakov arrived intact* [at the city of Shechem] ... *and he encamped before the city* (*Bereishis* 33:18). *Sfas Emes* explains this as follows: Yaakov arrived at the status of *sheleimus* when he encamped in front of Shechem, an event that according to *Chazal* occurred as the sun set on *erev Shabbos*. All of the Patriarch's struggles with Lavan and Esav were preludes to the *sheleimus* that he attained when Shabbos arrived. Similarly, all of our challenges during the week enable us to achieve a taste of the *sheleimus* of the World to Come on Shabbos.

(*Vayishlach* 5639)

◈ Freedom from the *Yetzer Hara*

ודבר זה נוהג בכל אדם כי מקודם צריכין ללחום עם היצה״ר ולפרוש עצמו ממנו. ולגבור נגד כל המחשבות והרצונות אשר לא לה׳ המה. ואז נעשה בן חורין והוא בן עוה״ב. כי מי שהוא בן חורין מיצה״ר ואינו משועבד לסט״א. הוא בן עוה״ב. והוא בחי׳ שבת. מנוחה בלי מלחמה ועבודה.

By describing Shabbos as a microcosm of the World to Come, *Chazal* may have been referring to the significant lessening of the *yetzer hara's* capacity to tempt us to sin on Shabbos. Just as in the World to Come, the evil inclination no longer exists, so too, to some extent every Shabbos, our temptation to sin may diminish. (*Vayeishev* 5635)

◈ The Light of the Seven Days (אוֹר שִׁבְעַת הַיָּמִים)

והכל ענין אחד כי הוא הארה מעין עוה״ב בחי׳ שמינית וכן מילה ביום השמיני. וכן שבת הוא אור שבעת הימים שנמשך הוספות מן השורש למעלה מעולם הטבע. והוא בחי׳ הגאולה.

While the natural world is subject to certain parameters — such as the ordinary length of a week being no more than seven days — Shabbos, which is a microcosm of the World to Come, is symbolized by the number eight. Since Shabbos is מֵעֵין עוֹלָם הַבָּא, *a microcosm of the World to Come,* it enjoys a measure of Divine blessings beyond anything that we could attain during the finite weekday world. Indeed, it is on this day of boundless *berachos* that we enjoy the *neshamah yeseirah* — the extra dimension of the soul. It is to this other-worldly aspect of Shabbos (represented by the number eight) that the author of the *zemer* (כָּל מְקַדֵּשׁ שְׁבִיעִי) may be referring when he describes Shabbos as אוֹר שִׁבְעַת הַיָּמִים, *the light of the seven days* (the heavenly and supernatural source of the *berachos* that we enjoy on this day).

(*Vayigash* 5659)

אכן בכל ש"ק שניתן מנוחה לבנ"י שביתות המעשה לכן הוא מעין עוה"ב ויכולין להרגיש מהארת אור הגנוז לכן נק' שבת אור שבעת הימים.

Expounding upon this theme (specifically, the connotation of אוֹר שִׁבְעַת הַיָּמִים, *the light of the seven days*; cf. *Yeshayahu* 30:26), we note that when *Klal Yisrael* pronounced נַעֲשֶׂה וְנִשְׁמַע, *we will do and we will listen* (and understand Hashem's Word), they were not only indicating their willingness to obey without attaining complete comprehension of Hashem's Will. They also were delineating the historical sequence of their future relationship with Hashem. For most of history, indeed until the completion of the sixth millennium (refer to *Rosh Hashanah* 31a), we were destined to perform the Divine Will without necessarily comprehending the inner significance of Torah and *mitzvos* (נַעֲשֶׂה). Only upon the completion of this historical cycle, when entering the seventh millennium (during the age of *Mashiach*), will we be able to fully comprehend the rationale for all that we had been observing previously (נִשְׁמַע). Then we will enjoy the אוֹר שִׁבְעַת הַיָּמִים, *the light* (and clarity) *of the seven days* (we will comprehend in the seventh millennium all that we have observed obediently during the first six millennia).

This sequence — first observing and only subsequently understanding the Divine Will — can also only be deduced from the juxtaposition of the conclusion of *Parashas Va'eschanan* (*Devarim* 7:11), where the Torah writes, הַיּוֹם לַעֲשׂתָם, *it is today* (in This World) *to perform them* (that you must observe *mitzvos*) and the commencement of *Parashas Eikev*, וְהָיָה עֵקֶב תִּשְׁמְעוּן, *This shall be the reward when you hearken [to these ordinances]*. It is only at the end that you will truly listen (and comprehend) all that you have been observing. As Bilaam prophesied, כָּעֵת יֵאָמֵר לְיַעֲקֹב וּלְיִשְׂרָאֵל מַה פָּעַל אֵל, *Even now it is said to Jacob and Israel what God has wrought* (*Bamidbar* 23:23) — there will be a time (in the Future World) when it will be said (understood) by *Klal Yisrael* what God has done.

On Shabbos, however, an occasion which is a microcosm of the World to Come, we are able to discern some of the reasoning behind the Torah's Commandments even during our life span in This World. Consequently, Shabbos is described as אוֹר שִׁבְעַת הַיָּמִים, *the light of the seven days* — the moment of clarity when we can comprehend the Divine Will even before the climax of history. (*Eikev* 5643)

⟡ The Light of Torah

וכמו כן כל המצות הם לזכך חומריות בגוף. כמ״ש חז״ל רצה הקב״ה לזכות את ישראל כו׳. והוא בבחי׳ נר מצוה כמ״ש לעיל. אבל שבת שהוא מעין עוה״ב הוא בחי׳ אור תורה כמ״ש חז״ל אין דומה מאור פניו של אדם בשבת לימות החול ואפילו עם הארץ אימת שבת עליו.

Whereas in This World, *mitzvos* fulfill the vital role of purifying our body to serve Hashem, and ultimately to study His Torah, in the World to Come, we will (by virtue of our enhanced spirituality) have earned the distinction of being able to *directly* appreciate the great light that emanates from the Torah.[1] Shlomo *HaMelech* (*Mishlei* 6:23) makes this distinction between נֵר מִצְוָה, *a mitzvah is a lamp* – the luminary (the source of light) that every *mitzvah* provides – and תּוֹרָה אוֹר, *the Torah is light* – the light of the Torah itself. Whereas in This World we can only approach the light of Torah through the luminary of *mitzvos* (which help purify our bodies from the excessive materialism that pervades This World), in the World to Come and on Shabbos, which is מֵעֵין עוֹלָם הַבָּא, one can approach the radiant light of Torah directly.

Chazal allude to the unusual radiance that we all assume on Shabbos when they relate, אֵינוֹ דוֹמֶה מָאוֹר פָּנָיו שֶׁל אָדָם בְּשַׁבָּת לִימוֹת הַחוֹל, *a person's countenance on Shabbos does not resemble his appearance during the week* (*Yalkut Bereishis* 16). In fact, we are told that even an *am ha'aretz* perceives a certain aura on Shabbos. Consequently, he is afraid to deceive someone or, in some instances, deliberately sin.

(*Ki Sisa* 5654)

1. Refer to *Niddah* 61b discussing whether מִצְוֹת בְּטֵלוֹת לֶעָתִיד לָבֹא, *mitzvos will no longer pertain in the World to Come*. In this context, the *Sfas Emes* is not necessarily involving himself in this halachic controversy. Rather he is simply suggesting that we will be able to benefit from the great luminescence of Torah without first having to resort to the medium of *mitzvos*.

☙ *Tefillas Mussaf* – The "Supernatural Prayer"

וזהו מוסף שבת. כמ״ש תמידין כסדרן מוספים כהלכתן. כי התמידים יש להם סדר מסודר. והשבתות וי״ט יש מוסף שהוא שינוי שלא בהדרגה ולמעלה מן הטבע. לכן איתא שבת הוא מעין עוה״ב ... וזה מנוחה ונחלה דרשו חז״ל מנוחה זו שילה נחלה ירושלים. כי ירושלים היא בחי׳ יהודה ודהע״ה שהיא בנין קבוע כמ״ש ירושלים בין הגוים שמתי׳. והיא חומה המבדלת בין ישראל לעמים. אכן בחי׳ משכן שילה הוא מקום שאין התנגדות האומות מגיע שם כלל וזהו בחי׳ השבת שנקרא מנוחה.

One of the most significant consequences of the other-worldly atmosphere of Shabbos is our newly-found capacity to *daven* an additional prayer, *Tefillas Mussaf*. The unique nature of this additional prayer is alluded to in *Tefillas Mussaf* itself when we pray, וַתְּצַוֵּנוּ ה׳ אֱלֹהֵינוּ לְהַקְרִיב ... תְּמִידִים כְּסִדְרָם וּמוּסָפִים כְּהִלְכָתָם, *HASHEM, our God, commanded us to sacrifice ... the daily sacrifice according to its order* (ordinary routine) *and the Mussaf offerings according to their laws* (halachic regulations). By utilizing the term כְּסִדְרָם, *according to its* (established) *order*, only in reference to the daily sacrifice (*korban tamid*) and not for the *mussaf*, we are implying that the *Mussaf tefillah* is based on supernatural parameters (rather than the natural order). It follows that it is only on Shabbos and *Yom Tov*, occasions that simulate the supernatural ambiance of the World to Come, that we can pray *Mussaf*. (*Vayechi* 5647)

☙ Sanctifying This (Material) World

כל ימי חיי לרבות גם בעוה״ז. כמו שיהי׳ לעתיד יום שכולו שבת. ואז נכון יהי׳ הר בית ה׳ גם בעוה״ז. וכל האבות ע״ז שמו כל לבם ונפשם והקב״ה רצה למלאות רצונם וכמו שהי׳ אח״כ בקבלת התורה ומצות ובנין ביהמ״ק ויהי׳ נגמר הכל בשלימות לימות המשיח בב״א. ולכן הוצרך לגלגל סיבת גלות מצרים כי ע״י יציאת מצרים הי׳ הכנה לכל זה ... והנה מנוחת שבת היא מעין עוה״ב. והוא באמת זכר ליציאת מצרים שע״י יציאת מצרים זכינו לשבת שניתנה במכה אחר יצ״מ.

Just as in the World to Come, the entire universe, earth as well as heaven, will be suffused with *kedushah*, so too, on Shabbos, which is

מֵעֵין עוֹלָם הַבָּא, the material world will be imbued with sanctity. As Dovid *HaMelech* pleads, שִׁבְתִּי בְּבֵית ה׳ כָּל יְמֵי חַיַּי, (*Permit me*) *to dwell in the House of* HASHEM *all of the days of my life* (*Tehillim* 27:4). By using the expression כָּל יְמֵי חַיַּי, *all of the days of my life*, Dovid is beseeching Hashem that he should be able to dwell in the House of Hashem even during his life span in This World. This, too, was the primary objective of the *Avos*, that the entire universe — the earth as well as the heavens — be imbued with *kedushah*. Ultimately, their dream was realized and *Olam Hazeh* indeed became a worthy receptacle for the *Shechinah*. Think of some of the greatest moments of Jewish history — *Matan Torah*, as well as the building of the *Beis HaMikdash*. During these seminal moments in the history of *Klal Yisrael*, Hashem's Presence was evident on earth as well as in heaven. Of course, the greatest manifestation of *kavod Shamayim* (Hashem's honor) on this earth, is yet to come — during the long-awaited Messianic Era.

To some extent, this dream of sanctifying the earth with the *kedushah* of heaven is realized every Shabbos, the day described by *Chazal* as being a miniaturized version of the World to Come. Just as in the Future World the entire earth will be consecrated, so too, the *kedushah* of Shabbos may permeate even the most secular aspects of This World.

Utilizing this approach, we gain new insight into *Chazal's* designation of Shabbos as being זֵכֶר לִיצִיאַת מִצְרָיִם, *a remembrance of the Exodus*. It was only through *yetzias Mitzrayim* that we merited one of the first observances of Shabbos at the waters of Marah (refer to *Rashi, Shemos* 15:25, as well as *Rashi, Devarim* 5:12), and ultimately, many of the other seminal moments of Jewish history when the *Shechinah* graced this earth as well as heaven. (*Vayeishev* 5654)

Receiving Reward in This World

ואין פריעת שכר בעוה״ז כי עוה״ב אין בו מציאות בעוה״ז. זולת במצות שבת יוכל להיות קצת שכר בעוה״ז. כי הוא מעין עוה״ב ע״י שמצות שבת הוא שביתות המעשה ולכן יש בו נשמה יתירה. וז״ש אתה מענג נפשך ואני נותן לך שכר ע״ש במד׳.

Despite the generally accepted principle of שְׂכַר מִצְוָה בְּהַאי עָלְמָא לֵיכָּא, *There is no reward for performance of mitzvos in This World* (refer to

Chulin 142a), there is one exception to this rule. We may be rewarded even during our life span in This World for observing the *mitzvos* associated with Shabbos. While *Olam Hazeh* is generally considered to be an inappropriate environment to enjoy the eternal and indescribable spiritual reward reserved for the World to Come,[1] by observing the *mitzvos* of Shabbos, on the day when we are blessed with the presence of the *neshamah yeseirah* and a day which itself is a microcosm of *Olam Haba*, we may merit to be rewarded even in This World. Moreover, by abstaining from many forms of *Melachah* on Shabbos, we help create an environment that is sufficiently spiritual for us to enjoy some of the reward that would ordinarily be reserved for the World to Come. In the words of the *Midrash* (cf. *Devarim Rabbah* 3:1), אַתָּה מְעַנֵּג נַפְשְׁךָ וַאֲנִי נוֹתֵן לְךָ שָׂכָר, *You delight* (by participating in the *mitzvos* of Shabbos) *and I will reward you.* (*Eikev* 5639)

הטעם דשכר מצוה בהאי עלמא ליכא. כי א״י לקבל שכר עוה״ב עד אחר כל השלימות כמ״ש אין כלי מחזיק ברכה אלא שלום. וכל השלימות א״א להשיג בזה העולם לכן שכרו בעקב. אכן בשבת קודש ע״י הביטול שמבטלין הכל יכולין להשיג הארה מעוה״ב. כמ״ש שבת מעין עוה״ב ... רמז למ״ש שבש״ק יש ענין שכר בעוה״ז ג״כ. ולכן רמז האר״י ז״ל ביומו תתן שכרו ר״ת שבת שבשבת יש קבלת שכר כנ״ל.

Utilizing this approach, we may better appreciate why the Shabbos is frequently described as a day of *shalom*, a day of perfection and completion (refer to our chapter on this theme). Whereas in This World we lack the *sheleimus* to be able to truly benefit from Hashem's blessings (and consequently we are generally rewarded for our *mitzvos* in the World to Come), on Shabbos, by virtue of the *neshamah yeseirah*, we reach a level of spiritual completion (*sheleimus* derived from *shalom*). This enables us to enjoy some of the reward that would normally be withheld until the World to Come. As *Chazal* note, לֹא מָצָא הַקָּדוֹשׁ בָּרוּךְ הוּא כְּלִי מַחֲזִיק בְּרָכָה

1. A possible explanation for our inability to enjoy any true reward in This World may be because *Olam Hazeh* (ever since Adam partook of the fruit of the Tree of Knowledge of Good and Evil) has been a constant blend of good and evil. In such an environment, it is virtually impossible to enjoy the infinite spiritual reward that awaits us in *Olam Haba*. However, on Shabbos, the day that simulates the World to Come, a day of undiluted good , we may merit to enjoy the reward for performance of *mitzvos* (*Eikev* 5648).

אֶלָּא הַשָּׁלוֹם ..., HASHEM *found no better receptacle for His Blessings than [the attribute of] peace* (*Uktzin* 3:12). In fact, the *Ari HaKadosh* suggested that the first letters of the term בְּיוֹמוֹ תִתֵּן שְׂכָרוֹ, *on its day you shall grant its reward* (*Devarim* 24:15), spell (when rearranged) Shabbos, alluding to our capacity to enjoy the reward normally reserved for *Olam Haba* on Shabbos. (*Eikev* 5642)

"Severance Pay" for a Mission Accomplished

שבת הוא מעין עוה"ב ולכן יש בו בחי' הענקה לבנ"י והוא בחי' הנשמה יתירה לכל א' כפי עבודתו בימי המעשה. וכמו שזכו בנ"י אחר העבודה במצרים לקבלת התורה שהיא ג"כ הענקה כמו כן בכל גלות הגם שבא ע"י החטאים מ"מ דין הענקה להם.

While the Torah mentions the concept of giving a severance gift, *hanakah* (similar to severance pay) to a departing Jewish servant (*Devarim* 15:14), according to the *Midrash* (*Yalkut Devarim* 898), we may deduce from here that in the World to Come, Hashem will reward generously those who follow His Will – when they have completed their life's mission. It follows that if a Jewish slave, who may have been originally sold because he had stolen and was unable to compensate the victim of his theft, nonetheless receives a form of severance pay, then certainly those who have lived a purposeful life in This World deserve generous compensation, once they have successfully completed their mission.

Not only at the conclusion of a well spent life but even as a week of *avodas Hashem* draws to a close and we enjoy the Shabbos (which is a microcosm of the World to Come), we are granted a beautiful gift – the *neshamah yeseirah*.[1] (*Re'eh* 5659)

1. The *Sfas Emes* suggests that other Divine gifts that were granted to us after a period of servitude may also be understood as being a form of *hanakah*. For example, the Torah was presented to us after many generations of slavery in Egypt. In fact, he concludes, when each of the *galus* periods reaches its conclusion, *Klal Yisrael* will enjoy an appropriate form of *hanakah*.

◆§ Eliciting Our *Penimiyus* (Inner Spark of *Kedushah*)

רק שעיקר העבודה לפתוח נקודה זאת. ובשבת נפתח זה השער כמ״ש שער החצר הפנימית כו׳ ששת ימי המעשה יהיה סגור וביום השבת יפתח. וכמו שראינו קדושת שבת בין הימים. אף שהוא תוך הזמן אעפ״כ הוא מעין עוה״ב.

To appreciate how it is possible that Shabbos attains the distinction of being described as מֵעֵין עוֹלָם הַבָּא, *a microcosm of the World to Come,* we turn to the prophet Yechezkel who describes the inner gate of the Future *Beis HaMikdash* in these terms: וּבְיוֹם הַשַּׁבָּת יִפָּתֵחַ, *it will be opened on the Shabbos day* (*Yechezkel* 46:1). By extension, we suggest that the *navi* is alluding to the inner recesses of our heart that contain a sacred Divine spark, which may be dormant all week but comes to the surface on Shabbos. It is this capacity to evoke the innermost recesses of our *neshamah* (and consequently utilize our full spiritual potential) that resembles the World to Come, a world dominated by *kedushah v'taharah.*

(*Vayigash* 5635)

◆§ Opening the Inner Gates

דכ׳ יפתח ה״א לך את אוצרו הטוב. מכלל שיש אוצר לפנים מאוצר. ולבנ״י מוכן אוצר הטוב כמ״ש ששת ימי המעשה יהי׳ סגור וביום השבת יפתח. שאין ימי המעשה מוכנים לקבל הארת שער החצר הפנימי רק יום השבת ... וז״ש יפתח ה״א לך. ולכן השבת אות מיוחד לבנ״י כמ״ש שבת וישראל מעידין זה על זה. ואיתא עוה״ז דומה לפרוזדור בפני עוה״ב ובנ״י שהם בני עוה״ב נפתח להם הטרקלין. וכן בש״ק שהיא מעין עוה״ב נפתח בו שער הפנימי ...

Among the *berachos* accruing to *Klal Yisrael* if it faithfully observes Torah and *mitzvos* is יִפְתַּח ה׳ לְךָ אֶת אוֹצָרוֹ הַטּוֹב, HASHEM *will open for you His storehouse of goodness* (*Devarim* 28:12), an allusion not only to material blessings but to the great spiritual gift of *Olam Haba.* While

This World is merely a corridor, the World to Come resembles the palace itself. When found deserving, *Klal Yisrael* merits that the palace doors are open on its behalf. Even in This World, every Shabbos, a day which is a microcosm of the World to Come, those inner gates are opened for the Jewish people. As *Chazal* describe Shabbos, מַתָּנָה טוֹבָה בְּבֵית גְּנָזַי, *a good gift in My treasure house* (cf. *Beitzah* 16a). Similarly, the prophet Yechezkel speaks (46:1) of the inner gates of the *Beis HaMikdash*, which only open on Shabbos. (*Ki Savo* 5659)

◆§ The World of *Machshavah* (Thought)

ועיקר הי׳ הפנימיות כמ״ש לחשוב מחשבות לעשות. להעלות המעשה להמחשבה. וז״ש עבדי אתה הוא בעובדא. אשר בך אתפאר הוא ברוחא ובמחשבה כדכ׳ בך. וז״ש חכם לב בכם יבואו ויעשו שיהי׳ העבודה מלבר ומלגאו ... וכן הוא בכל עבודת ימי המעשה מתקיים בש״ק אשר בך אתפאר. לכן צריכין לקשט המעשים בימי המעשה לזכור ביום השבת כענין המשל שכתוב במדרשים. מה שאתה יכול לקבוע אבנים טובות קבע שעתידה ליתן בראשה של מלך. והעיקר הוא ההכנה בעוה״ז לעוה״ב שכולו שבת שאז יתקיים אשר בך אתפאר. ובש״ק יש מעין זה.

We turn to the erection of the *Mishkan* for yet another approach to the resemblance between Shabbos and *Olam Haba*. When designating artisans to construct the *Mishkan*, Moshe takes pains to choose individuals who were not only noted for their craftsmanship and skill but also for their capacity as thinkers. As the Torah stipulates, וְלַחְשֹׁב מַחֲשָׁבֹת לַעֲשֹׂת, *to think those thoughts which lead to action* (*Shemos* 35:32). Similarly, Moshe called upon וְכָל חֲכַם לֵב בָּכֶם יָבֹאוּ וְיַעֲשׂוּ, *Any individual who possesses a wise heart* (the motivator and progenitor of great thoughts) *should come and do* (deeds) (ibid. 35:10).

The relationship between Shabbos and the weekdays (as well as This World and the World to Come) may also be understood in those terms. While during our lifetime in This World we focus on perfecting our deeds, it is in the World to Come that we reap abundant reward for our *mitzvos* and enjoy the most unprecedented intimacy with Hashem. (It is there that we can plumb the depths of the Torah and grasp some of its intimate secrets.) Even in This World on Shabbos, the microcosm of the World to

Come, it is through our attempts at perfecting our *maasei hamitzvos* (*mitzvah* performance) during the weekdays, that we can attain that level whereby our thoughts are consecrated (imbued with *kedushah*) on Shabbos.

Yeshayahu (49:3) delineates this relationship between deeds and thoughts by saying, עַבְדִּי אָתָּה יִשְׂרָאֵל אֲשֶׁר בְּךָ אֶתְפָּאָר, *You are My servant, Israel, in whom I take pride.* Whereas during the week we function primarily as servants of Hashem, focusing on performing exemplary deeds, on Shabbos our very personality and entire character (as the term בְּךָ, *in you,* implies) are also a source of pride and joy to Hashem. In this spirit, the *Midrash* implies that the *mitzvos* that we perform during the week may be compared to precious stones that will eventually become part of a monarch's crown. While during the week, we prepare those crown jewels (our *mitzvos* and *maasim*), it is on Shabbos that they are arranged and set so beautifully onto the King's crown.

(Adapted from *Vayakhel* 5643)

◈ Children and Servants (Shabbos and the Festivals)

דאיתא בזוה״ק פ׳ בא שפרעה הרשע קשר בנ״י תחת מצרים בג׳ קישרין והקב״ה בזכות שלשה אבות קטיר קשורין ע״ש שדרש בכור השפחה בכור השבי בכור בהמה. ונאמר עתה שכמו כן הקב״ה וב״ש לטובה קשר אותנו להיות לו לעבדים בג׳ קשרים והם ג׳ המועדות ... ובענין זה יש לפרש הפסוק עבדי אתה כו׳ על המועדות. אשר בך אתפאר רומז על השבת שהוא למעלה מהמועדות והוא בחי׳ בנים לכן שבת מעין עוה״ב שאז יתקיים זאת בתכלית. לכן כתיב אתפאר לשון עתיד. ועתה לא יש התגלות רק בחינת עבדים. רק בשבת שהוא מעין עוה״ב נמצא מבחי׳ זו ג״כ רשימה גם עתה.

According to the *Zohar HaKadosh* (*Parashas Bo*), Pharaoh sought to subjugate *Klal Yisrael* and to prevent them from leaving Mitzrayim by tying them down[1] through three different methods. These forces of

1. The *Zohar* is apparently alluding to three forms of spiritual coercion that Pharaoh utilized to prevent the Jewish people from rising above the moral abyss that Mitzrayim represented. By putting roadblocks in the path of their *ruchniyus* revival, Pharaoh sought to prevent their physical liberation as well.

tumah (defilement, refer to footnote) designed to constrain the Jewish people from leaving Egypt were known as the בְּכוֹר הַשֶּׁבִי (the firstborn captive), בְּכוֹר הַשִּׁפְחָה (the firstborn maid), and בְּכוֹר הַבְּהֵמָה (the firstborn animal), respectively. To remedy the effect of these three spiritual "knots" (קְשָׁרִים), Hashem granted us the Three Festivals (*Shalosh Regalim*), which testify to the permanent bond that exists between us and Hashem. In fact, on each of these occasions, we recite *Hallel* which opens with the words, הַלְלוּ עַבְדֵי ה׳, *Praise (Hashem) servants of HASHEM.* Similarly, the Torah reiterates three times that we are servants of Hashem: עֲבָדַי הֵם, *they are My servants* (*Vayikra* 25:42); כִּי לִי בְנֵי יִשְׂרָאֵל עֲבָדִים, *the Jewish people are servants of Mine* (ibid. 25:55); and עֲבָדַי הֵם, *they are My servants* (ibid.), corresponding to the triple bond that ties us to Hashem.

On Shabbos, however, we assume, a different (and even more significant) role — that of children of Hashem. Whereas in This World there is no more exalted role than that of becoming Hashem's servants, in the World to Come and on Shabbos, where we assume an intimacy with Hashem that resembles that of *Olam Haba*, we rise to the level of becoming children of Hashem.

The *pasuk* cited (*Yeshayahu* 49:3) in the previous *dvar Torah* reinforces this theme. עַבְדִּי אָתָּה יִשְׂרָאֵל, *You are My servant, Israel,* a relationship borne out by the Three Festivals, אֲשֶׁר בְּךָ אֶתְפָּאָר, *in whom I will glory* in the Future World, when your primary role will be that of children of Hashem. (*Pesach* 5643)

◆ Removing All Barriers

ויהודה המכין למטה כח החרישה שיוכל אח״כ לירד השפע מן השמים ובכח יוסף נגמר הפעולה ונקרא קוצר. אכן לעתיד יהי׳ אחדות למטה כמו למעלה ואז יהיה יהודה עיקר ... ואיתא כי שבת הוא מעין עוה״ב לכן בשבת זכור ושמור בדיבור אחד נאמרו והם ב׳ בחי׳ הנ״ל. ויתכן לרמז בחריש ובקציר תשבות על ב׳ בחי׳ הנ״ל יהודה ויוסף זכור ושמור. שמור הוא בלב. זכור בפה בהתגלות. וזה הרמז עזור לשובתים בשביעי בחריש ובקציר עולמים כי הם ב׳ עולמות.

To appreciate another aspect of the association between Shabbos and the World to Come, we turn to the dramatic reunion of Yosef and his brothers. *Chazal* (*Yalkut Bereishis* 150) react to this great moment in the history of *Klal Yisrael* by citing the *pasuk,* וְנִגַּשׁ חוֹרֵשׁ בַּקֹּצֵר, *the plower will approach the reaper* (*Amos* 9:13). According to them this *pasuk* alludes not only to the present moment when Yosef and Yehudah are reunited but also to their future relationship. While Yehudah, who had just concluded his dramatic appeal that his brother Binyamin be released, assumes the role of the "plower" (preparing the way for the good tidings that would ensue), it is Yosef *HaTzaddik,* the "reaper," who completes the task begun by his brother (by releasing Binyamin).

Perhaps, these lofty thoughts of *Chazal* refer to different approaches in the realm of *avodas Hashem.* Yehudah's role is to initiate the process of preparing the universe so that it be a suitable habitat for the *Shechinah,* analogous to the plower of a barren field. Yosef *HaTzaddik,* in his great merit, consummates the process (reaping) by ensuring that Hashem's blessings be showered upon this earth (which had been prepared for His Presence through the efforts of Yehudah). This presupposes a two-step process, which generally occurs in *Olam Hazeh* – first, "plowing," preparing the world for the *Shechinah,* followed by "reaping," actually enjoying the bountiful harvest of blessings coming from Hashem. God willing, the time will come when This World will have attained such a lofty level of *kedushah* that even without prior preparation it will be the perfect dwelling place for Hashem. Then there no longer will be a distinction between the initial efforts of Yehudah (the plower) and Yosef (the reaper). As the *pasuk* reads, "the plower will *approach* the reaper."

To some extent, on Shabbos, the gap between our initial efforts at evoking Hashem's *berachos* and our actual enjoyment of these blessings will no longer exist. On that day of such intense sanctity, when the Presence of the *Shechinah* visibly permeates the earth as well as the heavens, it will be possible to "reap" the bountiful rewards of heaven without first plowing and preparing the earth. On Shabbos too, which is מֵעֵין עוֹלָם הַבָּא, *a microcosm of the World to Come,* to some extent, the plower and reaper, Yehudah and Yosef, unite.

Utilizing this approach, we may derive a new explanation of the *pasuk,* בֶּחָרִישׁ וּבַקָּצִיר תִּשְׁבֹּת, *you should rest (from) plowing and harvesting* (*Shemos* 34:21), which homiletically may refer to the sequential process of first "plowing" and preparing the universe to later "reap" Hashem's *berachos.* While this two-phased process is necessary during the weekdays, on Shabbos we rest from this sequence and more expeditiously "reap" Hashem's bountiful harvest. Similarly, the stanza in the *zemer*, עֲזוֹר לַשּׁוֹבְתִים בַּשְּׁבִיעִי בֶּחָרִישׁ וּבַקָּצִיר עוֹלָמִים, *assist those who rest on the seventh day from plowing and the reaping of two worlds*, may also allude to the similarity between the World to Come and Shabbos — even during our life span in This World. In each instance, we rest from the usual sequence whereby spiritual plowing invariably precedes reaping.

(Adapted from *Vayigash* 5652)

כי כל ימי המעשה דכתיב ששת ימים תעבוד. תעשה מלאכה. ואעפ"כ יש קדושה גנוזה גם בעשי' ממש והוא בחי' מלאך ושליח כי כל דבר יש בו חיות מהשי"ת ונשתלח לעולם כדי לעשות רצון השי"ת שיש מצות בכל מעשה האדם. רק שנתלבש בעניני עוה"ז וצריך שמירה יותר אל תמר בו. רק לידע כי גם זה מחיות השי"ת כי שמי בקרבו כו' ועבדתם את ה' כו' הוא בחי' שבת בלי התלבשות המעשה כי שבת מעין עוה"ב ואז והסירותי מחלה מקרבך כו'. וזה שא"צ בקשה על שום דבר בשבת.

This same concept — the removal of all "barriers" between us and Hashem — is alluded to by the Torah when it suggests two different approaches how we can perceive Hashem. At times it is by seeking His Presence in the midst of the material world. As the Torah states, הִנֵּה אָנֹכִי שֹׁלֵחַ מַלְאָךְ לְפָנֶיךָ, *Behold I will send an emissary before you* (*Shemos* 23:20), an allusion to Hashem's management of the universe during the week when His Presence is often veiled by His "emissary" (the material world that He has created during the six weekdays). Even then, though the *Shechinah's* Presence may be veiled, our challenge is to find Him amidst His Universe. As the next *pasuk* continues, אַל תַּמֵּר בּוֹ, *Do not exchange Him* (do not confuse the surface materialism), כִּי שְׁמִי בְּקִרְבּוֹ, *for My Name is in its midst* (beneath the outer surface of materialism).

However, on Shabbos, Hashem manages His universe in a manner that we may be privileged to perceive His Presence more directly. On that day, which is a microcosm of the World to Come (when His Presence will be revealed to all mankind), the Torah says: וַעֲבַדְתֶּם אֵת ה' אֱלֹהֵיכֶם, *you will* (directly) *serve HASHEM, your God* (*Shemos* 23:25).

Utilizing the foregoing approach, we can appreciate why in the Shabbos *Shemoneh Esrei* there are no explicit references to our material needs. On this day when all material barriers between us and Hashem are dismantled – a day which resembles the intense spirituality of the World to Come – (under ideal circumstances) our material concerns are addressed without explicitly petitioning Hashem for their resolution. As the above *pasuk* (23:25) continues, וַהֲסִרֹתִי מַחֲלָה מִקִּרְבֶּךָ, *I will remove illness from your midst* (merely by serving Hashem). *(Mishpatim* 5631)

◆§ Restoring Sinai's Crowns

ולכן איתא כי בשבת קודש מחזיר מרע"ה הכתרים לישראל. דמתאחדין בשבת ברזא דאחד. והנה שבת הוא מעין עוה"ב. ולעתיד עתיד מרע"ה להחזירם לנו כמ"ש בגמ' ושמחת עולם על ראשם. שמחה שמעולם על ראשם. ושבת שהוא מעין עוה"ב זוכין ג"כ לשמחה זו.

נראה שבשבת לא קלקלו ע"י החטא. ולכך שבת מעין עוה"ב כמ"ש בלוחות ראשונות חירות כו'. וכן איתא בחטא אדם הראשון שנתקבל בשבת. ג"כ כנ"ל שלא הגיע החטא לבחי' שבת. והוא ששבת במקום הגניזה כמ"ש מתנה טובה יש לי בבית גנזי כו' וכיון שנגנז לא הגיע קלקול החטא לשבת כנ"ל.

To apppreciate yet another dimension of the other-worldly nature of Shabbos, we recall the *Chazal* stating that when the Jewish people erected the Golden Calf, they forfeited the crowns that they had first received at Sinai (refer to *Shabbos* 88a stating that when *Klal Yisrael* affirmed their commitment to Torah with the renowned words, נַעֲשֶׂה וְנִשְׁמַע, every Jew was granted two crowns). However, *Chazal* also offered a measure of comfort, noting that these crowns will be restored in the Future World.

We suggest that some semblance of these crowns is enjoyed by the Jewish people every Shabbos, a day which resembles the World to Come. To appreciate why this is the case, we cite the *pasuk*, תּוֹרָה צִוָּה לָנוּ מֹשֶׁה מוֹרָשָׁה קְהִלַּת יַעֲקֹב, *The Torah commanded to us by Moshe is the heritage of the congregation of Yaakov* (*Devarim* 33:4). While it is true that in the aftermath of the sin of the *Egel* all of the crowns that *Klal Yisrael* forfeited were granted to Moshe, whenever we are able to unite as one harmonious nation (*kehillas Yaakov*), we are able to retrieve these crowns. There is no better opportunity to unite than on Shabbos, the day described by the *Zohar* as דְאִתְאַחֲדַת בְּרָזָא דְאֶחָד, *She* (Shabbos) *becomes united in the secret of Oneness.* (*Terumah* 5658)

Alternatively, we propose that on Shabbos, a day which is a microcosm of the World to Come, *Klal Yisrael* is restored to its status prior to the sin of the *egel*. Just as prior to the Golden Calf, we existed in a virtually sin-free environment, so too, on Shabbos we return to this pristine, sin-free world. In such an environment, we deserve to enjoy those hallowed crowns of *Matan Torah* again.

To help comprehend why every Shabbos we are somehow able to transcend the world in which we currently live in favor of a sin-free environment, we propose that sins can only leave an impact in that part of the universe that is visible and apparent. However, Shabbos, which is a gift from Hashem's hidden treasure house (refer to the chapter on "The Gift of Shabbos"), emanates from a "hidden" impenetrable universe that is beyond the reach of even the worst sin committed on this earth. Thus, even the sin of the *egel* left no impact on the Shabbos day.

(*Ki Sisa* 5632)

☙ Returning to the First Two Commandments

וצריך שלא להיות דבר המפסיק בינתים. וסמיך לפרשת השבת ויתן אל משה. כמ״ש במ״א כי בשבת יש הארה מלוחות הראשונים. שזהו כוחו של מרע״ה דכ׳ ומשה יקח את האהל. ובשבת מחזירן לבנ״י ומתחדש אותו הארה בכל שבת. ובכל שבת חוזר הקב״ה ונותן מתנה זו למשה שהוא הדעת של כלל בנ״י. ואיתא ב׳ דברות שמעו בנ״י מהקב״ה בעצמו ואח״כ אמרו דבר אתה עמנו. והי׳ בזה הלימוד שכחה. וע״ז מבקשין ישקני מנשיקות פיהו ע״ש במדרש שיה״ש שהשיב להם הקב״ה אין זה עתה רק לעתיד ועל לבם אכתבנה ע״ש. והנה שבת מעין עוה״ב. לכן יש בו הארת ב׳ הדברות מפי של הקב״ה.

In the previous *dvar Torah* we discussed how the crowns that were given to the Jewish people at the time of *Matan Torah* are restored every Shabbos. In a similar vein,we suggest here that on Shabbos we return to the exalted spiritual level that our forefathers enjoyed when they heard the first two commandments, אָנֹכִי ה׳ אֱלֹהֶיךָ and לֹא יִהְיֶה לְךָ, directly from Hashem. Whereas the other eight commandments, which Moshe transmitted to the Jewish people (as well as the rest of the Torah), are frequently forgotten (unless we review their contents diligently), the first two commandments transmitted *directly* by Hashem are less likely to be forgotten. In fact, the opening verse of *Shir HaShirim* reflects *Klal Yisrael's* passionate desire to return to the halcyon moments at Sinai when Hashem gave the first two commandments: יִשָּׁקֵנִי מִנְּשִׁיקוֹת פִּיהוּ is literally translated, *Let Him kiss me with the kisses of His mouth* (*Shir HaShirim* 1:2), which according to the *Midrash* is an allusion to the first two commandments transmitted from the "mouth" of Hashem (i.e., His Divine Command) to the Jewish people. Hashem responds that this degree of intimacy is not possible in This World and it is only in the World to Come that the intimacy enjoyed at Sinai will once again be afforded to *Klal Yisrael*. Nevertheless, on Shabbos, which is a microcosm of the World to Come, *Klal Yisrael* is on so exalted a level that it is able to return to the level of intimacy with Hashem that they enjoyed when the first two commandments were transmitted. Consequently, on Shabbos we not only study Torah but we may be able to retain much more readily what we had learned.

It is significant that the positive and negative commandments associated with Shabbos, *Zachor* and *Shamor*, parallel the first two of the *Aseres HaDibros* — אָנֹכִי (a positive commandment) and לֹא יִהְיֶה לְךָ (a negative commandment) — supporting our contention that every Shabbos the milieu of the first two commandments is restored. (*Ki Sisa* 5661)

◆§ Only Through Effort

ואיתא במד׳ תורה וא״י ועוה״ב אין זוכין רק ע״י יסורין. וגם שבת הוא מעין עוה״ב. לכן כפי היגיעה בימות החול זוכין לשבת וכמ״ש במרה נצטוו. כי אחר גלות מצרים זכו לשבת.
לכן שבת מעין עוה״ב וזכו לזה אחר יצ״מ. לכן שבת זכר ליצ״מ.
דא״א לקבל הארה מעין עוה״ב רק ע״י יסורים. ולכן הוא זכר ליצ״מ.

Drawing the analogy between Shabbos and the World to Come even further, we note that in both instances *yesurim* (suffering) may be a prerequisite.[1] Just as the supreme spiritual bliss of *Olam Haba* can only

1. The millennia of suffering that the Jewish people have suffered throughout the long *galus* at the hands of various tyrannical regimes are an essential component of the *yesurim* that we experience in This World prior to reaping the infinite reward of *Olam Haba* (*Shemos* 5658).

be attained through the suffering that we first experience in This World, so too, the other-worldly ambiance of Shabbos can only be attained through the many challenges of the weekdays. It is by struggling and ultimately prevailing over the *yetzer hara* that we merit the microcosm of the World to Come that Shabbos represents. How appropriate that the *mitzvah* of Shabbos was first transmitted to the Jewish people almost immediately after *yetzias Mitzrayim* (at Marah). It was through the relentless persecution that our forefathers suffered in Egypt that they now merited the Shabbos.[1] (*Shemos* 5634, 5658)

◆§ A World Without *Melachah* (A World of Pure Thoughts)

וכמו דאיתא שיתא שלפי שנין הוי עלמא וחד חרוב.פי׳ כיון שיהי׳ אז הכל הדיקדוק הדין והמשפט. לכן אין העולם מתקיים. כמו כן שבת מעין עוה״ב נאסר בו כל העבודה. ורק הרצון והמחשבה לשמים.

To obtain a new perspective on Shabbos being a microcosm of the World to Come (and of the prohibition of *Melachah* – refer to the chapter on this topic), we recall the *maamar Chazal* (*Rosh Hashanah* 31a), שִׁיתָּא אַלְפֵי שְׁנֵי הֲוָה עָלְמָא וְחַד חָרוּב, *the universe will exist for six millennia and (then) it will be destroyed for one millennium.* Whereas during the first six millennia (corresponding to the Six Days of Creation) the universe, to a large extent, perseveres on the basis of Divine kindness, during the seventh millennium which corresponds to Shabbos (a day of perfection, *sheleimus*), the world is judged on the basis of strict justice (*middas hadin*). On that basis, the universe is deemed no longer worthy of existence (in its present form). Similarly, every Shabbos, which is a microcosm of the World to Come (represented by the seventh millennium), a day of supreme spirituality (in the words of the *Zohar*, יומא דנשמתין ... ולא דגופא, *a day of the soul not the body*), we are held to a higher standard. Instead of the universe being judged on the basis of

1. Perhaps for this reason the Torah (in the second rendition of the *Aseres HaDibros, Devarim* 8:15) attributes *shemiras Shabbos* to the Exodus. It was only through the suffering that we endured in Mitzrayim that *Klal Yisrael* merited to receive the *mitzvah* of Shabbos (author's note).

Divine kindness, its very existence (in a physical sense) is contingent on the perfect behavior of its inhabitants. Inasmuch as perfection (at least in the contemporary world) is not possible, rather than allow the universe to continue in its present physical form (*olam hamaaseh),* Hashem "destroys" the material world – symbolized by the thirty-nine forms of *melachah.* Simultaneously, he replaces it with a new (even loftier) world based on spirituality, the world of *machshavah,* of thought, and of an intense desire to serve Hashem. (*Va'eira* 5636)

☙ Forgetting About *Melachah*

וברש"י שבת שבתון מנוחת מרגוע ולא עראי. פי' שלא יהי' השביתה עיכוב המלאכה לפי שעה רק לשכוח מכל ענין המלאכה. שבאמת שבת קודש הוא הכנה לעוה"ב. כמ"ש חז"ל שהוא מעין עוה"ב. וצריך האדם להתלמד לשכוח כל המעשים בבוא יום השבת. וכמו כן יזכה בנקל למנוחת עוה"ב.

Whereas in the previous *dvar Torah* we portrayed a new world – one of *machshavah* supplanting the material world on Shabbos – here we will focus on the role played by every individual in ensuring that Shabbos indeed becomes מֵעֵין עוֹלָם הַבָּא, *a microcosm of the World to Come.*

Evidently, the transformation from the material environment of the weekdays to the "taste" of *Olam Haba* that characterizes Shabbos cannot occur by itself. On the contrary, it is critical that at the beginning of Shabbos we take the initiative in forgetting the many material concerns of This World. As *Rashi* states, מְנוּחַת מַרְגּוֹעַ וְלֹא מְנוּחַת עֲרָאִי, resting from *Melachah* should be perceived as *"a permanent rest, not (merely) a temporary reprieve."* Drawing upon the analogy to the World to Come that we have been making throughout this chapter, we suggest that just as in the World to Come, all of This World's material concerns are forgotten, so too, with the advent of Shabbos one must leave behind all of *Olam Hazeh's melachos.* In fact, there may be an association between the degree to which one forgets about *Olam Hazeh* at the beginning of Shabbos and one's capacity to enjoy the World to Come's totally spiritual ambiance.

(*Ki Sisa* 5638)

◆ Forgetting *Olam Hazeh*/ Remembering the Divine Spark

דכ׳ שמעי בת וראו כו׳ ושכחי עמך. שצריך האדם להשתמש במדת זכירה ושכחה. לשכוח הבלי עולם ולזכור בחלק אלקות שהיא בו בעצם. וזהו זכור ושמור. והנה שבת היא מעין עוה״ב ולעתיד ישתכח כל עוה״ז ויתדבקו בשורש העליון ומעין זה בכל שבת קודש. וכמו כן לבן ותכלת.

In the previous *dvar Torah* we noted that every Shabbos, we make every effort to set aside and even forget — the many material concerns (and *melachos*) that frequently dominate This World. Extending this theme even further, we propose that just as in the World to Come we will forget every aspect of *Olam Hazeh* in favor of the overwhelming spirituality of that world, so too, when Shabbos arrives. Every Shabbos, we gain the capacity to forget the many fleeting matters of This World and to discover our own enormous spiritual potential.

In fact, the dual nature of the commandment of Shabbos, *Zachor V'Shamor*, may allude to a dual process — the forgetting and the remembering that occurs every Shabbos. On one hand, *Shamor*, guarding oneself from the fleeting vanities of This World by forgetting *Olam Hazeh*, and at the same time *Zachor*, recalling the Divine Spark that we all possess.[1]

This double charge given by Hashem to *Klal Yisrael* — to leave behind our inadequate past and simultaneously remember our immense innate spiritual potential — is aptly stated in *Tehillim*: שִׁמְעִי בַת וּרְאִי ... וְשִׁכְחִי עַמֵּךְ וּבֵית אָבִיךְ, *Hear, O daughter* (the Jewish people) *and see ... forget your nation and your father's house* (45:11). (*Shelach* 5659)

ושבת קודש ניתן לישראל יום א׳ לעזוב כל עניני עוה״ז והוא מעין עוה״ב כמ״ש חז״ל והוא סימן כפי מה שמדבק האדם עצמו בקדושת שבת יש לו חלק לעוה״ב והוא קבלת מלכות. ובימי המעשה קבלת מצות כנ״ל.

---

1. Refer to the complete text of *Sfas Emes* where he suggests that the dual components of *tzitzis*, *techeiles* (sky blue wool) and *lavan* (wool that is not dyed) also represent these two challenges: forgetting the material concerns of This World and drawing closer to our own Divine Spark.

In fact, there may be a direct association between the degree to which one "clings" (מְדַבֵּק עַצְמוֹ) to the *kedushah* of Shabbos and his portion that he will enjoy in the World to Come. Those individuals who are truly attached to the Shabbos, to the extent that they put aside all of their worldly concerns when Shabbos arrives, are indicating already in This World that they deserve a portion in the World to Come. Moreover, there may be a correlation between the extent to which one clings to Shabbos' sacred ambiance and the extent of his portion in the World to Come. (*Eikev* 5633)

◈ The Song of the Future World

במדרש קח את הלוים כמה נימין הי׳ בכנור שבע ולימות המשיח ח׳ ולעתיד עשרה בנבל עשור כו׳. כי השירה תליא בזמן. ולכן בכל יום יש שיר אחר כי ההתחדשות שיש בכל יום נותן השירה כמ״ש ז״ל כי השמש אומרת שירה וזורחת ע״ש בפסוק שמש בגבעון דום. כי בכל יום יש הארה אחרת כדאיתא בשם האר״י ז״ל כי אין כל יום דומה לחבירו מבריאת עולם ... וכמו כן שבת מעין עוה״ב לכן מזמור שיר ליום השבת כתיב בי׳ עלי עשור. ושבת הוא בחי׳ שיר השירים שכולל כל השירים של ימי המעשה.

Even the song dedicated to the Shabbos day, מִזְמוֹר שִׁיר לְיוֹם הַשַּׁבָּת (*Tehillim* 92), reflects the other-worldly nature of Shabbos. *Chazal* relate (*Arachin* 13b) that the harp in *Olam Haba* will consist of ten strings (whereas in This World there are seven strings on the Temple's harp and in the Messianic age there will be eight strings). However, every Shabbos, we read Dovid's exhortation to praise Hashem עֲלֵי עָשׂוֹר, *on the ten-stringed instrument.*

It is no coincidence that each epoch of *Klal Yisrael's* history requires its unique *shirah*. In fact, every day of the week enjoys its own song.[1] As the *Ari HaKadosh* noted, every day since Creation is distinct from any of its counterparts. To herald the uniqueness of each day (and the sense of renewal that we experience with each new day), we offer

1. Perhaps it is for this reason that *Leviim* are disqualified from performing certain aspects of the Divine Service — particularly to sing the *shir shel yom* — on the basis of age alone. The ability to sing Hashem's praises is very much predicated on our song being timely in nature. A Levite who has concluded his years of service is no longer as well poised to evoke the freshness and vitality that every day brings (adapted from *Beha'aloscha* 5653).

tribute to Hashem with a different *shirah* each day of the week. It is on Shabbos, a microcosm of the World to Come, that we can best evoke the joy and the distinct ambiance of *Olam Haba*. (*Beha'aloscha* 5653)

◆§ Removing Old Garments/ Donning New Garments

לכן בהתגלות הארת השבת והארת הנשמה יתירה באדם בורחת כל הסט״א. והוסר כל החושך המכסה הפנימיות. וע״ז תקנו רצה והחליצנו. החליצנו כולל שניהם. הסרת מלבושים דחול וללבוש מחלצות דקדושה. כי שבת מעין עוה״ב וכמו דכתיב הסירו הבגדים הצואים כו׳ והלבש אותו מחלצות כן הוא בשבת מעין זה.

By comparing Shabbos to *Olam Haba, Chazal* may be providing an additional source for the tradition that we wear distinct (and better) garments on Shabbos than during the week (refer to *Shabbos* 113a). Upon entering the World to Come our "garments" that we had worn in This World (i.e. our ties to *Olam Hazeh*) are first removed and only then do we don our new garments (the mantle of *ruchniyus* that graces the soul), which are more suited to *Olam Haba*. [Refer to *Zechariah*, הָסִירוּ הַבְּגָדִים הַצֹּאִים מֵעָלָיו ... וְהַלְבֵּשׁ אֹתְךָ מַחֲלָצוֹת, *remove the besmirched clothing from him ... and dress him with fresh clothing* (3:4). This may be an allusion to first severing the soul's ties to the material world followed by the *neshamah's* immersion in the sacred milieu of the World to Come.] Similarly, every Shabbos we first remove our weekday garments and only then don our fresh (and distinct) Shabbos clothing. When we recite in *Birchas HaMazon*, רְצֵה וְהַחֲלִיצֵנוּ (at the beginning of the special paragraph pertaining to Shabbos), the term וְהַחֲלִיצֵנוּ may allude to both aspects of the transformation that we experience with the advent of every Shabbos. On one hand, is the removal of the worn garments of the week (according to this approach, וְהַחֲלִיצֵנוּ means "to remove").[1] However, it also refers to the new garments that we don in

1. This interpretation of חָלַץ as *remove* is used, for example, in the Torah in the verse, וְצִוָּה הַכֹּהֵן וְחִלְּצוּ אֶת הָאֲבָנִים ..., *The Kohen shall command, and they shall remove the stones ...* (*Vayikra* 14:40). Also regarding *yibum*, וְנִגְּשָׁה יְבִמְתּוֹ אֵלָיו ... וְחָלְצָה נַעֲלוֹ מֵעַל רַגְלוֹ ..., *then his sister-in-law shall approach him ... she shall remove his shoe from on his foot ...* (*Devarim* 25:9).

honor of Shabbos (related to מַחֲלָצוֹת). (*Ki Sisa* 5649)

◆§ A Day of Joy

והענין הוא כי בעוה״ז אין השמחה והשירה בשלימות כמ״ש חז״ל ישמח ה׳ במעשיו לעתיד. אכן יש זמנים שבנ״י יכולין להרגיש משמחה ושירה העתידה. וז״ש בתפלת שבת ישמחו במלכותך שומרי שבת. כי בהשמחה לעתיד במלכותו ית׳. יהי׳ לבנ״י חלק גדול. בזכות שהם שומרי שבת. ולכן כיון ששבת הוא מעין עוה״ב. יכולין להרגיש מעין אותה השמחה העתידה. לכן דרשו חז״ל וביום שמחתכם על השבת. שהוא מעין עולם שכולו שבת. ואז ישמח ה׳ במעשיו.

By describing Shabbos as a microcosm of the World to Come, *Chazal* may have been alluding to the great joy that will pervade the universe in the Future World. Whereas in This World, our happiest moments are often tinged with sadness, in *Olam Haba* there will be no finite limits to our *simchah*. In fact, the boundless joy that *Klal Yisrael* will then enjoy may be in large part attributed to their determination to always observe the laws of Shabbos. As we read in the *Mussaf Shemoneh Esrei*, יִשְׂמְחוּ בְמַלְכוּתְךָ שׁוֹמְרֵי שַׁבָּת, *Let those who observe the Shabbos rejoice in Your coronation* (during the Messianic Era when all mankind will acknowledge Hashem's sovereignty).

While the full measure of the joy that Hashem shares with His subjects is reserved for the World to Come [as we read in *Tehillim* (104:31), יִשְׂמַח ה׳ בְּמַעֲשָׂיו, *HASHEM will rejoice with His creations*], nonetheless on Shabbos, which is a replica of the World to Come, we can perceive some of the joy with which the universe will be suffused in *Olam Haba*. To support our contention that even in This World we can experience true joy on Shabbos, we cite the *Chazal*, וּבְיוֹם שִׂמְחַתְכֶם אֵלּוּ שַׁבָּתוֹת, *the day of your joy, refers to Shabbos* (*Yalkut Bamidbar* 724).

(*Beshalach* 5652)

◆§ The Soul's Revelation

ופנימיות הענין הוא שיין המשומר בענביו הוא עצמו כח הנשמה המסתרת בגוף. וא״י לשלוט בה מגע נכרי כי היא סתומה. ועלי׳ נאמר עין לא ראתה זה יין המשומר. ולעתיד צדיקים יושבין ועטרותיהם בראשיהם הוא התגלות הנשמה בשלימות. אך כי שבת הוא מעין עוה״ב לכן יש בו מעט התגלות הנשמה כמ״ש חז״ל נשמה יתירה בשבת קודש. לכן מקדשין על היין לרמוז על התגלות הנשמה כנ״ל. ולכן יין צריך שמירה ממגע נכרי.

To appreciate the relationship between Shabbos and the World to Come, we need to consider the meaning of some of the metaphors utilized by *Chazal* to describe *Olam Haba*. For example, they relate that the treasures of the Future World are compared to יַיִן הַמְשׁוּמָּר בַּעֲנָבָיו מִשֵּׁשֶׁת יְמֵי בְרֵאשִׁית, *wine that has been preserved in its grapes since the Six Days of Creation* (*Berachos* 34b). Our rabbis also portray the World to Come as a beautiful spiritual realm, wherein the *tzaddikim* repose wearing crowns on their heads (*Berachos* 17a). These (very esoteric) metaphors may be the mechanism which *Chazal* use to allude to the revelation of the soul. Whereas in This World, the soul is concealed in the body, just as wine is preserved in the outer casing of the grape, in *Olam Haba* the wine will be extracted from the grape (the soul will be revealed). When *Chazal* speak of the righteous resting in *Olam Haba* with their resplendent crowns on their heads, they too may be alluding to the emergence of the soul from its previous plight of being subsumed within the body. Whereas previously the crown jewel of every one of us, the *neshamah*, was recessed deep within our persona (גוף), in the Future World those crowns will be very apparent and, in fact, be worn proudly over our heads.

This phenomenon — the emergence of the soul from its previously "subdued" role — while primarily occurring in the Future World, to some extent occurs every Shabbos, the day which is a microcosm of the World to Come. This wondrous occurrence is materially assisted through the presence of the *neshamah yeseirah*, the extra dimension of the soul that we enjoy every Shabbos.

Based upon this approach we may be able to derive additional justification for the requirement that *Kiddush* be recited over wine. By doing so, we are alluding to our hidden capacity for spirituality — to evoke the *neshamah* that emerges every Shabbos, just as wine will emerge from its "grapes" in *Olam Haba.* (*Ki Sisa* 5653)

◆§ Our True Personality (צִיוּר רוּחָנִי) Emerges

והנה שבת אמרו חז"ל שהוא מעין עוה"ב ולכן נתגלה בו מעין ציור וצלם הנ"ל לכן אמרו אין דומה מאור פניו של אדם כו'.

In the previous *dvar Torah,* we emphasized the emergence of the *neshamah* on Shabbos. Expanding upon that theme, we propose that our true inner spiritual personality, submerged to some extent all week long, is revealed on Shabbos.

To appreciate this point, we turn to the Torah's description of the impact of *mitzvos* on all of us — אֲשֶׁר יַעֲשֶׂה אֹתָם הָאָדָם וָחַי בָּהֶם, *which man shall carry out and by which he shall live* (*Vayikra* 18:5). The word בָּהֶם, *with them,* can be explained that through observance of *mitzvos* a person's true personality is created and he will live בָּהֶם, through them. While it may appear that our body, consisting of 248 limbs and 365 sinews, is our true essence, in reality, the body is only the outer casing concealing the true persona — our inner spiritual self, which is formed by the 248 positive commandments and 365 negative commandments. As the foregoing *pasuk* indicates, it is through *mitzvos asei* and *lo saasei* that this dynamic inner personality develops.While our *guf* decomposes after death, our true self formed through *mitzvos* not only remains after our passing but actually emerges as the dominant force in the World to Come — once the soul has been liberated from the body's exterior casing.

We are privileged to evoke our true self — our dynamic inner spiritual personality — not only in the World to Come but also on Shabbos, which is מֵעֵין עוֹלָם הַבָּא. As *Chazal* relate (*Yalkut Shimoni, Bereishis* 16), a person's countenance on Shabbos is different than during the week.

(*Acharei* 5653)

Satiating the Soul (Replicating the Manna)

והנה נשאר מזה משהו לדורות כמ״ש מלא העומר כו׳ למשמרת כו׳. ונראה כי סעודת שבת שהוא מעין עוה״ב והוא נחלת יעקב. כמ״ש והאכלתיך נ״י אביך שהיא נחלה בלי מצרים. פי׳ שהמאכל עצמו יש בו חירות. ולכן נקרא סעודתא דמהימנותא והוא מעין אכילת המן.

By declaring that Shabbos is a microcosm of the World to Come, *Chazal* may have been alluding to the resemblance between eating the manna and partaking of the Shabbos meals. One of the outstanding characteristics of the manna was that it primarily satiated the soul rather than the body.[1] In the same vein, every Shabbos, a day of such rarefied spirituality that it simulates the World to Come, when we partake of the Shabbos meals, we benefit spiritually as well as physically (refer to the chapter on *Shalosh Seudos* for further discussion of these concepts).

The Torah implies that some remnant of the manna's immense spiritual powers will be enjoyed by future generations of the Jewish people. As the *pasuk* states, מְלֹא הָעֹמֶר מִמֶּנּוּ לְמִשְׁמֶרֶת לְדֹרֹתֵיכֶם, *a full omer worth of it* (manna) *should be preserved for your* (future) *generations* (*Shemos*

1. Refer to the full text of the *Sfas Emes* where he discusses at length the justification for this distinctive characteristic of the manna. In particular, he notes that the Torah emphasizes that the manna should be *seen* [לְמַעַן יִרְאוּ אֶת הַלֶּחֶם, *in order that they see the bread* (*Shemos* 16:32)]. Rather than merely partake of the manna , our forefathers were encouraged to look at and absorb its full spiritual impact, as well as its physical attributes. In the words of the *Sfas Emes*, שהיה להם פקיחת עין השכל וסתימת עין הגשמי, *they partook of the manna with an open intellect and a closed* (minimal) *craving for material pleasure enjoyed.*

16:32). We suggest that this phenomenon occurs every Shabbos when we partake of the spiritual nurturement provided by the *Shalosh Seudos.*
(*Beshalach* 5654)

◆§ An Ideal Opportunity to Liquidate Amalek

פי׳ שע״י השבת יום מנוחה שמתדבקין בני ישראל בנקודה הפנימיות שהוא ענין העלאת הנרות כו׳. ע״ז והיה בהניח כו׳. כי בנ״י היו ראוין בעת יצ״מ להיות כל הנהגתם למעלה מהטבע כמו שיהי׳ לעתיד. רק ע״י זה הרשע עמלק ימ״ש שעירבב אותנו קודם גמר התיקון כמ״ש בדרך. לכן צריכין כל אלו היגיעות וגליות המרים. ולכן בש״ק שמתעורר הנהגת ישראל שלמעלה מהטבע. כמ״ש שהוא מעין עוה״ב. ע״ז מתעורר בשבת שנאת עמלק. ובכל שבת יש קצת מחיית עמלק כפי שמירת שבת שבישראל.

כמ״ש בשבת יעשה כולו תורה. ועמלק אין לו מגע רק בעשי׳. לכן כשיש ביטול המעשה נמחה זכר עמלק. כמו שיהי׳ לעתיד ליום שכולו שבת.

וכשיהי׳ יום מנוחה אז יתבטל השקר. וז״ש והי׳ בהניח כו׳ תמחה כו׳ זכר עמלק. ומעין זה בכל שבת. יום מנוחה. מעין עוה״ב. יום שכולו שבת. ושבת סהדותא אקרי לכן הוא זמן מחיית עמלק.

A particularly significant benefit resulting from the other-worldly atmosphere of Shabbos is that we enjoy an increased capacity to perform the *mitzvah* of eliminating Amalek. To appreciate the relationship between Shabbos and *mechiyas Amalek,* we recall that *Parashas Shekalim* which discusses *Klal Yisrael's* generous contribution of the half-shekel coin (and, by extension, the entire theme of generously giving *tzedakah*) always precedes *Parashas Zachor,* which is devoted to the elimination of Amalek. This juxtaposition of *parshiyos* suggests that as a result of generously giving *tzedakah,* we are able to evoke the Divine Spark (נְקוּדָה פְּנִימִיּוּת) that is always latent in every soul.

Moreover, there is another prerequisite for successfully eliminating Amalek — striving to lead a supernatural life (לְמַעְלָה מִן הַטֶּבַע). In fact, prior to Amalek's surprise attack upon the nascent Jewish nation (which had just departed from Mitzrayim), we were poised to lead such a lifestyle. However, our brush with Amalek while we were en route towards this laudable objective [as the *pasuk* reads, אֲשֶׁר קָרְךָ בַּדֶּרֶךְ, *he chanced upon you while you were on the road* (*Devarim* 25:18), which may be rendered homiletically, "While you were on the road towards a more spiritual life"] forced us to adopt a more natural course. Under those conditions – living in This World – it is difficult to successfully combat and eliminate this rogue nation. However on Shabbos, the day which is a microcosm of the World to Come, we are able to develop so intense a loathing for Amalek (and the ideology of this nation that poses so immense a threat to *Klal Yisrael's* vitality) that we are, in some fashion, successfully able to eliminate Amalek.[1] [2]

In fact, there may be a relationship between the prohibition of *Melachah* (refer to our chapter on this theme) and our increased capacity to eliminate Amalek on Shabbos. It is only in a material (*Melachah*-driven) world that Amalek enjoyed to capacity to harm *Klal Yisrael*. However, in the more spiritual world which we adopt every Shabbos we stand a better chance of eliminating our greatest foe, *Amalek*. Extending our analogy between Shabbos and *mechiyas* Amalek even further, we propose that the very name Shabbos, which is synonymous with the concept of *shalom* (*peace*, the prevalent attribute in the World to Come), is the antithesis of Amalek with whom we are commanded to wage an eternal battle.

In a similar vein, Amalek who epitomizes deceit (*sheker*) can only exist in This World (which is often known as the עלמא דשקרא, *the world of falsehood*). However, in the Future World – and every Shabbos which is a microcosm of the World to Come – Amalek has no basis. The Torah may be alluding to our increased capacity to eliminate Amalek on Shabbos by saying, וְהָיָה בְּהָנִיחַ ה׳ אֱלֹהֶיךָ לְךָ ... תִּמְחֶה אֶת זֵכֶר עֲמָלֵק, *When* H*ASHEM* *will let you rest* (on Shabbos) ... *you will eliminate any remembrance of Amalek* (*Devarim* 25:19). In fact, there may be a direct

1. While every Shabbos we do not actually perceive a distinct reduction in Amalek's capacity to harm the Jewish people, the *Sfas Emes* may be referring to the grave spiritual threat posed by Amalek which may lessen as a result of the intense *kedushah* of Shabbos.

2. The Torah alludes to Amalek's eventual elimination in the Future World by stating, תִּמְחֶה אֶת זֵכֶר עֲמָלֵק מִתַּחַת הַשָּׁמָיִם, *You will wipe out the memory of Amalek from beneath the heavens* (*Devarim* 25:19). In other words, when the time will come that even the earth will be described as being תַּחַת הַשָּׁמָיִם, *below the heavens* (and totally dominated by the spirituality emanating from heaven), then Amalek will no longer have a place on the face of the earth (adapted from *Zachor* 5641).

relationship between the degree of our *shemiras Shabbos* and our capacity to wipe out Amalek. (*Zachor* 5636, 5643, 5657)

Why We Don't Sound the *Shofar* on Shabbos Rosh Hashanah

דהנה כ׳ שער החצר הפנימית כו׳ וביום השבת יפתח וביום החודש. וכיון דנכסה פתיחה דר״ח צריכין לעורר שער הנפתח בשבת בכח השופר ... ולכן בשבת א״צ לתקיעות שופר. כי כל כח השופר לעורר שער השבת כנ״ל.

In this *dvar Torah* we will present an innovative approach, based on the relationship between Shabbos and the World to Come, to explain why the *shofar* is not sounded when Rosh Hashanah occurs on Shabbos.[1]

To help resolve this issue we turn to Yechezkel's (46:1) renowned description of the inner gates of the (future) *Beis HaMikdash* which will only be opened on Shabbos and on Rosh Chodesh. Even in contemporary times, prior to the rebuilding of the Temple, we draw inspiration from the (inner) gates of our *neshamah* that open every Shabbos and Rosh Chodesh. While this sense of renewal holds true for every Rosh Chodesh, there is one exception, Rosh Hashanah. On this first day of the month of Tishrei (and first day of the year) we go to great lengths to hide that a new month is commencing. As we read, תִּקְעוּ בַחֹדֶשׁ שׁוֹפָר בַּכֶּסֶה לְיוֹם חַגֵּנוּ, *Sound the shofar on the first day of the month, on the* (*hidden*) *day of our festival* (*Tehillim* 81:4).

Consequently, we are unable to evoke that sense of renewal and inspiration that would ordinarily be derived from the gate of Rosh Chodesh. Lacking this powerful means of coming close to Hashem that we enjoy on every other Rosh Chodesh, we turn to the *shofar* to help us draw inspiration from the gates that open on Shabbos.[2] However, when Rosh Hashanah occurs on Shabbos, we no longer require the *shofar's*

1. Refer to *Rosh Hashanah* 29b where the Gemara justifies this ruling on the basis of גְּזֵירָה שֶׁמָּא יַעֲבִירֶנּוּ אַרְבַּע אַמּוֹת בִּרְשׁוּת הָרַבִּים, *We are concerned that* (if one were permitted to sound the *shofar* on Shabbos), *one would come to carry four cubits in a public thoroughfare.* In this *dvar Torah* the *Sfas Emes* is offering a homiletical approach to this issue. (Cf. *Days of Awe*, pp. 191-196 for further discussion of this theme.)

2. Perhaps the *shofar*, described by *Tehillim* as being בַּכֶּסֶה, *hidden*, is a very potent and effective means of eliciting inspiration from the gate that opens on Shabbos.

assistance in eliciting inspiration from the gate of Shabbos. On Shabbos Rosh Hashanah, the gate of Shabbos opens even without benefit of the *shofar*.

(*Rosh Hashanah* 5660)

✤ The Root (Source) of All *Shabbosos*

וע"ז אומרים בתפלת שבת ושני לוחות אבנים הוריד בידו וכתוב בהם שמירת שבת. דיש זכור ושמור זכור בפה שמור בלב וכתיבות הלוחות הוא החקיקה בלבות בנ"י כמ"ש כתבם על לוח לבך וע"י החטא לא יכלו לקבל הלוחות.

Throughout this chapter, we have explored in detail the association between Shabbos and *Olam Haba*. In this concluding *dvar Torah* we take note of an annual occasion that simulates the World to Come to an even greater extent than the weekly Shabbos – Yom Kippur. This day when we abstain from all food and drink (as well as all forms of *Melachah*) is so spiritual in nature that it can truly be described as the שׁוֹרֶשׁ כָּל הַשַּׁבָּתוֹת, *the root of all Shabbosos*. In a similar vein, the entire Divine Service of Yom Kippur in the *Beis HaMikdash* was conducted by the *Kohen Gadol*, a most distinguished member of *Klal Yisrael*, and took place largely in the *Kodesh Kadashim*, the most exalted site on earth.

(*Yom Kippur* 5653)

Shabbos – Shalom

In this chapter we will discuss the relationship between the concept of *Shalom,* generally translated as *peace,* as well as the concept of *sheleimus,* completion, which is closely associated with *shalom.* In particular, we will discuss the renowned statement of the *Zohar* that *Shalom* is one of the names of the Shabbos day (*Zohar, Korach* 352b).

⁂ The Perfect Receptacle for Berachos (*Keli Machazik Berachah*)

דאיתא אין כלי מחזיק ברכה אלא שלום. ולכן כתיב ויברך כו' את יום השביעי שבת שנקרא שלום ומיני' מתברכין כל שיתא יומין. ולא נתן הקב"ה ברכת כל יום ביומו כי אין מחזיקין ברכה ימי המעשה רק השבת שהוא שלום.

Chazal (*Uktzin* 3:12) note that there is no better receptacle for Hashem's blessings than the attribute of *Shalom.* It is because Shabbos is known as *Shalom* that the entire week's *berachos* are reserved for Shabbos. Rather than bless whatever Hashem created on the day of its creation, Hashem blessed the Shabbos and through the Shabbos, He blessed the entire week. It is no coincidence that Hashem reserved all of the universe's *berachos* for Shabbos, the day that epitomizes the attribute of *Shalom.*

To appreciate why Shabbos was selected as the source of each day's *berachos,* we recall that true *sheleimus* can only be attained by focusing on the spiritual aspect of everything. It is only on Shabbos, the day of such *sheleimus,* that these *berachos* can be truly effective. (*Naso* 5650)

במדרש ויכלו השמים כו׳ שנעשו כלים. דכל מה שברא הקב״ה לכבודו ברא. ולכן בשבת ע״י הביטול שנתבטל הבריאה אליו ית׳ שלא יהי׳ דבר נפרד בפ״ע. ונתברר שהכל הכנה להיות כלי לתשמישו ית׳ אז שורה ברכה כמאמר חז״ל כלי מחזיק ברכה והוא השבת שנקרא שלום. ומזה מתקיים בכל שבת.

Moreover, it was on Shabbos, when the entire process of Creation had been completed — and when the full glory of Hashem was revealed — that the universe became the true receptacle of Hashem's Blessings. Whereas during the first Six Days of Creation, when different aspects of Creation emerged daily, one might have (*chas v'shalom*) overlooked the Creator and instead focused on the sheer beauty of His Creations, no such mistake could be made upon beholding the finished universe. It was then, on the first Shabbos, that the universe could truly benefit and "contain" Hashem's *berachos.* It was then that the attribute of *Shalom* prevailed. (*Bereishis* 5645)

◆§ Deflecting Evil (Deflecting *Mazikin*)

אך הקב״ה הוא שלימות העולם. וזה בחי׳ ש״ק שנק׳ שלום כידוע בזוה״ק בע״ש ביה״ש נבראו מזיקין ורצו לשלוט בעולם רק שהקב״ה השפיע קדושת ש״ק ונשבתו המזיקין. והיינו שסוף ימי המעשה הוא בחסרון שחסר השלימות. וע״ז אמרו מה הי׳ העולם חסר מנוחה פי׳ השלימות ובא שבת והשלים.
ונק׳ שלום ע״י דמתעברין מיני׳ כל סט״א ונגלה הברית בזמן.

To appreciate further why Shabbos is the perfect receptacle for Hashem's *berachos,* we turn to the first *erev Shabbos,* when according to *Chazal* (*Avos* 5:6) demons (*mazikin*) were created. The *Zohar* notes that these forces of evil were prepared to dominate the newly-completed universe and were only prevented from doing so by the advent of

Shabbos. Returning to the analogy of a vessel, which we employed in the previous *dvar Torah,* we suggest that at the completion of the Six Days of Creation — when the *mazikin* threatened to hold sway over the universe — the world, despite its brilliance, was no more than a beautiful utensil that nonetheless contained a fatal flaw, a significant hole which prevented it from retaining anything of substance. It was only when the *mazikin* were prevented from taking over at the beginning of Shabbos that the world now attained *sheleimus* and, indeed, emerged as the ideal receptacle for Hashem's *berachos.*

Not only at the very inception of the universe, but even today, every Shabbos the forces of evil (known as the *sitra achara*) are neutralized, giving additional credence to the name *Shalom.*

(*Korach* 5636; *Pinchas* 5652)

איתא גולל אור מפני חושך ובהסרת הערלה הנשמה מאירה באדם וגולל חושך מפני אור ואז נקרא תמים ושלם וכמו כן שבת נקרא שלום דסט״א אתעברית בשבת ומאיר הנשמה.

The phrase recited during the daily *Maariv* prayer, גּוֹלֵל ... וְחֹשֶׁךְ מִפְּנֵי אוֹר, *He removes the darkness in the presence of the light,* may allude to the inception of the first Shabbos, when the forces of evil (depicted as darkness) gave way to the light of the *neshamah yeseirah,* the extra spiritual dimension of Shabbos (refer to our chapter on *Tefillos* and Kindling the Shabbos Lights for further discussion of this theme).

(*Lech Lecha* 5662)

⸎ The Source of All Time

וכמו כן שבת כולל כל הזמן וששת ימי המעשה ונקרא שלום ובו הברכה על כל הזמנים.

ויש זמן הכולל כל הזמנים והוא שבת שלום.

Assuming that all blessings are derived from the source of *berachah* (מְקוֹר הַבְּרָכָה), we suggest that the many *berachos* with which Hashem blesses the six weekdays are all derived from the Shabbos, the day of the week that incorporates every aspect of each of the weekdays – a concept known as *kollel.* Consequently, Shabbos, the source of all of the weekdays' *berachos,* is itself depicted as *Shalom,* a time of peace, which is the perfect receptacle for all of Hashem's *berachos.*

(*Lech Lecha* 5648; *Chayei Sarah* 5658)

◆§ The Heavenly Roots of Time

ולכן בשבתות וימים טובים שנקראו מועדי ה׳ יש בהם ידיעת הבורא ית׳ שהם ימי תמימים. כמ״ש שבת נקרא שלום. שכל הבריאה מתדבק בשרשו לכך נקראו תמימים.

Chazal describe Shabbos and *Yom Tov* as being יְמֵי תְמִימִם, *perfect days.*[1] To appreciate this reference and to derive some insight into the process of *hashgachah pratis, Divine guidance* (and intervention), we suggest that every day of the week not only exists as an independent entity here on earth, but also enjoys heavenly roots (a concept known as *shoresh*).While the weekdays are also associated with their heavenly *shoresh,* it is on Shabbos and *Yom Tov* that the relationship between the concept of time here on earth and its heavenly equivalent are much more apparent. It is on these days that the temporal presence on earth clings most intensely to its true heavenly source. Hence, the term *yemei temimim,* days of perfection, in which the apparent presence of time as it exists on earth is intimately connected to its perfect (and supernatural) heavenly source.

It is through these *yemei temimim,* perfect days in which the presence of Hashem is much more apparent to us, that the entire process of Divine Providence operates. Inasmuch as these days are so closely associated with their heavenly roots, allowing an extraordinary degree of *hashgachah pratis* to take place, then all of the other days which are linked to Shabbos and *Yom Tov* also benefit from this phenomenon. In other words, Shabbos amd *Yom Tov* act as a funnel through which Hashem's *hashgachah* is manifested not only on those days but also every day.[2]

1. This term is derived from the *pasuk,* יוֹדֵעַ ה׳ יְמֵי תְמִימִם, *Hashem knows the days of the perfect* (*Tehillim* 37:18). In fact, one attains a degree of *yedias Hashem, intimate knowledge of Hashem,* on Shabbos and *Yom Tov* that is generally unattainable during the week.

2. It follows that *tzaddikim,* who throughout life are conscious of their Heavenly roots every day of the week – and always enjoy the same degree of intimacy with Hashem as if it were

The term *Shalom,* implying perfection, is an ideal metaphor to describe succinctly the intimate connection between these sacred days and their perfect roots in Heaven — a process by which every day of the year becomes an opportunity to benefit from Divine Providence.

(*Chayei Sarah* 5640)

Using this concept, we can appreciate why so many of the *mitzvos* of Shabbos are observed as pairs. Thus, we partake of *lechem mishneh,* the Double Bread, and commemorate both *Zachor V'Shamor,* the positive and negative commandments associated with Shabbos, to remind us that the physical presence of Shabbos that we enjoy on earth is only one aspect of this greatest of days. It is by appreciating the heavenly roots of Shabbos that its sanctity can be truly enjoyed and valued.

We Lack Nothing on Shabbos

וכמו כן בכל פרט איש ישראל כפי כח שמירת שבת שבו שמשליך כל מחשבת מלאכת חול בביאת הש״ק. כמו כן נשלם אצלו ג״כ עבודת הבורא ית״ש. הגם שהוא חסר השלימות. השבת נותן לו שלימות. ולכן הגם שהיו זריזין במלאכת המשכן. כשבא שבת כאלו נשלם המשכן ששבת שלום משלים המלאכה כמ״ש. וז״ש למעט שבת ממלאכת המשכן.

Perhaps most simply by stating that *Shalom* (related to *sheleimus,* completion) is one of the names of Shabbos, *Chazal* are emphasizing that when Shabbos arrives, we may consider it as if all our objectives that we sought to complete during the past week — and all of the activities necessary to accomplish those objectives — have been completed.

In this light, we may appreciate why the *Mishkan* could not be erected on Shabbos. While it is certainly true that the building of the Sanctuary represented the highest form of creativity,[1] on Shabbos every

Shabbos — are always pursuing a lifestyle of *temimus* (perfection). In this vein, *Chazal* use the same metaphor *yemei temimim,* the perfect days to describe the lifespan of *tzaddikim* (such as Sarah *Imeinu*), as well as for Shabbos and *Yom Tov.*

1. Perhaps this is the reason why the 39 categories of *Melachah* that are prohibited on Shabbos are derived from the *Mishkan.* We may assume that these forms of work represent the highest forms of creativity. Moreover, just as Hashem rested on Shabbos from creativity (rather than physical labor), so too, when celebrating the weekly Shabbos, we desist from these modes of creativity.

form of work – even the most rarefied – has reached its *sheleimus* and requires no further effort on our part. As *Rashi* notes, כָּל אַכִין ... מִעוּטִין לְמַעֵט שַׁבָּת מִמְּלֶאכֶת הַמִּשְׁכָּן, *All appearances of* אַךְ *[in the Torah] ... are exclusions. [In this case,] it serves to exclude Shabbos from the work of the Mishkan* (*Shemos* 31:13, s.v. אך). In other words, just as our mundane weekdays' activities are considered completed upon the arrival of Shabbos, so too, the *Melachah* that was required to build the *Mishkan* was also completed at the beginning of Shabbos. (*Ki Sisa* 5661)

The Source of All *Berachos* – Attaining Personal *Sheleimus*

ולכן כמו שבנ״י מעידין בש״ק עליו ית׳. כן השבת עדות על בני ישראל. [דזה] שזוכין להעיד העדות הוא עצמו עדות על תיקונם ושלימותם. ובכל שבת ושבת ניתוסף איזה הארה לנפש הישראלי. וזה ענין ושמעה קול אלה כו׳ ראה כו׳ ידע. כל אחד לפי מדריגה שלו. ובימי המעשה צריכין להמשיך כל המעשים אחר מה שקיבל הנפש בשבת קודש שלא להיות אם לא יגיד כו׳.

In the previous *dvar Torah,* we noted that the universe and all our efforts to sustain it reach completion on Shabbos. In reality, the same process occurs for each individual Jew as well. While we generally assume that by observing Shabbos, *Klal Yisrael* attests to Hashem's creation of heaven and earth, the converse is also true. When we observe Shabbos properly, the Shabbos itself testifies to the level of *sheleimus* attained by the Jewish people. The mere fact that we successfully bear witness to Creation every Shabbos, in itself is an indication of the level of perfection that we have attained on this blessed day.

Homiletically, we may derive this thought from the *pasuk* discussing the responsibility borne by any individual to testify in *beis din* (when summoned by the plaintiff): וְשָׁמְעָה קוֹל אָלָה וְהוּא עֵד אוֹ רָאָה אוֹ יָדָע אִם לוֹא יַגִּיד וְנָשָׂא עֲוֹנוֹ, *If he accepted a demand for an oath, and he is a witness – either he saw or he knew – if he does not testify he shall bear his iniquity* (*Vayikra* 5:1). This may be interpreted homiletically as follows: If he heard the voice (of Hashem) [וְשָׁמְעָה קוֹל] by testifying [וְהוּא עֵד] (to His Creation on Shabbos), either by seeing or knowing [אוֹ רָאָה אוֹ יָדָע] (recognizing his new-found potential), if he doesn't feel drawn [אִם לוֹא יַגִּיד] during the weekdays to exploit the renewed Divine Presence in his midst, then (God forbid) he will bear his sin [וְנָשָׂא עֲוֹנוֹ] (suffer the consequences).

In other words, it is our sacred responsibility to exploit the phenomenal spiritual growth that we enjoy as a result of testifying to Creation on Shabbos. Then we must integrate this new-found spirituality into our lives during the week ahead. (*Vayikra* 5649)

◈ Returning to One's Roots

ולכן בשבת שיש הארת נשמה יתירה. הוא הזמן להעיד על הבורא. שבת סהדותא איקרי. לפי שהוא יומא דנשמתין. ונקרא שלום שנדבק החלק בהשורש.

The term *Shalom,* implying *sheleimus,* reminds us of the invaluable opportunity that we enjoy every Shabbos to return to our roots (a theme discussed throughout *Sfas Emes* and in many of the essays of this volume). While a certain component of our *neshamah* descends to This World (and becomes an integral part of us), the soul's true roots remain in heaven (even during our life span in *Olam Hazeh*). On Shabbos, fortified by the presence of the *neshamah yeseirah,* we are able to link that aspect of the soul that is present on earth with its counterpart in heaven. What greater *sheleimus* than connecting our *neshamah* on earth with its roots in heaven. (*Vayikra* 5661)

וכן בזמן ניתן לבנ״י שבתות ויו״ט שהם ימי תמימים וזה שנק׳ שבת שלום. והנה צריכין לקבל נשמה יתירה בש״ק הרמז ...

Utilizing this approach, we gain insight into the Torah's plea, תָּמִים תִּהְיֶה עִם ה׳ אֱלֹהֶיךָ, *You shall be wholehearted* (*complete*) *with* H*ASHEM*, *your God* (*Devarim* 18:13). By ensuring that our physical presence on earth is inseparably linked to its spiritual roots in heaven, we can achieve this status of *temimus* (perfection).

It is well-known in the realm of Jewish thought (*machshavah*) that there are three distinct categories to which all natural phenomena belong:

עוֹלָם, *olam* (the universe); שָׁנָה, *shanah* (year, the dimension of time); and נֶפֶשׁ, *nefesh* (the soul). To achieve *temimus,* we need to exploit one aspect of these three dimensions. Thus, in the realm of the universe (*olam*), there is no location on earth that is more conducive to attain this objective than *Eretz Yisrael* and the sacred site of the *Beis HaMikdash.*[1] Likewise, in the realm of the soul (*nefesh*), of all Hashem's subjects, no nation is better equipped to achieve the objective of *temimus* than the Jewish people, especially because of its observance of *bris milah* (a practice that promotes moral purity) and through its immersion in Torah. Of greatest pertinence to our discussion is the dimension of time (*shanah*), the Shabbos and *Yom Tov* which are described as being יְמֵי תְמִימִם, *days of perfection* (unparalleled opportunities for us to "reconnect" with our heavenly antecedents). It is because of this capacity to realign our presence on earth with its heavenly origins that the Shabbos is known as *Shalom,* a time of true perfection. (*Shoftim* 5660)

◆§ A Day of Complete Unity

ולכן שבת קודש נק׳ שלום שאז מתבטלין כולם אל השורש. וז״ש בשבת זכר למעשה בראשית כי ששת ימי בראשית נתאחדו בש״ק כמ״ש בו שבת כו׳ אשר ברא ק׳ לעשות. לעשות כל יום ויום בחי׳ שלו. וזהו פי׳ מעשה בראשית שאז היו דבקים כולם בראשית ואחדות. ובימי החול מנהיג כל א׳ את שלו.

והוא פשוט מצות שבת שמבטל כל אחד מעשה ידיו ואינו עושה מלאכה ובזה נעשה שלום וזה מקיים העולם.

In this *dvar Torah* we will consider the consequences of returning to one's roots (the theme of the previous piece). Whereas it is entirely possible that at times any one of Hashem's creations may contravene the effects of another one of His creations (water, for example, extinguishes fire), on Shabbos, when all of nature returns to its heavenly roots, all competition and rivalry between various aspects of *masseh bereishis* ceases. As we recite in *Kaddish,* עֹשֶׂה שָׁלוֹם בִּמְרוֹמָיו, *He Who*

1. This capacity of these sacred locations to help us align our roots on earth with their counterparts in heaven may be particularly appreciated in light of *Chazal's* observation that the *Beis HaMikdash* on earth is located "parallel" to its counterpart in heaven (cf. *Rashi, Shemos* 15:17, s.v. מכון).

makes peace in His heights — which refers to Hashem's heavenly servitors. The angel whose function it is to supervise fire and the one appointed over water subordinate their own interest in favor of fulfilling the Divine Will. (A classic example of such harmony occurred in Mitzrayim, when fire and water coexisted harmoniously as part of the plague of בָּרָד, *hail*.) We voice a similar thought in the *Pesukei D'zimrah* of Shabbos, אֵין אֹמֶר וְאֵין דְּבָרִים בְּלִי נִשְׁמָע קוֹלָם, *There is no speech and there are no words, their sound is not heard* (*Tehillim* 19:4). Whatever "disputes" may occur between the *malachim* empowered over aspects of this universe during the weekdays yields to silence on Shabbos, when their sole function is to harmoniously perform the Divine Will.

Likewise, mortals, who all week long may be pursuing their own individual objectives (materially or even in the pursuit of *avodas Hashem*), subordinate their own agenda every Shabbos (by abstaining from *Melachah*). By doing so, they too promote a spirit of *achdus* (unity) and *shalom*.

Just as we describe the process of bringing together Hashem's servitors as an act of *shalom* (עֹשֶׂה שָׁלוֹם בִּמְרוֹמָיו), so too, by inducing all of Hashem's Creations to unite for the common purpose of fulfilling His Will, the Shabbos deserves the distinction of being called *Shalom*.

With this approach, we can appreciate why Shabbos — the one day in which Hashem ceased creating — is described as זֵכֶר לְמַעֲשֵׂה בְרֵאשִׁית, *a remembrance of Creation*. While it is true that nothing was created on the seventh day, it was not until then that all of Hashem's creations coexisted and worked harmoniously to fulfill His Will. It was only then that we could justifiably speak of *masseh bereishis*, a complex and completed act of Creation that is united as it was at the *reishis*, the very beginning of Creation. (Adapted from *Emor* 5664; *Korach* 5635)

הרמז הוא על בחי׳ יוסף שהוא שלום והוא בחי׳ שבת שהוא כלל שבעת הימים באחדות אחד ולכן מעלה הכל אל השורש. וז״ש ביוסף בן שבע עשרה שנה הי׳ רועה את אחיו. אבל בשבטים כ׳ לרעות את צאן ודרשו חז״ל נקוד על את לרעות את עצמן. אלא היו באחדות כראוי כי הם בחי׳ פרט.

The relationship between the six weekdays, with their distinctive contributions, and Shabbos, a time when all disparate elements of Creation harmonize to serve Hashem, may be analogous to that of Yosef and his brothers. Just as Yosef *HaTzaddik* embodied within himself the traits of all the other *shevatim*,[1] so too, the Shabbos contains the unique aspects of each of the other days. (*Mikeitz* 5651)

☙ Knowing One's Unique Function (Raison D'etre)

והוא בחי׳ שבת שנק׳ שלום בכח הנשמה יתירה שמתדבק האדם לשורשו ומקומו לכן נק׳ יום מנוחה ושמחה. אך איתא יש קונה עולמו בשעה אחת. פי׳ כדאיתא כל אדם יש לו עולם בפ״ע ...

On Shabbos we enjoy the capacity not only to return to our roots but also to appreciate the purpose of our existence. Every individual was created for a unique purpose, which only he can fulfill. The renowned comment of *Chazal*, יֵשׁ קוֹנֶה עוֹלָמוֹ בְּשָׁעָה אַחַת, *there are those who can acquire their own universe in one moment* (*Avodah Zarah* 17a), may refer not only to every individual's portion in the World to Come but also to the unique challenges that only he can overcome — and by doing so he justifies his creation.[2] It is by rising to these challenges and fulfilling his life's mission that he merits his *Olam Haba*, his portion in the World to Come.

There is no better opportunity to meet this challenge and to understand the true purpose of one's existence than on *Shabbos Kodesh* when we are graced with the presence of the *neshamah yeseirah*. Shabbos has earned the distinction of being called a day of *menuchah v'simchah*, rest and joy, because it is then that we return to our roots and grasp our raison d'etre.

What greater sense of *sheleimus* and of *shalom* can be achieved every Shabbos than successfully defining one's purpose and understanding the very challenges that we must face during our lifetime. (*Pinchas* 5645)

1. The relationship between Yosef and his brothers is discussed many times in the writings of *Sfas Emes*. In this context, we present one allusion to the preeminent role of Yosef *HaTzaddik*. Whereas Yosef is depicted as the רֹעֶה אֶת אֶחָיו, *the shepherd who was grazing with* (and on behalf of) *his brothers* (i.e. he was sustaining them), they are described by *Chazal* in the following terms: שֶׁלֹּא הָלְכוּ אֶלָּא לִרְאוֹת אֶת עַצְמָם, *they merely went* (to Shechem) *to graze for themselves* (to advance their own spiritual growth). Rather than denigrating these great *tzaddikim*, by utilizing this metaphor, *Chazal* are suggesting that each of Yaakov's sons nurtured his own individual traits, whereas Yosef was concerned with his brothers' growth.

2. According to this approach, the term עוֹלָם is related to העלם, *hidden*. It is only by overcoming those challenges that appeared to be beyond our grasp that we have justified our existence and earned our true unique portion in *Olam Haba*.

◆§ Finding Hashem Amidst the Natural World

וזהו ל״ב אלקים דעובדא דבראשית. ונראה דל״ב חוטין שבציצית רומזין לל״ב אלקים. וד׳ שרשים ד׳ חוטי תכלת הם אלקים דבראשית ברא. וג׳ אלקים דפ׳ ויכולו שהם כוללים כל הל״ב ... והנשארים הם כח מעשיו שהגיד לעמו ... ושבת קודש כולו תורה וצריכין להתבונן בו בשורש שלמעלה מבריאת מ״ב. ולכן נק׳ שבת שלום שמו של הקב״ה ויש בו אחדות כמ״ש דאתאחדת ברזא דאחד.

Whereas during the week, Hashem's Presence is felt in the universe that He created, it is only on Shabbos, the most spiritual of days when *Klal Yisrael* is totally devoted to studying Torah, that we can appreciate His Presence most acutely.

To illustrate our contention that there is a significant difference between our awareness of *HaKadosh Baruch Hu* all week long and on Shabbos, we note that the term אֱלֹהִים appears 32 times during the story of Creation. Of these references, 28 are cited in the context of the Six Days of Creation, while the first reference, בְּרֵאשִׁית בָּרָא אֱלֹהִים, refers to the Presence of Hashem which filled the universe before Creation. The three other references to Hashem's Name can be found in the context of the first Shabbos, in the *parashah* of וַיְכֻלּוּ, *Thus the heaven and the earth were finished ...* (*Bereishis* 2:1-3).[1]

This relationship between the numbers twenty-eight and four also appears in reference to *tzitzis*. As we know, there are eight strands on each of the four corners of the garment. Of these thirty-two threads, four of them consist of *techeiles* while 28 were comprised of *lavan* (ordinary white wool). Just as the 28 references to Hashem's Name in the story of Creation allude to the natural world of the six weekdays in which Hashem's Presence may be veiled, so too, the *tzitzis* are placed on the fringes of our garments, to indicate that during the week we can

1. David *HaMelech* may be alluding to these 28 references to Hashem's Name in the context of the natural world created during the Six Days of Creation by describing Creation with these words: כֹּחַ מַעֲשָׂיו הִגִּיד לְעַמּוֹ, *The strength of His deeds He told to His nation* (*Tehillim* 111:6). The numerical equivalent of the term כֹּחַ used to describe Creation is identical with the number 28, alluding to the 28 references to Hashem's Name in the Torah's account of the Six Days of Creation.

only grasp some small measure of Hashem's greatness. It is only those four strands that are dyed with *techeiles*, resembling the sky and ultimately the heavenly Throne of Hashem (כִּסֵּא הַכָּבוֹד), that allow us to feel the more intimate Presence of the *Shechinah*. It is well-known that Korach dramatized his feud with Moshe by dressing his co-conspirators in cloaks that consisted entirely of *techeiles* — which, from his perspective, were exempt from *tzitzis*. According to Korach, there was no distinction between the natural world in which Hashem's Presence is veiled during the weekdays and the overwhelming *kedushah* of Shabbos. For him, the entire world was already suffused, and visibly so, with Godliness. Our challenge, however, is to connect the otherwise mundane environment of the six weekdays to Shabbos.

With this approach, we gain new insight why the term *Shalom* is used to describe Shabbos (as well as being one of Hashem's Names). It is on this day that we can best relate to the One and Only Creator of the universe (אֶחָד וּמְיוּחָד), and to the Ultimate and Perfect (related to *sheleimus* and *shalom*) source of the entire universe, Hashem. By disputing the concept of Shabbos (as related in *Zohar, Parashas Korach*), Korach was challenging an essential mission of every Jew to look beyond This World and turn to Hashem, the Perfect Creator.

(Adapted from *Korach* 5656)

◆§ The Completion (and Purpose) of Creation

ולכן נק׳ השבת שלום שהוא תכלית הבריאה. כמ״ש מה הי׳ העולם חסר מנוחה בא שבת נגמרה המלאכה. ולכן נקראו בנ״י השולמית שהם כלי לקבל אותה הנקודה.

It was not until the first Shabbos that the universe was truly complete. As *Chazal* note, מַה הָיָה הָעוֹלָם חָסֵר? מְנוּחָה, *What was the universe lacking? Rest* (*Bereishis Rabbah* 10:9). It wasn't until the *Menuchah* of Shabbos became evident that the universe was considered to be complete. As we pray every Friday evening, תַּכְלִית מַעֲשֵׂה שָׁמַיִם וָאָרֶץ, [*Shabbos is*] *the completion* (and true purpose) *of the creation of heaven and earth*. It is because of this *sheleimus*, the sense of completion that Shabbos brought, that this day earned the distinction of being called *Shalom*. (*Beshalach* 5648)

◈ The Divine Imprint

ושבת הוא הכלל וע״ז הכלל חתם השי״ת שמו כמ״ש יום הששי ויכולו השמים ר״ת שם הוי׳.

While the universe was virtually completed at the conclusion of the Six Days of Creation, the sense of *sheleimus*, of completion and perfection, was still lacking. It was not until the advent of Shabbos, when the *Shechinah's* Presence was felt, that the world attained perfection. In fact, the first letters of the opening passage of *Kiddush* (based on the *parashah* of וַיְכֻלּוּ describing the first Shabbos), יוֹם הַשִּׁשִּׁי וַיְכֻלּוּ הַשָּׁמַיִם (*the sixth day and heaven was completed*), spell out the Name of Hashem (consisting of the letters *yud, hey, vav, hey*).

Chazal describe the arrival of Shabbos as being analogous to the imprint of a seal (*chosam*) on a ring. It was only when the beautiful but still unfinished universe received the Divine Imprint of Shabbos — the seal of the ring — that true *Shalom* was attained. (*Pinchas* 5651)

◈ The *Chasimah* (Sealing) of the World

כי חתימת אות ברית קודש נק׳ שלום כמו שבת שנק׳ שלום כי השלמת הבריאה הי׳ בו כמ״ש מה הי׳ העולם חסר מנוחה באת שבת כו׳. ואיתא במד׳ בראשית המשל טבעת שחסר בו חותם ע״ש.

In the previous *dvar Torah* we noted that Shabbos represents the Divine Imprint on the universe that Hashem had created. Elaborating upon this theme, we propose that *maaaseh bereishis* may be compared to the writing (*kesivah*) of a document whose author is as yet unidentified. It was not until the advent of the first Shabbos, when the universe appeared in its full splendor (and after the First Man had been created) that Hashem's Presence in His universe could be fully appreciated. Thus Shabbos, the *chasimah* (sealing) and true purpose of the entire process of Creation, truly deserves the distinguishing title of *Shalom*. For it was only then that the universe attained a sense of *sheleimus* (completion and closure). (*Pinchas* 5661)

⁂ Perceiving the Divine Spark

והכלל כי הנקודה ממנו ית׳ שמחי׳ כל נק׳ שלום. ולכך כלי מחזיק ברכה הוא להיות בנקודה זו והיא נק׳ שבת ולכך ויברך כו׳ כי מחזיק ברכה כנ״ל.

The term *Shalom* derived from *sheleimus* reminds us of the Divine Spark that maintains this universe. Just as Hashem is the epitome of perfection, so too, His Presence in This World is the source of all of its *berachos*. We perceive this Divine Spark best on Shabbos, a day which embodies the attribute of *Shalom* more than any other occasion. Consequently, Shabbos was designated as the ideal receptacle for Hashem's *berachos*. As the Torah writes, וַיְבָרֶךְ אֱלֹהִים אֶת יוֹם הַשְּׁבִיעִי, *God blessed the seventh day* (*Bereishis* 2:3). (*Pinchas* 5631)

⁂ A Day Without Coercion

אבל שבת שלום מתגלה הנהגה עליונה מלך שהשלם שלו פי׳ הכל משלימין ושמחים במלכותו שהוא מלך האמת. ולכן שבת זכר ליצ״מ שהוא זמן חירות ולכן יש בו ברכה ולכן השבת ניתן לבני ישראל שהם בני חורין ויכולין לקבל ברכת השבת וז״ש ישמחו במלכותך שומרי שבת.

Whereas all week long, the natural world is compelled to serve Hashem, on Shabbos it does so of its own free will, as we shall elucidate. It is because of this peaceful acquiescence to implement Hashem's design for the universe — rather than its more natural reluctant compliance with the Divine Will occurring during the weekdays — that Shabbos earns the accolade of *Shalom*, a time of peace and Divine blessings.

To elaborate, we recall the comment of *Chazal* (*Bereishis Rabbah* 10:6) that every entity that Hashem created — even a simple blade of grass — is compelled to fulfill its Divinely-ordained function by an angel that supervises it and "strikes it" until it acts according to the preordained Divine Plan for His universe. In this vein, *Koheles* writes, כִּי גָבֹהַּ מֵעַל גָּבֹהַּ

שֹׁמֵר וּגְבֹהִים עֲלֵיהֶם, *for there is One higher than high Who watches and there are high ones above them* (5:7). The שֹׁמֵר, *watchman*, is a metaphor for those forces ensuring that the natural world implements Hashem's bidding and they are high above high. In many instances, Hashem's creations are compelled to act in a manner that is the antithesis of their true desire by the forces that are positioned above them. In fact, the term מַעֲשֵׂה בְרֵאשִׁית (generally translated as "the act of Creation") may be related to מְעוּשָּׂה, *force* (cf. *Gittin* 88b, a divorce that is acquired through coercion). It is only through a process of subordination to superior elements in the hierarchy of Creation that Hashem's Master Plan for the universe is effectuated. This process of subordination and the entire management of the universe itself is a beautiful tribute to Hashem and bears witness to the symmetry with which He created the world.

On Shabbos, however, this process of maintaining the universe occurs without any need for compulsion. On this day of consummate freedom (as we say, זֵכֶר לִיצִיאַת מִצְרָיִם, *a remembrance of the Exodus*), the natural world of its own free will performs the bidding of Hashem – and with great joy. As we recite in the Shabbos *Mussaf Shemoneh Esrei*, יִשְׂמְחוּ בְמַלְכוּתְךָ שׁוֹמְרֵי שַׁבָּת, *They shall rejoice in Your kingdom, those who observe the Shabbos.* (*Noach* 5663)

◆§ More on *Shalom* and Unity

וכן הוא בזוה״ק דפליג על שבת שנק׳ שלום ואחיד במחלוקת ע״ש. כי בודאי יש מקום לחילוקי דיעות שנמצא בבנ״י כמ״ש כשם שאין פרצופיהם שוה כך אין דיעותיהם שוות. והענין עפ״י מ״ש אא״ז מו״ר ז״ל על המשנה אם אין אני לי מי לי כי כל אדם נברא לתקן דבר מיוחד שאין אחר יכול לתקן וכן בכל זמן וזמן מיוחד תיקון אחר. עכ״ז כשאני לעצמי מה אני שצריך כל אחד לבטל חלק פרטי שלו אל הכלל ע״כ דפח״ח. וענין זה נוהג בעולם שנה נפש. כי בששת ימי בראשית נברא בכל יום ענין מיוחד לא ראי זה כראי זה. אך השבת הוא הכולל כל הימים והוא כלי מחזיק ברכה ע״י שיש בו האחדות לכן הוא קיום כל הימים כדאיתא באת שבת באת מנוחה ונגמרה המלאכה כי אם אין שלום אין כלום.

In previous *dvrei Torah*, we suggested that the Shabbos day acts as a unifying force motivating disparate elements of Hashem's heavenly servitors, as well as individuals here on earth to set aside their various differences in favor of performing the Divine Will.

To give us some insight into how this unity can be achieved, consider the following argument: Far from obliterating individual differences, the Torah recognizes the unique contribution offered by every Jew. As it says in *Pirkei Avos*, אִם אֵין אֲנִי לִי מִי לִי וּכְשֶׁאֲנִי לְעַצְמִי מָה אֲנִי, *If I am not for myself, who will be for me, [but] if I am [only] for myself, what am I?* (1:14). According to the *Chiddushei HaRim*, the *mishnah* is emphasizing the unique contribution that every Jew offers to the community. In fact, each of us was created for the singular purpose of contributing something to the universe that none of our peers is capable of duplicating. Moreover, even מַחֲלוֹקֶת לְשֵׁם שָׁמַיִם, a *controversy for God's sake*, reflects sincere differences in interpreting the Torah and are welcomed. In the same manner that our individual personalities and physiques differ, so too, there is room for different opinions regarding matters of *Halachah*. However, as the *mishnah* continues, *if I am only for myself, what am I?* teaches us that it is critical that our unique contribution be offered for the purpose of benefitting the entire community, rather than for our own self-advancement. This synthesis of individual initiative with the community's larger interests already began at Creation. During each of the Six Days of Creation, another aspect of Hashem's universe was revealed. However, it was only on Shabbos that each of the individual components of the universe reached its fullest potential and achieved its true and unique function when its contribution became part of the larger completed universe.[1]

By unifying each of the disparate elements of the universe and, by extension, each member of *Klal Yisrael* — while simultaneously permitting them to retain their individual identity — the Shabbos day has earned the distinction of being called *Shalom*. (*Korach* 5647)

1. The *Sfas Emes* demonstrates that a similar relationship exists between the extraordinary role played by every Jew and the unique status of the *tzaddik*, who embodies the best traits of every individual. Likewise, the outstanding features and the grace of every location on earth is somehow captured by and subsumed within the unparalleled beauty of *Eretz Yisrael* and especially Yerushalayim .

◆ Unity Among Disparate Factions of *Klal Yisrael*

ובשבת קודש הוא מעין זה ונקרא שלום כמ״ש יעקב ובניו ינוחו בו. ובו מתאחדין כל הדעות. ולכן בתפלת מנחת שבת חשיב י״ב מנוחות מנוחה וקדושה כו׳ אהבה נדבה כו׳ שלום כו׳. והוא כלל כל הי״ב שבטים. שנעשין אחד.

To elaborate on the theme that Shabbos, the day when *Shalom* prevails, affords the Jewish people an unparalleled opportunity to unite factions that previously had been at odds, we recall the Shabbos *Minchah Shemoneh Esrei* where we emphasize, יַעֲקֹב וּבָנָיו יָנוּחוּ בוֹ, *Yaakov and (all of) his children will rest on it* (Shabbos). Despite differences that may have existed between Yaakov's children during the weekdays, on Shabbos these differences are submerged in favor of peace and harmony. As further indication of our belief that Shabbos harmonizes all factions of the Jewish people, twelve different expressions are utilized to connote the *Menuchah* of Shabbos, including מְנוּחַת שָׁלוֹם וְשַׁלְוָה, *a rest [that is derived from] peace and serenity* — the ambiance that we enjoy on Shabbos. *(Vayigash* 5647)

◆ Achieving Unity Within Oneself

וזה המחלוקת באדם עצמו שמדה זו ממשיכו לכאן וזה לכאן. ובש״ק שזוכין לסייעתא דשמיא שורש העליון בהארת נשמה יתירה נק׳ יום מנוחה שבו מתאחדין כל המדות להיות אחד.

Whereas in previous *divrei Torah* we discussed how the Shabbos motivates unity among otherwise discordant elements both here on earth and in heaven, there is another aspect of unity as well — internal harmony. Each individual personality consists of a delicate blend of varying attributes (such as fear/awe of Hashem and love of Hashem). Moreover, during the weekdays it is entirely possible that each of the attributes do not operate harmoniously. Thus our perception of *ahavas Hashem* (love of Hashem) may motivate us to act in a certain fashion, while our sense of *yiras Hashem* (fear/awe of Hashem) may have the opposite effect. It is only on Shabbos when we enjoy the presence of the *neshamah yeseirah* that these otherwise clashing attributes, as well as the *middos* operating within us, are able to coalesce and join forces in the interests of Divine Service. It is in this sense that Shabbos deserves the distinction of being a day of *Menuchah* (internal peace and harmony) and a time of true *Shalom*. (*Korach* 5649)

☙ Sanctifying the Mundane (*Kedushah* of Eating *L'shem Shamayim*)

וכזה ממש הוא בשבת קודש שנק׳ שלום כדאיתא בזוה״ק דרוחא דקודשא שיורד בשבת יש לו חלק בסעודת שבת ע״ש בפ׳ ויקהל פי׳ הפסוק ביני ובין בני ישראל כו׳. ולכן נק׳ פריסת סוכת שלום. והכלל בכל מקום שיש התחברות התחתונים אל השורש בעליונים זה בחי׳ השלום ... ושבתות ויו״ט הם מעלין כל הזמנים ולכן סעודת שבת נק׳ סעודתא דמהימנותא שע״י נמשך כל האכילות שבימי המעשה אל השורש. ושמעתי מפי מו״ז ז״ל במ״ש באכילת מעשר ואכלת לפני ה׳ אלקיך כו׳ למען תלמד ליראה. נלמד מזה כי אכילת מצוה בקדושה מביא האדם לידי יראה וכן הוא באכילת שבת עכ״ד.

In a previous *dvar Torah* we suggested that one aspect of the *sheleimus* (derived from *Shalom*) of Shabbos is our capacity, while living in *Olam Hazeh*, to evoke the heavenly roots of our *neshamah*. A significant ramification of this new-found capacity to link our heavenly origins (*shoresh*) with our presence in This World, is the sanctification of every aspect of Shabbos *Kodesh* – what appears to be mudane as well as the spiritual. Thus eating, an activity which during the week is generally not perceived as being sacred, assumes the aura of *kedushah* on Shabbos and can lead us to an even closer relationship with Hashem.

To support our contention that on Shabbos even the secular becomes sacred, the *Chiddushei HaRim* cited the *pasuk* discussing the impact of eating *maaser sheni* in Yerushalayim: לְמַעַן תִּלְמַד לְיִרְאָה אֶת ה׳ אֱלֹהֶיךָ כָּל הַיָּמִים, *so that you will learn to fear* HASHEM, *your God, all the days* (*Devarim* 14:23) – as a result of eating *maaser sheni* you will learn to fear Hashem for all of the days. Evidently, engaging in a physical activity, such as eating, *l'shem Shamayim* leads us to a more intense level of fear of Hashem. In fact, the Talmud (*Yevamos* 93a) interprets the foregoing *pasuk* as referring to Shabbos and *Yom Yov* whose meals bring us closer to Hashem. In a similar vein, the *Zohar* notes that the spirit of *kedushah* that graces us every Shabbos actually "partakes" of the Shabbos meals.

What greater manifestation of our capacity every Shabbos to elicit our heavenly roots and to invest anything that we do with an aura of *kedushah* than the sanctification of every aspect of this day — the apparently mundane meals as well as the obviously spiritual component.

(*Tzav* 5651)

The Spiritual Dimension of All Creation

והוא באמת ענין שבת קודש שניתן לבנ״י כי בששת ימים עשה השמים וארץ כו׳. אעפ״כ שבת הוא השלמת כל המעשים כמ״ש רש״י ז״ל על ויכל כו׳ ביום השביעי כו׳ ופי׳ שיש נקודה קדושה תוך הבריאה שהיא למעלה מהעשי׳ והיא בחי׳ שבת שנותנת שלימות וחיות לכל הנבראים. לכן נק׳ שלום. וכמ״ש תכלית שמים וארץ. ששורש מעשה בראשית הוא בחי׳ שבת וניתן לבנ״י שמעשיהם בקדושה כנ״ל.

The concept of *sheleimus* (which may be the source of Shabbos being called *Shalom*) is by no means confined to the Shabbos day itself. On the contrary, the Shabbos is the source of perfection for the entire week. By not completing Creation and by not resting until the seventh day, Hashem made it clear that the true completion of all Creation occurs on Shabbos. While the physical aspect of each entity of *maaseh bereishis* was completed in its appropriate time, there exists a spiritual dimension to all that Hashem created — and that spiritual core was created on the first Shabbos. As *Rashi* notes (*Bereishis* 2:1), by saying וַיְכַל אֱלֹהִים בַּיּוֹם הַשְּׁבִיעִי מְלַאכְתּוֹ אֲשֶׁר עָשָׂה, *God completed on the seventh day His work which He had done*, the Torah is intimating that Creation was not completed until the arrival of the first Shabbos. As we pray every Friday evening, תַּכְלִית מַעֲשֵׂה שָׁמַיִם וָאָרֶץ, [*Shabbos is*] *the completion of the creation of heaven and earth*. It was only after the first Shabbos that the enormous potential of every component of the universe to be utilized for a higher spiritual purpose was achieved. It is this aspect of Shabbos which lends it an aspect of *ruchniyus* and consequently *sheleimus* that earns it the distinction of being called *Shalom*. (*Acharei* 5635)

◆§ The Linchpin of the Universe

ברית עולם פי׳ להכניס נקודת שבת להיות שורש הכל שיתמשך כל הבריאה אחר זאת הנקודה ואז נקראת ברית עולם ... וכ״כ על שבת שנקרא שלום כי שלימות הבריאה הוא שבת.

By describing Shabbos as a בְּרִית עוֹלָם, *an eternal covenant* (*Shemos* 31:16), the Torah may be suggesting that the entire universe (עוֹלָם) exists because of the spiritual dimension that Shabbos brings. Every entity can only exist on the basis of an inner mechanism that drives it. For the universe, that driving force — that spark — is Shabbos. By calling Shabbos, *Shalom*, we are implying that the *sheleimus* and consummation of the entire Creation was Shabbos. (Adapted from *Noach* 5634)

◆§ A Day of Inner Revelation

ובודאי הי׳ קרח ועדתו אנשים גדולים והיו נראין בהתגלות כאלו הם גדולים מאהרן הכהן. אבל כח הפנימיות גובר וזה הי׳ הסימן פרח מטה אהרן שיש לו חלק בנסתרות. ואיתא כהנים שומרים מבפנים ולוים מבחוץ שכן הי׳ משמרות הלוים וכחם ועבודתם בבחי׳ חיצוניות וכהן בפנימיות. וכתיב ששת ימי המעשה יהי׳ סגור וביום השבת וחודש יפתח שער החצר הפנימית. ולכן נקרא שבת שלום שיש בו התגלות הפנימיות. וימי המעשה הוא חלק התגלות ואינו שלום. וכמו כן הלוים היו בחי׳ ימי המעשה ולכן בנסוע הארון היו הלוים נושאין הארון וכלי המשכן כי הם אנשי המלחמה בחי׳ ימי המעשה. ושבת יום מנוחה כשהיו הארון והמשכן במקומם היו הכהנים עיקר.

To appreciate yet another dimension of Shabbos' *Shalom*, we recall the *Zohar's* assertion that Korach challenged the very institution of

Shabbos and, in particular, the association between Shabbos and *Shalom*.

Seemingly, Korach's entire function as a *Levi*, and especially as a bearer of the Ark, was ultimately the antithesis of the role of Aharon whose *kehunah* he challenged, as well as that of the Shabbos.

To explore the nature of Korach's insurrection and where precisely he strayed, we acknowledge the unique function of both *Kohanim* and *Leviim*. Whereas the Levites undoubtedly played a significant role – both in guarding the Temple and in transporting the *Aron* and other sacred utensils – their role was primarily on the surface (*chitzoniyus*). Thus, the *Leviim* guarded the Temple's *outer* perimeter while the *Kohanim* were stationed *inside* the *Beis HaMikdash* (cf. *Middos* 34a). Similarly, the Levites performed their function of transporting the Ark only during the weekdays (when the *Mishkan* may have been in transit) and particularly during times of war when the Ark might accompany Jewish armies into battle. As significant as the Six Days of Creation are, and despite the critical importance of waging battles on behalf of *Klal Yisrael*, these aspects of Jewish life are only the prelude to the true inner (*penimiyus*) values of Jewish life – the *Menuchah* that prevails after the battle has been concluded and the inner serenity that only Shabbos can bring.

By challenging the institution of Shabbos and the *Shalom* that is so closely associated with Shabbos, Korach was asserting the primacy of the Levites' function, *chitzoniyus*, over the *Kohanim's penimiyus*. No better symbol exists of the essential nature of inner values to Jewish life, and no better target for Korach, than the Shabbos, which exemplifies the inner treasures and true meaning of Judaism. The prophet Yechezkel (46:1) describes the inner gates of the Future Temple as being closed during the weekdays and only opened on Shabbos, the day which epitomizes inner meaning. To give further support to his contention that superficial values rather than *penimiyus* really matter, Korach and his cohorts robed themselves in impressive outer garments consisting of *techeiles* whose appearance resembles that of the sky and even the Heavenly Throne of Hashem. It is entirely possible that on the surface, Korach appeared to fill the role of a Jewish leader better than Aharon. However, by trouncing Korach's attempt at leadership, Moshe proves convincingly that it is *penimiyius*, not *chitzoniyus*, that ultimately prevails.

As discussed previously, the term *Shalom* refers not only to the concept of peace but is also a name of Hashem. Just as there are various names of Hashem — those that we are permitted to articulate and others which are hidden from us (too much associated with *penimiyus* for us to appreciate or comprehend) — so too, by challenging the concepts of *Shalom* and Shabbos, Korach was contesting many of the inner nuances of Hashem's Name, as well as the inner serenity of *Shabbos Kodesh.*

(Adapted from *Korach* 5652)

◆§ Korach's Revolt

בזוה״ק קרח חלק על שלום ושבת ע״ש. דאיתא מהו שבת שמא דקוב״ה. כי הקב״ה נקרא שלום לאשר לכל הנבראים נמשך חיות מנקודה אחת שנק׳ שלום ששלימות הכל בנקודה הנ״ל מהשי״ת המחי׳ כל. ואיתא קוב״ה לא יתיב על כורסיא יקירא עד דאתעבידת ברזא דאחד והוא בשבת שכל הנבראים עולים ונכללים בנקודה זאת שנק׳ רזא דאחד שהוא חיות פנימי שבכל הנבראים ובשורש הכל רק נקודה א׳ ונק׳ רזא דאחד.

According to the *Zohar* (3:176b), Korach's rebellion against Moshe *Rabbeinu* was, in actuality, intended to challenge the very institution of Shabbos and in particular, the association between Shabbos and *Shalom* (which, as noted previously, is also a Name of Hashem) .

To appreciate why Korach intended to disrupt the relationship between Shabbos and *Shalom,* we recall the similarity between *Shalom* and *sheleimus* (true perfection), the attribute by which Hashem created His universe and through which He maintains His world by the presence of His Divine Spark. It is only on Shabbos — and even then only by negating one's personal interest to that of the greater community — that one can approach the perfection and evoke the Divine Spark which is the Source of the universe's continued existence (refer to our commentary on the כְּגַוְנָא prayer — recited according to *nusach sefard* on Friday evening — for elaboration of this theme). By insisting that every Jew could exist independently of the larger community (rather than as part of a larger *Klal Yisrael*), Korach threatened the very core of the universe — the perfect Divine Spark — the *sheleimus* and *Shalom* which are the underpinnings of our world and the assurance of its continued existence.

(Excerpted and adapted from *Korach* 5631)

Finding One's Inner Self (*Penimiyus*)

רק ע״י חטא הראשון נתערב פסולת ובקבלת התורה הי׳ מוכן להיות תיקון השלם וע״י חטא העגל שוב מעשה פסולת וע״ז כ׳ שחת לו כו׳ בניו מומם שנעשו בעלי מומין. אבל בכח בתורה שנקראת תמימה יכול איש ישראל להיות תמים ... וז״ש תמים תהי׳ עם ה״א להיות לו חלק בזו הצורה הפנימיות וצורה זו מתגלה בש״ק לכן נק׳ שבת שלום שהיא בחי׳ הצור תמים.

When Hashem created man, He created an outer casing known as the body *(guf)* as well as a pure soul (*neshamah*) which, though not visible, is the true mechanism that, if man is deserving, drives his behavior. Unfortunately, as Adam and his descendants sinned (most notably by partaking of the Tree of Knowledge and by erecting the Golden Calf), their actions had the effect of corrupting this pristine inner core. It is this process of corrosion of our *penimiyus* that Moshe *Rabbeinu* decries in the song of *Haazinu*. He laments, הַצּוּר תָּמִים פָּעֳלוֹ ... שִׁחֵת לוֹ לֹא בָּנָיו מוּמָם, which may be translated, *The Creator's handiwork was perfect* (as He formed a perfect inner soul) ... [*nevertheless*] *His children became corrupted* (cf. *Devarim* 32:4-5). And it to this ideal state – "the perfect handiwork" that we were created (תָּמִים פָּעֳלוֹ) – that the Torah summons us with the cry of תָּמִים תִּהְיֶה עִם ה׳ אֱלֹהֶיךָ, *You shall be wholehearted with* H*ASHEM your God* (*Devarim* 18:13). This means that we must endeavor to return to the inner bliss and the state of perfection that we enjoyed when we were first created.

No better occasion exists to elicit our inner self and return to our indigenous *penimiyus* than *Shabbos Kodesh*. It is then when we attain the status of true perfection and completion (*sheleimus*) that allows us to call this blessed day, *Shalom*. (*Shoftim* 5661)

Linking Body and Soul

וכ׳ תן חלק לשבעה שבעת ימי בראשית וזה בכח השבת שהוא כח המסייע בבחי׳ ז׳ ימי הבנין. ולכן עונג שבת גם בגוף יש בו קדושה. ולכן נקרא שבת שלום. וגם לשמנה זו מילה בחי׳ עוה״ב כנ״ל.

Whereas during the week there exists a potential conflict between body and soul – in which the body strives for its material cravings and the soul seeks to attain *kedushah* – on Shabbos, even the *guf* attains an aura of sanctity. This newly-found *kedushah* of the body is reflected in the *mitzvah* of *oneg Shabbos*. On Shabbos, by eating and drinking, the body as well as the soul benefits from the sanctity of Shabbos. By putting to rest the latent conflict between these two critical components of body and soul, the Shabbos earns the distinction of being called *Shalom*. (*Tazria* 5657)

כי יש בו תיקון הגוף שהוא מעין עוה״ב. ולעתיד לבוא יהיו הגופות מתוקנים ממש כמו נשמות. ובש״ק יש מעין זה תיקון הגופות קצת לכל א׳ כפי הכנת מעשיו בימי המעשה זוכה בשבת לנשמה יתירה שהוא ע״ש תוקף התפשטות כחה בגוף.

To appreciate better why this innate conflict between body and soul ceases every Shabbos, we recall that Shabbos is described as being מֵעֵין עוֹלָם הַבָּא, *a semblance of the World to Come* (*Berachos* 57b). Just as in that Future World any distinction between the spiritual status of body and soul will cease, so too, in This World on Shabbos, the day when we are graced with the presence of the *neshamah yeseirah*, we are able to elevate our body to a level more commensurate to that of our soul. The extent to which this phenomenon occurs is directly proportionate to our efforts at preparing ourselves for the immense *kedushah* of Shabbos during the weekdays. (*Vayishlach* 5636)

A Replica of *Olam Haba*

והיא עצמה השלום שניתן לפינחס דשבת שלום איקר׳. והענין דשבת הוא מעין עוה״ב כי בעוה״ז חסר השלימות כמ״ש במ״א. ולכן שבת צריך הכנה. וזהו הודעה שקודם המתנה להיות מוכן לקבל הארה שלמעלה מעוה״ז. וז״ש לכן שמור הנני נותן כו׳.

To appreciate yet another dimension of the *Shalom* associated with Shabbos, we recall that Pinchas was granted the *berachah* of *Shalom*. As a result of this blessing, Pinchas was assured of living an other-worldly existence while still in *Olam Hazeh*. (According to *Chazal*,

Pinchas was assured of immunity from reprisals by his victims' supporters and of living a long life.) Just as Pinchas enjoyed *Olam Haba* while living in This World, so too, on Shabbos we live in an environment vastly different from that of the weekdays – in a replica of *Olam Haba* (מֵעֵין עוֹלָם הַבָּא).

Drawing the parallel even further between the *Shalom* enjoyed by Pinchas and the sense of *Shalom* that permeates the Shabbos, we note that in each instance this Divine grant is proclaimed in advance. Thus, Hashem instructs Moshe to inform Pinchas, לָכֵן אֱמֹר הִנְנִי נֹתֵן לוֹ אֶת בְּרִיתִי שָׁלוֹם, *Therefore, say: Behold I give him My covenant of peace* (*Bamidbar* 25:12). In the same spirit, Hashem insists that Moshe *Rabbeinu* inform *Klal Yisrael* about the Divine gift of Shabbos.

(Adapted from *Pinchas* 5646)

◆§ The Perfect Receptacle to Receive the Blessings of *Olam Haba*

כידוע שמקבלין לבוש חדש כי בלבוש זה של הגוף א״י לקבל עוה״ב. כמ״ש בזוה״ק כי עוה״ב א״י לסבול כחוט השערה מעוה״ז. רק בש״ק יש נשמה יתירה ויכולין לקבל קצת הארה מעוה״ב.

In previous *divrei Torah,* we emphasized that the term *Shalom* used to describe Shabbos is derived from both Shabbos' status as a microcosm of the World to Come, as well as being the perfect receptacle for Hashem's *berachos.* Here we will integrate each of these themes and propose that the Shabbos is the perfect receptacle for us to receive the blessings of *Olam Haba.* Because of this dual distinction, this unique day deserves to be known as a time of *Shalom.*

To elaborate, we note that it is virtually impossible to accept and appreciate the blessings of the World to Come as long as we are encumbered with the outer casing (לְבוּשׁ) of our body. It is only after achieving *sheleimus* through our distinguished behavior in This World and then receiving an entire set of "spiritual vestments" (לְבוּשׁ חָדָשׁ)[1] in the

1. These words of the *Sfas Emes* may allude to something discussed elsewhere in greater detail (see *Days of Awe,* pages 302-313). Whereas in This World the 248 positive and 365 negative commandments correspond to the respective limbs and sinews of the human body, in the *spiritual* milieu of *Olam Haba* we are actually sustained by those *mitzvos asei* and *lo saasei.*

World to Come that we can appreciate those *berachos*. In fact, according to the *Zohar*, the World to Come is so distinct from any of This World's experiences that it cannot tolerate even a scintilla (literally, a hairbreadth) of *Olam Hazeh*.

However, on Shabbos, which more than other occasion of This World resembles the World to Come, we are best able to appreciate and enjoy the great reward associated with *Olam Haba*. Shabbos, then is the perfect receptacle to receive the blessings of the World to Come and thus deserves the distinction of a being a day of *Shalom*. (*Eikev* 5642)

◌ Linking Hashem and *Klal Yisrael*

כי יש בו חלק להשי״ת וחלק לבנ״י לכן נקרא שלום שמחבר עליונים ותחתונים. ופ״א כתיב הטעם כי בו שבת והוא חלק הנותן ...

Anyone bringing together harmoniously two otherwise disparate elements deserves the distinction of *Shalom*, a peacemaker and conciliator. Whatever gap may have occurred during the weekdays between the Jewish people and Hashem is bridged on Shabbos. As the Torah states: בֵּינִי וּבֵין בְּנֵי יִשְׂרָאֵל אוֹת הִוא לְעֹלָם, *It is a sign forever* (of the relationship) *between Myself and the Jewish people* (*Shemos* 31:17).

To appreciate further how Shabbos brings us closer to Hashem, consider the two distinct reasons given for its observance. On one hand, the Torah states: כִּי בוֹ שָׁבַת מִכָּל מְלַאכְתּוֹ, *on it He rested* (abstained) *from all of His work* (*Bereishis* 2:3), which clearly attributes the Shabbos to Hashem's completion of *maaseh bereishis*. On the other hand, we are also commanded to observe Shabbos in commemoration of *yetzias Mitzrayim* — וְזָכַרְתָּ כִּי עֶבֶד הָיִיתָ בְּאֶרֶץ מִצְרַיִם ... עַל כֵּן צִוְּךָ ה׳ אֱלֹהֶיךָ לַעֲשׂוֹת אֶת יוֹם הַשַּׁבָּת, *And you shall remember that you were a slave in the land of Egypt ... therefore* Hashem*, your God, has commanded you to make the Sabbath day* (*Devarim* 5:15). By citing the significance from both Hashem's perspective (and relating it to an event that occurred even before the Jewish people's emergence), as well as what Shabbos means for the Jewish people, the Torah is emphasizing that Shabbos is a day that is permeated by *Shalom*. (*Shabbos HaGadol* 5647)

◆§ Linking Heaven and Earth

וזהו רמז ז׳ כפולות כדאיתא במד׳ כל מעשה שבת כפולים זכור ושמור משנה לחם שני כבשים כו׳. וזה עצמו ענין לחם משנה דכתיב בשבת שהחלק שלמטה מתאחד בשורש שלמעלה. לכן נקרא שבת שלום שמחבר עליונים לתחתונים ויש עליות נשמות למעלה וירידת נשמה יתירה למטה.

Whereas in previous *divrei Torah* we suggested that the Shabbos harmoniously links *Klal Yisrael* and Hashem, as well as our *guf* and *neshamah,* here we suggest that the Shabbos links our physical presence on earth with our heavenly roots. In fact, *Chazal* emphasize that many of the *mitzvos* of Shabbos are presented in the form of "pairs": for example, *Zachor V'Shamor, lechem mishneh,* as a well as the two lambs that were offered every Shabbos. These *mitzvos* may also represent the same theme — that every Shabbos our material presence here on earth is drawn closer to its heavenly roots.

In a similar vein, we find that on one hand the *neshamah yeseirah* descends from above every Shabbos. Simultaneously, our own souls here on earth ascend heavenwards as they attain ever higher levels of *kedushah.*

By linking harmoniously our mortal presence on earth with our heavenly roots, the Shabbos has earned the distinction of being known as *Shalom.* (*Beha'aloscha* 5651)

◆§ Developing A Harmonious Relationship Between Heaven and Earth

דאיתא מים תחתונים בוכין ונכרת להם ברית מלח למלוח כל קרבן כמ״ש רש״י פ׳ ויקרא. ומעין זה הברית הי׳ בעולם שנה נפש. ולפי שהתחתונים נתרחקו כמ״ש במד׳ והארץ היתה ... לכן עשה הקב״ה אות להיות גם בתחתונים מעין העליונים. והכה״ג נכנס לפני ולפנים תוך הפלטין וניזון במתנה כמ״ש עבודת ונתנה והוא שלא הדרך הטבע. וכמו כן בזמן השבת שיש בו כל אלו הבחי׳ כמ״ש במ״א ונקרא מתנה.

In the previous *dvar Torah* (and elsewhere) we elaborated on the capacity of Shabbos to link our roots on earth with their heavenly equivalent; here we will discuss the ability of this extraordinary day to reconcile heaven and earth. To appreciate this concept – and how the name *Shalom* may be derived from the "peacemaking" capacity of Shabbos – we turn to the story of *maaseh bereishis. Chazal* relate that when Hashem (on the second day of Creation) created the firmament, thus separating the waters below (on earth) from the waters above (in heaven), the water complained, pleading that it too desired to remain in Hashem's Presence. In response, Hashem arranged for certain individuals and certain sacred occasions when the *kedushah* of the heavens would be preserved and enjoyed on earth. An example of such an individual is the *Kohen Gadol*, who uniquely could enter the *Kodesh Kodashim*, Hashem's inner sanctum, every Yom Kippur. An example of such an occasion is the Shabbos, when a semblance of that *kedushah* [as the Torah states, לָדַעַת כִּי אֲנִי ה׳ מְקַדִּשְׁכֶם, *to know through the Shabbos that I am HASHEM Who makes you holy* (*Shemos* 31:13)] is present. It is this property of the Shabbos to bring the immense sanctity of heaven to earth, and to thus reconcile the waters on the earth itself, which felt removed from Hashem's Presence at Creation, that may earn it the distinction of being called *Shalom*, the "peacemaker." Similarly, Aharon, whose sacred personality and Divine Service in the innermost sanctum of the *Mishkan* linked together heaven and earth, is described as an אוֹהֵב שָׁלוֹם וְרוֹדֵף שָׁלוֹם, *lover and pursuer of peace* (*Avos* 1:12). (*Korach* 5657)

שהתחתונים מתרעמין למה העליונים נזונין מטמיון והתחתונים אם אינם יגיעים אין אוכלין. תו העליונים קרובים אל המלך והתחתונים נדחו ע״ש. והנה בשבת הוא יום מנוחה ונק׳ מתנה טובה וא״צ יגיעה והתחתונים מתקרבין ויש להם עלי׳ ולכן הוא שלום שעליונים ותחתונים נעשין אחד ביום השבת.

In a similar vein, *Chazal* relate that the earth (and all of its inhabitants, who are required to toil for their sustenance) envied the ease with which the angels and all of Hashem's servitors are nurtured. The Shabbos, a day in which the earth too is satiated with spirituality and consequently its residents don't require physical exertion to survive, is the ideal opportunity to relieve the concerns of mortals. It was on Shabbos that this latent conflict between Hashem's subjects in heaven and on earth was resolved. This new-found harmony reflects the ambiance of *Shalom* that permeates the Shabbos. (*Bereishis* 5653)

◈ Hashem's Name

ונותן השבת השלמה לכל הדברים המתבטלין להשבת. לכן נק׳ שבת שלום מעין שמו של הקב״ה שנק׳ שלום. וטעם שהוא הנותן שלימות לכל.

We may draw an analogy between the Shabbos day which is known by the name *Shalom* and (כביכול) *HaKadosh Baruch Hu* Whose Name is also *Shalom* (cf. *Shabbos* 10b). Just as Hashem's Presence motivates all of His creations to attain *sheleimus* (perfection, derived from *shalom*), so too, everything associated with *Shabbos Kodesh* achieves its fullest potential. Moreover, just as we can only attain our personal *sheleimus* by negating ourselves to Hashem, so is it through our *hisbatlus* (negation) to the sanctity of Shabbos that we can perceive that all our objectives are accomplished, which is a form of *sheleimus*.

(Adapted from *Yisro* 5641)

◈ Revealing Hashem's Name in the Universe

ובזוה״ק מאי שבת שמא דקוב״ה והוא שלום. ופי׳ שם הוא התגלות כבודו במעשה בראשית הרחוק ג״כ כי קודם הבריאה הי׳ ה׳ אחד. ובחי׳ הבריאה הוא שמו אחד כדי להראות שלימותיו. וכשכל הבריאה מתבטל להכלל שנקרא כנס״י. זה שמו אחד והוא כלי לעצמותו ית׳ והבן.

To appreciate the relationship between Hashem's Name *Shalom* and Shabbos, we refer to the renowned *pasuk*, ה׳ אֶחָד וּשְׁמוֹ אֶחָד, *Hashem is One and His Name is One* (*Zechariah* 14:9). We suggest that this *pasuk* alludes to two distinct periods of the Creation process. Whereas prior to Creation, Hashem was certainly unique, ה׳ אֶחָד (and alone, there being no other entity present to "challenge Him"), it was also true that there was no entity present to appreciate His Presence. As such, it could be said, in truth, that the Name of Hashem was not known. It was through the *sheleimus* (perfection) and sense of completion attained after the first Shabbos, when the entire universe in its full splendor testified to the greatness of its Creator, that it could be said, שְׁמוֹ אֶחָד, *His Name* (i.e., His Presence as perceived by His subjects) *is One*. It was only on Shabbos, a day of consummate *sheleimus* (related to *Shalom*) that Hashem's Name was revealed. Thus, it follows that the Shabbos is appropriately described as a day of *Shalom*, alluding not only to Hashem's Name but also to the *sheleimus* that enabled man to appreciate its Creator.

(Adapted from *Bereishis* 5631)

A Letter of Hashem's Name (the אות of Shabbos)

אבל העיקר תכלית כל הבנינים והצירופים הללו הוא להמשיך אותיות שמו ית' שהוא פנימיות התורה שכולה שמותיו של הקב"ה וב"ש. כענין שנאמר ועשו לי מקדש ושכנתי בתוכם. וזהו בחי' שבת שמא דקוב"ה שלום מלך שהשלום שלו. פי' שלום שבאות אחת משמו של הקב"ה נמצא כל השלימות. כמ"ש עושה שלום במרומיו.

In the previous *dvar Torah*, we noted the association that exists between *Shalom*, which is Hashem's Name, and the Shabbos day, which is known by the name *Shalom*.

Utilizing this approach, we may gain enhanced appreciation why Shabbos is called an אות [*os*], which may mean a *letter* (of the *aleph-beis*) as well as a *sign*. It is well-known that Hashem created the universe by utililizing various formulations of the sacred letters of the *aleph-beis* (cf. *Menachos* 29b and *Rashi*, s.v. אחת). According to the Gemara (*Berachos* 55a), Betzalel, the architect of the *Mishkan*, enjoyed the unique capacity to utilize the "tools" with which Hashem had created the universe for the purpose of erecting the *Mishkan*. Specifically, Betzalel was able to successfully apply the various formulations of the *aleph-beis* through which heaven and earth were created and that are the letters used to form the words and sentences of the Torah. Moreover, in light of the *Ramban's* observation (in the introduction to his commentary on the Torah) that the entire Torah consists of various combinations of Hashem's Name, Betzalel, by utilizing the letters of the *aleph-beis* to erect the *Mishkan* was, in reality, incorporating these formulations of the *Shem Hashem* into the *Mishkan*. As a result of this Divine gift, Betzalel was able to employ 39 different forms of creative activity while building the *Mishkan*.

On Shabbos, however, Betzalel's sacred mission of building the *Mishkan* yielded to the even more significant objective of asserting that Hashem created heaven and earth and rested on the seventh day. In fact, all of the forms of *Melachah* that were used to erect the *Mishkan* are precisely the categories of work that may not be performed on Shabbos. Not only did the nature of Betzalel's mission differ on Shabbos from that of the weekdays, but the method used to implement this mission was also changed. Instead of utilizing the various formulations of Hashem's Name to create the *Mishkan,* on this day even one letter of Hashem's Name, even an *os,* is sufficient to attain *sheleimus.*

(Adapted from *Ki Sisa* 5654)

◆§ Understanding Hashem's Ways (Deflecting the *Yetzer Hara*)

ושבת בחי' בן שאנו זוכין בשבת להתגלות דעת האדם שיסכים השכל לקיים רצון אבינו שבשמים בלי מלחמות. וזהו שנק' שבת שלום כי משפטי ה' אמת ובשמים הכל מעידין על צדקת הבורא וכ' ה' עוז לעמו יתן כו' יברך כו' בשלום.

As we discussed in several other essays, the Jewish people enjoy a dual relationship with Hashem. On one hand, we are His servants, especially during the six weekdays. Just as a servant loyally obeys his master — whether or not he comprehends the rationale for doing so — so are we obliged to serve Him despite our lack of comprehension of His ways. On Shabbos, however, our relationship with Hashem is that of children to a parent. In the same manner that a child is frequently able to attain enhanced understanding of a parent's motivations for his actions, so too on Shabbos we are able to plumb the depths of Torah. Consequently we achieve enhanced insight into Hashem's commandments.

Whereas during the week it is often necessary to engage the *yetzer hara* and to prevent the forces of evil from obstructing our attempts at *avodas Hashem,* on Shabbos, the day when we begin to appreciate the rationale for *mitzvos,* we no longer have to struggle in our quest to serve Hashem. On this day, when our intellect as well as our better instincts militate us to observe Torah and *mitzvos,* we rest from our ongoing battle with evil. On this blessed day we enjoy a sense of respite, a feeling of true *Shalom*.[1] (*Mishpatim* 5636)

Fusing the Six Weekdays Into One Combined Entity

כי כל יום מימי המעשה הוא דבר פרטי לא ראי זה כראי זה. אבל שבת נעשין מכל הימים כלי אחד. ולכן נק׳ שלום.

Yet another aspect of Shabbos' *sheleimus* (and why *Shalom* is one of Shabbos' names) is simply the timing of the first Shabbos, and every Shabbos thereafter at the conclusion of the Six Days of Creation. Whereas each of the first weekdays represent another aspect of Hashem's Creation, it is only Shabbos that represents the totality and completion of *maaseh bereishis*. Unlike any of the individual entities created during the Six Days of Creation, which may be challenged by a counterforce which has the effect of negating its creative potential (e.g., fire and water, plants and predator beasts that consume those plants), the Shabbos day itself faces no such challenge. Existing alone, in an environment of complete security and beyond the reach of any counterforce, the Shabbos truly epitomizes *Shalom*. (*Tzav* 5654)

Completing All of the Challenges of the Weekdays (and of *Galus*)

וז״ש שנכנס עם דמדומי חמה הוא דבר גדול כמ״ש ז״ל על הבורא ית׳ ויכל ביום השביעי. שיודע רגעיו ונכנס בו כחוט השערה. כביכול כך אבינו יעקב עבד ממש כל העבודה המיוחדת לימי המעשה עד גמירא. ולכן נכנס ממש כחוט השערה דמדייק המדרש מדכתיב ויבוא יעקב שלם. ושלום הוא שבת. כנראה שבא ממש בשבת כמ״ש ויכל ביום השביעי כנ״ל.

What greater sense of *sheleimus* (and *Shalom*) than the completion of all of the tasks that we must accomplish during the six weekdays.

1. The renowned *pasuk*, ה׳ עֹז לְעַמּוֹ יִתֵּן ה׳ יְבָרֵךְ אֶת עַמּוֹ בַשָּׁלוֹם, *Hashem will give His people strength, Hashem will bless His people with peace* (*Tehillim* 29:11), may be interpreted to reflect the association between our Divine Service during the week and that of Shabbos. Whereas

When Yaakov enters the city of Shechem after triumphing over Esav and Lavan, the Torah heralds his arrival as שָׁלֵם, *an act of completion.* Moreover, *Chazal* place great significance on the time of his arrival in Shechem – Friday evening at the very moment of the inception of Shabbos. Whereas ordinarily we are obligated to welcome Shabbos early (prior to the precise moment when it commences), the Patriarch could not rest until all of his challenges that he faced in *galus* had been successfully completed. Just as the first Shabbos – at the completion of Creation – did not begin until the precise moment when the Six Days of Creation ended, so too, Yaakov's undertakings were of such significance that he required every moment of the weekdays' ambiance to finish the tasks that he had set for himself while in *galus*. Only then could he rest and enjoy a sense of *sheleimus*, completion, having accomplished all that he sought to do. (*Vayishlach* 5637)

◆§ Becoming a "Man"

כל המדריגות עד בחי׳ אדם לכן הי׳ צריך מקודם לתקן בחי׳ תורת חי׳ בהמה וזה שם יעקב. וכמו שהאדם נברא בסוף ואמרו חז״ל כדי שיכנוס לשבת מיד. כן אחר שהוציא יעקב אע״ה בחי׳ אדם בשלימות שהוא שצורתו חקוקה תחת כסה״כ ... אח״ז כתיב בו שמירת שבת כמ״ש חז״ל בפסוק ויחן את פני העיר כי כשנגמר הצורה בשלימות הוא בחי׳ שבת שלום.

Refer to the previous *dvar Torah* in which we noted that there is a sense of *sheleimus* that we enjoy every Shabbos upon completing all the challenges that we face during the six weekdays. It was this sense of harmony and unity of all of Hashem's creations which became evident upon the completion of the universe that first Shabbos that gives this extraordinary day the name *Shalom* (related to *sheleimus*, completion and perfection). In this *dvar Torah* we will consider the impact that the advent of Shabbos leaves on the individual and how the name *Shalom* is derived from the extraordinary growth that we all (potentially) enjoy on Shabbos.

---

during the six weekdays of Creation, Hashem grants us the strength and capacity (through His Torah) to combat the *yetzer hara*, on Shabbos – in the merit of having prevailed during the week – we merit to serve Him in an ambiance of peace.

To appreciate the impact of Shabbos on the human being and how our enormous potential is elicited by the arrival of this day, we turn again to Yaakov *Avinu*. He is not described as having attained *sheleimus* until he enters the city of Shechem as Shabbos was about to begin. In fact, at that time he had attained so lofty a level of *kedushah* that, as *Chazal* relate, his profile was engraved on Hashem's throne (cf. *Chullin* 91b).

It was at that moment of having achieved *sheleimus* that Yaakov truly attained the status of being called a man (*adam*), and it was at that moment that Yaakov's name was changed to Yisrael (cf. *Bereishis* 32:29; 35:10). Drawing on the analogy of man versus lower forms of life (such as animals), we may assert that all that the Patriarch had accomplished *prior* to attaining *sheleimus* (for example, his many bouts with Esav and Lavan) can be compared to the "preparatory" status of an animal (which was created prior to man and whose *halachos* are discussed prior to *dinim* pertaining to man). On the other hand, all that he achieved *after* entering Shechem at the arrival of Shabbos reflects his new-found status as the אָדָם הַשָּׁלֵם, the consummate man. In fact, Yaakov, in reaching out to his estranged brother Esav, notes וָאֵחַר עַד עָתָּה, *and I have lingered until now* (*Bereishis* 32:5), which may be homiletically interpreted, "I utilized the 'rear' (אָחור) approach (in which he perceives only some aspect of the *Shechinah's* overwhelming *kedushah*) until now." (In the future, once Esav is vanquished, Yaakov will aspire to a greater level, fully intending to use the frontal approach – one of "intimacy" with Hashem – known as *panim*.)

The much-coveted distinction of becoming a man, who has truly utilized his potential for greatness, only occurred at the conclusion of all the travail that Yaakov experienced in *galus*. Just as the first man, Adam, was created almost immediately prior to the advent of Shabbos so that he could enter its rarefied ambiance as soon as he was born, likewise, Yaakov's new status as the אָדָם הַשָּׁלֵם (along with his new name Yisrael) was immediately exposed to the best possible environment in which to utilize these Divine gifts – the Shabbos. Yaakov's arrival in Shechem is described in the following terms: וַיִּחַן אֶת פְּנֵי הָעִיר, *he encamped before the city* (ibid. 33:18). This may be homiletically interpreted: He was blessed with *chein* (Divine favor) resulting from his new status as the consummate man.

By referring to Shabbos as a time of *Shalom*, the *Zohar* is alluding to the enormous potential for growth and *sheleimus* (to become a consummate man permeated with *kedushah*) that comes to the fore as we welcome Shabbos. Just as the first man was created on Shabbos, and Yaakov becomes the אָדָם הַשָּׁלֵם on Shabbos, so too, we elicit our own potential for greatness as Shabbos arrives. (*Vayishlach* 5653)

◆§ *Shalom* and *Shulamis* (Shabbos and *Yom Tov*)

ושבת כתב זוה״ק מאי שבת שמא דקוב״ה שלום. ובנ״י נקראו שולמית. ושמעתי מאא״ז מו״ר ז״ל טעם שהם מבררין שלימות הקב״ה אשר כל השלימות אליו. וגם אנו נאמר שביו״ט הוא בחי׳ שולמית כנ״ל ושבת שלום כנ״ל. ואמת שצריכין לידע שגם כח מעשינו רק מהשי״ת.

Whereas *Shalom* is one of the names of Shabbos, the Jewish people are described in similar terms as הַשּׁוּלַמִּית (cf. *Shir HaShirim* 7:1), *the perfect one,* since by their upright behavior they are the perfect vehicle to demonstrate to the world at large the *sheleimus* (perfection) of Hashem's creations. We suggest that in the same vein, the term *shulamis* may also refer to the *Yamim Tovim,* since the miracles they commemorate demonstrate to mankind the infinite perfection of Hashem.

(Adapted from *Pesach* 5632)

◆§ The Crown of a Good Name (Shabbos and *Yom Tov*)

וכן סדר הברכה מקדש השבת וישראל והזמנים. וכתבתי במ״א רמז המשנה ג׳ כתרים הם כתר כהונה תורה ומלכות. והם ג׳ רגלים. וכתר שם טוב עולה על גביהם והוא בחי׳ השבת שהוא שלום שמו של הקב״ה כדאיתא בזוה״ק מאי שבת שמא דקוב״ה.

In the previous *dvar Torah* we suggested a relationship between Shabbos and *Yom Tov* based on the assertion of the *Zohar* (*Korach* 352b) that *Shalom* is one of the names of Shabbos. In a similar vein, we propose another association between Shabbos and the *Yamim Tovim.* Recalling the *mishnah* stating: שְׁלֹשָׁה כְתָרִים הֵם: כֶּתֶר תּוֹרָה, וְכֶתֶר כְּהֻנָּה, וְכֶתֶר מַלְכוּת; וְכֶתֶר שֵׁם טוֹב עוֹלֶה עַל גַּבֵּיהֶן, *There are three crowns: the crown of Torah, the crown of the priesthood, and the crown of royalty; but the crown of a good name surpasses them all* (*Avos* 4:17), we suggest that each of the *shalosh regalim* (Three Pilgrimage Festivals) represents one of the attributes cited in the first segment of the foregoing *mishnah*. However, Shabbos, the day whose name *Shalom* is identical to that of *HaKadosh Baruch Hu*, represents the greatest crown, that of the good name.

(*Pesach* 5652)

☙ Motivating Us to Fear Hashem (*Yiras Shamayim*)

והנה בזוה״ק יתרו איתא כי עיקר השלימות הוא ליראי ה׳ כמ״ש אין מחסור ליראיו. ממשמע דאין מחסור שלום איקרי ע״ש. ולכן זכה אהרן למדת השלום אוהב ורודף שלום. כי שלום שמו של הקב״ה. ולפי שחל עליו יראת ה׳ טהורה לכן זכה אל השלום. ומה״ט נקרא עיר הקודש ירושלים על היראה והשלימות שנמצא בה. וגם בש״ק דחל יראת ה׳ על בנ״י כדאיתא אפי׳ ע״ה אימת שבת עליו לכן נק׳ שלום.

According to the *Zohar* (*Parashas Yisro*), true *sheleimus* is attained by those who fear Hashem. As we recite at the conclusion of *Birchas HaMazon*, יְראוּ אֶת ה׳ קְדֹשָׁיו כִּי אֵין מַחְסוֹר לִירֵאָיו, *Fear* HASHEM, *you – His holy ones – for there is no deprivation for His reverent ones* (*Tehillim* 34:10). Consequently, Aharon, who epitomized fear of Hashem in his role as *Kohen Gadol*, merited the attribute of *Shalom* (cf. *Avos* 1:12, where Aharon is described as an אוֹהֵב שָׁלוֹם וְרוֹדֵף שָׁלוֹם, *one who loves peace and pursues peace*). Similarly, the holy city of Yerushalayim, whose name is a composite of these two inseparable concepts of *yirah*, fear, and *shalom*, peace, is an ideal venue for achieving both fear of Hashem and true *sheleimus*.

The Shabbos day itself is a powerful force in motivating even the simplest Jew to enhance his level of *yiras Shamayim*. *Chazal* (*Demai* 4:1) relate that even an *am ha'aretz*, an unlearned individual, would be reluctant to be deceitful on Shabbos about matters of *halachah*, because of the fear of Hashem that he may acquire on this day. It is because of the additional element of *yiras Shamayim* permeating the entire day that Shabbos deserves the distinction of being called *Shalom*. (*Emor* 5652)

Free from the Influence of the (gentile) World

כי שבת הוא בחי' שלום ואין בו מגע נכרי. בשש צרות יצילך הוא בששת ימי המעשה דכתיב ויגע בכף ירכו דרשו חז"ל ביוצאי ירכו.

Just as Esav's angel was only able to injure Yaakov's thigh while the *tzaddik* himself emerged unscathed, so is the impact of the non-Jewish world confined to the six weekdays (which are peripheral to Shabbos). On Shabbos, when an atmosphere of *Shalom* prevails, the Jewish people, Yaakov's descendants, may be immune from any form of harm that may befall them. The *pasuk*, בְּשֵׁשׁ צָרוֹת יַצִּילֶךָּ, *He will save you from six travails* (*Iyov* 5:19), alludes to the predicaments that *Klal Yisrael* may experience during the six weekdays. On Shabbos, however, these concerns cease as we enjoy an atmosphere of *Shalom*, as the *pasuk* continues, וּבְשֶׁבַע לֹא יִגַּע בְּךָ רָע, *and in the seventh no harm will reach you.*

(*Vayishlach* 5659)

Vanquishing Amalek

וכתבנו שם עפ"י המדרש בראשית אמת אמר אל יברא עולם הזה דכולי' שקר ושלום אמר אל יברא דכולי' קטטה. אבן לבנ"י ניתן גם בעוה"ז אמת ושלום. בתורה והשבת. ע"י שהם בני עוה"ב. והוא עדות על בנ"י שיכולין להשיג אלה המדות בעולם שהם מוכנים לעולם הבא. ועשו ועמלק שעיקרו רק עוה"ז. לכן הם שקר ומלחמה.

In a previous *dvar Torah* we suggested that on Shabbos, the *yetzer hara's* capacity to subvert us and prevent us from serving Hashem diminishes. In a similar light, we suggest that Amalek, that rogue nation that was the first to threaten *Klal Yisrael* after we left Egypt, and continues in its various guises to threaten the Jewish people, loses some of its capacity for harm on Shabbos. While we are commanded, תִּמְחֶה אֶת זֵכֶר עֲמָלֵק, *you should wipe out the memory of Amalek* (*Devarim* 25:19), on Shabbos, the day which is a microcosm of *Olam Haba* (cf. *Berachos* 57b) when Amalek will no longer exist, merely by taking note of the sanctity of this day (in the form of *Kiddush* and *tefillah*), we help ensure Amalek's liquidation.

To elaborate on this theme and to help clarify why Amalek's threat dissipates every Shabbos, we recall *Chazal's* (*Bereishis Rabbah* 8:5) rendition of the reaction of the angels representing the forces of Truth and Peace to the imminent creation of the universe. In their words: "Truth objected to Creation because of the potential for deceit that the new universe would bring, while the element of Peace voiced similar objections noting that the new world would be full of strife." In fact, the world, when completed, did contain both elements of truth and virtue, especially in the person of *Klal Yisrael*, as well as all of the deceit and controversy that the *malachim* were concerned about in the form of Amalek. However, Amalek's persistent threat to the universe, as it continues to propagate a lifestyle defined by bloodshed and falsehood, is only viable in This World. On Shabbos, however, the day permeated by the values and aura of *Olam Haba*, the attribute of peace, *Shalom*, which is the very name of Shabbos, prevails.[1] (*Zachor* 5649)

◆§ The Perfect Antidote to Amalek – the Final Shabbos

וקבעו חז״ל לקרות פ׳ זכור בש״ק כי כמו שאמרו חז״ל אילו שמרו בנ״י שבת ראשונה לא שלטה בהם אומה ולשון דכתיב יצאו וכו׳ ויבוא עמלק כו׳. כמו כן בוודאי יהי׳ התיקון ע״י שמירת שבת. כי שבת נק׳ שלום שמא דקב״ה. וכבר נשבע שאין שמו שלם עד שימחה זרעו של עמלק ... ואם בנ״י היו מתקנים שבת ראשונה לא הי׳ נמצא ראשית של עמלק כלל. ועתה צריך להיות התיקון ע״י שבת האחרון יום שכולו שבת. כי שבת רומז לשבת בראשית ולשבת שלעתיד.

In the previous *dvar Torah* we suggested that every Shabbos Amalek's capacity to threaten *Klal Yisrael* is greatly diminished. In this *dvar*

1. Similarly, Amalek's penchant for falsehood can only be a viable threat in a universe without Torah. For *Klal Yisrael* , the recipients of Hashem's Torah, known as *Toras Emes*, the Torah of truth, we need not fear the impact of the deceit sown by Amalek.

Torah, we propose that it is in the merit of *shemiras Shabbos* that Amalek will ultimately be vanquished.

To appreciate the association between observing Shabbos and *mechiyas Amalek,* we turn to the first manifestation of *chilul Shabbos* cited in the Torah — when Dasan and Aviram defied Moshe's instructions and sought to gather manna on Shabbos. This breach in the sanctity of Shabbos was almost immediately followed by Amalek's lightning attack on *Klal Yisrael.* The relationship between these two events is emphasized by *Chazal* (cf. *Shabbos* 118b) who note that if the entire Jewish people had only observed the first Shabbos (after they were informed about the sanctity of this day), they would have remained immune from attack by any foe. We may assume that just as desecration of Shabbos prompted Amalek's emergence, so too, the merit of *shemiras Shabbos* will hasten his downfall. In fact, by designating the month of Nissan as a particularly opportune time for the Final Redemption (cf. *Rosh Hashanah* 11a), *Chazal* may have been motivated by the belief that immediately prior to *Mashiach's* arrival — in the month of Adar — the Jewish people will again observe Shabbos properly, thus rectifying the factor that prompted Amalek's first attack. To compensate for the first Shabbos whose desecration induced Amalek's attack, we will diligently observe the "ultimate" Shabbos (cf. *Tamid* 7:4, describing לְיוֹם שֶׁכֻּלּוֹ שַׁבָּת, *the day that is completely observed in the spirit of Shabbos,* an allusion to the Messianic Era), celebrated in the final month of the Jewish year, Adar, just before *Mashiach's* arrival. This sequence of future events is implied by the *pasuk* describing Amalek's destruction: וְהָיָה בְּהָנִיחַ ה׳ אֱלֹהֶיךָ לְךָ מִכָּל אֹיְבֶיךָ מִסָּבִיב ... תִּמְחֶה אֶת זֵכֶר עֲמָלֵק, *It shall be that when* H*ASHEM*, *your God, gives you rest from all your enemies all around ... you shall wipe out the memory of Amalek ...* (*Devarim* 25:19) — when you will rest (בְּהָנִיחַ) [from *melachah* on Shabbos], תִּמְחֶה אֶת זֵכֶר עֲמָלֵק, you will merit to erase the name of Amalek.

With this approach, we gain new insight into the designation of *Shalom* as one of the names of Shabbos. Perhaps this name refers to the "ultimate" Shabbos, that blessed day when Amalek will be finally vanquished. *Chazal* (cf. *Rashi, Shemos* 17:16) note that Hashem's Name is not considered to be complete (i.e., written in its complete form consisting of four sacred letters) until Amalek is destroyed.[1] It is this sense of

1. *Sfas Emes* notes an interesting parallel between the oath that Hashem had assumed to liquidate Amalek and the oath that He took to eternally preserve and protect the Jewish people. It is when each of these solemn promises have been realized — at the time of Amalek's liquidation and *Klal Yisrael's* redemption — that His Name will finally be complete.

completion and perfection (made possible by the destruction of Amalek, as well as our return to Sabbath observance) that the "ultimate" Shabbos will bring that is alluded to by the name *Shalom*. (*Zachor* 5650)

◆§ Hashem's Battles / Hashem's Peace

הענין הוא דשמו של הקב"ה שלום ומ"מ בשמו הוא נלחם. וכן הוא כל מלחמות ה' אהבה בסופה. וכן אחר כל המלחמות ביצ"מ היה בסוף השירה. וכן הוא בכל מחלוקת שהוא לשם שמים סופה להתקיים ... כי בתורה כ' וכל נתיבותי' שלום. פי' אפילו המלחמות שנעשין עפ"י התורה הם שלום. וכן הוא בששת ימים תאכל מצות שהם הקטנות ומלחמות שעם מצרים. ובשביעי עצרת שהוא כנופיא ושלימות שנעשה בסוף ע"י אלו המלחמות. והוא השירה שבשביעי של פסח. לכן איתא במד' כי שביעי של פסח כמו שבת. ושבת הוא שלום שמו של הקב"ה.

In the previous *dvar Torah,* we noted the asssociation between *Shabbos Kodesh* and the *sheleimus* that can only be attained with the obliteration of any final vestiges of Amalek. In a similar vein, we suggest that Shabbos is known as *Shalom,* the day of peace, because it represents the true peace that can only be obtained by first waging Hashem's battles (*milchamos Hashem*). As we read in *Pirkei Avos,* כָּל מַחֲלֹקֶת שֶׁהִיא לְשֵׁם שָׁמַיִם סוֹפָהּ לְהִתְקַיֵּם, *Any controversy that is pursued for Heaven's sake will have a constructive outcome* (5:20) – when true peace is achieved between the once-antagonistic parties. Whereas all week long our challenge may be to wage battle against all of our foes, on Shabbos, having prevailed in battle, we now celebrate the peace that eventually ensues. Consequently, *Shalom* is an appropriate name of Shabbos. In fact, the harmony that emerges after a successful battle against Hashem's foes, is itself an indication of the sincerity with which this struggle was conducted.

Extending the relationship between the initial battle that is conducted *l'shem Shamayim* and the peace that will eventually emerge, we cite the renowned *pasuk,* וְכָל נְתִיבוֹתֶיהָ שָׁלוֹם, *all of its paths are those of peace* (*Mishlei* 3:17). Not only the peace that results from the successful completion of hostilities, but even the battle itself conducted for Hashem's sake is in reality another form of *Shalom.*

This relationship between initial controversy followed by true peace is not just typical of the association between the challenges of the weekdays and the harmony of Shabbos. In particular, it represents the relationship between the first six days of Pesach in which we contended with the Egyptians, and the seventh day (which according to *Chazal, Shemos Rabbah* 19:8, is compared to Shabbos), when we witnessed their final defeat at the Reed Sea and in this new-found environment of peace sang Hashem's praises (*Shiras HaYam*). As the *pasuk* states, שֵׁשֶׁת יָמִים תֹּאכַל מַצּוֹת וּבַיּוֹם הַשְּׁבִיעִי עֲצֶרֶת לַה' אֱלֹהֶיךָ, *For a six-day period you shall eat matzos and on the seventh day shall be an assembly to* H*ASHEM, your God* (*Devarim* 16:8). This may be homiletically interpreted: "Six days you should be engaged in waging Hashem's battles,[1] and on the seventh day, you shall gather to sing Hashem's praises (the *Shirah*)."[2]

(Adapted from *Pesach* 5652)

1. According to this approach, the term *matzos* is related to וְכִי יִנָּצוּ אֲנָשִׁים, *if men shall fight* (*Shemos* 21:22).

2. For further discussion of the relationship between the struggles associated with the first days of Pesach and the triumph that we celebrate on the seventh day, refer to *The Three Festivals,* pgs. 107-111.

Index

תורה

BEREISHIS / בראשית

VAYIKRA / ויקרא

BAMIDBAR / במדבר

DEVARIM / דברים

נביאים

כתובים

TEHILLIM / תהלים

MISHLEI / משלי

IYOV / איוב

SHIR HASHIRIM / שיר השירים

RUTH / רות

EICHAH / איכה

תפילה